Multimedia: Making It Work, Second Edition

Multimedia is any combination of text, graphic art, sound, animation and video

Tay Vaughan

Osborne **McGraw-Hill**

Berkeley New York St. Louis San Francisco Auckland Bogotá Hamburg London Madrid Mexico City
Milan Montreal New Delhi Panama City Paris São Paulo Singapore Sydney Tokyo Toronto

Publisher
Lawrence Levitsky

Project Editor
Bob Myren

Computer Designer
Jani Beckwith

Illustrator
Marla Shelasky

Quality Control Specialist
Joe Scuderi

Osborne **McGraw-Hill**
2600 Tenth Street
Berkeley, California 94710
U.S.A.

For information on software, translations, or book distributors outside of the U.S.A., please write to Osborne McGraw-Hill at the above address.

Multimedia: Making It Work, Second Edition

34567890 DOC 998765

ISBN 0-07-882035-9

Series Design: Seventeenth Street Studios

In Memory of

CECIL TODD KNIGHT VAUGHAN

1921 - 1992

1937

CONTENTS AT A GLANCE

I INTRODUCTION

1	WHAT IS MULTIMEDIA?	2
2	INTRODUCTION TO MAKING MULTIMEDIA	22
3	MULTIMEDIA SKILLS AND TRAINING	32

II MULTIMEDIA HARDWARE

4	MACINTOSH AND WINDOWS PRODUCTION PLATFORMS	54
5	HARDWARE PERIPHERALS	68

III MULTIMEDIA SOFTWARE

6	BASIC TOOLS	98
7	MAKING INSTANT MULTIMEDIA	124
8	MULTIMEDIA AUTHORING TOOLS	146

IV MULTIMEDIA BUILDING BLOCKS

9	TEXT	192
10	SOUND	238
11	IMAGES	276
12	ANIMATION	304
13	VIDEO	318

V ASSEMBLING AND DELIVERING A PROJECT

14	PLANNING AND COSTING	358
15	DESIGNING AND PRODUCING	386
16	CONTENT AND TALENT	420
17	DELIVERING	438
18	CD-ROMS AND SOFTWARE PACKAGING	458
A	FONT MANUFACTURERS	484
B	MULTIMEDIA TRAINING PROVIDERS	492
C	MACROMEDIA PRODUCT REFERENCE	500
D	THE MACROMEDIA SHOWCASE CD-ROM	512
	INDEX	547

CONTENTS

PREFACE, *XVII*
ACKNOWLEDGMENTS, *XIX*
INTRODUCTION, *XXV*

INTRODUCTION

1 What Is Multimedia? **2**

DEFINITIONS, 5
CD-ROM AND THE MULTIMEDIA HIGHWAY, 7
CD-ROM and Multimedia, 7
The Multimedia Highway, 8
WHERE TO USE MULTIMEDIA, 10
Multimedia in Business, 10
Multimedia in Schools, 13
Multimedia at Home, 16
Multimedia in Public Places, 17
Virtual Reality, 19

2 Introduction to Making Multimedia **22**

THE STAGES OF A PROJECT, 24
WHAT YOU NEED, 25
Hardware, 25
Software, 26
Creativity, 27
Organization, 30

3 Multimedia Skills and Training **32**

THE MULTIMEDIA TEAM, 35
Project Manager, 36
Multimedia Designer, 38
Interface Designer, 40
Writer, 42
Video Specialist, 44
Audio Specialist, 46

Multimedia Programmer, 47
The Sum of the Parts, 48
TRAINING OPPORTUNITIES IN MULTIMEDIA, 49
Formal Training, 49
Internship and Fellowship Programs, 50
Multimedia Training Providers, 51

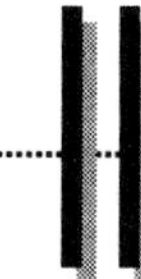

MULTIMEDIA HARDWARE

4 Macintosh and Windows Production Platforms **54**
MACINTOSH VERSUS PC, 57
THE MACINTOSH PLATFORM, 59
The Macintosh PowerPC, 60
Desktop CPUs, 61
PowerBook CPUs, 63
THE MULTIMEDIA PC PLATFORM, 64
Multimedia PC Level 2 Specification, 64

5 Hardware Peripherals **68**
CONNECTIONS, 70
Small Computer System Interface (SCSI), 71
The Media Control Interface (MCI), 72
MEMORY AND STORAGE DEVICES, 74
Floppy and Hard Disks, 76
SyQuest Drives and Optical Storage Devices, 78
CD-ROM Drives, 78
CD-ROM Recorders, 79
Videodisc Players, 79
INPUT DEVICES, 80
Keyboards, 80
Mice, 81
Trackballs, 81
Touchscreens, 82
Magnetic Card Encoders and Readers, 82
Graphics Tablets, 83
Scanners, 84
Optical Character Recognition Devices, 84
Infrared Remotes, 85
Voice Recognition Systems, 85
Digital Cameras, 85

OUTPUT HARDWARE, *86*

Audio Devices, 86

Monitors, 88

Video Devices, 90

Projectors, 90

COMMUNICATION DEVICES, *91*

Modems, 92

Networks, 92

Remote Application Sharing, 94

MULTIMEDIA SOFTWARE

6 Basic Tools **98**

PAINTING AND DRAWING TOOLS, *102*

CAD AND 3-D DRAWING TOOLS, *104*

IMAGE EDITING TOOLS, *106*

OCR SOFTWARE, *108*

SOUND EDITING PROGRAMS, *109*

ANIMATION, VIDEO, AND DIGITAL MOVIES, *111*

Video Formats, 112

QuickTime, 113

Microsoft Video for Windows, 117

Movie Players, 118

Movie Editors, 119

Compressing Movie Files, 120

HELPFUL ACCESSORIES, *122*

7 Making Instant Multimedia **124**

LINKING MULTIMEDIA OBJECTS, *127*

AppleEvents, 127

DDE and OLE, 128

WORD PROCESSORS, *129*

Microsoft Word for the Macintosh, 130

Microsoft Word for Windows, 131

WordPerfect for Macintosh, 131

WordPerfect for Windows, 133

Ami Pro, 133

Microsoft Works Multimedia Edition, 134

SPREADSHEETS, *134*

Lotus 1-2-3 for the Macintosh, 135

Lotus 1-2-3 for Windows, 135

Excel, 136

DATABASES, *136*

FileMaker Pro, 137

Superbase, 137

WindowBase, 137

Q+E Database/VB, 138

PRESENTATION TOOLS, *138*

Astound, 139

Persuasion, 140

PowerPoint, 140

DeltaGraph Professional, 141

CA-Cricket Presents, 142

Canvas, 142

Charisma, 143

SYSTAT, *143*

8 Multimedia Authoring Tools 146

TYPES OF AUTHORING TOOLS, *148*

The Right Tool for the Job, 150

Editing Features, 150

Organizing Features, 151

Programming Features, 151

Interactivity Features, 152

Performance Tuning Features, 153

Playback Features, 153

Delivery Features, 153

CARD- AND PAGE-BASED AUTHORING TOOLS, *153*

HyperCard (Macintosh), 155

SuperCard (Macintosh), 158

ToolBook (Windows), 160

Visual BASIC (Windows), 162

ICON-BASED AUTHORING TOOLS, *162*

Authorware Professional (Macintosh and Windows), 163

IconAuthor (Windows), 166

HSC Interactive (Windows), 167

TIME-BASED AUTHORING TOOLS, *168*

Action! (Macintosh and Windows), 168

Animation Works Interactive (Windows), 170

Cinemation (Macintosh), 172

Macromedia Director (Macintosh), 174

MediaBlitz! (Windows), 177

Producer (Macintosh and Windows), 179

PROmotion (Macintosh), 181

CROSS-PLATFORM TOOLS, *183*

PACo Producer (Macintosh), 184

Director Windows Player (Windows), 187

ConvertIt! (Macintosh and Windows), 188

MULTIMEDIA BUILDING BLOCKS

9 Text **192**

THE POWER OF MEANING, *195*

ABOUT FONTS AND FACES, *196*

Cases, 197

Serif Versus Sans Serif, 197

USING TEXT IN MULTIMEDIA, *200*

Designing with Text, 200

Choosing Text Fonts, 201

Menus for Navigation, 202

Buttons for Interaction, 203

Fields for Reading, 205

Symbols and Icons, 206

Animating Text, 208

COMPUTERS AND TEXT, *209*

The Font Wars, 209

Macintosh Bitmapped Fonts, 212

Installed Fonts in Windows and System 7, 213

Font Manufacturers, 213

Managing Your Fonts, 214

Character Sets and Alphabets, 215

THE ATYPI ORGANIZATION, *220*

FONT EDITING AND DESIGN TOOLS, *221*

ResEdit, 222

FONTastic Plus, 222

Fontographer, 223

Metamorphosis Professional, 224

FontStudio, 225

Making Pretty Text, 226

HYPERMEDIA AND HYPERTEXT, *228*

The Power of Hypertext, 231

Using Hypertext, 232

Searching for Words, 233

Hypermedia Structures, 234

Hypertext Tools, 236

10 Sound **238**

THE POWER OF SOUND, *240*

MULTIMEDIA SYSTEM SOUNDS, 242

MIDI VERSUS DIGITAL AUDIO, 243

Choosing Between MIDI and Digital Audio, 246

DIGITAL AUDIO, *246*

Preparing Digital Audio Files, 247

MAKING MIDI AUDIO, 253

Preparing MIDI Files, 257

Playing Back Your MIDI Sounds, 259

AUDIO FILE FORMATS, 259

WORKING WITH SOUND ON THE MACINTOSH, *260*

MIDI on the Macintosh, 261

Digital Audio on the Macintosh, 262

Audio in QuickTime, 263

WORKING WITH SOUND IN WINDOWS, 263

MIDI Under Windows, 264

Digital Audio Under Windows, 267

ADDING SOUND TO YOUR MULTIMEDIA PROJECT, 267

TOWARD PROFESSIONAL SOUND: THE RED BOOK STANDARD, 269

Space Considerations, 270

PRODUCTION TIPS, *270*

AUDIO RECORDING, *271*

Audio Editing, 272

Keeping Track of Your Sounds, 273

Testing and Evaluation, 274

Copyright Issues, 275

11 Images **276**

BEFORE YOU START TO CREATE, *278*

Plan Your Approach, 279

Organize Your Tools, 279

Multiple Monitors, 279

MAKING STILL IMAGES, *280*

Bitmaps, 281

Vector Drawing, 288

3-D Drawing and Rendering, 290

COLOR, 292

Working with Color, 292

Understanding Natural Light and Color, 292

Computerized Color, 293

Color Palettes/Color Lookup Tables, 296

IMAGE FILE FORMATS, *300*

Macintosh Formats, 300

Windows Formats, 300

Cross-Platform Formats, 302

12 Animation **304**

THE POWER OF MOTION, *306*

PRINCIPLES OF ANIMATION, *307*

Animation Techniques, 308

Animation File Formats, 310

MAKING ANIMATIONS THAT WORK, *310*

A Rolling Ball, 310

Creating an Animated Scene, 312

Font Animation, 315

13 Video **318**

USING VIDEO, *320*

Obtaining Video Clips, 322

HOW VIDEO WORKS, *322*

BROADCAST VIDEO STANDARDS, *325*

NTSC, 325

PAL, 326

SECAM, 326

HDTV, 326

INTEGRATING COMPUTERS AND TELEVISION, *327*

The First Step: Video Overlay Systems, 327

The Next Step: Digitized Video Playback, 330

Differences Between Computer and Television Video, 332

Working with Text and Titles for Television, 335

SHOOTING AND EDITING VIDEO, *335*

RECORDING FORMATS, *336*

S-VHS Video, 336

Component (YUV), 336

Component Digital, 337

Composite Digital, 338

Video Hardware Resolutions, 338

Consumer-Grade Equipment, 338

Editing with Consumer VCRs, 340

Professional Video Equipment, 341

VIDEO TIPS, 345

Shooting Platform, 345

Lighting, 345

Chroma Key or Blue Screen, 346

Composition, 347

VIDEO COMPRESSION, *348*

JPEG, 349

MPEG, 350

DVI, 350

Other Compression Methods, 351

Optimizing Video Files for CD-ROM, 351

Recording Computer Output, 352

Taking Care of Your Tapes, 353

ASSEMBLING AND DELIVERING A PROJECT

14 Planning and Costing **358**

PROJECT PLANNING, *361*

The Idea, 361

Idea Management Software, 367

Building a Team, 369

Pilot Projects and Prototyping, 371

Task Planning, 373

Scheduling, 374

ESTIMATING, *375*

Billing Rates, 378

Example Cost Sheets, 379

PROPOSALS AND BIDS, *379*

The Cover and Package, 383

Table of Contents, 383

Executive Summary, 384

Needs Analysis and Description, 384

Target Audience, 384

Creative Strategy, 384

Project Implementation, 384

Budget, 385

15 Designing and Producing **386**

DESIGNING, *389*

Designing the Structure, 389

Designing the User Interface, 401

A Multimedia Design Case History, 407

PRODUCING, *413*

Starting Up, 413

Working with Clients, 415

Tracking, 416
Open Code, 416
Hazards and Annoyances, 417

16 Content and Talent **420**

ACQUIRING CONTENT, *423*
USING CONTENT CREATED BY OTHERS, *424*
Locating Preexisting Content, 425
Copyrights, 426
Obtaining Rights, 426
USING CONTENT CREATED FOR A PROJECT, *430*
USING TALENT, *432*
Locating the Professionals You Need, 432
Working with Union Contracts, 433
Acquiring Releases, 435

17 Delivering **438**

TESTING, *441*
Alpha Testing, 441
Beta Testing, 442
Polishing to Gold, 442
PREPARING FOR DELIVERY, 444
Compressing and Joining Files, 446
File Archives, 446
DESIGNING INSTALLATION PROGRAMS, *449*
INSTALLATION ON A WINDOWS PLATFORM, *451*
EDI Install for Windows, 451
INSTALLATION ON A MACINTOSH PLATFORM, *453*
Using StuffIt InstallerMaker, 454

18 CD-ROMs and Software Packaging **458**

CD-ROM, 460
COMPACT DISC TECHNOLOGY, *462*
Compact Disc Standards, 463
Producing a CD, 473
PACKAGING YOUR PROJECT, *474*
Package Covers, 474
Package Shapes, 475
Basic Packaging, 476
Multimedia PC Packaging Standards, 477
CD Packaging, 478
Displaying System Requirements, 482

A Font Manufacturers 484

B Multimedia Training Providers 492

COLLEGE MULTIMEDIA PROGRAMS, *494*

OTHER MULTIMEDIA TRAINING PROVIDERS, *496*

C Macromedia Product Reference 500

MACROMEDIA—THE COMPANY, *502*

MARKET OPPORTUNITY, *503*

MACROMEDIA'S BUSINESS STRATEGY, *504*

TECHNOLOGICAL LEADERSHIP, *505*

MACROMEDIA PRODUCTS, *506*

Authorware Professional for Macintosh and Windows (Authoring), 506

Macromedia Director for Macintosh and Windows (Authoring), 507

MacroModel for Macintosh and Windows (3-D Graphics), 507

Action! for Macintosh and Windows (Presentation), 508

SoundEdit 16 and SoundEdit 8 (Sound), 508

Swivel 3D Pro, Three-D, ModelShop II, Life Forms (3-D Graphics), 508

ClipMedia for Macintosh and Windows (Content), 509

MACROMEDIA USERS, *509*

D The Macromedia Showcase CD-ROM 512

HOW TO USE THE SHOWCASE CD-ROM, *515*

Hybrid CD-ROMs, 515

For Macintosh Users, 515

For Windows Users, 517

WHAT'S ON THE PRODUCT SHOWCASE DISC, *519*

Multimedia Solution Demos, 519

Macromedia Programs, 522

Macromedia Services, 522

Ordering Information, 522

Compatability Information, 523

Working Models, 523

GNS Demo, 523

Other Great Demos, 523

DIRECTORY: MACINTOSH PARTITION, *524*

DIRECTORY: DOS/WINDOWS PARTITION, *538*

Index 547

Preface

The Revolution

There is an unstoppable revolution underway, made possible by the technology and ideas described in this book.

The way humans access and learn information, and the swiftly-changing way that information is packaged, have kindled an electronic revolution far more complex and powerful than the liberation of the printed word that occured 500 years ago in middle Europe. That last revolution, led by Gutenberg, Grolier, Aldus Manutius, and others who built and used printing presses, yielded powerful and long-lasting transformations to the human condition that far exceeded the imaginations of that day.

Someone among us, perhaps you, may become multimedia's Gutenberg, a creative, intellectual, or engineering talent who will truly alter the human condition.

Surfing at the leading edge of the wave of change, you have already abandoned the calm place behind the crest; ahead is the unknown.

The Calling

If, among your talents, you are able to discern the hazy silhouette of future tracks through the multimedia froth, we want your help to shape that which is to come. If you are a story teller, artist, musician, programmer, idea person or other creative talent with a sense of what multimedia is all about... if you can make order out of chaos... join the revolution and write personally to Tay Vaughan at Timestream, Inc., 6114 LaSalle Avenue, Suite 300, Oakland, California 94611 U.S.A.

Tay Vaughan
Oakland, California
May, 1994

Acknowledgments

I would like to thank my family and many colleagues who allowed me the time and space to write this second edition of *Multimedia: Making It Work*.

I could not have written this book without the steady and disciplined help of my colleague, Donna Booher. A professional editor with a quick mind, she lived for months in the storm of words, and fashioned in the lee a special place for calm discourse about good writing and the craft.

For this Second Edition, Helayne Waldman, Hank Duderstadt, Chip Harris, Joyce Edwards, and Michael Allen contributed greatly to making the work more complete; and Bill Pollock, Bob Myren, Rich Santalesa, Jeff Pepper, Kathy Hashimoto, Marla Shelasky, Jani Beckwith, Linda Medoff, Valerie Robbins, Cindy Brown, and Larry Levitsky at Osborne/McGraw-Hill kept me from falling off the deep end of my deadlines. For the original manuscript, I remain indebted to Eric Brown, Tom Sheldon, Frances Stack, Jill Pisoni, Madhu Prasher, Carol Henry, Linda Beatty, Theo Posselt, and especially to Ann Stewart, Graham Arlen, Kathy Gardner, Steve Goeckler, Steve Peha, Christine Perey, Pam Sansbury, and Terry Schussler, who helped me form the words.

I would also like to acknowledge my many friends in the computer and publishing industries who made this book possible. They have continued to send me quotes and multimedia anecdotes to enliven the book; many arranged for me to review and test software and hardware; many were there when I needed them. I would like to thank them all for the time and courtesy they afforded me on this project:

Eric Alderman, HyperMedia Group
Kurt Andersen, Andersen Design
Ines Anderson, Claris Corporation
Yasemin Argun, Corel Systems
Cornelia Atchley, Comprehensive Technologies
Dana Atchley, Network Productions
Pamela Atkinson, Pioneer Software
Patricia Baird, *Hypermedia Journal*
Gary Baker, Technology Solutions

Richard Bangs, Mountain Travel-Sobek
Sean Barger, Equilibrium
Heinz Bartesch, The Search Firm
Bob Bauld, Bob Bauld Productions
Jon Barrett, Dycam
Heinz Bartesch, The Search Firm
Thomas Beinar, Add-On America/Rohm
Bob Bell, SFSU Multimedia Studies Program
George Bell, Ocron
Andrew Bergstein, Altec Lansing
Bren Besser, Unlimited Access
Nancy Blachman, Variable Symbols
Dana Blankenhorn, *Have Modem Will Travel*
Brian Blum, The Software Toolworks
Michele Boeding, ICOM Simulations
Donna Booher, Timestream
Gail Bower, TMS
Susan Boyer, Blue Sky Software
Deborah Brown, Technology Solutions
Eric Brown, *NewMedia* magazine
Russell Brown, Adobe Systems
Stephanie Bryan, SuperMac
Ann Marie Buddrus, Digital Media Design
David Bunnell, *NewMedia* magazine
Jeff Burger, Creative Technologies
Bridget Burke, Gryphon Software
Dominique Busso, OpenMind Inc.
Ben Calica, Tools for the Mind
Doug Campbell, Spinnaker Software
Doug Camplejohn, Apple Computer
Tim Carrigan, *Multimedia* magazine
Herman Chin, Computer Associates
Angie Ciarloni, Hayes
Frank Colin, Equilibrium
David Collier, decode communications
Freda Cook, Aldus
Wendy Cornish, Vividus
Jeff Dewey, Luminaria
Jennifer Doettling, Delta Point
Hank Duderstadt, Timestream

Mike Duffy, The Software Toolworks
Joyce Edwards, Timestream
Mark Edwards, Independent Multimedia Developer
Dan Elenbaas, Amaze!
Kathy Englar, RayDream
Jonathan Epstein, *MPC World*
Kiko Fagan, Attorney at Law
Joe Fantuzzi, Macromedia
Terry Fleming, Timeworks
Patrick Ford, Microsoft
Marty Fortier, Prosonus
Kathy Gardner, Gardner Associates
Peter Gariepy, Zedcor
Bill Gates, Microsoft
Petra Gerwin, Mathematica
Jonathan Gibson, Form and Function
Karen Giles, Borland
Amanda Goodenough, AmandaStories
Danny Goodman, Concentrics Technology
Howard Gordon, Xing Technology
Catherine Greene, LightSource
Kim Haas, McLean Public Relations
Marc Hall, Deneba Software
Johan Hamberg, Timestream
Lynda Hardman, CWI - Netherlands
Tom Hargadon, Conference Communications
Chip Harris, Timestream
Trip Hawkins, 3DO/Electronic Arts
Randy Haykin, Apple Computer
Ray Heizer, Heizer Software
Dave Heller, Salient Software
Josh Hendrix, CoSA
Maria Hermanussen, Gold Disk
Allan Hessenflow, HandMade Software
Lars Hidde, The HyperMedia Group
Dave Hobbs, LickThis, Inc.
Petra Hodges, Mathematica
Elena Holland, Traveling Software
Mike Holm, Apple Computer
Bob Hone, Bob Hone Productions
Kevin Howat, Macromedia
Claudia Husemann, Cunningham Communications

Les Inanchy, Sony CD-ROM Division
Tom Inglesby, *Manufacturing Systems*
C. Carl Jaffe, Yale University School of Medicine
Scott Johnson, NTERGAID
Neele Johnston, Autodesk
JoAnn Johnston, Regis McKenna
Dave Kaufer, Waggener/Edstrom
David Kazanjian, AFTRA Actor
Jenna Keller, Alexander Communications
Trudy Kerr, Alexander Communications
Jeff Kleindinst, Turtle Beach Systems
Sharon Klocek, Visual In-Seitz
Lewis Kraus, InfoUse
Katrina Krebs, Micrografx
Kevin Krejci, Pop Rocket
Larry Kubo, Ocron
Howard Kwak, Pixel & Dot
Craig LaGrow, *Morph's Outpost*
Kimberly Larkin, Alexander Communications
Nicole Lazzaro, ONYX Productions
Bob LeVitus, LeVitus Productions
Steven Levy, *MacWorld*
Leigh-Ann Lindsey, Mathematica
Rob Lippincott, Lotus
Elliot Luber, Technology Solutions
David Ludwig, Interactive Learning Designs
John MacLeod, FastForward
Philip Malkin, Passport Designs
Basil Maloney, Winalysis
Kathy Mandle, Adobe
Audrey Mann, Technology Solutions
Robert May, Ikonic
Georgia McCabe, Applied Graphics Technologies
Kevin McCarthy, Medius IV
Charles McConathy, MicroNet Technology
Laurie McLean, McLean Public Relations
Bert Medley, "The NBC Today Show"
Art Metz, Metz, Inc.
Steve Michel, Author
Doug Millison, Morph's Outpost
Karen Milne, Insignia Solutions
Brian Molyneaux, Heizer Software

Rob Morris, VGraph
Glenn Morrisey, Asymetrix
Philip Murray, Knowledge Management Associates
Chuck Nakell, Inspiration Software
Kee Nethery, Kagi Engineering
Mark Newman
Terry Nizko, AimTech
Glenn Ochsenreiter, MPC Marketing Council
Jim O'Gara, Altsys
Eric Olson, Virtus
Karen Oppenheim, Cunningham Communications
Susan Pearson, Waggener/Edstrom
Sylvester Pesek, Optical Media International
Scott Pink, Bronson, Bronson & McKinnon
Shirley Rafieetary, Medius IV
Tom Randolph, FM Towns/Fujitsu
Steven Rappaport, Interactive Records
David Reid
Diane Reynolds, Graphsoft
Connie Roloff, Software Products International
Steve Rubenstein, *San Francisco Chronicle*
Marie Salerno, AFTRA
Jay Sandom, Einstein & Sandom
Pam Sansbury, Disc Manufacturing
Richard Santalesa, R&D Technologies
Anne Sauer, Fast Electronic U.S.
Melissa Scott, Window Painters
Sandy Scott, Soft-Kat
Karl Seppala, Gold Disk
Chip Shabazian, Ocron
Rochelle Schiffman, Electronics for Imaging
Adam Silver, Videologic
Chris Smith, VideoLabs
Brian Snook, Visual In-Seitz
Kent Sokoloff, Timestream
David Spitzer, Hewlett-Packard
Domenic Stansberry
Ann Stewart, Interactive Dimensions
Marty Taucher, Microsoft
Amy Tenderich, Norton-Lambert
Dave Terran, WordPerfect
Leo Thomas, Eastman Kodak

Terry Thompson, Timestream
Tom Toperczer, Imspace Systems
Ross Uchimura, GC3
David Vasquez, SFSU Multimedia Studies Program
Sally von Bargen, 21st Century Media
Helayne Waldman, National Educational Film & Video Festival
Arnold Waldstein, Creative Labs
Tom White, Roland U.S.
John Wilczak, HSC Software
Laura Williams, Waggener/Edstrom
Mark Williams, Microsoft
Shelly Williams, Prosonus
Hal Wine
Marcus Woehrmann, Handmade Software
Wendy Woods, *Newsbytes*
Chris Yalonis, Passport Designs
Frank Zellis, KyZen

Introduction

In a few years, multimedia computers will be an anachronism. All computers will readily integrate images, sounds, and motion video—and this capability will be built onto the motherboard as an essential part of what a computer is. In several years, these computers will be connected to worldwide networks with terabit-per-second transfer rates to make real-time sharing of high-quality images, sounds, and video practical. Intelligent software will make the technology of multimedia transparent at the user interface.

Multimedia computers *per se* may disappear when hardware and software platforms become more capable and we take sound, animation, and video features for granted, but the fundamental concepts and techniques required to work with these elements will not disappear. This is a book about the elemental parts of multimedia as much as about how to sew these parts together with current technology and tools. It is a book that shows you how to use text, images, sound, and video to deliver your messages and content in meaningful ways. It is about designing, organizing, and producing multimedia projects of all kinds and avoiding technical and legal pitfalls along the way. Above all, it is a practical guide to making multimedia, complete with tips, pointers, and answers.

This book first deals with the basic elements of multimedia. Hardware and software tools are described in detail. After the basics are covered, you are then introduced to the step-by-step creative and organizing process that results in a finished multimedia project. You will learn about the importance of text and how to make characters look pretty, about making graphic art on your computer and how to choose colors, and about how to digitize sound and video segments. You will learn about human interaction and how to design a user-friendly computer interface. You will even find a chapter about packaging your finished product.

I have written this book for people who make or want to make multimedia, for people who gladly take up new challenges and are unafraid of learning curves and intensely creative work. The words and ideas of this book are the harvest of many years in the computer industry and of hands-on experience deep in the factory where real multimedia is being made daily. The book is intended to be, above all, useful.

For focus, I chose two well-known computer environments to discuss in detail throughout the book: Apple Macintosh and Microsoft Windows—these are the most widely used computers today for making multimedia. But multimedia is by no means limited to these platforms, and most of the ideas discussed in the book are translatable to others.

I have made a great effort to include in this book references to as much multimedia software and hardware as I could, trying not to miss any players. Because, however, the industry is fast-paced and rapidly growing and because, while writing this book, I have rediscovered the finite limits of my own time, I am sure some have fallen into the bit bucket anyway. Immutable physical laws have prevented me from including the fine details of forty or fifty hardware and software manuals and technical resources into the pages allowed for this book; the distillation presented here should, however, provide you with pointers to further information and study. I have also made a great effort to double-check my words and statements for accuracy; if errors have slipped past, they are mine alone.

This is the second edition of *Multimedia: Making It Work*. While only a year has passed since the first edition was published, many changes have occurred, and I have not only attempted to bring the book's content up to date, I have reorganized much of it for a smoother read.

Some years ago, after completing a book about HyperCard, I swore never to write another. Writing a book is much like childbirth, I believe. In the beginning it gestates slowly, usually over a few months, then it ramps up inexorably and quickly toward deadline until all attention is focused upon the delivery itself and the pain and workload are great. Afterwards, you remember it was rough, but the pain itself becomes diffused in the post-partum release. I am glad to share my multimedia experiences with you, and hope that in reading this book you will become better at what you do.

Multi

Multimedia is any combination

[*Multimedia excites eyes, ears, fingertips, and, most importantly, the head.*]

When you **weave** together the sensual elements of multmedia -

interactive control

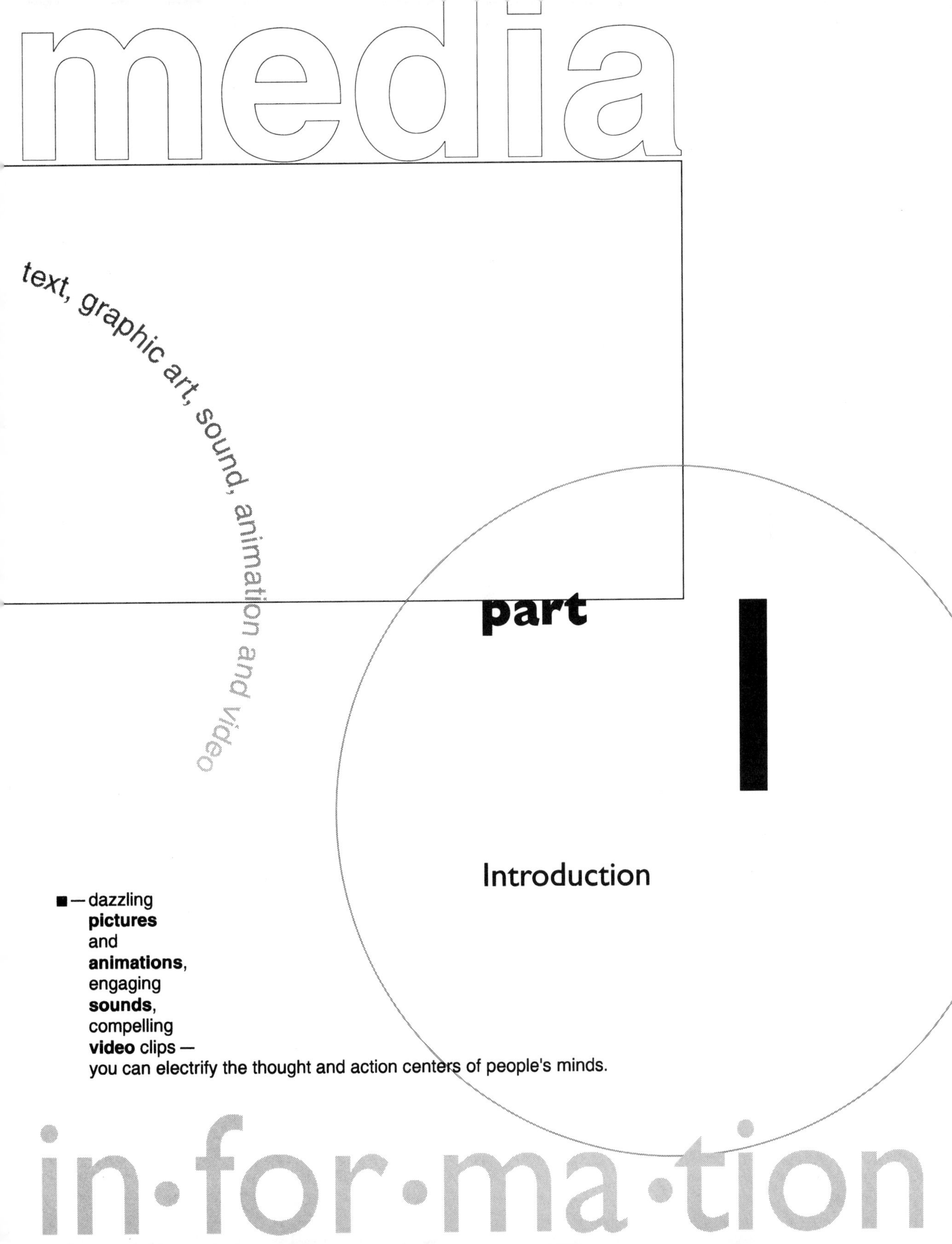

part I

Introduction

■ — dazzling
pictures
and
animations,
engaging
sounds,
compelling
video clips —
you can electrify the thought and action centers of people's minds.

Multi

Multimedia is any combination o

A revolution is taking place today in the way humans access, learn, and interact with information.

When you **weave** together the sensual elements of multmedia -

interactive control

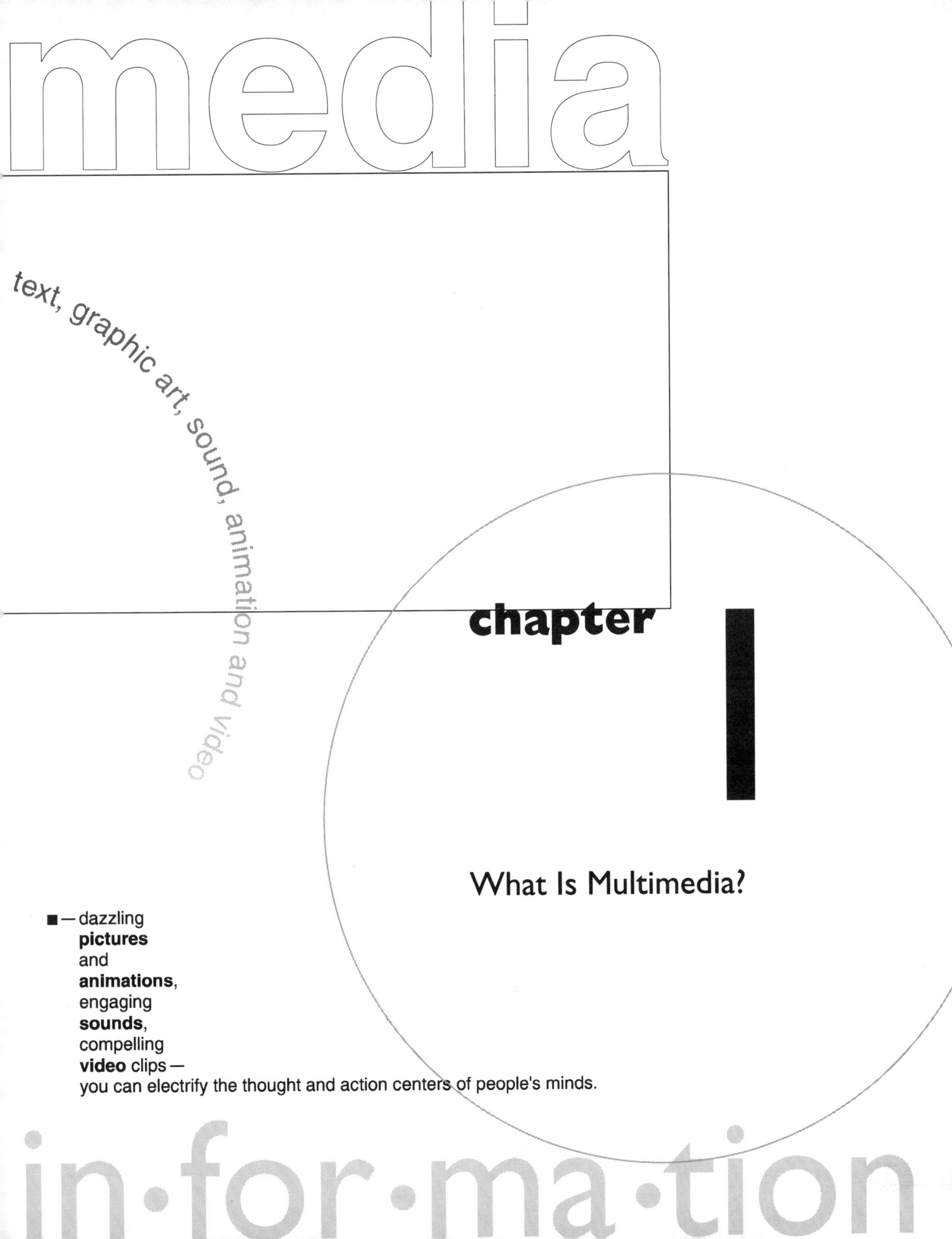

chapter 1

What Is Multimedia?

■ — dazzling
pictures
and
animations,
engaging
sounds,
compelling
video clips —
you can electrify the thought and action centers of people's minds.

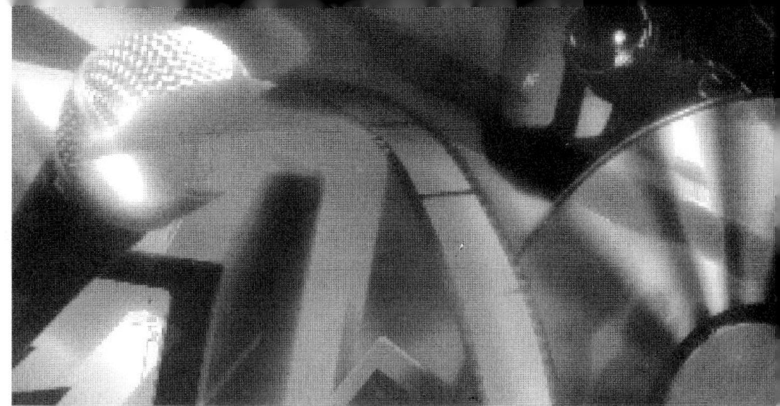

MULTIMEDIA is an eerie wail as two cat's eyes appear on a dark screen. It's the red rose that dissolves into a little girl's face when you press "Valentine's Day." It's a small window of video, showing an old man recalling his dusty journey to meet a rajah, laid onto a map of India. It's a catalog of fancy cars with a guide to help you buy one. It's a real-time video conference with three colleagues in Paris, London, and Hong Kong on your office computer. At home, it's an algebra or geography lesson for a fifth-grader. At the arcade, it's goggled kids flying fighter planes in sweaty virtual reality.

Multimedia is any combination of text, graphic art, sound, animation, and video delivered to you by computer or other electronic means. It is richly presented sensation. When you weave together the sensual elements of multimedia—dazzling pictures and animation, engaging sounds, compelling video clips, and raw textual information—you can electrify the thought and action centers of people's minds. When you give your audience interactive control of the process, they can be enchanted. Multimedia excites eyes, ears, fingertips, and, most importantly, the head.

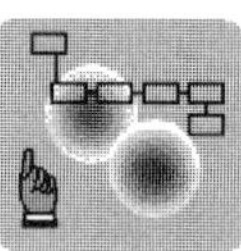

This book is about creating each of the elements of multimedia and weaving them together for maximum effect. This book is for computer beginners and computer experts. It is for serious multimedia producers and their clients as well. It is for desktop publishers and video producers who may need a leg up as they watch traditional methods for delivery of information and ideas evolve into new, technology-driven formats. This book is also for hobbyists, who want to make Photo CD albums and family histories; for mainstream businesses, where word-processed documents and spreadsheets are illustrated with audio, video, and graphic animation; for public speakers, who use animation and sound on large monitors and auditorium projection systems to present ideas and information to an audience; for information managers, who organize and distribute digital images, sound, video, and text; and for educators and trainers, who design and present information for learning.

The implementation of multimedia capabilities in computers is just the latest episode in a long series: cave painting, hand-crafted manuscripts, the printing press, radio and television.... These advances reflect the innate desire of man to create outlets for creative expression, to use technology and imagination to gain empowerment and freedom for ideas.

From a presentation to the European Software Publishers Association, Cannes, France, June 2, 1992, by Glenn Ochsenreiter, Managing Director, MPC Marketing Council

If you are new to multimedia and are facing a major investment in hardware, software, and the time to learn each new tool, take a gradual approach to these challenges. Begin by studying each element of multimedia and learning one or more tools for creating and editing that element. Get to know how to use text and fonts, how to make and edit colorful graphic images and animate them into movies, and how to record and edit digital sound. Read the computer trade periodicals that contain the most up-to-date information. Your skills will be most valuable if you develop a broad foundation of knowledge about each of the basic elements of multimedia.

Producing a multimedia project requires more than creative skill and high technology. You need organizing and business talent as well. For example, issues of ownership and copyright will be attached to some elements that you wish to use: text from books, scanned images from magazines, or audio and video clips. These require permission and often payment of a fee to the owner. Indeed, the management and production infrastructure of a multimedia project may be as intense and complicated as the technology and creative skills needed to complete it.

Definitions

Multimedia is, as described above, woven combinations of text, graphic art, sound, animation, and video elements. When you allow an *end user*—the viewer of a multimedia project—to control what and when the elements are delivered, it is called *interactive multimedia*. When you provide a structure of linked elements through which the user can navigate, interactive multimedia becomes *hypermedia*.

We define multimedia as anything that requires more than two trips to the car.

Robert May, President of Ikonic Interactive Multimedia, speaking to a MacWorld Conference audience, August, 1990

Although the definition of multimedia is a simple one, making it work can be complicated. Not only do you need to understand how to make each multimedia element stand up and dance, but you also need to know how to use multimedia computer tools and technologies to work them together. The people who weave multimedia into meaningful tapestries are *multimedia developers*.

The software vehicle, the messages, and the content presented on a computer or television screen constitute a *multimedia project*. If the project is shipped or sold to consumers or end users, typically in a box or sleeve, with or without instructions, it is a *multimedia title*.

A multimedia project doesn't have to be interactive to be called multimedia: users can sit back and watch it just as they do a movie or television. In such cases, a project is *linear*, starting at a beginning and running through to an end. When users are given navigational control to wander through the content at will, multimedia becomes *nonlinear* and interactive, and is a very powerful personal gateway to information.

Determining how a user will interact with and navigate through the content of a project requires great attention to the message you want conveyed, the *scripting* or *storyboarding* describing the parameters of the project, the artwork, and the programming. You can break an entire project with a badly designed interface. You can also break a project with inadequate or inaccurate content.

Multimedia elements are typically sewn together into a project using *authoring tools*. These software tools are designed to manage individual multimedia elements and provide user interaction. In addition to providing a method for users to interact with the project, most authoring tools also offer facilities for creating and editing text and images, and they have extensions to drive videodisc players, videotape players, and other relevant hardware peripherals. Sounds and movies are usually created with editing tools dedicated to these media, and then the elements are imported into the authoring system for playback. The sum of what gets played back and how it is presented to the viewer is the *human interface*. This interface is just as much the rules for what happens to the user's input as it is the actual graphics on the screen. The hardware and software that govern the limits of what can happen are the multimedia *platform* or *environment*.

Talking about multimedia is a lot like talking about love. Everybody agrees that it's a good thing, everybody wants it, wants to participate in it, but everybody has a different idea of what "it" really is. Right now, the industry reminds me of a bunch of teenagers dabbling in something that instinctively feels right, all the while wondering how and when they'll know for sure if they're really in "it," and what to do about it if they are.

Georgia McCabe, Senior Vice President, Applied Graphics Technologies

CD-ROM and the Multimedia Highway

Multimedia requires large amounts of digital memory when stored in an end user's library, or large amounts of bandwidth when distributed over wires or glass fiber on a network.

CD-ROM and Multimedia

CD-ROM (compact disc–read-only memory) has emerged during the last few years as the most cost-effective distribution medium for multimedia projects: a CD-ROM disc can be mass produced for less than one dollar and can contain as much as 72 minutes of excellent-quality full-screen video. Or it can contain unique mixes of images, sounds, text, video, and animation controlled by an authoring system to provide unlimited user interaction.

Discs can be pressed out of polycarbonate plastic as fast as cookies on a production line. By 1997, it is estimated that more than 20 million CD-ROM players will be installed on computers and hooked to television sets, like Sega, 3DO, and Kodak Photo CD systems.

In the long term, many experts view CD-ROM as an interim memory technology that will be replaced by new devices that do not require moving parts, such as flash memory. They also believe that as the data highway described below becomes more and more pervasive, copper wire, glass fiber, and radio/cellular technologies will prevail as the most commonly used delivery means for interactive multimedia.

Everybody in this market seems to be waiting for the other shoe to drop—and they all look pretty silly standing on one leg. Get on with it!

Jonathan Epstein, Publisher of *MPC World* magazine

The Multimedia Highway

Now that telecommunications networks are global, and as information providers and content owners determine the worth of their products and how to charge money for them, information elements will ultimately link up online as distributed resources on a data highway, like a toll road, where you will pay to acquire and use multimedia-based information. In the U.S., alliances are under way between the government, cable companies, telephone companies, computer companies, and existing data distribution networks such as Internet to build a National Information Infrastructure (NII).

Full-text content from books and magazines will be accessible by modem and electronic link; feature movies will be played at home; real-time news reports from anywhere on earth will be available; lectures from participating universities will be monitored for education credits; street maps of any city will be viewable—with recommendations for restaurants, in any language; online travelogues will include testimonials and video tracks. This is not science fiction; it is being implemented now. Each of these interfaces or gateways to information is a multimedia project just waiting to be developed.

In a few years, interactive multimedia will be delivered to many homes throughout the world. Interest from a confluence of entertainment megacorps, information publishers and providers, cable and telephone companies, and hardware and software manufacturers is already driving this inevitable evolution, and profound changes in global communications strategy are on the drawing boards. What will be piped through this new system are the very multimedia elements discussed in the chapters of this book: text, graphics, animation, sound, and video.

Giant companies with vast engineering and financial resources are beginning to design the digital data highway and to establish rules and fees for its use. Telephone companies like U.S. West are joining forces with cable TV interests like HBO; Paramount and other entertainment companies that own content easily converted to multimedia projects are teaming up with cable TV companies like Viacom—owner of MTV, Showtime, and Nickelodeon. Film studios like Disney and Warner Brothers are creating new divisions to produce interactive multimedia. Railroads like Union Pacific, with well-defined rights-of-way, are laying cable for the high-traffic superhighway links connecting major cities in the United States.

Some companies will own the routes for carrying data, while other companies will own the hardware and software interfaces at the end of the line, at offices and homes. Some will knit it all together and provide supply-on-demand and billing services. Regardless of who owns the roadways and the hardware boxes, multimedia producers will create the new literature and the rich information sent along it. This is a new and exciting industry coming of age, but one still faced with many growing pains.

First Person

I witnessed an amazing multimedia event in the fall of 1993. On an exuberant playing field at Las Vegas, 170,000 computer people and almost 2,000 exhibiting companies gathered to make deals and a lot of noise at the annual COMDEX trade show. This was the year of multimedia, the year when decades of creative and technical effort from thousands of brilliant hardware and software developers around the world would pay off–finally and clearly, there was a marketplace for their wares.

But one of the players marched onto the field like Darth Vader and stole the game ball. In front of a disbelieving and hostile press corps, Compton's NewMedia broadly declared multimedia to be their own invention–search and retrieval of text, picture, audio, and animated data, especially when delivered on CD-ROM. They passed out copies of their Patent No. 5,241,671 and said "Read it." And they outlined a program for multimedia developers whose work falls under the broad scope of the patent, possibly most developers: pay one percent of your net profits to Compton's NewMedia if you join our special program before June, 1994. After that, the price will go higher. "Why have government bureaucrats allowed you to patent something that we were doing in '86 and '87?" asked an attendee, gleaning cheers and hoots from the crowd. Another observer grabbed the mike to say, "I can't believe the arrogance that's standing in front of us and telling us that YOU invented the multimedia industry!" "What ISN'T covered by this patent?" asked another reporter, culling a one-word reply from executives on the podium: "text."

Compton's would like you to think that this is simply business as usual, and that the angry response to the announcement is simply a matter of naive developers who aren't used to playing hardball. Norm Bastins, Compton's general manager, was quoted by Amy Harmon in The Los Angeles Times saying "software developers historically do not like to pay licensing fees.... But it's time for the industry to grow up...."

Uh uh. Grown-ups today are making multimedia alliances and are nurturing the industry, not holding their colleagues hostage and demanding money. Grown-ups don't hold the game ball over the heads of the other players like spoiled schoolyard bullies, yelling "Mine, mine, mine!"

Don't get me wrong. Patents are good things; I even have one (No. 4,227,246). And the people I know in the multimedia industry don't mind paying real money for software, hardware, talent, content, and ideas that provide value. But Compton's has manipulated the system and taken advantage of patent examiners who were apparently unaware of the scope and breadth of prior art. Compton's gambit is a pushy, grabby, shockingly in-your-face

(continued)

First Person

maneuver that gives no credit to the many thousands who have contributed bleeding hard work to the multimedia industry for many years before autumn of 1989, when Compton's applied for their patent.

Laying claim to their "invention," Stanley Frank, CEO and president of Compton's, says "We simply want the public to recognize Compton's NewMedia as the pioneer in the industry...and be compensated for the investments we have made to make multimedia a reality for developers and end users." Few would deny that Compton's was a pioneer, but none of the pioneers I know is arrogant enough to profess being THE pioneer.

While initially stunned and affronted by Compton's claims of invention and their strategy for taxing multimedia, like mugging victims, the industry will emerge from a brief period of shock and get mad, real mad. "Compton's might have overlooked how closely knit this industry is," commented Randy Haykin, Strategic Marketing Manager for the New Media Division at Apple.

Just so. Multimedia developers typically know, help, and respect each other–they've been on the steep learning curve together. We are growing a new industry from hard work, sweat, all-nighters, and a coruscation of creative ideas and inventions. Indeed, what we are doing today will alter the fundamental ways people learn and entertain themselves for generations to come. We have a chance, now, to build the multimedia industry right. I submit that doing business with grace and with good will, not greed, is a very grown-up thing.

Portions excerpted from an opinion column by Tay Vaughan titled "The Compton's Patent: Who Owns Multimedia?" first printed in *NewMedia* magazine, January, 1994. (Note: In March, 1994, the U.S. Patent and Trademark Office rescinded this patent.)

Where to Use Multimedia

Multimedia is appropriate wherever people need access to electronic information of any kind. Multimedia enhances traditional text-only computer interfaces and yields measurable benefit by gaining and holding attention as well as interest. Multimedia improves information retention. When properly woven, multimedia can also be tremendously entertaining.

Multimedia also provides a way to reach out to people who are intimidated by computers by presenting information in ways they are more comfortable using. For example, a grandmother who refuses to touch a computer keyboard may see a store directory on a kiosk and start pressing buttons to find out what daily specials are featured. The following sections describe some of the ways multimedia is being used in business, in schools, in public places, and at home.

Multimedia in Business

Business applications for multimedia include presentations, training, marketing, advertising, product demonstrations, databases, catalogs, and network communications. Voice mail and video conferencing will soon be provided on many local and wide area networks (LANs and WANs).

After a morning of mind-numbing 35mm slide and overhead presentations delivered from the podium of a national sales conference, a multimedia presentation can make an audience come alive. Most presentation software packages let you add audio and video clips to the usual "slide show" of graphics and text material (see Chapter 7). Figure 1-1 is from a business presentation developed in Macromedia's Action! that plays background music as data scrolls across the screen; it includes a video clip of sunset at the Golden Gate Bridge to add impact.

Application: *Action!*
Macintosh Pathname: *MACROMEDIA :Product Demonstrations :Action! Demo :Action! GNS demo files :GNS Complete Presentation*
Windows Pathname: *SHOWCASE_CD \MACROMED \PRODEMS \ACTIONPC \PLAYACT.EXE*

Multimedia in training has become widespread. Flight attendants learn to manage international terrorism and security through simulation. Mechanics learn to repair engines. Salesmen learn about product lines and offer customers software for training. Fighter pilots practice full-terrain sorties before spooling up for the real thing. Figure 1-2 is from an animated project made with Macromedia's Director that describes the process of making steel.

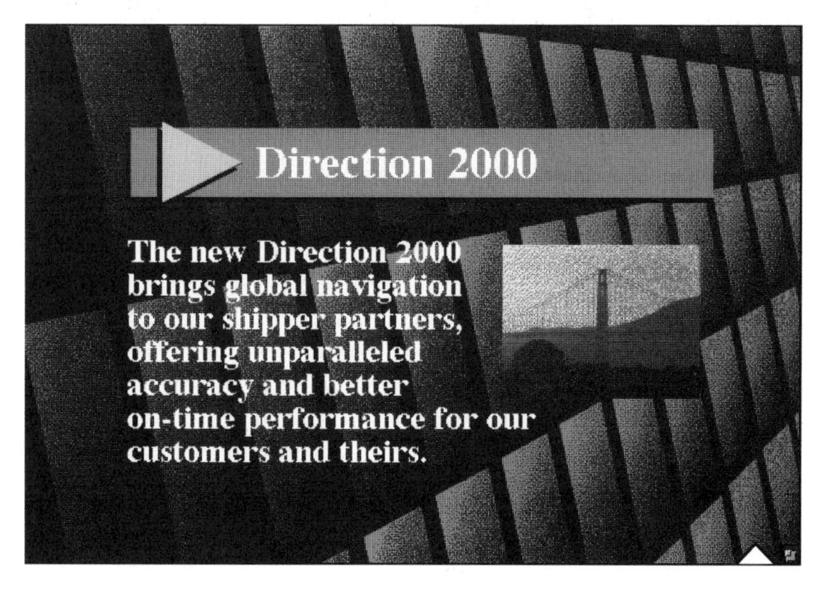

FIGURE 1-1 *Most presentation software provides animated text and graphics, and will allow you to attach audio and video components to your slide show.*

FIGURE 1-2 Animated instructional and training multimedia can contain as much information as a printed manual. Trainees can actually turn valves and flip switches to see what happens ■

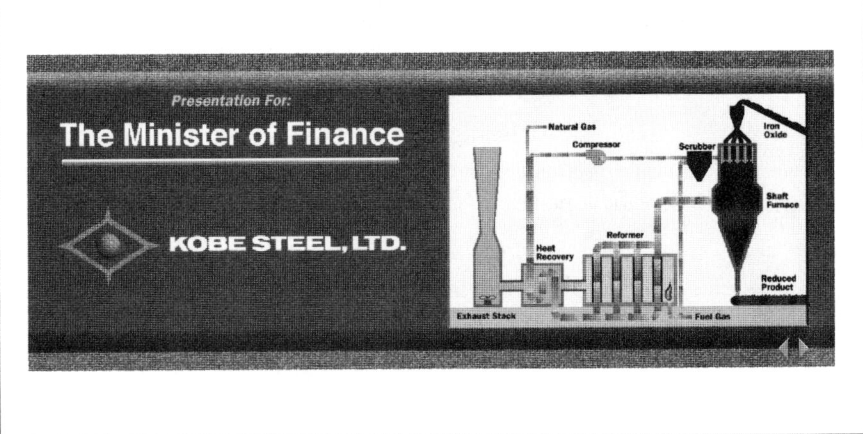

Application: *Director/Authorware*
Macintosh Pathname: *MACROMEDIA :SltnDems :KbeStl :KbeDem*
Windows Pathname: *SHOWCASE_CD \MACROMED \ATHWRDEM \NEWTONS \NEWTONLE.EXE*

Multimedia around the office has become more commonplace. Figure 1-3 shows VideoLabs' FlexCam, an inexpensive add-on video camera and stereo microphone unit. Such video capture hardware can be used for building employee ID and badging databases, for video annotation, and for real-time teleconferencing. As companies and businesses catch on to the power of multimedia, and the cost of installing multimedia capability decreases, more applications will be developed both in-house and by third parties to allow businesses to run more smoothly and efficiently.

Often, in businesses, CD-ROM drives are attached to a network server, and a single CD-ROM disc can be accessed by many users. At the beginning of 1993, almost twenty million PCs and PC clones were installed at businesses, compared to about three million Macintoshes. Of these computers, only about one in a hundred Intel-based machines had a CD-ROM drive aboard, while about four out of a hundred Macintoshes used in business were equipped with CD-ROM drives. Apple has teamed up with IBM and Motorola in an alliance once thought impossible to produce a new genera-

FIGURE 1-3

VideoLabs' FlexCam (neatly implemented by Worrell Designs of Minneapolis, MN) can be used for video capture and videoconferencing

tion of computers, the PowerPC (see Chapter 4), most of which will ship with a CD-ROM drive installed.

Multimedia in Schools

Schools are perhaps the most needy destination for multimedia. Many schools in the United States today are chronically underfunded and are occasionally slow to adopt new technologies, but it is in the schools that the power of multimedia can be maximized for the greatest long-term benefit to all. Multimedia will provoke radical changes in the teaching process in the coming decades, particularly as smart students discover they can go beyond the limits of traditional teaching methods. Indeed, in some instances, teachers may become guides and mentors along a learning path instead of the primary providers of information and understanding—the students, not teachers, become the core of the teaching and learning process. This is a sensitive subject among educators, so educational software is often positioned as "enrichening" the learning process, not as a potential substitute for traditional teacher-based methods.

An interactive episode of Wild Kingdom might start out with normal narration. "We're here in the Serengeti to learn about the animals." I see a lion on the screen, and think, "I want to learn about the lion." So I point at the lion, and it zooms up on the screen. The narration is now just about the lion. I say, "Well that's really interesting, but I wonder how the lion hunts." I point at a hunt icon. Now the lion is hunting and the narrator tells me about how it hunts. I dream about being the lion. I select another icon, and now see the world from the lion's point of view, making the same kinds of decisions the lion has to make—with some hints as I go along. I'm told how I'm doing, and how well I'm surviving. Kids could get very motivated from experiencing what it's like to be a lion, and from wanting to be a competent lion. Pretty soon they'd be digging deeper into the information resource, finding out about animals in different parts of the world, studying geography from maps displayed on the screen, learning which animals are endangered species...

Trip Hawkins, Chairman, Electronics Arts

Multimedia for learning takes many forms. Figure 1-4 shows Mercer Meyer's pioneering and award-winning "Just Grandma and Me," an animated story from Brøderbund, aimed at three- to eight-year-olds. Reading skills grow through word recognition: a mouse click on any word plays it back. The computer reads the story aloud, sometimes spelling words individually. Figure 1-5, at the other end of the educational continuum, shows the title screen from an advanced electronic teaching tool prepared by Yale University School of Medicine. It provides physicians with over 100 case presentations, and gives cardiologists, radiologists, medical students and fellows an opportunity for in-depth learning of new clinical techniques in nuclear cardiac perfusion imaging. Adults, as well as children, learn well by exploration and discovery.

Perhaps the most interesting use of multimedia in schools involves the students themselves. Late in 1993 in San Rafael, California, 12 Davidson Junior High School students put together perhaps the first interactive magazine for kids and called it the "San Rafael Community Express." They made original art using Fractal Design's Painter, interviewed students and townspeople, including the mayor, and made QuickTime movies (see Chapter 6). They wove their work into six sections on topics such as, "If you're a kid, how do you get treated at local restaurants?"

Supported by Kodak and Apple, Plugged In, a nonprofit organization dedicated to bringing new technologies to children of low-income communities, gave cameras to six students in East Palo Alto, California, who made

FIGURE 1-4

"Just Grandma and Me" is aimed at developing reading skills. It's also entertaining: click on the mailbox and a frog jumps out; the chimney coughs smoke; the telephone rings, and you hear Grandma's answering machine ■

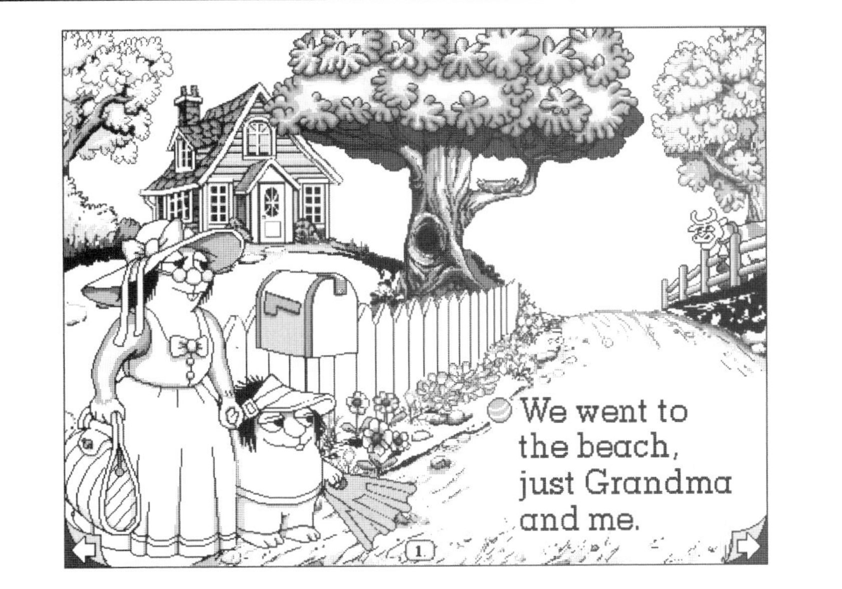

the award-winning "Escapes from the Zoo," a Portfolio format Photo CD that includes poignant first person views of their everyday lives.

FIGURE 1-5

This multimedia project from Yale University School of Medicine was written in SuperCard (see Chapter 8) ■

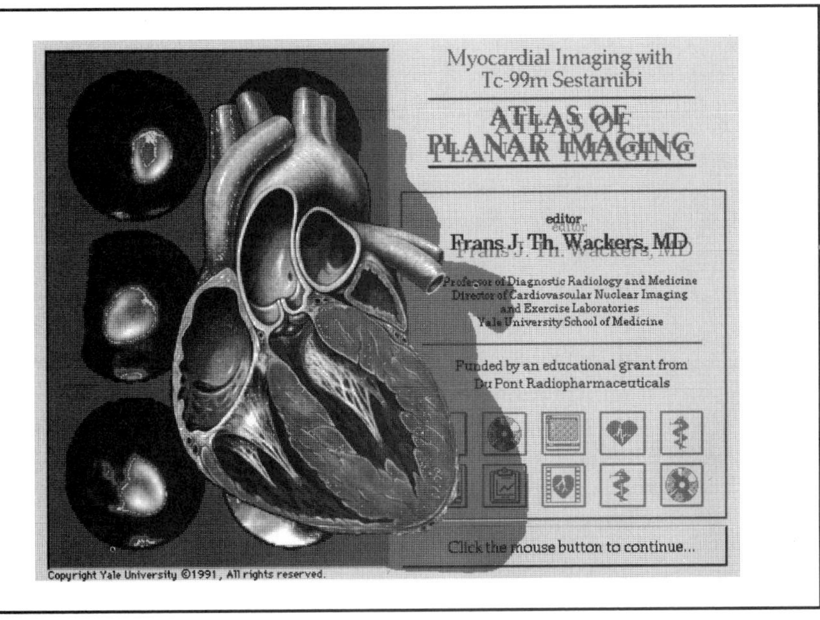

Laserdiscs currently bring the greatest amount of multimedia to the classroom. In 1994, more than 2,500 educational titles are available for grades K-12, the majority aimed at science and social science curricula. Use of laserdiscs will likely be supplanted as schools purchase more CD-ROM players and, later, as they become part of the National Information Infrastructure, when multimedia will arrive by glass fiber and network.

The technology is here to turn around the education system—all we lack is the will to make it happen.

David Bunnell, Editor in Chief, *NewMedia* magazine

Multimedia at Home

Eventually, most multimedia projects will reach the home via television sets or monitors with built-in interactive user inputs—either on old-fashioned color TVs or on new high-definition sets (see Chapter 13). The multimedia viewed on these sets will likely arrive on a pay-for-use basis along the data highway.

Today, however, the home consumer of multimedia either owns a computer with an attached CD-ROM drive or a set-top player that hooks up to the television, such as Kodak's Photo CD player, Philips's CD-I player, or Panasonic's 3DO player. Figure 1-6 shows several screens from an interactive Photo CD adventure travel disc aimed at home viewers; it was included in the 1994 catalog of treks and trips offered by Mountain Travel/Sobek of El Cerrito, California.

Many homes already boast Nintendo, Sega, or Atari game machines connected to the TV; newer game machines include CD-ROM drives and provide significantly more horsepower for displaying multimedia. There is increasing convergence of computer-based multimedia with entertainment and games-based media traditionally described as "shoot-em-up." Nintendo alone has sold over 100 million game players worldwide and more than 750 million games.

The Sega Channel (a joint venture of TCI, Time Warner, and Sega) will offer a library of games to home viewers. Prodigy, a dial-up computer information and shopping service with more than two million subscribers in 1993, will distribute set-top boxes. Interactive Network (IN) already provides interactive hand-held sets so home users can play along with televised sports and game shows, then send their scores to a national database for prizes.

Who lives in the multimedia consumer home? Late in 1993, Philips Consumer Electronics, makers of proprietary CD-I format set-top players,

FIGURE 1-6 A portfolio-formatted Kodak Photo CD disc lets you interactively browse through high-quality images shown on your television. Full stereo audio often accompanies the images

launched a 30-minute television infomercial to advertise and sell their set-top multimedia players to consumers. The target audience for this infomercial, according to Philips, was adults 30 to 50 years in age, 70 percent male and 30 percent female. This typical consumer has children between the ages of 2 and 11, is married, has been to college, earns more than $30,000 per year, and is open to new technology.

The home of the future will be very different when the cost of set-top players and multimedia televisions becomes mass-market affordable and the multimedia connection to the data highway is widely available. When the number of multimedia households increases from hundreds of thousands to many millions, a vast selection of multimedia titles and material will be required to satisfy the demands of this market, and vast amounts of money will be earned producing and distributing these products.

Multimedia lets you design a continuous discovery.

Sharon Klocek, Producer, Visual In-Seitz, Inc., ...while building parts, and parts, and parts

Multimedia in Public Places

In hotels, train stations, shopping malls, museums, and grocery stores, multimedia will become available at stand-alone terminals or kiosks to provide information and help. Such installations reduce demand on traditional information booths and personnel, add value, and they can work around the clock, even in the middle of the night, when live help is off-duty.

Figure 1-7 shows a menu screen from a supermarket kiosk that provides services ranging from meal planning to coupons. Hotel kiosks list nearby restaurants, maps of the city, airline schedules, and provide guest services such as automated checkout. Printers are often attached so users can walk away with a printed copy of the information. Museum kiosks are used not only to guide patrons through the exhibits, but to provide greater depth at each exhibit, allowing visitors to browse through rich, detailed information specific to that display.

CD-ROM

Application: *Director*
Macintosh Pathname: *MACROMEDIA :SltnDems :IntlgntH :Cascades CD Demo :Grocery Demo*
Windows Pathname: *SHOWCASE_CD \MACROMED \SLTNDEMS: \INTLGNTH: \CASCADES \GROCRYDM*

The power of multimedia in public places has been part of the human experience for many thousands of years: the mystical chants of monks, cantors, and shamans accompanied by potent visual cues, raised icons, and persuasive text has long been known to produce effective response. Scriabin,

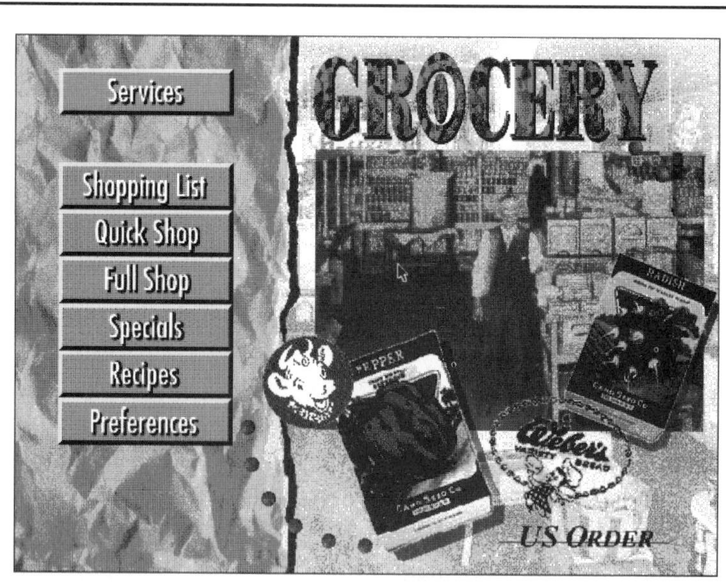

FIGURE 1-7 Kiosks in public places will make everyday life simpler

the 19th-century Russian composer, used an orchestra, a piano, a chorus, and a special color organ to synthesize music and color in his Fifth Symphony (Prometheus). Probably suffering from synesthesia (a strange condition where a sensory stimulus, such as a color, evokes a false response, such as a smell), Scriabin talked of tactile symphonies with burning incense scored into the work. He also claimed that colors can be heard. Table 1-1 lists the colors of his color organ.

Prometheus premiered before a live audience in Moscow in 1911, but the color organ had proved technologically too complicated and was eliminated from the program. Then Scriabin died suddenly of blood poisoning from a boil on his lip, so his ultimate multimedia vision, Mysterium, remained unwritten. He would have reveled in today's world of MIDI synthesizers (see Chapter 10), rich computer colors and video digitizers, and, though smell is not yet part of any multimedia standard, he would surely have researched that concept, too. The platforms for multimedia presentation have much improved since Scriabin's time.

Virtual Reality

In multimedia, where technology and creative invention converge you'll find virtual reality, or VR. Goggles, helmets, special gloves, and bizarre human interfaces attempt to place you "inside" a life-like experience. Take

Frequency (Hz)	Note	Scriabin's Color
256	C	Red
277	C#	Violet
298	D	Yellow
319	D#	Glint of steel
341	E	Pearly white shimmer of moonlight
362	F	Deep red
383	F#	Bright blue
405	G	Rosy orange
426	G#	Purple
447	A	Green
469	A#	Glint of steel
490	B	Pearly blue

TABLE 1-1 *Scriabin's Colors*

a step forward, and the view gets closer; turn your head, and the view rotates. Reach out and grab an object; your hand moves in front of you. Maybe the object explodes in a 90-decibel crescendo as you wrap your fingers around it. Or it slips out from your grip, falls to the floor, and hurriedly escapes through a mouse hole at the bottom of the wall.

VR requires terrific computing horsepower to be realistic. In VR, your cyberspace is made up of many thousands of geometric objects plotted in three-dimensional space: the more objects and the more points that describe the objects, the higher the resolution and the more realistic your view. As you move about, each motion or action requires the computer to recalculate the position, angle, size, and shape of ALL the objects that make up your view, and many thousands of computations must occur as fast as 30 times per second to seem smooth.

Using high-speed dedicated computers, multi-million-dollar flight simulators built by companies like Singer and RediFusion have led the way in commercial application of VR. Pilots of F-16s, Boeing 747s, and Rockwell space shuttles have made many dry runs before attempting the real thing. At the California Maritime Academy and other merchant marine officer training schools, computer-controlled simulators teach the intricate loading and unloading of oil tankers and container ships.

Figure 1-8 shows a rough model of the City of San Francisco rendered in Macromedia's ModelShop II at coordinates 37°48'0"North by 122°24'0" West. By adjusting the viewer's standpoint, the program will recompute the view. Note how jagged the lines are, particularly the curves of the suspension wires on the Bay Bridge at the left. With more points to define these objects, they would be much smoother, but it would also take significantly more time to render the view each time it changed. If you string together many rendered views into a movie, the result can be a realistic first-person fly-through or walk-through. Such tricks are very useful for architects, chemists, surgeons, and other professionals who wish to explore the virtual world they are working in. Most computer aided design (CAD) programs today offer three-dimensional capability (see Chapter 6); many even provide facilities for creating walk-throughs in digital movie formats.

CD-ROM

Application: *ModelShop II*
Macintosh Pathname: *MACROMEDIA :Product Demonstrations:Other 3D Demo App's:ModelShop II:Sample Models:San Francisco II*

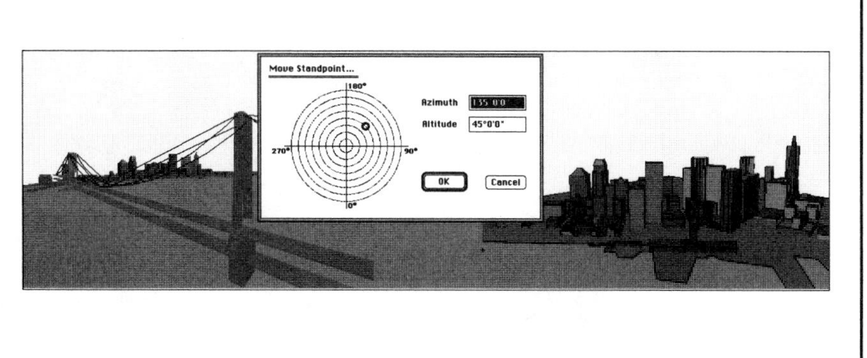

FIGURE 1-8

This city model is constructed and rendered from many individual geometric parts and shapes using MacroModel II.

Specialized public game arcades have been built recently to offer VR combat and flying experiences for a price. From Virtual World Entertainment in Walnut Creek, California and Chicago, Illinois for example, BattleTech is a 10-minute interactive video encounter with hostile robots. You compete against others, perhaps your friends, who share couches in the same Containment Bay. The computer keeps score in a fast and sweaty firefight. Similar "attractions" will bring VR to the public—particularly a youthful public—with increasing presence during the 1990s.

The technology and methods for working with three-dimensional images and for animating them is discussed in Chapters 11 and 12. VR is an extension of multimedia—it uses the basic multimedia elements of imagery, sound, and animation. Because it requires instrumented feedback from a wired-up person, VR is perhaps interactive multimedia at its fullest extension.

Multimedia is revolutionary and will change our lives. Markets are evolutionary, and consumers take incremental steps up the technology ladder. It will take about ten years for the multimedia seeds we plant today to fully bloom.

Sally von Bargen, 21st Century Media

Multi

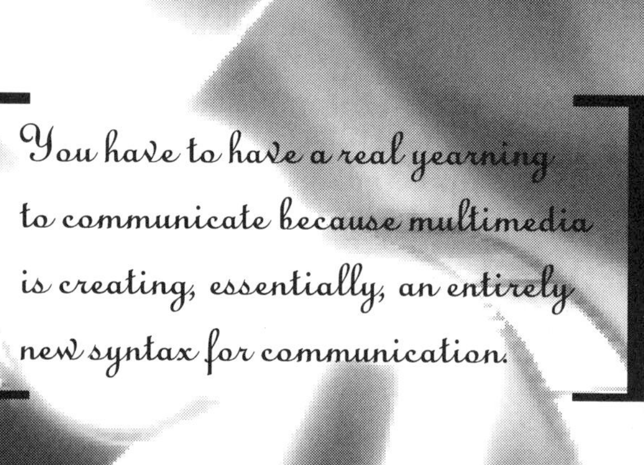

You have to have a real yearning to communicate because multimedia is creating, essentially, an entirely new syntax for communication.

good ideas

chapter 2

Introduction to Making Multimedia

You need hardware, software, and good ideas to make multimedia.

To make *good* multimedia, you need talent and skill.

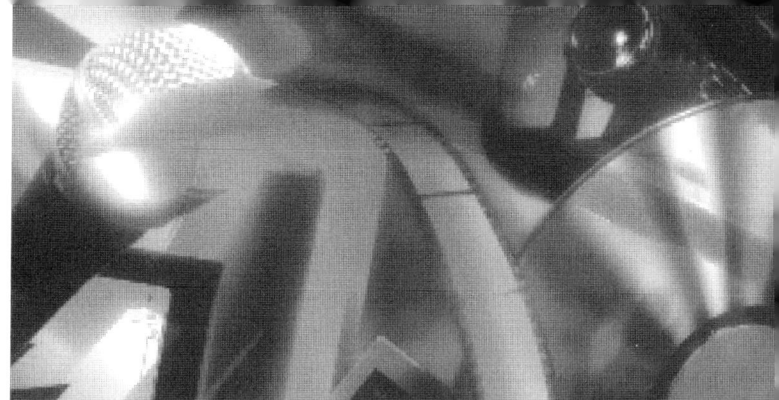

In Chapter 1 you learned what multimedia is, what it may become, and where you can experience it. In this chapter you will be introduced to the workshop where it is made. This chapter provides guidance and suggestions for getting started. Later, more detail is provided in Chapter 14. In Chapter 15 you will learn about producing, managing, and designing a project. In Chapter 16, you will learn about where to get material and content for your project, and in Chapters 17 and 18, you will learn how to test your work and ship it to end users. If you want to create multimedia yourself, from your own ideas and talents, check your skills against those described in Chapter 3.

The Stages of a Project

Most multimedia projects must be undertaken in stages. Some stages should be completed before other stages begin, and some stages may be skipped or combined. Here are the four basic stages in a multimedia project:

1. **Planning and Costing:** A multimedia project always begins with an idea or a need that you refine by outlining its messages and objectives. Identify how you will make each message and objective work within your authoring system. Before you begin developing, plan what writing skills, graphic art, music, video, and other multimedia expertise will be required. Develop a creative graphic look and feel, as well as a structure and navigation system that will let the viewer visit the messages and content. Estimate the time needed to do all elements, and prepare a budget. Work up a short prototype or proof-of-concept.
2. **Designing and Producing:** Perform each of the planned tasks to create a finished product.
3. **Testing:** Always test your multimedia programs to make sure they meet the objectives of your project, they work properly on the intended platforms, and they meet the needs of your client or end user.
4. **Delivering:** Package and deliver the project to the end user.

What You Need

You need hardware, software, and good ideas to make multimedia. To make *good* multimedia, you need talent and skill. You also need to stay organized, because as the construction work gets underway, all the little bits and pieces of multimedia content—the six audio recordings of Alaskan Eskimos, the Christmas-two-years-ago snapshot of your niece, the 41 articles still to scan with your optical character recognition (OCR) program—will get lost under growing piles of paper, cassettes, video tapes, disks, phone messages, permissions and releases, cookies, photocopies, and yesterday's mail. Even in serious offices, where people sweep all flat surfaces of paperwork and rubber bands at five o'clock, there will be mess.

You will need time and money (for consumable resources such as disks and other memory, for telephoning and postage, and possibly for paying for special services and time, yours included), and you will need to budget these precious commodities (see Chapter 14).

You may also need the help of other people. Multimedia is often a team effort: artwork is performed by graphic artists, video shoots by video producers, sound editing by audio producers, and programming by programmers (see Chapter 3). You will certainly wish to provide plenty of coffee and snacks, whether working alone or as a team. Late nights are often involved in the making of multimedia.

You have to have a real yearning to communicate because multimedia is creating, essentially, an entirely new syntax for communication. You must have an interest in human psychology because you need to anticipate the brainwaves of all the potential end users. What will they expect from the program now? What will they want to do with the program now? How can you integrate all the multimedia elements in a really elegant and powerful way? You should adopt a strategy that allows you to prototype and test your interactive design assumptions.

Ann Marie Buddrus, President, Digital Media Design

Hardware

This book will help you understand the two most significant platforms for producing and delivering multimedia projects: the Macintosh computer from Apple, and any Intel-based IBM-PC or PC clone computer running Microsoft Windows. These computers, with their graphical user interfaces and huge installed base of many millions of users throughout the world, are the most commonly used today for the development and delivery of multimedia. Certainly, detailed and animated multimedia is also created on Atari and Amiga computers and on specialized workstations from Silicon Graphics and even mainframes, but the Macintosh and the PC offer a compelling combination of affordability, software availability, and worldwide access. Regardless of the delivery vehicle for your multimedia—whether it is destined to play on a computer, on a television set-top box such as CD-I, 3DO, or Sega, or as bits moving down the data highway—most will probably be made on a Macintosh or on a PC. Or on one of the new-generation PowerPCs.

Hardware is discussed in greater detail in Chapter 4, and hardware peripherals such as monitors, disk drives, and scanners are described in Chapter 5. Audio hardware is discussed in Chapter 10 and video hardware is discussed in Chapter 13.

The basic principles for creating and editing multimedia elements are the same on Macintoshes and PCs. A bitmap is a bitmap, a digitized sound is a digitized sound, regardless of the methods or tools used to make and display it or play it back. Indeed, many software tools readily convert picture, sound, and other multimedia files (and even whole functioning projects) from Macintosh to PC/Windows format, and vice versa. In this book, this cross-platform icon will flag complicated or difficult issues in this area that need your special attention:

Multimedia, it's not just here, it's a $25,000 microcomputer and a $40,000 consulting fee.
Multimedia, it's not just here, it's twice the cost, three times the time, and half the results.
Multimedia, the zero billion dollar industry.

Chris Yalonis, VP Business Development, Passport Designs

Software

Multimedia software tells the hardware what to do. Display the color red. Move that tiger three leaps to the left. Slide in the words "Now You've Done It!" from the right and blink them on and off. Play the sound of cymbals crashing. Run the digitized movie of Captain Hook.

In this book, the discussion of software is divided into three parts, based on what the software is designed to do for you. In Chapter 6 you will learn about the basic software tools used to work with text, images, sounds, and video; you will also learn about handy tools for capturing screen images, translating between file formats, and editing your resources. Chapter 7 will show you how to use common tools, such as word processors, spreadsheets, and databases, for presenting instant multimedia—no special authoring systems are required. In Chapter 8, the increasingly wide selection of specialized multimedia authoring tools will be described in detail.

You do not have to be a programmer or a computer scientist to make multimedia work for you, but you do need some familiarity with terms and building blocks; even the simplest multimedia tools require a modicum of knowledge to operate. If someone asks to borrow a metric 13mm wrench, you should know they are probably working with a nut or a bolt. If someone sends you a file in Macintosh AIF format, you should know that you're getting digitized sound. Don't be afraid of the little things that so easily depress the uninformed. From plumbing to nuclear physics, learning just takes time and practice.

The Showcase CD-ROM from Macromedia included in this book contains examples and demonstrations of multimedia software applications and projects. When you come across the icon and pathnames shown below, it means that there is a file or application on the CD-ROM that illustrates a point made in the text of the book. The pathname describes where on the disc the example is located—see Appendix D for more details and a complete listing of all files available on the Showcase CD-ROM.

Application:	*Action*
Macintosh Pathname:	*MACROMEDIA :Product Demonstrations :Action Demo :Action demo disk :Action! Demonstration*
Windows Pathname:	*After installing the Showcase CD, click on the Action! Working Model Demo icon in the Windows Macromedia Showcase CD Program Group*

Creativity

Before you begin a multimedia project, you must first develop a sense of its scope and content. Let the project take shape in your head as you think through the various methods available to get your message across to your viewers.

The most precious asset you can bring to the multimedia workshop is your creativity. It's what separates run-of-the-mill and "underwhelming" multimedia from compelling, engaging, and award-winning products, whether for a short sales presentation viewed solely by colleagues within your firm or for a full-blown CD-ROM title.

You have a lot of room for creative risk-taking, because the rules for what works and what doesn't work are still being empirically discovered; there are few known formulas for the success of multimedia. Indeed, companies that produce a terrific multimedia title are usually rewarded in the marketplace, but their competitors reverse engineer the product, and six months later "knock-offs" using similar approaches and techniques appear on the market.

The evolution of multimedia is evident when you look at some of the first multimedia projects done on computers and compare them to today's titles. Taking inspiration from earlier experiments, developers modify and add their own creative touches to design their own unique multimedia projects. For example, "Just Grandma and Me" (see Figure 1-4 in Chapter 1) is an extension of techniques used in an earlier HyperCard children's game ("Cosmic Osmo"), which in turn is an extension of experiments with interactive virtual desktops in HyperCard. Click on the telephone and up pops a dialing directory, click on the calendar and see your schedule. Click on a flower and it grows. Click on Grandma, and she may warn you about sunscreen. Click on the umbrella, and it blows away in the wind.

It is very difficult to learn creativity. Some might say it's impossible—one is born with it. But like classical artists who work in paint, marble, or bronze, the better you know your medium, the better able you are to express your creativity. For multimedia, this means you need to know your hardware and software first. Once you are proficient with the hardware and software tools, what then can you build that will look great, sound great, and knock the socks off the viewer? The rhetorical answer is simply "How creative are you?" Check out Chapters 14 and 15.

First Person

The Credit Alligator usually appears late in a multimedia project and has nothing to do with MasterCard or Visa. This gnarly animal typically lives unseen in the delicate fringes of workgroup politics, but can appear with great distraction during beta testing, adding moments of personal tension and occasionally destroying friendships and business relationships.

After hard cash, the most satisfying remuneration for your sweaty effort and late-night creative contributions to a multimedia project is to see your name on the credit screen. Indeed, this visible credit is a special high-value currency because it can be added to your portfolio to help you land the next job; the more of this currency, the higher your potential wage. And the more likely you will remain employed doing the things you like to do.

Start building defenses against this alligator up front. When you negotiate the original contract with whomever pays the multimedia bill, be sure to include wording such as: "We shall be allowed to include a production credit display on the closing screen or in another

(continued)

First Person

mutually agreeable position in the finished work." If you are an individual who is contracting to a producer, be sure it is understood that IF there is a credit screen, your name will be on it.

*Not all clients will stand for a credit screen. Apple Computer, for example, uses many outside contractors to produce multimedia, but as a company policy rarely allows contributors to be credited by name. Some contractors and frustrated employees develop ingenious work-arounds and indirections to bury these important intellectual credits within their work. For example, in an excellent book written by a team of skilled Apple people and published officially by Addison-Wesley (*HyperCard Stack Design Guidelines *by Apple Computer, Inc.) you may discover a list of talented instructional designers, illustrators, writers, and editors in Figure 3-3, an unassuming bitmapped screen grab showing an "About" box. The real people that wrote the book are buried there, in the example credit screen.*

The Credit Alligator raises its head over the little things, too, and there are often no defenses. If your name begins with a letter that is toward the end of the alphabet, it may never appear first on the list of contributors, even if your contribution was major. Of course, if your name is Walsh or Young, you have endured this ordering system since first-grade lineups. Warning: reversing an alphabetic credit list from last to first will only create or heighten tension; to propose such a list is, in itself, ego-driven and self-serving. Learn to live with it.

The most treacherous place where the Credit Alligator lives is in the busy time of finalizing a project and going gold. If you are not participating in the final mastering but have contributed a piece or pieces to the project, you must trust the masterer to do it right. But it doesn't always happen right.

One company recently consulted on a job where their work represented the second-greatest contribution from a group of about fifteen contributors, all of whom had credit screens. Their contract required credit, but in the final version of the storyboard they discovered their screen buried at the end of a four-minute linear sequence of all the other credits and advertisements. They asked the producer to move it up. "Sorry," said the producer, "it was an oversight." Then in the last-minute process of resequencing, the producer also switched that company's custom music to his own company's credit screen, leaving our friend's screen attached to a pretty ugly left-over sound byte. Because the company was not included in the final feedback and approval loop, they discovered this "little mistake" only after mass replication. It's tough to change 50,000 shrink-wrapped CD-ROMs, so there was nothing to say.

Crediting creative talent is sensitive stuff. Avoid recurring bouts with the Credit Alligator by publicizing among your people your policy about credit screens. Talk about intellectual credit openly, not as a last-minute thing. Negotiate hard for inclusion of credit in all the projects you undertake for clients. Indeed, multimedia doesn't spring from the bankrolls of investors and publishers, but is the result of the hard work of talented real people.

From the monthly column "Alligators" by Tay Vaughan, first printed in *Morph's Outpost*, December, 1993.

warning *If you are managing a multimedia project, remember that creative talent is priceless, so be certain to reward it well. If you don't, you may find that your talent takes a job elsewhere, even at lower pay!*

Organization

It's essential that you develop an organized outline and a plan that is rational in terms of what skills, time, budget, tools, and resources are at hand. They should be in place before you start to render graphics, sounds, and other components, and they should continue to be monitored throughout the project's execution. Chapter 14 provides planning and costing models for a multimedia project, and Chapter 15 discusses the details of multimedia project management.

Multi

Multimedia developers come from all corners of the computer, art, literary, film, and audio worlds.

Are multimedia developers computer scientists?

no traditional mold

media

chapter 3

Multimedia Skills and Training

Or are they programmers, graphic artists, animators, storyboard craftspeople, **musicians,** instructional designers, or Renaissance authors?

A recent study reported that physicians, dentists, and computer scientists share highest honors for the most respected professions in the United States. Are multimedia developers computer scientists? Or are they programmers, graphic artists, musicians, animators, storyboard craftspeople, instructional designers, and/or Renaissance authors? However you define them, multimedia developers come from all corners of the computer, art, literary, film, and audio worlds. Video producers become expert with computer-generated animation and MIDI controls for their edit suites. Architects become bored with two-dimensional drafting and create three-dimensional animated walk-throughs. Oil field engineers get tired of FORTRAN and design mouse-driven human interfaces. Classical painters learn the electronic elements of red, green, and blue and create fantastic computer-based artwork. A multimedia developer might be any or all of these and typically fits no traditional management information systems (MIS) or computer science mold; many have never seen a line of COBOL code or booted up an IBM 3090 mainframe.

Consider Leonardo da Vinci, the Renaissance man who was scientist, architect, builder, creative designer, craftsman, and poet folded into one. To produce good multimedia, you will need a similar diverse range of skills—detailed knowledge of computers, text, graphic arts, sound, and video. These skills, the *multimedia skillset,* may be available in a single individual or, more likely, in a composite team of individuals. Complex multimedia projects are, indeed, often assembled by teams of artists and computer craftspeople, where tasks can be delegated to those most skilled and competent in a particular discipline or craft. Many job titles and collaborative team roles for multimedia development are being adapted from a mix of motion picture industry and computer software industry experiences.

When I was young, I started in "media" as a disc jockey and news director on radio. It was one medium. I then progressed to doing movies and slide shows with audio, calling it multiple media. When video took over from film, I moved into print media and paper, the original medium for mass communications when people knew how to read. Now, much of what I do starts out in electronic form on the PC, so I guess I'm into yet another medium. What I see being called "Multimedia" seems to be all of the above displayed on a CRT [cathode ray tube], and it all looks vaguely familiar as what I was doing years ago with projectors on walls. So I guess you might say that multimedia today is the same old stuff packaged in a modern box, it just doesn't use the walls...

Tom Inglesby, Editor of *Manufacturing Systems* magazine, who has seen it all

The Multimedia Team

A recent survey, developed by instructors David Vasquez and Helayne Waldman of the Multimedia Studies Program at the San Francisco State University Extension, defined major categories of multimedia production skills:

- *Project manager*
- *Multimedia designer* (including information designers, graphic designers, illustrators, animators, image processing specialists, instructional designers, and interface designers)
- *Writer*
- *Video specialist*
- *Audio specialist*
- *Multimedia programmer*

Often, individual members of multimedia production teams wear several hats: graphic designers may also do interface design, scanning, and image processing. A project manager or producer may also be the video producer. Depending on the scope and content of your project and the mix of people required, a team may also employ animators, art directors, composers and musicians, content developers, creative directors, digital special effects engineers, editors, photographers, researchers, videographers, and others.

Mere possession of the equipment does not make one into a videographer, film editor, set designer, scriptwriter, audio engineer, animator, and programmer. Some people do possess all of the innate talents required to produce decent multimedia, but few have mastered all the skills required to bring a major project to fruition. More typically, world-class productions are realized through the teamwork of a variety of talented people with specialized experience.

Jeff Burger, Creative Technologies, in "Sound Off," *NewMedia* magazine, March 1993

warning *A multimedia expert working alone will be hard-pressed to compete with a team of experts, and may be overwhelmed by the sheer amount of effort required to build a complex project single-handedly.*

Project Manager

A project manager's role is at the center of the action. He or she is responsible for overall development and implementation of a project as well as for day-to-day operations. Budgets, schedules, creative sessions, time sheets, illness, invoices, team dynamics—the project manager is the glue that holds everything together.

Mark Williams

Microsoft's *Cinemania* CD-ROM is a comprehensive, authoritative guide to the movies and the people who make them, and it's designed for computer-owning film lovers (see Figure 3-1). Producing Cinemania involved a core team headed by project manager Mark Williams with additional specialists, technicians, and assistants brought on board as needed.

At Microsoft, project managers are called program managers but it means exactly the same thing. The program manager has two major areas of responsibility: design and management. Design consists of devising a vision for the product and working out the complete functionality with the design team, and then putting that into a complete functional spec and adjusting it as necessary throughout the development of the product. The management side consists of scheduling and assigning tasks, running meetings, managing milestones—essentially overseeing all aspects of product development from beginning to end.

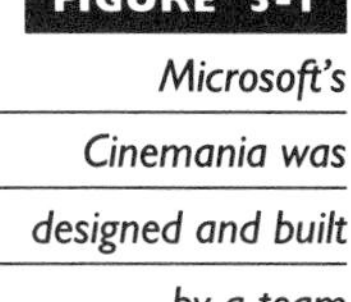

FIGURE 3-1 *Microsoft's Cinemania was designed and built by a team*

Our core team consisted of myself, a subject matter expert, which at Microsoft we call an editor, a graphic designer, and a programmer called a software development engineer. Another important team member was the product manager—the marketing person who represents the product to the outside world. We also found that it was very valuable to get early design input from the person who creates the online and printed help for the product and from the person who eventually manages the testing of the product.

In the production phase we brought in additional talent for scanning images, digitizing sound, proofreading, and other production tasks. We also utilized numerous specialists along the way, such as an audio producer to secure soundtrack material and, crucially, acquisitions specialists.

The acquisitions folks were vital to the effort because we were trying to get a variety of media from people who really didn't understand what we were doing. The second version has been much easier because the studios and license holders saw the product and can now visualize how it works.

Speccing the right content and being able to acquire it was critical. Our pictures and content are all of the highest quality and the design is clear and easy to use. Keeping a vision of the product in mind—making sure that the design really meets the needs of the end user—is very important. Constant usability testing gives us a way to keep the end user involved in the design process.

A good project manager must completely understand the strengths and limitations of hardware and software so that he or she can make good decisions about what to do and what not to do. Aside from that I'd say the most important skills are people skills (keeping your team happy and motivated), organizational skills, and attention to all the myriad details of a project. At the same time it's critical to keep the big picture, the vision, in mind so that everything that needs to get done does in fact get done.

PROJECT MANAGER/INTERFACE EXPERT

Multimedia company looking to immediately fill position on interactive television project for major telecommunications company. Project manager needed to manage production and design efforts on large-scale interactive television project for air in western United States.

- Must be adept and experienced at managing complex projects, preferably with large corporate accounts.
- Must have solid understanding of interactivity and experience with interactive media—ideally interactive television.
- Must have several years of experience with interface design or management thereof and have good design sensibilities.
- Communication skills a must; must be an articulate and effective communicator, an excellent listener, and act as a conduit for information between our team and the client's teams.
- Superior attention to detail and ability to coordinate large amounts of information a must.
- Prefer entertainment experience—ideally television or video production.
- Solid computer or digital media experience and knowledge a must.
- Travel required to visit focus groups and gather consumer information.
- Must function well in fast-paced team-oriented environment.
- Position must be filled immediately.

Multimedia Designer

The look and feel of a successful multimedia project is pleasing and aesthetic, inviting and engaging. Screens present an appealing mix of color, shape, and type. The project maintains visual consistency, using only those elements that support the overall message of the program. Navigation clues are clear and consistent, icons are meaningful, and screen elements are simple and straightforward. If the project is instructional, it's designed to be sensitive to the needs and styles of its learner population while demonstrating sound instructional principles and promoting mastery of subject matter. Who puts it all together?

Graphic designers, illustrators, animators, and image processing specialists deal with the visuals. Instructional designers make sure that the subject matter is clear and properly presented. Interface designers devise the navigation pathways and content maps. Information designers structure content, determine user pathways and feedback, and select presentation media based on an awareness of the strengths of the many separate media that comprise multimedia.

Kurt Andersen

Kurt Andersen has been an instructional designer for the past six years. Most recently, he was a senior designer at the George Lucas Educational Foundation, where he designed multimedia prototypes for middle school math and science curricula. Currently he is a consultant in the fields of multimedia and information design and development.

A multimedia designer often wears many hats, but most importantly he or she looks at the overall content of a project, creates a structure for the content, determines the design elements required to support that structure, and decides which media are appropriate for presenting which pieces of content. In essence, the multimedia designer (sometimes called an information designer) prepares the blueprint for the entire project: content, media, and interaction.

From an interactive standpoint, many multimedia projects are too passive—you click and watch. The challenge is to get beyond what is appealing visually and design products to be activity-based. A multimedia project needs to be truly interactive, and this means you have to have a clear picture of what goes on whenever the user interacts with the program.

Advances in technology are bringing us closer to this. For example, one of the most interesting things going on is the development of adaptive systems—systems that accept user input and modify themselves based on this input. In training projects, they're called intelligent tutors. Right now, we're working on a medical application that will analyze a patient's history and background to present information that is personalized to that particular patient.

I was recently a member of two different teams that developed multimedia prototypes for middle school science and mathematics at the George Lucas Educational Foundation. Our approach was to develop prototypes that might be distributed as exemplars of rigorous, engaging, effective multimedia design using leading edge technology. The real challenge was to create a program that presented mathematics so that users could play, explore, and develop their own conceptual schema around the concepts we were developing. We were also challenged to implement our ideas from a technological standpoint. For example, we wound up hooking up a high-end rendering machine so that we could do 3D graphics on the fly.

Multimedia designers need a variety of skills. You need to be able to analyze content structurally and match it up with effective presentation methods. You need to be an expert on different media types and be a capable media integrator, in order to create an overall vision. The ability to look at information from different points of view and a willingness to shift your own point of view to be empathetic with end users are absolutely essential. So are interpersonal skills, because you spend so much of your time interacting with other team members, with clients, and extracting information from subject matter experts. You must be able to "talk the talk" with all of them. Finally, you must understand the capabilities of your resources, both technological and human, and know when to push ahead and when to stop.

MULTIMEDIA DESIGNER/
PRODUCER

Seeking an experienced new media professional who loves inventing the future and enjoys the challenge of integrating complex information and media systems. Our ideal candidate has solid experience in interface design, product prototyping, and marketing communication. A knowledge of image manipulation is critical, as well as proven skills in Lingo scripting and the use of digital time-based authoring tools. We seek a team player with excellent communication skills and grace under pressure.

* Must have experience designing large information and/or entertainment systems.
* Must have experience creating system flows and program architectures.
* Must have solid organizational skills and attention to detail.

Interface Designer

Like a good film editor, an interface designer's best work is never seen by the viewer; it's "transparent." In its simplest form, an interface provides control to the people who use it. It also provides access to the "media" of multimedia—the text, graphics, animation, audio, and video—without calling attention to itself. The elegant simplicity of a multimedia title screen, the ease with which a user can move about within a project, the effective use of windows, backgrounds, icons, and control panels...these are the results of an interface designer's work.

Nicole Lazzaro

Nicole Lazzaro is an interface designer with ONYX Productions in Oakland, California and teaches interface design in the San Francisco State

University's Multimedia Studies Program. She spends her days thinking of new ways to design multimedia interfaces that feel more like real life.

The role of an interface designer is to create a software device that organizes the multimedia content, that lets the user access or modify that content, and that presents the content on screen. These three areas—information design, interactive design, and media design—are central to the creation of any interface, but of course they overlap.

In the real world, design responsibilities are often assigned differently depending on the project. An interface designer may also be the multimedia designer or the graphic designer. Sometimes all of the design is given to one person; sometimes it is divided among group members; and sometimes the interface springs from the group as a whole. In the best of all worlds everyone has input into the final vision, but realistically, everyone also has other responsibilities outside of interface design. The advantage of dedicating one team member experienced in a number of interface solutions to this particular task is to make sure the end user does not get left out of the equation. A good interface designer will create a product that rewards exploration and encourages use. You have to design the interface from the ground up, not just slap on some graphics and fancy icons after most of the programming is done.

A crucial skill is being familiar with a lot of multimedia interfaces so that you are able to visualize ideas as they are discussed. What is the best way to represent this function? Will this program look better using a hierarchical menu or a book metaphor? What will be the user's experience? Being familiar with film or video editing can be helpful, because telling a story with sounds and images is what most multimedia experiences are all about. From a visual perspective, cinematography and film editing are, I think, the closest parallels to what we would call interface design. These techniques can seamlessly change a point of view or tell a story more effectively and are being used by interface designers today. Knowing an authoring system is also crucial, so you can develop your ideas in some interactive fashion and be able to present them to your design group. Having basic drawing skills also helps, because then you can describe how a screen looks using pencil and paper. Also, know how to do user testing, and do lots of it!

The most challenging interface I ever designed was for a project called Take Control, developed by InfoUse of Berkeley [see Figure 3-2]. It's an AIDS education project for people with mental retardation. It was exciting for me to do because we had an important message, and the audience had very special needs. We wanted to use interactive media to give our users control over their own learning. But the people we were trying to reach might not know what a computer was or how to operate one—and they might not know how to read. So we decided to base the interface on what we could guarantee our audience had experienced before: real life and television. We chose to map people's natural tendency to reach out and point, and made this be the way to control the navigation and content delivery using a touch screen. We limited the use of text and created "buttonless" menus from stills of the actual video. Because we poured the content into three characters, the learner could touch and follow them to hear what they had to say. Using a touch screen to directly manipulate video images literally lets us achieve the best interface design, it was as transparent as possible!

Artist/Designer needed to create graphics for interactive multimedia titles aimed at children. Solid experience in graphic design, including knowledge of Adobe Photoshop and Adobe Premiere. Must have superior illustration ability. Must have experience in animation. Experience in video graphics (Paintbox, Hari, etc.) a plus.

Writer

Multimedia writers do everything writers of linear media do, and more. They create character, action, and point of view—a traditional scriptwriter's tools of the trade—and they also create interactivity. They write proposals, they script voice-overs and actors' narrations, they write text screens to deliver messages, and they develop characters designed for an interactive environment.

FIGURE 3-2 *A book metaphor was used in Take Control—users can touch a picture for details or close the book by touching the hand*

Writers of text screens are sometimes referred to as content writers—they glean information from content experts, synthesize it, and then communicate it in a clear and concise manner. Scriptwriters write dialog, narration, and voice-overs. Both often become involved in overall design.

Domenic Stansberry

Domenic Stansberry is a writer/designer currently working with Adair & Armstrong on an interactive drama for Brøderbund. He has also written for documentary film and published two books of fiction.

The role of the writer changes with each different project, depending on the people you're working with. But multimedia writing is always different from writing a film or video script. In a film or video you're plotting a story the way a dramatist or novelist would. With multimedia, it can be more difficult: you're still thinking dramatically, but in smaller, more discrete units that have to interrelate to each other, that have to be compiled into a puzzle of sorts.

In traditional drama there are characters and an inevitability about what happens to those characters. You build circumstances that have certain significance for your characters as they go on to meet their destiny. In multimedia, we plot out stories that can go many different ways. This is inherently contradictory to the way we've thought about dramatic structure. Intelligent writers are still working hard to invent interactive dramatic structures: we see some attempts in games, which are obstacle driven. The user needs to perform a task and is presented with an obstacle—a need to overcome the obstacle and move on. This is not unlike the position a character takes in a story or movie where characters are presented with physical or psychological obstacles and must find a way to get beyond them. It's really too bad that writers are not brought in on more game projects...the quality of the interaction would be much higher.

I work best when I am involved at the conceptual level of a project, but in many projects, it is the flowcharts that are generated first. Then as the writing process unfolds, you find that the flowchart doesn't work because the material isn't what the flowchart wants it to be. When you're working on a dramatic script, you have to make the characters and the drama work first, before you start doing flowcharts. So if the writer is invited into the process at Step 7 and handed a flowchart, you're going to run into a problem. Another problem lies in working with people who are mainly from computer backgrounds. They are used to the writer as a writer of documentation—someone who comes in at the end of a project and writes a manual about how the product works. Computer people are often very uncomfortable with media people playing a role at the heart of the creative process. You need to develop a sense about where other team members are coming from when you are brought on to a project, and try to educate them if necessary.

But in the final analysis, the producer or project manager has got to be the person to handle conflict in differing team member's visions. A good producer will get the most out of the team members by getting team members to work not against each other but together toward their strengths. There are bound to be competing visions on a project, and in the best case scenario, the team members will work out their differences through a consensus process. But if they can't, the producer has to have a guiding vision.

MULTIMEDIA WRITER needed for multimedia kiosk in retail outlet. Must be familiar with interactive design and user interface issues. Background in marketing or copywriting a plus. Ability to work under tight deadlines in a team environment essential. Candidates will be asked to provide writing samples.

Video Specialist

A video specialist on a multimedia project may be just one person and a camcorder. Or, for projects requiring extensive amounts of sophisticated video, a video specialist may be responsible for an entire team of videographers, sound technicians, lighting designers, set designers, script supervisors, gaffers, grips, production assistants, and actors. In a multimedia project, a video specialist must be a seasoned professional, skilled in managing all phases of production, from concept to final edit. Team production of video can be very expensive and may be more than necessary to produce good multimedia projects today.

Since the early 1990s, digital video presentation methods such as Apple's QuickTime or Microsoft's Video for Windows (see Chapter 6) have married increasingly capable hardware and software so that editing and preparing video on Macintoshes and PCs has become affordable to multimedia developers. In addition to knowing the basics about shooting good video, multimedia video specialists must also be thoroughly familiar with the tools and techniques used for digital editing on computers.

Hank Duderstadt

Hank Duderstadt has worked as an independent video producer, director, and video editor specializing in promotions/commercials, corporate marketing, education, broadcast programming, and multimedia production.

A multimedia video specialist does much more than just shoot and edit video. He or she must understand the potentials and limitations of the medium, how these limitations affect the video production itself, and how to get the most out of the video. He or she must also understand interactivity and how it will affect the video. Shooting in traditional styles, you will end up with footage that doesn't work, and there is always a tendency to overcompensate, ending up with video that is little more than gimmicky. With experience, you learn the tricks that make a video look larger than it really is without looking gimmicky.

When you are shooting footage that will end up on CD-ROM, you have to realize in all probability it won't be full screen, full motion. At best it could be half-screen size at 20 frames per second; or at worst, the size of a postage stamp, with 10 frames per second. Wide panoramas and complex camera moves get lost or don't work. The best shots are medium to close-ups. While video may play back in a limited screen size using today's technology, full screen video will soon become a reality, so shoot your material on the best format available—BetaSP is ideal— and allow time to grab library shots that also work with larger screen displays.

Another thing to decide is whether to build sets, or just shoot your talent in front of a blue screen, compositing later with computer-generated environments. If this is the case, it's important to know exactly what the environment looks like before you shoot, so the talent can be easily incorporated into the scene.

Programs like Premiere, MetaFlo, Video Graffiti, and After FX are equal to, and often surpass what you might find at a traditional video production facility, but, don't let the ability to do all these incredible things overwhelm your vision. It's very easy to create video that loses the viewer because the editor became so thrilled with all the fancy effects!

> **VIDEO SPECIALIST** wanted for multimedia production. Must have strong background in video direction and editing. Good understanding of shooting for interactive programming required. Strong background working with blue screen a plus.

Audio Specialist

The quality of audio elements can make or break a multimedia project. Audio specialists are the wizards who make a multimedia program come alive, designing and producing music, voice-over narrations, and sound effects. They perform a variety of functions on the multimedia team, and they may enlist help from one or many others: composers, audio engineers, or recording technicians. Audio specialists may be responsible for locating and selecting suitable music and talent, scheduling recording sessions, and digitizing and editing recorded material into computer files (see Chapter 10).

Chip Harris

Chip Harris studied trumpet and electronic music composition at the Peabody Conservatory of Music, and he has worked with the noted composer Jean Eichelberger Ivy. He has recorded releases on major and independent labels, including Atlantic, RCA, and Warner Bros., has composed music for CD-ROM titles for Virgin Games and Timestream, and has created soundtracks for Clio and Joey award-winning spots.

What makes a good soundtrack—the music, voice over, and sound effects—is the same, whether the final mix is delivered in analog or digital format. In digital multimedia, though, you have to worry about how much space is available for a project, and you do a lot of figuring to optimize the sample rates that particular sounds are digitized at to still sound decent. It helps to know little tricks, like what kinds of sounds still sound OK at lower sample rates, because you can save considerable amounts of space.

An audio specialist needs a hybrid of talents and interests. Working with multimedia, you need to have more creative and technical knowledge than a traditional sound artist/engineer. A composer, for example, should know the capabilities and limitations of not only the musical instruments for which he is writing, but also the electronic environment. The only way I think you can acquire this knowledge is through hours and hours of hands-on experience and endless button-pushing and experimentation.

> **MULTIMEDIA**
> **AUDIO SPECIALIST**
> Audio Specialist needed for multimedia project.
>
> Must have strong background in studio recording techniques—preferably with time spent in the trenches as an engineer in a commercial studio working on a wide range of projects. Must be comfortable working with computers and be open and able to learn new technology and make it work with high quality results. Familiarity with standard recording practices, knowledge of music production, and the ability to work with artists a definite plus. Requires fluency in MIDI; experience with sequencing software, patch librarians, and synth programming; and a knowledge of sampling/samplers, hard disk recording, and editing. In addition to having a solid technical foundation, you must be able to survive long hours in the studio riding faders and pushing buttons.

Multimedia Programmer

A multimedia programmer or software engineer integrates all of the multimedia elements of a project into a seamless whole using an authoring system or programming language (see Chapter 8). Multimedia programming functions range from coding simple displays of multimedia elements to controlling peripheral devices, such as laser disc players, and managing complex timing, transitions, and record keeping. Creative multimedia programmers can coax extra (and sometimes unexpected) performance from multimedia authoring and programming systems. Without programming talent, there can be no multimedia. Code, whether written in HyperTalk, OpenScript, Lingo, Authorware, or C++, is the sheet music played by a well rehearsed orchestra.

Hal Wine

Hal Wine is a programmer familiar with both the Macintosh and Windows environments. In his many years of experience, he has worked in most of the important areas of computing and for many of the leading computing companies. He currently is a consultant in the San Francisco Bay Area.

The programmer on a multimedia team is called on to perform a number of tasks, from assisting producers in organizing their code more effectively to enhancing the production and playback tools. The most important skill a multimedia programmer can bring to a team is the ability to quickly learn and understand systems. And not just understand the various calls, but know why those calls are needed. In other words, to be able to read between the lines of the technical manuals, so that your solutions are harmonious with the philosophy and intent of the system designers.

Multimedia products are displayed on a large variety of display systems, and the enhancement needed often requires going behind the normal system safeguards to meet the objective. Such programming requires a thorough understanding of the target operating system and device capabilities to produce a robust solution.

While multimedia authoring tools are continually improving, they are still evolving. Many times a producer will want to do something slightly beyond the built-in capabilities of the tools, and the programmer will build extensions to the authoring and presentation suite in order to add the desired capability or effect.

Many of the workers on a multimedia team have come to computing from a background in another discipline such as graphic art or journalism, and while they may have strong creative skills, most can benefit from learning more about computing techniques. Often, a multimedia programmer acts as a teacher and technical coach to the team. This implies having better than average communication and comprehension skills, both verbal and written, and the ability to listen!

I often come in to handle "emergencies" in multimedia projects, rather than participate in the whole project's life cycle. This provides me with maximum variety in my own work, which really keeps me on my toes. Sometimes I'll be working for several clients simultaneously. The down-side is that I miss out on a lot of the creative synergy; but even so, coming in at the spur of the moment, trying to understand the parameters of the problem, and producing robust solutions quickly leads to quite a bit of creativity, too! Knowing how to make your own latte is also useful.

INTERACTIVE PROGRAMMER needed to work on multimedia prototyping and authoring tools for CD-ROM and interactive television projects.
- Thorough knowledge of HyperTalk and C/C++, Macintosh environment required.
- 3DO and MPC knowledge desirable.
- Must have working familiarity with digital media, particularly digital video.
- Must have a demonstrated track record of delivering quality programming on tight schedule.
- Must function well in fast-paced team-oriented environment.

The Sum of the Parts

Successful multimedia projects begin with selecting "team players." But selection is only the beginning of a team-building process that must continue through a project's duration. *Team-building* refers to activities that help a group and its members function at optimum levels of performance by creating a work culture incorporating the styles of its members: you should encourage communication styles that are fluid and inclusive, and you should develop models for decision making that respect individual talents, expertise, and personalities. This is not easy, but repeated studies have shown that workgroup managers with well developed "team" skills are more successful than managers who dive headlong into projects without attention to team dynamics. While it is usually a project manager who initiates team-building, all team members should recognize their role; gentle collaboration is a key element of successful projects.

Training Opportunities in Multimedia

Staying at the leading edge is very important. If you remain knowledgeable about what's new and expected, you will be more valuable to your own endeavors and to prospective clients. But be prepared for steep learning curves and difficult challenges in keeping your own skills and those of your employees current and in demand.

tip *If you are looking for skilled multimedia people, try placing a Help Wanted ad in one of the special-interest group forums on CompuServe, America OnLine, AppleLink, or a local or national bulletin board such as those operated by the Boston Computer Society (BCS) or the Berkeley Macintosh User Group (BMUG). Job seekers will also find these forums valuable.*

Formal Training

College-level academic programs as well as fee-based commercial programs run by private companies and organizations have become big business. Multimedia is booming, and many people want to learn the new tools and techniques. Arizona State, New York University, Andrews University in Michigan, Georgia Tech, University of Toronto, San Francisco State University, and others offer degree programs or continuing education units in interactive technologies. A list of some universities and colleges offering academic programs in multimedia can be found in Appendix B.

Bob Bell

Bob Bell is currently Director of the Multimedia Studies Program at San Francisco State University, Extended Education Division. He believes that a comprehensive education in multimedia must include more than a mastery of software applications.

Although we are very respectful of the need for programs dealing with the technology, we believe that the future for the development of the field is related to the development of what *Economist* magazine recently called "technobohemians." So we are trying hard not to be a training school per se, but to establish the atmosphere of the French *atelier* or studio. We must examine the very structure of this multimedia phenomenon and its potential effects on society and social discourse. I have grave concerns that multimedia remain a democratic, open-ended means of expression. This is one of our primary commitments.

Getting into multimedia, it would certainly help to have more than a nodding acquaintance with how computers function. But it's not necessarily essential. Someone who is involved with law as it relates to multimedia may not require the technology competence. At the moment, our program at San Francisco State reflects the way the film business is organized. There are five independent but interrelated activities: development, finance, production, marketing, and distribution. It's under these categories that our courses are structured. We see many students leave our program with a very specialized set of skills in just one of these areas.

As multimedia educators, we have a marvelous opportunity here to explore and perhaps inflect the next wave of human development and understanding. We must strive to keep the educational process moving forward before exclusivity sets in. We must keep questions open. This will require, more than ever, an educated electorate and practicing professionals who care about these issues.

Internship and Fellowship Programs

One way to get your feet wet in multimedia is to intern at a company producing multimedia titles or custom multimedia programs. Most academic programs offer students unpaid and occasionally paid internships, and some companies will accept interns who are not affiliated with any academic program. The greatest value of an internship lies in its ability to help you develop a portfolio of work that you can bring around to prospective employers. Employers are looking for multimedia developers with proven competence. Multimedia fellowships (where students study free or are paid a stipend) are more difficult to find but may become increasingly available as multimedia carves a niche in the academic world.

Helayne Waldman

In 1990, a special fellowship program was set up by the Bay Area Video Coalition (BAVC) in San Francisco, California and the MacArthur Foundation. Helayne Waldman was co-director of the Interact Program at BAVC for two years and recalls how this program jump started more than a few multimedia careers.

Our goals for the Interact Program were twofold, really. On the one hand we wanted to provide a fellowship program for professionals in related fields—graphic arts, video and film, software development, and education. We wanted to bring a team of professionals together and teach them how to transition their already well developed skills into a larger skillset that encompassed multimedia. At the same time we were committed to offering that training at no cost to the fellows.

Our second goal was to introduce the nonprofit sector in the San Francisco Bay Area to the power of multimedia. Project teams were matched up with nonprofit clients such as the National Task Force on AIDS Prevention, SeniorNet, Strategies for Media Literacy, and the California Academy of Sciences. Under the direction of myself and codirector Kurt Andersen, and with the support of BAVC executive director David Bolt, teams of fellows created laserdisc-based prototypes for these organizations to try out, play with, and show to their constituents. One of the prototypes, The Critical Eye: Inside TV Advertising, actually turned into a product for middle and high school students. This helped generate exposure for the Interact participants, most of whom have leveraged their experience into new multimedia work.

Multimedia Training Providers

More than 500 training providers also offer highly focused, specialized instruction about a variety of multimedia tools—HyperCard, Macromedia Director, Adobe Premiere, Aldus Persuasion, LinkWay, Authorware, SoundEdit Pro, Photoshop, Action!, Swivel 3D, Morph, and others. Appendix B contains an abbreviated list of some of these training providers.

Multi

[*The environment will improve; good ideas, not hardware, will drive the multimedia industry.*]

Selection of the proper platform for developing your multimedia project may be based on

environment

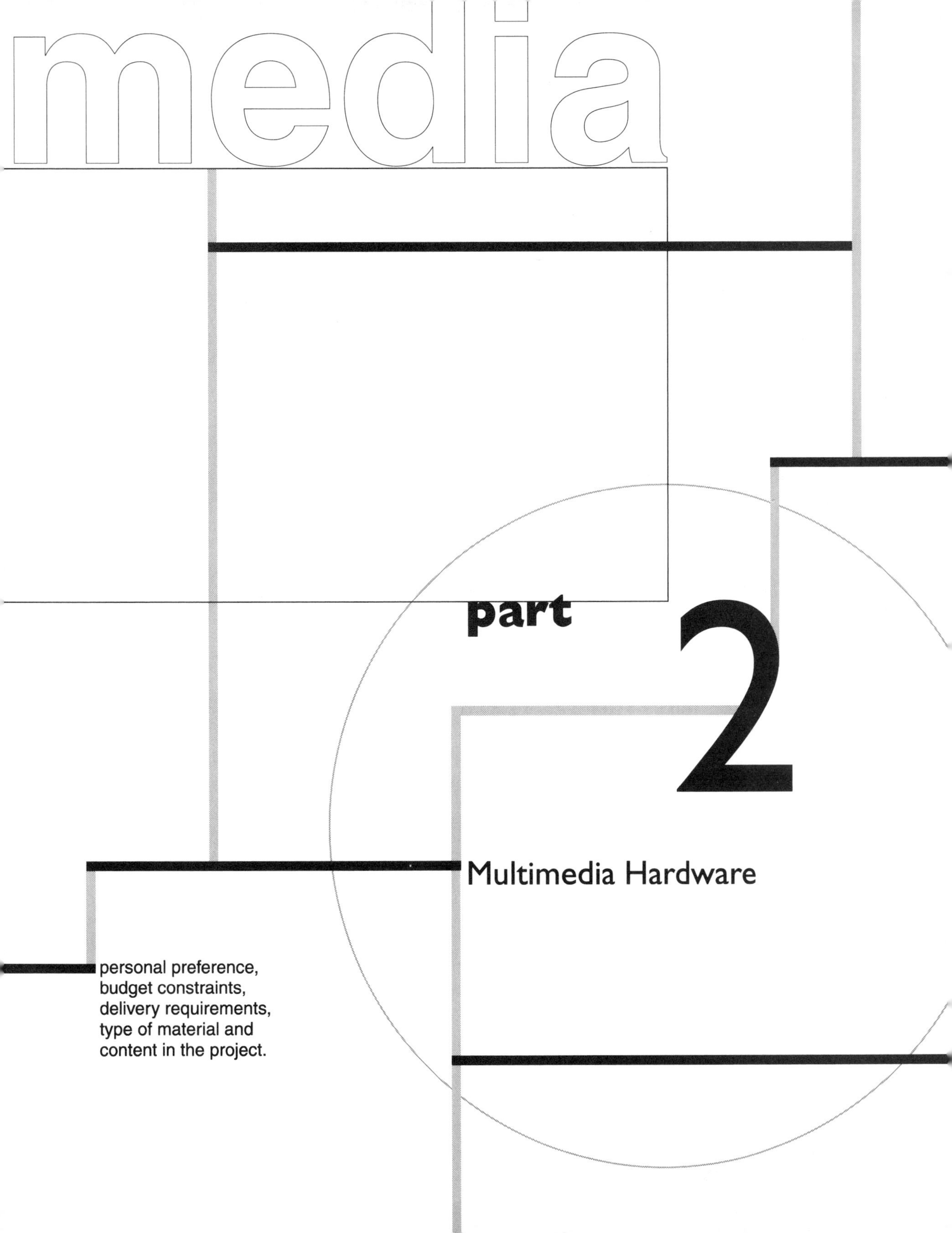

part 2

Multimedia Hardware

personal preference,
budget constraints,
delivery requirements,
type of material and
content in the project.

Multi

Since its inception, the Macintosh has been, by definition, a multimedia computer.

Selection of the proper platform
for developing your multimedia project may be based on

environment

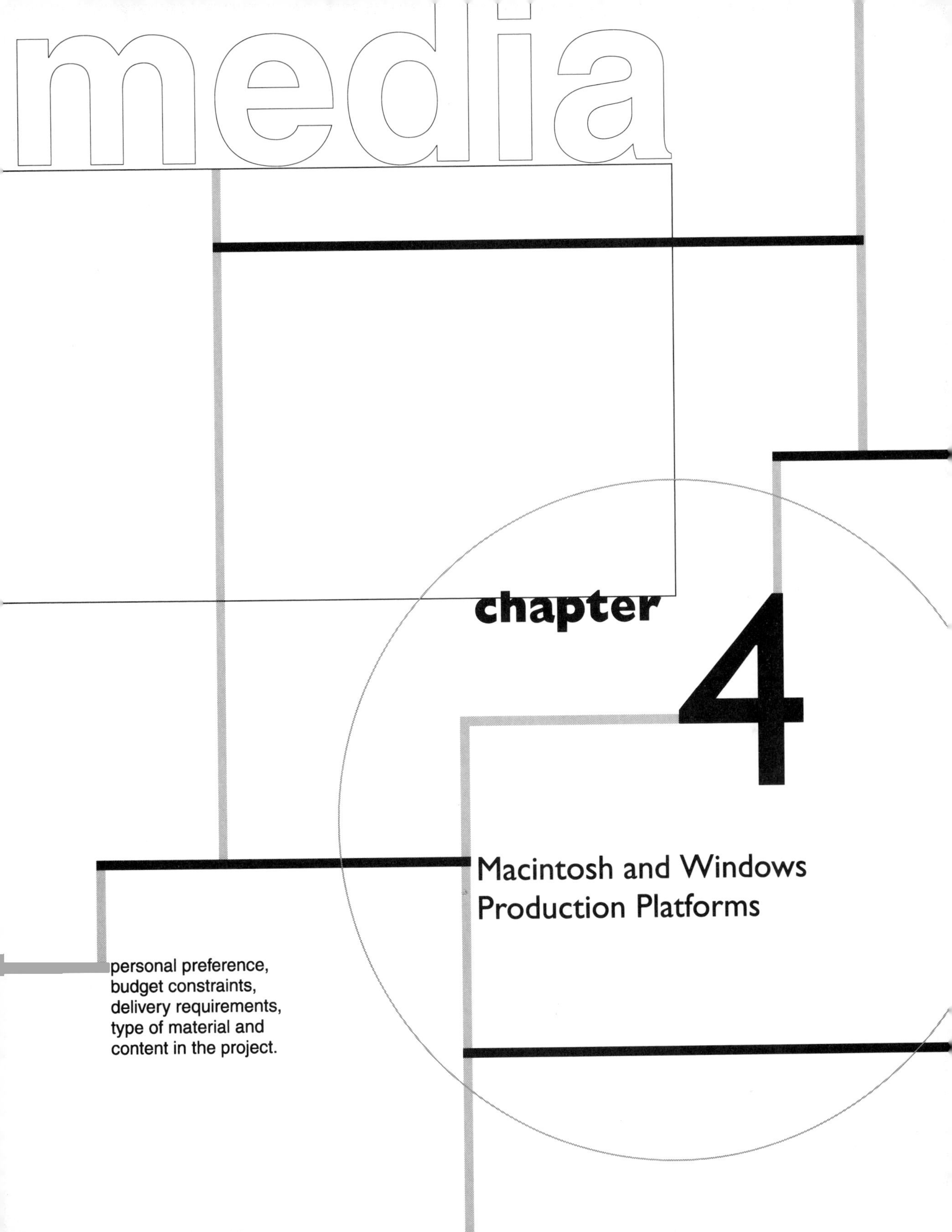

chapter 4

Macintosh and Windows Production Platforms

personal preference, budget constraints, delivery requirements, type of material and content in the project.

SELECTION of the proper platform for developing your multimedia project may be based on your personal preference of computer, your budget constraints, project delivery requirements, and the type of material and content in the project. Most multimedia developers today agree, nonetheless, that multimedia development is smoother on the Macintosh than in Windows, even though projects destined to run in Windows must then be ported across platforms. Hardware and authoring software tools for Windows are improving, however, so it will not be long before you can produce the same multimedia project with equal ease in either the Windows or Macintosh environment.

Soon, also, there will be other multimedia production environments that achieve widespread notice. In 1991, Apple, IBM, and Motorola formed an alliance to design and build a new generation of computers that use reduced instruction-set computing (RISC) microprocessors. This PowerPC hardware family bridges both Macintosh and PC environments. Apple and IBM have funded two new companies in order to produce operating system software that maximizes the performance benefits of the new platform: Taligent, to create a completely new object-oriented operating system; and Kaleida Labs, to create standards for multimedia products. This high-investment joint effort by two of the computer industry's leaders will bear fruit in the latter half of this decade.

Vaughan's Rule for Keeping Up:

Upgrade to proven products that lie in the calm water slightly behind the leading edge of the wave

The rationale for trading in my workhorse Macintosh IIci for a Quadra 840AV in 1993 was that I can get at least three years of good use out of a computer that will remain at or near the top of the line long enough to justify its cost. Apple's RISC-based PowerPC, which began shipping in 1994, is more than twice as powerful as my Quadra. But that power will be available mainly to applications that have been written specifically for the PowerPC chip in native code. Indeed, it is rumored that some applications, until they are redesigned by their vendors, will actually run slower on the PowerPC than on my Quadra. You can capsize at the frothy leading edge of technology, where the Surf Alligators live.

Macintosh Versus PC

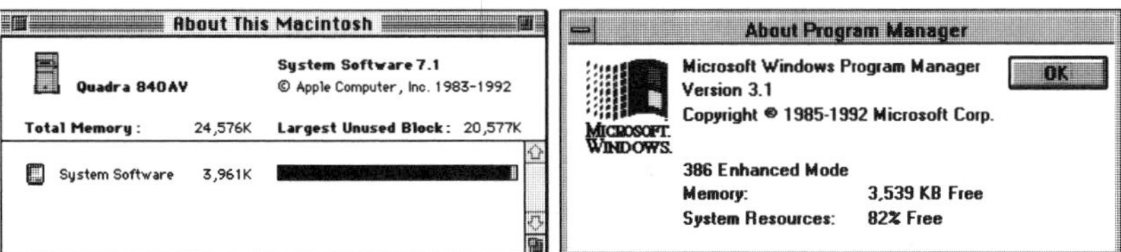

Since its inception, the Macintosh has been, by definition, a multimedia computer. At the famous roll-out of the Macintosh in January, 1984, at Apple's annual shareholders' meeting, the new device actually introduced itself in a crudely synthesized voice:

> Hello. I'm Macintosh. It sure is great to get out of that bag... Unaccustomed as I am to public speaking, I'd like to share with you a maxim I thought of the first time I met an IBM mainframe: Never trust a computer you can't lift! Obviously, I can talk, but right now I'd like to sit back and listen. So it is with considerable pride that I introduce the man who's been like a father to me, Steven Jobs.

Whereas the Macintosh had good built-in audio right from the start, in 1984, IBM personal computers could not process sound without very expensive add-on components. With its focus on business computing, the PC remained for many years able to provide only system beeps and limited sound effects on a tiny (and tinny) on-board speaker. Recently, due primarily to the demands of game software, lower-cost sound boards and software have become available for PCs. Other multimedia tools and hardware, such as video digitizers, are now readily available in PC marketing channels.

Hardware and software vendors are understandably attracted to the PC world because there have been many more PCs sold than Macintoshes (see Table 4-1). For many multimedia vendors, each PC computer represents a potential upgrade sale. Until IBM redesigned the PC to use proprietary hardware (the PS/2 series), the functionality of the AT-bus PC could be copied or *cloned* by other hardware manufacturers. Many computers from other manufacturers with widely varying features became available, offering more or fewer special capabilities according to that manufacturer's market strategy and production costs. Even today, not all PCs provide the sound and graphics features necessary to make and display multimedia.

The Multimedia Personal Computer, or MPC, is an industry-wide effort begun in the late 1980s to provide a standardized and capable multimedia computing environment for PCs. However, an MPC computer is not required for you to create multimedia presentations on PCs. Though few multimedia authoring and delivery tools are designed strictly for the DOS environment, some of these are quite extensive. But more multimedia tools are becoming available for Windows—and many multimedia applications are being ported from the Macintosh to Windows.

When enhanced with Windows, a sound board, and SuperVGA graphics, the PC readily challenges the Macintosh in delivering excellent audio and visual presentations. An MPC computer, moreover, will always provide

Platform	1993 Installed Base	Estimated 1994 Installed Base	Estimated 1995 Installed Base
MPC (or equivalent)	2,300,000	3,000,000	4,500,000
Macintosh	1,175,000	2,000,000	4,000,000
Total	3,475,000	**5,000,000**	**8,500,000**

TABLE 4-1 *CD-ROM Installed Base for Macintosh and MPC* ■

sound capability, a CD-ROM player, access to the Media Control Interface (MCI) for extensions to video overlay boards and other peripherals, and minimum CPU and memory configuration.

The multimedia toolset is currently biased in one direction: from Macintosh to Windows. If you create a multimedia project using an authoring tool such as Director or Authorware on a Mac, you can convert it to run in Windows; if you make a QuickTime movie with Premiere or VideoShop on the Mac, you can convert it to play as an .AVI file in Windows; you can convert a HyperCard stack using ConvertIt! to run it as a ToolBook book or you can import the stack through Windowcraft and run it in Windows. Crossing platforms in either direction, however, can be a trauma of font, palette, and format inconsistency; crossing against the present Mac/Windows bias may put you into the intensive care ward.

We need to move about four or five megabytes of information per second to satisfy the heavy requirements of multimedia. To achieve this rate, you need to optimize storage technology, CPU processing power, and bandwidth. When there are solutions for each of these elements, multimedia will come of age.

Charles McConathy, President of MicroNet Technology, suppliers of high performance data storage systems

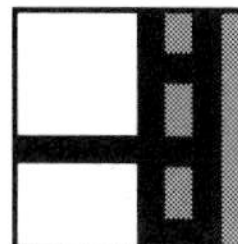

tip *In producing your multimedia projects, pay attention to your budget for computation and rendering time. If you've planned a great deal of 3D animation, you may want to invest in a second computer dedicated to processing these images. It can take from several hours to many days for a complex series of objects to be computed and rendered into a three-dimensional presentation, and if you have only one central processing unit (CPU), other tasks will likely be on hold in the meantime.*

The Macintosh Platform

All Macintoshes can play sound. The latest generation of Macintoshes includes hardware and software for digitizing sound without additional hardware: the LC, IIsi, IIvx, Centris, Quadra, Performa, and PowerBooks have built-in microphone jacks. For most Macintoshes, 8-bit, 16-bit, and 32-bit graphics capability is available. The AV series of Macintoshes can digitize video as well as sound. Unlike the Windows environment, where users can operate an application with keyboard input, the Macintosh requires a mouse. The Macintosh operating system allows easy, flexible storage and retrieval of the information and/or graphics files needed during your production process.

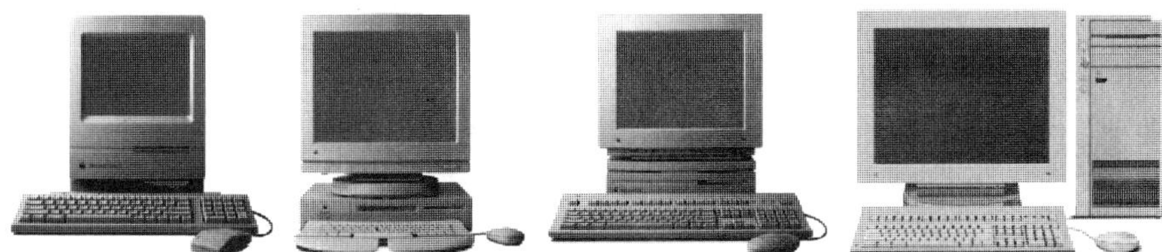

Nevertheless, there is significant variation in the ways you can set up your Macintosh hardware and software. What you need to develop your project depends entirely on the project's delivery requirements, its content, and the tools you need for production. Of course, the ideal production station is the newest, fastest, and most flexible computer you can get your hands on, but such a configuration may be beyond the scope of your budget. Thankfully, acceptable performance is not limited to the top-of-the-line configuration—many simple multimedia projects have been produced in black and white on a Macintosh Plus.

The Macintosh PowerPC

Apple introduced the first Macintosh computers based on PowerPC reduced instruction-set computing (RISC) microprocessors in 1994. RISC technology has typically been used in engineering workstations and commercial database servers designed for raw computational power, but Apple formed an alliance with IBM and Motorola to design and build this new family of RISC-based CPUs (central processing units), around which Apple is designing new RISC-based Macintosh models.

PowerPCs utilize the familiar Macintosh interface, support nearly all current Macintosh printers, networking cards, and other hardware accessories, and share data and coexist with other Macintosh models (and PCs) on a network. Apple is not the only manufacturer to incorporate PowerPC technology into personal computers, but from both a user's and a developer's perspective, Apple's PowerPC-based models look, act, and feel like familiar Macintosh systems.

Vaughan's One-Way Rule:

Once you've tried it, you can't go back

In 1987, a few weeks after HyperCard was released by Apple, I went to work there, designing and building the guided tour for an information management tool used in-house by Apple. I said I didn't know the software; they said that's OK, nobody else does, either. They gave me a cubicle with my name on it, a Macintosh Plus with a 20MB hard disk, and I was up and running.

The Macintosh II had been shipping for a short while, and every department at Apple was attempting to get this latest and hottest CPU—but most units were going to the retail channel. There were about three Macintosh IIs among about 40 of us.

One afternoon, I sat at a Macintosh II, inserted my 800K disk, and ran my HyperCard stack. I couldn't believe it! The screen-to-screen dissolves and special effects I had carefully programmed on the Macintosh Plus went by so fast I couldn't see them. I had to reprogram everything, with a special test to check for CPU speed. If it was a fast machine, I programmed the visual effects to run slower; on a slow machine, faster. But the sad part was that I not only wanted this faster machine, I felt I needed it! I had had the same experience moving from a 300-baud modem to 1200-baud, and, later, from a 14-inch monitor to a 21-inch monitor.

Desktop CPUs

Quadras

The Macintosh Quadra series is currently the top of the line. At its heart is a 68040 microprocessor running at clock speeds of 25 MHz (Quadra models 605, 610, 660AV, 700, 900), 33 MHz (Quadra models 650, 800, 950), or 40MHz (Quadra 840AV). These machines come with a built-in 8-bit video capability (256 colors) that can be increased to 16-bit (32,768 colors) or 24-bit (millions of colors) by simply adding video random access memory (VRAM).

Quadras include internal NuBus and/or processor-direct expansion slots. Custom hardware cards in the processor-direct slot (PDS) can be used to increase the power of the CPU through accelerator or memory cache cards. Add-on cards in the NuBus expansion slots allow the addition of a second monitor, access to full-motion video, and the highest quality audio production. For this reason, if you will be developing serious multimedia projects on your Macintosh, you should select a model that provides NuBus slots.

Quadras come with built-in LocalTalk, and many have built-in Ethernet connections for networking.

The Quadra 660AV and 840AV include a special digital signal processor (DSP) chip that enables software-driven high-speed modem communications (using Apple's GeoPort Telecom Adapter) and software-driven audio and video digitizing.

SIs, LCs, and Centris

The SI and LC series Macintoshes have allowed more people to own a Macintosh than ever before. These two machines support a 68030 microprocessor and provide reasonable computation speed at 20 MHz. These are not the fastest machines on the block, but they can definitely be reasonable products for the investment. NuBus expansion slots are limited on these two machines, but they can be set up for production and/or delivery stations. Many have been sold with Apple's low-end 12-inch color monitor that offers only a 512×384-pixel display in 256 colors. Accessory hardware and VRAM kits are available to increase the display resolution to 640×480 pixels.

The Centris models were designed to make high-performance CPUs affordable to businesses and professional users. All use the Motorola 68040 microprocessor and operate at 20 or 25MHz. The Centris 650AV includes a DSP chip and has capabilities similar to the Quadra 840AV.

Performas

The Performa line of lower-priced Macintoshes is sold through consumer outlets and department stores. These computers are intended for first-time and home computer users. The 300i CD-ROM player is included in the Performa 600CD. With the exception of the Performa 475 and 476, these all run with Motorola 68030 processors at 25 or 33MHz, and do not ship with floating point coprocessors (Motorola 68882 chips). For CAD and 3D work, you should install a coprocessor for faster computations and renderings.

Older Macintosh Models

Discontinued Macintoshes can work great, and Macintosh II series computers are still the backbone of many multimedia development houses! For developing multimedia, however, avoid the older, slower Macintosh computers with Motorola 68020 and 68000 microprocessors—they are too slow and frustrating for production multimedia authoring, but they can often be used for word processing, database tasks, and project management.

The IIvi and IIvx were developed to include either a built-in CD-ROM, a magneto-optical (MO) drive, or a half-height hard disk in addition to the internal hard disk. The series is designed to take advantage of multimedia capabilities on the Macintosh. They are fast (a Motorola 68040 microprocessor operating at 32 MHz) and can be expanded with up to 20MB on-board RAM. They include a microphone and can be used with high-performance video monitors.

The IIfx provides six expansion slots for special hardware such as video digitizers and high-end sound boards. It is fast enough for good multimedia, but all video and Ethernet connections must be added with cards in the NuBus slots.

The IIci and IIcx are small-footprint computers. Though considered "older" models, they still make excellent multimedia production platforms. Again, NuBus expansion slots are necessary for Ethernet and full-motion video cards (only three slots are available in these small-footprint machines). The IIci has an on-board video port for built-in 8-bit (256-color) graphics display.

PowerBook CPUs

With the introduction of the liquid crystal display (LCD)-screen PowerBook series of Macintosh laptop computers, you can take your multimedia on the road. As serious production platforms for multimedia, however, PowerBooks are inadequate.

An external monitor can be attached to a PowerBook, but there are no NuBus slots for video and sound enhancement cards. Moreover, it is not uncommon for a multimedia developer to have five or more windows open on the screen simultaneously, and the PowerBook screen simply does not have enough room for all these windows. Most PowerBooks use a 640×400 gray-scale screen, not the 640×480 size most commonly used for multimedia. The color PowerBook 180c (and the Duo 270c) provide a full 640×480 pixel backlit active-matrix color screen. These units are great for showing multimedia while you are on the road.

The Duo series of PowerBooks is designed to be connected to a "dock" to convert the laptop into a full-bore desktop model, complete with external monitor, extra disk drives, floppy drives, and even NuBus slots.

An ounce on the desk is a pound in my hand.

Dana Blankenhorn's First Law of Laptops, Editor,
Have Modem Will Travel

The Multimedia PC Platform

The MPC computer is not a hardware unit per se, but rather a standard that includes minimum specifications to turn Intel-microprocessor-based computers into multimedia computers. In fact, there are two MPC standards: MPC Level 1 and MPC Level 2. The MPC standard is maintained by the Multimedia PC Marketing Council, 1730 M Street NW, Suite 707, Washington, DC 20036 USA.

The MPC Level 1 minimum standard workstation consists of a 386SX microprocessor, at least 2MB of RAM, a 30MB hard disk, a CD-ROM drive, VGA video (16 colors), an 8-bit audio board, speakers and/or headphones, and Microsoft Windows software with the MultiMedia Extensions package. This minimum-configuration MPC is not powerful enough to develop serious multimedia, and it is hardly powerful enough to play multimedia at all.

The more realistic MPC Level 2 minimum standard was released in 1993. This Specification defines the minimum system functionality for Level 2 compliance but is not intended as a recommendation for a particular system configuration.

Multimedia PC Level 2 Specification

The functional specifications for an MPC Level 2 platform are provided verbatim below.

HARDWARE SPECIFICATIONS:

- CPU—Minimum requirement: 25MHz 486SX (or compatible) microprocessor.
- RAM—Minimum requirement: 4MB of RAM (8MB recommended).
- Magnetic Storage Requirements: 3 1/2-inch high density (1.44MB) floppy disk drive. 160MB or larger hard drive.
- Optical Storage Requirements: CD-ROM drive capable of sustained 300K per second transfer rate. No more than 40 percent of the CPU bandwidth may be consumed when maintaining a sustained transfer

rate of 150K per second. Average seek time of 400 milliseconds or less. 10,000 hours MTBF. CD-ROM XA ready (mode 1 capable, mode 2 form 1 capable, mode 2 form 2 capable). Multisession capable. MSCDEX 2.2 driver or equivalent that implements the extended audio APIs. Subchannel Q support (P, R–W optional). At 300K per second sustained transfer rate it is recommended that no more than 60 percent of the CPU bandwidth be consumed. It is recommended that the CPU utilization requirement and recommendation be achieved for read block sizes no less than 16K and lead time of no more than is required to load the CD-ROM buffer with 1 read block of data. It is recommended that the drive have on-board buffers of 64K and implement readahead buffering.

- Audio Requirements: CD-ROM drive with CD-DA (Red Book) outputs and volume control. 16-bit Digital-to-Analog Converter (DAC) with: Linear PCM sampling; DMA or FIFO buffered transfer capability with interrupt on buffer empty; 44.1, 22.05 and 11.025KHz sample rate mandatory; stereo channels; no more than 10 percent of the CPU bandwidth required to output 22.05 and 11.025KHz; it is recommended that no more than 15 percent of the CPU bandwidth be required to output 44.1KHz. 16-bit Analog-to-Digital Converter (ADC) with: Linear PCM sampling; 44.1, 22.05, and 11.025KHz sample rate mandatory; DMA or FIFO buffered transfer capability with interrupt on buffer full; microphone input. Internal synthesizer capabilities with multi-voice, multi-timbral capacity, 6 simultaneous melody notes plus 2 simultaneous percussive notes. Internal mixing capabilities to combine input from three (recommended four) sources and present the output as a stereo, line-level audio signal at the back panel. The four sources are: CD Red Book, synthesizer, DAC (waveform), and (recommended but not required) an auxiliary input source. Each input must have at least a 3-bit volume control (8 steps) with a logarithmic taper. (4-bit or greater volume control is strongly recommended.) If all sources are sourced with –10dB (consumer line level: 1 milliwatt into 600 ohms = 0dB) without attenuation, the mixer will not clip and will output between 0dB and +3dB. Individual audio source and master digital volume control registers and extra line-level audio sources are highly recommended. CD-ROM XA audio capability is recommended. Support for the IMA adopted ADPCM software algorithm is recommended. Guidelines for synthesizer implementation are available on request from the Multimedia PC Marketing Council at the above address.

- Video Requirements: Color monitor with display resolution of 640×480 with 65,536 (64K) colors. The recommended performance goal for VGA+ adapters is to be able to blit 1, 4, and 8 bit-per-pixel DIBs (device independent bitmaps) at 1.2 megapixels/second given 40 percent of the CPU. This recommendation applies to run-length encoded images and nonencoded images. The recommended performance is needed to fully support demanding multimedia applications including the delivery of video with 320×240 resolution at 15 frames per second and 256 colors.
- User Input Requirements: Standard 101-key IBM-style keyboard with standard DIN connector, or keyboard that delivers identical functionality utilizing key combinations. Two-button mouse with bus or serial connector, with at least one additional communication port remaining free.
- I/O Requirements: Standard 9-pin or 25-pin asynchronous serial port, programmable up to 9600 baud, switchable interrupt channel. Standard 25-pin bi-directional parallel port with interrupt capability. 1 MIDI port with In, Out, and Thru, must have interrupt support for input and FIFO transfer. IBM-style analog or digital joystick port.

SYSTEM SOFTWARE: Multimedia PC system software must offer binary compatibility with Windows 3.0 plus Multimedia Extensions or Windows 3.1

Minimum Full System MPC Configuration

A full Multimedia PC Level 2 system requires the following elements and components, all of which must meet the full functional specifications outlined in the previous section.

- CPU: 25MHz 486SX or compatible microprocessor.
- RAM: 4MB of RAM (8MB recommended).
- Magnetic Storage: Floppy drive, hard drive (160MB minimum).
- Optical Storage: CD-ROM double-speed with CD-DA outputs, XA ready, multisession capable.
- Audio: 16-bit DAC, 16-bit ADC, music synthesizer, on-board analog audio mixing.
- Video: Display resolution of at least 640×480 with 65,536 (64K) colors.

- Input: 101-key keyboard (or functional equivalent), two-button mouse.
- I/O: Serial port, parallel port, MIDI I/O port, joystick port.
- System Software: Binary compatibility with Windows 3.0 plus Multimedia Extensions or Windows 3.1.

Minimum Upgrade Kit Configuration

The Multimedia PC Marketing Council has also specified criteria for upgrade kits. A Multimedia PC Level 2 Upgrade Kit requires the following elements and components, all of which must meet the full functional specifications outlined in the preceding section.

- Optical Storage CD-ROM double-speed with CD-DA outputs, XA ready, multisession capable.
- Audio: 16-bit DAC, 16-bit ADC, music synthesizer, on-board analog audio mixing.
- I/O: MIDI I/O port, joystick port.
- Providing system software with Upgrade Kits is optional.

warning *Not all CD-ROM players will play Kodak's Photo CD multisession discs. If you plan to digitize and transfer images using Photo CD, you need a CD-ROM player capable of reading the Photo CD format; this is not specified in the MPC Level 1 standard, but it is required with Level 2.*

MPC systems are available in prepackaged configurations from a variety of vendors, including Tandy, Zenith, NEC, NCR, and Fujitsu America. Manufacturers who sell MPC computers guarantee that software written to the MPC standard, usually labeled with the MPC mark, will play on their machines.

Because the MPC is a standard, not a computer, you can assemble your own clone with components from various suppliers and meet the standard. Upgrade kits that typically include a CD-ROM player and a sound board are available from many hardware vendors.

Our motto is "Plug it in and see if it smokes."

Robert May of Ikonic Interactive Multimedia, speaking to a MacWorld Conference audience, January, 1991, on the complexities of board compatibilities on the PC platform

Multi

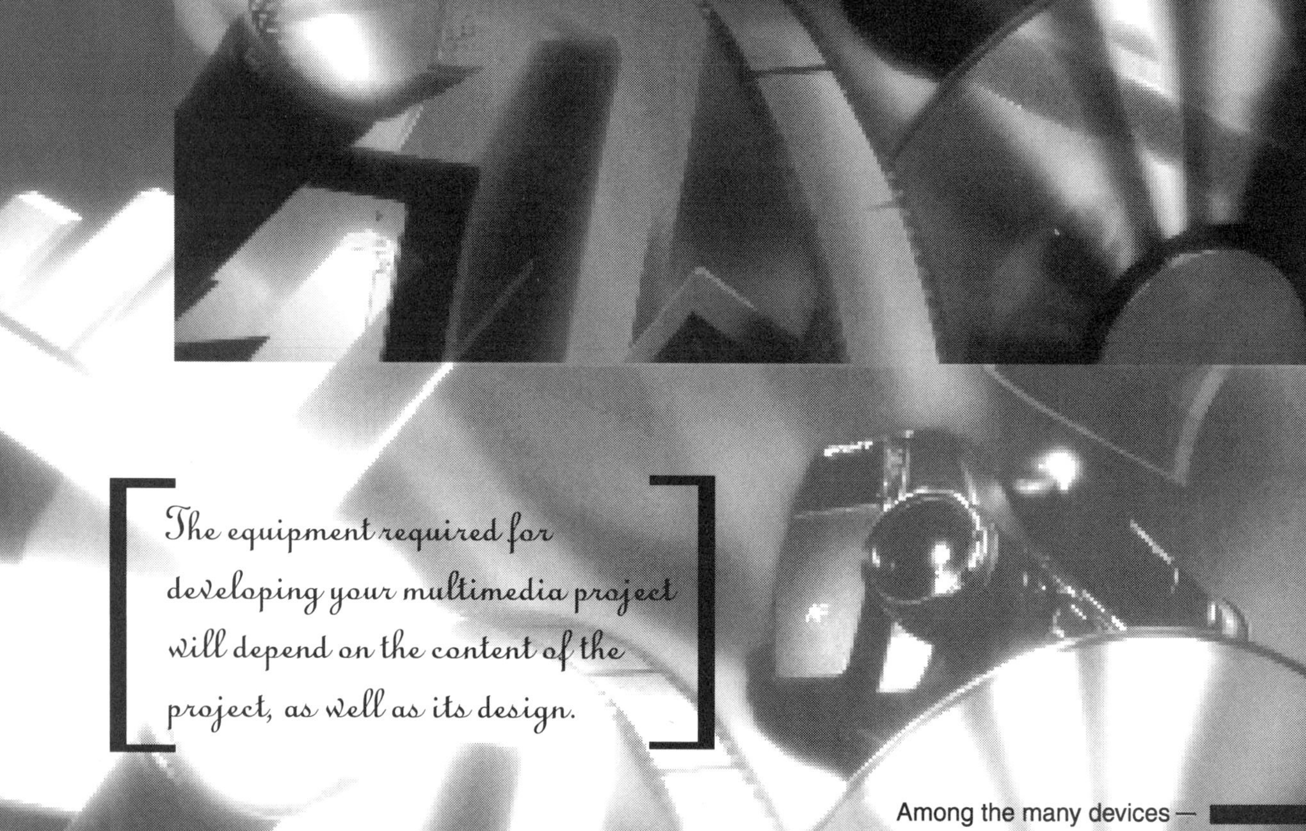

[The equipment required for developing your multimedia project will depend on the content of the project, as well as its design.]

Among the many devices —

communicate

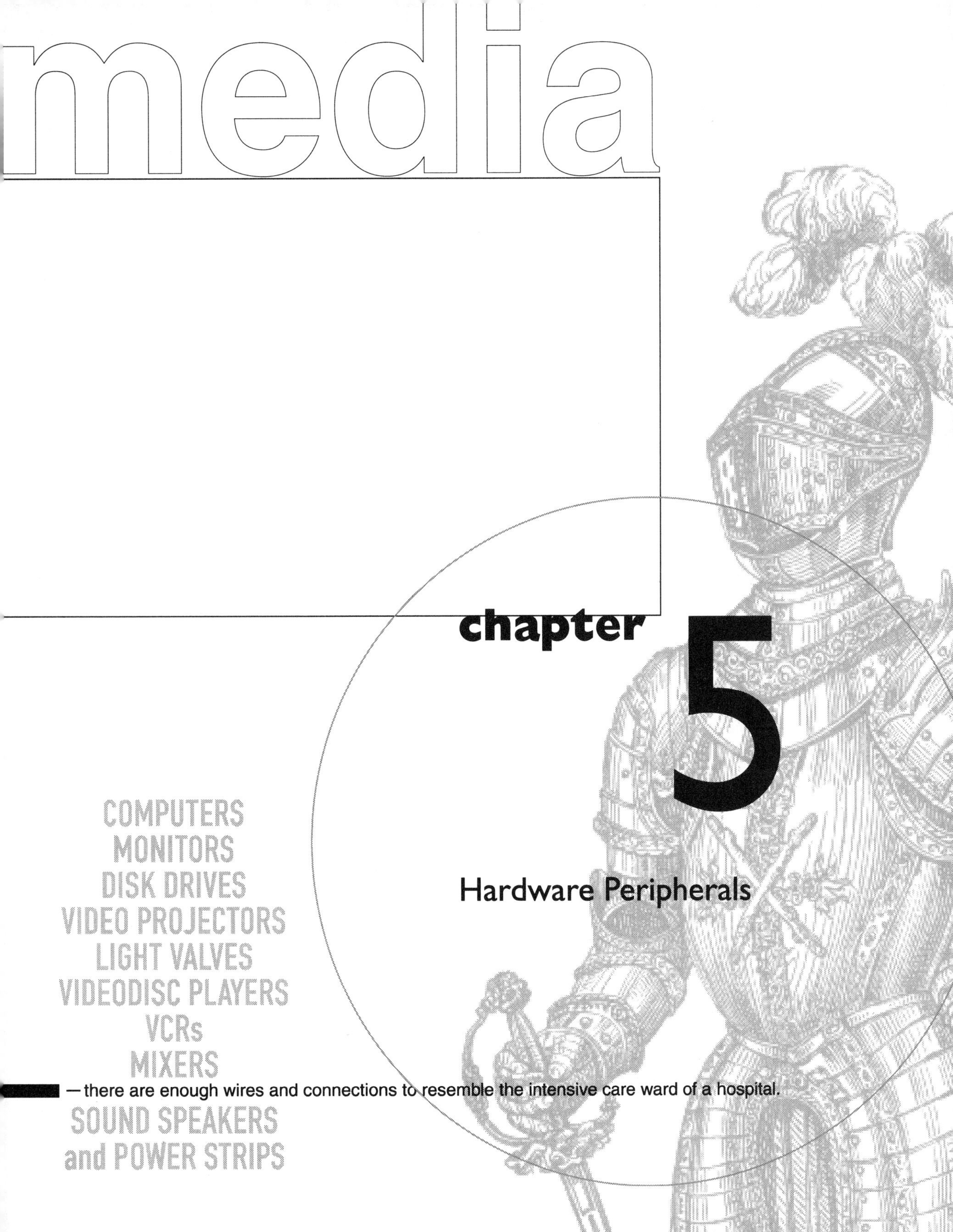

media

chapter 5

Hardware Peripherals

COMPUTERS
MONITORS
DISK DRIVES
VIDEO PROJECTORS
LIGHT VALVES
VIDEODISC PLAYERS
VCRs
MIXERS
— there are enough wires and connections to resemble the intensive care ward of a hospital.
SOUND SPEAKERS
and POWER STRIPS

THE following sections describe the hardware components necessary to translate a user's commands, queries, and responses into computer activity, to deliver and display a multimedia project, to store a project, and to communicate with co-workers and others during its production.

Connections

At conferences where multimedia presentations are shown, the human speakers usually sit facing the audience, while the audience is treated to a view of the backside of the speakers' computers. Among the many devices—computers, monitors, disk drives, video projectors, light valves, videodisc players, VCRs, mixers, sound speakers, and power strips—there are enough wires and connections to resemble the intensive care ward of a hospital. Sometimes an attempt is made to drape these power and data hoses with a curtain.

The equipment required for developing your multimedia project depends on the content of the project as well as its design. You will certainly need as fast a computer as you can lay your hands on, with lots of RAM and disk storage space. If you can find content such as sound effects, music, graphic art, clip animation, and QuickTime or AVI movies to use in your project, you may not need the extra tools for making your own. Typically, however, multimedia developers have separate equipment for digitizing sound from tapes or microphone, scanning photographs or other printed matter, and making digital still or movie images from videotape. Each device used for making or delivering multimedia must be "connected."

Small Computer System Interface (SCSI)

The Small Computer System Interface (SCSI) has been built into all current models of the Macintosh and lets you add peripheral equipment such as disk drives, scanners, CD-ROM players, and other peripheral devices that conform to the SCSI standard. You can connect as many as eight devices (ID numbers 0 to 7) to the SCSI port, but one of them must be the computer itself with ID 7, and one is usually your internal hard disk with ID 0.

If you are developing on a Macintosh, you need to set up your SCSI devices carefully, because SCSI cabling is very sensitive to length and to resistance. Follow the instructions in your Macintosh user's guide for proper termination and ID number assignment for SCSI devices. Having more than one external SCSI device can make your system "delicate," and even more will make it "fragile." The configuration below, which includes several external disk drives, a CD-ROM player, and a flat-bed scanner, took several hours to hook up and is fragile:

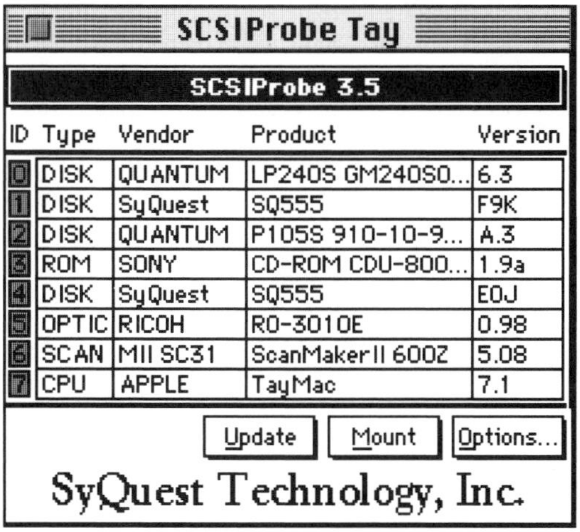

SCSIProbe Tay

SCSIProbe 3.5

ID	Type	Vendor	Product	Version
0	DISK	QUANTUM	LP240S GM240S0...	6.3
1	DISK	SyQuest	SQ555	F9K
2	DISK	QUANTUM	P105S 910-10-9...	A.3
3	ROM	SONY	CD-ROM CDU-800...	1.9a
4	DISK	SyQuest	SQ555	E0J
5	OPTIC	RICOH	RO-3010E	0.98
6	SCAN	MII SC31	ScanMakerII 600Z	5.08
7	CPU	APPLE	TayMac	7.1

Update Mount Options...

SyQuest Technology, Inc.

When your Macintosh is not happy with your chain of SCSI peripherals, it is not forgiving, and it will refuse to boot up. Often you will need to adjust cable lengths and reconfigure terminating resistors, then try again. Make sure that IDs assigned to peripherals are neither 0 nor 7 and that the same ID number is not assigned to two different devices.

SCSI interface cards can also be installed in PCs, and up to seven external peripheral devices, such as hard disks, CD-ROM drives, tape drives, printers, scanners, rewritable cartridge drives, and magneto-optical drives, can be connected to each installed card. But not all PC SCSI cards and software drivers recognize Macintosh-formatted media (such as Syquest cartridges or magneto-optical discs).

When a SCSI device is connected to the interface card in a PC, it is mounted to the system as another drive letter. Thus, you may have floppy disk drives mounted as drives A: and B:, a hard disk as drive C, and SCSI-based external devices as drives D, E, F, G, etc. While usually connected to a hard disk controller card in the PC, the internal disk drive C can also be a SCSI device, connected to a SCSI card. Specialized software such as Corel SCSI from Corel is available to maximize the flexibility of a PC-based SCSI system by providing drivers that work with hundreds of hardware devices from many different vendors.

The Media Control Interface (MCI)

As illustrated in Figure 5-1, Windows provides Media Control Interface (MCI), a unified, command-driven method for software to talk to related multimedia peripheral devices. With MCI, any hardware (or software) device can be connected to a computer running Windows. Using the appropriate drivers (normally supplied by the device manufacturer), you can control the device with simple command strings or codes sent to the MCI.

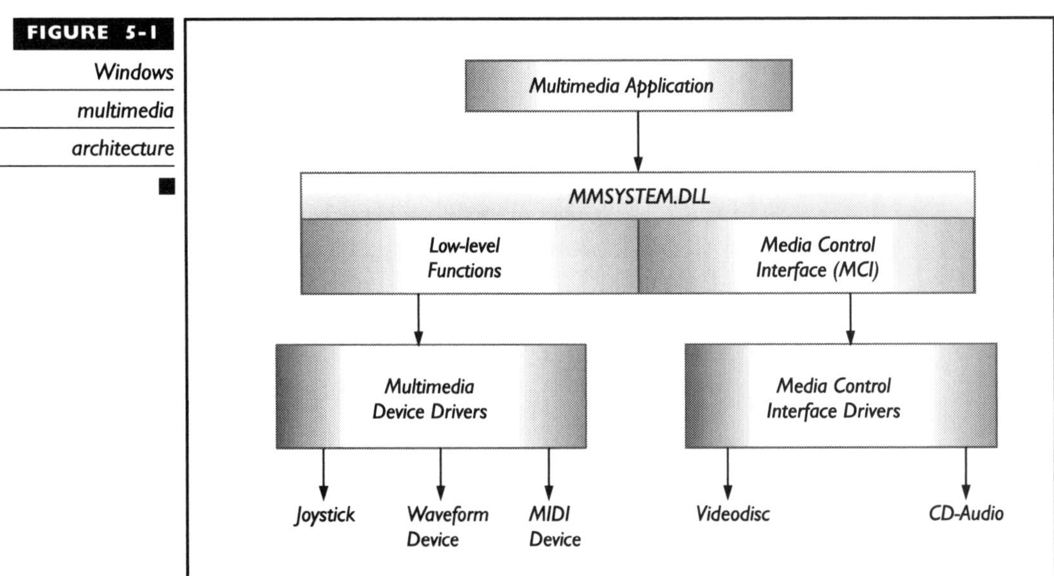

FIGURE 5-1 Windows multimedia architecture

Device Type	Description
avi	Audio Video Interleaved (Microsoft Video for Windows)
cdaudio	CD-Audio player (Red Book)
dat	Digital audio tape player
digitalvideo	Digital video in a window
mmmovie	Multimedia Movie Player (Macromedia Director)
other	Any undefined MCI device
overlay	Video overlay device
scanner	Image scanner
sequencer	MIDI sequencer
vcr	Videotape recorder or player
videodisc	Videodisc player
waveaudio	Waveform (digitized) audio device

TABLE 5-1 *Device Types Supported by Windows MCI* ■

Windows 3.0 does not include the MCI high-level interface, but MCI is available in Microsoft's Multimedia Development Kit (MDK).

Table 5-1 lists the device types supported by Windows MCI. Applications with internal scripting languages such as Visual Basic and ToolBook can easily be programmed to send MCI commands to these devices.

The cdaudio, sequencer, and waveaudio device drivers are delivered with Windows 3.1; the mmmovie driver for Director animation and the videodisc driver for the Pioneer LD-V4200 player are available in the MDK. The AVI component for playing digital video was not available until the end of 1992. Manufacturers of some peripheral equipment, such as video overlay boards, also supply their own MCI drivers.

Multimedia devices and drivers are managed by the [mci] and [drivers] sections of the Windows SYSTEM.INI file. By reading the SYSTEM.INI text file when it starts up, Windows knows what multimedia devices are present in your system; this information is critical. When you install multimedia software in Windows, the setup program will actually write the appropriate lines of data into the SYSTEM.INI file for you. Typical multimedia entries in the SYSTEM.INI file might look like this:

```
[mci]
CDAudio=mcicda.drv          ;for playing CD-Audio
WaveAudio=mciwave.drv       ;for playing digital sound files
```

```
Sequencer=mciseq.drv        ;for MIDI sequencing
MMMovie=mcimmp.drv          ;for Director animations (old)
Videodisc=mcipionr.drv      ;for Pioneer videodisc player
Animation=mcimmp.drv        ;for Director animations
AVIVideo=mciavi.drv         ;for Audio Video Interleaved

[drivers]
timer=timer.drv
midimapper=midimap.drv
MIDI=sb16fm.drv
Aux=sb16aux.drv
Wave=sb16snd.drv
MIDI1=sb16snd.drv
VIDC.MSVC=msvidc.drv
VIDC.RT21=indeo.drv

[sndblst.drv]
Port=220
MidiPort=330
Int=7
DmaChannel=1
HDmaChannel=5

[AVI Codecs]
mssq=mssqcomp.drv MS-Grid Compressor

[speaker.drv]
CPU Speed=28
Volume=983
Version=774
Enhanced=1
Max seconds=3
Leave interrupts enabled=0
```

Memory and Storage Devices

As you add more memory and storage space to your computer, you can expect your computing needs and habits to keep pace, filling the new capacity. So enjoy the weeks that follow a memory storage upgrade or adding an additional hard disk; the honeymoon eventually ends.

Vaughan's Rule of Capacity:

You never have enough memory or disk space

To estimate the memory requirements of a multimedia project—the space required on a floppy disk, hard disk, or CD-ROM, not the random access memory (RAM) used while your computer is running—you must have a sense of the project's content and scope. Color images, text, sound bites, video clips, and the programming code that glues it all together require memory; if there are many of these elements, you need even more. If you are making multimedia, you also need to allocate memory for storing and archiving working files used during production, original audio and video clips, edited pieces, final mixed pieces, production paperwork and correspondence, and at least one backup of your project files, with a second backup stored at another location.

Adequate storage space for your production environment can be provided by large-capacity hard disks, a server-mounted disk on a network, Syquest removable cartridges, optical media, tape, floppy disks, banks of special memory devices, or any combination of the above.

SyQuest 44MB removable cartridges are currently the most widely used portable medium among multimedia developers and professionals. These cartridges fit into a letter-sized mailer for overnight courier service. One or many cartridges may be required for storage of each project, and you should plan to keep backups elsewhere. Rewritable 128MB 3 1/2-inch magneto-optical disks (about the same dimensions as a floppy disk but slightly fatter) are becoming popular.

It is important to remember that if you are faced with budget constraints, you can certainly produce a multimedia project on a slower or minimally configured computer. On the other hand, it is profoundly frustrating to face memory (RAM) shortages time after time, when you're attempting to keep multiple applications and files open simultaneously. It is also frustrating to wait the extra seconds required of each editing step when working with multimedia material.

On the Macintosh, the minimum RAM configuration for serious multimedia production is about 16MB; 20MB configurations are adequate, but even 32MB and 64MB systems are becoming common, because while digitizing audio or video, you can store much more data much more quickly in RAM. And some software can quickly chew up available RAM—for example, Photoshop (5MB minimum, 10MB better), Director (2MB minimum, 10 to 20MB better), and Macromedia's 3D (1MB minimum, 5 to 8MB better). Figure 5-2 illustrates the allocation of RAM in a 24MB Macintosh system with many applications open simultaneously.

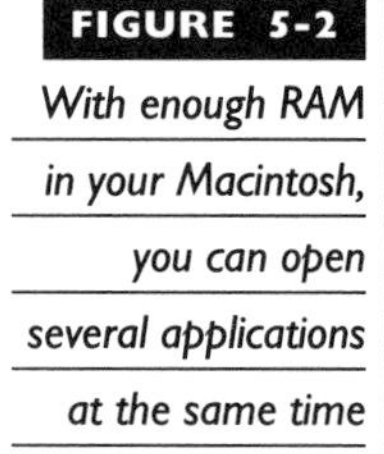

FIGURE 5-2 With enough RAM in your Macintosh, you can open several applications at the same time

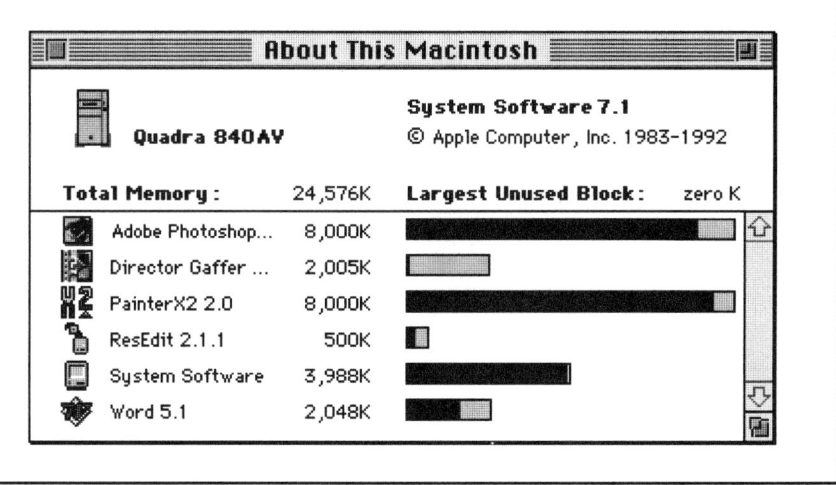

On a Multimedia PC (MPC) platform, multimedia authoring can also consume a great deal of memory—you may need to open many large graphics and audio files, as well as your authoring system, all at the same time to facilitate faster copying/pasting and then testing in your authoring software (see Chapter 4 for more on MPC). While 2MB is the minimum under the MPC-1 standard, 8MB is better, and 20MB may be required. Windows itself barely runs in 2MB of RAM!

Floppy and Hard Disks

Floppy disks and hard disks are mass-storage devices for binary data, data that can be easily read by a computer. Hard disks can contain much more information than floppy disks, and they operate at far greater data transfer rates.

A *floppy disk* is made of flexible mylar plastic coated with a very thin layer of special magnetic material. The disk is *formatted* to create *tracks* and *sectors* where data can be written. As the disk spins, data is written along each track in spots that become magnetically charged or not (either "on" or "off"). The data is then readable from the disk as a string of binary information. Disks are made in different sizes and with different data *densities* for use in various drive mechanisms.

Floppy disks for the Macintosh are the 3.5-inch size developed by Sony, and they provide either 800K storage on a double-density (DD) disk or 1.44K storage on a high-density (HD) disk. Older single-density (SD) disks are rarely used today. For DOS-based Windows computers, disks may be either

5.25-inch or 3.5-inch, providing 360K, 720K, 1.2MB, 1.44MB, or 2.88MB of storage. Table 5-2 lists these formats for the Macintosh and Windows.

cross platform *There are still a great many older Macintoshes and DOS machines in use that can only read the older-format disks.*

The most common floppy disk medium used for distribution of software is the high-density (HD) 1.44MB 3.5-inch floppy disk, although it is not uncommon for software vendors to ship two sets of disks—the 1.44MB 3.5-inch and the 1.2MB 5.25-inch sizes—in the same package with their product. More recently, however, many vendors are shipping only 1.44MB disks, with instructions to the user to call and ask for overnight shipment of the older format if it is required.

Hard disks are the most common mass-storage device used on computers. A *hard disk* is actually a stack of hard metal platters coated with magnetically sensitive material, with a series of recording heads or sensors that hover a hairsbreadth above the fast-spinning surface, magnetizing or de-magnetizing spots along formatted tracks using technology similar to that used by floppy disks and audio and video tape recording. Hard disks range from 20 megabytes (20,000,000 bytes) to more than three gigabytes (3,000,000,000 bytes) of storage capacity. For making multimedia, you need a large-capacity hard disk drive (see Vaughan's Rule of Capacity earlier in this chapter).

Most computers are sold with a hard disk installed, and the system software *boots* or starts up from this hard disk. External hard disks, most commonly SCSI devices, are also available at greater expense (they require their own power supply and electronics).

Disk Size (Inches)	Nominal Capacity	Actual Capacity	Platform/System
5.25	360K SD	368,640 bytes	DOS 2.0 or later
3.5	400K SD	N/A	Macintosh HFS (discontinued)
3.5	720K DD	737,280 bytes	DOS 3.2 or later
3.5	800K DD	816,128 bytes	Macintosh (all)
5.25	1.2MB HD	1,228,800 bytes	DOS 3.0 or later
3.5	1.44MB HD	1,474,560 bytes	DOS 3.3 or later
3.5	1.44MB HD	1,474,560 bytes	Macintosh (later than Macintosh IIx)
3.5	2.88MB	2,949,120 bytes	DOS 5.0 or later

TABLE 5-2 *Floppy Disk Formats for Macintosh and Windows* ■

SyQuest Drives and Optical Storage Devices

SyQuest drives are similar to hard drives except that the disk is a removable cartridge. They are among the most useful external and portable storage devices available for multimedia today. These are Winchester disk drives that use removable cartridges of 44MB or 88MB storage capacity, and they are almost as quick as other hard disks. Blank 44MB cartridges currently cost approximately $50 each.

Magneto-optical (MO) drives use a high-power laser to heat tiny spots on the metal oxide coating of the disk. While the spot is hot, a magnet aligns the oxides to provide a 0 or 1 (on or off) orientation. Like SyQuests and other Winchester hard disks, this is rewritable technology, because the spots can be repeatedly heated and aligned. Moreover, this medium is normally not affected by stray magnetism (it needs both heat and magnetism to make changes), so these disks are particularly suitable for archiving data. The most popular format uses a 128MB-capacity disk (about the size of a 3.5-inch floppy) that costs about $40 at current prices. Larger format magneto-optical drives with 5.25-inch cartridges offering 650MB to 1.3Gb of storage are available.

CD-ROM Drives

Compact Disc Read Only Memory (CD-ROM) drives have become an integral part of the multimedia development workstation and are an important delivery vehicle for large, mass-produced projects. A wide variety of developer utilities, graphic backgrounds, stock photography and sounds, applications, games, reference texts, and educational software are available only on this medium.

First Person

Somewhere in my basement is an old drive that used 256K, 8-inch floppy disks. I often carried these big floppies from workplace to workplace in a sneaker network (by tennis shoe, that is, not wire or glass fiber). I was astounded and pleased when the new 5.25-inch disks came out, then amazed by the high-technology 3.5-inch disks that fit in a shirt pocket. The higher-density floppies kept pace with the growing sizes of my project files, until I switched to color and began including sound and animation. For a while, segmenting and joining large files across several disks worked around the constraint, but it was tedious. So I finally went to 44MB Syquest cartridges, then to 128MB magneto-optical disks; both are currently the standard storage medium for multimedia producers on the sneaker net.

CD-ROM players have typically been very slow to access and transmit data (150K per second, which is the speed required of consumer audio CDs), but new developments have led to double-, triple-, and quadruple-speed drives designed specifically for computer (not Red Book Audio) use. See Chapter 18 for a detailed discussion of CD-ROMs.

CD-ROM Recorders

With a special compact disc recorder, you can make your own CDs using special CD-recordable (CD-R) blank optical discs to write a disc in most of the formats of CD-ROM and CD-Audio (see Chapter 18). The machines are made by Sony, Philips, Ricoh, Kodak, JVC, Yamaha, and Pinnacle. Software, such as TOPIX from Optical Media, Inc., lets you organize files on your hard disk(s) into a "virtual" structure, then writes them to the CD in that order. CD-R discs are made differently than normal CDs but can play in any CD-Audio or CD-ROM player. They are available in either a "63-minute" or "74-minute" capacity — for the former, that means about 560MB, and for the latter, about 650MB. These *write-once* CDs make excellent high-capacity file archives, and are used extensively by multimedia developers for premastering and testing CD-ROM projects and titles. Once the data is written onto these CDs, that part of the disc cannot be overwritten or changed.

Videodisc Players

Videodisc players (commercial, not consumer quality) can be used in conjunction with the computer for superior delivery of multimedia applications. The requirements of your project and your budget will dictate your choice of player.

You can design a custom videodisc to operate at three different levels: Level I, Level II, or Level III.

Level I

All code that enables user interaction is recorded in an information channel on the videodisc itself. When delivering a Level I application, all the end user needs is a videodisc player and a monitor; a computer is not required. Programmed interaction with the videodisc is managed using the remote control unit for the videodisc player.

Level II

Your project's program code is downloaded to the videodisc player's on-board RAM via an interface cable. Your code often remains in the player's static RAM, even when the player is turned off. The computer is used only to load your controlling software into the videodisc player. A high level of programming expertise is required to develop a Level II project.

Level III

The computer provides direct and immediate control of the player via an RS-232 interface cable. Level III is most commonly used for multimedia development; it allows the widest range of alternatives for interface design and user interaction. A computer must be attached for running your project.

Input Devices

A great variety of input devices—from the familiar keyboard and handy mouse to touchscreens to voice recognition setups—can be used for development and delivery of a multimedia project. If you are developing your project for a public kiosk, use a touchscreen. If your project is for a lecturing professor who likes to wander about the classroom, use a remote hand-held mouse. If you create a great deal of original computer-rendered art, consider a pressure-sensitive stylus and a drawing tablet.

Keyboards

A keyboard is the most common method of interaction with a computer. Keyboards provide various tactile responses (from firm to mushy), and they have various layouts depending on your computer system and keyboard model. Most provide the common QWERTY typewriter layout (in the U.S.), large keys with roman letter labels and raised dots on the F, J, and 5 keys so that number-processing software can use these and the surrounding keys to emulate a calculator pad (on the Macintosh, the raised dot keys are D, K, and 5). For users who spend substantial time doing numeric entries and accounting, a numeric keypad is an essential part of the keyboard. Function keys let users perform special operations or *macros* with a single keystroke. Keyboards are typically rated for at least 50 million cycles (the number of times a key can be pressed before it might suffer breakdown).

On PCs, keyboards connect to circuitry on the motherboard. The most common keyboard for PCs is the 101 style (which provides 101 keys), although many styles are available with more or fewer special keys, light-emitting diodes (LEDs), and other features, such as a plastic membrane cover for industrial or food-service applications.

Macintosh keyboards connect to the Apple Desktop Bus (ADB), which manages all forms of user input—from digitizing tablets to mice. Three Macintosh keyboards are available: the Apple Standard, the Apple Extended, and the Apple Adjustable Keyboard that can be split into two sections adjustable to 30 degrees. Standard keyboards provide a common typewriter layout with a few extra keys for special Macintosh tasks. Extended keyboards have an added row of function keys for access to special commands specific to an application or operating system (such as PAGEUP or PRINTSCREEN).

Mice

A mouse is the standard tool for interacting with a graphical user interface (GUI). All Macintosh computers require a mouse; on PCs, mice are often an option. Even though the Windows environment accepts keyboard entry in lieu of mouse point-and-click actions, your multimedia projects should typically be designed with the mouse or touchscreen in mind.

Of the several technologies used by mice to generate cursor location and command information, the most common is the rolling ball mouse. These use a heavy, rubber-coated steel ball enclosed within a compact plastic case. Inside the case are two slotted cog wheels that rub against the steel ball and rotate as the ball spins across a smooth surface. These wheels drive the circuitry built into the mouse that signals position changes to the computer.

The buttons on the mouse provide additional user input, such as pointing and double-clicking to open a document, or the click-and-drag operation, in which the mouse button is pressed and held down to drag (move) an object or to select an item on a pull-down menu. The Apple mouse has one button; PC mice may have as many as three.

Trackballs

Trackballs are similar to mice, except that the cursor is moved by using one or more fingers to roll across the top of the ball. The trackball does not need the flat space required by a mouse; this is important in small confined environments and for portable laptop computers. Trackballs have at least two buttons: one for the user to click or double-click, and the other to provide the press-and-hold condition necessary to select from menus and drag objects.

Touchscreens

Touchscreens are monitors that usually have a textured coating across the glass face. This coating is sensitive to pressure and registers the location of the user's finger when it touches the screen. The TouchMate system measures the pitch, roll, and yaw rotation of the monitor when pressed by a finger, it determines how much force was exerted and the location where the force was applied, and it has no coating (details on TouchMate are described in the following "First Person"). Other touchscreens use invisible beams of infrared light that criss-cross the front of the monitor to calculate where a finger was pressed. Pressing twice on the screen in quick succession simulates the double-click action of a mouse. Touching the screen and dragging the finger, without lifting it, to another location simulates a mouse click-and-drag. A keyboard is sometimes simulated using an onscreen representation so users can input names, numbers, and other text by pressing "keys."

Touchscreens are not recommended for day-to-day computer work, but they are excellent for multimedia applications in a kiosk, at a trade show, or in a museum delivery system—anything involving public input and simple tasks. When your project is designed to use a touchscreen, the monitor is the only input device required, so you can secure all other system hardware behind locked doors to prevent theft or tampering.

Magnetic Card Encoders and Readers

Magnetic (mag) card setups are useful when you need an interface for a database application or multimedia project that tracks users. You need both a card encoder and a card reader for this type of interface. The encoder connects to the computer at a serial port and transfers information to a magnetic strip of tape on the back of the card. The card reader then reads the information encoded on the card. A visitor to a museum, for example, slides an encoded card through a reader at any exhibit station and is rewarded with personalized or customized response from an intelligent database or presentation system. French-speaking visitors to a Norwegian museum, for instance, could hear an exhibit described in French.

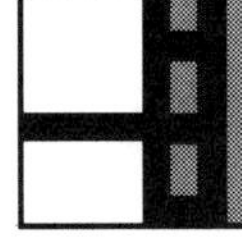

tip *When you design a project to use mag cards or pen scanners, always provide immediate feedback to an action by the user, such as a beep response or a displayed message.*

First Person

One of the more seductive rewards for working on the steep and slippery learning curves of multimedia is an occasional overwhelming introduction to a new idea or invention, the kind of encounter characterized by a neck-wrenching flash of wonderment as you stop in your tracks for a double-take. "How does that work?"

The TouchMate from Visage, Inc., is just such an invention. It's about two inches high, sits under your monitor, and requires only a 12-volt power supply and a cable to the RS-232 serial port of your PC. There are no electrical or data connections between the device and the monitor, no occluding membranes glued to glass, and no LEDs buried in a protruding bezel.

So how does TouchMate work if it's not connected to the screen? It translates tiny three-dimensional changes in monitor position caused by pressure on the screen into screen coordinates. This is the same sort of awesome blackbox science that enables inertial navigation systems to guide a 747 from New York to Paris, hands-free. TouchMate combines well understood sensor hardware with the mathematics of force vectors.

The top of TouchMate, where the monitor sits, is mounted on three-dimensional springs, allowing it to move with equal freedom in all directions relative to the base. Internal sensors constantly measure the distance between the top and the base. Each sensor consists of two parallel plates that form a capacitor, one attached to the top of TouchMate and one attached to the base. Two sets of these sensor plates are located in each corner, mounted at a 45-degree angle, providing a total of eight sensors.

When the monitor (sitting on the TouchMate) is touched, the force of the touch causes a slight change in the distance between TouchMate's top and base, typically on the order of one thousandth of an inch. This causes the distance between each set of sensor plates to change slightly, changing the capacitance across the plates. TouchMate uses the change in capacitance across each sensor to determine the amount the top plate moved in the x, y, and z directions and the amount it rotated in each direction (roll, pitch, and yaw). Firmware then calculates what level of force was exerted to cause this movement and the location where the force was applied.

Graphics Tablets

Flat-surface input devices are attached to the computer in the same way as a mouse or trackball. A special pen is used against the pressure-sensitive surface of the tablet to move the cursor. Graphics tablets provide substantial control for editing finely detailed graphic elements, a feature very useful to graphic artists and interface designers. Tablets can also be used as input devices for end users: you design a printed graphic, place it on the surface of the tablet, and let users work with a pen directly on the input surface. On a floor plan, for instance, visitors might draw a track through the hallways and rooms they wish to see and then receive a printed list of things to note along the route. Some tablets are pressure-sensitive and are good for drawing: the harder you press the stylus, for example, the wider or darker the line you draw. Graphic artists who try these usually fall prey to Vaughan's One-Way Rule, "Once you've tried it, you can't go back," (see Chapter 4) and never return to drawing with a mouse.

Scanners

A scanner may be the most useful piece of equipment you encounter in the course of producing a multimedia project. There are flat-bed and hand-held scanners; most commonly available are gray-scale and color flat-bed scanners that provide a resolution of 300 or 600 dots per inch. Hand-held scanners can be useful for scanning small images and columns of text, but they may prove inadequate for your multimedia development.

Be aware that scanned images, particularly those at high resolution and in color, demand an extremely large amount of storage space on your hard disk, no matter what instrument is used to do the scanning.

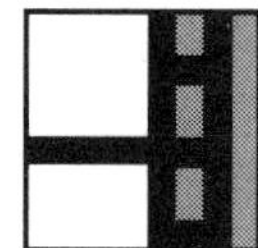

tip *Always scan images at the highest resolution possible. When a scanned image is reduced to lower resolution in an image editing program such as Photoshop or PhotoStyler, you get a better quality result if your original document was scanned at the highest resolution possible.*

Scans let you make clear electronic images of existing artwork, such as photos, ads, pen drawings, and cartoons, and they can save many hours when you are incorporating proprietary art into your application. Scans also can give you a starting point for your own creative diversions. Scanners enable you to use optical character recognition (OCR) software, such as OmniPage from Caere or Perceive from Ocron, to convert printed matter to ASCII text files in your computer.

Optical Character Recognition Devices

Barcode readers are probably the most familiar optical character recognition devices in use today—mostly at markets, shops, and other point-of-purchase locations. Using photo cells and laser beams, bar code readers recognize the numeric characters of the Universal Product Code that are printed in a pattern of parallel black bars on merchandise labels. With OCR or "barcoding," retailers can efficiently process goods in and out of their stores and maintain better inventory control.

An OCR terminal can be of use to a multimedia developer, because it is a tool that recognizes not only printed characters but soon handwriting as well. This facility may be beneficial at a kiosk or in a general education environment where user friendliness is a goal. Indeed, the popularity of the new Personal Digital Assistants (PDAs) such as Apple's Newton (that learns to recognize handwriting) attests to the demand for a more personal and less technical interface to data and information.

Uses of OCR are growing with the widening application of image-based computing. The ability to recognize characters is critical to making images such as faxes and scanned documents useful, and the technology is rapidly becoming easier to use and more affordable. As a result, more and more computer users will be applying it to new needs in the coming years.

Larry Kubo, VP of Marketing, Ocron, Inc.

Infrared Remotes

An infrared remote unit lets a user interact with your project while he or she is freely moving about. Remotes work like mice and trackballs, except they use infrared light to direct the cursor. Remote mice work well for a lecture or other presentation in an auditorium or similar environment, when the speaker needs to move around the room.

Voice Recognition Systems

Voice recognition systems facilitate hands-free interaction with your project. These systems usually provide a unidirectional cardioid, noise-cancelling microphone that automatically filters out background noise. Most voice recognition systems currently available can trigger common menu events such as Save, Open, Quit, and Print, and you can teach the system to recognize other commands that are more specific to your application. Systems available for the Macintosh and Windows environments typically must be taught to recognize individual voices and then be programmed with the appropriate responses to the recognized word or phrase. The Macintosh AV computers include voice recognition capability; add-on sound boards such as the SoundBlaster-16 or Diamond Sonic Sound and others provide this feature for PCs.

Digital Cameras

To take pictures with digital cameras instead of film cameras, you need video technology hardware (see Chapter 13). The XAPSHOT SV camera, for example, can record up to 50 images (300-line video fields) on a reusable

2-inch floppy disk. Images can be played back directly from the camera to any standard TV monitor or used with a digitizer for computer input. Software controls the image capture, image adjustment, and save functions of the digitizer. Once the image is saved in the computer environment, of course, it can easily be exported to various applications, incorporated into desktop publishing setups, used to enhance a database, or added as a graphic image to a multimedia presentation.

Output Hardware

Presentation of the audio and visual components of your multimedia project requires hardware that may or may not be included with the computer itself: speakers, amplifiers, monitors, motion video devices, and capable storage systems. The better the equipment, of course, the better the presentation. There is no greater test of the benefits of good output hardware than to feed the audio output of your computer into an external amplifier system—suddenly the bass sounds become deeper and richer, and even music sampled at low quality may sound acceptable.

Audio Devices

All Macintoshes are equipped with an internal speaker and a dedicated sound chip, and they are capable of audio output without additional hardware and/or software. The Macintosh II series and later models provide stereo sound; Quadras can sample sounds at rates up to 44.1 kHz. Older Macintish models are limited to a 22.05 kHz sampling rate.

Digitizing sound on your Macintosh requires an external microphone and sound editing/recording software such as SoundEdit Pro from Macromedia, Alchemy from Passport, or SoundDesigner from DigiDesign. If your Macintosh model does not support external microphones, an external digitizer (such as MacRecorder from Macromedia) can be connected to the modem port; this device can be used not only for digitizing voice, but also for digitizing from cassette tape players, radios, VCRs, and other analog sound sources. Connect your microphone or external digitizer, open your sound editing software, select a sampling rate, and play the desired music or sound or speak into the microphone. To record a stereo audio file with MacRecorder, you need to use two MacRecorder systems, one attached to the modem port and the other to the printer port. High-end audio boards that digitize in stereo at a 16-bit sample size and 44.1 kHz (such as DigiDesign's AudioMedia board) are also available for the Macintosh. After editing your sound file, you can save it to disk and then import it into your multimedia authoring system.

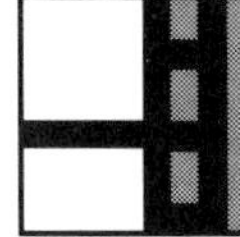

tip *Design your project to use many shorter duration audio files rather than a single, long file. This simplifies the redaction of your project within your authoring system, and it may also improve performance because you load shorter segments of sound into RAM at any one time.*

PCs are not capable of multimedia audio until a sound board is installed. MPC computers (see Chapter 4) are configured for sound from the start. Upgrade kits that include sound boards and CD-ROM players are available from many sources. WaveEdit is a simple sound production and editing system for the MPC. WaveEdit is available in Microsoft's Multimedia Development Kit, and it provides recording and editing features sufficient for most projects. It also provides a utility for converting files from Windows to Macintosh and vice versa.

IBM PS/2 computers have four levels of audio recording and playback capability: voice, music, stereo, and high-quality music. Recording and editing are handled through IBM's Audio Visual Connection (AVC) development environment and employ IBM's M-Audio Capture/Playback Adapter or another compatible microchannel soundboard. If you have installed the Windows operating system on your PS/2 computer, you can also use Media Control Interface (MCI) capturing software and playback capability. Sound in multimedia projects is discussed in detail in Chapter 10.

tip *The quality of your audio recordings is greatly affected by the caliber of your microphone and cables. A unidirectional microphone helps filter out external noise, and good cables help reduce noise emitted from surrounding electronic equipment.*

Amplifiers and Speakers

Often the speakers you use during a project's development will not be adequate for its presentation. Speakers with built-in amplifiers or attached to an external amplifier are important when your project will be presented to a large audience or in a noisy setting. Altec Lansing's three-piece amplified speaker system, for example, is designed for multimedia presentations and is small and portable. It includes its own digital signal processing (DSP) circuitry for concert hall effects; it has a mixer for two input sources (the computer's digital output and the CD-ROM player's audio output can be blended); and it uses a subwoofer sensitive to 35 Hz.

warning *Always use magnetically shielded speakers to prevent color distortion on nearby video displays.*

Monitors

The monitor you need for development of multimedia projects depends on the type of multimedia application you are creating as well as what computer you're using. A wide variety of monitors is available for both Macintoshes and PCs. High-end, large-screen graphics monitors are available for both; they are expensive.

Serious multimedia developers often attach more than one monitor to their computers, using add-on graphics boards. Many authoring systems allow you to work with several open windows at a time, so you can dedicate one monitor to view the work you are creating or designing, while you perform various editing tasks in windows on other monitors. Figure 5-3

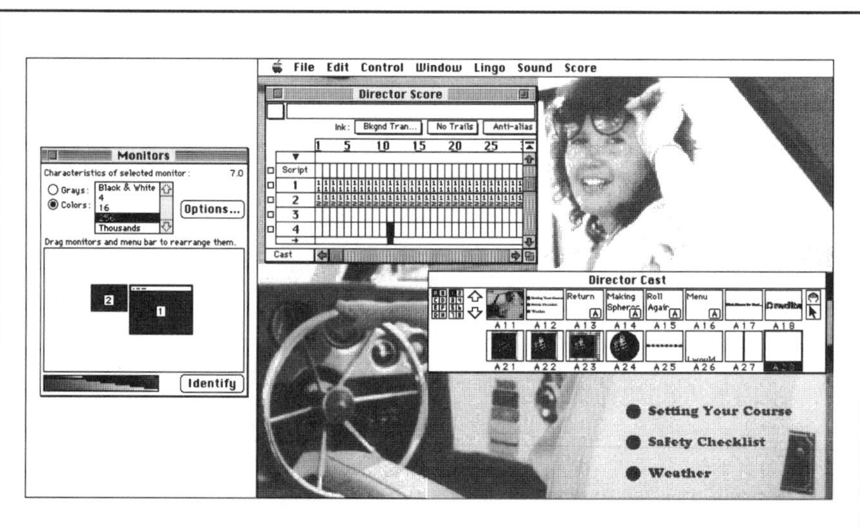

FIGURE 5-3 *Without a second monitor, you can have difficulty editing your project and viewing it at the same time*

illustrates Macromedia's authoring environment, Director, using one monitor with editing windows that overlap a work view. Developing in Director is best with at least two monitors, one to view your work, the other to view the "score." A third monitor is often added by Director developers to display the "cast." See Chapter 8 for more about Director.

tip *Always develop your project using the screen resolution of the destination platform.*

It is important to develop your application on monitors of the same size and resolution as those to be used for its delivery. A variety of monitors can be used for both development and delivery.

The maximum number of colors you can display on your monitor depends on the graphics card or amount of video RAM (VRAM) installed in the computer. Older Macintosh II systems provide 8-bit (256-color) capability, but you can expand this to 24-bit (millions of colors) by adding a 24-bit board in a NuBus slot. The newer Macintoshes typically provide 16-bit capability (more than 32,000 colors), and you can add VRAM to the motherboard for larger monitors and more colors. On PCs, monitor displays are typically 8-bit (256 colors), but you can easily upgrade to 16-bit (32,000+ colors), or 24-bit (millions of colors) boards. Of course, the more colors displayed, the slower the system performance. Accelerator cards for video display are also available.

First Person

A bunch of us worked on a guided tour project destined for Sun SparcStations. SparcStations have large monitors with a screen resolution of 1024×768 pixels, but, because we were most proficient with Macintosh graphics tools, we created most of the bitmapped artwork on Macintosh 13-inch, 640×480-pixel RGB monitors. Though the Macintosh software deftly managed the big image sizes, the process was very tiresome to the artists, because the 640×480 monitors provided only a window onto the larger bitmap. We had to scroll the window back and forth over the larger image to see what we were doing. Dragging and dropping was a horror show.

Finally, we installed a 19-inch monitor and set up a Macintosh with a high-resolution video card. It was better, but there were not enough of them to go around. In the end, about 75 percent of the artwork was done in scrolling windows on the Macintosh, and it turned out great.

Large monitors do not necessarily increase the real estate available to you for your graphics and information display: 35-inch monitors, or even the 50-foot projection displays common to auditoriums, may still provide just 640×480 pixels of resolution. The large monitors that do effectively increase the real estate also require higher-resolution boards in Macintosh or PC expansion slots. Again, these are expensive.

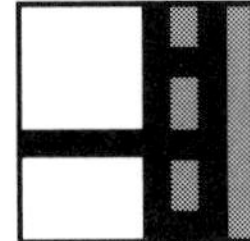

tip *To improve performance while running in 24-bit mode, you can often convert some graphic elements to 8-bit images without degradation; this increases the redraw speed for that image. Don't animate with very large bitmaps, regardless of their color depth, and use minimal gradients or shadings.*

Video Devices

No other contemporary message medium has the visual impact of video. With a video digitizing board installed in your computer, you can display a television picture on your monitor. Some boards include a frame grabber feature for capturing the image and turning it into a color bitmap, which can be saved as a PICT or TIFF file (see Chapter 11) and then used as part of a graphic or a background in your project.

Display of video on any computer platform requires manipulation of an enormous amount of data (see Chapter 13). When used in conjunction with videodisc players, which give you precise control over the images being viewed, video cards let you place an image into a window on the computer monitor; a second television screen dedicated to video is not required. And video cards typically come with excellent special effects software.

There are many video cards available today. Most of these support various video-in-a-window sizes, identification of source video, setup of play sequences or segments, special effects, frame grabbing, and digital movie making. In Windows, video overlay boards are controlled through the Media Control Interface (MCI). On the Macintosh, they are often controlled by external commands and functions (XCMDs and XFCNs) linked to your authoring software.

Good video greatly enhances your project; poor video ruins it. Whether you deliver your video from tape using VISCA controls, from videodisc, or as a QuickTime or AVI movie, it is critical that your source material be of high quality.

Projectors

If you're showing your material to more viewers than can huddle around a computer monitor, you will need to project it onto a large screen or even a white-painted wall. Cathode-ray tube (CRT) projectors, liquid crystal display (LCD) panels attached to an overhead projector, stand-alone LCD projectors, and light-valve projectors are available to splash your work onto big-screen surfaces.

CRT projectors have been around for quite a while—they are the original "big-screen" televisions. They use three separate projection tubes and lenses (red, green, and blue), and the three color channels of light must "converge" accurately on the screen. Setup, focusing, and aligning is important to getting a clear and crisp picture. CRT projectors are compatible with the output of most computers as well as televisions.

LCD panels are portable devices that fit in a briefcase. The panel is placed on the glass surface of a standard overhead projector available in most schools, conference rooms, and meeting halls. While the overhead projector does the projection work, the panel is connected to the computer and provides the image, in thousands of colors and, with active-matrix technology, at speeds that allow full-motion video and animation. Because LCD panels are small, they are popular for on-the-road presentations, often connected to a lap-top computer and using a locally available overhead projector.

More complete LCD projection panels contain a projection lamp and lenses, and they do not require a separate overhead projector. They typically produce an image brighter and sharper than the simple panel model, but they are somewhat larger and cannot travel in a briefcase.

Light-valves compete with high-end CRT projectors, using a liquid crystal technology in which a low-intensity color image modulates a high-intensity light beam. While these units are expensive, the image from a light valve projector is very bright and color-saturated and can be projected onto screens as wide as 30 feet or more.

Communication Devices

Many multimedia applications are developed in workgroups comprising instructional designers, writers, graphic artists, programmers, and musicians located in the same office space or building. The workgroup members' computers typically are connected on a local area network (LAN). The client's computers, however, may be thousands of miles away, requiring other methods for good communication.

Communication among workgroup members and with the client is essential to the efficient and accurate completion of your project. Normal U.S. Postal Service mail delivery is too slow to keep pace with most projects; overnight express services are better. And when you need it immediately, a modem or network is required.

In the workplace, use quality equipment and software for your communications setup. The cost—in both time and money—of stable and fast networking will be returned to you.

Modems

Modems can be connected to your computer externally at the serial port or internally as a separate board. Internal modems often include fax capability. Be sure your modem is Hayes-compatible. The Hayes AT (named for the ATTENTION command that precedes all other commands) standard command set allows you to work with most software communications packages.

Modem speed, measured in *baud*, is the most important consideration. Because the multimedia files that contain the graphics, audio resources, video samples, and progressive versions of your project are usually large, you need to move as much data as possible in as short a time as possible. Today's standards dictate at least a 9600-bps (bits per second) modem. Transmitting at 2400 bps, a 350MB file may take as long as 45 minutes to send, but at 9600 bps, you can be done in 6 or 7 minutes. Most modems follow the CCITT V.32 or V.42 standards that provide data compression algorithms when communicating with another, similarly equipped, modem. Compression saves significant transmission time and money, especially over long distance. Be sure your modem uses a standard compression system (like V.32) and not a proprietary one.

Copper telephone lines and the switching equipment at the phone companies' central offices can handle modulated analog signals up to about 28,000 bps on "clean" lines. Modem manufacturers that advertise data transmission speeds higher than that are counting on hardware-based compression algorithms to crunch the data before sending it, decompressing it upon arrival at the receiving end. If you have already compressed your data into a .SIT, .SEA, .ARC, or .ZIP file, then you may not reap the benefits from the higher advertised speeds, because it is difficult to compress an already compressed file. For truly higher transmission speeds, you need to use Integrated Services Digital Network (ISDN), Switched-56, T1, ATM, or another of the telephone companies' Digital Switched Network services.

Networks

Local area networks (LANs) and wide area networks (WANs) can connect the members of a workgroup. In a *LAN*, workstations are usually located within a short distance of each other, on the same floor of a building, for example. *WANs* are communication systems spanning great distances, typically set up and managed by large corporations and institutions for their own use or to share with other users.

LANs allow direct communication and sharing of peripheral resources such as file servers, printers, scanners, and network modems. They use a variety of proprietary technologies, most commonly LocalTalk, Ethernet,

First Person

Around midnight, I got a phone call from a client in Europe. His investors were meeting later that day, and he needed the project now and not in two days by DHL courier. Compressed, the code was less than a megabyte. So I went to my office and cranked up the modem, dialed the overseas phone number, and connected. The modem software estimated a total transmission time of 73 minutes, and we started the XMODEM protocols. While the little packets of data were humming out across the continent and an ocean, I made a peanut butter sandwich and kept an eye on the Bytes Remaining counter as it worked its way down in ratchets of 1024. It was hypnotic.

Annoying spikes and glitches in the phone system had always plagued my modem calls with intermittent transmission failures that required starting over. With about four minutes to go, I began suffering hot flashes and a pounding heart, and I found myself riveted to the monitor with head in hands, cheering the system on. "Don't crash now! Just a little more! Pretty please with icing! Nice baby!" All the possible scenarios of disaster paraded in front of me: a shipping calamity in the English channel causing the transatlantic cable to break at 30 fathoms; a street cleaning truck taking out the electric power pole on the street outside; mice chewing through the antenna leads of a lonely microwave station high in the Colorado Rockies... Everything suddenly seemed so fragile. But we made it!

3COM, and token-ring, to perform the connections. They can usually be set up with twisted-pair telephone wire, but be sure to use "data-grade" wire—it makes a real difference, even if it's a little more expensive. Bad wiring will give you a never-ending headache of intermittent and often untraceable crashes and failures.

LocalTalk can transfer data at a rate of 230.4 kilobits per second, and network connections are made through the printer's serial port on the Macintosh and with a dedicated network card on the PC. LocalTalk is perhaps the simplest and least expensive network to set up, but its transfer rate is slow compared to other LAN systems: Ethernet is ten times faster. LocalTalk limits to 32 the number of users, or *nodes,* in a zone, although zones can be chained together to accommodate an aggregate of 254 computers. For any more than a dozen or so workgroup members, Ethernet, 3COM, or token-ring are recommended, but these require dedicated cards for both Macintoshes and PCs (although the newer Macintoshes have Ethernet built in). These systems operate at transfer rates of ten megabits per second.

WANs are expensive to install and maintain, but other methods for long-distance communication are available without a dedicated telephone network. Global store and forward mail and file transfer services are available from CompuServe, America OnLine, AppleLink, Connect, and a host of electronic bulletin board systems (BBSs). Here, messages and files can be uploaded to private electronic mailbox (e-mail) addresses and downloaded later by the recipient. You pay for a local telephone call and the length of time you are connected to the service (usually at a reasonable hourly rate). If you are working with people in various time zones (an artist in New York, a programmer in San Francisco, and a client in Singapore), all can communicate and share information with other locations at any time of day or night.

Remote Application Sharing

Timbuktu Remote from Farallon allows application sharing between two Macintoshes by modem. In Windows, CloseUp from Norton-Lambert and pcAnywhere from Symantec provide the same service. These special programs let the connected computers "conference" with one another. You can view what the remote computer is showing on its screen, as well as operate it with a keyboard and mouse from your own, distant computer. Though activities such as screen drawing and refreshing are slow (limited by your modem speed), remote application sharing can be extremely useful for team problem solving and collaboration. Only screen and keyboard information is sent down the wire, while all processing is performed on the local system. LapLink Remote from Traveling Software allows you to communicate between Macintoshes and PCs.

Multi

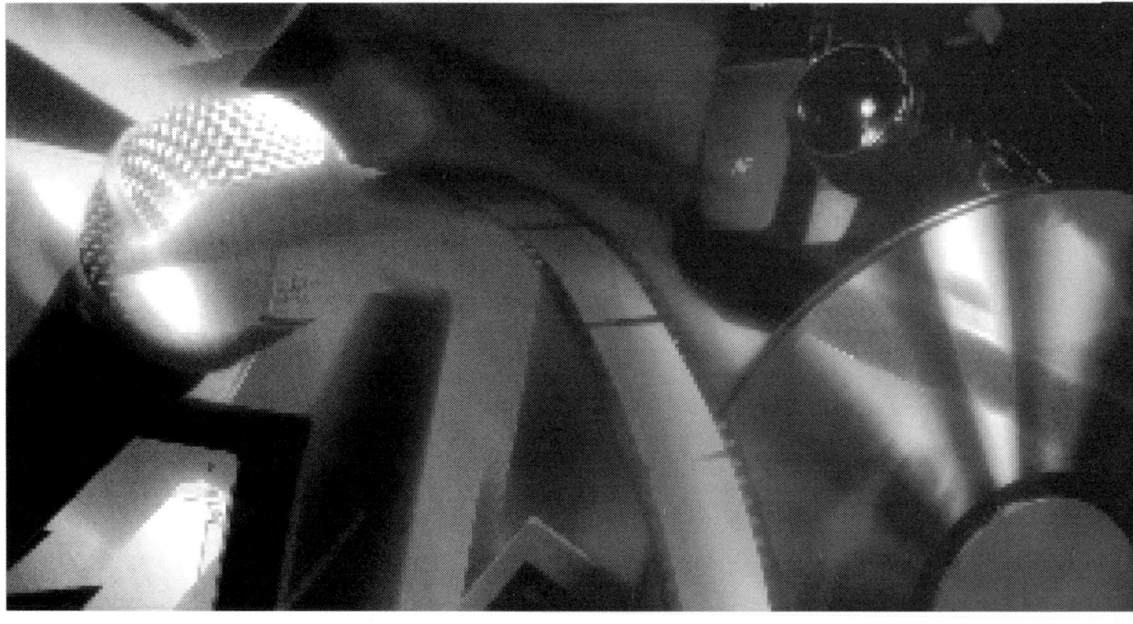

Making good multimedia is picking a successful route through the software swamp.

The software in your multimedia toolkit, and your skill at using it...

test and review

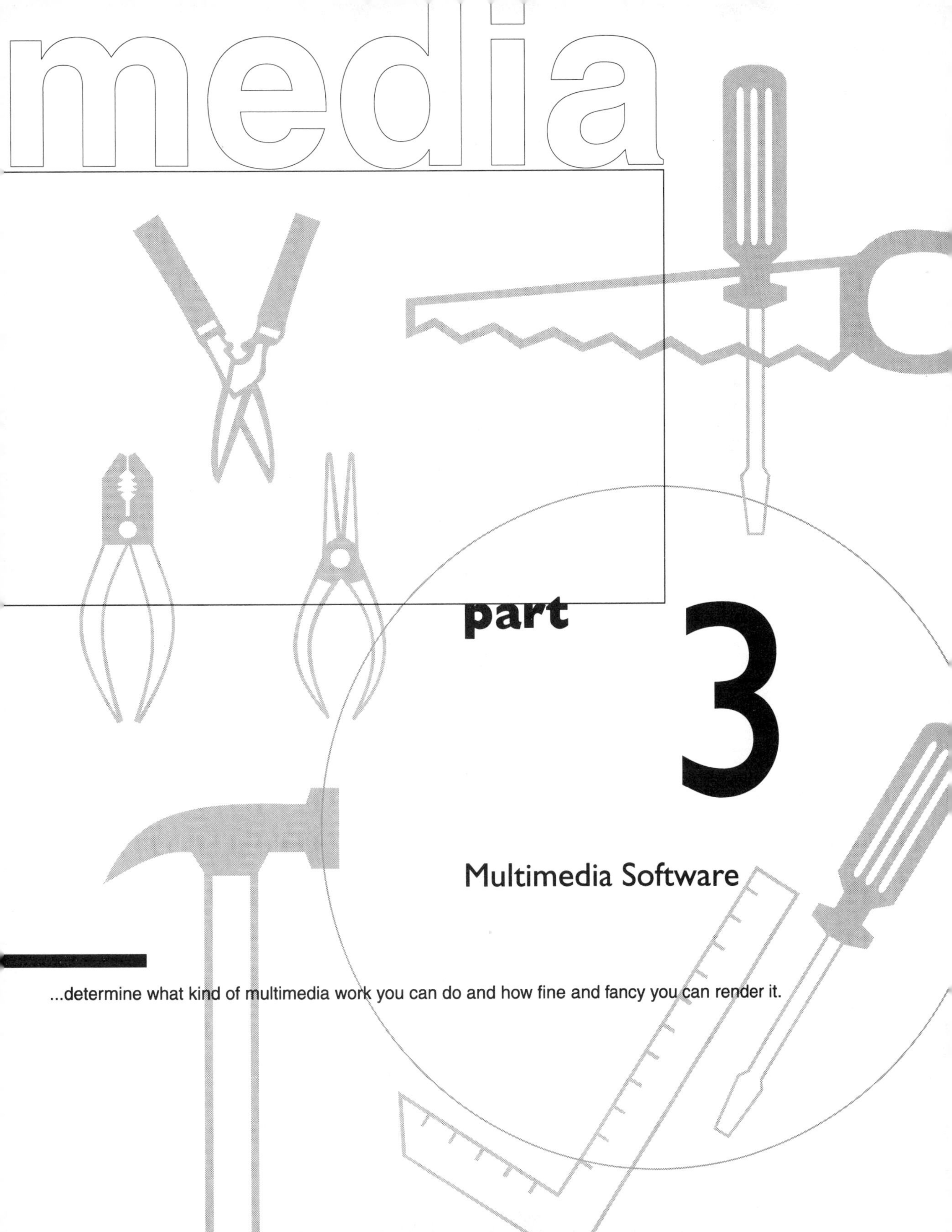

media

part 3

Multimedia Software

...determine what kind of multimedia work you can do and how fine and fancy you can render it.

Multi

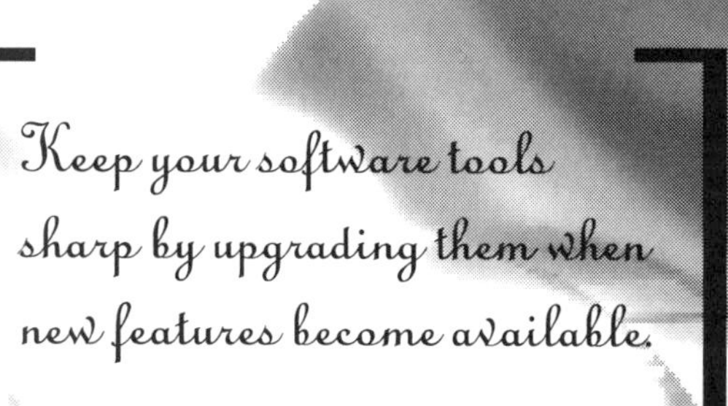

Keep your software tools sharp by upgrading them when new features become available.

The software in your multimedia toolkit, and your skill at using it...

test and review

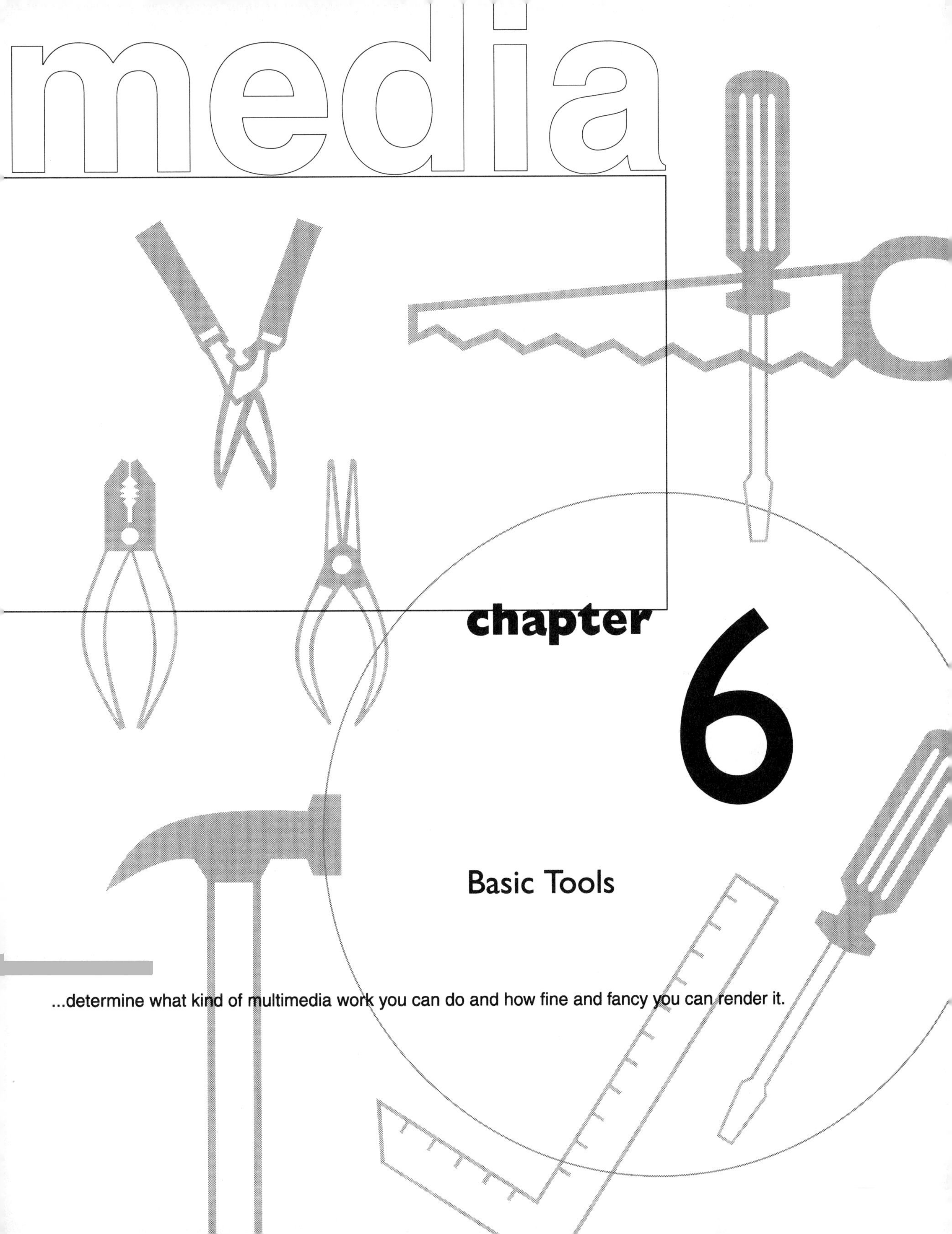

media

chapter 6

Basic Tools

...determine what kind of multimedia work you can do and how fine and fancy you can render it.

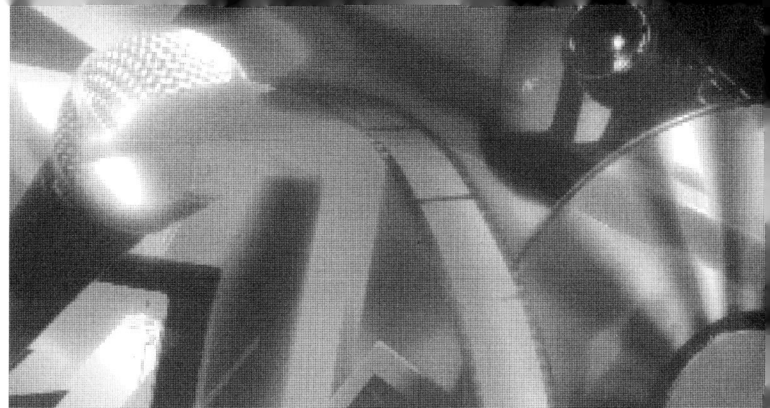

THE basic tool set for building multimedia projects contains one or more authoring systems and various editing applications for text, images, sounds, and motion video. A few additional applications are also useful for capturing images from the screen, translating file formats, and moving files among computers when you are part of a team—these are tools for the housekeeping tasks that make your creative and production life easier. The software in your multimedia toolkit, and your skill at using it, determine what kind of multimedia work you can do and how fine and fancy you can render it. Making good multimedia is picking a successful route through the software swamp. The alligators rise up out of nowhere to nip you in the knees.

Keep your software tools sharp by upgrading them when new features become available, by thoroughly studying and learning each tool, by reading tips and tricks in the computer magazines and trade press, and by observing the practices and products of other multimedia developers.

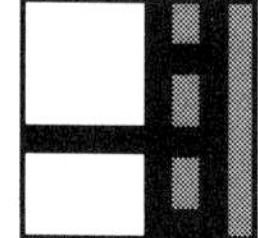

tip *Always fill out the registration card for your new software and return it to the vendor. If the vendor pays attention to product marketing, you will receive upgrade offers and often special newsletters with helpful information.*

The tools used for creating and editing multimedia elements on both the Macintosh and Windows platforms, listed in the following table, support the authoring systems described in Chapter 8. This is only a representative list of recommendations, not an exclusive one.

PAINTING AND DRAWING

Canvas
Charisma
ColorStudio
Corel Draw
Cricket Draw
Cricket Graph
Cricket Paint
DeltaGraph Pro
Designer
DeskDraw
DeskPaint
Fractal Design Painter
Harvard Graphics
Illustrator
ImageStudio
MacDraw Pro
MacPaint
PixelPaint Pro
Professional Draw
Studio 1/8/32
SuperPaint
Windows Draw

CAD AND 3-D

3-D Studio
addDepth
AutoCAD
Claris CAD
Infini-D
Life Forms
MacroModel
MiniCad+
ModelShop
RayDream Designer
StrataVision
Super 3D
Swivel 3D
Three-D
VersaCAD
Virtus WalkThrough

IMAGE EDITING

Color It!
ColorStudio
Composer
Digital Darkroom
Gallery Effects
JagII
Ofoto
Photoshop
PhotoStyler
Picture Publisher

OCR AND TEXT

OmniPage
Perceive
TypeAlign
Typestry
TypeStyler

SOUND EDITING

Alchemy
AudioShop
AudioTrax
Encore
Master Tracks Pro
Midisoft Studio
Sound Designer II
SoundEdit Pro
TurboTrax
WaveEdit

VIDEO AND MOVIE-MAKING

Animator Pro
Elastic Reality
MediaMaker
MetaFlo
Morph
MoviePak
Premiere
Screen Machine
SuperVideo
VideoFusion
Video Grafitti
VideoMachine
VideoShop
VideoSpigot
Videovision
VideoWare HSC

ACCESSORIES

Capture
ClipMedia
CompileIt
ConvertIt!
DeBabelizer
DiskDoubler
Fetch
FreezeFrame
Hijaak
Image Alchemy
ImagePals
Kai's Power Tools
Kudo Image Browser
Media Cataloger
MediaDOCS
MediaOrganizer
MusicBytes
Photo Disc
PICTpocket
ResEdit
Shoebox
SmartPics
SnapPRO!
StuffIt
upDiff
Wraptures

The following tools are featured on the Macromedia Product Showcase CD-ROM included in this book: Life Forms, MacroModel, ModelShop, Swivel 3D, Three-D, SoundEdit Pro, MediaMaker, and ClipMedia

Each new tool has a learning curve.

David Spitzer, Learning Products Engineer, Hewlett-Packard

Painting and Drawing Tools

Painting and drawing tools are perhaps the most important items in your toolkit because, of all the multimedia elements, the graphic impact of your project will likely have the greatest influence on the end user. If your artwork is amateurish, or flat and uninteresting, both you and your users will be disappointed.

First Person

When I left graduate school, I joined the Carpenters Union and built highway bridges, apartment houses, and fine custom homes. The wholesale tool supply store that catered to the trade had one wall covered with more than a hundred different hammers–some for nailing big nails, some for tiny upholstery tacks, some for metal work, others with a hatchet on one side for shingles, or with a waffled striking head that would drive slick and wet nails under the roughest conditions. They all came in different weights and handle lengths and shapes. I tested a few framing hammers and chose a 24-ounce waffle-head that felt good. With it, I could drive 16d nails in a single stroke. It was a Vaughan hammer.

Next day at noon, the union steward took me aside and quietly told me that The Rules limited hammer weight to 22 ounces; the older guys couldn't keep up. My hammer was illegal, and if he saw it the next day, I'd be sent back to the hiring hall. "Sorry," I said, "Jeez, I didn't know." He let me leave early so I could get to the tool store before it closed.

In producing multimedia, no tool is illegal. You should use the best tools that fit your talent, needs, and budget.

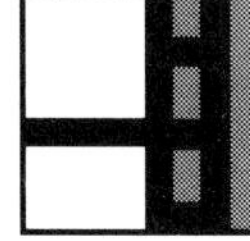

tip *Look in Chapter 15 for suggestions for designing effective graphical screens.*

Painting software is dedicated to producing excellent bitmapped images. Drawing software is dedicated to producing line art that is easily printed to paper using PostScript or another page markup system such as QuickDraw on the Macintosh. Drawing packages include powerful and expensive computer-aided design (CAD) software, which is increasingly used for rendering three-dimensional artwork.

Some software applications combine both drawing and painting capabilities, but many authoring systems can import only bitmapped images. The differences between painting and drawing (that is, between bitmap and drawn images) are described in Chapter 11. Typically, bitmapped images provide the greatest choice and power to the artist for rendering fine detail and effects, and bitmaps are used in multimedia more often than drawn objects. The anti-aliased character shown in the bitmap of Color Plate 5 is an example of the fine touches that improve the look of an image.

Look for these features in a drawing or painting package:

- An intuitive graphic interface with pull-down menus, status bars, palette control, and dialog boxes for quick, logical selection
- Scalable dimensions, so you can resize, stretch, and distort both large and small bitmaps

- Paint tools to create geometric shapes from squares to circles and from curves to complex polygons
- Ability to pour a color, pattern, or gradient into any area
- Ability to paint with patterns and clip art
- Customizable pen shapes and sizes
- Support for scalable text fonts and drop shadows
- Undo capabilities, to let you try again
- Painting features such as smoothing coarse-edged objects into the background with anti-aliasing (see Color Plate 5); airbrushing in variable sizes, shapes, densities, and patterns; washing colors in gradients; blending; and masking
- Zooming, for magnified pixel editing
- All common color depths: 1-, 4-, 8-, and 16- or 24-bit color, and gray-scale
- Good color management and dithering capability among color depths using various color models such as RGB, HSB, and CMYK
- Good palette management when in 8-bit mode
- Good file importing and exporting capability for image formats such as PIC, GIF, TGA, TIF, WIN, AVC, PCX, EPS, PTN, and BMP

If you are new to multimedia and to these tools, you should take time to examine more than one software package. Find someone who is already familiar with these applications. You will spend many days learning to use your painting and drawing software, and if it does not fit you and your needs, you will be unhappy. Many artists learn to use a single, powerful tool well.

CAD and 3-D Drawing Tools

Because they consist of drawn or vector graphics, computer-aided design (CAD) images are easily manipulated mathematically in the computer. They can be resized, rotated, and, if there is depth information, spun about in space, with lighting conditions exactly simulated and shadows properly drawn—all by computer number crunching. With CAD software, you can

First Person

During the early 1980s, I founded an accredited maritime school at Pier 66 in San Francisco, and we offered courses in everything from high-tech composite plastics and welding to Rules of the Road and celestial navigation. We also ran several marine trade certification programs. When I talked with Ford, General Motors, Cummins, and Caterpillar about setting up a course for marine diesel mechanics, I was surprised at their competitive interest in supporting the program. It turned out that a widely publicized survey had shown that a mechanic trained to work on a particular brand of engine will stick with it for life, loyally recommending and supporting that brand.

The same holds true for software. By the time you master an application, you have spent many hours on its learning curve. You will likely stay with that product and its upgrade path rather than change to another.

watch a drawing go from 2-D to 3-D elevation and stand in front of your work and view it from any angle, making judgments about its design. You can create animated walk-throughs and even sun studies based on geographic location, time of day, and time of year. You can generate realistic 3-D renderings for movie presentations. Figure 6-1 shows a simple floor plan rendered to 3-D perspective by MiniCad+.

Each rendered 3-D image takes from a few seconds to a few hours to complete, depending upon the complexity of the drawing and the number of drawn objects included in it. If you wish to turn a sequence of these renderings into a visually smooth animation movie, walk-through, or flyby, plan to set aside many hours of computation time on your computer.

tip *If there are small errors or things you would like to change in a rendered movie sequence, it may take less time to edit each frame by hand, using an image editing program, than to re-render the corrected original.*

There are other ways to develop a 3-D look to your images. Set up a photo shoot. Make a stage using a black or white nonreflective cloth for a background, and place an object or scene in the center. You can then use a video camera and capture board (or a still camera and scanner to digitize developed photographs) to make an image of the scene. Lighting effects and shadows—very important to the 3-D effect—can be adjusted as you work by using inexpensive hand-held flashlights (some flashlights even let you focus the beam and vary the intensity for good spot effects). When you have finished, you can clean up the image in an editing program.

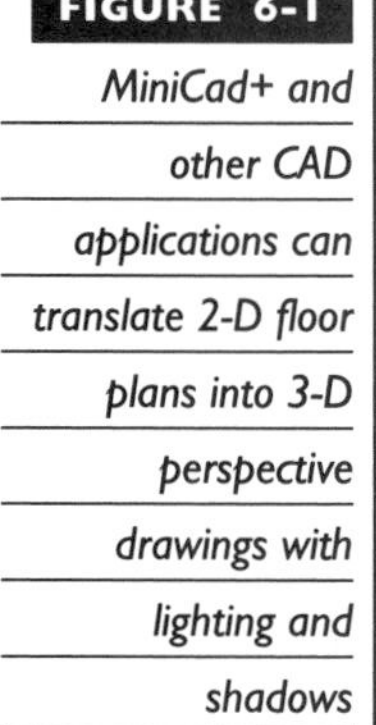

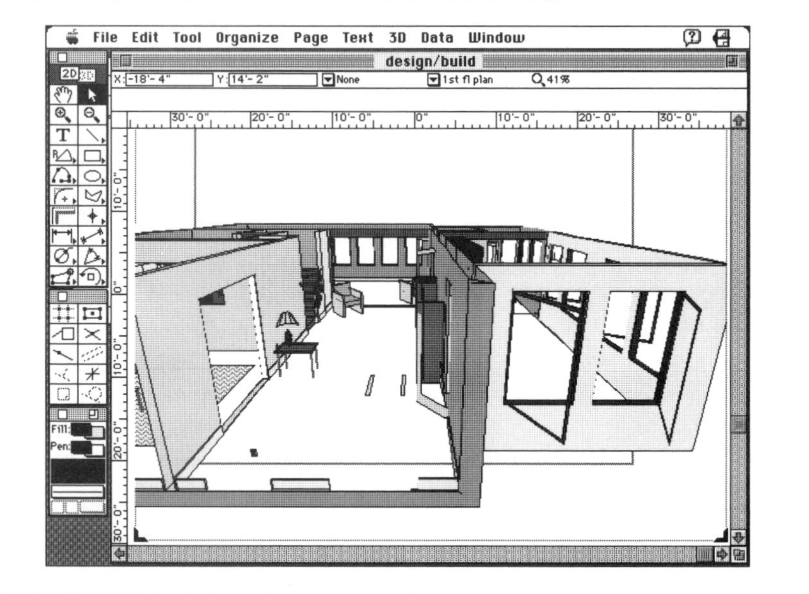

FIGURE 6-1 MiniCad+ and other CAD applications can translate 2-D floor plans into 3-D perspective drawings with lighting and shadows

Image Editing Tools

Image editing applications are specialized and powerful tools for enhancing and retouching existing bitmapped images usually destined as color separations for print output. These programs are also indispensable tools for rendering the images used in multimedia presentations. Increasingly, modern versions of these programs also provide many of the features and tools of painting and drawing programs and can be used to create images from scratch as well as images digitized from scanners, video frame-grabbers, digital cameras, clip art files, or original artwork files created with a painting or drawing package.

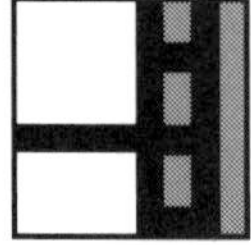

tip *If you want to print an image to a 300-dpi laser printer for collateral reports and attractive print-matter icons, work with the image in the image editing application at 300 dpi in black and white (every black pixel will be a very fine laser printer dot). Then resize the image to one-fourth its size (leaving the resolution set at 300 dpi), and save it as a PICT or TIFF file for importing into your word processor. The result is a finely detailed black-and-white picture printed at the highest resolution of your laser printer.*

Here are some features typical of image editing applications and of interest to multimedia developers:

- Multiple windows provide views of more than one image at a time
- Conversion of major image-data types and industry-standard file formats
- Direct inputs of images from scanner and video sources
- Employment of a virtual memory scheme that uses hard disk space as RAM for images that require large amounts of memory
- Capable selection tools, such as rectangles, lassos, and magic wands, to select portions of a bitmap
- Image and balance controls for brightness, contrast, and color balance
- Good masking features
- Undo and restore features
- Anti-aliasing capability, and sharpening and smoothing controls
- Color-mapping controls for precise adjustment of color balance
- Tools for retouching, blurring, sharpening, lightening, darkening, smudging, and tinting
- Geometric transformations such as flip, skew, rotate, and distort, and perspective changes
- Ability to resample and resize an image
- 24- or 16-bit color, 8- or 4-bit indexed color, 8-bit gray-scale, black and white, and customizable color palettes
- Ability to create images from scratch, using line, rectangle, square, circle, ellipse, polygon, airbrush, paintbrush, pencil, and eraser tools, with customizable brush shapes and user-definable bucket and gradient fills
- Multiple typefaces, styles, and sizes, and type manipulation and masking routines
- Filters for special effects, such as crystallize, dry brush, emboss, facet, fresco, graphic pen, mosaic, pixelize, poster, ripple, smooth, splatter, stucco, twirl, watercolor, wave, and wind (see Color Plate 7).

Gallery Effects, stand-alone image editing tools or "plug-ins" from Silicon Beach/Aldus, offers 16 excellent effects to transform images; these effects also work directly within Photoshop, PhotoStyler, ColorStudio, Digital

Darkroom, and Fractal Design Painter. Kai's Power Tools offers more effects and has powerful built-in algorithms for making fractal images.

Image editing programs usually come with plug-in modules allowing you to warp, twist, and otherwise "filter" your images for special effects, but painting/drawing applications such as Brøderbund's TypeStyler, Pixar's Typestry, and Adobe's TypeAlign are designed to manipulate typefaces in a graphical way. Figure 6-2 shows text being drawn and manipulated using TypeAlign. The custom-tortured characters can be captured as a bitmap and incorporated into your project.

OCR Software

Often you will have printed matter and other text to incorporate into your project, but no electronic text file. With optical character recognition (OCR) software, a flatbed scanner, and your computer, you can save many hours of rekeying printed words, and get the job done faster and more accurately than a roomful of typists.

OCR software turns bitmapped characters into electronically recognizable ASCII text. A scanner is typically used to create the bitmap. Then the software breaks the bitmap into chunks according to whether it contains

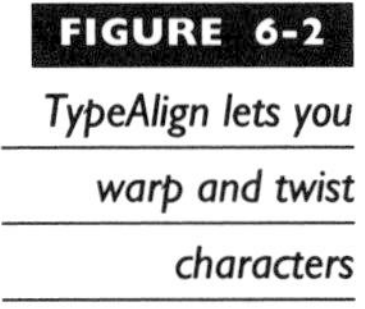

FIGURE 6-2

TypeAlign lets you warp and twist characters

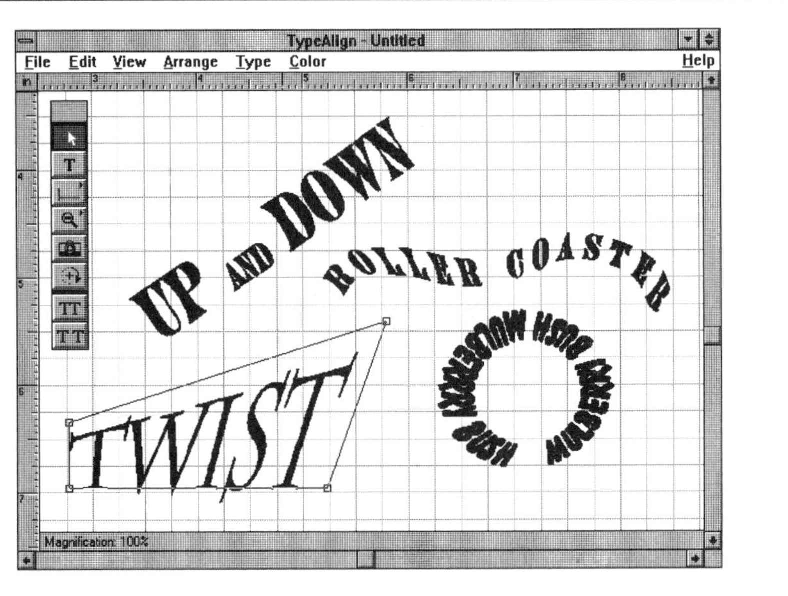

text or graphics, by examining the texture and density of areas of the bitmap and by detecting edges. The text areas of the image are then converted to ASCII characters using probability and expert system algorithms. Most OCR applications for Macintosh and Windows claim about 99 percent accuracy when reading 8- to 36-point characters at 300 dpi and can reach processing speeds of about 150 characters per second.

Perceive, a Windows OCR application from Ocron, offers a learning mode for recognizing any typeface, European language, or special symbols, and it will provide formatted output to most popular word processors.

Figure 6-3 shows a document in the process of bitmap-to-character conversion by OmniPage Pro (Macintosh version) from Caere.

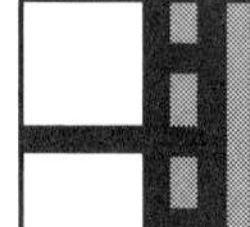

tip *Many OCR applications are also bundled with hand-held scanners that are usually less expensive than flat-bed scanners.*

Sound Editing Programs

Sound editing tools for both digitized and MIDI sound let you see music as well as hear it. By drawing a representation of a sound in fine increments, whether a score or a waveform, you can cut, copy, paste, and otherwise edit

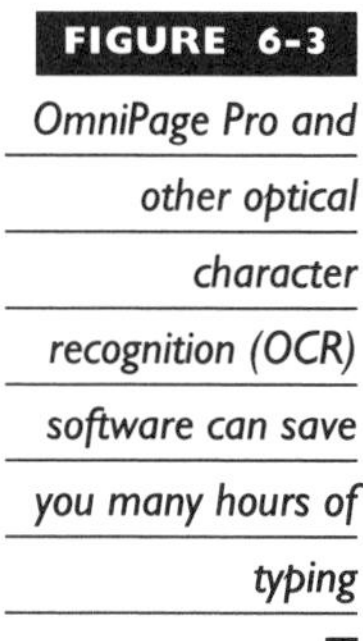

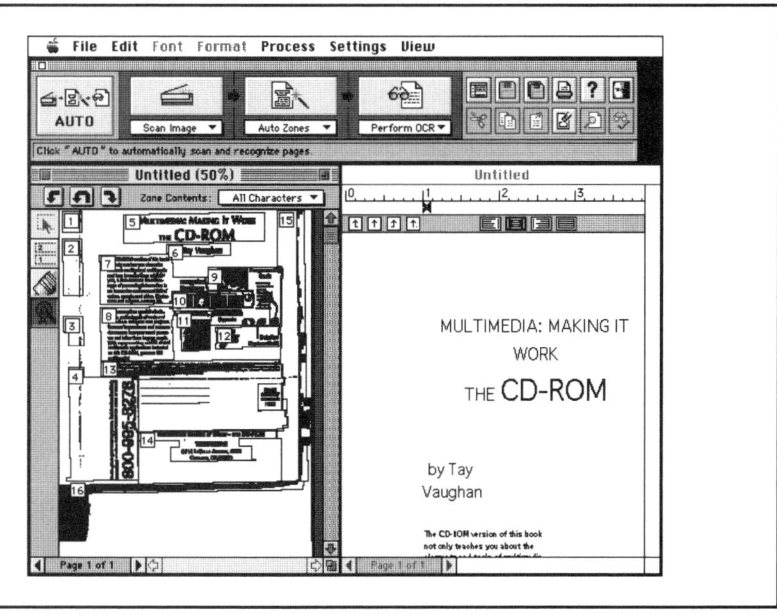

FIGURE 6-3 *OmniPage Pro and other optical character recognition (OCR) software can save you many hours of typing*

segments of it with great precision—something impossible to do in real time (that is, with the music playing). The basics of computerized sound for both the Macintosh and Windows environments are discussed in Chapter 10.

System sounds are shipped with both Macintosh and Windows systems (see Figure 10-1 in Chapter 10), and they are available as soon as you install the operating system. System sounds are the beeps used to indicate an error, warning, or special user activity. On the Macintosh you get Droplet, Indigo, Quack, Simple Beep, Sosumi, and Wild Eep. In Windows you get chimes, chord, ding, and tada. With Windows Multimedia Extensions installed, you get bells, blocks, clock, gong, jawharp, laser, ohoh, siren, and water. Using sound editing software, you can make your own sound effects and install them as system beeps, to the delight (or perhaps dismay) of colleagues and neighbors.

For digital waveform sounds, Windows ships with the Sound Recorder program, which provides some rudimentary features for sound editing; and the Windows Multimedia Development Kit ships with a simple editor, WaveEdit, shown in Figure 6-4. The Macintosh, however, does not ship with sound editing tools, so Macintosh users need to invest in an editor such as SoundEdit Pro from Macromedia, Alchemy or AudioTrax from Passport, or Sound Designer II from DigiDesign.

cross platform *WaveEdit in Windows can convert Macintosh AIFF sound file formats, but most Macintosh digital sound editing applications cannot import or convert Windows .WAV files.*

Although you can usually incorporate MIDI sound files into your multimedia project without learning any special skills, using editing tools to make your own MIDI files requires that you understand the way music

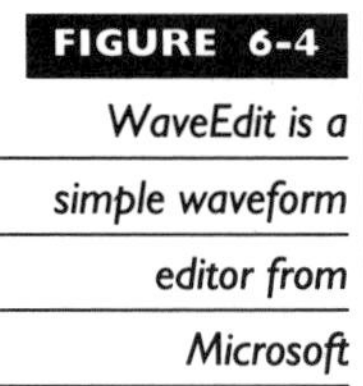

FIGURE 6-4

WaveEdit is a simple waveform editor from Microsoft

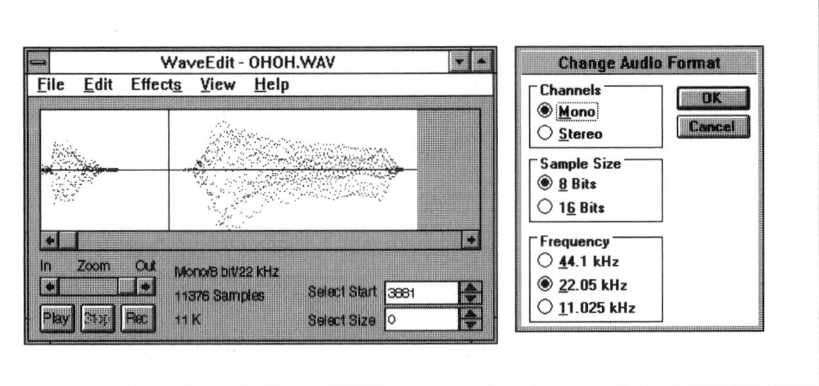

is sequenced, scored, and published; see Chapter 10 for details. You need to know about tempos, clefs, notations, keys, and instruments. And you will need a MIDI synthesizer or device connected to your computer. Many MIDI applications provide both sequencing and notation capabilities, and some, such as Alchemy (see Figure 6-5) and AudioTrax, let you edit both digital audio and MIDI within the same application.

Animation, Video, and Digital Movies

Animations and digital video movies are sequences of bitmapped graphic scenes (*frames*), rapidly played back. But animations can also be made within the authoring system by rapidly changing the location of *objects* or *sprites* to generate an appearance of motion. Most authoring tools adopt either a frame- or object-oriented approach to animation, but rarely both (see Chapter 12 for more about animation).

Movie-making tools take advantage of QuickTime (Macintosh) and Microsoft Video for Windows (also known as AVI, or Audio Video Interleaved) technology and let you create, edit, and present digitized motion video segments, usually in a small window in your project. To make movies from video you need special hardware to convert the analog video signal to digital data (see Chapter 13). Movie-making tools such as

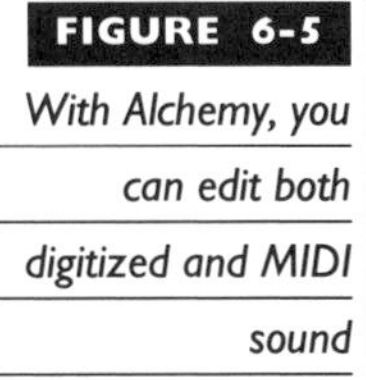

FIGURE 6-5 With Alchemy, you can edit both digitized and MIDI sound

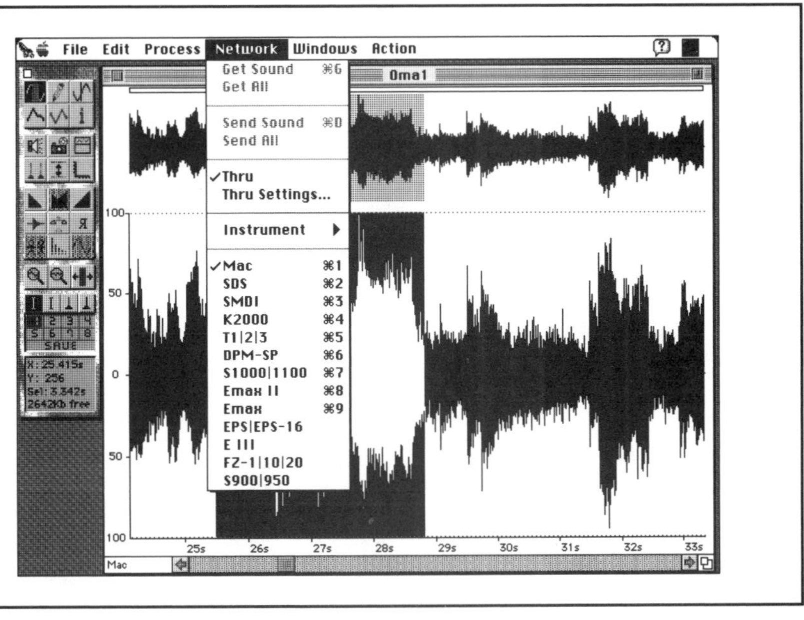

Premiere(see Figure 6-6) let you edit and assemble video clips captured from camera, tape, other digitized movie segments, animations, scanned images, and from digitized audio or MIDI files. The completed clip, often with added transition and visual effects, can then be played back—either stand-alone or windowed within your project.

Morph, a popular software application for the Macintosh (see Color Plate 12) allows you to dynamically blend two still images, creating a sequence of in-between pictures that, when played back rapidly in QuickTime, metamorphoses the first image into the second. A racing car transforms itself into a tiger; a mother's face becomes her daughter's.

warning *Because only de facto animation standards exist today, you will want to use editing tools that allow you to save to a format that can be efficiently shared with other applications and your authoring system. On the Macintosh, PICS files are perhaps the most common animation format. On PCs, the most common animation files are Macromedia's MMM format and Autodesk's FLI and FLC formats. QuickTime and AVI use their own proprietary formats.*

Video Formats

Formats and systems for storing and playing digitized video to and from disk files are available with QuickTime and AVI. Both systems depend on special algorithms that control the amount of information per video frame that

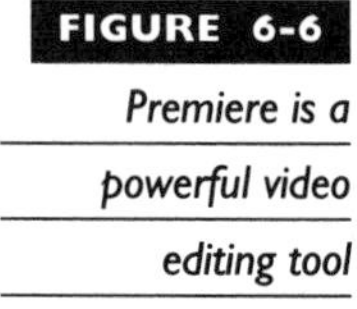

FIGURE 6-6

Premiere is a powerful video editing tool

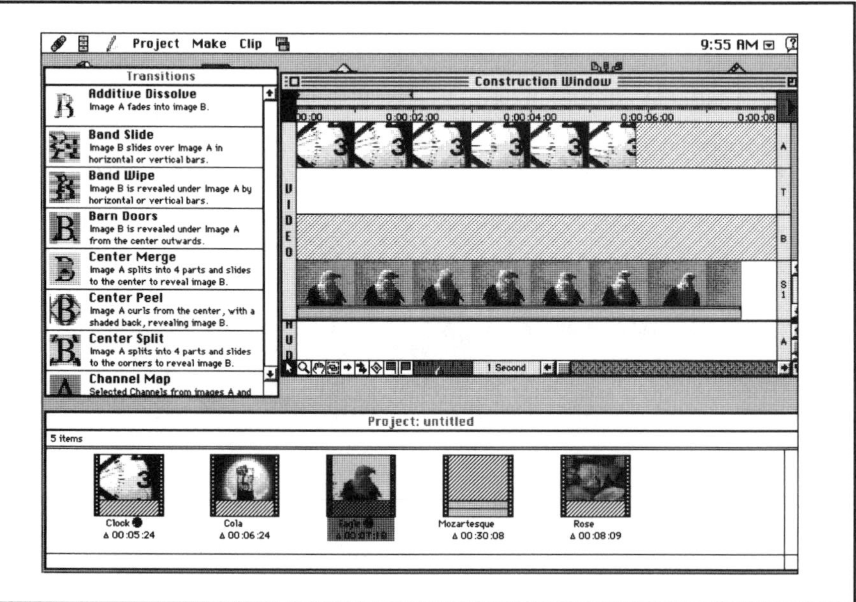

is sent to the screen, as well as the rate at which new frames are displayed. Currently, neither technology provides full-screen images at 30 frames per second (NTSC television standard) without the aid of special add-on boards; neither the PC nor the Macintosh have the processing horsepower. Both technologies provide a methodology for *interleaving* or blending audio data with video data so that sound remains synchronized with the video. And both technologies allow data to stream from disk into memory in a buffered and organized manner.

QuickTime is an organizer of time-related data in many forms. Classic videotape involves a video track with two tracks of audio; QuickTime is a multitrack recorder in which you can have an almost unlimited range of tracks. Digitized video, digitized sound, computer animations, MIDI data, external devices such as CD-ROM players and hard disks, and even the potential for interactive command systems are all supported by the QuickTime format. With QuickTime, you can have a movie with five different available languages, titles, MIDI cue tracks, or the potential for interactive commands.

In Windows, the Media Control Interface (MCI) is a more traditional organizing vehicle. MCI provides a uniform command interface for managing audio and video that interleaves audio and video together in the file, hence the Audio Video Interleaved name for the technology. MCI is discussed in greater detail in Chapter 5.

DVI (Digital Video Interactive) is proprietary technology from Intel and IBM, and it may have a place in your multimedia toolkit. Facing the inevitable performance limits of both platforms, DVI offers a dedicated hardware solution for compressing video and audio information and playing it back full-screen with excellent quality.

The QuickTime and Microsoft Video for Windows (AVI) formats are discussed in greater detail below.

QuickTime

QuickTime is Apple's software-based architecture for seamlessly integrating sound, animation, and video (data that changes over time) into any Macintosh with a color-capable processor (Motorola 68020 or greater). QuickTime lets you create, compress, view, control, and edit QuickTime movie files in a consistent fashion across all applications.

QuickTime is a devious plot, by Apple and other hardware vendors, to get you to buy lots of STUFF.

Bob Levitus, author, after ordering a Quadra 950, gigabyte hard drive, and 64MB RAM upgrade, all needed to complete his book about QuickTime

QuickTime Building Blocks

QuickTime includes four elements, described in the following paragraphs, that work in unison:

- A system software extension
- A set of compression algorithms
- A standard "movie" file format
- A standard human interface for defining the dynamic data capture, compression, and playback characteristics.

QuickTime System Software

The QuickTime system-level software extension consists of three pieces: the Movie Toolbox, the Image Compression Manager (ICM), and the Component Manager.

- The Movie Toolbox is a set of high-level system software services that make it easy for your applications to incorporate support for movies.
- The ICM shields applications from the intricacies of compression and decompression, by using device- and algorithm-independent services. This compression manager lets you take advantage of new and improved compression schemes from within many QuickTime-savvy applications without having to buy an upgrade for your applications. Display details such as clipping, scaling, crossing screens, and fast dithering are supported automatically via the ICM. With QuickTime's dithering capabilities, you can create a movie in 24 bit, and play it back in 1, 8, 16, or 24 bits with the same playback speed.
- The Component Manager allows external resources (for example, digitizing cards, VCRs, and compression software extensions) to register their capabilities with the system at run time. With an appropriate QuickTime component installed in the System Folder, any piece of QuickTime hardware is transparent to end user applications. An application merely makes a request to the Component Manager for a piece of hardware (for instance, "digitizer card with X capabilities"), and the Component Manager takes care of locating components of that type.

QuickTime Compression Schemes

QuickTime 1.6.1 features six compression schemes or *codecs* (coder-decoders): Photo Compressor (JPEG), Video Compressor, Animation Compressor, Graphics Compressor, Apple Cinepak, and YUV Compressor.

APPLE PHOTO-JPEG COMPRESSOR The Photo Compressor implements a JPEG-based algorithm. The JPEG compressor generally yields compression ratios in the range of 10:1 to 25:1 without visible degradation of the image. This compression scheme is used for still images, and for video that has been compressed using hardware compression. Without the power of a compression board, this codec slows the video down to unacceptable rates. With it, compression ratios of up to 180 to 1 are possible, as is full-screen, full-motion (60 fields per second) video.

APPLE VIDEO COMPRESSOR The Video Compressor uses a proprietary algorithm developed by Apple. It is the most basic QuickTime compressor and supports both spatial and temporal compression and takes about three times as long to compress a full-screen image as it does to decompress the same image. Compression ratios range from 5:1 to 25:1 and can typically play back about 15 frames per second in a small 160×120 pixel window on a Macintosh IIsi.

APPLE ANIMATION COMPRESSOR The Animation Compressor is based on Run Length Encoding (RLE). It can operate in a lossless or lossy mode (described in "Compressing Movie Files," later in this chapter) and takes about twice as long to compress a full-screen image as it does to decompress the same image. Ratios vary, depending on the content of the images. As the name implies, this codec is optimized for animation. The Apple Animation Codec displays animation at acceptable speeds on low-end Macintosh systems and allows complex animation to be previewed on a Macintosh system without first having to lay them to videotape one frame at a time. It also offers the unique ability to play the movie within an irregular mask—a useful feature when, for example, you want to layer a moving face into an otherwise still image.

APPLE GRAPHICS COMPRESSOR The Graphics Compressor is similar to the Apple Animation Codec, but is optimized for 8-bit graphics, with a faster compression speed but slower decompression speed. This compressor may not be appropriate for CD-ROM playback, where decompression speed is important.

APPLE CINEPAK Compared to the Video Codec above, the Apple Cinepak Compressor significantly increases the image quality, playback size, frame rate, and compression of digitized video. While taking substantially longer to compress a movie (30 seconds to two minutes per frame), the software-only Cinepak Compressor can play back a movie on a Macintosh IIsi in a 240×180 pixel window at 15 frames per second off of CD-ROM. On more powerful Macintosh systems, frame sizes and frame rates can reach quarter screen (320×240 pixels) and 24 frames per second. With QuickTime 1.6.1, Cinepak playback to 16-bit destinations (thousands of colors) is now of higher quality. The dithering algorithm has been significantly improved. This codec was developed by SuperMac and also exists in AVI files.

YUV CODEC A YUV Compressor/Decompressor Component stores data in YUV 4:2:2 format. The compression algorithm is not lossless, but the image quality is extremely high. The compression ratio is 2:1. The YUV codec is useful with certain video input solutions, and it is also useful as an intermediate storage format if users are applying multiple effects or transitions to an image.

OTHER COMPRESSION SCHEMES Version 1.6.1 of QuickTime includes the Kodak Photo CD codec, the Compact Disc Video codec, and the SuperMac codec. Third-party developers are designing new and improved schemes for compression. Real Time Video (RTV), for example, is a software-only decompression scheme from NewVideo Corporation to permit Intel DVI files to be played back on Macintosh computers without special and expensive hardware.

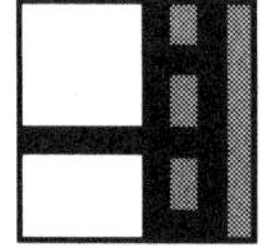

tip *Every QuickTime compressor is designed for a specific data type. You should test your movie with an assortment of compressors before choosing the one best suited.*

QuickTime Movie File Format

Along with operating system calls and compression schemes, Apple developed a new file format, the "movie." Think of a QuickTime movie as a container for one or many "tracks," each containing information about time-related data. A QuickTime movie track points to a stream of data stored on your hard drive or on a CD-ROM. The track uses the movie's time coordinate system and begins at the beginning of the movie, but the track's data may not begin until some time value other than 0 is reached. The track is, in essence, a media edit list. Unlike traditional analog video, your

QuickTime movies may contain any combination of video, animation, audio, MIDI, text, and even interactive command tracks, each with different start and stop points, to produce a single movie.

The movie format provides a standard method for the Macintosh toolbox to interact with your text, sound, animation, and video files, to synchronize them and ensure that they play back consistently on any QuickTime–enabled Macintosh. The movie format also defines the characteristics of your movie's "poster"—a single frame that represents, as an icon, the movie as a whole, as well as the portion of the movie to be used as a preview.

Another feature unique to QuickTime is its ability to support internal interactive commands as well as source material. Using an application that can support this capability, such as Motion Works IQ, a stand-alone interactive QuickTime movie can be built that needs only a simple movie player to run. Likewise, this feature has also been used to create "Navigable Movies," which allow users to look at any angle of a room or space as if they were actually there. The process of creating such a film requires a video camera on an automated pan/tilt head controlled by a Mac. This camera is used to take frames of the room from every possible angle. The resulting frames (which are recorded in a continuous movie) are then linked and given interactivity with another application.

In addition to creating a new file format, QuickTime also expands the PICT file format within the operating system to take advantage of the Photo-JPEG compressor. Using a program that knows about QuickTime, you can compress a graphic image with any QuickTime software or hardware compressor on your computer. One plus to this system is that a program able to open a simple PICT image needs no changes to be able to open an Apple Photo-JPEG compressed image. Updated application programs can save a small thumbnail version of a PICT image along with the PICT file. The new QuickTime-savvy Open... dialog box can then display these thumbnails as you browse your hard drive or CD-ROM content.

Most multimedia authoring systems for Macintosh can make and play QuickTime movies, and other programs such as SYSTAT (see Chapter 7) can export animations as QuickTime files. Other software, such as Microsoft Word and Lotus 1-2-3 for Macintosh, will play QuickTime movies.

Microsoft Video for Windows

Audio Video Interleaved (AVI) is Microsoft-developed software that plays full-motion interleaved video and audio sequences in Windows, without specialized hardware, at about 15 frames per second in a small window. With acceleration hardware, you can run AVI video sequences at 30 frames per second. Video data are interleaved with audio data within the file that contains the motion sequence, so the audio portion of the movie remains synchronized to the video portion.

Like Apple's QuickTime, AVI provides the following features:

- Playback from hard disk or CD-ROM
- Playback on computers with limited memory; data are streamed from the hard disk or CD-ROM player without using great amounts of memory
- Quick loading and playing, because only a few frames of video and a portion of audio are accessed at a time
- Video compression to boost the quality of your video sequences and reduce their size

AVI includes two tools to capture and edit video sequences and play them back: VidCap and VidEdit, respectively. AVI also includes data preparation tools (BitEdit, PalEdit, and WaveEdit), MCIAVI.DRV (the MCI driver for AVI), MediaPlayer, and sample video sequences.

Movie Players

With QuickTime players (SimplePlayer or Popcorn, for example), and with the Windows MediaPlayer (with AVI installed), you can view and edit movies. You can play a movie forward or backward, and resize it. You can also cut and copy frames from one movie and paste them into another. Popcorn, a freeware QuickTime player and editor supplied by Aladdin Systems for the Macintosh, is illustrated in Figure 6-7.

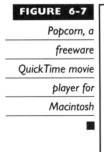

FIGURE 6-7 *Popcorn, a freeware QuickTime movie player for Macintosh*

With Wild Magic, Apple's extension for playing QuickTime movies in PICT-supporting applications, you can paste movies into documents in other applications and play them there. Windows's Media Player (see Figure 6-8) can run either as a stand-alone Windows application or as an embedded object in other applications and documents, using OLE. AddImpact! from Gold Disk is a Windows tool for playing back multimedia files from within an OLE-ready application document (see Figure 6-9).

Movie Editors

With the invention of QuickTime and Video for Windows, desktop video publishing (DVP) on Macintoshes and PCs became a digital process (see Chapter 13 for a discussion of the analog process). Improved compression and decompression techniques allow quarter-, half-, and full-screen/full-motion movies instead of the small, 160×120 pixel-sized movies characteristic of earlier digital video experiments.

With desktop editing software and an appropriate video digitizing board, you can digitize video clips, edit the clip offline, add special effects and titles, mix sound tracks, and save the finished product as digital file on magnetic or optical media.

Video digitizing boards for making Macintosh QuickTime movies from videotape are available from SuperMac, RasterOps, Radius, Fast, and others. The Targa board from TrueVision, VideoBlaster from Creative Labs, Super VideoWindows SL from New Media Graphics, and other boards are available for making AVI movies for Windows.

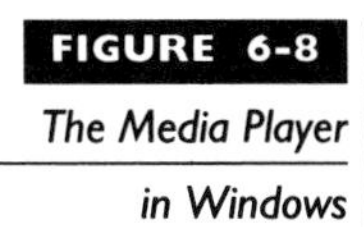

FIGURE 6-8 The Media Player in Windows

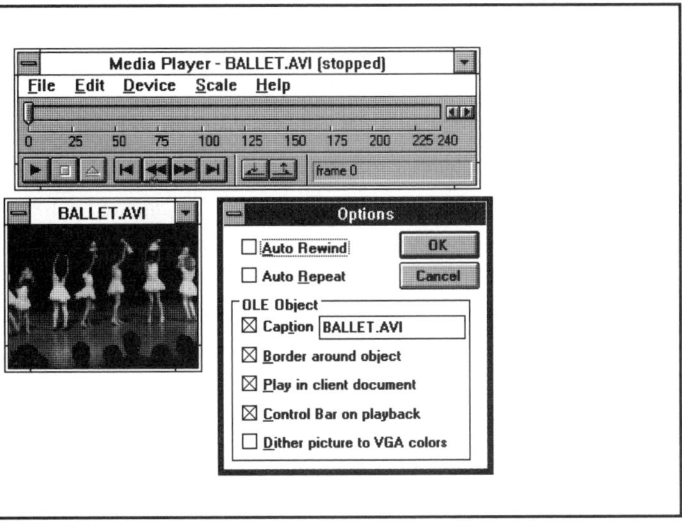

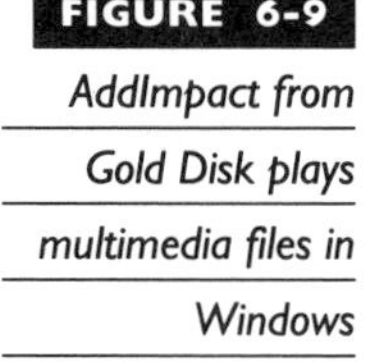

FIGURE 6-9

AddImpact from Gold Disk plays multimedia files in Windows

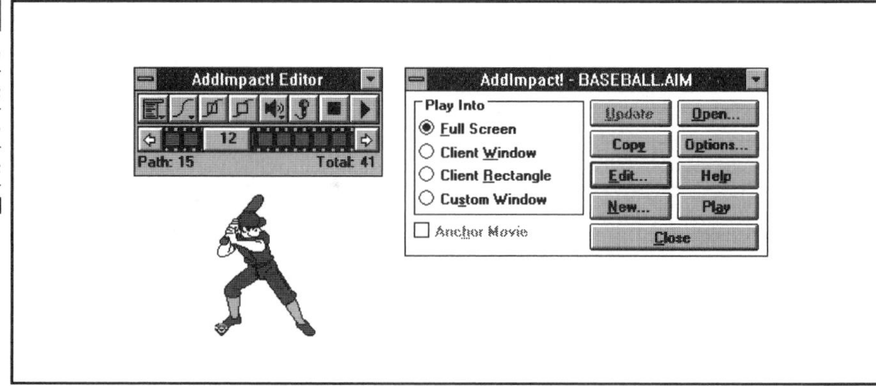

Specialized video editors have been designed around this technology for both the Macintosh and PC environments—for example, DIVA's VideoShop, Adobe's Premiere, and Fast's VideoMachine. These applications let you mix video clips, audio recordings, animation, still images, and graphics to create QuickTime or AVI movies. You arrange your clips linearly, cutting and pasting, and layering them into transitions with special effects such as dissolves, page turns, spins, tinting, distorting, and replicating. A familiar push-button control panel is used for stop, rewind, play, fast-forward, record, and single-stop, and these applications display time references, frame counts, and audio and transparency levels. Figure 6-10 shows a movie being edited in Premiere, with visual effects and sounds.

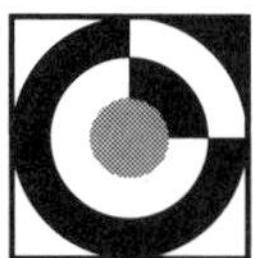

warning *Digital video editing and playback requires an immense amount of free disk space, even when the video files are compressed.*

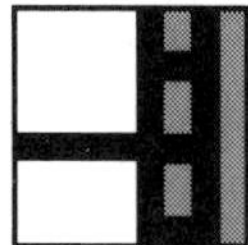

tip *Because digital movie data must stream rapidly and without interruption from your disk drive, be sure that you defragment and optimize your disk with a utility such as Norton's Speed Disk before recording and playing back your movie files. If your movie file is fragmented, the read head of the disk drive may need to pause sending data while it physically moves to wildly different locations on the disk; a defragmented file lets the head read sequentially from one adjoining sector to the next.*

Compressing Movie Files

Image compression algorithms are critical to the delivery of motion video and audio on both the Macintosh and PC platforms. Without compression,

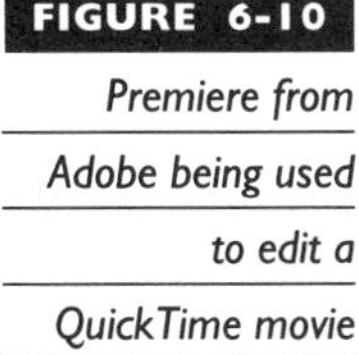

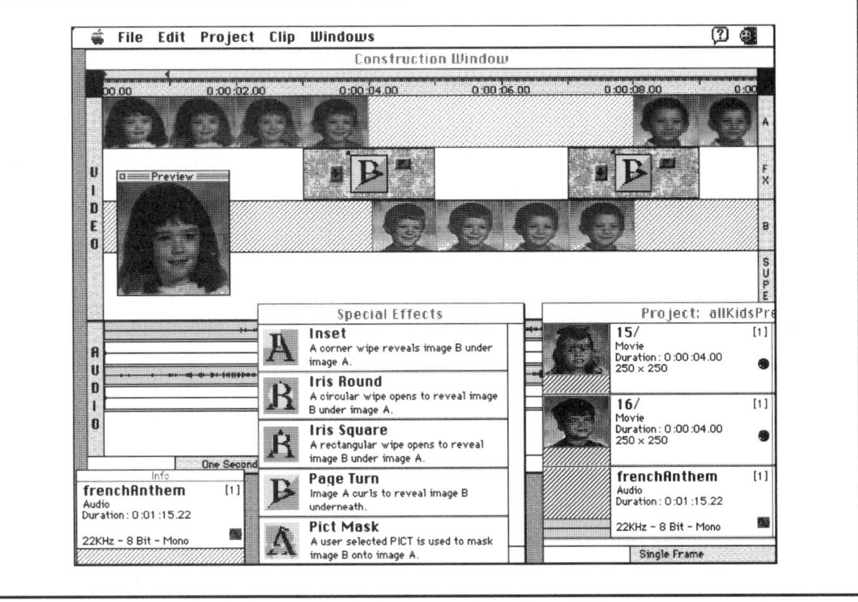

FIGURE 6-10 Premiere from Adobe being used to edit a QuickTime movie ■

there is simply not enough bandwidth on the Macintosh or PC to transfer the massive amounts of data involved in displaying a new screen image every one-thirtieth of a second. A compression ratio of 5:1 allows use of CD-ROM players to deliver streamed images at transfer rates of 150K per second (see Chapter 13); higher ratios allow transmission of video images over telephone lines. To understand compression, consider these three basic concepts:

COMPRESSION RATIO The compression ratio represents the size of the original image divided by the size of the compressed image—that is, how much the data are actually compressed. Some compression schemes yield ratios that are dependent on the image content: a busy image of a field of multicolored tulips may yield a very small compression ratio, and an image of blue ocean and sky may yield a very high compression ratio. Video compression typically manages only the part of an image that changes from image to image (the *delta*).

IMAGE QUALITY Compression is either lossy or lossless. *Lossy* schemes ignore picture information the viewer may not miss, but that means the picture information is in fact lost—even after decompression. And as more and more information is removed during compression, image quality decreases. *Lossless* schemes preserve the original data precisely—an important consideration in medical imaging, for example. The compression ratio typically affects picture quality because, usually, the higher the compression ratio, the lower the quality of the decompressed image.

COMPRESSION/DECOMPRESSION SPEED You will prefer a fast compression time while developing your project. Users, on the other hand, will appreciate a fast decompression time to increase display performance.

Helpful Accessories

No multimedia toolkit is complete without a few indispensable utilities to perform some odd, but oft-repeated, tasks. These are the comfortable and well-worn accessories that make your computer life easier.

Traditional PC application software developers must create the basic motivating applications and tools for the creative and content communities.

Bill Gates, Chairman of Microsoft Corporation, in his keynote address to the International Conference on Multimedia and CD-ROM, March 10, 1992

On both the Macintosh and in Windows, a screen grabber is essential. Because bitmapped images are so common in multimedia, it is important to have a tool for grabbing all or part of the screen display so you can import it into your authoring system or copy it into an image editing application. Screen grabbing to the Clipboard, for example, lets you move a bitmapped image from one application to another without the cumbersome steps of first exporting the image to a file and then importing it back into the destination application. Figure 6-11 shows dialog boxes from Capture (for the Macin-

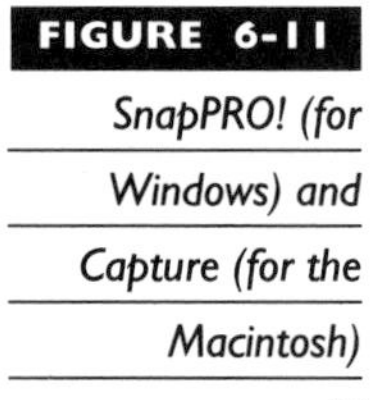

FIGURE 6-11 *SnapPRO! (for Windows) and Capture (for the Macintosh)*

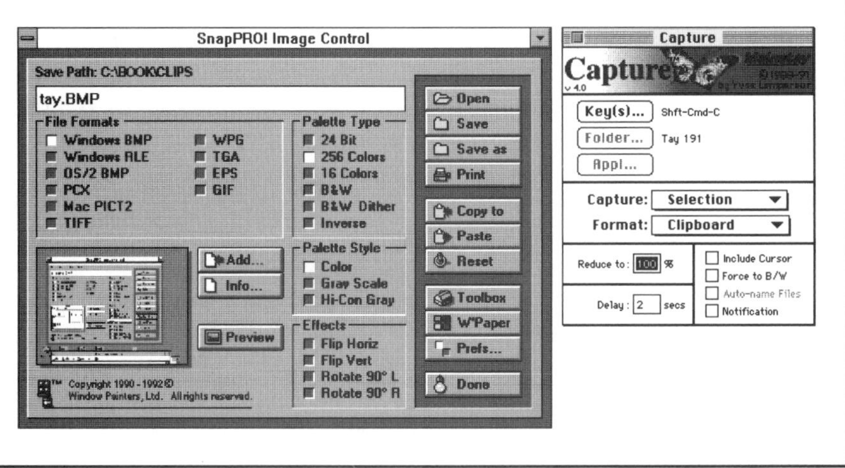

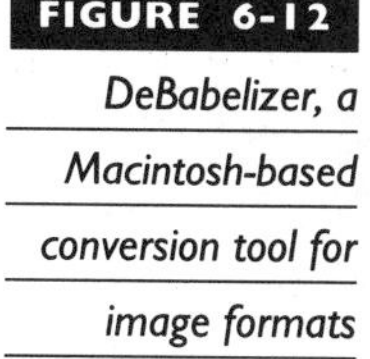

FIGURE 6-12

DeBabelizer, a Macintosh-based conversion tool for image formats

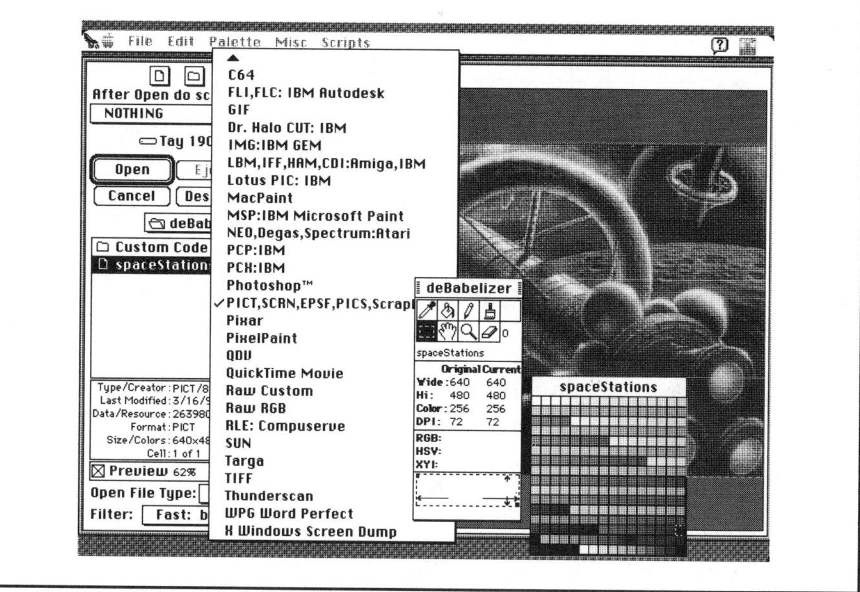

tosh) and SnapPRO! (for Windows). Both let you grab screen images and save them on the Clipboard or in optional PICT, TIFF, or other file formats.

Format converters are also indispensable for projects in which your source material may originate on Macintoshes, PCs, UNIX workstations, Amigas, or even mainframes. This is an issue particularly with image files, because there are many formats and many compressions schemes. Figure 6-12 illustrates deBabelizer, a Macintosh-based image converter and editor from Equilibrium Software. For the PC, Image Alchemy from Handmade Software will translate among some 60 image file formats.

Multi

Common desktop presentation tools are becoming more multimedia powerful...

sound and animation

media

In another few years,

most personal computers sold will be able to produce at least the sound and animation elements of multimedia.

chapter 7

Making Instant Multimedia

THERE is no reason to buy a dedicated multimedia authoring package if your current software (or an inexpensive upgrade) can do the job. Indeed, not only can you save money by doing multimedia with tools that are familiar and already at hand, but you also save the time spent on arduous and sometimes lengthy learning curves involved in mastering many dedicated authoring systems. Common desktop presentation tools are becoming more multimedia powerful, while dedicated multimedia authoring systems are offering simplified, easy-to-use versions (see Chapter 8).

In another few years, most personal computers sold will be able to produce at least the sound and animation elements of multimedia. In the meantime, manufacturers of popular software for word processing, spreadsheet management, database management, graphing, drawing, and presentation are adding capabilities for sound, image, and animation to their products. Already you can call a voice annotation, picture, or QuickTime or AVI movie from some word processing applications. You can click a cell in a spreadsheet to enhance its content with graphic images, sounds, and animations. Your database can include pictures, audio clips, and movies. Your presentation software can easily generate interesting titles, visual effects, and animated illustrations for your product demo. With these multimedia-enhanced software packages, you get many more ways to effectively convey your message than just a slide show.

To enliven your material and provide interesting illustrations, you can add multimedia elements to familiar tools such as word-processed documents, spreadsheets, and presentation aids. But where do you get these elements? You can either make your images, sounds, and animations from scratch, or you can import them from collections of clip media. You can also license rights to use resources or content, such as pictures, songs and music, and video from their owners. Importing from stock material limits you somewhat, but it may be all that you need, and these collections can yield quick and simple multimedia productions. If you make your multimedia elements from scratch or edit existing material, you'll need to have special software and hardware tools to customize the images, sounds, and animations, but the results are more spectacular and dramatic.

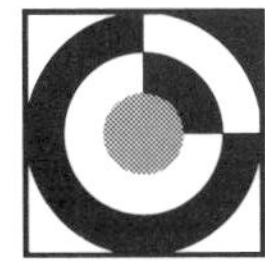

warning *You need special multimedia tools for digitizing your sounds and creating animations and movies before you can attach these objects to your word, data, or presentation documents. These tools are discussed in Chapter 6.*

Some multimedia projects may be so simple that you can cram all the organizing, planning, rendering, and testing stages into a single effort, making instant multimedia.

Here is an example: The topic at your weekly sales meeting is sales force performance. You want to display your usual spreadsheet so the group can see real names and numbers for each member of the team, then you want to show a multicolored 3-D bar graph for visual impact. Preparing for your meeting, you annotate the cell containing the name of the week's most productive salesperson, using sounds of applause taken from a public-domain CD-ROM, or a recording of your CEO saying "Good job!" or a colleague's "Wait till next week, Pete!" At the appropriate time during the meeting, you click that cell and play the annotation. And that's it—you have just made and used instant multimedia.

The following overviews do not include all products in each category of software tools, but they will give you a good sense of how multimedia might be applied in your everyday life working with computers. You will also find some tips and advice on using them in your multimedia projects.

Linking Multimedia Objects

The elements of multimedia (and other digitized information) are often treated as discrete *objects* that have particular characteristcs or *properties*. With objects described in a common format using object-oriented programming systems (OOPs), text, bitmapped images, sounds, and video clips can be dynamically linked among applications and documents or even embedded in them. This object-oriented approach to information management is supported on both Macintosh and Windows platforms.

AppleEvents

On the Macintosh, AppleEvents lets applications communicate with each other, sharing data and commands. InterApplication Communication (IAC) works with AppleEvents to automatically update documents that are linked with the "publish-and-subscribe" features of AppleEvents.

When you *publish* an application and then edit the data in it, the changes you make are copied to all of the *subscribers* to that data, even across a network. Publish-and-subscribe uses a transition file called the *edition file.*

You can *subscribe* to a spreadsheet table in a word processing document, for example, and when you change the spreadsheet, the word processing document gets changed automatically. Or you can embed a PICT image or QuickTime file in one application and change it in another, and the changes will appear in both applications—the two applications talk directly to each other.

To use publish-and-subscribe in System 7, follow these steps:

1. Select data that you want to place into another application or document.
2. From the Edit menu, choose "Create Publisher." This brings up a dialog box asking you to name the Edition file that will connect the Publisher to the other documents subscribing to this data.
3. After you have created the Edition file, go to the document or application where you want to use the data and select "Subscribe To..." from the Edit menu.

Now you have placed a *live* copy of the data in your document; whenever you modify the original publisher data, the subscriber is automatically updated, too.

DDE and OLE

Dynamic Data Exchange (DDE) and *Object Linking and Embedding* (OLE, pronounced olay) are two methods for linking data objects between Windows applications. For example, let's say you want to advertise your new mousetrap design with a flashy graphic—an illustration showing your mousetrap compared to other mousetraps on the market—and some text describing its extraordinary features. First, you make a colorful picture in a graphics application such as Micrografx Designer; then you create a bar chart comparing the number of mice in a spreadsheet program such as Excel; and finally, you paste all your elements into a word processor such as Microsoft Word.

cross platform *QuickTime for Windows supports OLE, so QuickTime movies made on the Macintosh can be integrated into Windows applications that support OLE.*

When two applications share data through DDE, they are in a *conversation.* DDE allows data to be transmitted between a *client* (the application that initiates the conversation) and a *server* (the application responding to the client). Data can be transmitted as a *hot link* so that modifications in the server application are also updated in the client application, or as a *cold link* so that data in the client application is independent of the server after it has been imported.

Paste Special

Formats:
Native
Link
ObjectLink
Ami Text Format
Rich Text Format
Text
Picture
Bitmap

OK
Cancel

OLE lets you embed or link data objects created in different Windows applications. An *embedded* object becomes a part of the file into which it is pasted, independent of the original application where it was created. A *linked* object, on the other hand, is changed automatically in a *container* file that *points* to the original file when the original file is updated. Linking is a useful feature for data that may be modified after it has been placed into other files.

warning *Using OLE, make sure that your linked files aren't moved to other directories, or the links may be broken. OLE 2.0 (and later versions) have improved the ability to track links between containers and objects, but the best way to ensure that your object isn't "lost" is to* embed *it in a file.*

Word Processors

Many word-processed documents are ultimately printed to paper, but many are also delivered on a server, floppy disk, or to an electronic mailbox. If your document will be viewed by others on a computer, consider attaching multimedia voice notes, pictures, or animated illustrations to emphasize your point or to clarify something that is difficult to express in words. The first-person example in the following section illustrates use of multimedia elements (in this case, QuickTime graphics) embedded into the working draft of a manuscript. The manuscript is shown, and the graphics, along with a note to the editor.

First Person

Working draft of Chapter 4, Revision 2, reads ...

My father said that Mommy was still in a coma and my little brother was sleeping. We should go home now. So we went out the back way to the physician's parking lot: down the elevator and past the noisy kitchen with its racks of trays, white-uniformed cooks, piles of canned goods, and the steamy smells of institutional stew. The green screen door slammed indelibly into my five-year-old memory, and the attendant waved to my dad; he probably didn't know we were there on family business. It was all pretty serious.

We found Mommy's car behind the police station. I stayed in my seat while my father got out and walked very slowly around the twisted metal. He was calculating the impact forces, visualizing the accident in slow motion freeze frames, and at one point, he leaned in through the broken glass and ran his hand across the dent in the steel glove compartment where my brother had smashed his face. He went around only the one time, then got back in. "She must have been doing about forty when she hit the pole," he offered as if I were an adult, and we drove out the narrow circular drive alongside the station house. It was a crisp, clear, football-and-pumpkins Saturday afternoon in October.

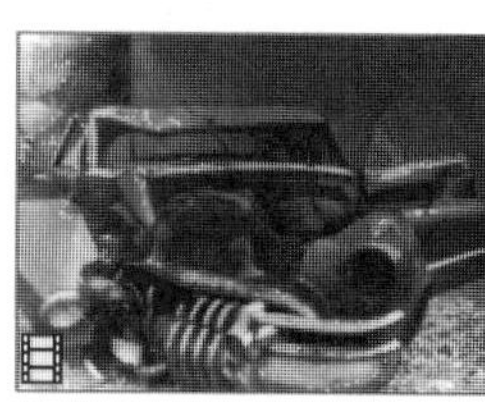

Editorial note to Sally: Per your comment last week, pick a good illustration from the file of images that I have attached. One of them should fit the bill... Thanks! See you next week.

Microsoft Word for the Macintosh

Microsoft's latest version of Word for the Macintosh offers special features of multimedia interest. You can make and import black-and-white, gray-scale, and color PICT files, and place them in your document. You can import digitized sounds, and you can record voice comments from an internal microphone or with MacRecorder, saving the recording (with a portion of the text as an identifier) for playback. Annotations can be searched for sound effects and content, edited, and even saved as separate files in any of four formats.

Word for the Macintosh also allows you to add a plug-in module to the Word Commands folder, so you can attach a QuickTime movie with a menu

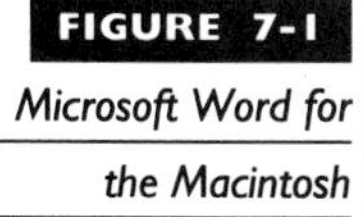

FIGURE 7-1 *Microsoft Word for the Macintosh*

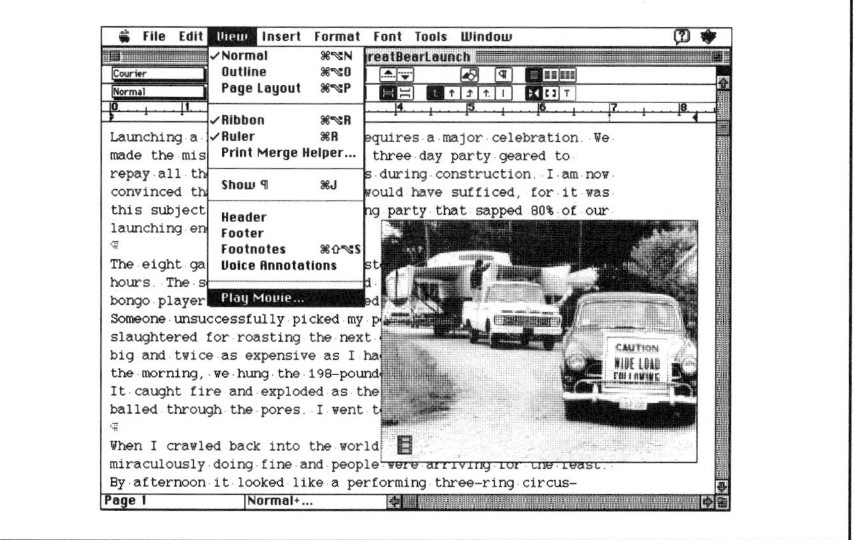

command (see Figure 7-1); control the movie's playback characteristics (forward, backward, start, and stop); and perform simple editing with cut, copy, and paste commands. The QuickTime plug-in for version 5.0 was not shipped with the Word product before May, 1992, but you can obtain it direct from Microsoft for a nominal shipping charge or free from bulletin boards and online services.

Microsoft Word for Windows

Word for Windows allows you to insert various objects into your text, including pictures, sounds, clip art, and movies. Figure 7-2 shows a movie object placed within a Word document using AddImpact (from Gold Disk). AVI movies can also be played as Object Linking and Embedding (OLE) objects from your Word document. With Word for Windows you can also create links to other programs using Dynamic Data Exchange (DDE). Figure 7-3 demonstrates graphic information from an Excel spreadsheet linked to a Word document using the automated DDE feature of Word for Windows.

WordPerfect for Macintosh

In WordPerfect's Macintosh version, a tool palette and drawing commands allow you to create and edit graphics with the standard Macintosh drawing tools, as well as to create Bézier curves and polygons; there's also a free rotation tool. A color editor lets you blend, rainbow, and complement

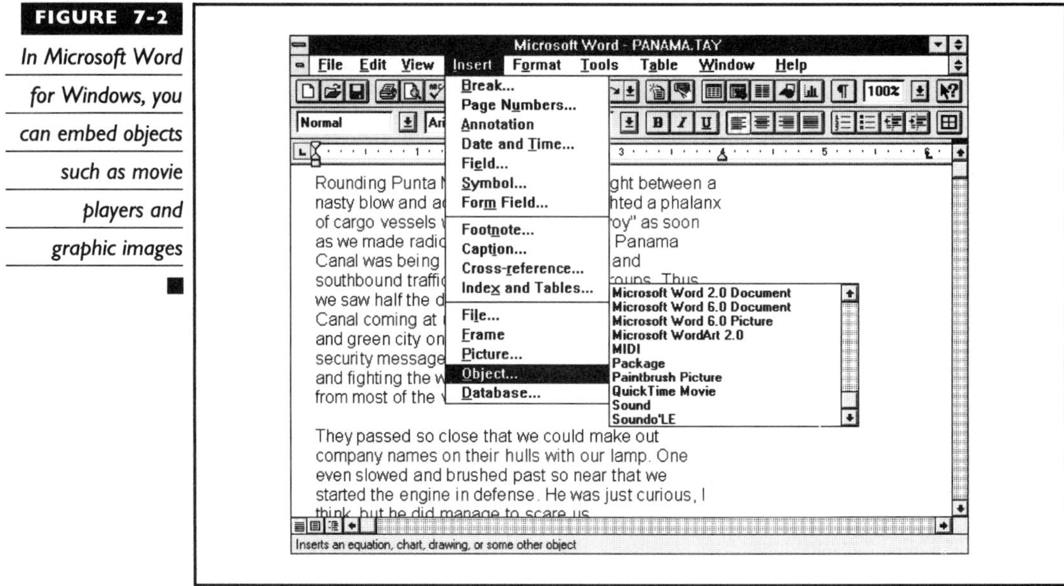

FIGURE 7-2 *In Microsoft Word for Windows, you can embed objects such as movie players and graphic images*

colors. You can edit, size, scale, and crop graphic images, and then click and drag them anywhere in your document while text automatically reformats around them.

WordPerfect for Macintosh offers a QuickTime movie playing facility (see Figure 7-4). The movie is represented by its poster, usually the first frame of

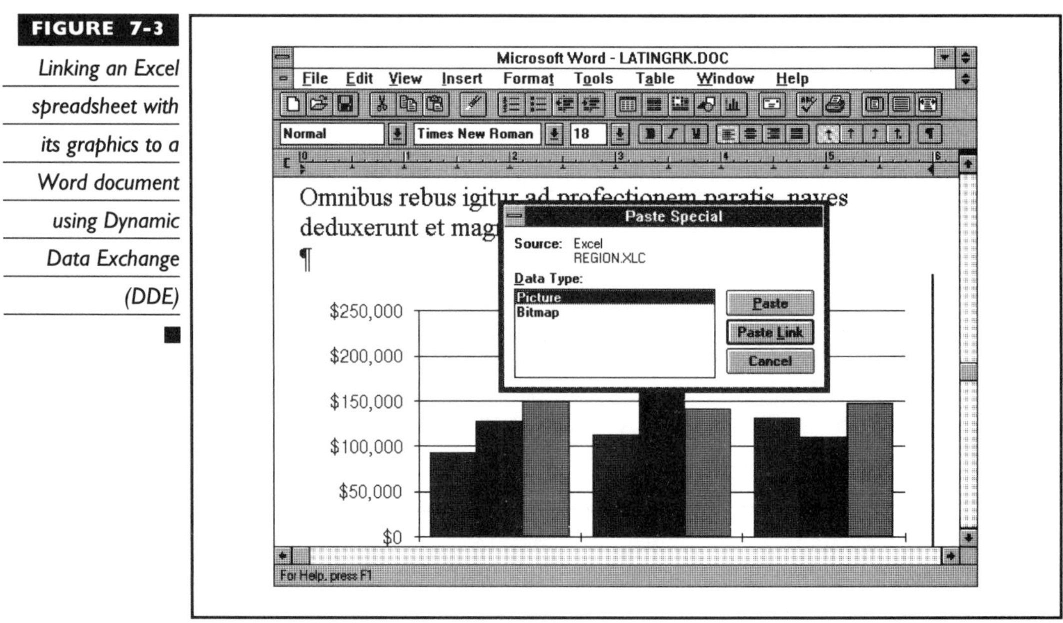

FIGURE 7-3 *Linking an Excel spreadsheet with its graphics to a Word document using Dynamic Data Exchange (DDE)*

FIGURE 7-4

WordPerfect for Macintosh provides a QuickTime player

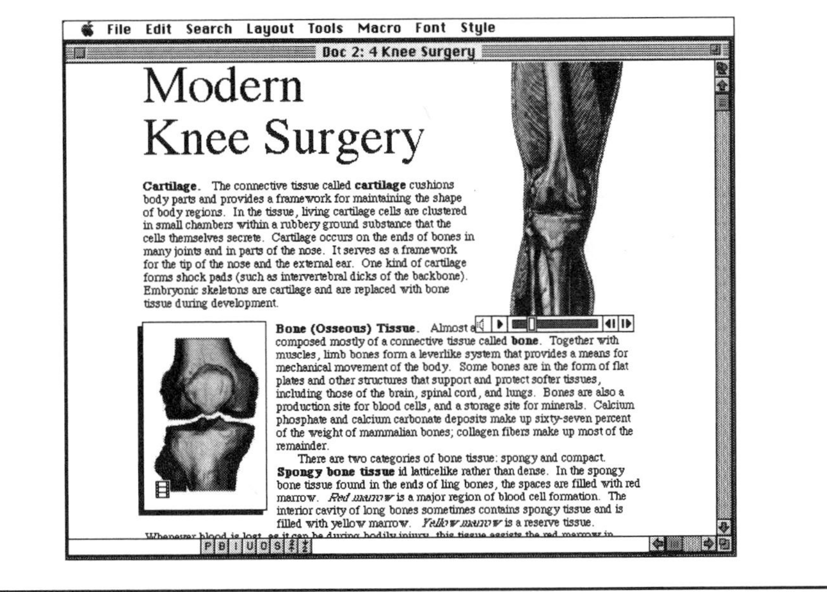

the movie. You can represent your movie as a character, anchor it to a page or paragraph, move it, add a caption, or put a frame around it, just as you can with graphics. There is a movie controller that gives you many options, such as custom playback or changing the poster.

tip *For voice annotation in WordPerfect, you can put sounds and voice into the audio track of a QuickTime movie, and they will play back just fine.*

WordPerfect for Windows

Using DDE, WordPerfect for Windows can share data with other DDE-compatible programs that use DDE links. If data is changed in a linked program, it is automatically updated in the WordPerfect document to which it is linked. A figure editor makes it easy to add graphics to your documents. You can view, retrieve, create, modify, and size figures, and save or import them into your document. WordPerfect for Windows works with the common graphic formats for DOS, as well as Windows metafiles and bitmaps.

Ami Pro

With its Windows DDE and OLE capabilities, Ami Pro from Lotus can link to other applications and embedded objects, such as sounds and AVI movies. Using DDE, you can paste a link in Windows bitmap or metafile format into an empty selected frame. You can even create a macro to control another application through DDE. As shown in Figure 7-5, with OLE you can link or embed objects into a frame in an Ami Pro document.

Microsoft Works Multimedia Edition

The multimedia version of Microsoft Works ships on a compact disc designed for MPC users. This version of Works offers a word processor, spreadsheet, database, and charting/drawing tools rolled into a single integrated application. The tutorial is comprised of many help-specific animation and sound files. As with other multimedia-capable applications, Microsoft Works Multimedia Editor can embed objects using OLE.

Spreadsheets

Spreadsheets have become the backbone of many users' information management systems. A spreadsheet organizes its data in columns and rows. Calculations are made based on user-defined formulas for, say, analyzing the survival rates of seedlings, or the production of glass bottles in Russia, or a household's consumption of energy in ergs per capita. Spreadsheets can answer what-if

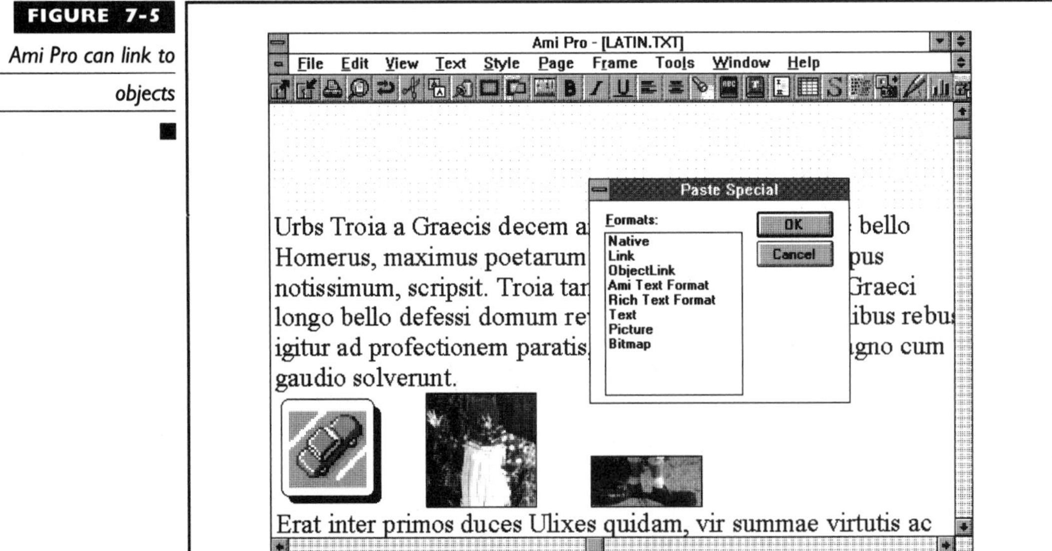

FIGURE 7-5 Ami Pro can link to objects

questions, build complex graphs and charts, and calculate a bottom line. From Alaska to Zimbabwe, spreadsheets have become a ubiquitous computer tool.

Most spreadsheet applications provide excellent chart-making routines; some allow you to build a series of several charts into an animation or movie, so you can dramatically show change over time or under varying conditions. Full-color curves that demonstrate changing annual sales, robbery and assault statistics, or birth rates may have a far greater effect on an audience than will a column of numbers.

The latest spreadsheets let you attach special notes and drawings, including full multimedia display of sounds, pictures, animations, and video clips.

Lotus 1-2-3 for the Macintosh

Lotus 1-2-3 for the Macintosh lets you rearrange graph elements by clicking and dragging, and use a menu to access data from the outside world through Apple's Data Access Manager. You can place bitmapped pictures and QuickTime movies anywhere in your spreadsheet. There is a complete color drawing package for placing lines, circles, arrows, and special text on top of the spreadsheet to help illustrate its content (see Figure 7-6).

Lotus 1-2-3 for Windows

Lotus 1-2-3 for Windows features Multimedia SmartHelp, which provides an interactive guided tour demonstrating the features of 1-2-3, and step-by-step instructions showing you how to create animated movies.

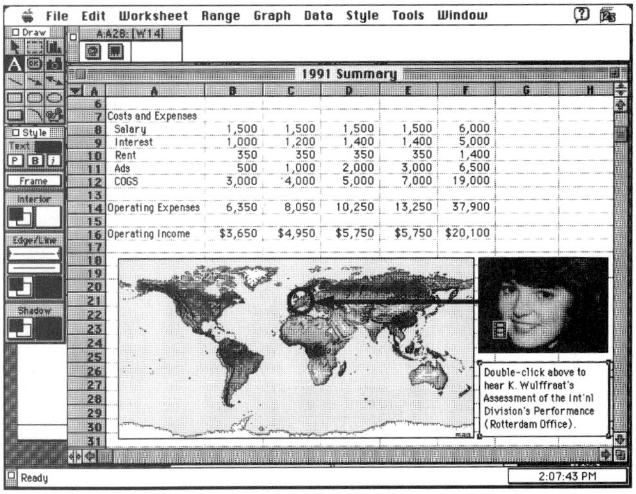

FIGURE 7-6 *Lotus 1-2-3 for Macintosh manages images and movies*

Excel

Using a special template document, you can create a slide show with Microsoft Excel (in both the Macintosh and Windows versions) to present worksheets, charts, and graphics. You can apply video and audio transition effects between slides, adjusting speed and the method of slide advance. The SLIDES.XLA file must be installed in the Windows version, and the Slide-show Add-In file for the Macintosh. QuickTime and AVI movies can be linked to Microsoft Excel documents. Figure 7-7 shows the Windows version of Excel's Edit Slide dialog box being used to embed material from Ami Pro, an OLE-capable word processor. Notice the transition effects and speed controls available for placement between slides.

Databases

A database program can store, sort, retrieve, and organize many types of information. Like spreadsheets, databases can exist in a digital environment without ever needing to be printed to paper. Images, sounds, and movies are treated as objects and can be stored, retrieved, and played by many databases.

During the coming years, it is likely that multimedia databases will become the primary method by which corporate users interact with multi-media elements.

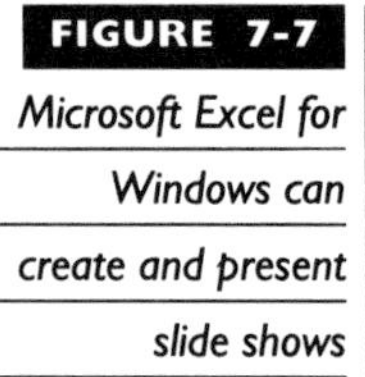

FIGURE 7-7 *Microsoft Excel for Windows can create and present slide shows*

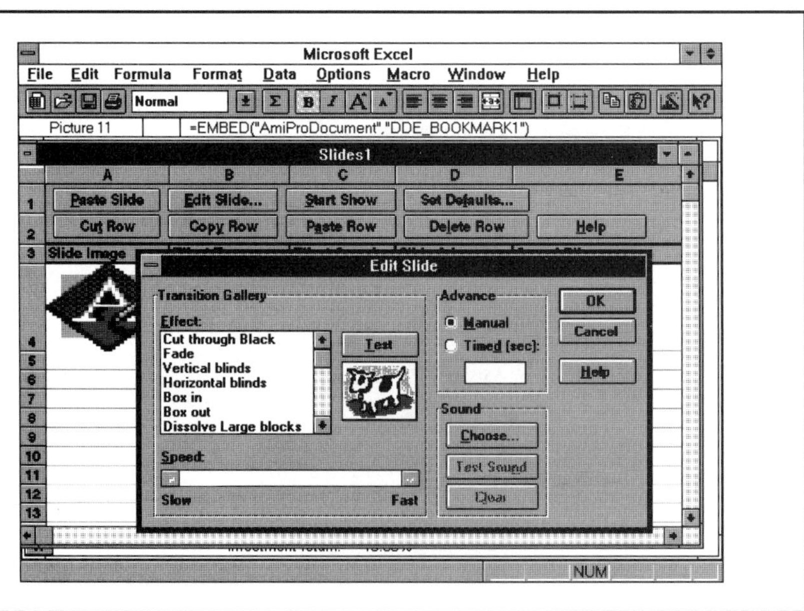

FileMaker Pro

Claris's FileMaker Pro rates high in ease-of-use and cross-platform capability with both Windows and Macintosh versions (see Figure 7-8). FileMaker Pro has a relatively simple interface, yet it is powerful enough to handle moderately complex operations. You can use the built-in graphics tools and record sound from within the application, or you can import images, sounds, and QuickTime movies from other applications.

Superbase

Superbase, from Software Publishing Corporation, allows you to add pictures and sound to database records. Superbase supports OLE and DDE applications, so data created in other applications, such as Harvard Graphics or AutoCAD, can be linked to a Superbase file. Super Basic Language (SBL), Superbase's event-driven procedural database management language, allows you to customize and supplement Superbase's range of features.

WindowBase

WindowBase from Software Products International is a relational database management system for Windows. It provides graphics tools for creating boxes and lines, and it lets you insert bitmap graphics created in other programs.

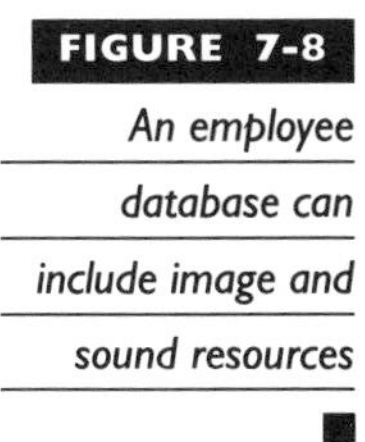

FIGURE 7-8 An employee database can include image and sound resources

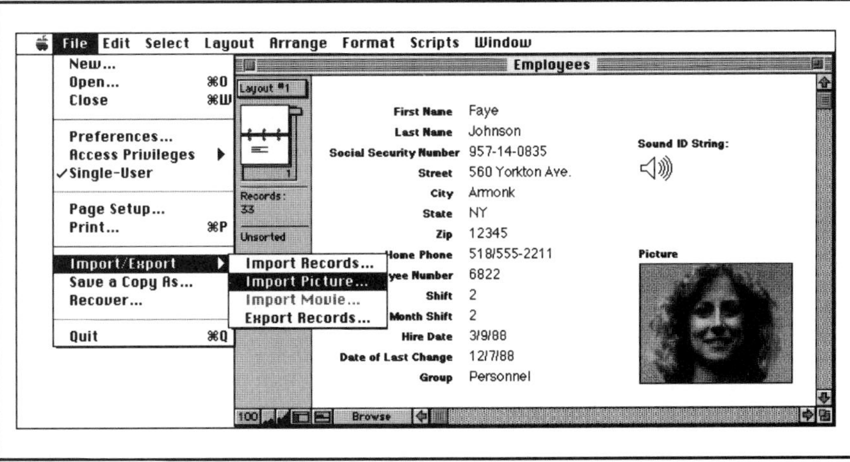

Q+E Database/VB

Q+E Database/VB is a set of custom Visual Basic controls from Pioneer Software (Visual Basic is an authoring system described in Chapter 8). This application lets you create programs to build and manage dBASE-compatible databases by adding custom database controls and functions to the standard set of controls available in Visual Basic. The controls and functions handle most database programming tasks, such as designing forms, reports, and queries for you, so you can create database programs without having to write a single line of code. As shown in Figure 7-9, images can be managed by Q+E Database/VB.

Presentation Tools

Presentation software was originally developed to computerize the creation of graphical business presentations, for both printed output (including laser-printed transparencies shown on overhead projectors) and 35mm slides. These graphical presentations are also useful for live presentations that use a computer to deliver messages and content. Presentation software might, indeed, be considered authoring software, because the publishers of today's products are making them more and more multimedia-capable.

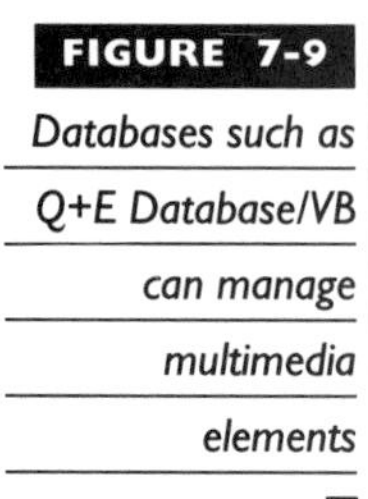

FIGURE 7-9

Databases such as Q+E Database/VB can manage multimedia elements

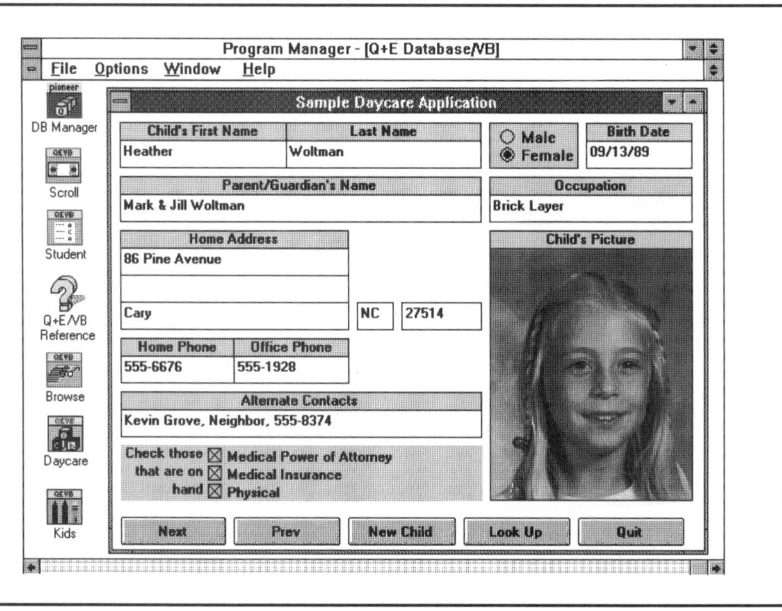

The line between multimedia authoring and desktop presentation software is already a wide gray area. As system tools make multimedia easier to understand and implement, it will become more common in mainstream applications. The same thing happened in desktop publishing. Initially, people were buying PageMaker to dress up office memos. Now, virtually all word processors have basic page layout capabilities, and the dedicated "publishing" products are targeted at professionals. Multimedia authoring is headed the same way.

Karl Seppala, Macintosh Product Line Manager, Gold Disk, Inc.

Magicians use live props that often run across the stage or fly out of hats, as well as other attention-grabbing effects, to direct viewers' attention away from tricks and sleight of hand. In contrast, multimedia presenters use the same delivery techniques (the smoke and mirrors of computerized visual effects) to focus their viewers' attention on presentation content, so that the content will be remembered even when it's competing with a heavy lunch or a dimly lit conference room.

Presentation tools are used to create overhead presentations and slide shows, and they add synchronized audio, self-running animations, and video to the multimedia presentation armamentarium. There is an emerging gray area between presentation tools and multimedia authoring systems, as software publishers develop methods to accommodate the needs of computer-based presenters, and as large-scale video and LCD panel projection systems become more common. The following applications described in this section include tools from the classic genre of presentation software; dedicated presentation organizers designed from the ground up to manage multimedia resources are discussed as authoring systems in Chapter 8.

Astound

Astound from Gold Disk lets you create attention-getting presentations that combine text, images, sound effects, and QuickTime movies. Astound excels at combining objects from different applications. You can do simple edits to objects, sounds, and QuickTime movies within the application, saving you the time and hassle of going back and forth between applications. Astound's animation features can create animated effects easily, with some built-in transition and interactivity options, as well as a time-line feature that lets you control when objects enter and leave the screen.

Persuasion

Persuasion is available from Aldus for both Macintosh and Windows environments. It's a complete desktop presentation toolkit for producing overhead transparencies, 35mm slides, and printed materials, including speaker notes and audience handouts. It includes tools for outlining, word processing, drawing, charting, and formatting, and it works in either black and white or color. Persuasion will also present in various slide show formats for on-screen viewing. This slide show feature lets you move manually or automatically through an entire presentation using the computer screen, which is useful for creating self-running demos. In slide show mode, users can choose from many transition effects, such as wipes and dissolves, that can be assigned either to entire slides or to layers within individual slides (see Figure 7-10).

On the Macintosh, Persuasion is System 7 savvy and is QuickTime-compatible.

PowerPoint

PowerPoint from Microsoft (for both Macintosh and Windows) is a tool for preparing presentations. It offers a complete drawing and text package with an automatic or manual slide show feature. In the Windows version, you can embed graphics and data from other applications into PowerPoint,

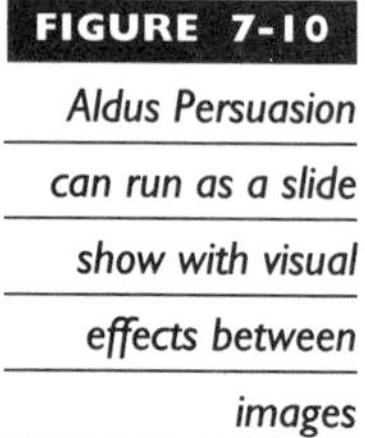

FIGURE 7-10 Aldus Persuasion can run as a slide show with visual effects between images

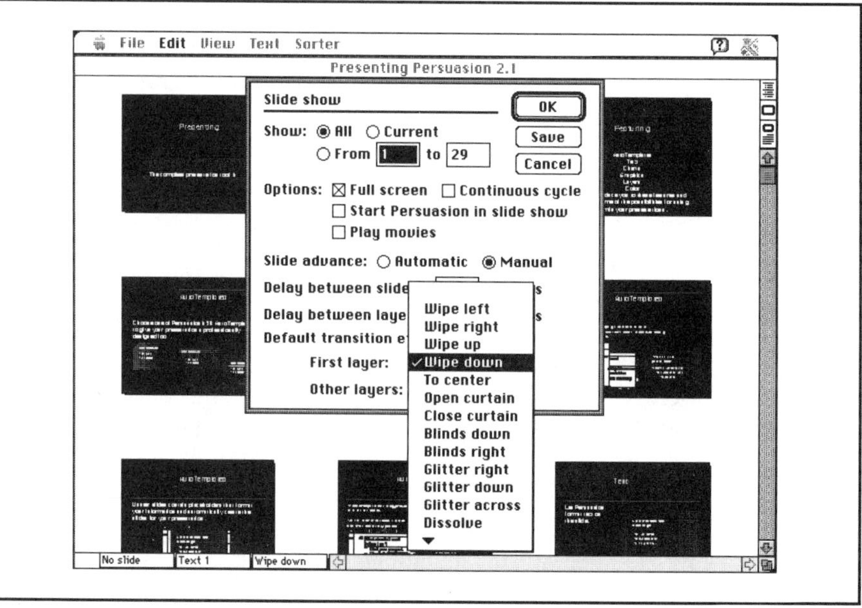

as well as copy bitmapped images, slides, and presentations from PowerPoint into other applications. And you can build live links between PowerPoint and other applications. The Windows version supports Multimedia Extensions for Windows by using OLE in conjunction with the Media Control Interface (MCI) command set; it lets you link objects such as AVI files and embedded sound.

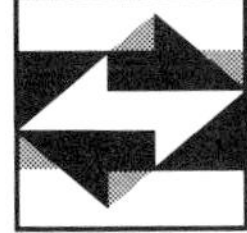

cross platform *An Apple File Exchange Translator lets you convert Macintosh PowerPoint files into Windows PowerPoint files and vice versa. The Microsoft PowerPoint HG translator for Apple File Exchange is available from Microsoft for a nominal shipping fee.*

DeltaGraph Professional

DeltaGraph Professional from DeltaPoint, Inc., is a comprehensive and flexible charting, graphics, and presentation application for the Macintosh (see Figure 7-11). Large data sets can be organized over multiple pages using the Data Notebook feature. Text outlining makes it easy to create organization and bullet charts. Data can be imported from and linked to many third-party file formats. You can adjust axis scaling, tick marks, legends, labels, perspective, and 3-D rotations. You can create fully customized presentations with the slide show feature, and you can add sound effects and visual transition effects as well as QuickTime movies.

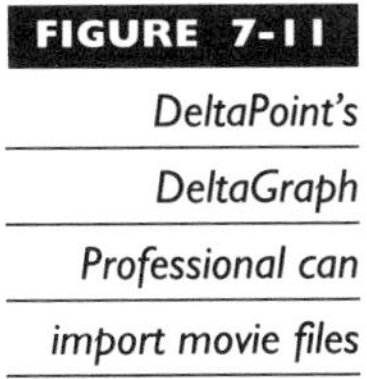

FIGURE 7-11

DeltaPoint's DeltaGraph Professional can import movie files

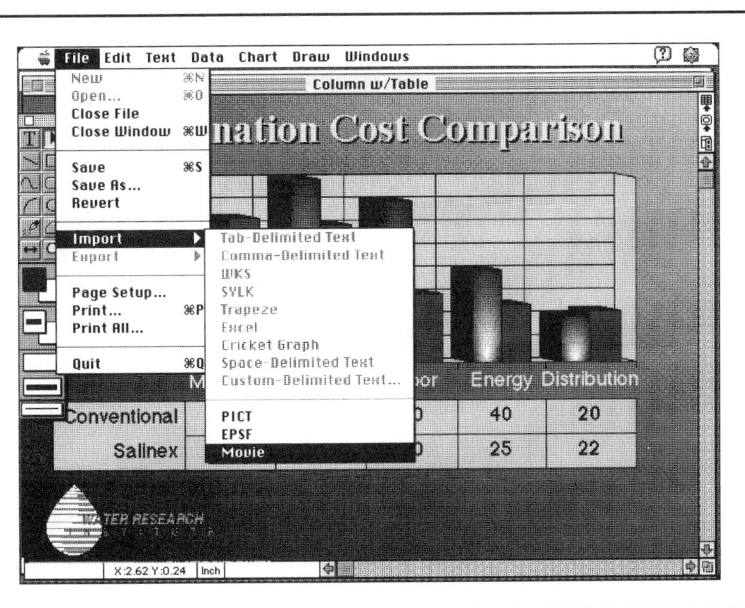

CA-Cricket Presents

CA-Cricket Presents from Computer Associates offers object-oriented drawing tools, integrated graphs and tables, and a text editor—on both Macintosh and Windows platforms. (The Macintosh version comes with an outline processor, templates, and a facility to automatically turn your content into a presentation based on text and images copied from an Acta outline.) It imports clip art, charts, and objects from other drawing, graphics, and painting applications. CA-Cricket Presents will run in slide show mode, with special effects for blending one slide into the next.

Canvas

Typically classified as a Macintosh graphics or drawing tool, Deneba's Canvas can also create on-screen presentations. For a slide show, Canvas lets you fill the screen with its still images and graphics, add text, and insert and control QuickTime movies from any slide. You can save your Canvas slide show in QuickTime movie format (see Figure 7-12). In this way, you can distribute your show for playback as a video presentation on any QuickTime-compatible Macintosh using Simple Player or Popcorn (see the "Movie Players" section in Chapter 6).

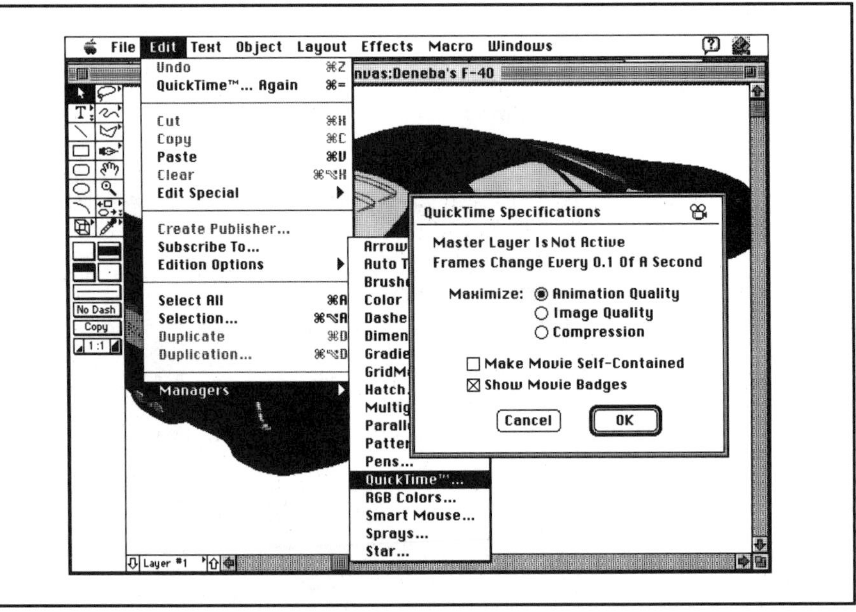

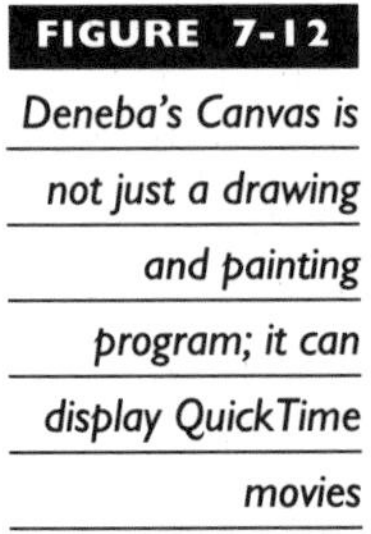
FIGURE 7-12 Deneba's Canvas is not just a drawing and painting program; it can display QuickTime movies

Charisma

Charisma from Micrografx is a Windows-based business graphics product that provides powerful charting, drawing, and dynamic presentation capabilities (see Figure 7-13). It offers DDE and OLE support, as well as support for large data files. It includes statistical algorithms for technical charting: linear, exponential, and logarithmic regression analysis. The slide show feature provides more than 21 transition effects, and a memory cache holds most recent slides for instant recall.

SYSTAT

SYSTAT from SYSTAT, Inc., is a Macintosh application that provides graphical visualization of data and extensive statistical analysis, letting you experiment with different graphical views of the same data (see Figure 7-14). The 24-bit graphing options include linear, quadratic, step, spline, polynomial, LOWESS, exponential, and log smoothing; confidence intervals and ellipses; scatterplot matrices; single, multiple, stacked, and range bar graphs; single and grouped box plots; stem-and-leaf diagrams; histograms; log and power scales; Voronoi tessellations; geographic projections; Chernoff faces;

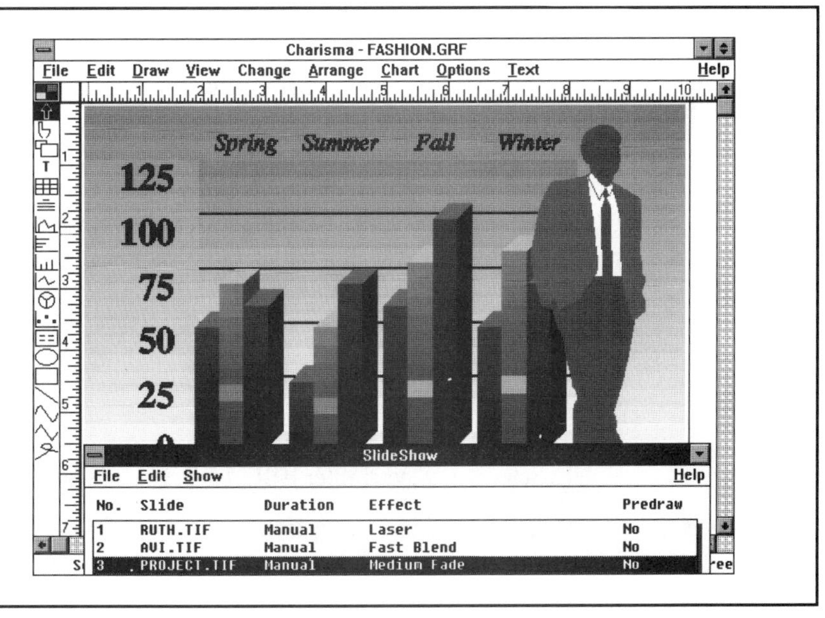

FIGURE 7-13 Charisma by Micrografx uses a playlist for organizing slide shows

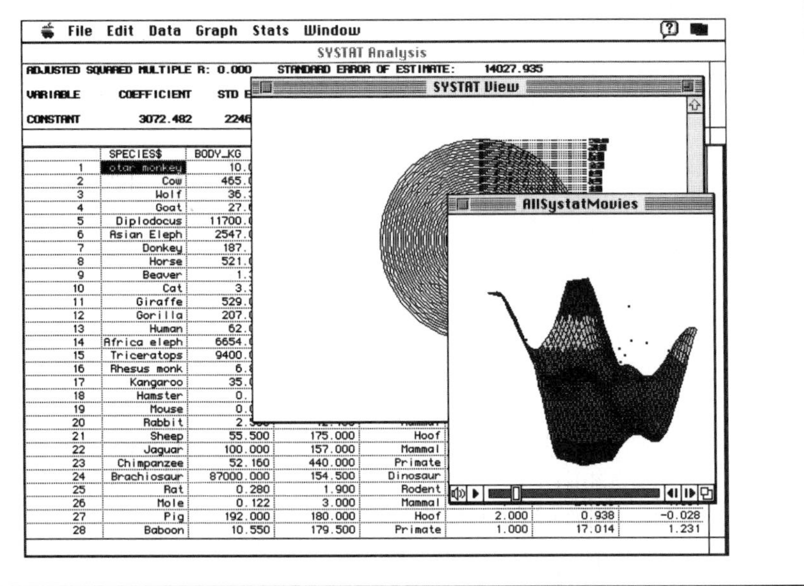

FIGURE 7-14 *SYSTAT can provide animated graphic visualizations of changing data*

star plots; Andrews' Fourier plots; pie charts; contour plots; control charts; 3-D data; and function plots. You can save graph specifications to be reused, and you can cut, copy, and paste your graphs into other Macintosh applications.

You can save your SYSTAT charts, graphs, and data in QuickTime movie file formats. This is useful because changing data is often better understood when presented in movie form, where you can see what is happening over time. This is powerful multimedia.

The simplest way to make a SYSTAT movie is to use a Graph menu item to set up a single graph; enter **MOVIE** as the argument for the graph option that you want to vary. In the ten-frame example below, DEATH_RT is plotted against BIRTH_RT with a LOWESS smoother of increasing TENSION:

1. Open your data file.
2. Select Plot/Plot from the Graph menu.
3. Select a Y variable: **DEATH_RT**.
4. Select an X variable: **BIRTH_RT**.
5. Click the Smooth option and choose LOWESS. Type **MOVIE** in the Tension box.
6. Click OK.

7. When the dialog box appears, you can control how the variable option(s) are used. Start by selecting the option to control: TENSION.
8. Specify an Initial Value: **0.05**.
9. Specify a Final Value: **0.95**.
10. Specify the number of frames: **10**.
11. Click OK. Then specify the filename and folder location for the movie.

To make the example illustrated in Figure 7-14, SYSTAT determined and executed ten PLOT commands with steadily increasing values for TENSION and made a QuickTime movie.

The Movie dialog box also provides special options for gradually changing eye perspective coordinates and vertical and horizontal scaling.

Multi

Authoring tools are used for designing interactivity and the user interface...

Multimedia authoring tools provide the important framework for organizing and editing the elements of your multimedia project

interactivity

media

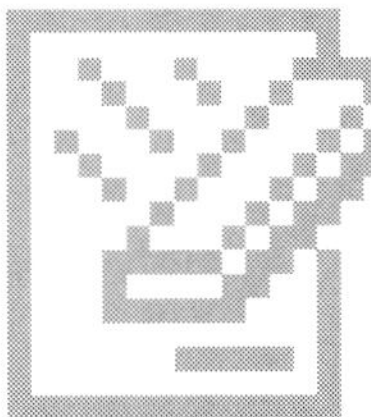

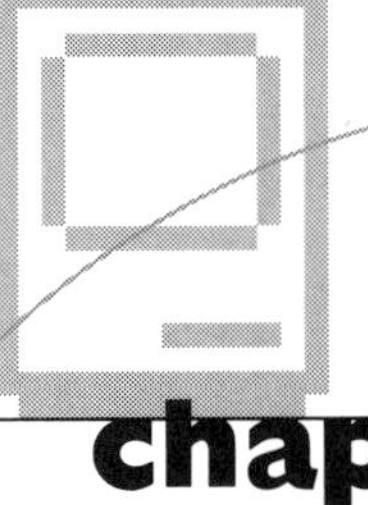

chapter 8

Multimedia Authoring Tools

including graphics, sounds, animations, and video clips.

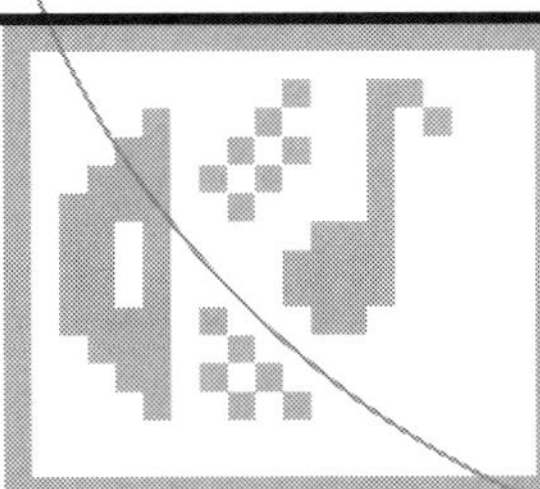

MULTIMEDIA authoring tools provide the important framework you need for organizing and editing the elements of your multimedia project, including graphics, sounds, animations, and video clips. Authoring tools are used for designing interactivity and the user interface, for presenting your project on screen, and for assembling multimedia elements into a single, cohesive project.

Authoring software provides an integrated environment for binding together the content and functions of your project. Authoring systems typically include the ability to create, edit, and import specific types of data; assemble raw data into a playback sequence or cue sheet; and provide a structured method or language for responding to user input. With multimedia authoring software, you can make

- Video productions
- Animations
- Demo disks and interactive guided tours
- Presentations
- Interactive kiosk applications
- Interactive training
- Simulations, prototypes, and technical visualizations

Types of Authoring Tools

This chapter arranges the various authoring tools into groups based on the metaphor used for sequencing and organizing multimedia elements and events:

- Card- or page-based tools
- Icon-based, event-driven tools
- Time-based and presentation tools

CARD- OR PAGE-BASED TOOLS In these authoring systems, elements are organized as pages of a book or a stack of cards. Thousands of pages or cards may be available in the book or stack. These tools are best used when the bulk of your content consists of elements that can be viewed individually, like the pages of a book or cards in a card file. The authoring system lets you link these pages or cards into organized sequences. You can jump, on command, to any page you wish in the structured navigation pattern. Card- or page-based authoring systems allow you to play sound elements and launch animations and digital video.

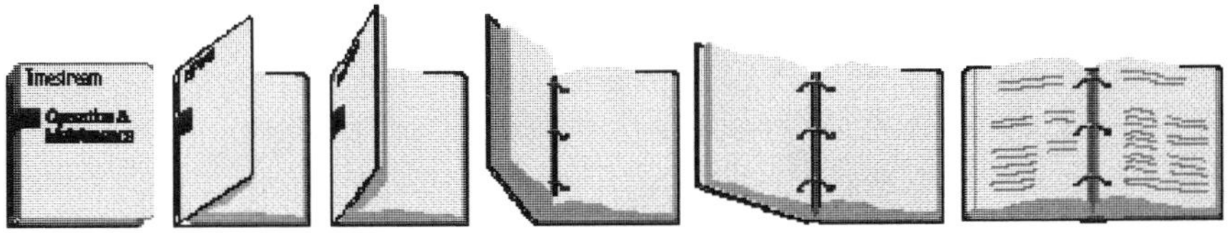

ICON-BASED TOOLS In these authoring systems, multimedia elements and interaction cues (events) are organized as objects in a structural framework or process. Icon-based, event-driven tools simplify the organization of your project and typically display flow diagrams of activities along branching paths. In complicated navigational structures, this charting is particularly useful during development.

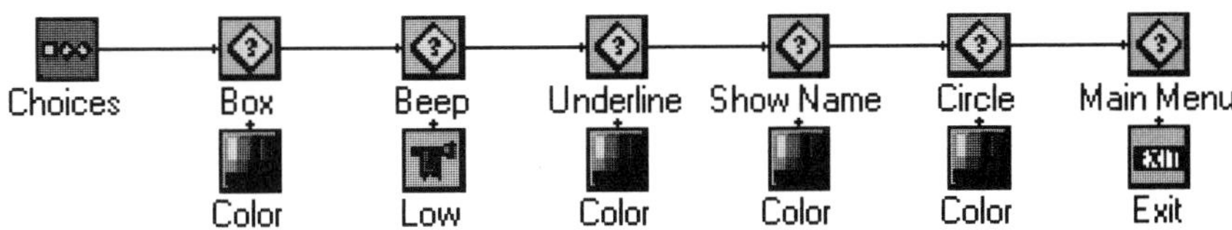

TIME-BASED TOOLS In these authoring systems, elements and events are organized along a time line, with resolutions as high as 1/30 second. Time-based tools are best to use when you have a message with a beginning and an end. Sequentially organized graphic frames are played back at a speed that you can set. Other elements (such as audio events) are triggered at a given time or location in the sequence of events. The more powerful time-based tools let you program jumps to any location in a sequence, thereby adding navigation and interactive control.

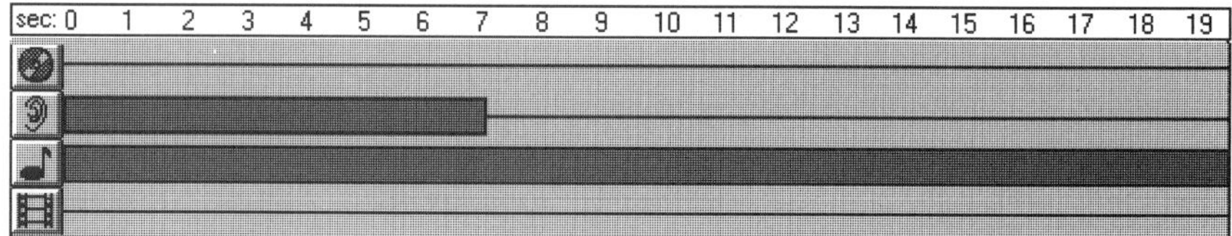

The Right Tool for the Job

Each multimedia project you undertake will have its own underlying structure and purpose and will require different features and functions. In the best case, you must be prepared to choose the tool that best fits the job; in the worst case, you must know which tools will at least "get the job done." Authoring tools are constantly being improved by their makers, who add new features and increase performance with upgrade development cycles of six months to a year. It is important that you study the software product reviews in computer trade journals, as well as talk with current users of these systems before deciding on the best ones for your needs.

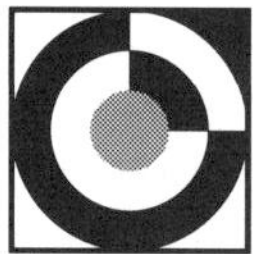

warning *Because multimedia authoring systems are constantly being updated, make sure you purchase and use the latest version of software.*

Editing Features

The elements of multimedia—images, animations, text, digital and MIDI sounds, and video clips—need to be created, edited, and converted to standard file formats, and the specialized applications described in Chapter 6 provide these capabilities. Also, editing tools for these elements, particularly text and still images, are often included in your authoring system. The more editors your authoring system has, the fewer specialized tools you will need. In many cases, however, the editors that come with an authoring system will offer only a subset of the substantial features found in dedicated tools. According to Vaughan's Law of Multimedia Minimums (see Chapter 10), these features may very well be sufficient for what you need to do; on the other hand, if editors you need are missing from your authoring system, or if you require more power, it's best to use one of the specialized, single-purpose tools described in Chapter 6.

Organizing Features

The organization, design, and production process for multimedia (described in Chapters 14 and 15) involves storyboarding and flowcharting. Some authoring tools provide a visual flowcharting system or overview facility for illustrating your project's structure at a macro level. Storyboards or navigation diagrams, too, can help organize a project. Because designing the interactivity and navigation flow of your project often requires a great deal of planning and programming effort, your storyboard should describe not just the graphics of each screen, but the interactive elements as well. Features that help organize your material, such as those provided by SuperEdit, Authorware, IconAuthor, and other authoring systems, are a plus.

Programming Features

Multimedia authoring systems offer one or more of the following approaches, which are explained in the paragraphs that follow:

- Visual programming with cues and icons
- Programming with a scripting language
- Programming with traditional tools, such as Basic or C
- Document development tools

Visual programming with icons is perhaps the simplest and easiest authoring process. If you want to play a sound or put a picture into your project, just drag the element's icon into the playlist. Or drag it away to delete it. Visual authoring tools such as Action, Authorware, IconAuthor, and Passport Producer are particularly useful for slide shows and presentations.

Authoring tools that offer a scripting language for navigation control and for enabling user inputs—such as HyperCard, SuperCard, Macromedia Director, and ToolBook—are more powerful. The more commands and functions provided in the scripting language, the more powerful the authoring system. Once you learn one of these languages, you will be able to learn other scripting languages relatively quickly; the principles are the same, regardless of the command syntax and keywords used. Many scripting languages on both platforms are similar to HyperTalk, the underlying scripting language of HyperCard.

A scripted handler to generate a system beep may be very similar, regardless of platform:

```
on mouseUp                -- HyperTalk (Macintosh)
  beep
end mouseUp

to handle buttonUp        -- ToolBook (Windows)
  beep 20
end buttonUp
```

As with traditional programming tools, look for an authoring package with good debugging facilities, robust text editing, and online syntax reference. Other scripting augmentation facilities are advantages, as well. In complex projects, you may need to program custom extensions of the scripting language for direct access to the computer's operating system. On the Macintosh, this means being able to use external commands and functions (XCMDs and XFCNs) written in C or Pascal. On PCs you will need to call dynamic link libraries (DLLs) and the Windows Media Control Interface (Windows MCI) device drivers.

A powerful document reference and delivery system is a key component of some projects. Some authoring tools offer direct importing of preformatted text, indexing facilities, complex text search mechanisms, and hypertext linkage tools. These authoring systems are useful for development of CD-ROM information products, online documentation and help systems, and sophisticated multimedia-enhanced publications.

Interactivity Features

Interactivity empowers the end users of your project by letting them control the content and flow of information. Authoring tools should provide one or more levels of interactivity:

- *Simple branching,* which offers the ability to go to another section of the multimedia production (via an activity such as a keypress, mouse click, or expiration of a timer)
- *Conditional branching,* which supports a go-to based on the results of IF-THEN decisions or events
- *A structured language* that supports complex programming logic, such as nested IF-THENs, subroutines, event tracking, and message passing among objects and elements

Performance Tuning Features

Complex multimedia projects require exact synchronization of events—for example, the animation of an exploding balloon with its accompanying sound effect. Accomplishing synchronization is difficult because there is a wide variance in performance among the different computers used for multimedia development and delivery. Some authoring tools allow you to lock a production's playback speed to a specified computer platform, but others provide no ability whatsoever to control performance on various systems. In many cases, you will need to use the authoring tool's own scripting language or custom programming facility to specify timing and sequence on systems with different (faster or slower) processors. Be sure your authoring system allows precise timing of events.

Playback Features

As you build your multimedia project, you will be continually assembling elements and testing to see how the assembly looks and performs. Your authoring system should let you build a segment or part of your project and then quickly test it as if the user were actually using it. You will spend a great deal of time going back and forth between building and testing, as you refine and smooth the content and timing of the project.

Delivery Features

Delivering your project may require building a run-time version of the project using the multimedia authoring software. A run-time version allows your project to play back without requiring the full authoring software and all its tools and editors. Often, the run-time version does not allow users to access or change the content, structure, and programming of the project. If you are going to distribute your project widely, you should distribute it in the run-time version. Make sure your authored project can be easily distributed (see Chapter 17 for more about delivery).

Card- and Page-Based Authoring Tools

Card- and page-based authoring systems provide a simple and easily understood metaphor for organizing multimedia elements. Because graphic images typically form the backbone of a project, both as navigation menus and as content, many developers first arrange their images into logical sequences or groupings similar to the chapters and pages of a book, or cards in a card catalog. Navigation routines become, then, simply directives to go to a page or card that contains appropriate images and text, and associated sounds, animations, and video clips.

Page-based authoring systems are object-oriented: the objects are the buttons, text fields, graphic objects, backgrounds, pages or cards, and even the project itself. The characteristics of objects are defined by properties (highlighted, bold, red, hidden, active, locked, and so forth). Each object may contain programming script, usually a property of that object, that is activated when an event (such as a mouse click) related to that object occurs. Events cause messages to pass along the hierarchy of objects in your project; for example, a mouse click message can be sent from a button to the background, to the page, and then to the project itself. As the message travels, it looks for handlers in the script of each object; if it finds a matching handler, the authoring system then executes the task specified by that handler.

Most page-based authoring systems provide a facility for linking objects to pages or cards (by automatically programming branching go-to statements for navigating by mouse clicks), but learning to write your own scripts and understanding the message-passing nature of these authoring tools is essential to making them perform well. Following are some typical messages that might be passed along the object hierarchy of the HyperCard, SuperCard, and ToolBook authoring systems:

HyperCard and SuperCard Message	ToolBook Message
closeCard	leavePage
closeStack	leaveBook
idle	idle
mouseDown	buttonDown
mouseStillDown	buttonStillDown
mouseUp	buttonUp
newBackground	newBackground
openCard	enterPage
openStack	enterBook

Now let's look at specific examples. To go to the next card or page when a button is clicked, you would place a message handler into the script of that button. (In the languages demonstrated below, handlers begin with "on" or "to handle.") Here is an example in HyperTalk:

```
on mouseUp
  go next card
end mouseUp
```

Here is an example in OpenScript (ToolBook):

```
to handle buttonUp
  go next page
end buttonUp
```

The handler, if placed in the script of the card or page, will execute its commands upon receiving a "mouseUp" or "buttonUp" message occurring at any location on the card or page—not just while the cursor is within the bounds of a button.

Most card- or page-based authoring systems require a special intermediate file that also receives scripted message handlers and acts as a repository for special routines and resources that are available to all projects being executed by the application. In HyperCard, this file is called Home; in SuperCard, this is the Shared File; in ToolBook, you may have one or more System Books.

HyperCard (Macintosh)

Apple Computer, Inc.
20525 Mariani Avenue
Cupertino, CA 95014

Shipped with every Macintosh sold since 1987, HyperCard is the most widely available programming system and multimedia authoring tool for the Macintosh. Since 1991, however, only a run-time version of HyperCard is bundled with new Macintoshes; the fully functional version for authoring must be purchased from Apple. HyperCard comes with ready-to-use template stacks (including an address book, datebook, graph maker, phone dialer, and scanned art) to shorten the learning curve for novice multimedia developers.

With HyperCard you create projects called *stacks* that are made up of cards. *Cards* can share the same background graphics, buttons, and text; and cards and shared backgrounds, as well, may contain graphic images, buttons, and text fields. HyperCard offers various card sizes (ranging from 64×64 pixels to 1280×1280 pixels); multiple windows (up to 18 at a time); styled text; AppleEvents support for links to programs running locally or across a network; hypertext support; support for black-and-white, gray-scale, or color PICT-based resources; QuickTime animation; and a powerful scripting language, HyperTalk, with user-definable menus and shared code libraries.

HyperCard includes an editor for bitmapped graphics. Color PICT images can be edited and placed into HyperCard stacks, but they must be scanned or made in a color drawing or painting application. HyperCard provides graphics tools for drawing, filling, and editing rectangles, ovals, polygons, lines, and text. Five styles of text fields (transparent, opaque, rectangle, shadow, and scrolling) can contain text in various fonts and styles. The program offers several methods for printing images and text reports.

You can organize your content by linking a card to any other card using scripts attached to buttons, fields, or other HyperCard objects. HyperTalk scripts, however, can do more than just link information. You can perform computational tasks, sense and respond to user input, create character, icon, and motion animations, launch other applications, and control external multimedia devices.

Figure 8-1 demonstrates use of HyperCard's card and background layers: When the gray foreground cover is wiped away with an "eraser," the background graphic image is revealed. This requires programming in HyperTalk to remove the cover beneath the special eraser cursor and to post elapsed time. The program handlers are in a transparent button over the image; they are as follows:

```
on mouseEnter
  global showFlag, totTime
  if showFlag is "True" then exit to HyperCard
  set cursor to "Eraser"
  put 0 into thisTime
  repeat while the mouseLoc is within the rect of bg btn "Frame"
    set cursor to "Eraser"
    if the mouse is down then
      lock screen
      choose eraser tool
      unlock screen
      put the ticks into startTime
      subtract 60 from startTime
      repeat
        click at the mouseLoc
        if the mouse is up then exit repeat
      end repeat
      put the ticks - startTime into thisTime
```

```
      put round((thisTime + totTime)/60) into bg fld "Timer"
add thisTime to totTime
      lock screen
      choose browse tool
      unlock screen
    end if
  end repeat
  set cursor to hand
end mouseEnter

on mouseLeave
  set cursor to hand
  choose browse tool
end mouseLeave
```

An animated earth is made up of 18 characters and rotates underneath a marker using font animation (see Chapter 12) to point out the habitat of the monkey species that is hidden below the cover. When enough of the cover is erased so the user can recognize the monkeys, the user releases the mouse button and chooses a name from a menu. If the name is incorrect, a sound plays and a cat appears and wags its tail (the cat is a button icon), and the user can continue. If the user selects the correct

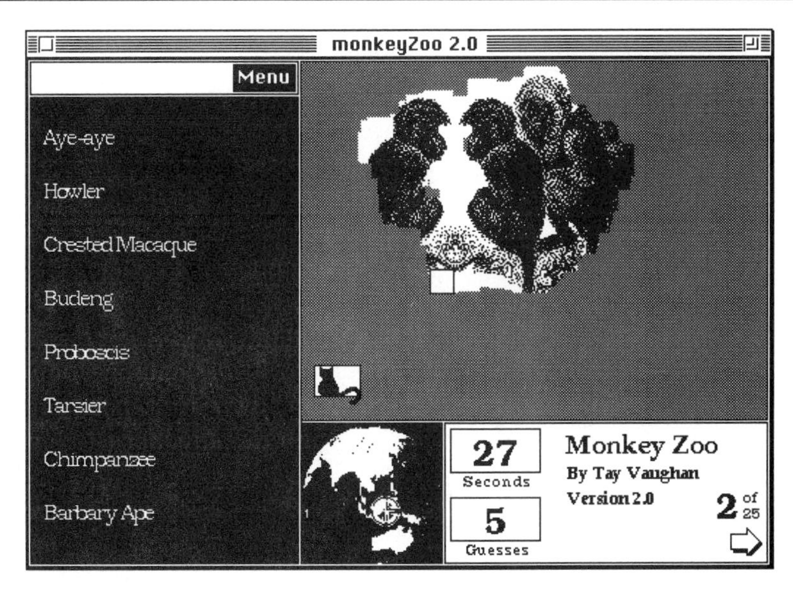

FIGURE 8-1 The globe and the cat are animated in HyperCard, as the foreground cover is erased to reveal the image beneath

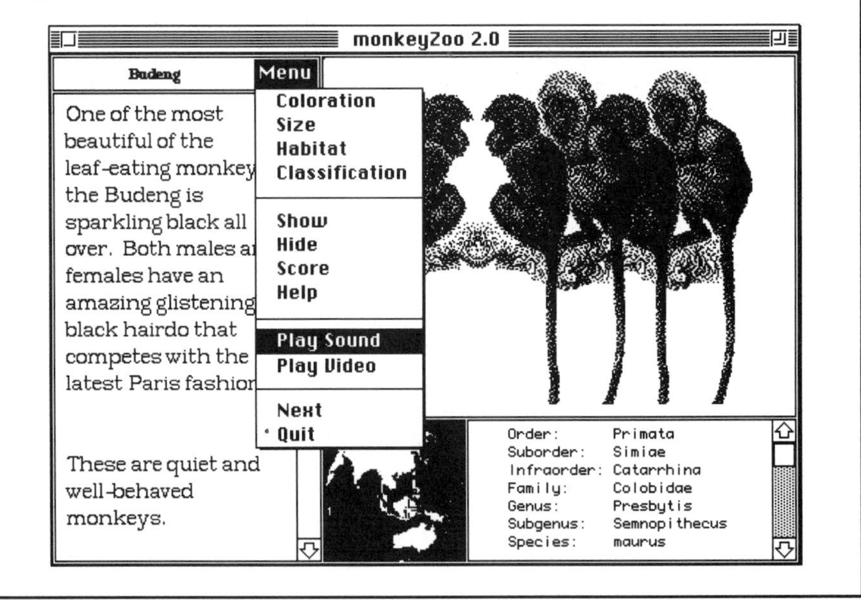

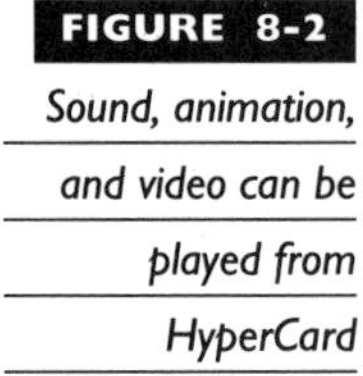
FIGURE 8-2 *Sound, animation, and video can be played from HyperCard*

monkey, an encyclopedia of information about that species is presented, and a pull-down menu (see Figure 8-2) provides access to a sound bite or video clip before going on. There are 25 monkeys, and the program keeps score.

SuperCard (Macintosh)

Aldus Corporation
411 First Avenue South
Seattle, WA 98104

SuperCard is an authoring application for the Macintosh used to produce sophisticated multimedia presentations, front-ends to databases, and computer-based education and training projects. With SuperCard you can build integrated, stand-alone Macintosh applications that include multiple windows of any type, full-color graphic objects with attached scripts, and a wide variety of other standard Macintosh interface elements. Unlike HyperCard, a SuperCard project contains windows, and windows contain backgrounds and cards that in turn contain drawn and bitmapped graphics, buttons, and text fields. SuperCard can convert HyperCard stacks to SuperCard format.

SuperCard is shipped as two applications: SuperCard and SuperEdit. SuperCard is optimized for running the projects you create in SuperEdit. SuperEdit is optimized for assembling applications. SuperCard, however, does have a powerful run-time editor built in, so developers typically design their screens and content layout first in SuperEdit, and then fine-tune the project and its scripts using SuperCard's editor.

SuperCard lets you create any of the seven standard types of Macintosh windows, and can contain many different custom windows that can be opened at any time and in any combination. A scrolling window may accommodate cards as large as 32,767×32,767 pixels—virtually 30 feet by 30 feet; if you make your window, say, 640×480 pixels, you can then scroll across the "geography" of the larger card. Custom windows from other projects can also be open at the same time, so you can move among applications with ease. You can create custom menus and add scripts to provide them with functionality. Figure 8-3 shows a SuperCard project with many custom windows being edited in SuperEdit.

SuperCard supports both drawn and bitmapped graphics—both can be created in SuperCard or in other Macintosh applications and imported into SuperCard. Graphic objects can have scripts attached to them, so you can create buttons of any shape. With an AutoTrace tool, bitmaps can be converted to drawn object polygons and to irregularly shaped buttons.

SuperCard provides animation commands within its scripting language, and can generate PICS and STEP animation files. The program will run at all color depth monitor settings, but it cannot import images with color depths greater than 8 bits (256 colors).

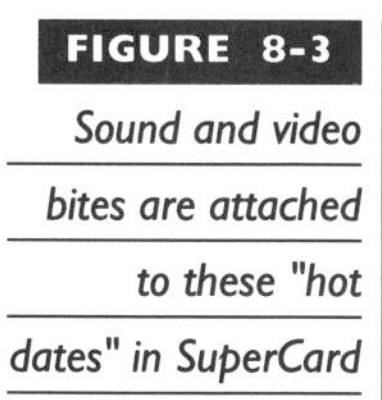

FIGURE 8-3 Sound and video bites are attached to these "hot dates" in SuperCard

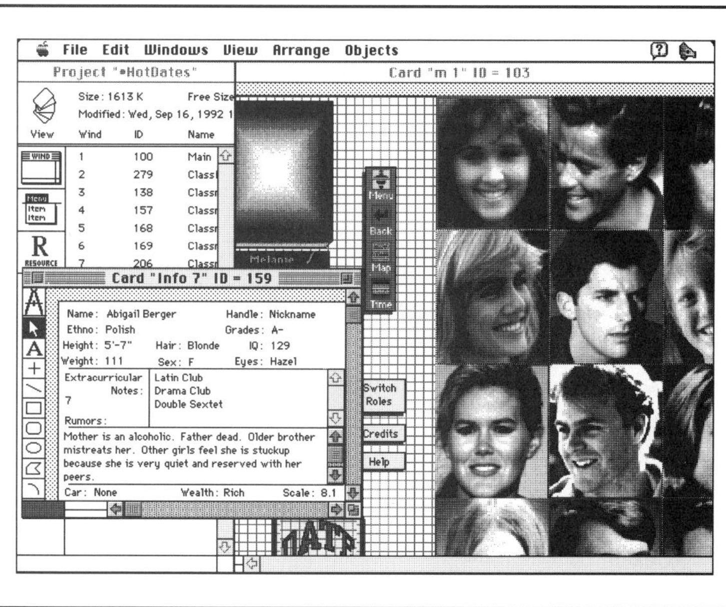

ToolBook (Windows)

Asymetrix Corporation
110 110th Ave. N.E., Suite 717
Bellevue, WA 98004

ToolBook offers a Windows graphical user interface and object-oriented programming environment for building projects, or books, to present information graphically as drawings, scanned color images, text, sounds, and animations. A book is divided into pages and is stored as a DOS file. Pages can contain text fields, buttons, and both drawn and bitmapped graphic objects. You assemble a book from pages and link the pages together; ToolBook's OpenScript programming then performs interactive and navigational tasks and defines how objects behave.

Hot words in text fields can have a script attached; these hot words provide a hypertext feature in ToolBook to connect related information that appears in different places throughout a book, or other books that can be opened. Clicking a hot word makes the word respond like a button.

ToolBook has two working levels: Reader and Author. You run a book's scripts at Reader level. At Author level, you use commands to create new books, create and modify objects on pages, and write scripts. ToolBook offers linking options for buttons and hot words, so you can create navigation scripts by identifying the page to go to. There is also a script recorder feature to record actions and translate them into OpenScript statements. ToolBook provides built-in tools for debugging, and if you are an experienced programmer, you can extend OpenScript by writing additional functions and Dynamic Link Libraries (DLLs). Scripts may be as large as 64K.

You can control image drawing and display speed, and you can paste or import large bitmaps, device-independent bitmaps (DIBs), and graphics from other applications. Graphics filters allow importing of .DRW, .EPS, .TIF, .BMP, .DIB, and Windows metafile files. You can store 16- or 256-color palettized bitmaps outside of the ToolBook application and display them in child, pop-up, or overlapped windows. You can create Windows-style buttons, list boxes, and dialog boxes, and you can translate Windows messages into OpenScript messages.

With the Multimedia Resource Kit (MMRK) for ToolBook, developers have access from within OpenScript to the Windows MCI for controlling external devices. The MMRK provides more than 250 prescripted graphic objects to copy and paste into your own project to control multimedia devices. These widgets look and feel similar to the controls on CD players, VCRs, and other consumer electronic devices. From OpenScript you also have access to the timer services of Windows, as well as object notification when a particular multimedia task is complete so that you can trigger other actions. You can link to and control any multimedia hardware or software that has a Windows DLL or a Windows driver. Devices supported by the MMRK include CD-ROM (for both digital data and Red Book Audio), laserdisc players, animation software, waveform audio cards, video overlay boards, and MIDI sequencers.

ToolBook supports Windows's multiple instance capability, so you can open two or more ToolBook windows at the same time, and the books can interact under script control. In this way you can, for example, display a control panel in one window and show the controlled animation, video, or bitmap in another. In Figure 8-4, four ToolBook windows are open at one time.

ToolBook provides DDE support, so you can open other Windows applications and control them from within your own project. Windows callback support and message translation, as well as support for any standard DLL, are available in OpenScript.

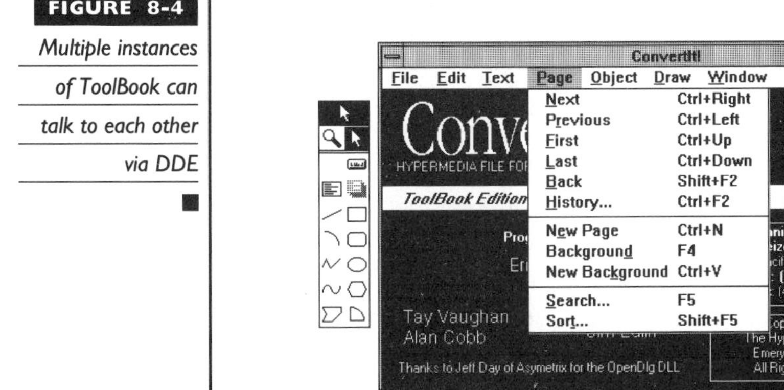

FIGURE 8-4 *Multiple instances of ToolBook can talk to each other via DDE*

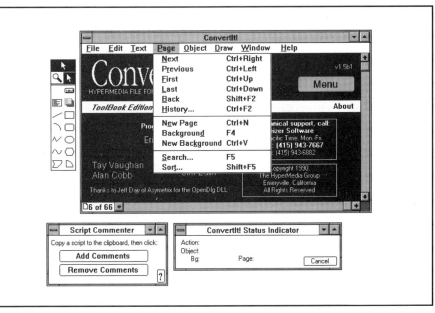

Visual BASIC (Windows)

Microsoft Corporation
One Microsoft Way
Redmond, WA 98052

Visual Basic is a programming system for Windows that is often used to organize and present multimedia elements. It is made up of *controls* (objects) that reside on *forms* (or windows). Visual Basic uses language code syntactically similar to BASICA or GW-BASIC. The program is *event-driven*—that is, code is attached to objects and remains idle until called to respond to user- or system-initiated events, such as a mouse click or system timeout. You use controls to create the user interface of an application, including command buttons, option buttons, check boxes, list boxes, combo boxes, text boxes, scroll bars, frames, file and directory selection boxes, timers, and menu bars.

Visual Basic provides flexible response to mouse and keyboard events (including drag and drop), can show and hide objects, and provides access to the Windows Clipboard, DDE, and OLE facilities (see Chapter 7 for more about DDE and OLE). There are also powerful debugging commands to help isolate and correct code errors. When your Visual Basic project is complete, you can convert it into an executable .EXE file to run as a stand-alone Windows file.

Multimedia enhancements to Visual Basic are available with the Professional Toolkit extensions. These offer additional custom controls: a Grid control for adding tables with rows and columns; a Child control for multiple document interfaces (MDI) child windows; a Graph control for creating graphs; and a Windows MCI control for incorporating audio, video, and animation elements using Windows MCI. Controls can be stored as special files with the extension .VBX.

The MCI.VBX lets you control CD players, VCRs, music files, laserdiscs, and full-motion video, using a control panel containing Play, Pause, Stop, Rewind, Next, Record, Eject, and other buttons drawn on a Visual Basic form. Figure 8-5 shows a Visual Basic controller for audio CD with a sample of code. At the left of this code sample is the Visual Basic Toolbox palette for creating controls.

Icon-Based Authoring Tools

Icon-based, event-driven tools provide a visual programming approach to organizing and presenting multimedia. First you build a structure or flow-

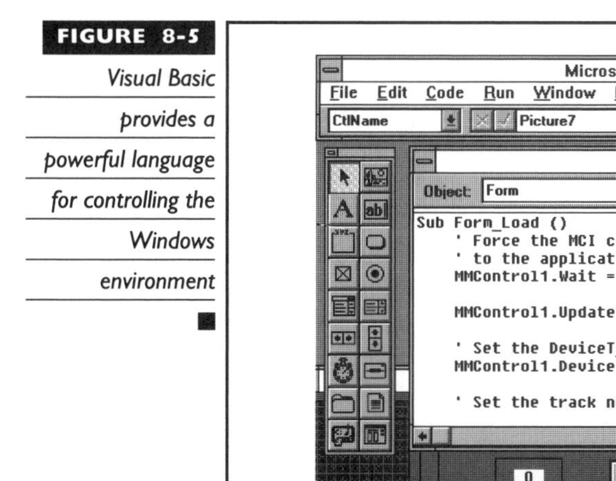

FIGURE 8-5 *Visual Basic provides a powerful language for controlling the Windows environment*

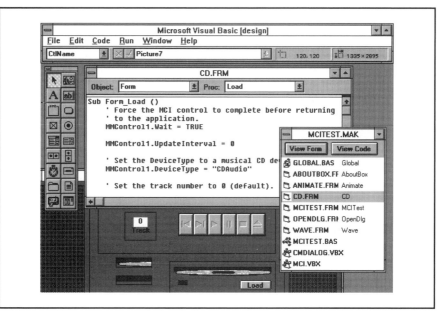

chart of events, tasks, and decisions, by dragging appropriate icons from a library. These icons can include menu choices, graphic images, sounds, and computations. The flowchart graphically depicts the project's logic. When the structure is built, you can add your content: text, graphics, animation, sounds, and video movies. Then, to refine your project, you edit your logical structure by rearranging and fine-tuning the icons and their properties.

Authorware Professional (Macintosh and Windows)

Macromedia
600 Townsend, Suite 310W
San Francisco, CA 94107

With Authorware Professional, nontechnical multimedia authors can build sophisticated applications without scripting. By placing icons on the flow line, you can quickly sequence events and activities, including decisions and user interactions. Authorware is useful as a design tool for storyboarding, because it lets you change sequences, add options, and restructure interactions by simply dragging and dropping icons. You can print out your navigation map or flowchart, an annotated project index with or without associated icons, design and presentation windows, and a cross-reference table of variables. Developers who use both Macintoshes and PCs can work with almost identical interfaces, authoring functions, media-editing capabilities, and data management on both platforms.

Authorware offers more than 200 system variables and functions for capturing, manipulating, and displaying data, and for controlling the operation of your project. Variables include interaction, decision, time, video, graphics, general, file, and user; functions include math, string, time jump, video, graphics, general, file, and user. You can paste variables and functions into calculation windows, option slots, or presentation windows, and you can control the format of variables embedded in selected display text. Authorware provides links to external user functions written as DLLs in Windows, or XCMDs and XFCNs on the Macintosh.

Application:	*Authorware*
Macintosh Pathname:	*MACROMEDIA :Product Demonstrations :APM Demo :Authorware Professionsl*
Windows Pathname:	*After installing the Showcase CD, click on the appropriate icon in the Windows Macromedia Showcase CD Program Group for Newton's Apple APW Demo, City of Novato APW Demo, and Authorware Working Model Demo.*

Authorware has a complete set of tools for incorporating and editing multimedia elements (graphic images, sounds, animations, and movies) created with other software. For text you can mix fonts, styles, sizes, modes, and colors, and you can draw graphic objects (polygons, ovals, rectangles, rounded rectangles, and lines) and fill them with up to 36 patterns. Authorware will import files in PICT, DIB, TIFF, EPSF, Windows metafile, and Windows bitmap formats. Graphics can be displayed with numerous transition effects. Authorware provides its own waveform sound editor, SoundWave, and it supports AIFF, SND, PCM, and Windows Waveform and MIDI formats. Path animation routines and QuickTime movies can be fine-tuned, and multiple layering is supported to govern which animated object overlaps another. Video can be displayed in still or motion in resizable, movable video windows with variable-speed playback.

In Authorware, design icons (1 through 8 in the illustration that follows) denote a special function that is performed when the icon is encountered during interaction with a user. Start/Stop Flag icons (9 and 10) are used while testing and debugging in the authoring mode. Multimedia icons (11 through

13) control playback of graphic animations, sound, and video. All the icons in the illustration are described next.

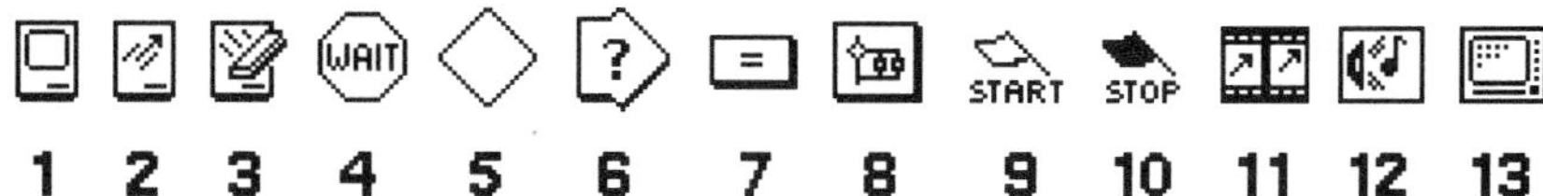

- Display icons (1) put text and/or graphics on the screen.
- Animation icons (2) move the objects of a preceding Display icon from one point to another in a given amount of time or at a specified speed.
- Erase icons (3) erase the text and/or graphics displays.
- Wait icons (4) interrupt file flow until the user presses a key or clicks the mouse, or until a specified amount of time elapses.
- Decision icons (5) select which icons (from a set of attached icons) to use next.
- Interaction icons (6) present options or questions and then, based on the user's response, select and branch to attached icons for feedback to the user.
- Calculation icons (7) perform arithmetic or special control functions, execute user-written code, jump to other files, or jump to other applications.
- Map icons (8) organize and modularize the file by providing space to put more icons. Each Map icon provides its own flow line on which you can place other icons, including additional Map icons.
- Start Flag icons (9) begin running a file from an intermediate location.
- Stop Flag icons (10) stop a file from running.
- Movie icons (11) provide for playing PICS, FLI, and FLC frame animations.
- Sound icons (12) provide many options for loading sounds and controlling their playback.
- Video icons (13) provide control of video players and playback of video segments and their sound tracks.

Figure 8-6 shows the layout of an online magazine published on CD-ROM using Authorware for Macintosh as the authoring system. Note that Interaction icons branch to other topics.

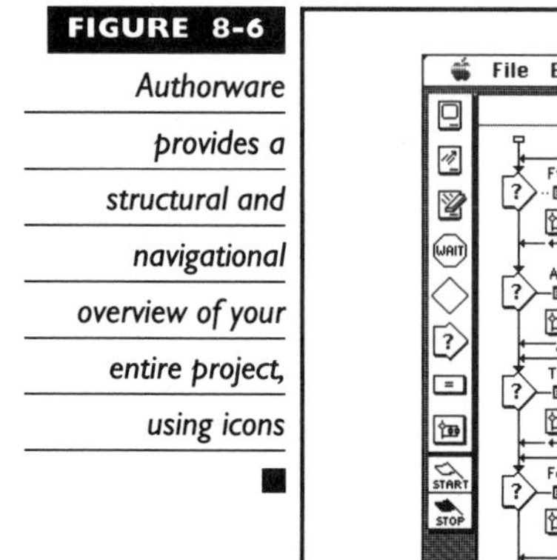

FIGURE 8-6

Authorware provides a structural and navigational overview of your entire project, using icons

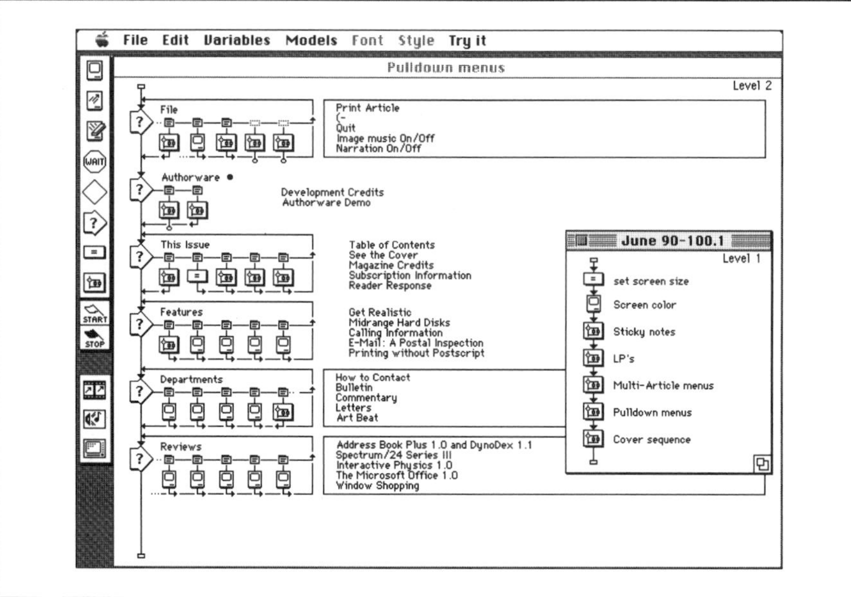

conAuthor (Windows)

AimTech
20 Trafalgar Square
Nashua, NH 03063

IconAuthor's visual programming environment enables nonprogrammers to create applications by building structures and then adding content to the building blocks. To build the structures, icons representing functions or tasks are moved from an icon library and connected to a flowchart (see Figure 8-7). You combine the icons into a logical sequence that depicts the flow of your project.

When you have built your structure, you can then add content, including text, graphics, animation, and/or full motion video. IconAuthor provides an integrated set of graphic, text, animation, and video editors to let you create screens as well as special effects such as wipes, zooms, and fades. With Rezolution, the graphic editing utility in IconAuthor, you can display graphic images in various resolutions for CGA, EGA, VGA, and Super VGA monitors. Rezolution can also convert between palettes of 2, 8, 16, and 256 colors.

IconAuthor uses the Windows MCI for management of videodisc and videotape devices, can read and write to dBASE database files, and supports DDE and access to DLLs.

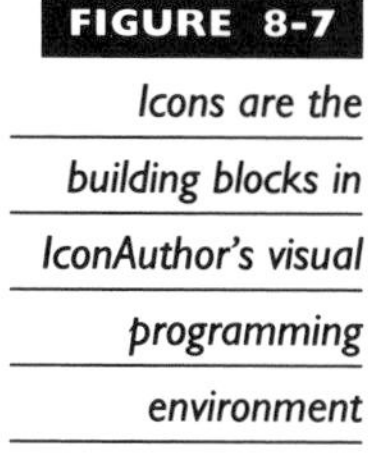

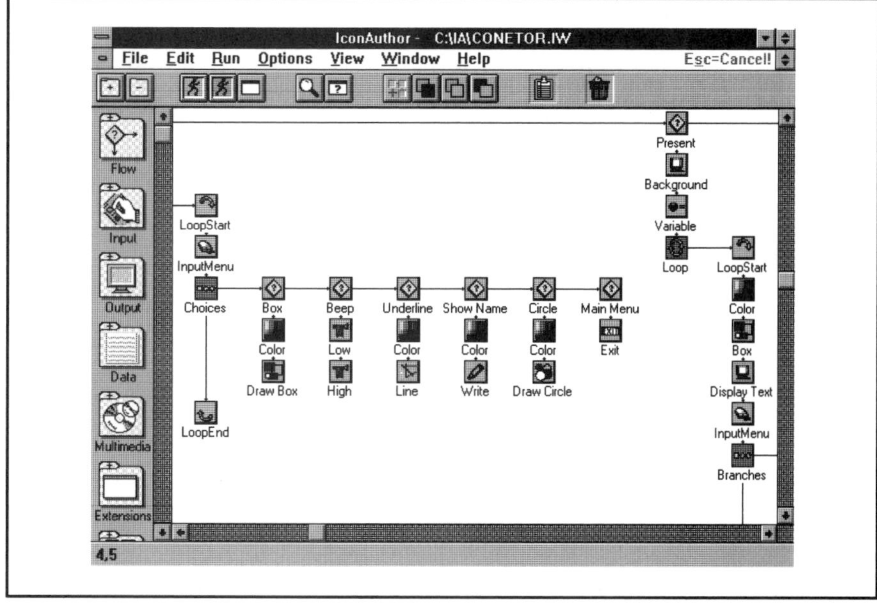

FIGURE 8-7 *Icons are the building blocks in IconAuthor's visual programming environment*

HSC Interactive (Windows)

HSC Software
1661 Lincoln Blvd. #101
Santa Monica, CA 90494

Under a publishing and distribution agreement, HSC Interactive is distributed as a less-expensive (but still powerful) subset of IconAuthor's full-featured professional authoring system. HSC Interactive includes IconAnimate, an animation editor, and RezSolution, a screen capture program.

You get the following features in the HSC program:

- Icon library containing powerful programming functions
- Ability to save any part of a project's structure as a user-defined icon
- Loops and unlimited branching capability for navigation design
- Support for Windows MCI function calls
- Automatic time capabilities to allow input timeouts, test timing, or elapsed timing
- Overlay features to combine graphics, text, and video on the same screen

- Multiple fonts, styles, and sizes
- Special effects such as 3-D, solid, or natural drop shadows, with screen blends up to 16.8 million colors
- Ability to import WMF, PCX, RLE, and BMP bitmap graphic files

Time-Based Authoring Tools

Time-based authoring tools are the most common of multimedia authoring tools. Each uses its own, distinctive approach and user interface for managing events over time. Many use a visual time line for sequencing the events of a multimedia presentation, often displaying layers of various media elements or events alongside the scale in increments as precise as 1/30th of a second. Others arrange long sequences of graphic frames, and add the time component by adjusting each frame's duration of play.

Action! (Macintosh and Windows)

Action! is from Macromedia (see the section on Authorware for this company's address). Action! creates on-screen multimedia presentations with motion, sound, text, graphics, animations, and QuickTime. Action! is for speakers, salespeople, business presenters, and educators who need to create high-impact, on-screen presentations quickly. This is a multimedia presentation package; it uses a time line to organize the elements.

Application:	*Action*
Macintosh Pathname:	*MACROMEDIA :Product Demonstrations :Action Demo :Action demo disk :Action! Demonstration*
Windows Pathname:	*After installing the Showcase CD, click on the Action! Working Model Demo icon in the Windows Macromedia Showcase CD Program Group.*

Action! presentations are made up of scenes, each being a single slide in a sequence of slides. Scenes typically last from a few seconds to a minute or more, and incorporate motion and sound while the scene plays. Transitions can be applied to objects in a scene so they can appear and disappear.

You compose and arrange a scene using both the Timeline and the Control Panel (see Figure 8-8). The Timeline is a visual ruler incremented in units of

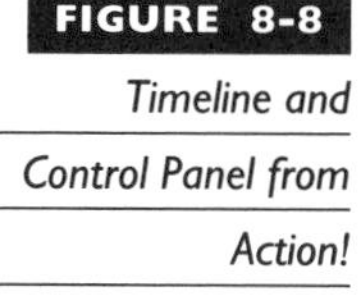

FIGURE 8-8

Timeline and Control Panel from Action!

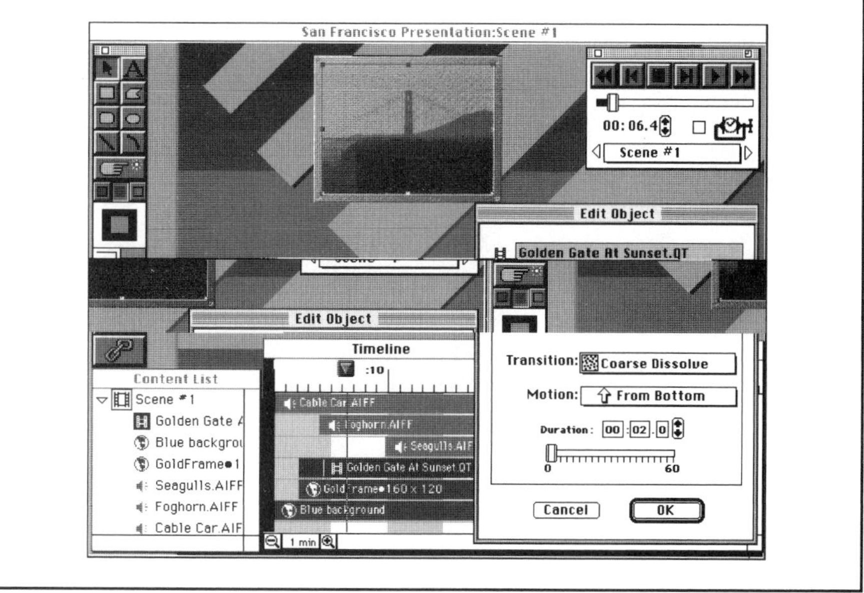

time; you drag and drop your multimedia objects onto the time line. The VCR-like Control Panel lets you move back and forth within the scene and navigate to other scenes.

A scene includes text, graphic objects, and sounds. Action! provides built-in text and drawing tools, and you can import these elements and sounds from other files and sources. Using MacRecorder, you can import sounds directly into the presentation. Action! for the Macintosh can also import and animate slides using PICT files generated in other applications, such as Persuasion or PowerPoint; the Windows version will import slides from applications such as Aldus Persuasion, Microsoft PowerPoint, SPC Harvard Graphics, and Lotus Freelance Graphics. QuickTime and AVI are supported. Each object on a slide can be programmed with its own motion and timing, so a pie chart generated in Microsoft Excel, for example, can be imported, and then programmed with Action! so that the pie segments fly into place. Animations for text and graphic objects are made by defining a spline-based path and directing the target object to travel along it. Action! supports QuickTime, so you can add digital video clips; these can be placed in a scene with other graphics that move in front of or behind the movie. Any object in a scene can be a button that controls the sequence of scenes.

A Content List displays the entire presentation in outline form for quick editing. A Scene Sorter displays each scene as a preview or thumbnail, and lets users rearrange scenes quickly. The Scene Sorter can also be used to set the background of several scenes at once.

Action! comes with a library of templates that can simplify presentation development. Simply change the template's text and graphics to suit your own needs—the animations will remain as original—and then save your new presentation.

Action! for Windows offers a Datamotion charting feature. Datamotion lets you incorporate animated 2-D and 3-D charts created in other applications such as Microsoft Excel and Lotus 1-2-3. Using the Windows DDE feature, whenever data are changed in the source application, Action! will update the Datamotion chart to reflect the new values. Action! for Windows includes MIDI and CD-Audio sound support through the Windows MCI, and supports TrueType fonts.

The Windows version includes a run-time player application to enable users to play an Action! presentation even if they don't own Action!.

Animation Works Interactive (Windows)

Gold Disk, Inc.
20675 South Western Ave. #120
Torrance, CA 90501

Animation Works Interactive for Windows is an authoring tool for creating complex animations and multimedia presentations synchronized with digital audio, MIDI, and CD-Audio. It is a frame-based tool with three authoring modules: a Cel Editor, a Background Editor, and a Movie Editor. Animation Works Interactive supports the Windows MCI to control devices and peripherals. In Figure 8-9 you see the Movie Editor, where you assemble actors on a background that can move along complex paths.

The Background Editor is a 256-color paint program. It can import GIF, DIB, and BMP bitmap files, and it exports DIB files.

With the Cel Editor, you create sequences of incrementally different images; an "onion-skin" feature shows the semitransparent images of previous frames while you create the next. With other special capabilities—color transparencies, auto-zoom, and auto-rotate—the Cel Editor lets you create flying titles and logos.

The Movie Editor lets you combine the actors and backgrounds, and sequence them with sounds and screen-wipe effects, using a Cue Sheet (shown in Figure 8-10) to display frames and interactivity in a tabular format. A Storyboard view, also shown in Figure 8-10, lets you view each frame. Interactivity is attached to the path of an actor: you can pause, wait for mouse clicks or keypresses, control the branching of your project, cause

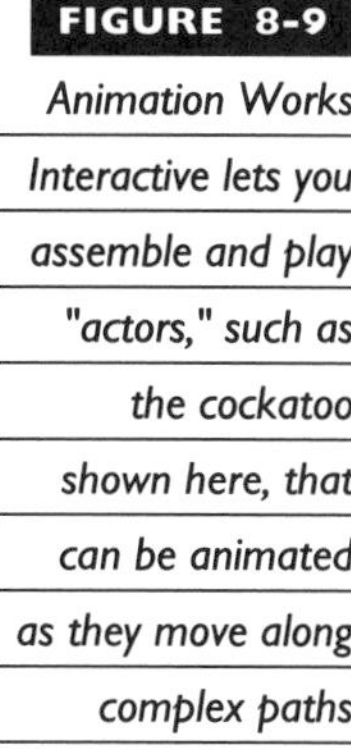

FIGURE 8-9

Animation Works Interactive lets you assemble and play "actors," such as the cockatoo shown here, that can be animated as they move along complex paths

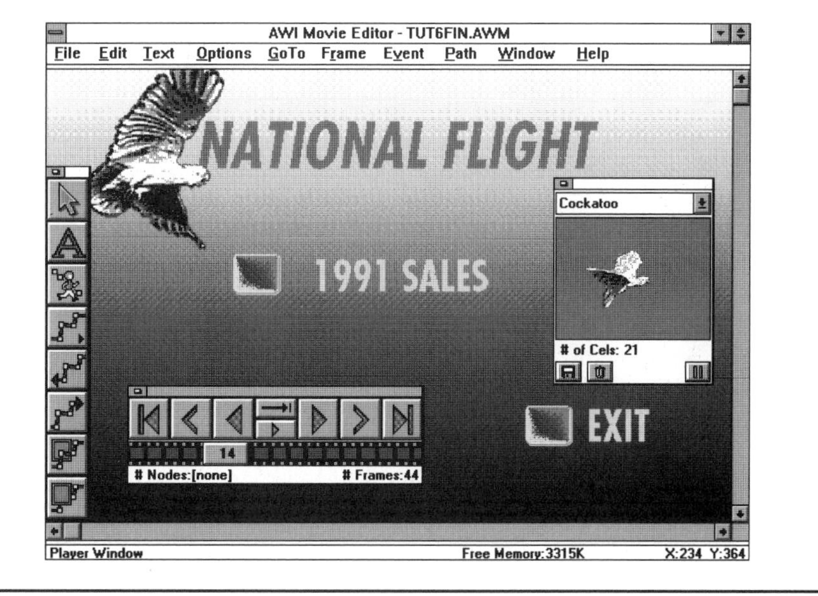

a sound to be played, execute a Windows MCI command, or even launch another application.

FIGURE 8-10

Animation Works Interactive uses a Cue Sheet to program sequences of action in the Storyboard view

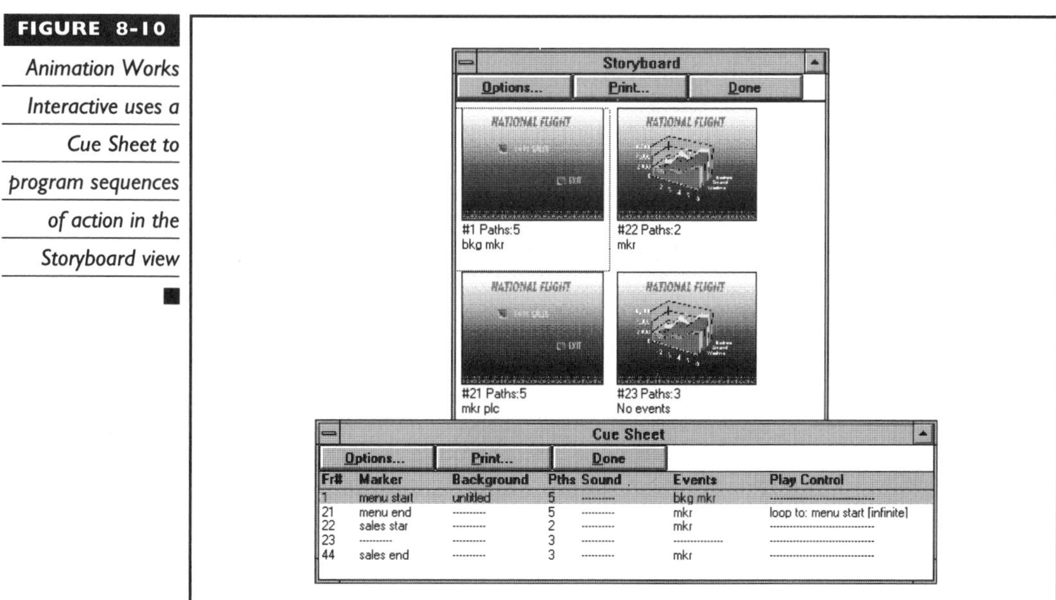

A special Animation Works Interactive feature allows you to compile your animations in a compression format, so your project can be played back at high speed.

Cinemation (Macintosh)

Vividus
651 Kendall Avenue
Palo Alto, CA 94306

Cinemation is an animation and presentation tool used to add motion to slides created in applications such as Microsoft PowerPoint and Aldus Persuasion. Cinemation animation sequences integrate text, still images, animations, digital audio, QuickTime movies, and other Cinemation files. You can also directly capture and edit digital audio to add to your project.

Cinemation includes a 24-bit color paint program for creating and editing images. A special ghosting feature displays any series of frames through a transparent easel, so you can paint in between frames or align objects using other frame images as a reference. Animations are created within Cinemation through either real-time recording of an object being moved around the screen or through a feature called Fill In Motion. Fill In Motion automatically fills in the motion of an object between two frames (see Chapter 12 for details about "tweening"). Cinemation also provides fill-in motion for cropping, scaling, and rotating an object.

Cinemation displays animation as a sequence of frames, or *filmstrip* (shown at the bottom of Figure 8-11). Frames can have sounds attached to them, and special effect transitions (wipes, dissolves, reveals, cuts) will operate when a frame is displayed. Sounds that begin playing at a specific frame will continue playing until the sound ends, another sound is played, or a STOP command is encountered. Frames and visual objects can have event links attached to provide control over the flow of a presentation:

- A pause can be applied to a frame. Pauses include waiting for a specified number of seconds to pass; until the mouse or an object in the frame is clicked; until the currently playing sound or QuickTime movie is finished playing; or until Cinemation has finished loading all the remaining frames to accelerate their playback.
- Links can direct playback to other frames in the presentation. This includes branching playback to the next or previous frame in the filmstrip, to a specified frame, to another file, to the last frame displayed, or halting altogether.

FIGURE 8-11

A Cinemation filmstrip

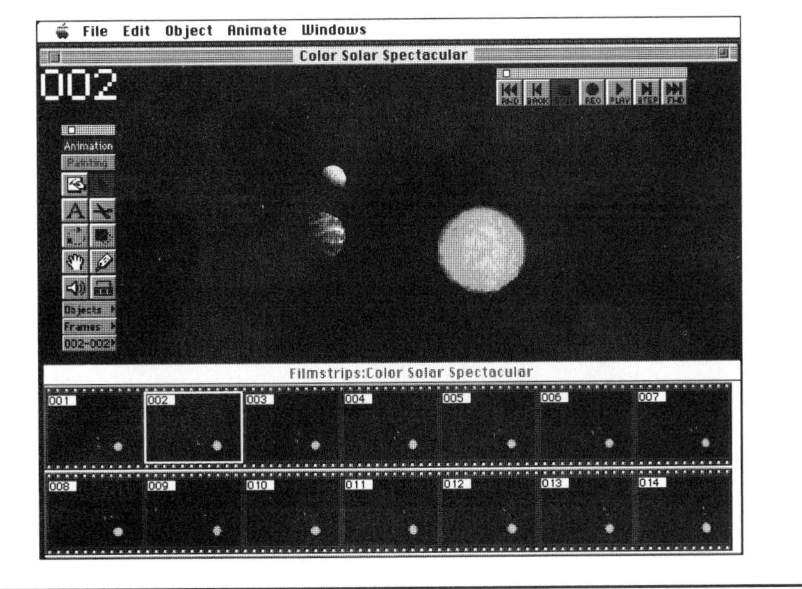

The sequencing of a presentation is managed through an Organizer, which allows you to manipulate named groups of frames all at once. Groups can be quickly rearranged or even temporarily disabled during playback. Organizer can also call sequences from other presentations.

If you are using traditional slide-based presentation tools, you can add animated effects with the AutoMotion feature. AutoMotion automatically animates presentations created in PowerPoint or Persuasion. For example, you can add animations or sound to Persuasion scrapbook files by importing them and then converting each slide into an individual Cinemation frame. You then add custom effects or apply one of Cinemation's AutoMotion templates to the text and graphic objects on the slide. AutoMotion can also be used in conjunction with templates to create animated slides.

To help you get started building your productions, Cinemation comes with over 12MB of clip animation, art, sounds, and music created by professional artists and composers. Collections of clips include business subjects, creatures, transportation, marquees, and buttons. Sounds include music loops, intros, finales, and button clicks.

For HyperCard users, Cinemation includes a MovieWindow XCMD that plays Cinemation productions from within HyperCard. The MovieWindow XCMD can also be used to obtain detailed control over user interaction, branching, and object positions using HyperTalk.

Once you have built your Cinemation project, you can distribute it with the included CinePlayer run-time engine, so that users who do not own

Cinemation can still play your project. You can also export Cinemation presentations into QuickTime format, for importing or pasting into other applications.

Macromedia Director (Macintosh)

Director is from Macromedia (see the section on Authorware for this company's address). Director is a powerful and complex multimedia authoring tool with a broad set of features used to create multimedia presentations, animations, and interactive multimedia applications. It requires a significant learning curve, but, once mastered, is among the most powerful of multimedia development tools. Director contains two major components: Overview and Studio.

Overview is an icon-oriented, simple-to-use tool for building linear multimedia presentations. You can import, arrange, and rearrange—in icon form—graphics, sounds, animations, and text. Overview also provides an Auto Animate feature for rapidly creating animated text and simple 2-D charts.

Serious production work (or anything interactive) requires the Studio component. In Studio, you assemble and sequence the elements of your project using a Cast and a Score.

Application:	*Director*
Macintosh Pathname:	*MACROMEDIA :Product Demonstrations :Director Demo :MacroMind Director 3.1.1 (SD)*
Macintosh Pathname:	*MACROMEDIA :Director 4.0 Save Disabled :Director 4.0 Demo*
Windows Pathname:	*After installing the Showcase CD, click on the Showcase CD Version 2 icon in the Windows Macromedia Showcase CD Program Group.*

Cast

The Cast is a multimedia database containing up to 512 elements—still images, sound files, text, palettes, QuickDraw shapes, programming scripts, QuickTime movies, and even other Director files. As shown in Figure 8-12, you not only can import a wide range of data types and multimedia element formats directly into this Cast, but also create multimedia elements from scratch using Director's own tools and editors.

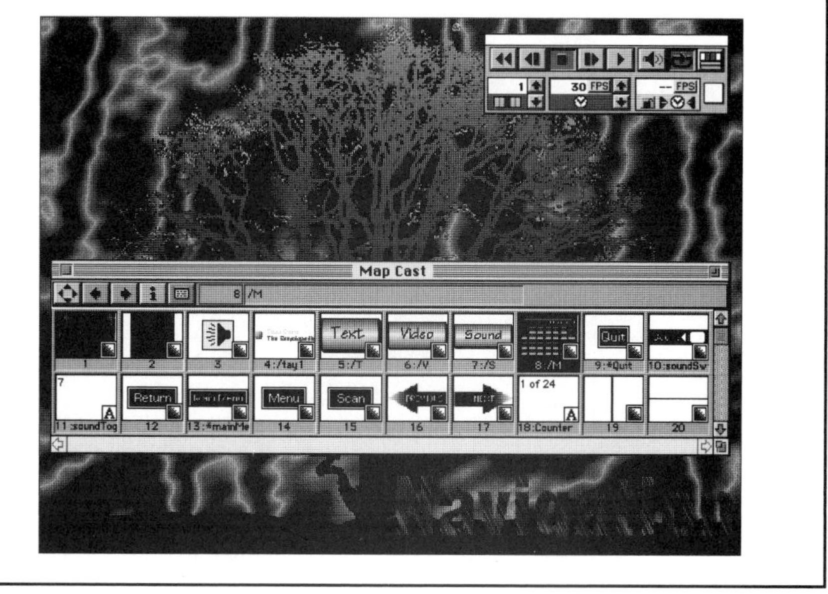

FIGURE 8-12 *Director's Cast feature contains all the multimedia elements of your project*

A full-featured painting tool lets you create bitmapped artwork in any color depth. You can create gradients, tile patterns, and animated transformations (such as rotations and skews) of artwork. Other tools edit and create QuickDraw shapes, text, QuickTime movies, palettes, and scripts.

Score

Once you have imported or created the multimedia elements for your project and placed them into your Cast, you tie these Cast members together using the Score facility. Score is a sequencer for displaying, animating, and playing Cast members, and it is made up of frames that contain Cast members, tempo, a palette, timing, and sound information in up to 24 channels. Each frame is played back on a "stage" at a rate specified in the tempo channel. The Score provides elaborate and complex visual effects and transitions, adjustments of color palettes, and tempo control. In Figure 8-13, the frames are the vertical bands, and the channels are the horizontal bands.

Animations, for example, are made by placing a graphic or *sprite* onto the stage and changing its location slightly over several or more frames. When the frames are played back at tempo, the sprite moves. You can synchronize animations with sound effects by highlighting a range of frames and selecting the appropriate sound from your Cast.

FIGURE 8-13 *Director's Score feature sequences and sets the tempo for playback*

Lingo

Director utilizes Lingo, a full-featured scripting language, to enable interactivity and programmed control. A built-in script editor offers Lingo debugging facilities. Because you can attach scripts to individual elements of the Cast, you can copy and paste complete interactive sequences. Lingo also uses XObjects, which are special code segments used to control external sound and video devices. Several XObjects and extensive examples of their use are shipped with Macromedia Director. You can also use many HyperCard XCMDs and XFCNs to extend the program's functionality for special purposes.

Using Lingo scripts, you can chain together separate Director documents and call other files as subroutines. You can also import elements into your Cast using pointers to a file. This allows you to share the same elements among many Casts; when your Score calls for that element, it is loaded into RAM from the file. Chaining and sharing let you create Director projects as large or complex as your storage medium will accommodate.

QuickTime Support

Director provides extensive support for QuickTime. You can import existing QuickTime movies directly into the Cast and have them play as part of your production at any time. A special QuickTime window lets you use the standard QuickTime controller to preview and perform simple editing with imported QuickTime movies. There are also special Lingo commands and functions that provide specific interactive control of many aspects of the QuickTime movies, including their location, playback rate, and audio volume.

With Director you can also create animations and save them in QuickTime format. Export options provide control of the exported QuickTime movie's size and frame rate.

Playback and Delivery

For noninteractive productions, you can use the Accelerator (included with Director) to compile your animations into a special high-speed playback format—a useful feature when you wish to record animations on videotape or play them back on slower computers. You can use the Player (also included with Director) to create run-time versions of your project for delivery to users who do not own Director.

Director is available in a CD-ROM version containing the following features:

- An assortment of animations, graphics, QuickTime movies, sound effects, and music clips
- The Macromedia KnowledgeBase, containing expert technical advice, common technical support questions and answers, and valuable tips and hints
- Working models of Swivel 3D_ Pro, ModelShop_ II, and SoundEdit_ Pro
- Advanced examples of Lingo scripting, ready to copy, paste, and customize

MediaBlitz! (Windows)

MediaBlitz! is a set of applications that together give novice users a simple way to edit, sequence, and play multimedia presentations. MediaBlitz! from Asymetrix (see the section on ToolBook for this company's address) was created in Asymetrix's own Multimedia ToolBook authoring system. As a result, developers can easily include MediaBlitz! sequences in ToolBook applications. MediaBlitz! is made up of three tools: ClipMaker, ScoreMaker, and ScorePlayer.

ClipMaker (Figure 8-14) lets users create multimedia elements, or clips, that can be named and stored in files. Clips can be pointers to media elements stored in data files; references to start and stop points in external peripheral devices such as videotape players; or parameters such as the display coordinates for animation sequences. MediaBlitz! supports digital audio, MIDI, CD-Audio, animation, and Windows bitmap images.

Once you have created your collection of clips (images, sounds, and animations), ScoreMaker (Figure 8-15) graphically represents a time line along which you can assemble the clips by dragging them with the mouse. ScoreMaker lets you align elements for synchronous play in one-second resolutions with overlapping, simultaneous, and sequential elements. You can then save the score as a text file describing the sequence of events. Presentations are played back using ScorePlayer, a simple tool that plays a selected score.

MediaBlitz! is shipped with over 4MB of multimedia clip files, including digitized audio, MIDI files, animations, and color images. Users receive an additional 6MB of multimedia clips when they register their product with Asymetrix.

Though MediaBlitz! provides no interactivity of its own, its sequenced presentations can be interactively controlled by other ToolBook projects. From ToolBook, you can launch clips and complete MediaBlitz! scores.

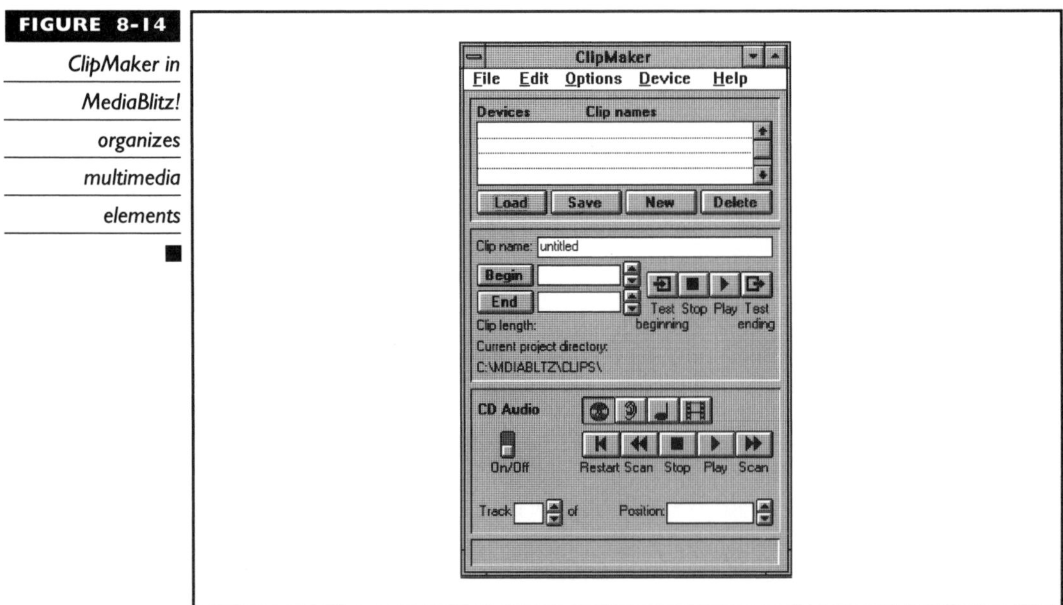

FIGURE 8-14 ClipMaker in MediaBlitz! organizes multimedia elements

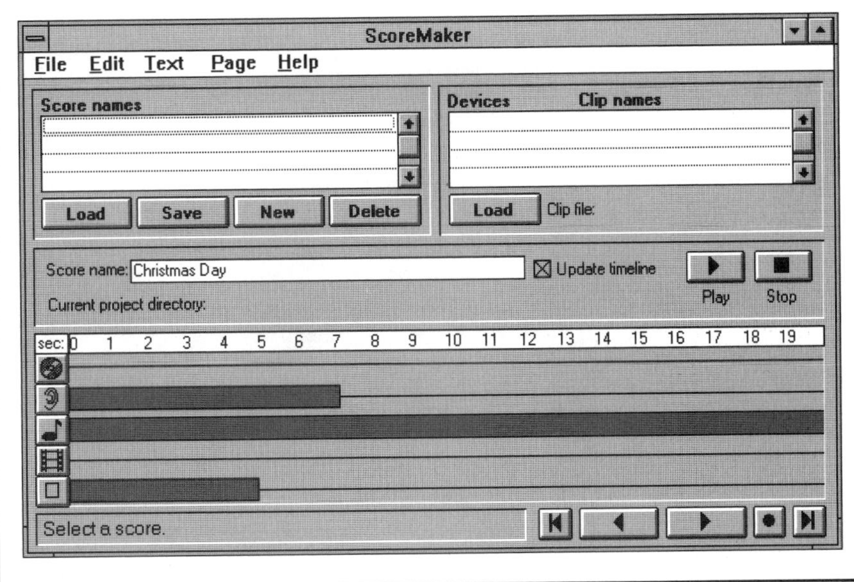

FIGURE 8-15 *The ScoreMaker feature of MediaBlitz! displays multimedia clips along a time line*

Producer (Macintosh and Windows)

Passport Designs, Inc.
100 Stone Pine Road
Half Moon Bay, CA 94019

Passport Producer is a time-based media integration and assembly tool designed for creating synchronized presentations. You can combine nearly any type of data—including still images, animations, QuickTime movies, digital audio, MIDI, and CD-Audio—into the program's SMPTE-based time line environment. (SMPTE time codes are discussed in Chapter 13.) Producer also lets you integrate slides containing text and graphics for titling. Producer's approach to synchronization provides very consistent playback, regardless of the speed of the host computer.

Producer uses a graphical time line or Cue Sheet, shown in Figure 8-16. The Cue Sheet is somewhat different from time lines in other multimedia authoring tools, because it displays the time scale along a vertical axis and uses tracks along a horizontal axis to score multiple simultaneous data elements (this orientation can be rotated). The time line can be scaled to various resolutions and can show time in several ways: in units of hours-minutes-seconds-hundredths of seconds (00:00:00.00) and in SMPTE time codes.

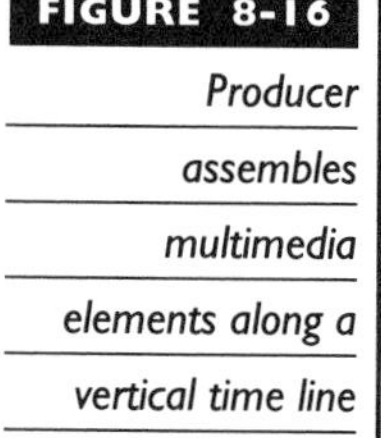

FIGURE 8-16 *Producer assembles multimedia elements along a vertical time line*

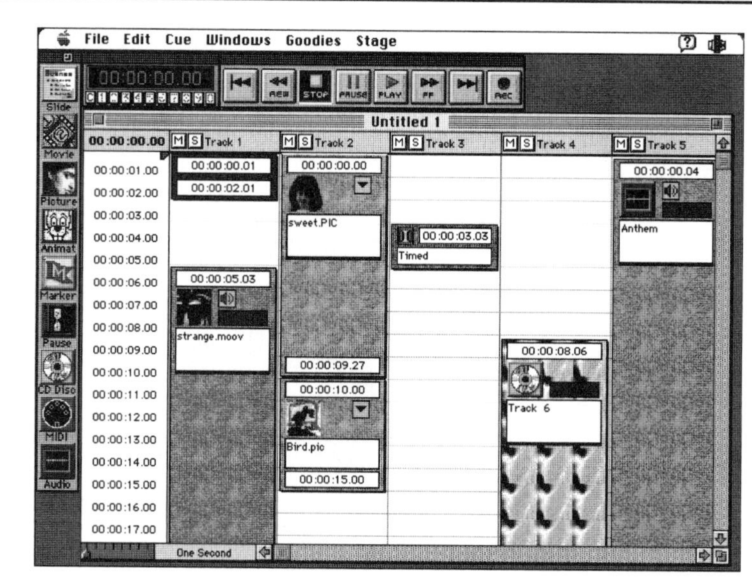

The Cue Sheet lets you integrate various media elements (*cues*). Each cue occupies a single track, matched to a location in time. Cues are created by clicking on an icon in a Cue Palette and dragging it into the Cue Sheet. Producer then opens up a dialog, where you can select a disk file containing the data file you wish to attach to that cue. Once created, each cue is displayed with a representation of the type of data, an image thumbnail, the name of the cue's data file, the starting and ending time within the Cue Sheet, and a number of controls that allow you to set the volume for a cue's audio, the speed at which animation or QuickTime cues are played, and the portion of a cue's content that is used.

Multiple cues can be quickly aligned to one another and resized in a number of ways, by dragging the mouse or typing settings into dialogs. The Cue Sheet can also be printed as a storyboarding aid. Producer lets you open multiple Cue Sheets and cut, copy, and paste cues among different presentations.

Audio cues can be created using 8- or 16-bit AIFF, Sound Designer, MIDI type O, or MIDI type 1 files, or using CD-Audio tracks. Also, with Producer you can input digital audio cues directly through a microphone or audio digitizer, and input MIDI cues through MIDI devices such as a keyboard or sequencer. Image and animation cues can be media elements from any presentation software that saves files in TEXT, PICT, or PICS formats. In addition, still images can have transitions applied to them as they appear on the screen. Producer also supports QuickTime movies, and will convert

PICT, PICS, and AIFF files into QuickTime movie format before assignment as a cue. Cues can be edited using built-in media editors, or Producer can launch third-party editing applications.

Producer also supports two special cue types: marker and pause. *Marker* cues are used to identify specific locations on the Cue Sheet, to navigate quickly to different locations, and to act as guides for precise alignment of other cues. *Pause* cues can be set to delay your presentation for a specified number of seconds, or until the mouse is clicked, a key is pressed, or a MIDI event is received.

Producer presentations are displayed on screen using a user-defined "stage." The stage can be a single-color background or an image imported from any graphics program. Producer's stage can be as big as any one monitor's display, or it can span several displays at once, making it useful for creating multimedia video walls. Visual cues can be located anywhere on the stage, as well as stretched and resized to fit specific areas. Playback control is provided by a VCR-like panel, and a separate time-counter panel gives you precision time management within the Cue Sheet.

You can use Producer for multitrack recording, soundtrack production, and for combining MIDI music with live instruments and vocals. Producer works with most popular MIDI sequencing and audio editing software and can be used as a complete postproduction system for audio.

Producer is a powerful tool for creating and displaying linear presentations in which synchronization is of primary importance; with its integrated SMPTE time code, Producer is an ideal tool for musicians and video specialists. But user interaction is limited to pausing and to controlled inputs from the MIDI channels.

PROmotion (Macintosh)

Motion Works International
1020 Mainland Street, Suite 130
Vancouver, B.C.
Canada V6B 2T4

PROmotion is a tool for creating and editing color animations that sequence multimedia data elements in frames (see Figure 8-17). You can import PICT, PICS, digital audio, and QuickTime files for sequencing. A full-featured 24-bit paint tool is provided for advanced animation editing, and you can directly record digital audio with a microphone or sound digitizer; special effects such as volume fading, amplifying, echo, and reversing can be applied.

FIGURE 8-17 PROmotion sequences multimedia elements and clips along a time line

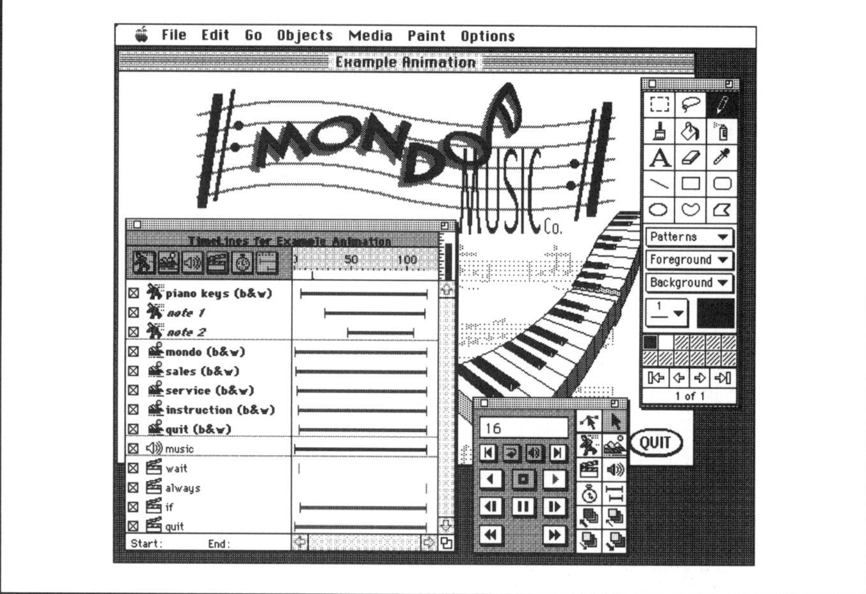

Animation features include cel tweening and sequencing (see Chapter 12), anti-aliasing, and automatic scaling. Multicel animations are called *actors,* and can be treated as single objects in the sequencer. You create a project by placing actors and backgrounds on the screen. You create animations by moving the actors with sophisticated path editing tools, shown in Figure 8-18. Animations are controlled using the Media Controller, a VCR-like panel.

For interactivity, PROmotion allows you to establish conditions, called *cues,* that trigger interactive events. You can attach cues to a frame or range of frames for pausing, controlling branches, changing the playback frame rate, playing a QuickTime movie, or sending a message to other AppleEvents-aware applications. PROmotion supports more than 200 Apple Events, so it can be commanded by other applications to play back projects.

Once you've created a project using PROmotion, you can distribute it as a run-time application. As a QuickTime movie, the project can be played from within programs such as word processors, presentation tools, and spreadsheets. You can also make your project into a custom After Dark screensaver.

You can record your project to videotape using a print-to-video feature; PROmotion supports Control-S, Control-L, and Sony VISCA device control protocols.

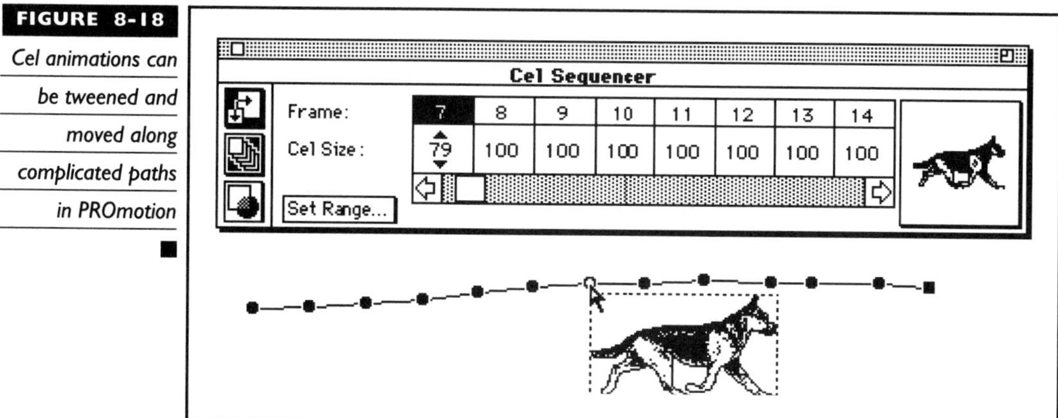

FIGURE 8-18 Cel animations can be tweened and moved along complicated paths in PROmotion

Cross-Platform Tools

Authorware, Director, and Producer are multimedia applications that run on both Macintosh and Windows platforms, and their files are either convertible to run in either environment or are "binary-compatible." A *binary-compatible file* can be read and used by Macintoshes or PCs or across a network. Other applications, such as PACo Producer, Windows Player, and ConvertIt!, are designed specifically to create files that are playable across platforms. Microsoft's QuickTime converter for AVI and Apple's QuickTime for Windows (see Chapter 6) will create a file on the Macintosh that can be played in Windows. most converters currently work from the Macintosh to Windows.

You face two major hurdles when you move multimedia projects across platforms; these hurdles have to do with the different schemes Macintosh and Windows computers use to manage text and colors.

If your project uses only bitmapped images and sounds, the text issue is moot. But if you use text in fields or require user entry of text, you will face size and shape issues (see Chapter 9). The Macintosh and Windows environments each use different fonts (even when the fonts have the same name), so you may wish to experiment with your fonts before converting a project.

Each platform also uses its own character set; some special characters may appear as different characters on the other platform. The following Macintosh characters do not always map across platforms, and you will have to use a substitute character:

Macintosh Character	Suggested Substitute
• (bullet)	*(asterisk)
" " (smart quotes)	" (normal quote)
≠ (does not equal)	<>
≤ (less than or equal to)	<=
≥ (greater than or equal to)	>=
. . . (ellipsis)	... (three periods)

Here are some important suggestions for working with text in cross-platform applications:

- For text in boxes, center the text, leaving plenty of space or margin to avoid possible word-wrap on the other platform.
- Avoid outline and shadow styles on the Macintosh. They are not currently supported in Windows, and may default to boldface.
- When the look of a larger-size font is extremely important, turn it into a bitmap, by screen capturing before you convert.
- If you use TrueType fonts or Adobe ATM, the fonts must be installed and available on both platforms.

Colors can also be difficult to manage in cross-platform projects, because both computer platforms employ different palette mapping systems. The colors you use on the Macintosh, for example, may not appear the same on the PC. When you convert a Macintosh 256-color graphics file to Windows, all colors are mapped to their nearest equivalents, so the results you get will depend on the color palettes used on each platform. The results of converting a Macintosh 256-color palette to a Windows 16-color palette are usually disappointing. Color palettes are discussed in detail in Chapter 11.

tip *Rather than dithering a 256-color bitmap to 16 colors with unattractive results, try using gray-scale images, instead.*

PACo Producer (Macintosh)

Company of Science and Art
14 Imperial Place #203
Providence, RI 02903

PACo Producer compresses and plays animations, digital videos, and audio files. PACo Producer can compress files containing data in PICT, PICS, QuickTime, and SoundEdit formats. It creates compressed, platform-independent files that can be played back on Macintosh, Windows, and XWindow (Silicon Graphics Indigo and Sun SparcStation) computers. Because PACo files are decompressed with software during playback, no special hardware is required.

The exact same PACo file can be played on any supported platform without special conversions, so multiplatform distribution of a CD-ROM is possible using but a single universal project data file. PACo files can also be played back on older, Motorola 68000-based Macintoshes—unlike QuickTime files, which require faster microprocessors for playback.

PACo files can be played back at any location on the screen, and a special QuickScale feature allows images to be enlarged up to four times normal size (see Figure 8-19). PACo uses built-in data buffering techniques that allow low-memory environments to play back unlimited-length files. Files can be played into an off-screen buffer for special inking effects, and they can be played at a frame rate synchronized to the refresh rate of the current monitor, to help prevent tearing of frames. Files can also be played back at color depths different from the PACo file's original data.

PACo Producer compresses multimedia data elements, including PACo files, QuickTime files, and SoundEdit files, at 5-kHz, 7-kHz, 11-kHz and 22-kHz resolutions, into the PACo file format. It can also create 1-, 2-,

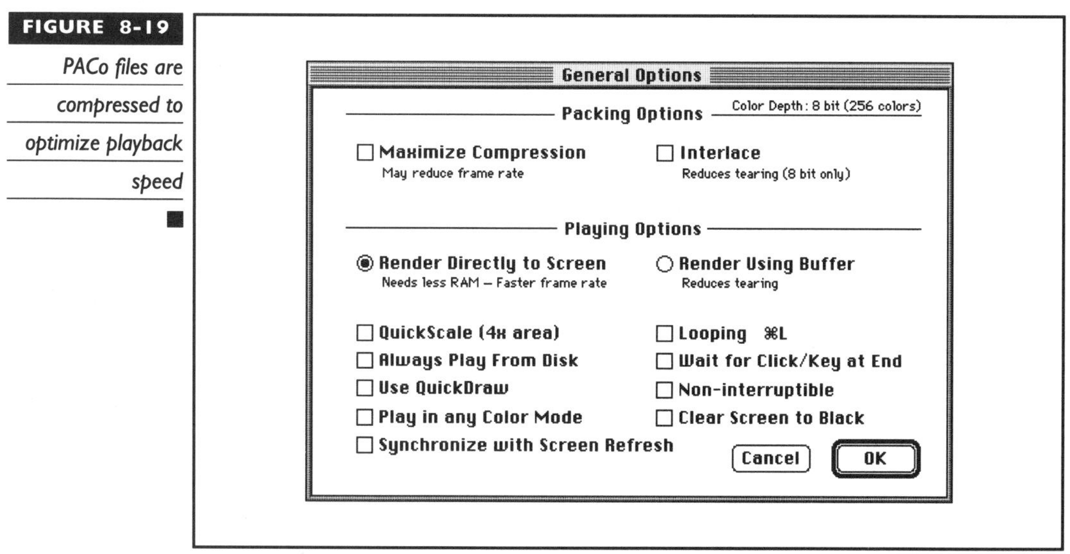

FIGURE 8-19 *PACo files are compressed to optimize playback speed*

4- and 8-bit PACo files using source material of any color depth, and scaling and dithering while converting. Figure 8-20 shows a QuickTime animation file and a sound bite being integrated and compressed to PACo file format.

PACo Producer can be used as a stand-alone player to view existing PACo files, but you can also create stand-alone, executable PACo files for the Macintosh. PACo's XPlayPACo external command (XCMD) lets you integrate PACo files into interactive presentations made with other Macintosh authoring tools (HyperCard, Director, SuperCard, and Authorware). XPlay-PACo can play PACo files on all Macintosh models, in color or black and white, depending upon the model.

PACo Producer includes a CD-ROM Simulator utility that creates a profile of playback speed as if your project were being played back from a CD-ROM, even though you are playing it back from hard disk. Thus you can test the performance of your project before mastering it to CD-ROM.

The PACo Windows Player allows PACo files (created on the Macintosh) to be played in Windows. It can be launched from other applications or run by itself, and includes a DLL for enabling playback control from Windows authoring environments such as Visual Basic, Authorware, and ToolBook. The PACo XWindow Player allows PACo files to be played on UNIX-based

FIGURE 8-20 *A QuickTime animation file and a sound bite are integrated and compressed to PACo file format*

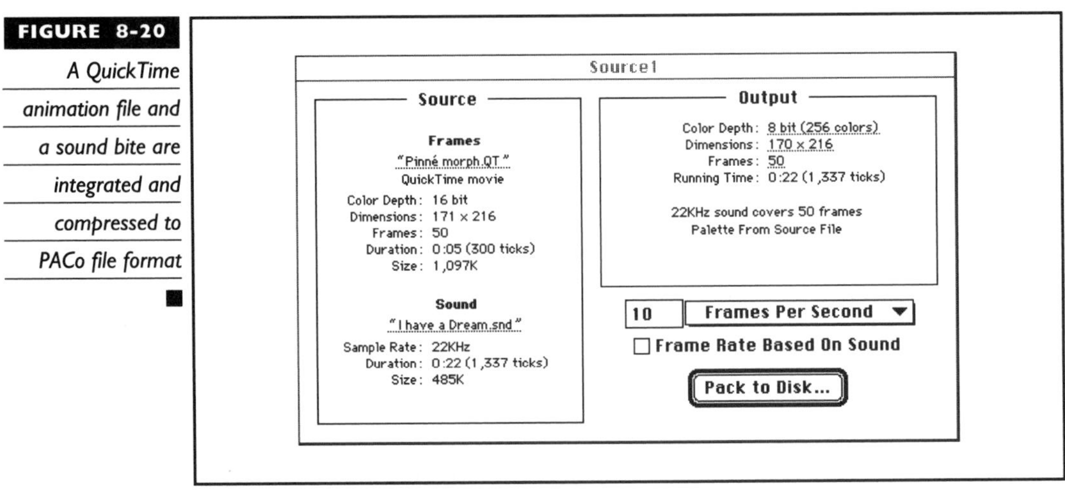

computers running the XWindow display system. The XWindow Player can be executed using command-line arguments to specify playback parameters; it can be launched from other applications; or it can run by itself in its own window or in a window created by another XWindow application.

Director Windows Player (Windows)

The Windows Player is another Macromedia product (see the section on Authorware for this company's address). The Player lets you play, in Windows, interactive multimedia applications created in Director (on the Macintosh). There are tools to convert Director files to a Windows format, to test playback, and to create executable .EXE run-time files. The Windows Player also includes development guidelines for authoring Director files so they will run properly in Windows. The Windows Player includes Gaffer, a Macintosh utility that converts a Director file into the Windows MMM format. Once it's converted, you must then transfer the file to the PC using shared media, telecommunications, or a network.

Application:	*Director*
Macintosh Pathname:	*MACROMEDIA :Product Demonstrations :Director Demo :MacroMind Director 3.1.1 (SD)*
Macintosh Pathname:	*MACROMEDIA :Director 4.0 Save Disabled :Director 4.0 Demo*
Windows Pathname:	*After installing the Showcase CD, click on the Showcase CD Version 2 icon in the Windows Macromedia Showcase CD Program Group.*

Windows MMM files can be made into stand-alone executable .EXE files, or Projectors. *Projectors* support the interactivity of Director's Lingo language. Groups of converted Director files can be bundled into a single Projector, for simple user selection and playback. The Windows Player attempts a best-guess mapping of Macintosh fonts and point sizes to Windows, to provide similar appearance on both platforms.

The Windows Player and Projectors can be launched from other Windows applications, such as ToolBook, and the MMM files can be used in the Macromedia Action! system. The Windows Player supports Windows MCI to control external devices such as videotape players, laserdisc players, video-in-a-window cards, and audio compact discs.

ConvertIt! (Macintosh and Windows)

Heizer Software
1941 Oak Park Blvd. #30
Pleasant Hill, CA 94523

ConvertIt!, developed by The HyperMedia Group, translates HyperCard stacks that run on the Macintosh to ToolBook books that run in Windows (see Figure 8-4 earlier in this chapter). ConvertIt! translates all of HyperCard's objects into ToolBook objects, and it converts most of a HyperCard stack's HyperTalk scripts into functional ToolBook OpenScript. This software development tool aids in porting language-driven, object-oriented applications (HyperCard, SuperCard, and ToolBook) running on the same or disparate platforms.

HyperCard's buttons, fields, field text, object properties, and bitmapped graphics are described and exported to a text file using HIFF (Hypermedia Interchange File Format) conventions. This intermediate HIFF text file is then transferred to the DOS/Windows platform over a network, by disk conversion (Apple File Exchange), or by direct serial uploading/downloading. The HIFF file, once on the PC, is read by the ToolBook ConvertIt! book (CVTIT.TBK), which reconstructs the HyperCard stack.

The export function of ConvertIt! describes the elemental parts of a HyperCard stack in the generic HIFF file format, and the importing function of the program reconstitutes these parts in ToolBook. ConvertIt! uses the source application to generate the descriptive HIFF file, and it uses the target application to reconstruct the file.

Multi

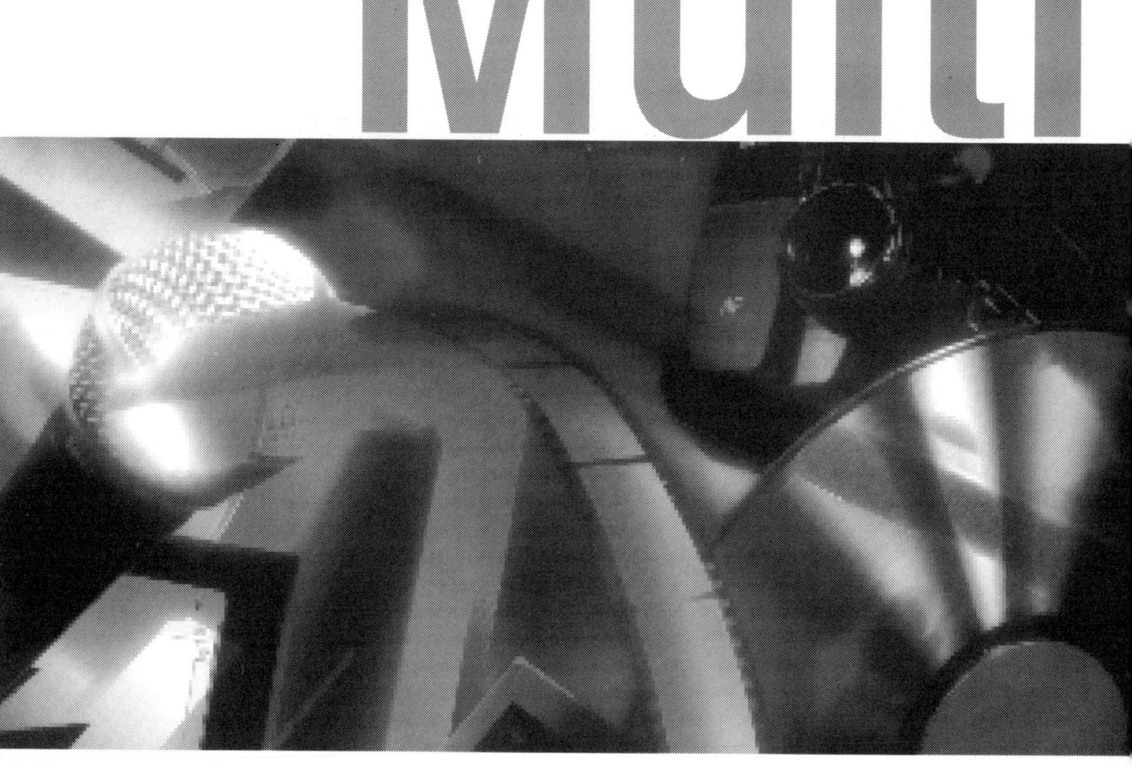

[*Today's poets and songwriters concentrate text by distilling prose into a very few words heavy with meaning.*]

6,000 years ago.......................................

words have
meaning

MESOPOTAMIA

Babylonia

part 4

Multimedia Building Blocks

..........................meaningful marks were scraped onto mud tablets and left to harden in the sun.

EGYPT

Multi

Words and symbols in any form, spoken or written, are the most common system of communication.

6,000 years ago..

words have meaning

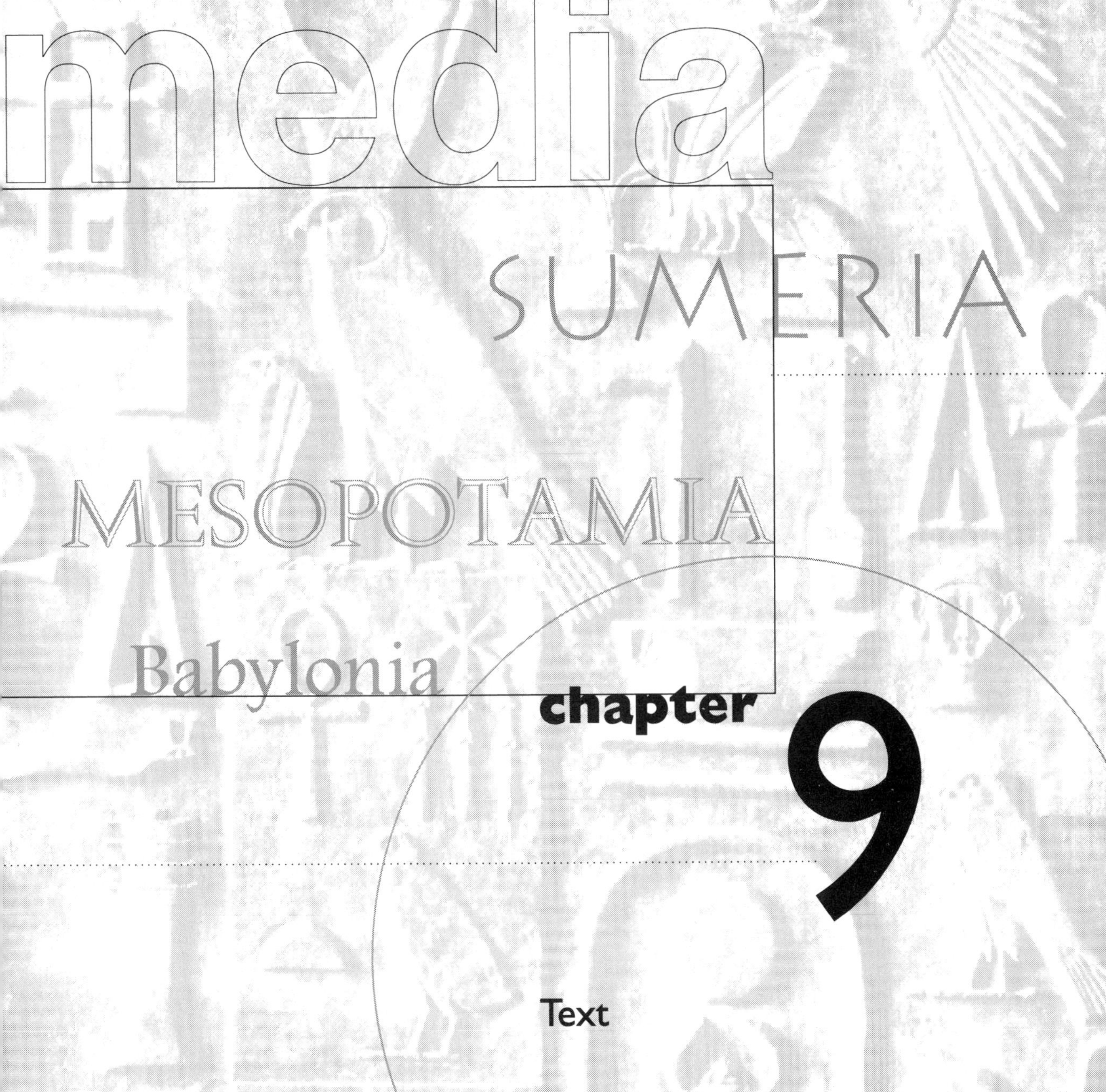

media

SUMERIA

MESOPOTAMIA

Babylonia

chapter 9

Text

........................meaningful marks were scraped onto mud tablets and left to harden in the sun.

EGYPT

HUMANS have only recently developed text and symbols for use in communication. That remarkable development really began about 6000 years ago in the Mediterranean Fertile Crescent—in Mesopotamia, Egypt, Sumeria, and Babylonia—where meaningful marks were scraped onto mud tablets and left to harden in the sun. Only members of the ruling classes and the priesthood were allowed to read and write the pictographic signs and cuneiforms.

The earliest messages delivered in written words typically contained information vital to the management of people, politics, and taxes. Because this new medium did not require rote memorization by frail human gray matter, written messages became popular among the elite. Unlike their human counterparts, these new messages were less likely to perish due to dysentery, acts of God, or amnesia. Even if your message were intercepted by foes or competitors, it would still be indecipherable except by those few who had acquired reading skills. In fact, you probably attended school with most of the other people in your society who could read your message; reading, writing, and power politics in those days were naturally intertwined. In some former eras it was a capital offense to read unless you belonged to the proper social class or possessed a patent granted by your rulers.

Today, however, text and the ability to read it are doorways to power and knowledge. Reading and writing have become a skill pervasive within most modern cultures. Now, depending upon your proficiency with words, you may be awarded a doctorate instead of the death penalty. And, as has been the case throughout history, text still delivers information that can have potent meaning.

With its penchant for interactivity, multimedia too often ignores the power of narrative, of stories. There's really something to be said for documents with a beginning, middle, and end.

Steven Levy, author of *Hackers and Artificial Life*,
editor/columnist for *MacWorld*

The Power of Meaning

Even a single word may be cloaked in many meanings, so as you begin working with any medium it is important to cultivate accuracy and explicitness in the particular words you choose. In multimedia, these are the words that will appear in your titles, menus, and navigation aids.

Today's poets and songwriters concentrate text by distilling lengthy prose into a very few words heavy with meaning. Advertising wordsmiths render the meaning of entire product lines into an evocative single word, logo, or tag line. Multimedia authors weave words, symbols, sounds, and images, and then blend text into the mix to create integrated tools and interfaces for acquiring, displaying, and disseminating messages and data, using computers.

"Barbie," "beef," and "lite" may each easily trigger a rush of different meanings. A piercing cry in the night, the sight of fire engines leaving your street as you steer your car into your neighborhood, the scent of drying kelp along the seashore, the feel of rough pine bark against your chest as you climb, fingernails on a chalkboard—all these raw sensory messages are important only because of what they mean to you. Indeed, you alone know the words that will stop you dead in your tracks with anger, or, better, soothe you seductively over a quiet dinner for two. These words have meaning.

All of these examples demonstrate the following multimedia principle: It's important to design labels for multimedia title screens, menus, and buttons using words that have the most precise and powerful meanings to express what you need to say. Understand the subtle shadings. GO BACK! is more powerful than Previous; Quit is more powerful than Close. TERRIFIC! may work better than That Answer Was Correct.

Experiment with the words you plan to use by letting others try them. If you have the budget, set up a focus group to have potential users experience your words. Watch them work. See if users flinch, balk, or click the Help button in confusion. See if they can even find Help.

Words and symbols in any form, spoken or written, are the most common system of communication. They deliver the most widely understood meaning to the greatest number of people—accurately and in detail. Because of this, they are vital elements of multimedia menus, navigation systems, and content. You will reward yourself and your users if you take the time to use excellent words. Let your poet loose!

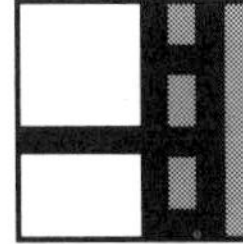

tip *Browse through a thesaurus. You will be surprised at the number of synonyms and related words that are closely associated to the word you start with, and you will certainly find the one word that most perfectly fits your need. The majority of today's popular word processors ship with a bundled electronic thesaurus.*

About Fonts and Faces

A *typeface* is a family of graphic characters that usually includes many type sizes and styles. A *font* is a collection of characters of a single size and style belonging to a particular typeface family. Typical font *styles* are boldface and italic. Other style attributes, such as underlining and outlining of characters, may be added by your computer software. Type sizes are usually expressed in points; one *point* is .0138 inches or about 1/72 of an inch. The font's size is the distance from the top of the capital letters to the bottom of the descenders in letters such as *g* and *y*. Helvetica, Times, and Courier are typefaces; Times 12-point italic is a font. In the computer world, the term "font" is commonly used when typeface or face would be more correct.

A font's size does not exactly describe the height or width of its characters. This is because the *x-height* (the height of the lowercase letter *x*) of two fonts may vary, while the height of the capital letters of those fonts may be the same (see Figure 9-1). Computer fonts automatically add space below the descender (and sometimes above) to provide appropriate line spacing, or *leading* (pronounced "ledding"). There can be significant variation among fonts.

Leading can be adjusted in most programs on both the Macintosh and in Windows. Typically you will find this fine-tuning adjustment in the Paragraph menu, though this is not an official standard. No matter where your application has placed the controls for leading, you will need to experiment

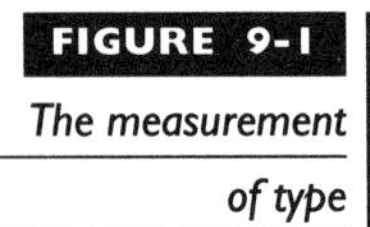

FIGURE 9-1 The measurement of type

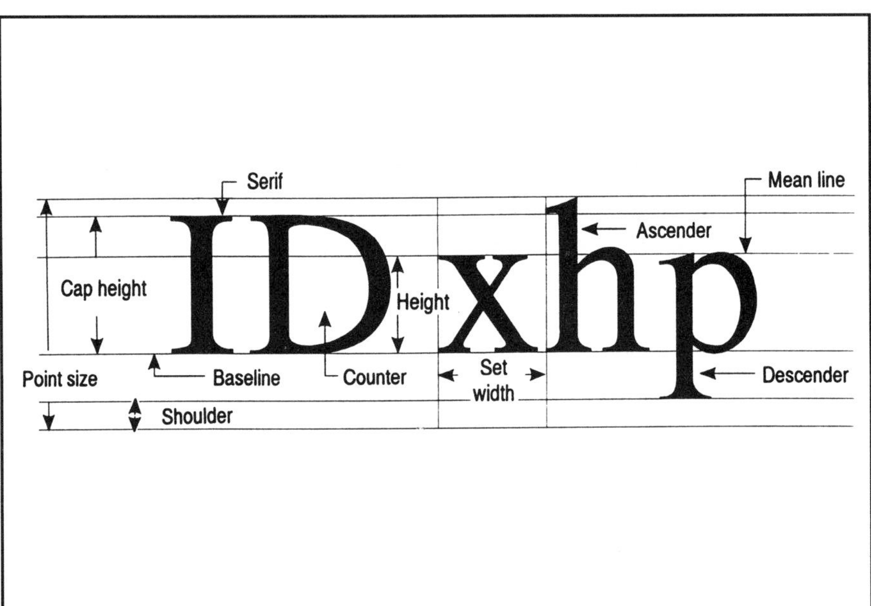

with them to achieve the best result for your font. Figure 9-2 illustrates common methods of adjusting leading for both the Macintosh and Windows.

When it draws or *rasterizes* the letter *A* on the screen or in printed output, the computer must know how to represent the letter. It does this according to the hardware available and according to your specification from a choice of available typefaces and fonts. High-resolution monitors and printers can make more attractive-looking and varied characters. And today's wide selection of software fonts makes it easier to find the right typeface and font for your need. Here are some examples of the same letter displayed using different fonts:

A A A A A A A A A

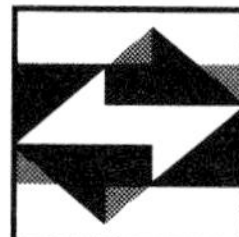

cross platform *Characters identified in a particular font (say, Courier 12-point) do not look the same on a Macintosh as they do on Windows display monitors. Typically, what is called 12-point on a Macintosh will be a 10- or 9-point size in Windows. And the actual shape of the characters will be different (see Figure 9-3).*

Cases

In centuries when type was set by hand, the type for a single font was always stored in two trays, or cases; the upper tray held capital letters, and the lower tray held the small letters. Today a capital letter is called *uppercase,* and a small letter is called *lowercase.*

In some situations, such as for passwords, a computer is case sensitive. But nowadays, in most situations requiring keyboard input—on the Macintosh or in Windows—the computer recognizes both the upper- and lowercase forms of a character to be the same. In that manner, the computer is said to be *case insensitive.*

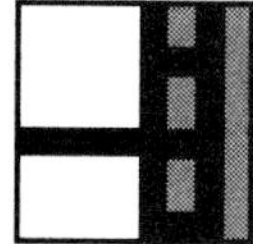

tip *Studies have shown that words and sentences with mixed upper- and lowercase letters are easier to read than words or sentences in all caps.*

Serif Versus Sans Serif

Typefaces can be described in many ways, just as a home advertised by a realtor, a wine described by a food critic, or a political candidate's platform

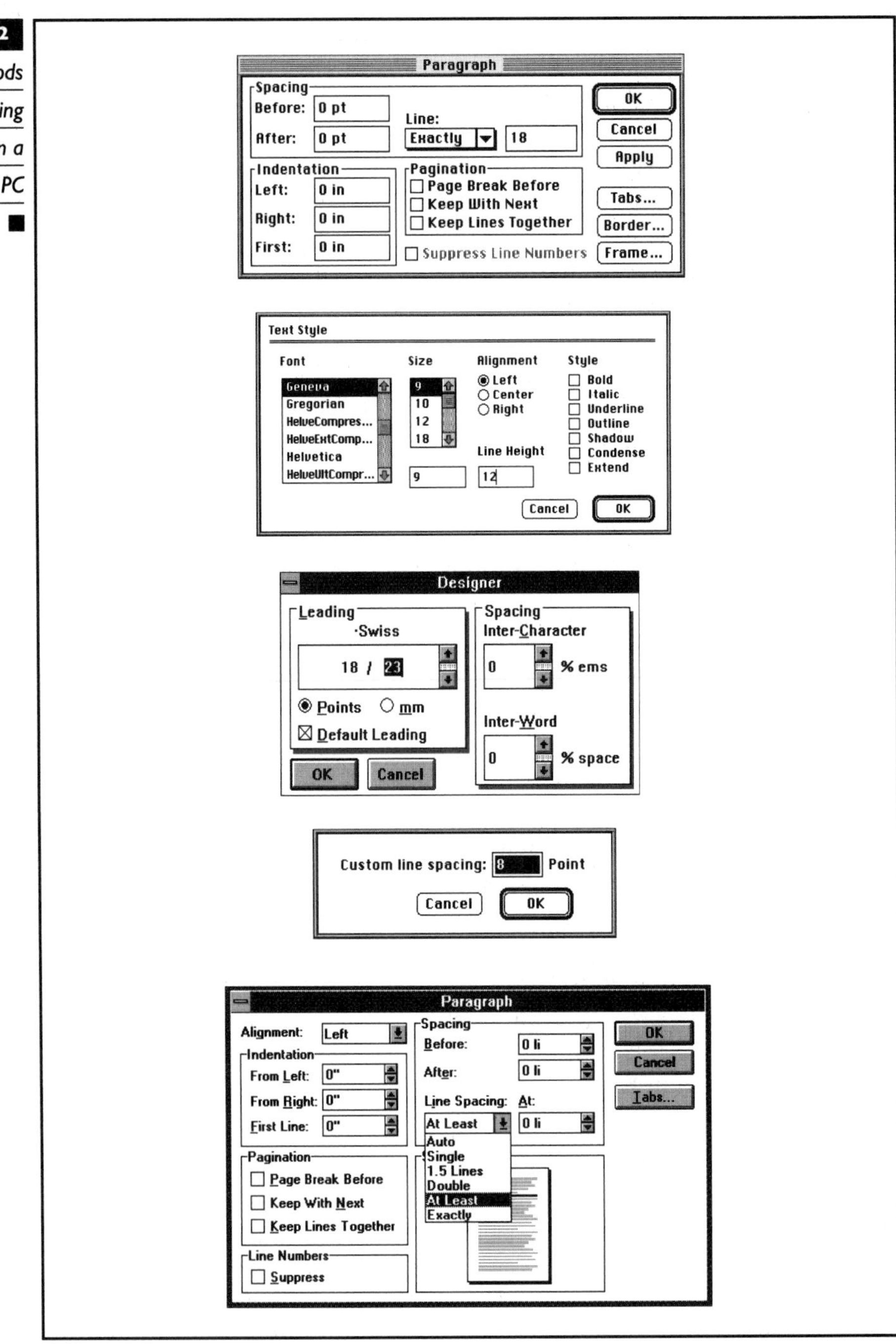

FIGURE 9-2 Common methods for adjusting leading on a Macintosh and PC

can all be described in many ways. Type has been characterized as feminine, masculine, delicate, formal, capricious, witty, comic, happy, technical,

FIGURE 9-3 Examples of Courier typeface on the Macintosh and on the PC

10 point Courier | 10 point Courier
12 point Courier | 12 point Courier
18 point Courier | 15 point Courier

10 point | 10 point

Macintosh | Windows

newsy—you name it. But one approach for categorizing typefaces is universally understood, and it has less to do with the reader's response to the type than it does with the type's mechanical and historical properties. This approach uses the terms serif and sans serif.

Serif versus sans serif is the simplest way to categorize a typeface; the type either has a serif or it doesn't (*sans* is French for "without"). The *serif* is the little flag or decoration at the end of a letter stroke. Times, New Century Schoolbook, Bookman, and Palatino are examples of serif fonts. Helvetica, Arial, Optima, and Avant Garde are sans serif. Notice the difference between serif and sans serif in the following illustration:

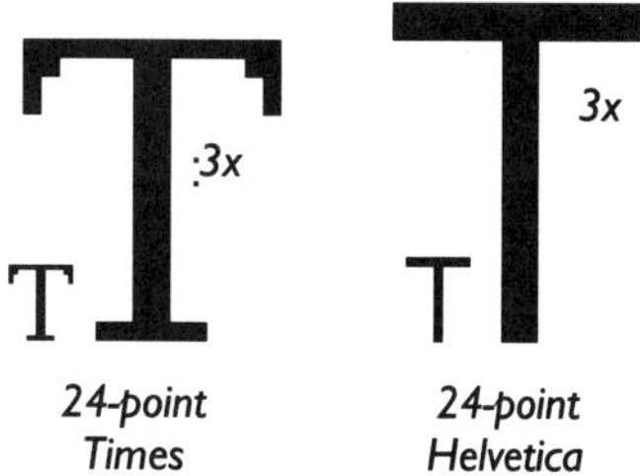

On the printed page, serif fonts are traditionally used for body text because the serifs are said to help guide the reader's eye along the line of text. Sans serif fonts, on the other hand, are used for headlines and bold statements. But the computer world of standard, 72-dpi monitor resolution is not the same as the print world, and it can be argued that sans serif fonts are far more legible and attractive when used in the small sizes of a text field on a screen. Indeed, careful selection of a sans serif font designed to be legible in the small sizes (such as Geneva on the Macintosh or Small Fonts in Windows) makes more sense when you are presenting a substantial amount of text on the screen. The Times font at 9-point size may look too busy and actually be difficult and tiring to read. And a large, bold serif font for a title or headline can deliver a message of elegance and character in your graphic layout. Use what is right for your delivery system, which may not necessarily be the same as what is right when you print the material to paper.

Using Text in Multimedia

Imagine designing a project that used no text at all. Its content could not be at all complex, and you would need to use many pictures and symbols to train your audience how to navigate through the project. Certainly voice and sound could guide the audience, but they would quickly tire of this—greater effort is required to pay attention to spoken words than to browse text.

A single item of menu text accompanied by a single action (a mouse click, keystroke, or finger pressed to the monitor) requires little training and is clean and immediate. Use text for titles and headlines (what it's all about), for menus (where to go), for navigation (how to get there), and for content (what you see when you get there).

tip *In designing your navigation system, bring the user to a particular destination with as few actions and as short a wait as possible. If the user never needs the Help button to get there, you are doing everything right!*

Designing with Text

If your messages are part of a user-driven, interactive project in which the user works within a real-time framework, you can pack a great deal of text information into the screen before it becomes overwhelmingly busy. Users can travel along your navigational pathways, stopping to scroll through text fields and pausing to study your screen in detail. Here is where you must strike a balance: too little text requires annoying page turns and unnecessary user activity; too much text makes the screen overcrowded and unpleasant. Be polite to the user.

On the other hand, if you are providing public-speaking support, the text will be keyed to a live presentation where the text accents the main message. In this case, use large fonts and few words with lots of white space. Let the audience focus on the speaker at the podium, rather than spend its time reading fine points and subpoints projected on a screen.

Computer screens provide a very small workspace for developing complex ideas. At some time or another, you will need to deliver high-impact or very concise text messages on the computer screen in as condensed a form as possible. From a design perspective, your choice of font size and the number of headlines you place on a particular screen must be related both to the complexity of your message and to its venue.

Choosing Text Fonts

Picking the fonts to use in your multimedia presentation may be somewhat difficult from a design standpoint. Here again, you must be a poet, an advertising psychologist, and also a graphic designer. Try to sense the potential reaction of the user to what is on the screen. Here are a few design suggestions that may help:

- Pick the fonts that seem right to you for getting your message across, then double-check your choice against other opinions. Learn to accept criticism.
- For small type, use the most legible font available. Decorative fonts that cannot be read are useless.
- Use as few different faces as possible in the same work, but vary the weight and the size of your typeface using italic and bold styles where it looks good.
- In text blocks, adjust the leading for the most pleasing line spacing. Lines too tightly packed are difficult to read.
- Vary the size of a font in proportion to the importance of the message you are delivering.
- In large-size headlines, adjust the spacing between letters (called *kerning*) so that the spacing feels right. Big gaps between large letters can turn your title into a toothless waif. You may need to kern by hand, using a bitmapped version of your text.
- To make your type stand out or be more legible, explore the effects of different colors, and of placing the text on various backgrounds. Try reverse type for a stark, white-on-black message.
- Use anti-aliased text where you want a gentle and blended look for titles and headlines. This can give a more professional appearance.

Anti-aliasing dithers the edges of the letters, creating a soft transition between a letter and its background. Color Plate 5 shows an example of anti-aliased text.

- If you are using centered type in a text block, keep the number of lines to a minimum.
- For attention-grabbing results, try graphically altering and distorting the text. Wrap your word onto a sphere, bend it into a wave, or splash it with rainbow colors. Font editing tools such as ResEdit, Fontographer, FONTastic Plus, Metamorphosis Professional, and FontStudio are discussed later in this chapter. Also, paint and drawing packages for customizing text and bitmaps are discussed in Chapter 6.
- Experiment with drop shadows. Place a transparent copy of the word on top of the original and offset the original up and over a few pixels. Then color the copy gray (or any other color). The word may become more legible and provide much greater impact.
- Surround headlines with plenty of white space.

Menus for Navigation

An interactive multimedia project typically consists of a body of information through which a user navigates by pressing a key, clicking a mouse, or pressing a touchscreen. The simplest menus consist of text lists of topics. You choose a topic, click it, and go there. As multimedia and graphical user interfaces become more pervasive in the computer community, certain intuitive actions are being widely learned. For example, if there are three words on a computer screen, the typical response from the user, without prompting, is to click one of these words to evoke activity. This click-to-act function is becoming widely understood by computer users. Sometimes the menu items are surrounded by boxes or made to look like push buttons. Or, to conserve space, text such as Throw Tomatoes, Play Video, and Press to Quit is often shortened to Tomatoes, Video, and Quit. Nonetheless, the intention remains clear to the user.

Text is very helpful to provide perpetual cues about location and menu-jumping for users. When users must click up and down through many layers of menus to reach their goal in your project's body of information, they may not get lost, but they will certainly suffer from the "You can't get there from here" syndrome. This is especially true if your project moves slowly from screen to screen en route to that goal. If Throw Tomatoes leads to Red or Green, then to California or Massachusetts, then to President or Vice President, then to Forehead or Chest, then to Arrested or Got Away, and so on, the user can end up tangled in the branches of a navigation tree. However, if an interactive textual or symbolic list of the branches taken (all the way from the beginning) is continuously displayed, the user can at any time skip intervening steps in a nonlinear manner, or easily return to one of the previous locations in the list. The more locations included in the list, the more options for navigation are available. Navigation methodologies are discussed in greater detail in Chapter 15.

tip *Avoid more than two levels of GO BACKs or RETURNs. Too much tunneling in and out will frustrate users with repetitive activity and discourage exploration. Display a perpetual menu of interactive text or symbolic cues, so users can always extricate themselves from any place in the tunnel.*

Buttons for Interaction

In most modern cultures a doorbell is recognized by its context (next to the door itself, possibly lit); but if you grew up in an apartment high-rise, you may have seen 50 or more buttons at the entrance. Unless you knew that yours was the third from the top on the left, you could find your button only by reading the printed or scrawled name beside it. And certainly your Aunt Barbara needed this text cue to avoid having to push the Help button, which in this case rang in the building superintendent's apartment.

In multimedia, buttons are the objects that do things when clicked. In an object-oriented authoring system you can click other objects, such as blocks of text, a pretty blue triangle, or a photograph, and these too will produce an action. But buttons, per se, were invented with the single role of being pushed or prodded with cursor, mouse, key, or finger—to manifest properties such as highlighting or other visual effects. Buttons and the art of button design and human interaction are discussed in detail in Chapter 15. For now, remember that the rules for proper selection of text and fonts in your projects apply to buttons as well as headlines, bullet items, and blocks of text.

When I was four years old, a button was the little plastic knob mounted in brass next to the front door. When I pushed it, a muffled ringing sound worked its way through the house from the kitchen. Sometimes I would push the button a lot and somebody would always come to the door. As an adult, I'm still pushing buttons to make things happen.

Ann Stewart, Multimedia Producer, Timestream, Inc.

The predesigned buttons supplied with your authoring system are useful, but they offer you little opportunity to fine-tune the label text. Character-

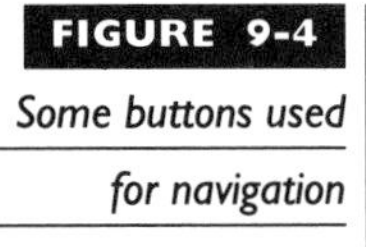

FIGURE 9-4 *Some buttons used for navigation*

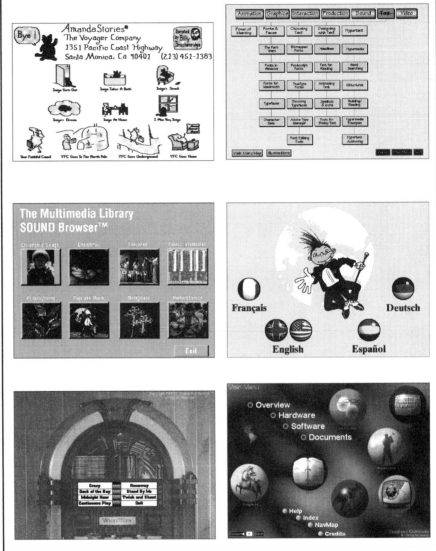

and word-wrap, highlighting, and inverting are automatically applied to your buttons, as needed, by the authoring system. Default buttons and styles may seem overused to you, but by using common button styles, shapes, and borders, you increase the probability that users will know what to do with the buttons—especially when they are also well labeled. Figure 9-4 shows a variety of buttons used in multimedia projects.

warning *The text that labels your buttons is generated by the same routines that draw text into fields. So make sure that the fonts you select for your buttons are available in the environments in which you will run your software. Your button fonts will need to travel with your project. See "Installed Fonts in Windows and System 7" later in this chapter for a list of fonts shipped with System 7 and Windows 3.1. These are perhaps safest for button labeling.*

Pick a font for buttons that is, above all, legible, then adjust the text size of the labels to provide adequate space between the button's rim and the text. You can choose from many styles of buttons and several standard methodologies for highlighting. You will want to experiment to get the right combinations of font, spacing, and colors for just the right look.

In most authoring platforms, it is easy to make your own buttons from bitmaps or drawn objects. In a message-passing authoring system, where you can script activity when the mouse button is up or down over an object, you can quickly replace one bitmap with another highlighted or colored version of the bitmap to show that the button has been "pushed." Making your own buttons from bitmaps or drawn objects gives you greater design power and creative freedom, and also ensures against the missing font problem. On the other hand, this custom work will require a good deal more time.

Whether default or custom, treat the design and labeling of your buttons as an industrial art project: buttons are the part of your project the user touches.

Fields for Reading

You are already working uphill when you design text to be read on the screen. Experiments have shown that reading text on a computer screen is slower and more difficult than reading the same text in hard copy or book form. Indeed, many users, it seems, would rather print out their reports and e-mail messages and read them on paper than page through screens of text. Reading hard copy is still more comfortable.

Unless the very purpose of your multimedia project is to display large blocks of text, try to present to the user only a few paragraphs of text per page. Use a font that is easy to read rather than a prettier font that is illegible.

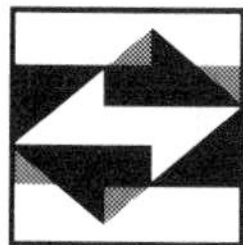

cross platform *The amount of text that will fit in a field is commonly limited by memory constraints. In most authoring systems on the Macintosh, this limit is 32K; under Windows it is often 64K. If your text exceeds this limit (32K allows about 4000 eight-character words), you will need to provide another mechanism for document paging. In some authoring systems there is significant degradation of performance when scrolling through large amounts of text in a scrolling field.*

Portrait Versus Landscape

The taller-than-wide orientation common to traditional hard copy simply cannot be displayed on a monitor that is wider than it is tall and that provides only standard 640×480 pixel resolution. (The taller-than-wide orientation is called *portrait*; this is the 8.5×11-inch size unique to the United States or the internationally designated standard A4 size, 8.27×11.69 inches. The wider-than-tall orientation is called *landscape*.) Shrinking an 11-inch portrait page of text into 480 pixels of monitor height yields illegible chicken tracks. If you are working with a block of text that is taller than what will fit on a computer monitor's short page, there are four possible solutions:

- Put the text into a scrolling field.
- Put the text into a single field in a project window that the user can move up or down upon command. This is most appropriate when you need to present text with page breaks identical to the printed document.
- Break the text into fields that fit on monitor-sized pages, and design control buttons to flip through these pages.
- Design your multimedia project for a special monitor that is taller than it is wide (portrait). Such "page view" monitors are expensive; they are used for print-based typesetting and layout.

Symbols and Icons

Symbols are concentrated text in the form of stand-alone graphic constructs. Symbols convey meaningful messages. The Macintosh trashcan symbol, for instance, tells you where to throw away old files; the Windows hourglass cursor tells you to wait while the computer is processing. Though you may think of symbols as belonging strictly to the realm of graphic art, in multimedia you should treat them as text—or visual words—because they carry meaning. Symbols such as the familiar trashcan and hourglass are more properly called *icons*; these are symbolic representations of objects or processes common to the graphical user interfaces of many computer operating systems.

Certainly text is more efficient than imagery and pictures for delivering a precise message to users. On the other hand, pictures, icons, moving images, and sounds are most easily recalled and remembered by viewers. With multimedia, you have the power to blend both text and icons (as well as colors, sounds, images, and motion video) to enhance the overall impact and value of your message.

Words are shared by millions of people, but the special symbols you design for a multimedia project are not; these symbols must be learned before they can be useful message carriers. Some symbols are more widely used and understood than others, but readers of even these symbols had to grow accustomed to their meanings. Learning a system of symbols can be as difficult as lessons in any foreign language.

Here are some symbols you may already know:

And here are some symbols you may not have learned—the 12 signs of the zodiac:

warning *Do not be seduced into creating your own language of symbols and icons.*

When HyperCard was first introduced in 1987, there was a flurry of creative attempts by graphic artists to create interesting navigational symbols to alleviate the need for text. The screens were pure graphic art and power—all lines and angles and stunning shadows. But many users were frustrated because they could not get to the data right away and had to first wade through help and guidance material to learn the symbols. In this context, it is clearly safer, from a product design point of view, to combine symbols with text cues. This ensures the graphic impact of the symbols but allows prompting the user on their meaning. The Macintosh trashcan icon, incidentally, also has a 9-point text label, Trash, just in case people don't get the idea from the symbol.

FIGURE 9-5

Some navigation symbols used in page-based and time-based multimedia presentations

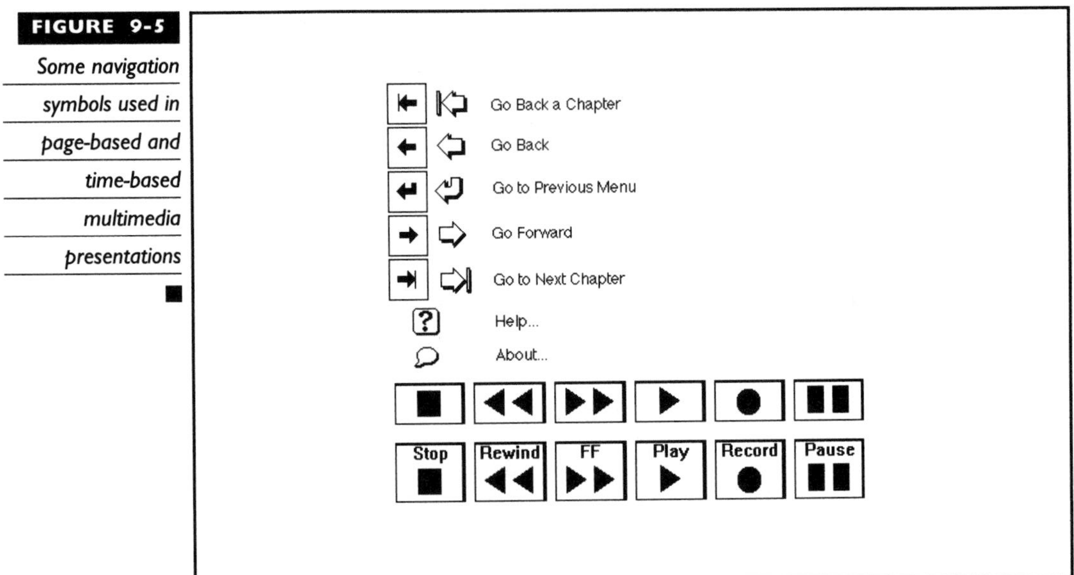

Nonetheless, a few symbols have emerged in the interactive multimedia world as an accepted lexicon of navigation cues that do not need text. These symbols are by no means universal, but Figure 9-5 shows some that have roots in early HyperCard development and others that have roots in the consumer electronics world of tape recorders and VCRs. Even for these common symbols, text labels are usually added to the graphic icons to avoid uncertainty.

Animating Text

There are plenty of ways to retain a viewer's attention when displaying text. For example, you can animate bulleted text and have it "fly" onto the screen. You can "grow" a headline a character at a time. For speakers, simply highlighting the important text works well as a pointing device. When there are several points to be made, you can stack up keywords and flash them past the viewer in a timed automated sequence (as in the famous Burma Shave highway ads). You might fly in some keywords, dissolve others, rotate or spin others, and so forth, until you have a dynamic bulleted list of words that is interesting to watch. But be careful—don't overdo the special effects or they will become boring. An example of font animation can be found in Chapter 12.

Computers and Text

Very early in the development of the Macintosh computer's monitor hardware, Apple chose to use a resolution of 72 pixels per inch. This matches the standard font resolution (72 points per inch) of the printing industry and allows desktop publishers and designers to actually see on the monitor what their printed output will look like (called "What You See Is What You Get," or WYSIWYG). In addition, Apple made each pixel square shaped, providing even measurements in all directions. Until the Macintosh was invented, and the VGA video standard for the PC, pixels were typically taller than they were wide. The aspect ratio for EGA, for example, is 1.33:1, taller than wide. VGA monitor resolutions for both Macintosh II and Windows display 640 pixels across the screen and 480 pixels down the screen (called 640×480 resolution), and the pixels have an aspect ratio of 1:1 (square).

The 640×480, square-pixel screen has become the most common for production of multimedia. This resolution also allows full-screen bitmaps created on the Macintosh platform to be easily ported to Windows, and vice versa.

The Font Wars

In 1985, the desktop publishing revolution was spearheaded by Apple and the Macintosh computer, in combination with word processing and page layout software products that enabled a high-resolution 300-dpi laser printer using special software to "draw" the shapes of characters on the basis of the geometry of the character. This special software was Adobe's PostScript page description and outline font language. It was licensed by Apple and included in the firmware of Apple's LaserWriter laser printer.

Because PostScript fonts describe each character (or illustration or digitized image) in terms of mathematical constructs (Bézier curves), each character can be scaled. This makes the characters look right whether they're drawn at 10 points or 100 points, whether the printer is a 300-dpi LaserWriter or a high-resolution 1200-, 2400-, or even 3600-dpi image setter suitable for the finest print jobs. And the characters can be drawn much faster than in the old-fashioned way of looking up the shapes in a bitmap table containing a representation of every character in every size. PostScript quickly became the de facto industry font and printing standard for desktop publishing and played a significant role in the early success of Apple's Macintosh computer.

There are two kinds of PostScript fonts: Type 1 and Type 3. There are currently over 6,000 different Type 1 typefaces available. Type 1 fonts contain *hints,* which are special instructions for grid fitting to help improve resolution. Hints can apply to a font in general or to specific characters at a particular resolution. Type 3 fonts do not work with Adobe Type Manager (described in the next section), Adobe's system for displaying outline fonts on both Macintosh and Windows screens. Type 3 fonts are rarely used by multimedia developers.

Other companies followed Adobe into the desktop publishing arena with their own proprietary and competitive systems for scalable outline fonts. In May, 1989, Apple announced an independent effort to develop a "better and faster" quadratic curves outline font methodology, called TrueType. In addition to printing smooth characters on printers, TrueType would draw characters to a low-resolution (72-dpi) monitor. Today TrueType ships with the new System 7 operating software. Both System 7 and Windows support TrueType fonts. Even if you're using TrueType, you can install PostScript and other outline fonts from other manufacturers with the proper drivers—type languages are not exclusive.

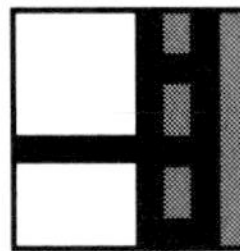

tip *On the Macintosh, if you have installed multiple bitmapped, TrueType, and PostScript versions of the same font, the system will attempt first to use the bitmaps, then the TrueType version, then a PostScript Type 1 version. If the selected font is not available, the system will use a default font.*

Though reverberations of the Postscript-versus-TrueType war continue to oscillate through the computer and publishing industries, multimedia developers really only need to be concerned about how these scaled fonts look on monitors, not about how they are printed to paper. TrueType and PostScript (with ATM) outline fonts allow text to be drawn at any size on your computer screen without *jaggies*:

The Jaggies

Adobe Type Manager

Adobe Type Manager (ATM) is required to display Type 1 PostScript fonts at all sizes without jaggies. This software is available for both the Macintosh and Windows. Once it's installed, ATM works automatically with word processing, page layout, spreadsheet, and graphics applications, including multimedia authoring systems.

In Windows, the ATM software requires about 450K of disk space, and each Type 1 PostScript outline font will take up another 40K. Using the ATM Control Panel (see Figure 9-6), you can add to and take away from your list of installed fonts.

On the Macintosh, you need to install the proper ATM driver into your System Extensions folder and the ATM desk accessory into your Control Panels folder. You also must place the outline fonts, sometimes called *printer fonts,* into your System folder.

Small Typefaces

In the early days of both Macintosh and Windows, a bitmap for the font and size was always required in the system in order to display text without jaggies. A collection of special, memory-hungry bitmaps was required to display fonts outside the normal range installed on the computer. TrueType and PostScript/ATM, using mathematical formulas, allow you to display smooth-edged type of any size and style on your monitor without requiring a collection of bitmap files.

Unfortunately, this helpful innovation does not come without a penalty. The smaller fonts (12-point and less) are not as legible on your monitor when drawn by mathematical formula as they are when drawn from bitmaps. TrueType and PostScript/ATM do their best to render the small sizes, but

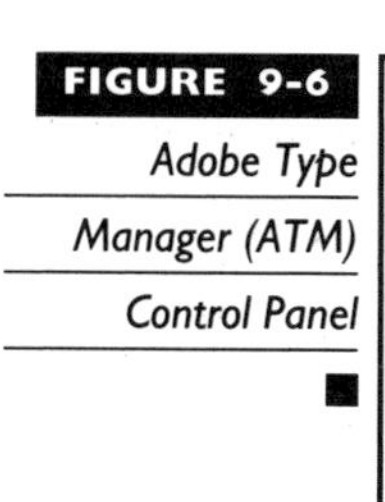

FIGURE 9-6 Adobe Type Manager (ATM) Control Panel

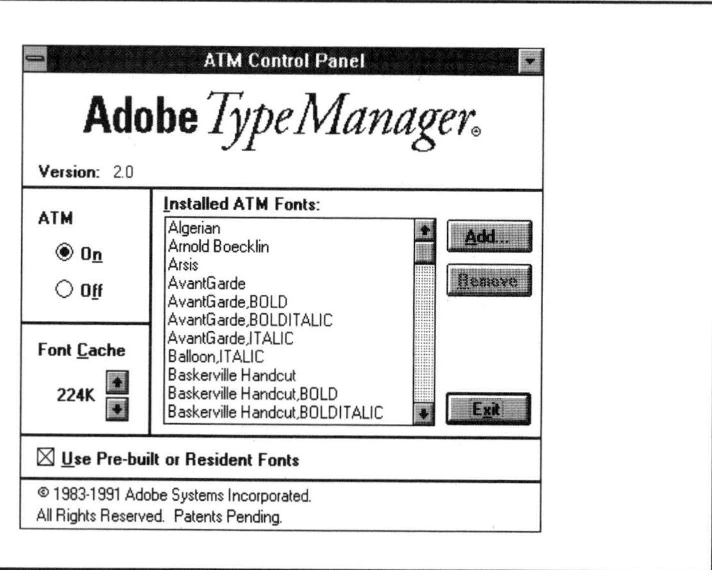

are hard pressed to compete with the clarity of font bitmaps. These were carefully hand-tweaked by real type designers to provide optimum legibility at 72 dots per inch (dpi). Moving a single pixel in a small letter can make a subtle but critical difference.

Windows contains a bitmapped font for VGA resolution called Small Fonts, which provides reasonable legibility for fonts as small as 5 points. On the Macintosh, you may wish to use bitmapped small fonts in lieu of TrueType or PostScript/ATM. Figure 9-7 shows examples of the same font drawn to the computer screen. The first line is drawn with a bitmap, the second line with PostScript using ATM, and the third line is drawn with TrueType.

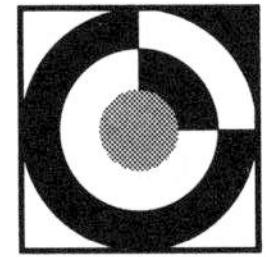

warning *Bitmapped, TrueType, and PostScript fonts do not display (or print) exactly the same, even though they may share the same name and size. Different formulas are used by the three technologies. This means that word wrapping in a text field may change. Text fields created under ATM, for example, will look different after ATM is disabled. So if you build a field or a button that precisely fits text displayed with PostScript, be aware that if you then display it with the same font in TrueType, the text may be truncated or wrapped, wrecking your layout.*

Macintosh Bitmapped Fonts

FONT and NFNT resources are the two major ways of representing bitmapped fonts (screen fonts) for the Macintosh.

- FONT resources contain a series of bitmaps that typically represent characters in the Macintosh character set. FONT resources can contain scanned images and other pictures just as easily as they can contain the alphabet, numerals, and punctuation marks. FONT resources come in families, so it is possible to display text on the screen (and print it on dot-matrix printers) in several styles. You can edit FONT resources using ResEdit (described later in this chapter in "Font Editing and Design Tools").
- NFNT resources also represent bitmaps, but they include color information and use a more flexible method for identifying the font.

Another resource, the FOND resource, "owns" sizes of a particular font and contains kerning tables and other important information. The FOND resource has a unique ID number, from which the ID numbers of its member FONTs are calculated. To calculate the ID number of a particular FONT

FIGURE 9-7

The same font displayed by different technologies

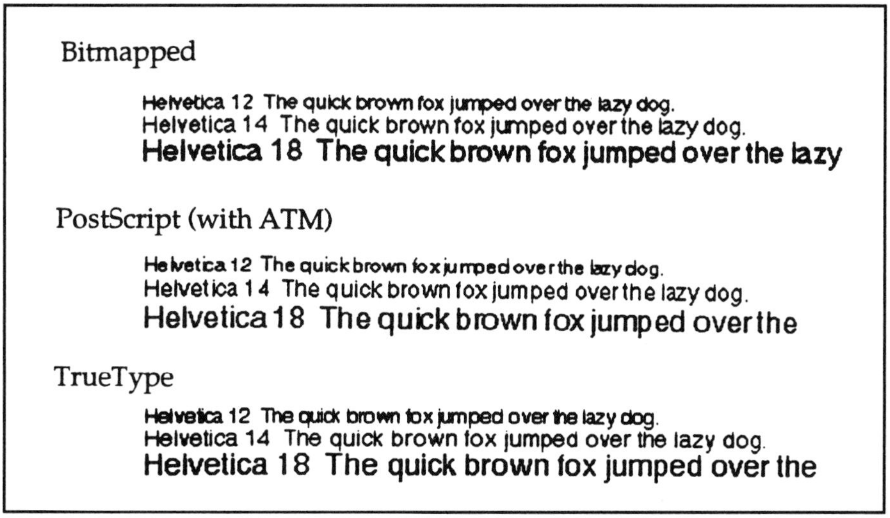

Bitmapped

Helvetica 12 The quick brown fox jumped over the lazy dog.
Helvetica 14 The quick brown fox jumped over the lazy dog.
Helvetica 18 The quick brown fox jumped over the lazy

PostScript (with ATM)

Helvetica 12 The quick brown fox jumped over the lazy dog.
Helvetica 14 The quick brown fox jumped over the lazy dog.
Helvetica 18 The quick brown fox jumped over the

TrueType

Helvetica 12 The quick brown fox jumped over the lazy dog.
Helvetica 14 The quick brown fox jumped over the lazy dog.
Helvetica 18 The quick brown fox jumped over the

resource, take the ID number of the parent FOND, multiply by 128, and add the point size of the FONT.

ID numbers of FOND resources range from 0 (Chicago, the default Macintosh System font) through 255. Apple reserves ID numbers from 0 through 127 for its own use. Unfortunately, there are a great many bitmap fonts (many more than 255), so occasional ID number conflicts will occur. Version 3.8 and later versions of the Font/DA Mover, a desk accessory available with Macintosh System software, attempt to resolve such collisions, as do some third-party System enhancement packages, such as Font Harmony from Fifth Generation Systems.

Installed Fonts in Windows and System 7

Before you can use a font, it must be recognized by the computer's operating system. Table 9-1 lists the fonts included in Windows and System 7. If you want to use other fonts, you will need to install them. In Windows, plotter fonts are carryovers from earlier Windows versions; they support pen-drawn characters found in architectural and engineering drawings.

Font Manufacturers

Collections of fonts are available through retail channels or directly from the manufacturers. A list of font manufacturers and descriptions of their products is provided in Appendix A.

Fonts Installed in Macintosh System 7	Fonts Installed in a VGA System in Windows 3.1
Chicago (TrueType)	Modern (Plotter)
Courier (TrueType)	Script (Plotter)
Courier Bold (TrueType)	Roman (Plotter)
Courier 9, 10, 12, 14, 18, 24 (Bitmap)	Small Fonts (Bitmap)
Geneva (TrueType)	Symbol 8, 10, 12, 14, 18, 24 (Bitmap)
Geneva 10, 14, 18, 20, 24 (Bitmap)	MS Serif 8, 10, 12, 14, 18, 24 (Bitmap)
Geneva Italic 9 (Bitmap)	Courier 10, 12, 15 (Bitmap)
Helvetica (TrueType)	MS Sans Serif 8, 10, 12, 14, 18, 24 (Bitmap)
Helvetica Bold (TrueType)	Arial (TrueType)
Helvetica 10, 12, 14, 18, 24 (Bitmap)	Arial Bold (TrueType)
Monaco (TrueType)	Arial Bold Italic (TrueType)
Monaco 12 (Bitmap)	Arial Italic (TrueType)
New York (TrueType)	Courier New (TrueType)
New York 9, 10, 12, 14, 18, 20, 24 (Bitmap)	Courier New Bold (TrueType)
Palatino 12, 14, 18, 24 (Bitmap)	Courier New Italic (TrueType)
Symbol (TrueType)	Courier New Bold Italic (TrueType)
Symbol 9, 10, 12, 14, 18, 24 (Bitmap)	Times New Roman (TrueType)
Times (TrueType)	Times New Roman Bold (TrueType)
Times Bold (TrueType)	Times New Roman Bold Italic (TrueType)
Times Bold Italic (TrueType)	Wingdings (TrueType)
Times 9, 10, 14, 24 (Bitmap)	Symbol (TrueType)
	Symbol B (Bitmap)

TABLE 9-1 *Fonts Included in Windows and System 7*

Managing Your Fonts

Never assume that the fonts you have installed on your computer will also be installed on a user's computer. Choose a system of type management and stick with it so that you will never face the nightmare of your carefully picked fonts being replaced by an ill-suited default font (see First Person, top of next page). If your work is being distributed to sites that may not have the fonts you are using, or if you do not license these fonts for distribution with your work, be sure to bitmap the special font text you use for titles, headlines, buttons, and so forth. For text to be entered by users, it is safest to stay with the installed Windows or System 7 fonts because you know they are

First Person

We had a short break between sessions to install the software for a panel discussion about multimedia. Four of us brought disks with discussion material. Our moderator installed her HyperCard stack first, and we heard her wail, "Something's wrong with my fonts!" We all looked at her ugly 48-point Geneva and felt sorry for her; we knew her mistake. The beautiful fonts she had installed on her home system were not installed on the Macintosh used for the presentation, and she had failed to bring the fonts along, separately or in the resource fork of her stack. By then, it was too late, anyway.

universally available. In Windows, use the TrueType fonts installed during the Setup procedure.

tip *Always be sure your fonts travel with your application when you are delivering software to run on a hardware platform other than the one where the application was created. To avoid many font display problems, particularly for menus and headlines, you may wish to snap a picture of your text with a screen capture utility, and use this image, or bitmap, instead of text that you type into a text field (Chapter 12 describes bitmaps and how to capture and edit images). This will ensure that the screen always looks right, regardless of what hardware platform you use or what fonts are installed.*

Character Sets and Alphabets

Knowing that there is a wide selection of characters available to you on your computer and understanding how you can create and use special and custom-made characters will broaden your creative range when you design and build multimedia projects.

The ASCII Character Set

The American Standard Code for Information Interchange (ASCII) is the 7-bit character coding system most commonly used by computer systems in the United States and abroad. ASCII assigns a number or value to 128 characters, including both lower- and uppercase letters, punctuation marks, Arabic numbers, and math symbols. Also included are 32 control characters used for device control messages, such as carriage return, line feed, and form feed. The ASCII character set is illustrated in Figure 9-8.

ASCII code numbers always represent the same letters of the English alphabet, so that a computer or printer can process that letter independent of what it will look like on the screen or printout. To a computer working

FIGURE 9-8

The 128 standard characters of ASCII

00	NUL	16	DLE	32	SP	48	0	64	@	80	P	96	‘	112	p
01	SOH	17	DC1	33	!	49	1	65	A	81	Q	97	a	113	q
02	STX	18	DC2	34	"	50	2	66	B	82	R	98	b	114	r
03	ETX	19	CD3	35	#	51	3	67	C	83	S	99	c	115	s
04	EOT	20	DC4	36	$	52	4	68	D	84	T	100	d	116	t
05	ENQ	21	NAK	37	%	53	5	69	E	85	U	101	e	117	u
06	ACK	22	SYN	38	&	54	6	70	F	86	V	102	f	118	v
07	BEL	23	ETB	39	'	55	7	71	G	87	W	103	g	119	w
08	BS	24	CAN	40	(	56	8	72	H	88	X	104	h	120	x
09	HT	25	EM	41	)	57	9	73	I	89	Y	105	i	121	y
10	LF	26	SUB	42	*	58	:	74	J	90	Z	106	j	122	z
11	VT	27	ESC	43	+	59	;	75	K	91	[	107k		123	{
12	FF	28	FS	44	,	60	<	76	L	92	\	108	l	124	|
13	CR	29	GS	45	-	61	=	77	M	93	]	109	m	125	}
14	SO	30	RS	46	.	62	>	78	N	94	^	110	n	126	~
15	SI	31	US	47	/	63	?	79	O	95	–	111	o	127	DEL

with the ASCII character set, the number 65, for example, always represents an uppercase letter A. Characters when displayed and printed are then further enhanced by applying various fonts and typefaces.

ASCII was invented and standardized for analog teletype communication early in the age of bits and bytes. The capabilities of the technology have now moved far beyond the original intent of the standard, but because millions of installed computers and printers use ASCII, it is difficult to set any new standards for text without the expense and effort of replacing existing hardware. At least, for these 128 characters, most computers and printers share the same values.

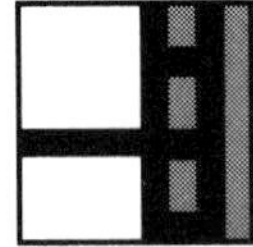

tip *On the Macintosh, use KeyCaps, a desk accessory delivered with the System and found in the Apple Menu, or PopChar, a shareware program, to examine the fonts available to your Macintosh System. Press* OPTION *or* OPTION-SHIFT to examine the extended character set. In Windows, use the Character Map accessory to view and access characters, especially those not on the keyboard (see Figure 9-9).

The Extended Character Set

A byte, which consists of eight bits, is the most commonly used building block for computer processing. ASCII uses only seven bits to code its 128 characters; the eighth bit of the byte is unused. This extra bit allows another 128 characters to be encoded before the byte is used up, and computer systems today use these extra 128 values for an extended character set. The extended character set is most commonly filled with ANSI (American National Standards Institute) standard characters, including often-used symbols, such as ¢ or ∞, and international diacritics or alphabet characters, such as ä or ñ. The Windows extended character set is shown in Figure 9-10.

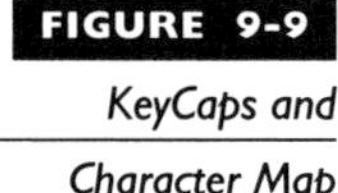

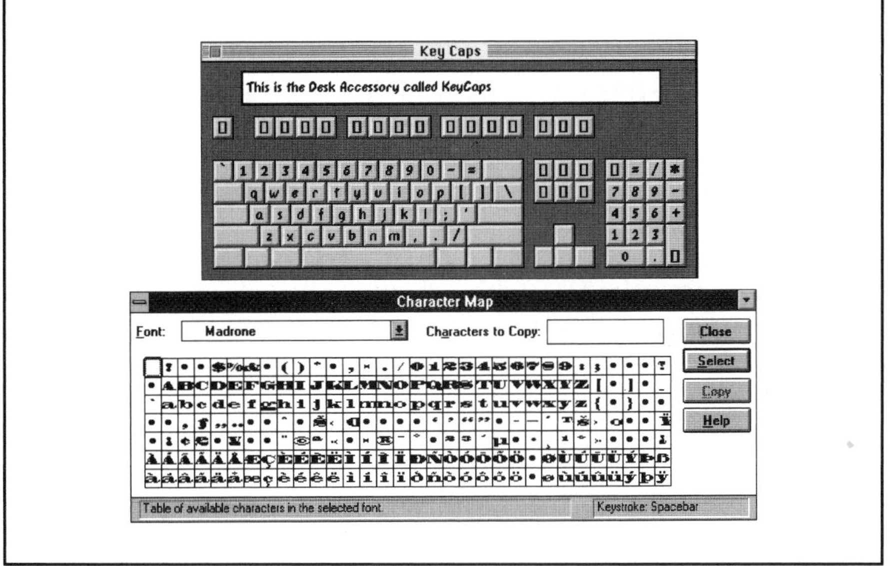

FIGURE 9-9 KeyCaps and Character Map

cross platform *The rules for encoding extended characters are not standardized. Thus ASCII value 165, for example, may be a bullet (•) character on the Macintosh; the character for Japanese yen (¥) in Windows (ANSI); or a capital N with a tilde (Ñ) in DOS.*

Languages in the World of Computers

In modern western languages, words are made up of symbols or letters strung together, representing as a whole the sounds of a spoken word. This is not so for eastern languages such as Chinese, Japanese, and Korean (and the ancient languages of Sumeria, Egypt, and Mesopotamia). In these languages, an entire concept might be represented by a single word symbol that is unrelated to a specific phonetic sound.

0-31	The first 32 characters of ASCII are reserved for "Control Characters"																														
32-63		!	"	#	$	%	&	'	(	)	*	+	,	-	.	/	0	1	2	3	4	5	6	7	8	9	:	;	<	=	>	?
64-95	@	A	B	C	D	E	F	G	H	I	J	K	L	M	N	O	P	Q	R	S	T	U	V	W	X	Y	Z	[	\	]	^	_
96-127	`	a	b	c	d	e	f	g	h	i	j	k	l	m	n	o	p	q	r	s	t	u	v	w	x	y	z	{	|	}	~	I
128-159	I	I	I	I	I	I	I	I	I	I	I	I	I	I	I	I	I	‘	’	I	I	I	I	I	I	I	I	I	I	I	I	I
160-191		¡	¢	£	¤	¥	¦	§	¨	©	ª	«	¬	-	®	¯	°	±	²	³	´	µ	¶	·	¸	¹	º	»	¼	½	¾	¿
192-223	À	Á	Â	Ã	Ä	Å	Æ	Ç	È	É	Ê	Ë	Ì	Í	Î	Ï	Ð	Ñ	Ò	Ó	Ô	Õ	Ö	×	Ø	Ù	Ú	Û	Ü	Ý	Þ	ß
224-256	à	á	â	ã	ä	å	æ	ç	è	é	ê	ë	ì	í	î	ï	ð	ñ	ò	ó	ô	õ	ö	÷	ø	ù	ú	û	ü	ý	þ	ÿ

FIGURE 9-10 The Windows system font character set. The extended character set (values higher than 127) uses the ANSI standard

The letters or symbols of a language are its alphabet. In English, the alphabet consists of 26 Roman or Latin letters; in Japanese, the Kanji alphabet comprises more than 3000 kanas, or whole words. The Russian alphabet, made up of Cyrillic characters based on the ancient Greek alphabet, has about the same number of letters as a Roman alphabet. All languages, from Navajo to Hebrew, have their own unique alphabets.

The written Japanese language consists of three different types of character sets, namely: kanji, katakana, and hiragana. Kanji was originally taken from the Chinese language and is essentially a pictographic representation of the spoken word. Each kanji has two different readings, "on-yomi" and "kun-yomi," respectively the "Chinese rendering" and the "Japanese rendering." Both are used depending on the conjugation of the kanji with other kanji.

Due to certain incompatibilities between the Japanese spoken word and kanji, two sets of kana or phonetic syllabary (alphabet) were developed. Katakana is the "square" kana and is used today for writing only foreign words or onomatopoeic expressions. Hiragana is the "cursive" kana and can be used alone to represent a certain word or combined with kanji to form other words and sentences. Romaji, a more recent addition to the alphabets of Japan, allows for the phonetic spelling of the Japanese language using the Roman characters familiar to the western world.

Ross Uchimura, Executive Vice President, GC3 Ltd., a cross-cultural expert

Most modern alphabets share one very important attribute: the graphic shapes and method for writing the Arabic numbers 0 1 2 3 4 5 6 7 8 9. This is a simple system for representing decimal numbers, which lends itself to easy reading, writing, manipulation, and calculation. Expressing and performing

16 + 32 = 48

is much easier in Arabic numbers than in Roman numerals:

XVI + XXXII = XLVIII

Use of Arabic notation has gradually spread across the world to supplant other systems, although Roman numerals are still used today in western languages in certain forms and contexts.

Translating or designing multimedia (or any computer-based material) into a language other than the one in which it was originally written is called *localization.* This process deals with everything from the month/day/year order for expressing dates to providing special alphabetical characters on keyboards and printers. Even the many western languages that share the Roman alphabet have their own peculiarities and often require special characters to represent special sounds. For example, German has its umlaut (ä); French its various accents (é), the cedilla (ç), and other diacritics; and Spanish its tilde (ñ). These characters are typically available in the extended character set of a font.

UNICODE As the computer market has become more international in the past ten years, one of the resulting problems has been handling the various international language alphabets. It was at best difficult, and at times impossible, to translate the text portions of programs from one script to another. For example, the differences between the Roman script used by western European writers and the Kanji script used by Japanese writers made it particularly challenging to transfer innovative programs from one market to another.

Since 1989, a concerted effort on the part of linguists, engineers, and information professionals from many well-known computer companies has been focused on a new 16-bit architecture for multilingual text and character encoding. Called *Unicode*, this new standard can accommodate up to about 65,000 characters and will ultimately include the characters from all known languages and alphabets in the world.

First Person

When I was in Germany some years ago I read a curious report in the Frankfurter Allgemeine *about a fellow who was suing the local electric utility for not correcting the spelling of his name to its proper form in the German alphabet. His name had an umlaut in it (Wörm), but his bill always read Woerm. In German, the letter ö sounds different from the letter o, so I can't say I blamed him. At first he didn't pay his bill, claiming that he wasn't that person; then the courts told him to pay anyway. So he initiated a civil suit to protect his name.*

It seems the utility was using a new IBM system with a high-speed chain printer to produce the monthly bills, and none of the umlaut characters were available on the ASCII-based chain. By long-standing convention, when you are limited to the English alphabet, the letter e immediately follows any umlautless vowel, to indicate that the umlaut should be there but isn't. Today, with high-speed laser printers and special fonts, the problem has probably gone away.

The current Unicode standard includes more than 18,000 Han characters (ideographs for Japanese, Chinese, and Korean), and future releases will include obsolete alphabets such as cuneiform, hieroglyphs, and ancient Han characters. In addition, character space will be reserved for users and publishers to create their own scripts, designed especially for their own applications. For example, a carpenter might develop a script that included a character meaning "half-inch sheetrock," another character meaning "three-quarter-inch plywood," and so forth.

Microsoft, Apple, Sun, IBM, Xerox, NeXT, Lotus, and Novell (among others) are participating in the creation of this standard, and both Microsoft and Apple have plans to incorporate Unicode into future releases of their operating systems. For more information about Unicode, contact

Unicode Consortium
c/o Metaphor Computer Systems
1965 Charleston Road
Mountain View, CA 94043

The ATypI Organization

The Association Typographique Internationale (ATypI) was founded as a nonprofit organization in 1957 by a small group of typographers, type designers, type manufacturers, and educators, under the direction of Charles Peignot. He was the president of the Deberny & Peignot type foundry in Paris (and has a popular typeface named after him).

The Association's primary objective is to provide a forum in which the designers and manufacturers of type and font products can work together to prevent the unauthorized copying of their products. As the Association's interests have widened and the range of its activities has expanded, ATypI membership has increased to over 400 individual and corporate members.

ATypI was instrumental in working with the World Intellectual Property Organization (WIPO) to produce special intellectual property protection for typeface designs. This resulted in the Vienna Agreement for the Protection of Typeface Designs, which has been signed by three nations. Work continues today to obtain two further signatory nations, which will bring this agreement into international force. In anticipation of a successful international resolution, ATypI has established an international depository of typeface designs at the St. Bride Printing Library in London.

In today's world, countless people are using type and typography without realizing that the letters were painstakingly designed by an artist or craftsman, and computer programs are readily available to anyone who wants to create new digital descriptions of character shapes. The education of designers and manufacturers, and the adequate protection of their products, is as important as it has ever been.

ATypI has recognized the dangers of font software piracy and, to support the efforts of its membership, acts as the general sponsor of the Font Software Anti-Piracy Initiative. This Initiative provides education for users of font software and ensures that the terms of a license and the value of a copyright are understood. ATypI also lends the moral support of the Association to the copyright holders' efforts to defend their intellectual property rights. This activity is a logical extension of the Association's original purpose in the world of digital desktop design and publishing.

ATypI has evolved into an international organization that exists to promote all aspects of typography: legal protection of authors, aesthetic standards, information, and education. Membership is open to anyone involved with type in any form. There are three membership levels: manufacturer, individual, and student. In the United States, for an application contact ATypI, c/o Mark Batty, President and CEO, ITC, 866 Second Avenue, New York, NY 10017, (212) 371-0699, Fax (212) 752-4752, AppleLink address: Typeface.

Font Editing and Design Tools

Special font editing tools can be used to make your own type, so you can communicate exactly an idea or graphic feeling. With these tools, professional typographers create distinct text and display faces. Graphic designers, publishers, and ad agencies can design instant variations of existing typefaces.

cross platform *Most of the current font editors are optimized for the Macintosh platform, but your new or edited fonts can be easily converted among the various font formats of PostScript Type 1 and Type 3 and TrueType. Well-known font editing software for the Macintosh is also becoming available in the Windows environment.*

Typeface designs fall into the category of industrial design and have been determined by the courts in some cases to be protectable by patent. For example, design patents have been issued for Bigelow & Holmes' Lucida, ITC Stone, and for Adobe's Minion. Be sure to read the above section on "The ATypI Organization" in this chapter.

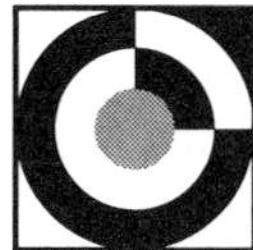

warning *If your project includes special fonts, be sure that your license agreement with the font supplier allows you to distribute them with your project.*

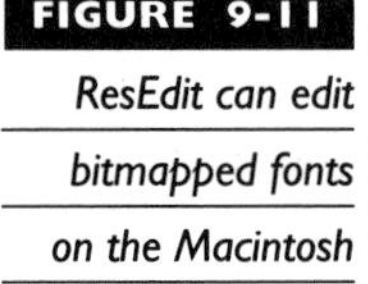

FIGURE 9-11

ResEdit can edit bitmapped fonts on the Macintosh

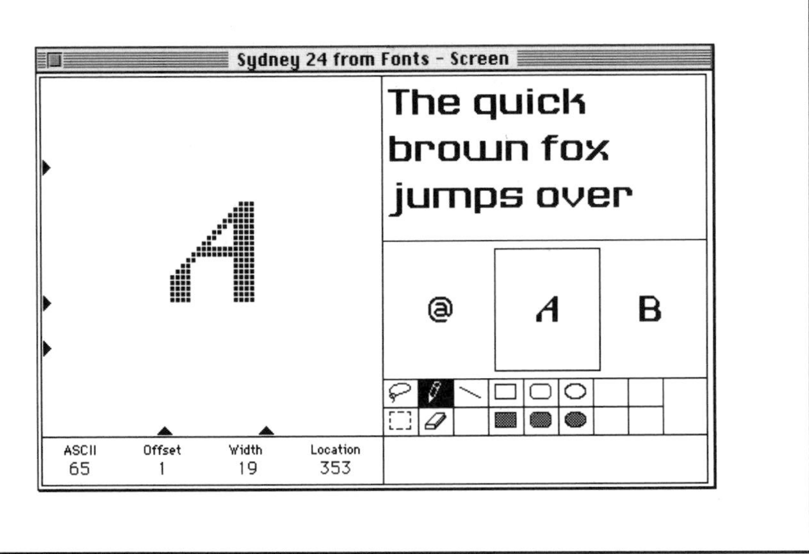

Occasionally in your projects you may require special characters. With the tools described in the paragraphs that follow, you can easily substitute characters of your own design for any unused characters in the extended character set. You can even include several custom versions of your client's company logo or other special symbols relevant to your content or subject right in your text font.

ResEdit

ResEdit is a resource editor available from Apple that is useful for creating and changing graphic resources such as cursors, icons, dialog boxes, patterns, keyboard maps, and bitmapped fonts on the Macintosh. It can be used to edit or create new FONT resources for storing the bitmaps of screen fonts. If you need to make small adjustments to a screen font or create special characters, as illustrated in Figure 9-11, try ResEdit.

FONTastic Plus

FONTastic Plus, supplied by Altsys, only works with Macintosh bitmapped fonts; it lets you edit existing fonts or create new ones. (See Appendix A for more information on font manufacturers.) The character editing window is similar to ResEdit's font editor. As illustrated in Figure 9-12, simple tools let you draw the pixels that make up the characters of

FIGURE 9-12

FONTastic Plus bitmapped font editor for Macintosh

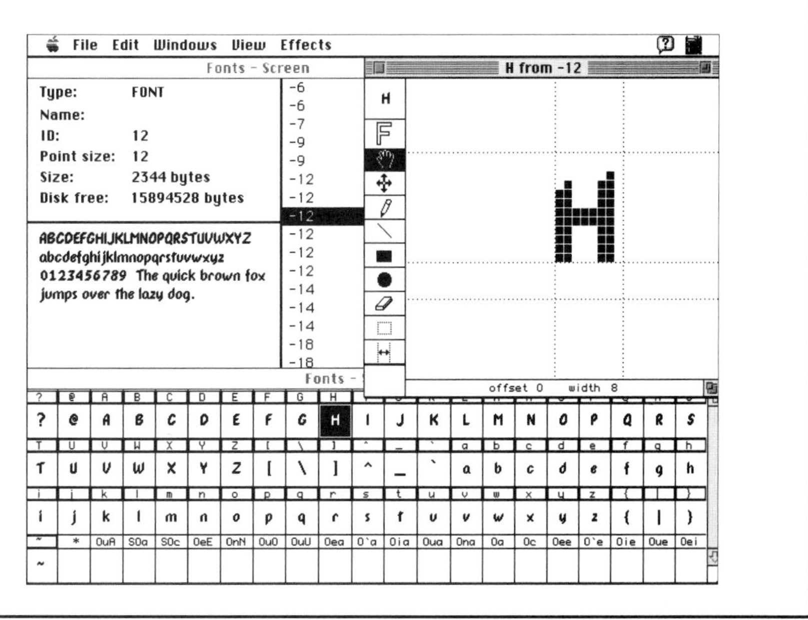

your font. You can change a font's style, rotate it, or flip it. FONTastic Plus is still available directly from Altsys, although its functions have been incorporated into the much more powerful Fontographer product, described next.

Fontographer

Fontographer, supplied by Altsys Corporation (see Appendix A), is a specialized graphics editor for both Macintosh and Windows platforms. You can use it to develop PostScript language fonts for Macintosh, IBM-compatible PCs, and NeXT workstations, as well as TrueType fonts for the Macintosh and PC. Designers can also modify existing typefaces, incorporate PostScript artwork, automatically trace scanned images, and create designs from scratch. A sample Fontographer screen is shown in Figure 9-13.

Fontographer's features include a freehand drawing tool to create professional and precise inline and outline drawings of calligraphic and script characters, using either the mouse or alternative input methods (such as Wacom pressure-sensitive pen systems, Kurta digitizing tablets, and CalComp DrawingBoard II). Fontographer allows the creation of multiple font designs from two existing typefaces, and you can design lighter or heavier fonts by modifying the weight of an entire typeface.

Fontographer for Windows opens any PostScript Type 1 or TrueType font for the PC, and lets you create condensed, expanded, and oblique versions of the same font or modify any of those fonts to suit your design needs. One character, several characters, or entire fonts can be scaled, rotated, and skewed to create new and unique typefaces. A metric window provides complete control over character width, spacing, offset, and kerning. The current Windows version of Fontographer does not make Multiple Master fonts (PostScript fonts that allow you to adjust a range of certain characteristics for a set of characters, for example, serif to sans serif or condensed to extended) or Type 3 PostScript fonts, and it does not have an Option-Copy, Paste feature for bringing drawings through the Clipboard from FreeHand or Illustrator. Nor can the current version read a Macintosh Fontographer database; font transfer is accomplished through Type 1 PostScript.

Metamorphosis Professional

This program, nicknamed Meta Pro and supplied by Altsys Corporation, converts PostScript fonts (except those made by The Art Importer and Parafont) into editable outlines and PostScript Type 1 fonts. It can convert fonts that are on your computer's hard disk, on an AppleShare server, in the ROM or RAM memory of your printer, and on the hard disk of your printer. Meta Pro can produce output in many different formats: a TrueType font

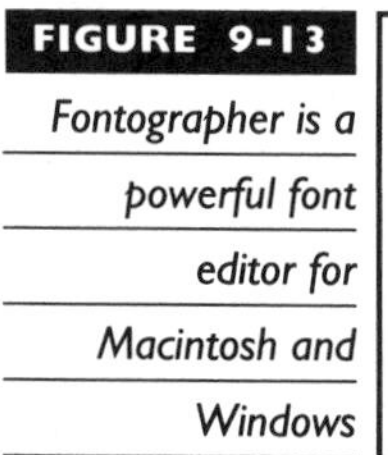

FIGURE 9-13 Fontographer is a powerful font editor for Macintosh and Windows

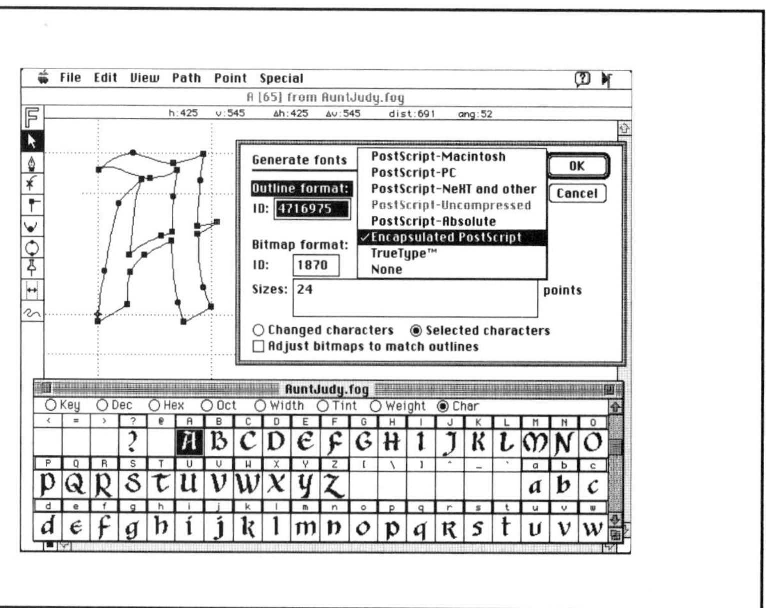

in Macintosh format; a TrueType font in Windows format; a fully standard, hinted Type 1 PostScript file that is ATM compatible; a Windows/ATM-compatible Type 1 PostScript font for IBM PCs running ATM in Windows; and a PICT file.

FontStudio

FontStudio, supplied by Letraset (see Appendix A), is a complete typeface creation and modification tool for the Macintosh. It works with PostScript, TrueType, and LetraFont (Letraset's own version of PostScript) fonts. Whether you're creating a font from scratch, importing and modifying an existing font, or using a scanned image as a template, FontStudio provides control over outline printer fonts and onscreen bitmap fonts, as shown in Figure 9-14. FontStudio can save as PostScript Type 1, Type 3, or TrueType, and you can also convert fonts from one format to another. It also has a built-in autohinter to ensure that your fonts look great at all point sizes and at low resolution.

After autohinting a font (or just individual characters), FontStudio allows you to manually tweak the hints for optimal onscreen appearance and output. You can edit outline shapes by manipulating curve control points (see Figure 9-14) and view the actual results on the characters displayed in a second window, where the character is automatically scaled by TrueType to a number of sizes. Though application designers may rely less and less on

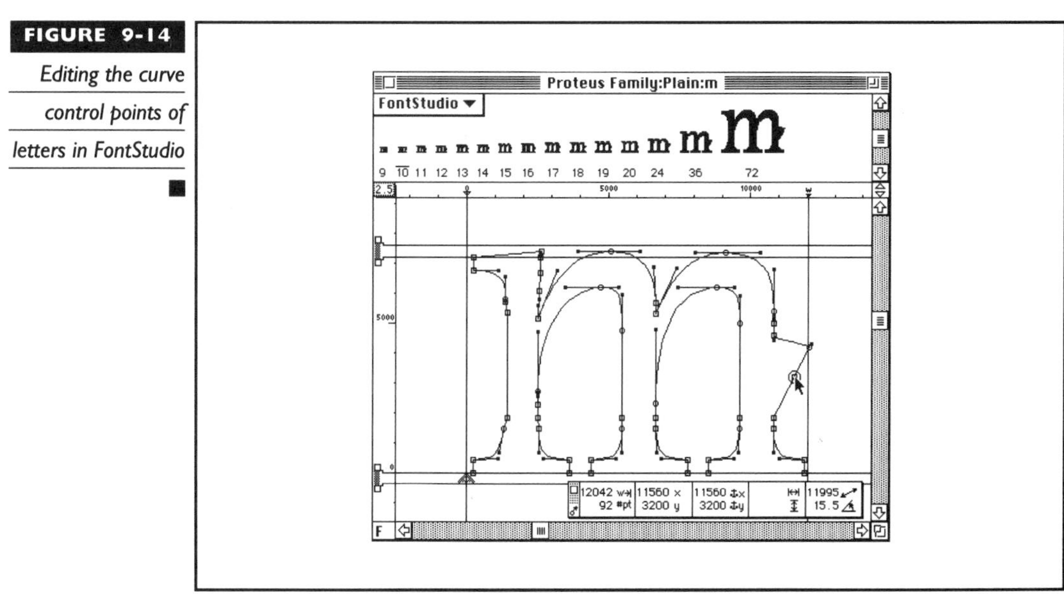

FIGURE 9-14 *Editing the curve control points of letters in FontStudio*

installed bitmaps since the advent of PostScript and TrueType, FontStudio also allows generation of bitmap fonts with a choice of rasterizers.

Making Pretty Text

To make your text look pretty, you need a toolbox full of fonts and special graphics applications that can stretch, shade, shadow, color, and anti-alias your words into real artwork. Pretty text is typically found in bitmapped drawings where characters have been tweaked, manipulated, and blended into a computer graphic image. Simply choosing the font is the first step. Most designers find it is easier to make pretty type starting with ready-made fonts, but some will create their own custom fonts using font-editing and design tools such as Fontographer, FONTastic, and FontStudio, described in the preceding sections.

With the proper tools and a creative mind, you can create endless variations on plain-old type, and you can not only choose, but customize the styles that will fit with your design needs.

When they first invented typesetting there were variants cut of each character so text would look as if it had been handwritten by a monk! Desktop designers have been fighting so hard to get their setting to look like it's come from a Berthold system, that most of the new potential of desktop typography has been overlooked.

David Collier, Author of *Collier's Rules for Desktop Design and Typography* (Addison-Wesley, 1990)

Most image-editing and painting applications let you make text using the fonts available in your system. You can colorize the text, stretch, squeeze, and rotate it, and you can filter it through various "plug-ins" to generate wild graphic results.

Figure 9-15 is an image with text created in Photoshop. The rose was scanned from a photograph, separated from its background (1), and placed onto black (2). A 200-point word, "Rose," was typed in bold black Peignot Light onto a white background without anti-aliasing (3). Then a rainbow of hues was "stolen" from the little strip on Photoshop's color wheel by screen capturing, and the strip was duplicated horizontally until it would be large enough to cover the entire word (4). Selecting and dragging the rainbow of colors on top of the word, the rainbow was laid onto the black letters by removing white from the underlying image using Photoshop's Composite Controls—note the lower right-hand slider is moved one value to the left, from 255 to 254 (5). The characters of the word were then selected along

FIGURE 9-15 *Image editing applications let you make pretty text*

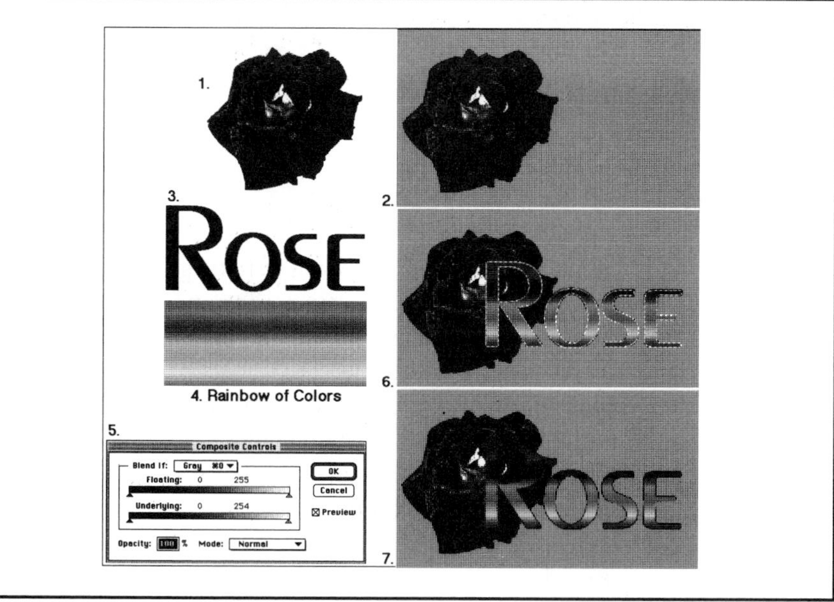

their edges by selecting all the white background with the "Magic Wand" tool, then "inverting" that selection (Invert in the Select menu). The rainbow word was dragged on top of the red rose (6), and a two-pixel border around it was selected (Border in the Select menu). Then the word was finally "anti-aliased" onto the background using the Blur filter, blurring just the border of the word (7).

3-D modeling programs allow you to create a character, add depth to it or extrude it, shade and light it, and manipulate it into other shapes. The character here was generated in just this way and, when animated using Macromedia's Director, spins in place:

Applications such as Brøderbund's TypeStyler, Pixar's Typestry, Ray-Dream's addDepth, and Adobe's TypeAlign are designed to manipulate typefaces in a graphical way. Figure 9-16 shows text being drawn and manipulated using TypeAlign and addDepth. The custom-tortured characters can be captured as a bitmap and incorporated into your project. Figure 9-17 shows the elements of Typestry, with a wire-frame drawing of the characters and a rendered bitmapped image of the wire frame under the chosen lighting conditions. Typestry allows you to wrap colored patterns onto your text and place it on a background.

Hypermedia and Hypertext

Multimedia—the combination of text, graphic, and audio elements into a single collection or presentation—becomes *interactive multimedia* when you give the user some control over the information that is viewed and when it is viewed. Interactive multimedia becomes *hypermedia* when its designer provides a structure of linked elements through which a user can navigate and interact.

When a hypermedia project includes large amounts of text or symbolic content, this content can be indexed and its elements then linked together to afford rapid electronic retrieval of the associated information. When words are keyed or indexed to other words, you have a *hypertext system*; the text part of this term represents the project's content and meaning, rather than the graphical presentation of the text.

FIGURE 9-16 TypeAlign and addDepth let you warp and twist characters

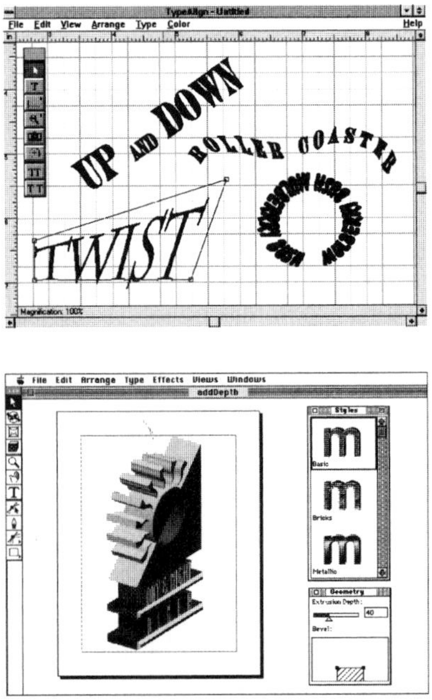

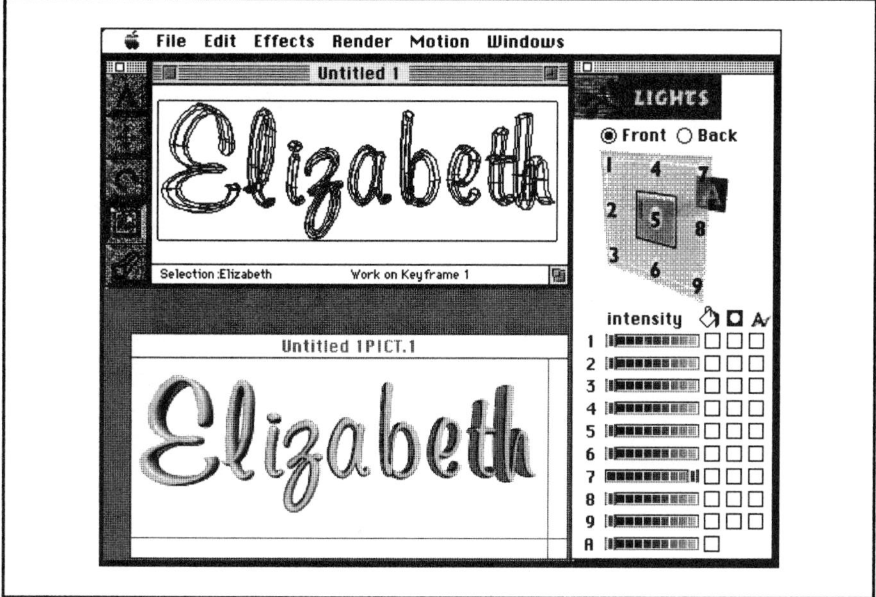

FIGURE 9-17 Typestry can render letters into complex shapes with shading and shadows

When text lives in a computer instead of on printed pages, the computer's powerful processing capabilities can be applied to make the text more accessible and meaningful. The text can then be called *hypertext*; because the words, sections, and thoughts are linked together, the user can navigate through text in a nonlinear fashion, quickly and intuitively.

Using hypertext systems, you can electronically search through all the text of a computer-resident book, locate references to a certain word, and then immediately view the page where the word was found. Or you can create complicated Boolean searches (using terms such as AND, OR, NOT, and BOTH) to locate the occurrences of several related words, such as "Elwood," "Gloria," "mortgage," and "happiness" in a paragraph or on a page. Whole documents can be linked to other documents. Figure 9-18 shows the results of a search on the terms "solenoid" and "harness guide" in an InnerView database. The terms are shown highlighted after being found together in the text of an engine repair manual.

A word can be made *hot,* as can a button, thus leading the user from one reference to another. Click on the word "Elwood," and you may find yourself reading a biography or resume; click on "mortgage," and a calculator pops up. Some authoring systems (HyperCard and ToolBook, for example) incorporate a hypertext facility that allows you to identify words in a text field using a bold or colored style, then link them to other words, pages, or activities, such as playing a sound or video clip related to that hot word. You cannot do this kind of nonlinear and associative navigation in a sequentially organized book. But

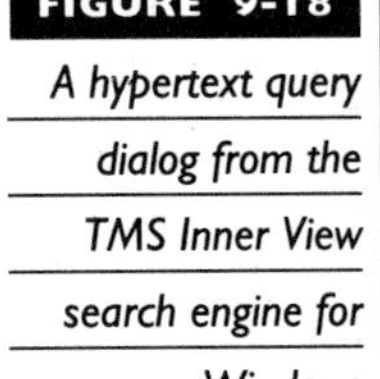

FIGURE 9-18

A hypertext query dialog from the TMS Inner View search engine for Windows

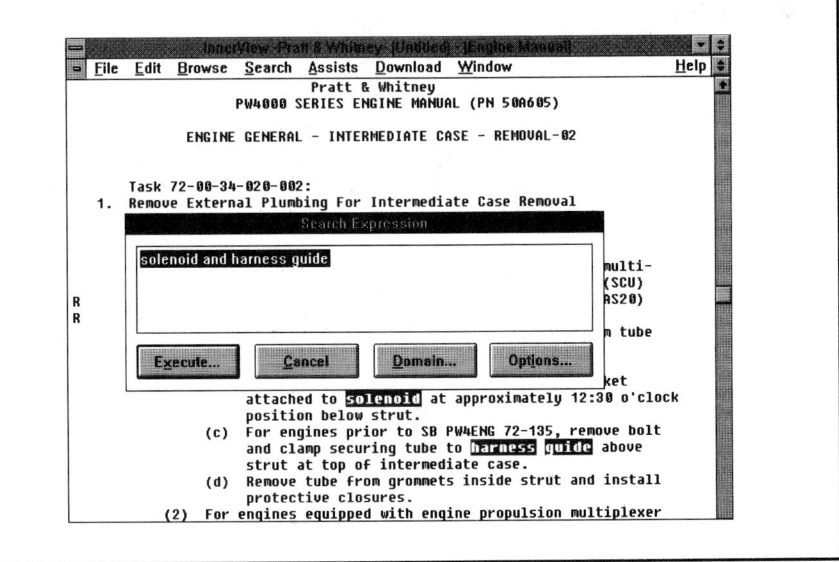

on a CD-ROM, where you might have more than 100,000 pages of text to investigate, search, and browse, hypertext is invaluable.

Because hypertext is the organized cross-linking of words not only to other words but also to associated images, video clips, sounds, and other exhibits, hypertext often becomes simply an additional feature within an overall multimedia design. The term "hyper" has come to imply that user interaction is a critical part of the design, whether for text browsing or for the multimedia project as a whole.

In 1945, Vannevar Bush wrote a seminal eight-page article, "As We May Think," for the *Atlantic Monthly*. This short treatise, in which he discusses the need for new methodologies for accessing information, has become the historic cornerstone of hypertext experimentation. Doug Englebart (inventor of the mouse) and Ted Nelson (who coined the term "hypertext" in 1965) have actively championed the research and innovations required of computer technology for implementing useful hypertext systems, and they have worked to combat the historic inertia of linear thought. Nelson would claim that the very structure of thought is neither sequential nor linear and that computer-based hypertext systems will fundamentally alter the way humans approach literature and the expression of ideas during the coming decades.

But the argument to this theory of associative thought is that people are, indeed, more comfortable with linear thinking and are easily overwhelmed by too much freedom, becoming quickly lost in the chaos of nonlinear gigabytes. As a practical reminder, it is important to always provide location markers, either text-and-symbol menus or illustrative maps, for users who travel the threads of nonlinear systems.

Bush identified the problem—and the need to provide new ways to access information—but was he right about how the mind works? I suspect a purely associative model of human memory and mental processes is too simplistic.

Philip Murray, *From Ventura to Hypertext*, Knowledge Management Associates, Danvers, MA, 1991

The Power of Hypertext

In a fully indexed hypertext system, all words can be found immediately. Suppose you search a large database for "boats," and you come up with a whopping 1623 references or *hits*—among them, Noah's Ark (open boat in water), television situation comedies (*The Love Boat*), political criticisms of cabinet members who challenged the status quo (rocked the boat), cabinet members who were stupid (missed the boat), and Christmas dinner trimmings (Grandmother's gravy boat). So you narrow your search and look for "boats" and "water" when both words are mentioned on the same page; this time you get 286 hits. "Boats," "water," and "storms" gets you 37; "boats," "water," "storms," and "San Francisco," one single hit. With over a thousand hits, you are lost. With one hit, you have something! But you still may not find what you are looking for:

> The *storm* had come and gone quickly across the Colorado plains, but *water* was still puddled at the foot of the house-high bank of mud that had slid into town when the dam burst. In front of the general store, which had remained standing, four strong men carefully lifted a tiny *boat* onto the large dray wagon borrowed from the woodcutters. On a layer of blankets in the bilge of the *boat*, the undertaker had carefully laid out the remains of both the Mayor and his paramour. The Mayor had not drowned in the flood, but died of a heart attack in the midst of the panic. Children covered the *boat* with freshly cut pine boughs while horses were quickly harnessed to the wagon, and a strange procession began to move slowly down *San Francisco* Street toward the new cemetery...

The power of such search and retrieval systems provided by a computer for large volumes of data is immense, but clearly this power must be channeled in meaningful ways. Links among words or clusters of information need to be designed so that they make sense. Judgments must be made about relationships and the way information content is organized and made available to users. The lenses through which vast amounts of data are viewed must necessarily be ground and shaped by those who design the access system.

The hype about hypertext may be justified. It can provide a computer-supported information environment which can add to our appreciation of the text, can go some way towards aping the mental agility of the human mind, can allow navigation along patterns of association, can provide a non-linear information environment. But the problems of constructing non-linear documents are not few and can prove to be very complex.

Patricia Baird, editor of *Hypermedia*, a scientific journal published in the United Kingdom

The issue of who designs the lenses and how the designers maintain impartial focus is troubling to many scientists, archivists, and students of cognitive thinking. The scientists would remain "hermeneutically" neutral, they would balance freedom against authority and warn against the epistemological unknowns of this new intellectual technology. They are aware of the forces that allow advertising and marketing craftspeople to intuitively twist meanings and spin events to their own purposes, with actions that can affect the knowledge and views of many millions of people and thus history itself. But these forces remain poorly understood, are not easily controlled by authority, and will express themselves with immeasurably far-reaching, long-term impact on the shape of human culture.

The multimedia designer controls the filtering mechanisms and places the lenses within the multimedia project. A manufacturer, for instance, that presents its products using interactive multimedia can bring abundant information and selling power within reach of the user, including background information, collateral marketing material, pricing statistics, and technical data. The project design will be, of course, biased—to sell more of the manufacturer's products and generate more profit; but this bias is assumed and understood in these circumstances. When the assumptions and understandings of inherent bias in any information base break down, when fiction or incomplete data are presented as full fact, that is when the powerful forces of multimedia and hypermedia can have their greatest deleterious effect.

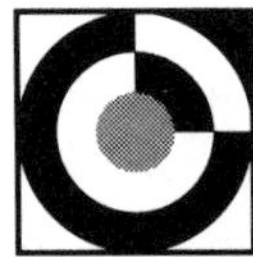

warning *Bad multimedia projects will not alter the collective view of history; really bad projects might.*

Using Hypertext

Special programs for information management and hypertext have been designed to present electronic text, images, and other elements in a database fashion. Commercial systems have been used for large and complicated mixtures of text and images, for example, a detailed repair manual for a Boeing 747 aircraft, a parts catalog for Pratt & Whitney jet turbine engines, an instant reference to hazardous chemicals, and electronic reference libraries used in legal and library environments. These hypertext databases rely upon proprietary indexing systems that carefully scan the entire body of text and create very fast cross-referencing indexes that point to the location of specific words, documents, and images. Indeed, a hypertext index by itself can be as large as 50 to 100 percent the size of the original document. Indexes are essential for speedy performance.

Commercial hypertext systems were developed historically to retrofit gigantic bodies of information. Licenses for use and distribution of these commercial systems are expensive, and the hypertext-based projects typically require the large mass-storage capability of one or many CD-ROMs and/or dedicated gigabyte hard disks. Simpler but effective hypertext indexing tools are available for both Macintosh and Windows, and they offer fairly elaborate features designed to work in concert with many multimedia authoring systems.

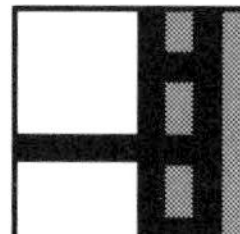

tip *Rather than designing an elaborate, fully cross-referenced hypertext system for your multimedia project, you can "hardwire" the links between the most salient words (highlight them in your text) so that a mouse click leads to a topic menu specific to the chosen word. Though this constrains the user's movement through the text, the user will not perceive it as such, and you can thus maintain strict control over your navigation pathways and design.*

Searching for Words

While the designer of a hypermedia database makes assumptions, he or she also presents users with tools and a meaningful interface to exercise the assumptions. Employing this interface, users can tailor word searches to find very specific combinations. Following are typical methods for word searching in hypermedia systems:

- **Categorical:** Selecting or limiting the documents, pages, or fields of text within which to search for a word or words.
- **Word relationship:** Searching for words according to their general proximity and order. For example, you might search for "party" and "beer" only when they occur on the same page or in the same paragraph.

- **Adjacency:** Searching for words occurring next to one another, usually in phrases and proper names. For instance, find "widow" only when "black" is the preceding adjacent word.
- **Alternates:** Applying an OR criterion to search for two or more words, such as "bacon" or "eggs."
- **Association:** Applying an AND criterion to search for two or more words, such as "skiff," "tender," "dinghy," and "rowboat."
- **Negation:** Applying a NOT criterion to search exclusively for references to a word that are not associated with the word. For example, find all occurrences of "paste" when "library" is not present in the same sentence.
- **Truncation:** Searching for a word with any of its possible suffixes. For example, to find all occurrences of "girl" and "girls," you may need to specify something like "girl#". Multiple character suffixes can be managed with another specifier, so "geo*" might yield "geo," "geology," and "geometry," as well as "George."
- **Intermediate words:** Searching for words that occur between what might normally be adjacent words, such as a middle name or initial in a proper name.

Hypermedia Structures

Two buzzwords used often in hypertext systems are link and node. *Links* are connections between the conceptual elements, that is, the *nodes* containing text, graphics, sounds, or related information in the knowledge base. Links connect Caesar Augustus with Rome, for example, and grapes with wine, and love with hate. The art of hypermedia design lies in the visualization of these nodes and their links so that they make sense, not nonsense, and can form the backbone of a knowledge access system.

Links are the navigation pathways and menus; nodes are accessible topics, documents, messages, and content elements. A *link anchor* is where you come from; a *link end* is the destination node linked to the anchor. Some hypertext systems provide unidirectional navigation and offer no return pathway; others are bidirectional.

The simplest way to navigate hypermedia structures is via buttons that let you access linked information (text, graphics, and sounds) that is contained at the nodes. When you've finished examining the information, you return to your starting location.

HyperWriter!, a powerful multimedia linking system from NTERGAID Inc., makes use of Windows' left and right mouse buttons for this navigation. The left button activates a link (takes you to the information node), and the right button returns you. A typical navigation structure might look like the following:

Pages of text with hot words linked to InfoBites only

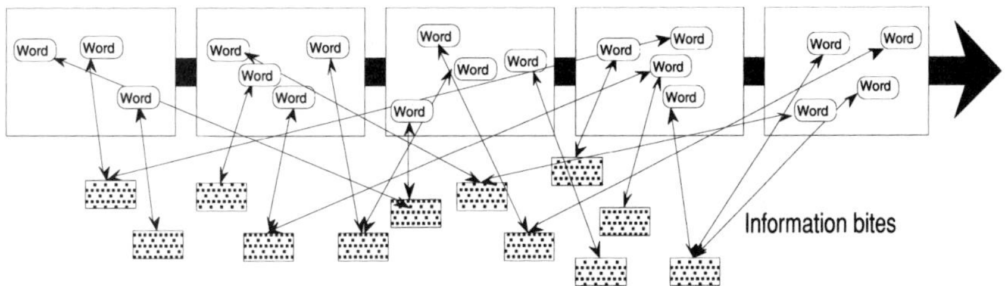

Navigation becomes more complicated when you add associative links that connect elements not directly in the hierarchy or sequence. These are the paths where users can begin to get lost if you do not provide location markers. A link can lead to a node that provides further links, as shown here:

Pages of text with hot words linked to InfoBites linked to pages and to other InfoBites

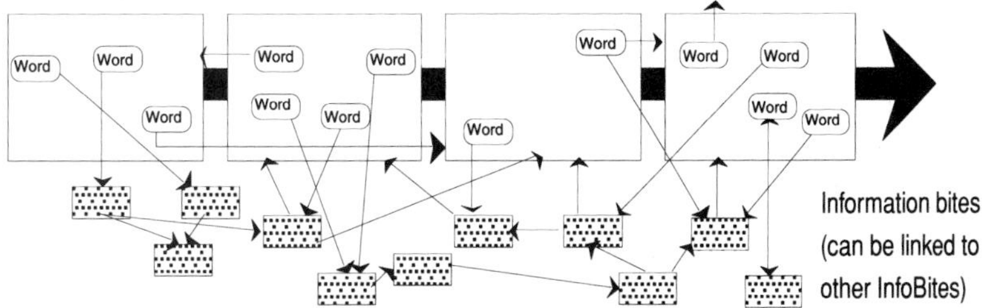

When you offer full-text search through an information base, there may be links between any number of items at your current node and any number of other nodes with items that meet your relationship criteria. When users are browsing freely through this system, and one page does not follow the next (as expected in the linear metaphor of books and literature), users can get lost in the associative maze of the designer's content:

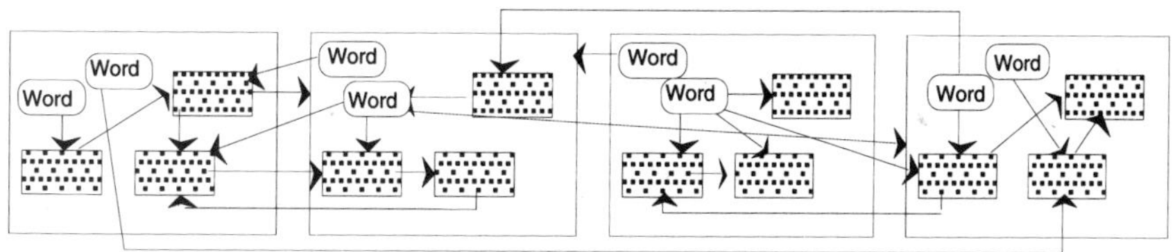

Documents containing pages of text with hot words linked to other documents, pages, InfoBites, and other hot words

Hypertext Tools

Two functions are common to most hypermedia text management systems, and they are often provided as separate applications: building (or authoring) and reading. The builder creates the links, identifies nodes, and generates the all-important index of words. The index methodology and the search algorithms used to find and group words according to user search criteria are typically proprietary, and represent an area where computers are carefully optimized for performance—finding search words among a list of many tens of thousands of words requires speed-demon programming. Search engines such as SmarText from Lotus (see Figure 9-19) and HyperWriter! from NTERGAID Inc. represent the technical core of hypertext.

Hypertext systems are currently used for electronic publishing and reference works, technical documentation, educational courseware, interactive kiosks, electronic catalogs, interactive fiction, and text and image databases. Today these tools are used extensively with information organized in a linear fashion; it still may be many years before the majority of multimedia project users become comfortable with fully nonlinear hypertext and hypermedia systems. When (and perhaps if) they do, the methodology of human thought and conceptual management—indeed, the way we think—will be forever changed.

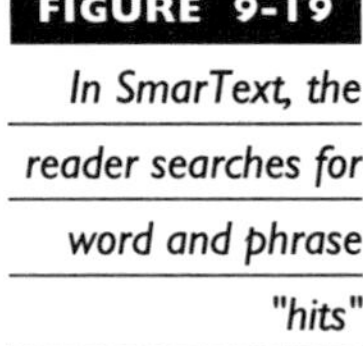

FIGURE 9-19

In SmarText, the reader searches for word and phrase "hits"

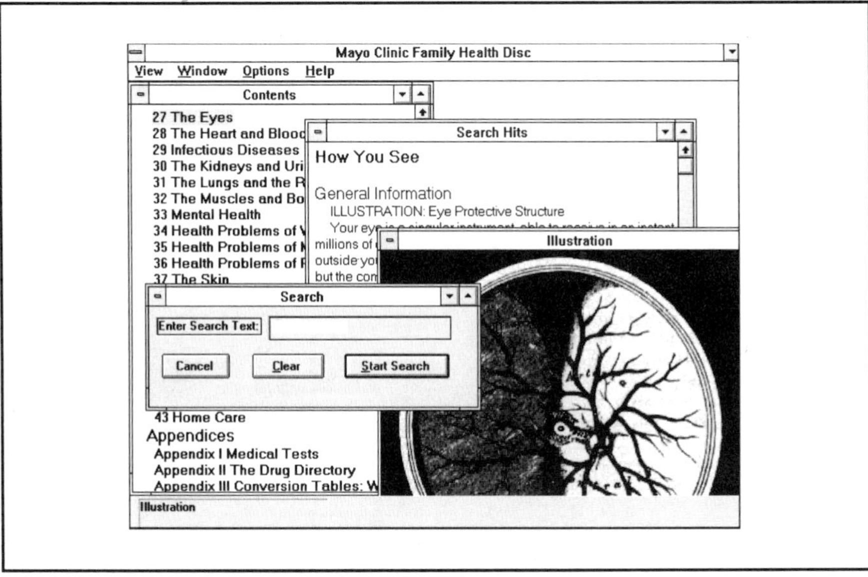

Multi

How you use the power of sound can make the difference between an ordinary multimedia presentation and a professionally spectacular one.

the power of sound

chapter 10

Sound

These waves spread like the ripples from a pebble tossed into a still pool and when they reach your eardrums, you experience the changes of pressure, or vibrations, as sound.

SOUND is perhaps the most sensuous element of multimedia. It is meaningful "speech" in any language, from a whisper to a scream. It can provide the listening pleasure of music, the startling accent of special effects, or the ambience of a mood-setting background. How you use the power of sound can make the difference between an ordinary multimedia presentation and a professionally spectacular one.

The Power of Sound

When something vibrates in the air by moving back and forth (such as the cone of a loudspeaker), it creates waves of pressure. These waves spread like the ripples from a pebble tossed into a still pool, and when they reach your eardrums, you experience the changes of pressure, or vibrations, as *sound.* In air, the ripples propagate at about 750 miles per hour, or Mach 1 at sea level. Sound waves vary in loudness (measured in decibels or dB) and in frequency or pitch (vibrations per second, measured in Hertz or Hz). Many sound waves mixed together form an audio sea of symphonic music, speech, or just plain noise.

Acoustics is the science of sound. Sound pressure levels (loudness or volume) are measured in decibels or dB; a decibel measurement is actually the ratio between a chosen reference point on a logarithmic scale and the level that is actually experienced. When you quadruple the sound output power, there is only a 6 dB increase; when you make the sound 100 times more intense, the increase in dB is not hundredfold, but only 20 dB. This scale makes sense because humans perceive sound pressure levels over an extraordinarily broad dynamic range. The decibel scale, with some examples, is shown in Table 10-1; notice the relationship between power (measured in watts) and dB.

dB	Watts	Example
195	25–40 million	Saturn rocket
170	100,000	Jet engine with afterburner
160	10,000	Jet engine at 7000 lbs. thrust
150	1,000	
140	100	
130	10	75-piece orchestra, at fortissimo
120	1	Large chipping hammer
110	0.1	Riveting machine
100	0.01	Automobile on highway
90	0.001	Subway train; a shouting voice
80	0.0001	Inside a 1952 Corvette at 60 mph
70	0.00001	Voice conversation; a freight train 100 ft. away
60	0.000001	Large department store
50	0.0000001	Average residence or small business office
40	0.00000001	Residential areas of Chicago at night
30	0.000000001	Very soft whisper
20	0.0000000001	Sound studio

TABLE 10-1 *Typical Sound Levels in Decibels (dB) and Watts* ■

Sound is energy, like the waves breaking on a sandy beach, and too much volume can permanently damage the delicate receiving mechanisms behind your eardrums. In terms of volume, what you hear subjectively is not what you hear objectively. The perception of loudness is dependent upon the frequency or pitch of the sound: at low frequencies, more power is required to deliver the same perceived loudness than a sound at the middle or higher frequency ranges. You may feel the sound more than hear it. For instance, when the ambient noise level is above 90 dB in the workplace, people are likely to make increased numbers of errors in susceptible tasks—especially when there is a high-frequency component to the noise. When the level is above 80 dB, it is quite impossible to use a telephone. Experiments by researchers in residential areas have shown that a sound generator at 45 dB produces no reaction from neighbors; at 45 to 55 dB, sporadic complaints; at 50 to 60 dB, widespread complaints; at 55 to 65 dB, threats of community action; and at more than 65 dB, vigorous community action. This research from the 1950s continues to provide helpful criteria for multimedia developers today.

There is a great deal more to acoustics than volume and pitch. If you are interested, there are many texts that discuss why middle C on a cello does not sound like middle C on a bassoon; or why a five-year-old can hear a 1000Hz tone played at 20 dB while an older adult with presbycusis (loss of hearing sensitivity due to age) cannot. Your use of sound in multimedia projects will not likely require highly specialized knowledge of harmonics, intervals, sine waves, notation, octaves, or the physics of acoustics and vibration, but you do need to know the following:

- How to make sounds
- How to record and edit sounds
- How to incorporate sounds into your work

Multimedia System Sounds

You can use sound right off the bat on both the Macintosh and in Windows because system beeps and warnings are available as soon as you install the operating system. These sound effects are limited, however.

On the Macintosh, you can choose one of several sounds for the system beep to indicate an error or warning: Droplet, Indigo, Quack, Simple Beep, Sosumi, and Wild Eep.

In Windows 3.1, system sounds include Chimes, Chord, Ding, and Tada. You can assign these sounds to system events such as Windows startup, warnings from other applications, or clicks outside of an open dialog box (which causes the default beep in Windows). If you install Microsoft's Multimedia Extensions software, additional sounds become available (Bells, Blocks, Clock, Gong, Jawharp, Laser, Ohoh, Siren, and Water).

If you are new to either platform (Mac or PC/Windows), your first multimedia sound experience might be simply finding one of these system sounds in the appropriate control panel (the Sound dialog box) and testing it out. To play sound with Windows, you need to have a sound board installed in your PC. You can also install the special SPEAKER.DRV file to play sound through the internal speaker of your PC. This driver is available on most bulletin boards and is free from Microsoft, but you will find the tiny internal speaker on the PC to be inadequate for multimedia performance. Figure 10-1 shows the Sound control panels in both Macintosh and Windows.

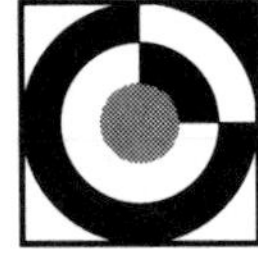

warning *The SPEAKER.DRV driver for playing Windows .WAV files through the on-board PC speaker automatically disables all interrupts. This means you can have no mouse or keyboard activity while the sound plays. You can adjust the driver to enable these interrupts, but this action decreases sound quality (which is not high to begin with). You will need to experiment to determine if using the PC speaker for your project provides satisfactory results.*

FIGURE 10-1

The Sound control panels from Macintosh System 7 and Windows 3.1 with Multimedia Extensions

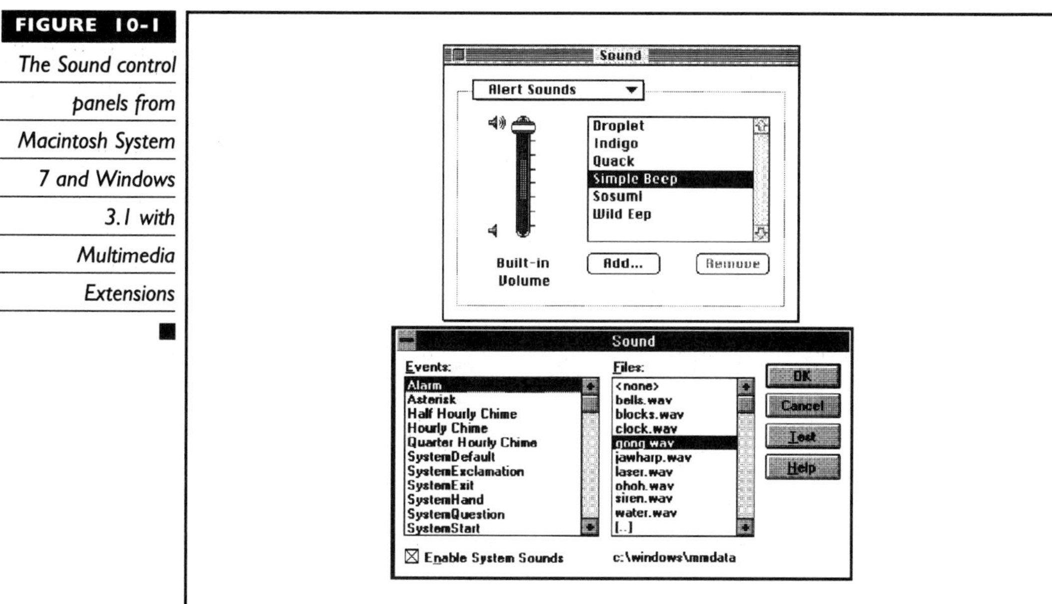

Using System 7 and newer Macintosh models with a connected microphone or any Macintosh with a sound digitizing device like MacRecorder, you can record and label new system sounds. This recording software is built into System 7:

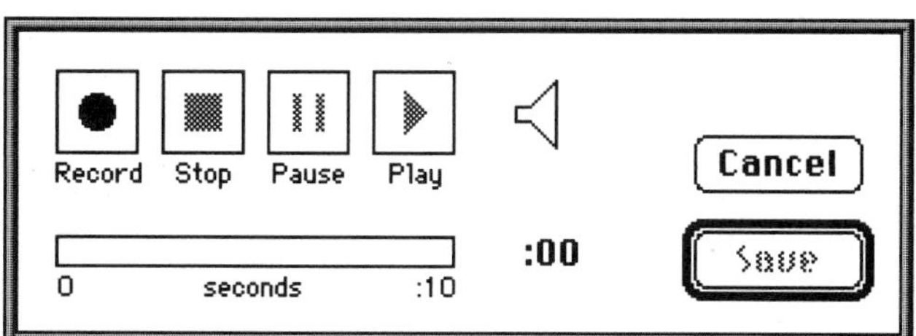

MIDI Versus Digital Audio

MIDI (Musical Instrument Digital Interface) is a communications standard developed in the early 1980s for electronic musical instruments and computers. It allows music and sound synthesizers from different manufacturers to communicate with each other by sending messages along cables connected to the devices. MIDI provides a protocol for passing detailed descriptions of a musical score, such as the notes, sequences of notes, and what instrument will play these notes. But MIDI data is not digitized sound—it is a shorthand representation of music stored in numeric form. A MIDI file is a list of time-stamped commands that are recordings of musical actions (the pressing down of a piano key or a sustain pedal, for example, or the movement of a control wheel or slider) that, when sent to a MIDI playback device, results in sound. A concise MIDI message can cause a complex sound or sequence of sounds to play on an instrument or synthesizer, so MIDI files tend to be significantly smaller (per second of sound delivered to the user) than equivalent digitized waveform files.

In contrast to MIDI data, *digital audio data* is the actual representation of a sound, stored in the form of thousands of individual numbers (called *samples*). The digital data represents the instantaneous amplitude (or loudness) of a sound at discrete slices of time. Because it is not device-dependent, digital audio sounds the same every time it is played. But that consistency comes at a price: large data storage files.

MIDI data are to digital audio data what vector or drawn graphics are to bitmapped graphics. That is, MIDI data is device-dependent; digital data is not. Just as the appearance of vector graphics differs depending on the printer device or display screen, the sounds produced by MIDI music files depend on the particular MIDI device used for playback. Similarly, a roll of perforated player-piano score sounds different played on a concert grand than on a honky-tonk piano. Digital data, on the other hand, sounds more or less identical regardless of the playback system. The MIDI standard is like Postscript, letting instruments communicate in a well understood language.

MIDI has several advantages over digital audio and two huge disadvantages. First, the advantages:

- MIDI files are much more compact than digital audio files, and the size of a MIDI file is completely independent of playback quality. In general, MIDI files will be 200 to 1000 times smaller than CD-quality digital audio files. Because MIDI files are small, they don't take up as much RAM, disk space, and CPU resources.
- In some cases, MIDI files may sound better than digital audio files if the MIDI sound source you are using is of high quality.
- You can change the length of a MIDI file (by varying its tempo) without changing the pitch of the music or degrading the audio quality. MIDI data is completely editable—right down to the level of an individual note. You can manipulate the smallest detail of a MIDI composition (often with sub-millisecond accuracy) in ways that are impossible with digital audio.

Now for the disadvantages: because MIDI data isn't sound, you can be certain that playback will be accurate only if the MIDI playback device is identical to the device used for production. Even with the General MIDI standard (see the "Making MIDI Audio" section, later in this chapter), the sound of a MIDI instrument varies according to the electronics of the playback device and the sound generation method it uses. Also, MIDI cannot easily be used to play back spoken dialog, although expensive and technically tricky digital samplers are available.

The pros and cons of working with digital audio are more or less the reverse of those for MIDI data and are described in Table 10-2.

In general, the most important advantage of digital audio is its consistent playback quality, but this is where MIDI is the least reliable. With digital audio you can be more confident that the audio track for your multimedia project will sound as good in the end as it did in the beginning when you created it. For this reason, it's no surprise that digital audio is used far more frequently than MIDI data for multimedia sound tracks.

There are two additional and often more compelling reasons to work with digital audio:

- A wider selection of application software and system support for digital audio is available for both the Macintosh and Windows platforms.
- The preparation and programming required for creating digital audio do not demand a knowledge of music theory; working with MIDI data usually does require a modicum of familiarity with musical scores as well as audio production.

Medium	Advantages	Disadvantages
MIDI	Compact file size. Low processor overhead. May sound better than digital audio in some circumstances. Lets you manipulate all details of a composition. Ability to scale time without changing pitch.	Unreliable playback except in controlled environments. Can't produce spoken dialog. More difficult to work with than digital audio. Usually requires some musical knowledge.
Digital audio	More reliable playback. Potentially highest audio quality.	Does not let you manipulate all details of a composition. Huge files. Significant processor overhead.

TABLE 10-2 *Pros and Cons of MIDI Versus Digital Audio* ■

Choosing Between MIDI and Digital Audio

In general, use MIDI data in the following circumstances:

- Digital audio won't work because you don't have enough RAM, hard disk space, or CPU processing power
- You have a high-quality MIDI sound source
- You have complete control over the playback hardware
- You don't need spoken dialog

In general, use digital audio in the following circumstances:

- You don't have control over the playback hardware
- You have the computing resources to handle digital files
- You need spoken dialog

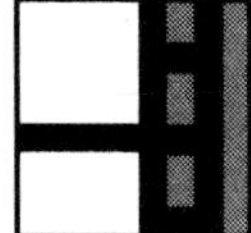

tip *It is possible to use both MIDI and digital audio together in the same project. Software tools, such as Passport's Alchemy and Producer, allow you to work with both types of data at the same time.*

Digital Audio

You can digitize sound from a microphone, a synthesizer, existing tape recordings, live radio and television broadcasts, popular CDs, and your favorite long-playing records. In fact, you can digitize sounds from any source, natural or prerecorded. The hardware and software requirements for digitizing sound are discussed in Chapters 4 and 6.

Digitized sound is *sampled sound*. Every *n*th fraction of a second, a sample of sound is taken and stored as digital information in bits and bytes. How often the samples are taken is the *sampling rate*, and the amount of information stored about each sample is the *sample size*. The more often you take a sample and the more data you store about that sample, the finer the resolution and quality of the captured sound when it is played back.

The three sampling frequencies most often used in multimedia are CD-Audio quality 44.1KHz (kilohertz), 22.05KHz, and 11.025KHz. Sample sizes are either 8 bits or 16 bits. The larger the sample size, the better the

FIGURE 10-2

It is impossible to reconstruct the original waveform if the sampling frequency is too low

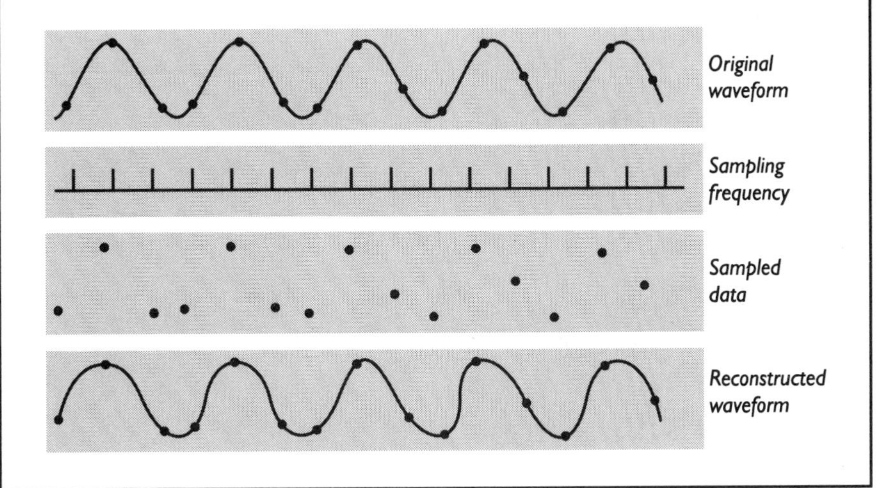

data describes the recorded sound. An 8-bit sample size provides 256 equal units to describe the dynamic range or amplitude—the level of sound at that time—of the slice of sound captured. A 16-bit sample size, on the other hand, provides a staggering 65,536 equal units to describe the dynamic range. As you can see in Figure 10-2, slices of analog waveforms are sampled at various frequencies, and each discrete sample is then stored either as 8 or 16 bits of data.

The value of each sample is rounded off to the nearest integer (*quantization*), and if the amplitude is greater than the intervals available, *clipping* of the top and bottom of the wave occurs. See Figure 10-3. Quantization can produce an unwanted background hissing noise, and clipping may severely distort the sound.

Preparing Digital Audio Files

Preparing digital audio files is fairly straightforward. If you have analog source material—that is, music or sound effects that you have recorded on analog media such as cassette tapes—the first step is to digitize the analog material by recording it onto computer-readable digital media. In most cases, this just means playing sound from one device (like a tape recorder) right into your computer, using appropriate audio digitizing software.

You want to focus on two crucial aspects of preparing digital audio files:

- Balancing the need for sound quality with your available RAM and hard disk resources
- Setting proper recording levels to get a good, clean recording

FIGURE 10-3

Examples of quantizing and clipping

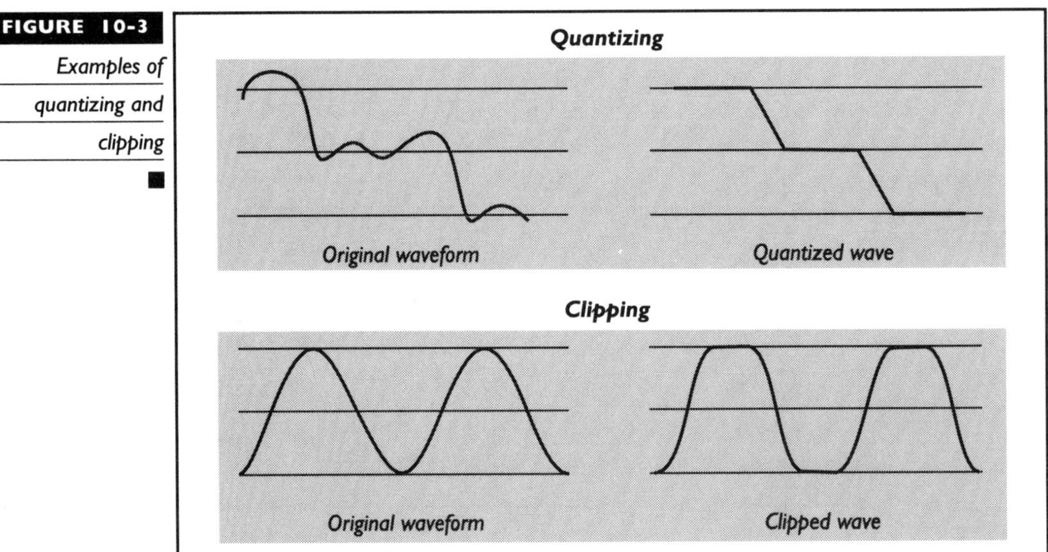

File Size Versus Quality

Remember that the sampling rate determines the frequency make-up of the recording. Sampling at higher rates more accurately captures the high-frequency content of your sound. *Resolution* determines the accuracy with which a sound can be digitized. Using more bits yields a recording that sounds more like its original.

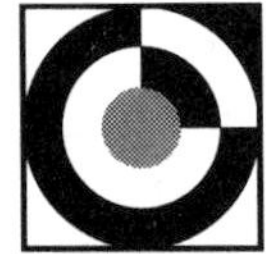

warning *The higher the sound quality, the larger your file will be.*

Stereo recordings are more lifelike and realistic, because human beings have two ears. Mono recordings are fine, but tend to sound a bit "flat" and uninteresting when compared with stereo recordings. Stereo sound files require twice as much storage space as mono files.

Table 10-3 provides some commonly available sampling rates and resolutions, with resulting file sizes.

Here are the formulas for determining the size (in bytes) of a digital recording. For a monophonic recording:

*sampling rate * duration of recording in seconds * (bit resolution / 8) * 1*

Sampling Rate	Resolution	Stereo or Mono	Bytes Needed for 1 Minute	Comments
44.1KHz	16-bit	Stereo	10.5MB	CD-quality recording; the recognized standard of audio quality.
44.1KHz	16-bit	Mono	5.25MB	A good trade-off for high-quality recordings of mono sources such as voice-overs.
44.1KHz	8-bit	Stereo	5.25MB	Achieves highest playback quality on low-end devices such as most of the sound cards in Windows PCs.
44.1KHz	8-bit	Mono	2.6MB	An appropriate trade-off for recording a mono source.
22.05KHz	16-bit	Stereo	5.25MB	Darker sounding than CD-quality recording because of the lower sampling rate, but still full and "present" because of high bit resolution and stereo.
22.05KHz	16-bit	Mono	2.5MB	Not a bad choice for speech, but better to trade some fidelity for a lot of disk space by dropping down to 8-bit.
22.05KHz	8-bit	Stereo	2.6MB	A very popular choice for reasonable stereo recording where full bandwidth playback is not possible.
22.05KHz	8-bit	Mono	1.3MB	A thinner sound than the choice just above, but very usable. Any Macintosh or any MPC can play back this type of file. About as good as listening to your TV set.
11KHz	8-bit	Stereo	1.3MB	At this low a sampling rate, there are few advantages to using stereo.
11KHz	8-bit	Mono	650K	In practice, probably as low as you can go and still get usable results. Very dark and muffled.
5.5KHz	8-bit	Stereo	650K	Stereo not effective.
5.5KHz	8-bit	Mono	325K	About as good as a bad telephone connection.

TABLE 10-3 *One-Minute Digital Audio Recordings at Common Sampling Rates and Resolutions* ■

For a stereo recording:

*sampling rate * duration of recording in seconds * (bit resolution / 8) * 2*

Thus the formula for a 10-second recording at 22.05 kHz, 8-bit resolution would be

*22050 * 10 * 8 / 8 * 1*

which equals 220,500 bytes. A 10-second stereo recording at 44.1 kHz, 16-bit resolution (meeting the CD-quality Red Book Audio standards—an international recording standard discussed later in this chapter) would be

44100 * 10 * 16 / 8 * 2

which equals 1,764,000 bytes. A 40-second mono recording at 11 kHz, 8-bit resolution would be

11000 * 40 * 8 / 8 * 1

which equals 440,000 bytes.

Mmm..Music, Mmm..Motion, Mmm..Megabytes!

Sharon Klocek, Producer, Visual In-Seitz, Inc., while clearing off her hard-drive.

Consumer-grade audio compact discs are recorded in stereo at a sampling rate of 44.1KHz and a 16-bit resolution. Fortunately, for hard disk storage requirements at least, user expectations of audio quality are somewhat lower for computer-based multimedia presentations than they are for Grammy Award-winning recordings (see Vaughan's Law of Multimedia Minimums in the "Production Tips" section of this chapter). Particularly on the Macintosh, 8-bit, 22KHz recordings are typical. Even lower rates are used for sound effects in many games.

tip *There is no benefit to digitizing audio at a higher specification than can be used by the target playback device. Although there is continuing improvement in the capability of both Macintoshes and PCs, most are currently limited to 8-bit resolution.*

Setting Proper Recording Levels

A distorted recording sounds terrible. If the signal you feed into your computer is too "hot" to handle, the result is an unpleasant crackling or background ripping noise. Conversely, recordings made at too low a level are often unusable because the amount of sound recorded does not sufficiently exceed the residual noise levels of the recording process itself. The trick is to set the right levels when you record.

Any good piece of digital audio recording and editing software will display digital meters to let you know how loud your sound is. Watch the meters closely during recording, and you'll never have a problem. Unlike analog meters that usually have a 0 setting somewhere in the middle and extend up into ranges like +5, +8, or even higher, digital meters peak out. To avoid distortion, do not cross over this limit. If this happens, lower your volume (either by lowering the input level of the recording device or the output level of your source) and try again. Try to keep peak levels between –3 and –10. Anytime you go over the peak, whether you can hear it or not, you introduce distortion into the recording.

Editing Digital Recordings

Once a recording has been made, it will almost certainly need to be edited. Figure 10-4 shows some of the edit tools in Passport's Alchemy software, and Figure 10-5 illustrates SoundEdit Pro's special effects menu. The basic sound editing operations that most multimedia producers need are described in the paragraphs that follow.

TRIMMING Removing "dead air" or blank space from the front of a recording and any unnecessary extra time off the end. Trimming even a few seconds here and there might make a big difference in your file size. Trimming is typically accomplished by dragging the mouse cursor over a graphic representation of your recording and choosing a menu command such as Cut, Clear, Erase, or Silence.

SPLICING AND ASSEMBLY Using the same tools mentioned for trimming, you will probably want to remove the extraneous noises that inevitably creep into a recording. Even the most controlled studio voice-overs require touch-up. Also, you may need to assemble longer recordings by cutting and pasting

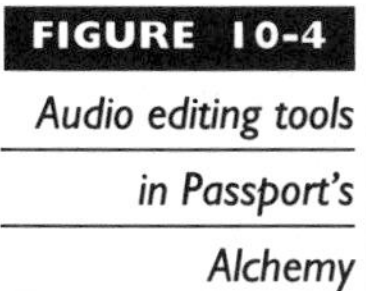

FIGURE 10-4 *Audio editing tools in Passport's Alchemy*

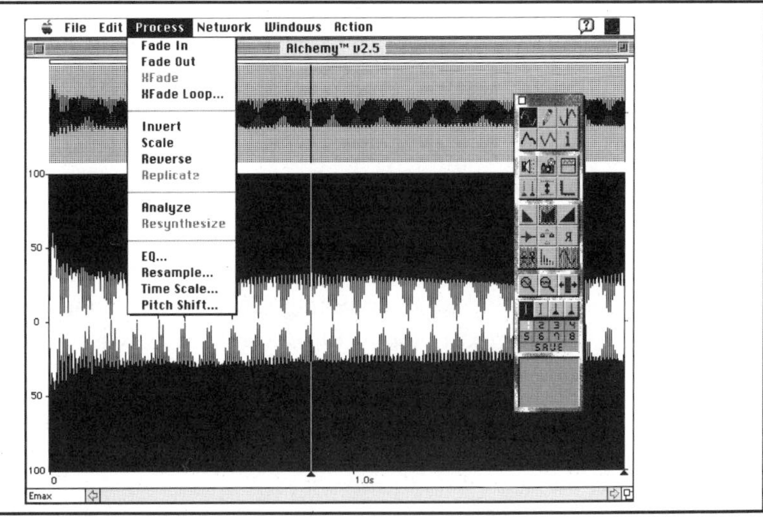

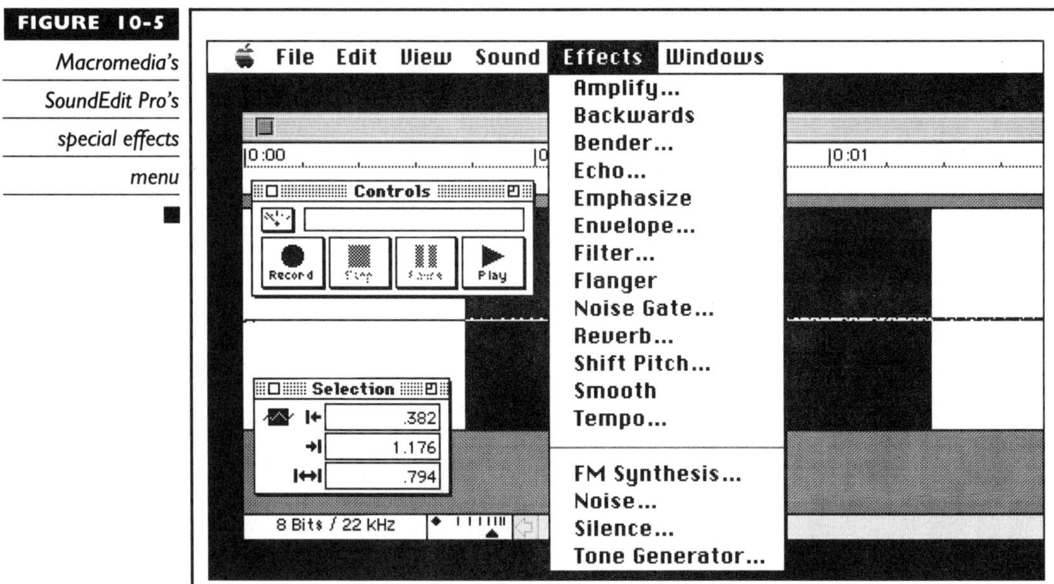

FIGURE 10-5 Macromedia's SoundEdit Pro's special effects menu

together many shorter ones. In the old days, this was done by splicing and assembling actual pieces of magnetic tape.

VOLUME ADJUSTMENTS If you are trying to assemble ten different recordings into a single sound track, there is little chance that all the segments will have the same volume. To provide a consistent volume level, select all the data in the file, and raise or lower the overall volume by a certain amount. Don't increase the volume too much, or you may distort the file.

FORMAT CONVERSION In some cases, your digital audio editing software might read a format different from that read by your presentation or authoring program. Most Macintosh sound-editing software will save files in SND and AIF formats, and most authoring systems will read these formats. In Windows, most editing software writes .WAV files. The Convert and WaveEdit utilities in Windows allow you to read the Macintosh .AIF format. (You can read more about formats in the "Audio File Formats" section later in this chapter.)

RESAMPLING OR DOWNSAMPLING If you have recorded and edited your sounds at 16-bit sampling rates but are using lower rates and resolutions in your project, you must resample or downsample the file. This process saves considerable disk space.

FADE-INS AND FADE-OUTS Most programs offer enveloping capability, useful for long sections that you wish to fade in or fade out gradually. This enveloping is important to smooth out the very beginning and the very end of a sound file.

EQUALIZATION Some programs offer digital equalization (EQ) capabilities that allow you to modify a recording's frequency content to sound brighter or darker.

TIME STRETCHING More advanced programs let you alter the length (in time) of a sound file without changing its pitch. This feature can be very useful, but watch out—most time-stretching algorithms will severely degrade the audio quality of the file if the length is altered more than a few percent in either direction.

DIGITAL SIGNAL PROCESSING (DSP) Some programs allow you to process the signal with effects such as reverberation, multitap delay, chorus, flange, and other special effects.

Being able to process a sound source with effects can greatly add to a project. To create an environment by placing the sound inside a room, hall, or even a cathedral brings depth and dimension to a project. But a little can go a long way—do not overdo the sound effects! Once a sound effect is processed and mixed onto a track, it cannot be further edited, so always save an original that you can tweak again if you are not happy.

REVERSING SOUNDS Another simple manipulation is to reverse all or a portion of a digital audio recording. Sounds, particularly spoken dialog, can produce a surreal, otherworldly effect when played backward.

Making MIDI Audio

Composing your own original score can be one of the most creative and rewarding aspects of building a multimedia project, and MIDI is the quickest, easiest, and most flexible tool for this task. Yet creating an original MIDI score is hard work. Knowing something about music, being able to play the piano, and having a lot of good ideas are just the prerequisites to building a good score; beyond that, it takes time and musical skill to work with MIDI.

Happily, you can always hire someone to do the job for you. In addition to the talented MIDI composers who charge substantial rates for their services, there are also many young composers available who want to get into multimedia. With a little research, you can often find a MIDI musician to work for limited compensation. Remember, however, that you often get what you pay for.

To make MIDI scores, you will need sequencer software (such as Midisoft Studio for Windows, illustrated in Figure 10-6), and a sound synthesizer (typically built into the sound board on PCs, but an add-on board or peripheral for the Macintosh). A MIDI keyboard is also useful to simplify the creation of musical scores. The MIDI keyboard is not, however, necessary for playback unless the keyboard has its own built-in synthesizer (most do) that you wish to specify for playback. Sequencer software lets you record and edit MIDI data and quantizes your score to adjust for timing inconsistencies (a great feature for those who can't keep the beat). The sequencer software records your actions on the MIDI keyboard (or another MIDI device) in real time and plays back exactly the notes you played on the keyboard; the software may also print a neatly penned copy of your score to paper. Sound boards and other hardware components of MIDI are discussed in Chapter 5.

A MIDI file can contain up to 16 channels of music data, so you can record many different instruments and play them back, each on a different channel. You can map your sequencer to play violin or harpsichord or sing as a celestial choir even though you enter the notes by keyboard. The master keyboard becomes simply an input device; and with a built-in synthesizer, it can also play back.

Instruments that you can synthesize are identified by a General MIDI numbering system that ranges from 0 to 127 (see Table 10-4). (The General MIDI Standard is described later in this chapter.) Until this system came along, there was always a risk that a MIDI file originally composed with, say, piano, electric guitar, and bass, might be played back with piccolo,

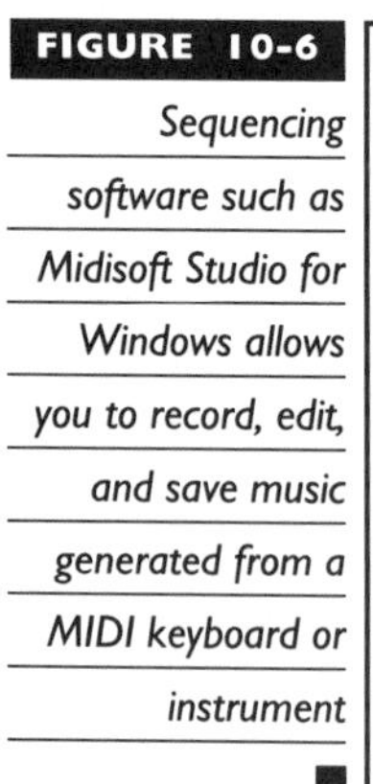

FIGURE 10-6 *Sequencing software such as Midisoft Studio for Windows allows you to record, edit, and save music generated from a MIDI keyboard or instrument*

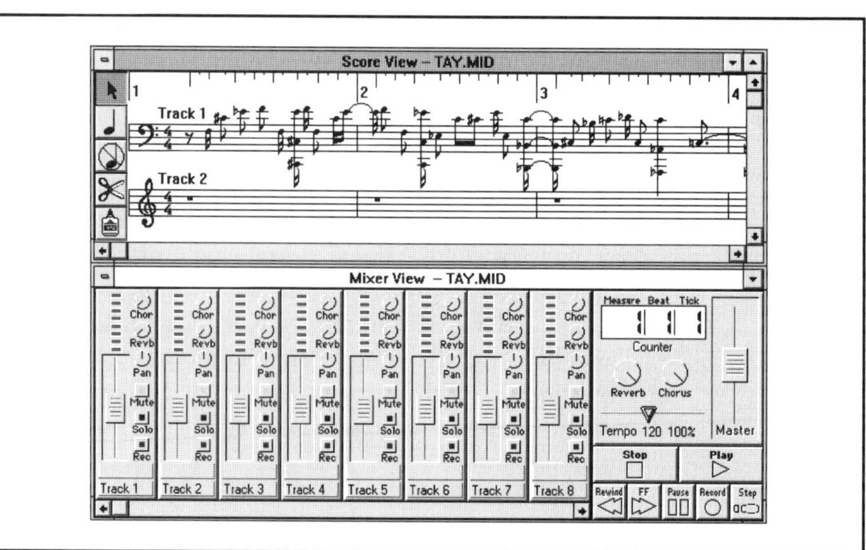

tambourine, and glockenspiel if the ID numbers were not precisely mapped to match your original hardware setup. This was usually the case when you played a MIDI file on a MIDI configuration different from the one that recorded the file. General MIDI offers not only de facto standard mapping of the most common musical instruments but also mapping for the master keyboard keys that represent drum and percussion sounds. MIDI is flexible, and you can always remap your sounds to nonstandard instruments. (Windows provides a control panel utility called MIDI Mapper to help with this.) Most multimedia sound boards for the PC and Macintosh follow the General MIDI specifications, and they have built-in synthesizers that can reproduce most of the sounds listed in Table 10-4.

ID	Sound	ID	Sound
0	Acoustic grand piano	33	Electric bass (finger)
1	Bright acoustic piano	34	Electric bass (pick)
2	Electric grand piano	35	Fretless bass
3	Honky-tonk piano	36	Slap bass 1
4	Rhodes piano	37	Slap bass 2
5	Chorused piano	38	Synth bass 1
6	Harpsichord	39	Synth bass 2
7	Clarinet	40	Violin
8	Celesta	41	Viola
9	Glockenspiel	42	Cello
10	Music box	43	Contrabass
11	Vibraphone	44	Tremolo strings
12	Marimba	45	Pizzicato strings
13	Xylophone	46	Orchestral harp
14	Tubular Bells	47	Timpani
15	Dulcimer	48	String ensemble 1
16	Hammond organ	49	String ensemble 2
17	Percussive organ	50	SynthStrings 1
18	Rock organ	51	SynthStrings 2
19	Church organ	52	Choir aahs
20	Reed organ	53	Voice oohs
21	Accordion	54	Synth voice
22	Harmonica	55	Orchestra hit
23	Tango accordion	56	Trumpet
24	Acoustic guitar (nylon)	57	Trombone
25	Acoustic guitar (steel)	58	Tuba
26	Electric guitar (jazz)	59	Muted trumpet
27	Electric guitar (clean)	60	French horn
28	Electric guitar (muted)	61	Brass section
29	Overdriven guitar	62	Synth brass 1
30	Distortion guitar	63	Synth brass 2
31	Guitar harmonics	64	Soprano saxophone
32	Acoustic bass	65	Alto saxophone

TABLE 10-4 *General MIDI Instrument Sounds* (continued)

ID	Sound	ID	Sound
66	Tenor saxophone	115	Wood block
67	Baritone saxophone	116	Taiko drum
68	Oboe	117	Melodic tom
69	English horn	118	Synth drum
70	Bassoon	119	Reverse cymbal
71	Clarinet	120	Guitar fret noise
72	Piccolo	121	Breath noise
73	Flute	122	Seashore
74	Recorder	123	Bird tweet
75	Pan flute	124	Telephone ring
76	Bottle blow	125	Helicopter
77	Shakuhachi	126	Applause
78	Whistle	127	Gunshot
79	Ocarina	**Percussion Keys**	
80	Lead 1 (Square)	35	Acoustic bass drum
81	Lead 2 (Sawtooth)	36	Bass drum 1
82	Lead 3 (Calliope lead)	37	Side stick
83	Lead 4 (Chiff lead)	38	Acoustic snare
84	Lead 5 (Charang)	39	Hand clap
85	Lead 6 (Voice)	40	Electric snare
86	Lead 7 (Fifths)	41	Low-floor tom
87	Lead 8 (Bass + lead)	42	Closed high-hat
88	Pad 1 (New Age)	43	High-floor tom
89	Pad 2 (Warm)	44	Pedal high-hat
90	Pad 3 (Polysynth)	45	Low tom
91	Pad 4 (Choir)	46	Open high-hat
92	Pad 5 (Bowed)	47	Low-mid tom
93	Pad 6 (Metallic)	48	High-mid tom
94	Pad 7 (Halo)	49	Crash cymbal 1
95	Pad 8 (Sweep)	50	High tom
96	FX 1 (Rain)	51	Ride cymbal 1
97	FX 2 (Soundtrack)	52	Chinese cymbal
98	FX 3 (Crystal)	53	Ride bell
99	FX 4 (Atmosphere)	54	Tambourine
100	FX 5 (Brightness)	55	Splash cymbal
101	FX 6 (Goblins)	56	Cowbell
102	FX 7 (Echoes)	57	Crash cymbal 2
103	FX 8 (Sci-Fi)	58	Vibraslap
104	Sitar	59	Ride cymbal 2
105	Banjo	60	High bongo
106	Shamisen	61	Low bongo
107	Koto	62	Mute high conga
108	Kalimba	63	Open high conga
109	Bagpipe	64	Low conga
110	Fiddle	65	High timbale
111	Shanai	66	Low timbale
112	Tinkle bell	67	High agogo
113	Agogo	68	Low agogo
114	Steel drums	69	Cabasa

TABLE 10-4 *General MIDI Instrument Sounds* (continued) ■

ID	Sound	ID	Sound
70	Maracas	76	High wood block
71	Short whistle	77	Low wood block
72	Long whistle	78	Mute cuica
73	Short guiro	79	Open cuica
74	Long guiro	80	Mute triangle
75	Claves	81	Open triangle

TABLE 10-4 *General MIDI Instrument Sounds* ■

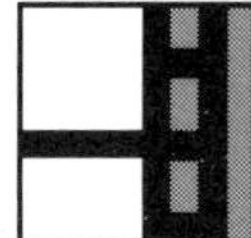

tip *Making MIDI files is as complex as recording good sampled files, so often it pays to find someone already set up with the equipment and skills to create your score rather than investing in both the hardware and learning curve.*

Preparing MIDI Files

Once you have gathered your audio material, you will need to edit it to precisely fit your multimedia project. As you edit, you will continue to make creative decisions. Because MIDI data is so editable, you can make many fine adjustments to your music.

Remember that a MIDI file contains not a digital representation of sound, but rather a series of commands that inform a MIDI playback device what sounds to play and when to play them. You must begin your MIDI files with "setup" messages at the beginning of each track, to initialize important playback values for each musical part. There are no hard-and-fast rules for assigning these setup parameters. Microsoft, for example, encourages MIDI authors to specify at least an initial program change value (to specify an instrument sound) and an initial volume level. In practice, this is not sufficient. The guidelines following may help.

All setup data should be placed on the first clock tick of the first beat of the first measure in each track. In some sequencers, that location is 1|1|1 on the counter; in other programs, it may be 1|1|0. Because setup information affects each MIDI channel, if a sequence contains two or more tracks that use the same MIDI channel, the setup information need only appear on one of those tracks.

Each track should always contain these two types of setup data:

- Program change message
- Volume message (Controller #7)

Other data might include the following:

- Pan message (Controller #10)—if stereo
- Reverb message (Controller #91)—-for effects
- Chorus message (Controller #93)—for effects
- Sustain pedal message (Controller #64)—for performance control
- Pitchbend message—for performance control

The program change message tells your MIDI device what instrument sound to use for a particular part. The volume, pan, reverb, and chorus messages specify amounts or levels for that respective function. Some MIDI devices respond to these messages; others do not and just ignore them. The sustain pedal message always has a value of 0 (off), to make sure any instruments that might have been left sustaining from a previously played piece will not adversely affect the current piece; otherwise, notes would play and then be unable to turn themselves off. The pitchbend message, too, always has a value of 0, to reset any instruments that might have used pitchbend in a previous piece.

When editing note information, especially deleting or erasing data, be careful not to delete wanted controller information. After making an edit, if you suddenly have "stuck" notes, you most likely have rubbed out a #64 controller pedal sustain off message. Simply go into the edit window for that controller and enter a zero (0=off) value at the appropriate point in the music.

The same applies with pitch bend. If, after editing a track containing pitch bend information, you have an instrument with a mind of its own deciding to play in a different and most unpleasant key, then you have probably zapped part of some pitchbend data, the very important part where the controller returns to the zero point or neutral position. A lot of times it will be obvious when a note stops in mid-bend, but sometimes you may be uncertain because the return to zero happens *after* a note has sounded, so there is no auditory clue as to the nature of the problem. Again, go into the edit window and make the appropriate repairs. Or even easier, with a performance driven controller such as pitchbend, go to a new track with the same MIDI channel and replay the pitch wheel until you're satisfied! Then merge this with the original track to restore pitchbend without having to redo your entire well-tempered performance. This trick can be applied to other controllers as well. In fact, sometimes it is preferable to have a separate track only for controller data when things start to get complicated in that area.

MIDI's true place in multimedia work may be as a production tool rather than a delivery medium. MIDI is by far the best way to create original music for multimedia projects, so use MIDI to get the flexibility and creative control you want. Then, once the music is completed and fits your project, lock it down for delivery by turning it into digital audio data.

tip *Test your MIDI files thoroughly by playing them back on a variety of hardware devices before you incorporate them into your multimedia project.*

Playing Back Your MIDI Sounds

The MIDI instrument sounds that you hear played back by your score are generated either from mathematical formulas (FM synthesis) or from short digital recordings of actual instruments (sample playback). The difference between the two presents a serious hardware choice and cost consideration. The Macintosh CPU and most MIDI sound boards for the PC provide only FM synthesis, which is less-expensive technology. You pay more for boards or MIDI libraries that provide realistic instrument sounds or sound effects, but the improvement in quality of sample playback is truly remarkable and, sadly, proportional to cost. If you are considering using MIDI sounds in your work and want to invest in this technology, you must assess the difference in quality yourself. Do this in a studio or showroom, because this is not a simple decision on what minimum quality will suffice; the difference in perceived quality is as stark as that between a 16-color VGA display and a 256-color Super VGA display.

MIDI is more susceptible to variance in the playback environment than is waveform sound. Because the quality of MIDI playback depends on the MIDI hardware installed, developers often create custom MIDI music using high-end hardware to improve, edit, and carefully synchronize the MIDI music to their projects. The developer can then play and digitize the MIDI score into a waveform sound file. The waveform sound requires greater storage space, but the music will have the same quality when it is played in most end-user environments. (Even if the product is downsampled, you may find the trade-offs acceptable.)

Audio File Formats

When you create multimedia, it is likely that you will deal with file formats and translators for text, sounds, images, animation, or digital video clips. A sound file's format is simply a recognized methodology for organizing the digitized sound's data bits and bytes into a data file. The structure of the file must be known, of course, before the data can be saved or later loaded into a computer to be edited and/or played as sound.

On the Macintosh, digitized sounds may be stored as data files (.AIF or .SND) or they may be stored as resources in the resource fork of the system or application. The Macintosh uses a unique dual-fork file structure, and you will need to know whether the file resides in a resource fork or as a stand-alone .AIF file.

In Windows, digitized sounds are stored as wave files (.WAV), the default and most common format. The Microsoft PCM (Pulse Code Modulation) format and Apple's Audio Interchange File Format (AIFF), or .AIF (sometimes .IFF), are also understood and translated to and from .WAV format by WaveEdit and Convert, programs supplied with Microsoft's Multimedia Extensions for Windows.

There are many ways to store the bits and bytes that describe a sampled waveform sound. The method used for Red Book Audio data files on consumer-grade CDs is Linear Pulse Code Modulation. The CD-I (compact disk-interactive) format, developed by Philips as a variant of the Red Book standard, uses Adaptive Delta Pulse Code Modulation (ADPCM) to deliver 2 hours of high-fidelity stereo music or as many as 20 hours of voice-quality monaural audio, per compact disc. This CD-I format provides for interleaving ADPCM audio data with screen graphics or video to allow synchronization of audio and image without extensive data buffering. It requires, however, a special CD-ROM XA (extended architecture) player.

Both Macintosh and Windows can make use of MIDI files. A MIDI interface is built into many sound boards on the PC (and is a requirement for MPC computers). On the Macintosh, a MIDI adapter is required for MIDI instrument input and output. On both platforms, MIDI sounds are typically stored in files with the .MID extension.

Working with Sound on the Macintosh

The original 128K Macintosh, released in January, 1984, was technically a capable multimedia machine. It displayed bitmapped graphics (albeit in black and white) and, more significantly, boasted 8-bit digital audio capability right on the motherboard. In fact, the very first Macintosh actually introduced itself by voice when it was first unveiled by Steve Jobs. (See Chapter 4 to read what it said.)

Here's a little history: In order to use the Apple moniker, the original founders of Apple Computer, Inc., worked out an arrangement with the Beatles (yes, *those* Beatles). One part of that agreement stipulated that Apple

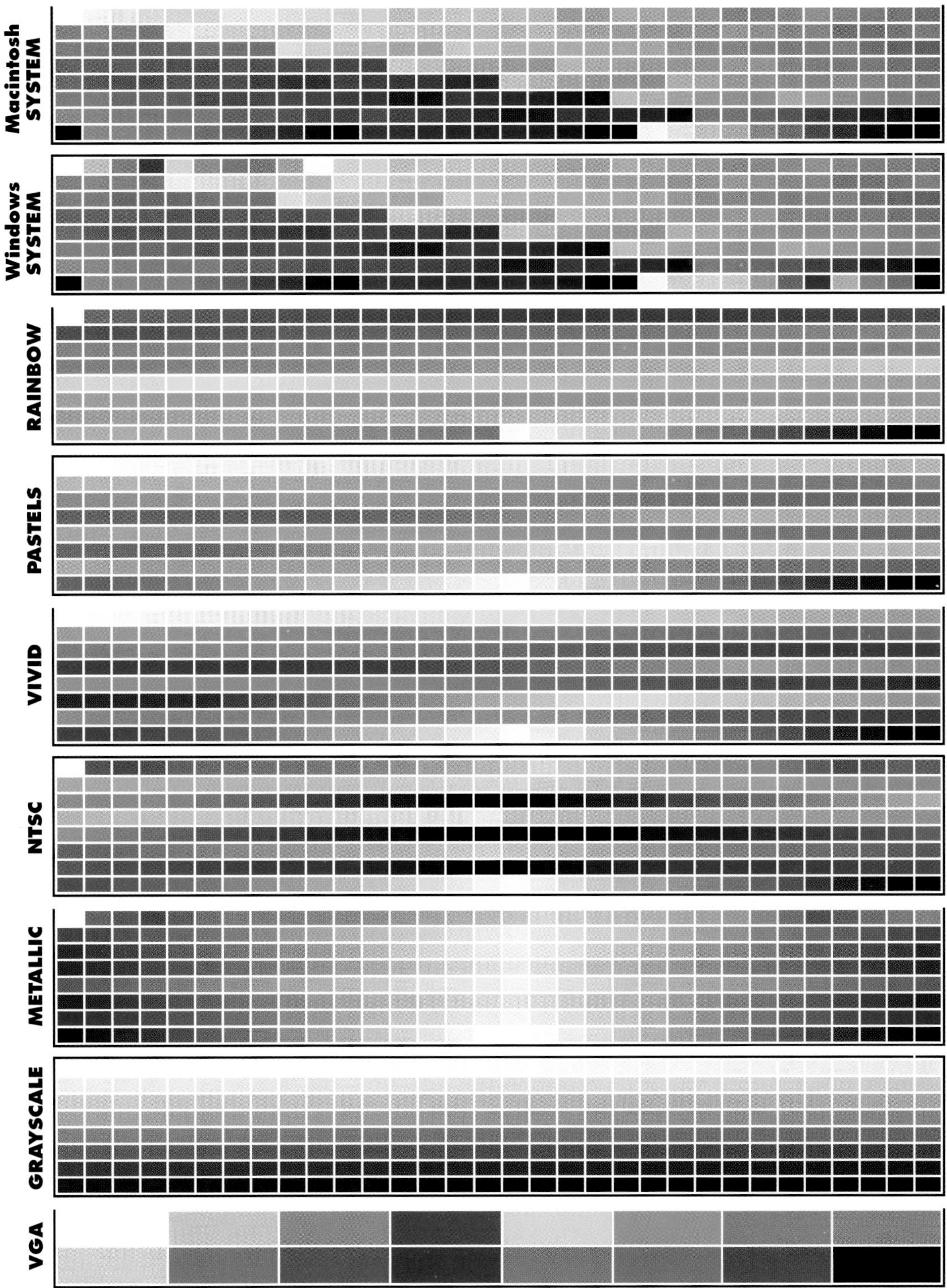

Color Plate 1:

These palettes of 256 colors (8-bit color depth) are provided in Macromedia's Director. Note the VGA palette: these are the colors available in 16-color VGA mode in Windows.

Color Plate 2:
The RGB (Red, Green, Blue) color space model used to specify the intensity of each color dot on a computer monitor. See Chapter 11 to learn about color on computers.

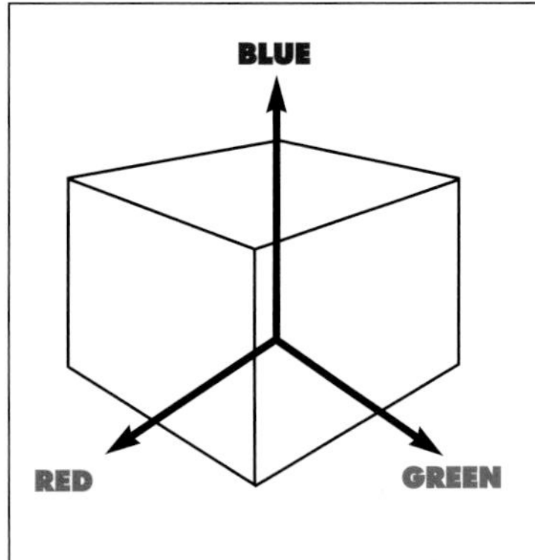

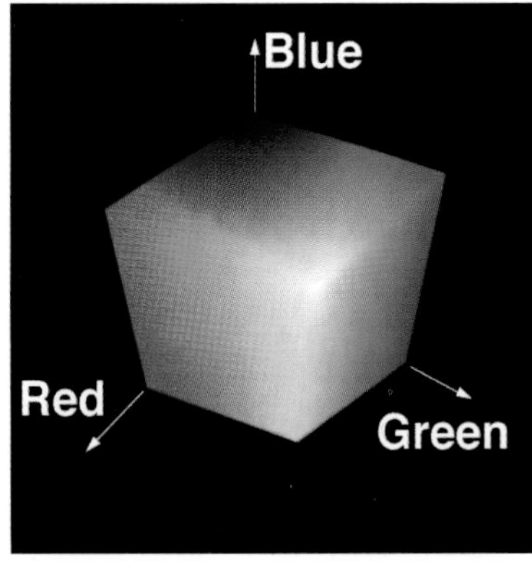

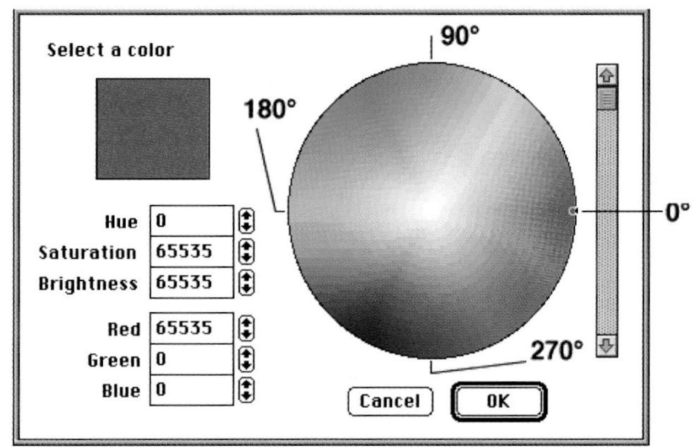

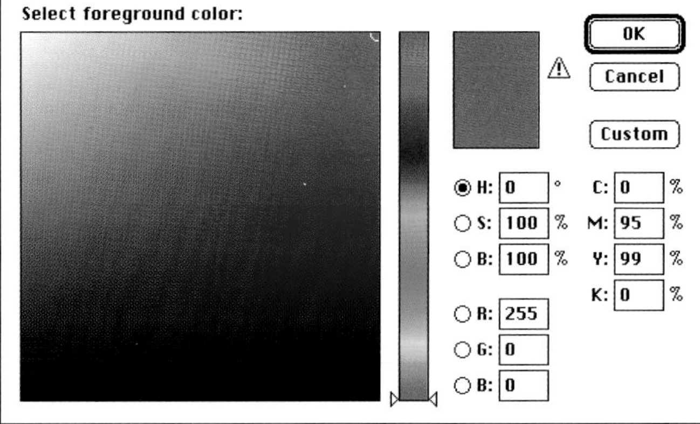

Color Plate 3:
Color pickers allow you to select a color using one or more different models of color space. The pickers shown above illustrate the RGB (red, green, blue), HSB (hue, saturation, brightness), and CMYK (cyan, magenta, yellow, black) models for choosing colors. These are described in Chapter 11.

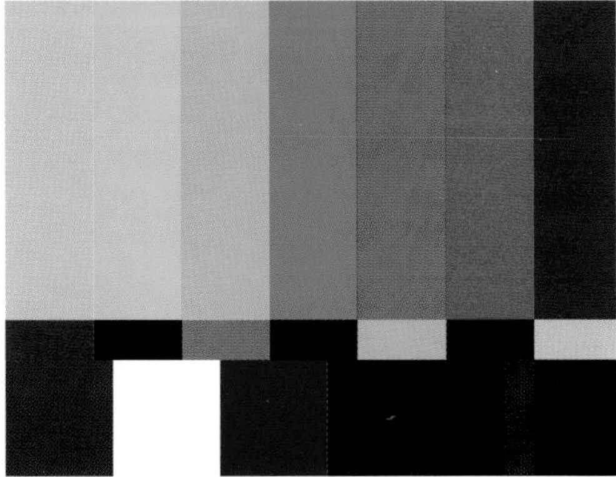

R: 204 G: 204 B: 204	R: 255 G: 255 B: 0	R: 0 G: 255 B: 255	R: 0 G: 255 B: 0	R: 255 G: 0 B: 255	R: 255 G: 0 B: 0	R: 0 G: 0 B: 255
R: 0 G: 0 B: 255	R: 19 G: 19 B: 19	R: 255 G: 0 B: 255	R: 19 G: 19 B: 19	R: 0 G: 255 B: 255	R: 19 G: 19 B: 19	R: 204 G: 204 B: 204

R: 8 G: 62 B: 89	R: 255 G: 255 B: 255	R: 58 G: 0 B: 126	R: 19 G: 19 B: 19	0 0 0	19 19 19	38 38 38	R: 19 G: 19 B: 19

Color Plate 4:
This SMPTE color bar pattern can be used at the beginning of a video tape for calibration. The RGB values of each bar are included so you can make your own screen using an image editing application. See Chapter 13.

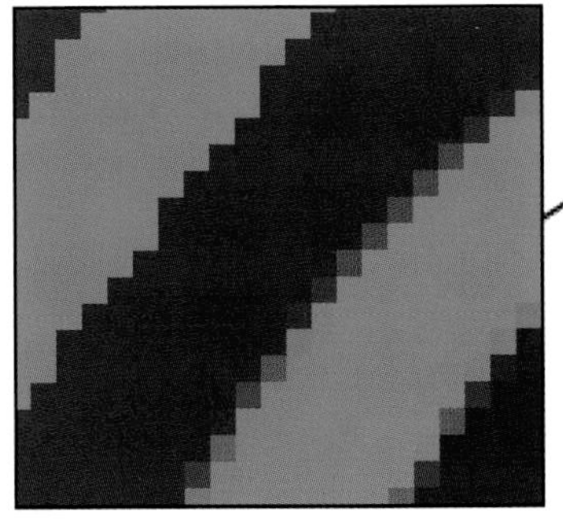

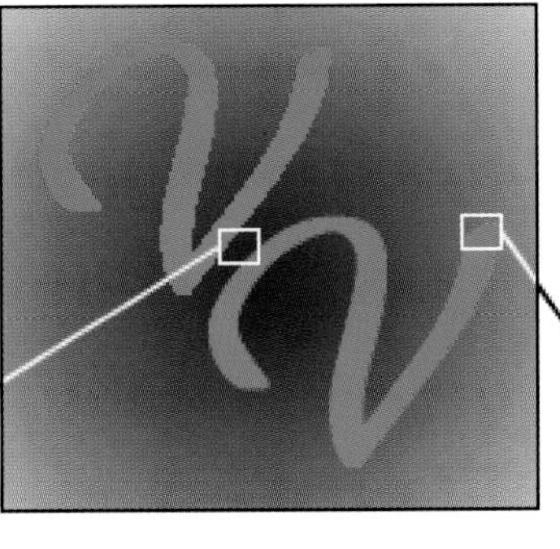

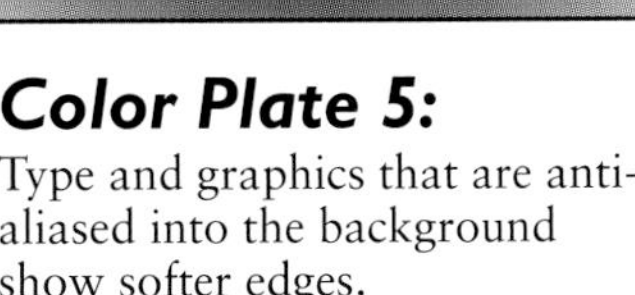

Color Plate 5:
Type and graphics that are anti-aliased into the background show softer edges.

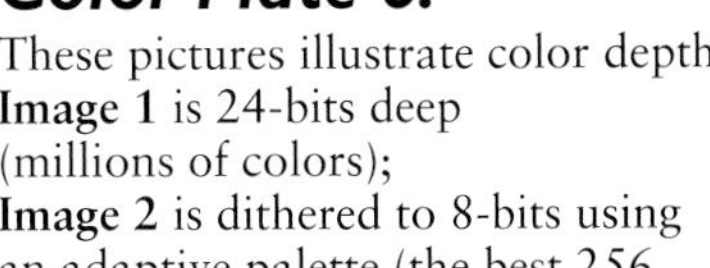

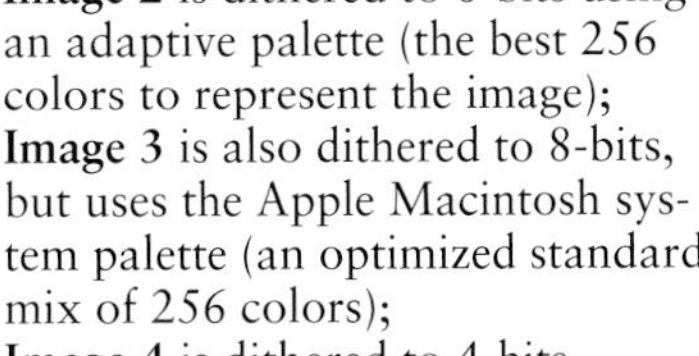

Color Plate 6:
These pictures illustrate color depth.
Image 1 is 24-bits deep (millions of colors);
Image 2 is dithered to 8-bits using an adaptive palette (the best 256 colors to represent the image);
Image 3 is also dithered to 8-bits, but uses the Apple Macintosh system palette (an optimized standard mix of 256 colors);
Image 4 is dithered to 4-bits (16 colors);
Image 5 is dithered to 8-bit grayscale (256 shades of gray);
Image 6 is dithered to 4-bit grayscale (16 shades of gray); and
Image 7 is dithered to 1-bit (two colors - in this case, black and white). Refer to Chapter 11.

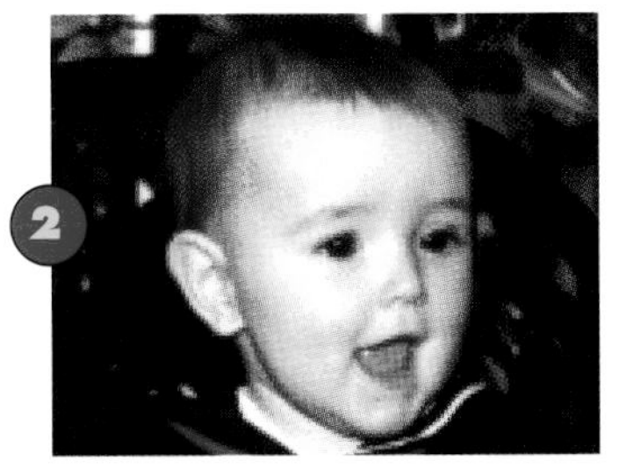

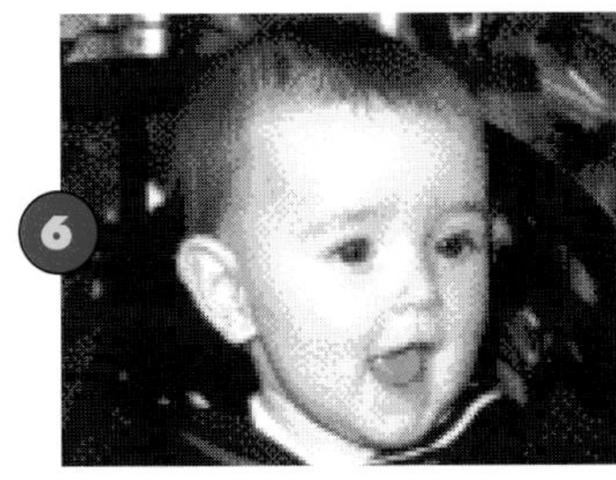

Color Plate 7:
Special effects for enhancing, altering, and manipulating bitmapped images are provided by most image editing applications, such as Picture Publisher (shown here, courtesy of Micrografx, Inc.), or as special plug-ins such as Kai's Power Tools for Photoshop.

Color Plate 8:
Both of these images were created on a computer using Fractal Design Painter with a pressure-sensitive stylus and special electronic watercolor effects. The lake scene is by Peter McCormick and the penguin by Peter and Caitlin Mitchell-Dayton.

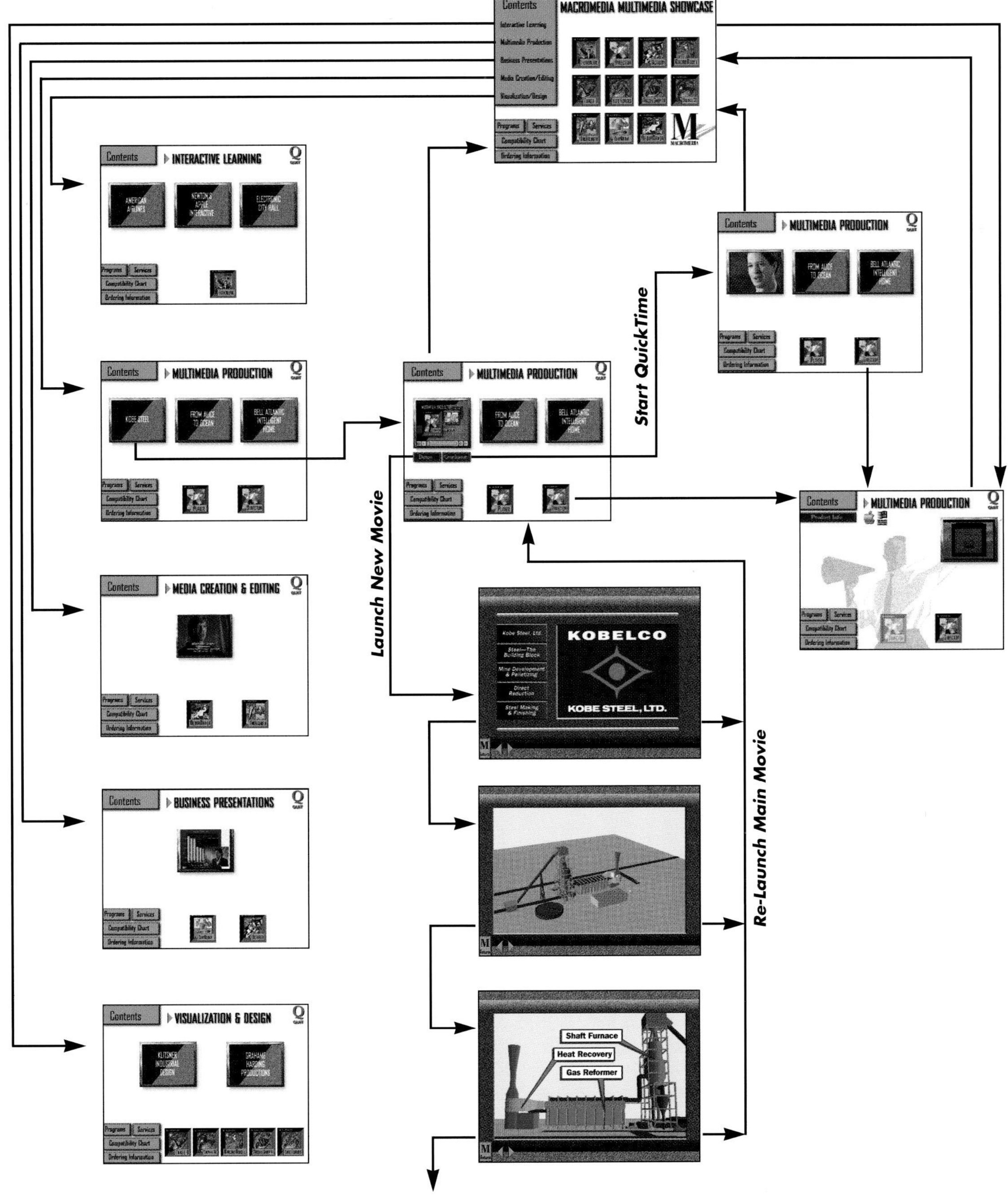

Color Plate 9:

A simplified navigation map for Macromedia's Product Showcase Version 2, a multimedia graphical user interface (GUI) written as a Director "movie" (see Chapter 8). It provides links to megabytes of information and content using mouse clicks on buttons or "hot" graphics. This map does not show the many sound narrations or QuickTime movies that play when a new screen opens or a button is clicked, nor does it show the myriad of possible routes through the content—there would be a confusing number of lines and arrows. Clearly, the linking of information in such easy-to-make GUIs demonstrates the power of multimedia. The Product Showcase Version 2 is included on the CD-ROM bound into this book.

Color Plate 10:
Eric James used only 48 custom colors in a 256-color palette to paint this credit screen. Shadows, embossing, and delicate highlighting can provide a subtle sense of depth and texture.

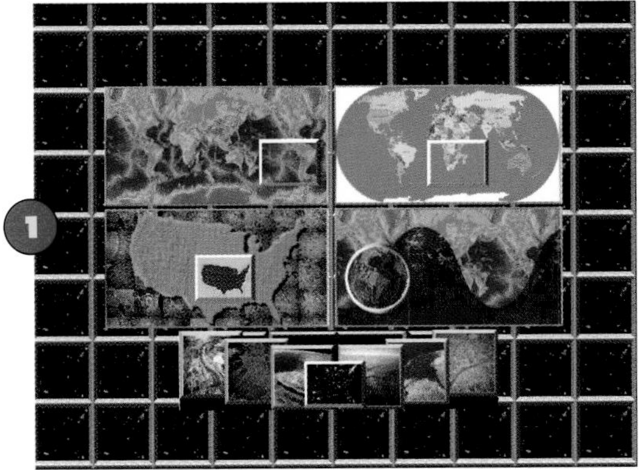

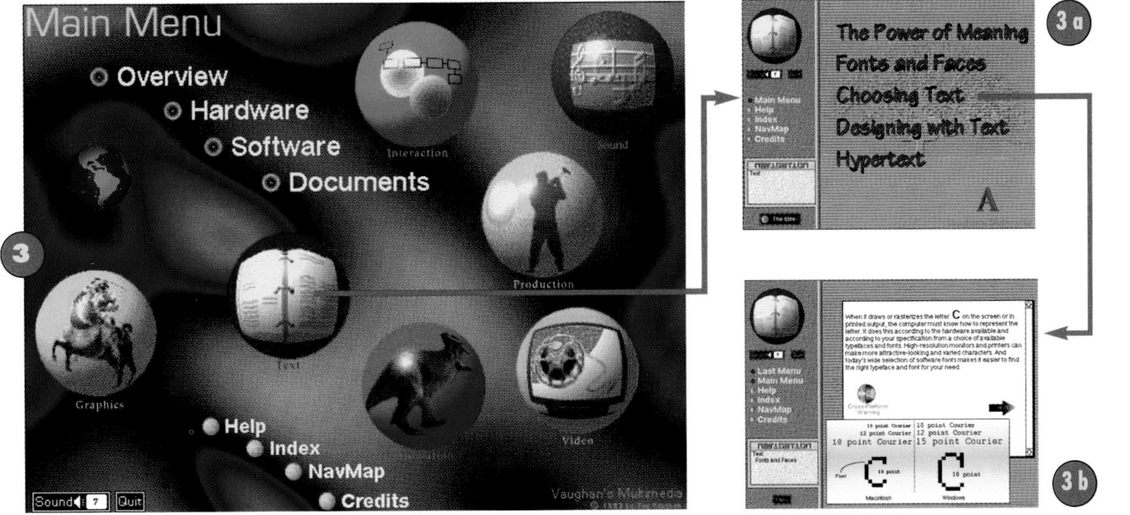

Color Plate 11:

There are many design approaches for buttons and interactive hot spots. **Screen 1** is from Small Blue Planet, The Real Picture Atlas (Now What Software); **screen 2** is from Wrath of the Gods (Luminaria); **screens 3, 3a, 3b**, and 5 are from the CD-ROM version of this book (available from Timestream, see the last page of this book); **screen 4** is from the Osborne/McGraw-Hill Catalog that is included on the CD-ROM bound into this book; **screen 5** shows the author and a few friends—click on any face for small-town secrets.

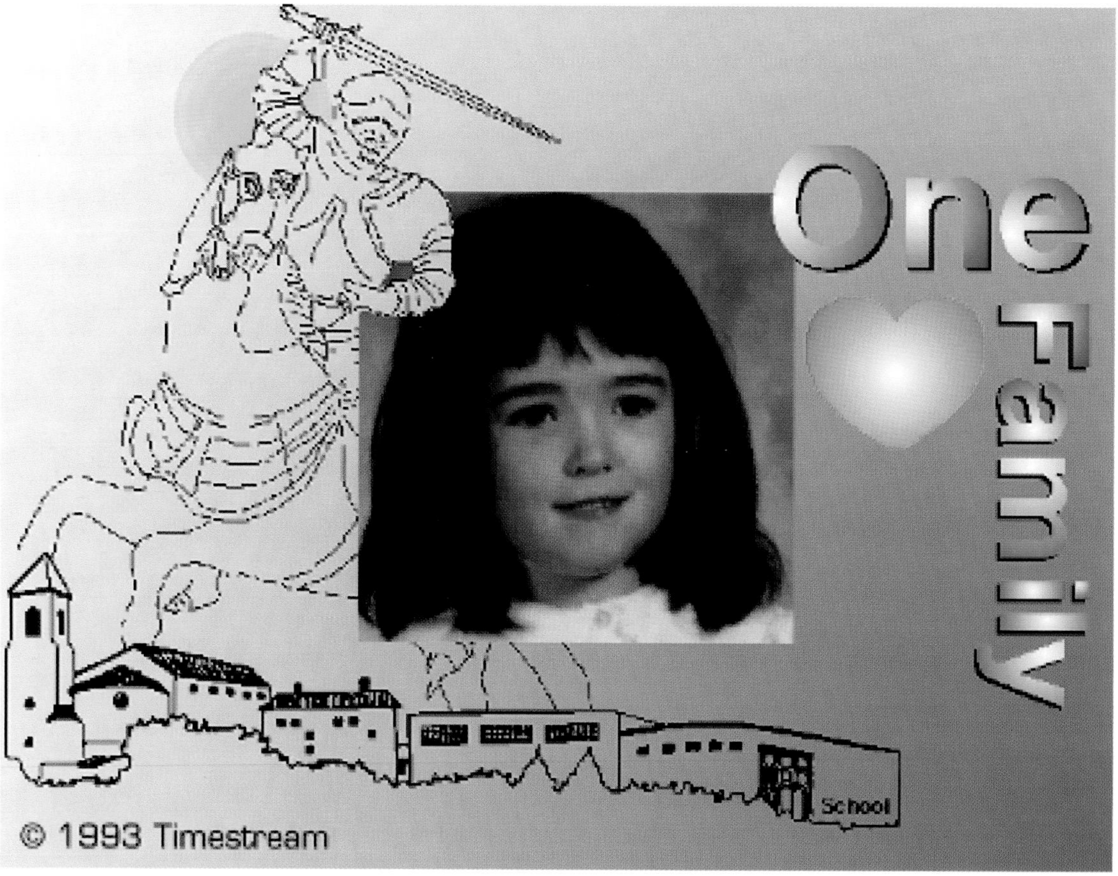

One
Family
School
© 1993 Timestream

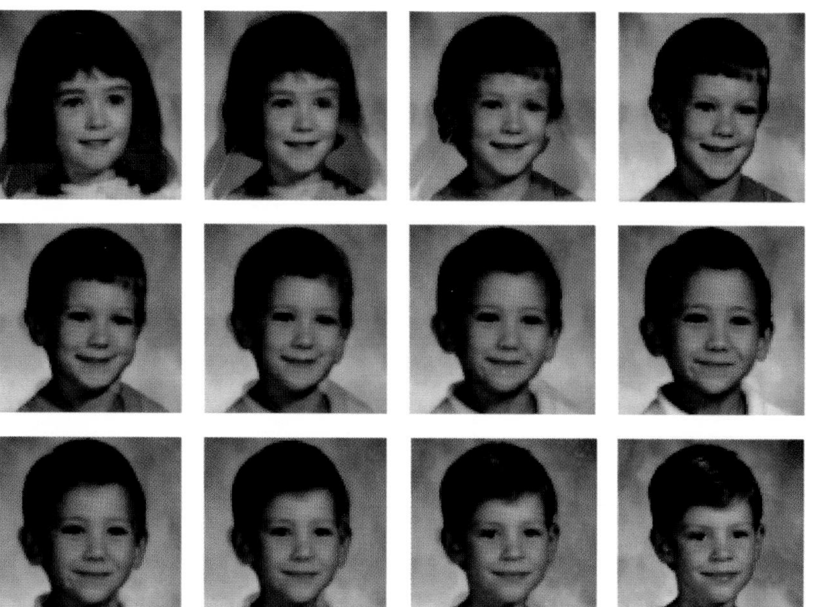

Color Plate 12:
Morphing software is available to seamlessly transform one image into another. This Color Plate illustrates a project where sixteen kindergartners were morphed into one another and then into their teacher. When a sound track of music and voices was added, it made a compelling QuickTime movie about how similar individuals are each to another.

Computer, Inc., would never venture into the music business. To Steve Jobs and Steve Wozniak, working out of their garage in the late 1970s on a machine that could barely manage a convincing system beep, that clause probably seemed a harmless one. Little did they know that less than ten years later their computer would become the most popular music computer in the world.

Over the years, many people have speculated that the agreement with the Beatles has kept Apple out of the music business and delayed development of system software for audio applications. Although Apple would doubtless deny this, the company did recently pay representatives of the Beatles about $30 million to settle the issue once and for all. As a result of the settlement, more powerful system software for audio applications may be forthcoming.

MIDI on the Macintosh

In the Windows environment, almost every major publisher of music and audio software has supported Microsoft's approach to MIDI. In contrast, many Macintosh developers are still not supporting Apple's MIDI Manager, the Macintosh software counterpart to the Windows MIDI Mapper. Many programs still rely exclusively on their own drivers. Even the publishers who have added support for the MIDI Manager don't aggressively encourage its use.

Despite the lag in development of compatible software, Apple's MIDI Manager is in wide use today, because it represents the only easy way of multitasking with MIDI. It may not possess MIDI mapping capabilities, but MIDI Manager does have additional features for interapplication communication and synchronization that are lacking in the Windows MIDI Mapper. Apple's software is, true to its name, a true manager of MIDI data and not just a data "mapper"; on the other hand, Microsoft's MIDI Mapper was designed to facilitate playback of MIDI data for multimedia. Thus the MIDI Manager is a more serious tool for synchronization and for multiple MIDI bus capabilities as well. (MIDI Manager supports both the Macintosh modem and printer ports, simultaneously.)

Apple's MIDI Manager interface is called PatchBay. With PatchBay you "patch" (route) the input and output of any number of MIDI applications to or from the Macintosh's serial ports, and even to or from other MIDI applications running at the same time under MultiFinder or System 7. Communication among the various clients is established by dragging "patch cords" (lines) between pairs of devices. Connections can be made between inputs and outputs, and to clock sources (for synchronization) as well. PatchBay is shipped with most MIDI applications. See Figure 10-7.

Many non-MIDI programs can now play back MIDI data from within the context of a multimedia presentation. It is even possible to use MIDI

FIGURE 10-7 *Apple's PatchBay utility for routing MIDI messages to the appropriate devices*

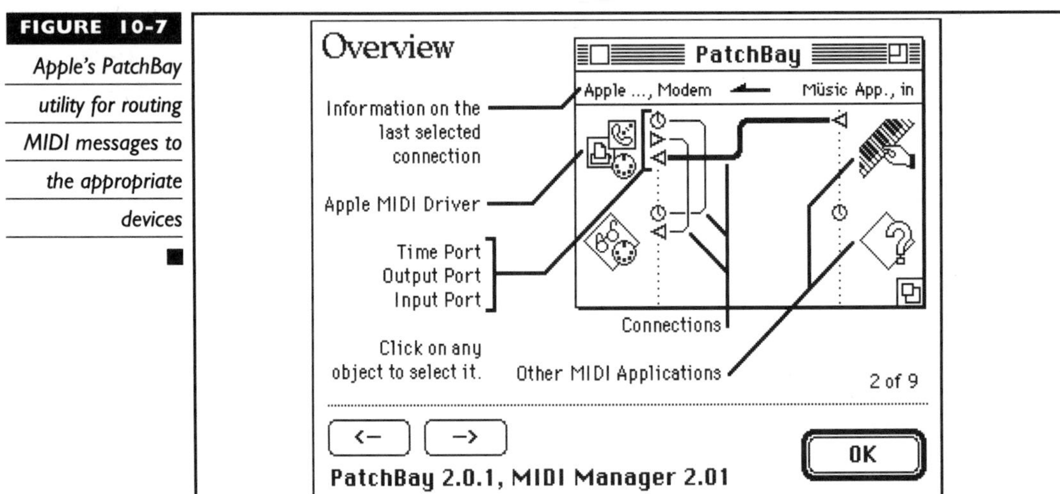

Manager's synchronization features to put visual events from one program in synch with MIDI events in another.

Digital Audio on the Macintosh

The Macintosh's role in creating digital audio (as with MIDI) has been shaped more by music and sound professionals than by the needs of more consumer-oriented multimedia developers. As with Windows-based PCs, Macintosh users must go to specialized add-in sound cards to break the 8-bit sound barrier. The procedure for using high-end audio cards with different multimedia applications is not as easy on the Macintosh as it is now under Windows, but more high-end audio systems are available for the Macintosh than for Windows. (This may not be so for long, however; because of their open architecture and massive cloning, PCs are less expensive and more expandable than Macintoshes.) There is increasing development of specialized multimedia add-in boards that provide both 16-bit stereo audio, in and out, and video. These boards will greatly simplify the task of adding high-end audio into Macintosh-based multimedia projects.

Using digital audio on the Macintosh has always been fairly easy to do. The primary format for sounds within applications is the SND (sound resource) format. Many applications can play back digital audio files from imported SND files.

Audio in QuickTime

Apple broke new ground, outpacing Microsoft, with the release of the QuickTime video technology. QuickTime is a standard file format for displaying digitized motion video from hard disk or CD-ROM without special hardware. (See Chapter 6 for a discussion of QuickTime.) Digital audio data is interleaved with video information in the file, and when it is played back, the audio stays synchronized to the motion picture. You can use QuickTime just to play stereo sounds; the video part of QuickTime is not required.

Working with Sound in Windows

Windows 3.1 includes standardized support for both digital audio and MIDI. To some extent (especially in the MIDI area), Windows has now surpassed the Macintosh in the area of basic audio support. Rather than just creating a utility, as Apple did with its MIDI Manager, and letting multimedia developers decide whether or not to use it, Microsoft has created an entire environment for MIDI—complete with MIDI file authoring guidelines for software developers.

All MPC machines now support 8-bit digital audio (*wave audio*), standardized MIDI playback, and CD-Audio. The MPC standard also requires manufacturers to provide a digital mixing system (albeit a simple one), so that all audio outputs (MIDI, wave audio, and CD-Audio) can be mixed together and directed to a single pair of audio outputs. Chapter 4 contains a complete listing of the MPC specifications.

First Person

In April 1992, Microsoft rolled out its new version of Windows 3.1 with speeches and a live MIDI performance at the Spring COMDEX/Windows World Trade Show in Chicago.

Tracy Hurst played the piano, and Steve Peha worked the electronic interface. As Tracy played "Striving for Glory: The Windows 3.1 Theme" on his Roland HP-5700, the music was instantaneously transcribed by Midisoft Studio, and the notes ran real-time across the 50-foot big screen, like sing-along bouncing balls. The show worked perfectly, and Windows Magazine later called it a tour de force for Windows multimedia. It was slick.

But I knew these people, who looked so professional and confident. I knew about the late nights, the crashed disk drives, the long drive from Boston, and the hurried runs to the nearest Radio Shack. This performance was not just about MIDI; it was about multimedia development in general. Hard work and technology are the substantial invisible part of the iceberg supporting multimedia's visible leading edge.

MIDI Under Windows

Microsoft's approach to MIDI has two parts. One part is the MIDI Mapper (see Figure 10-8), which directs the flow of MIDI data from application software to MIDI hardware devices. The second part is a set of MIDI file authoring guidelines for creating MIDI files that play back properly and on the widest possible variety of hardware devices.

Windows splits all MIDI devices into two categories: base-level MIDI devices and extended-level MIDI devices.

- *Base-level MIDI devices* can play back at least three melodic instrument parts with at least six notes playing at one time and a

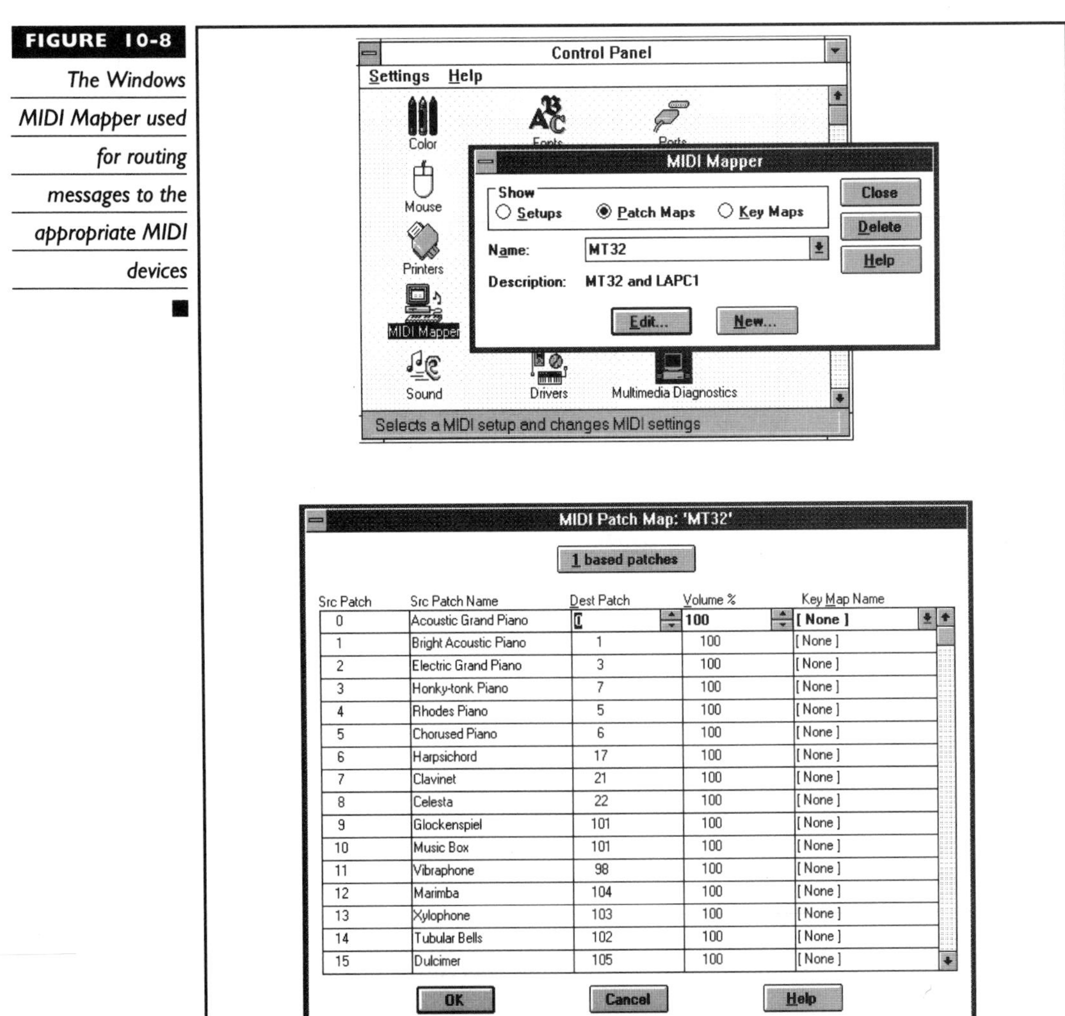

Src Patch	Src Patch Name	Dest Patch	Volume %	Key Map Name
0	Acoustic Grand Piano	0	100	[None]
1	Bright Acoustic Piano	1	100	[None]
2	Electric Grand Piano	3	100	[None]
3	Honky-tonk Piano	7	100	[None]
4	Rhodes Piano	5	100	[None]
5	Chorused Piano	6	100	[None]
6	Harpsichord	17	100	[None]
7	Clavinet	21	100	[None]
8	Celesta	22	100	[None]
9	Glockenspiel	101	100	[None]
10	Music Box	101	100	[None]
11	Vibraphone	98	100	[None]
12	Marimba	104	100	[None]
13	Xylophone	103	100	[None]
14	Tubular Bells	102	100	[None]
15	Dulcimer	105	100	[None]

FIGURE 10-8 *The Windows MIDI Mapper used for routing messages to the appropriate MIDI devices*

percussion track with at least three notes playing at one time. Most FM-based sound cards, such as the Sound Blaster Pro or Pro AudioSpectrum cards, are considered base-level devices.

- *Extended-level MIDI devices* can play back at least nine melodic instrument parts with at least sixteen notes playing at one time and a percussion track with at least sixteen notes playing at one time. Most sample-based sound cards, such as the Roland SCC-1 and Turtle Beach MultiSound cards, are extended-level devices.

General MIDI devices, such as the Roland SC-55 Sound Canvas and the Roland SCC-1 Sound Canvas Card, are considered extended-level devices—even though they have only 24-voice polyphony. *Polyphony* allows for more than one note to be played simultaneously (for example, a chord).

MIDI device manufacturers typically supply a MIDI driver to work with Microsoft's system-level MIDI commands. This frees software developers from having to write individual drivers for each piece of MIDI hardware.

MIDI Mapping

MIDI files created to adhere to Microsoft's guidelines are called device-independent MIDI files. Each file stores two arrangements of each piece. One arrangement is intended for extended-level devices, in MIDI channels 1 to 10, and a second arrangement is intended for base-level devices, in channels 13 to 16. (There are 16 different MIDI channels to work with. Each channel can be sent, or mapped, to a different hardware device.)

This is where the MIDI Mapper comes in. If you have a base-level device, you can set up a MIDI Mapper configuration that allows channels 13 to 16 to be sent to your device, while the other channels are sent elsewhere or ignored. If you have an extended-level device, you can use the Mapper to filter out the base-level channels. Ready-made MIDI maps may be supplied with your MIDI device. When the MIDI Mapper sees a MIDI message coming its way, it checks to see on which MIDI channel that message is being transmitted, and then it sends the message to the appropriate MIDI hardware device. For example, if you have a sound card in your PC that has an on-board synthesizer as well as a MIDI output, you can tell the MIDI Mapper to send certain MIDI channels to the synthesizer and other MIDI channels to the MIDI output, where they are sent to an external MIDI device.

In addition to the simple *channel mapping* just described, the MIDI Mapper also provides patch mapping and key mapping. *Patch mapping* is useful when you want to play, on a General MIDI device, MIDI files that were created on a different type of device containing a different set of sounds (or patches). By creating an appropriate patch map, the MIDI Mapper can change any patch from the source file into the correct patch on the destination MIDI playback device. *Key mapping* is similar to patch mapping; instead of mapping program change numbers from one device to another, key mapping maps notes (or "piano keys"). This is intended to resolve conflicts between the various key-based percussion mapping systems used on many different MIDI devices. MIDI channel 10 usually maps to the percussion sounds, in which each key plays the sound of a different instrument (see Table 10-4 for a list of these percussion keys).

Table 10-5 shows the channel and polyphony assignments that are part of the Microsoft guidelines for MIDI file authoring. By setting up your MIDI Mapper to correspond to this arrangement of channels, you can ensure that the MIDI file you create will sound as intended when played on another MPC system.

General MIDI Standard

Microsoft's guidelines also specify that device-independent MIDI files should be created to conform to the new General MIDI hardware standard for MIDI playback devices. This standard accomplishes the following:

- Dictates a standardized program change mapping system and a standardized set of sounds. This means, for example, that all General MIDI devices have a bassoon sound mapped to patch number 70, and that sound can be called up by transmitting a MIDI program change command with a value of 70 to any General MIDI device. In fact, all General MIDI devices have the same set of 128 orchestral sounds, synthesizer sounds, and special effects. The actual timbres may vary from instrument to instrument, but the types of sound (piano, bass, guitar, and so forth) are the same. (See Table 10-4 for the General MIDI numbering assignments.)

Channels	Assignment	Polyphony
1 to 9	These channels are reserved for extended-level melodic (nonpercussion) parts	16 notes
10	Reserved for extended-level percussion parts	16 notes
11	Unused	
12	Unused	
13 to 15	These channels are reserved for base-level melodic (nonpercussion) parts	6 notes
16	Reserved for base-level percussion parts	3 notes

TABLE 10-5 *MIDI Channel and Polyphony Assignments*

- Provides minimum polyphony and channel requirements. All General MIDI devices must be capable of playing 24 notes simultaneously and of receiving MIDI messages simultaneously on all 16 MIDI channels.
- Provides standardized percussion and instrument channel assignments and patch mapping. All General MIDI devices play instrument sounds on channels 1 to 9; channel 10 is for percussion instruments. All General MIDI devices use the same percussion sounds on the keyboard keys (MIDI note numbers) of MIDI channel 10.

Digital Audio Under Windows

Developing digital audio under Windows is much simpler than working with MIDI, but that's to be expected because digital audio data is much simpler in general than MIDI data. Microsoft has established a common file format called the wave audio format (.WAV files), a standardized method for playing back digital audio, as well as a requirement that all MPC machines have at least 8-bit digital audio capabilities.

Every software program that uses digital audio will have a simple method for incorporating .WAV files with other data. Just follow the instructions, and you're on your way.

Though every Macintosh provides at least 8-bit audio, in the PC world only MPC computers are guaranteed to have this capability. Indeed, many millions of Windows-equipped PCs have no digital audio capabilities at all. The component that gives a Windows PC its digital audio capabilities is the add-in sound card. At this writing, you can get 8-bit sound cards for under $200; 16-bit cards cost $300 to $350. The 16-bit cards are quickly becoming the multimedia standard. One manufacturer has a 16-bit card that you can get via mail order for only $30 more than the company's popular 8-bit card.

In addition to wave audio playback under Windows, Microsoft has also standardized the playback of CD-Audio (also called Red Book Audio). Through Microsoft's Media Control Interface (MCI) command set, multimedia users can control the playback of audio data from a compact disc.

Adding Sound to Your Multimedia Project

Whether you're working on a Macintosh or in Windows, you need to follow certain steps to bring an audio recording into your multimedia project. Here is a brief overview of the process:

1. Decide what kind of sound is needed (such as background music, special sound effects, and spoken dialog). Decide where these audio

events will occur in the flow of your project. Fit the sound cues into your storyboard, or make up a cue sheet.

2. Decide where and when you want to use either digital audio or MIDI data.
3. Acquire source material by creating it from scratch or purchasing it.
4. Edit the sounds to fit your project.
5. Test the sounds to be sure they are timed properly with the project's images. This may involve repeating steps 1 through 4 until everything is in sync.

When it's time to import your compiled and edited sounds into your project, you'll need to know how your particular multimedia software environment handles sound data. Each program handles it a bit differently, but the process is usually fairly straightforward: tell your software which file to play and when to play it. This is usually handled by an importing or "linking" process during which you identify the files.

cross platform *Not all presentation software can play digital audio and/or MIDI files. In most sophisticated animation environments, better support is often available. You can often count on being able to work with digital audio, but you may not be able to work very effectively with MIDI, especially on the Macintosh.*

cross platform *SuperCard imports a sound file but stores it in the data fork of the project. The sound cannot be exported or edited again without special tools. Be sure to archive your original SND or resource files before you import them.*

Conventional audio speakers were never designed with computer users in mind. Hooking up regular speakers to a PC is OK for low-quality mono signals, but now, with high-quality stereo audio cards coming onto the market, you need high-quality speakers to do your sound justice.

Andrew Bergstein, Marketing Director of Altec Lansing, manufacturers of patented computer audio systems and speakers

Multimedia authoring tools and environments are discussed in Chapter 8. Presentation, word processing, and spreadsheet applications that allow you to import sounds are discussed in Chapter 7. Here is some advice about using sound with various multimedia software.

Scripting languages such as OpenScript (ToolBook), the Media Control Interface (Windows), HyperTalk (HyperCard), and SuperTalk (SuperCard) provide a greater level of control over audio playback, but you'll need to know about the programming language and environment. Here's an example of OpenScript programming to control MIDI play:

```
On buttonDown
    midiOpen ("midifile.mid", 0, 1, notError)
    play it
    if notError<>nil
         send midiPlayError
    else
         wait until the file is done
         send done
    endIf
End buttonDown
```

In authoring environments, it is usually a simple matter to play a sound when the user clicks a button, but this may not be enough. If the user changes screens while a long file is playing, for example, you may need to program the sound to stop before leaving the current screen. If the file to be played cannot be found on the hard disk, you may need to code an entire section for error handling and file location. Sample code is generally provided in both printed and disk-based documentation for software that includes sound playback.

Toward Professional Sound: The Red Book Standard

The method for digitally encoding the high-quality stereo of the consumer CD music market is an international standard, ISO 10149. This is also known as the *Red Book standard* (derived simply from the color of the standard's book jacket). Developers of this standard claim that the digital audio sample size and sampling rate of Red Book Audio (16 bits at 44.1KHz) allow accurate reproduction of all sounds that humans can hear. Until recently, dedicated professional sound-studio equipment was used for this high-fidelity recording; today high-end sound boards are available that will record and play 16-bit sampled sound at 44.1KHz and at 48KHz. These boards are available for both Macintosh and PC platforms.

Space Considerations

The substantial amount of digital sound information that is required for high-quality sound takes up a lot of disk storage space, especially when the quantity is doubled for two-channel stereo. It takes about 1.94MB to store 11 seconds of uncompressed Red Book stereo sound.

If monaural sound is adequate for your project, you can cut your storage space requirement in half or get double the play time in the same memory space. With compression techniques, you might be able to store the sound in one-eighth the space, but you will lose some fidelity due to the rounding-off effects of quantization. Further, to conserve space you can try downsampling, or reducing the number of sample slices you take in a second. Many multimedia developers use 8-bit sample sizes at 22.05KHz sampling rates because they consider the sound to be good enough (about the quality of AM radio) and they save immense amounts of digital real estate by not using the Red Book standard.

The following formula will help you estimate your storage needs. If you are using two channels for stereo, double the result.

*(sampling rate * bits per sample) / 8 = bytes per second*

You face important trade-offs when deciding how to manage digitized sound in your multimedia project. How much sound quality can you sacrifice in order to reduce storage? What compression techniques make sense? Will compressed sound work in your authoring platform? What is good enough but not amateurish? Can you get away with 8 bits at 11.025KHz for voice mail, product testimonials, and voice-overs, and then switch to higher sampling rates for music? As with other elements of multimedia, you need to assess the sound needs of your project and make adjustments in quality and quantity to ensure that you get the most value from the limited space you have available.

Production Tips

A classic physical anthropology law (Leibig's Law of the Minimums) proposes that the evolution of eyesight, locomotor speed, sense of smell, or any other species trait will cease when that trait becomes sufficiently adequate to meet the survival requirements of the competitive environment. If the trait is good enough, the organism expends no more effort improving it. Thus, if consumer-grade electronics and a hand-held microphone are good enough for making your sound, and if you, your client, and your audience are all satisfied with the results, conserve your energy and money and avoid any more expenditure. And keep this Law of Minimums in mind when you make all your trade-off decisions involving other areas of high technology and multimedia, too.

> **Vaughan's Law of Multimedia Minimums:**
>
> There is an acceptable minimum level of adequacy that will satisfy the audience, even when that level may not be the best that technology, money, or time and effort can buy.

Audio Recording

Most multimedia developers record their sound material to cassette tapes as the first step in the digitizing process. With tape, you can do many takes of the same sound or voice, listen to all the takes, and pick the best one to digitize. By recording on inexpensive media rather than directly to disk, you avoid filling up your hard disk with throw-away stuff. If your project requires CD-quality digitized sound at 44.1KHz and 16 bits, then you should hire a sound studio. High-fidelity sound recording is a specialized craft, a skill learned in great part by trial and error, much like photography. If you decide to do it yourself at CD-quality levels, then be prepared to invest in an acoustically treated room, high-end amplifiers and recording equipment, and expensive microphones.

As already stated, there are many trade-offs involved in making multimedia. For example, if you are satisfied with 22.05KHz in your project or are constrained to this rate by storage considerations, any consumer-grade tape recorder of reasonable quality will do fine. This, of course, also applies to conversations recorded from the telephone, where a sampling rate of 11.025KHz is adequate. Noise reduction circuits and metal tapes are helpful to remove hiss, but at a sampling rate of 22.05KHz you are only going to be digitizing audio frequencies as high as about 11KHz anyway. Both the high and low ends of the audio hearing spectrum are therefore less important to you, and that is OK, because those areas are precisely the add-value focus of very elaborate and expensive consumer equipment.

Video cassette recorders (VCRs) usually have excellent stereo audio circuits, and many good multimedia sounds were first recorded and digitized using the audio tracks of video tape.

Digital Audio Tape (DAT) systems have now entered the consumer marketplace. They provide a tape-based 44.1KHz, 16-bit record and playback capability. You may, however, find that DAT is high-fidelity overkill for your needs, because the recordings are too accurate, precisely recording glitches, background noises, microphone pops, and coughs from the next room. A good editor can help reduce the impact of these noises, but at the cost of your time and money.

One day we'll have just one format for multimedia, just like in audio, where we have compact discs, cassettes, vinyl, eight track....."

Tim Carrigan, who is editor of *Multimedia,* a magazine published in the United Kingdom

Audio Editing

There is excellent waveform editing software available for both Macintosh and Windows platforms. On the Macintosh, you will need third-party editing software such as SoundEdit Pro from Macromedia; Alchemy and AudioTrax from Passport; or SoundTools from DigiDesign. Figure 10-9 shows a SoundEdit Pro display of the phrase, "Twinkle, twinkle, little star," as spoken by a three-year-old girl. Both syllables of the word *twin-kle* show up as discrete waveforms. Notice the clipping of the *-kle* in the second spoken *twinkle.* By copying and pasting words and even individual syllables, the content and meaning of entire sentences can be rearranged.

For Windows, MediaVision's Stereo Studio F/X and other waveform sound editors are available. With Microsoft's Multimedia Extensions for Windows you get the WaveEdit program.

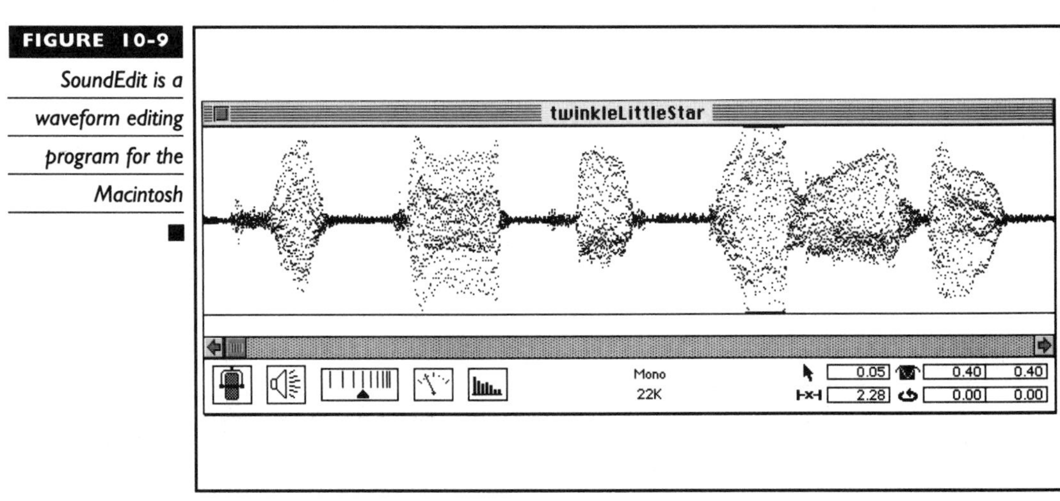

FIGURE 10-9 *SoundEdit is a waveform editing program for the Macintosh*

Indeed, excellent tools, some of which are shareware or public domain, are available for both platforms. With editing software you can manipulate your digitized sounds in a myriad of ways—cutting and pasting, adding special effects, mixing various sounds together, and, if you wish, literally putting words into people's mouths. AudioTrax from Passport blends both the sampled sound and MIDI worlds by combining a 2-track digital audio recorder with a 64-track MIDI sequencer. Midiscan software from Musitek can be used with a scanner to recognize notation and convert sheet music to multitrack MIDI files (see Figure 10-10). Other software lets you print your MIDI score.

Keeping Track of Your Sounds

Be sure your tape deck or recorder has a good counter built into it, so that you can mark and log the locations of various takes and events on the tape and quickly find them later. Get into the habit of jotting down the counter position and tape content whenever you record sounds.

In an elaborate project with many sounds, maintain a good database, keeping a physical track of your original material—just in case you need to revert to it when your disk drive crashes. This database is particularly important because you may need to give your sound files such unhelpful names as SND0094A.WAV or CHAPT1-3.WAV; these names won't contain many cues about the file's actual content, and you will need at hand a more descriptive cross-reference. You don't want to have to load and play all the

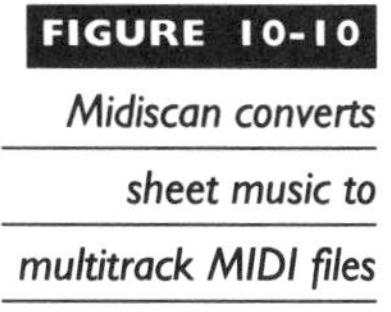

FIGURE 10-10 Midiscan converts sheet music to multitrack MIDI files

sound files from SND0080.WAV through SND0097.WAV just to find the one you need.

See Chapter 15 for suggestions about the management of such multimedia project resources.

Testing and Evaluation

Putting everything together can be tough, but testing and evaluating what you've done can be even tougher—especially if your project involves a complicated live presentation, or if you're shipping a commercial multimedia application.

The most serious challenge is synchronization of sound elements with presentation of visual images on computers that are faster or slower than the machine on which the sound elements were created. Unless you plan ahead, problems will not emerge until you begin testing on different computers.

Both digital audio and MIDI are time-based events, but most animation, computer-based video, and miscellaneous CPU tasks are not. A 60-second digital audio or MIDI file will play for the same length of time on a slow Macintosh Classic, a fast Quadra 900, a slow 386SX, or a fast 486/66. On the other hand, an animation on a 486/66 will run five to ten times faster than on a 386SX. If you time your music to animation running on a slow machine, then play it back on a faster machine, you may find that the music plays on after the speedier animation sequences are done. Since you can't make a slow machine run faster, the usual solution is to make a fast machine run slower.

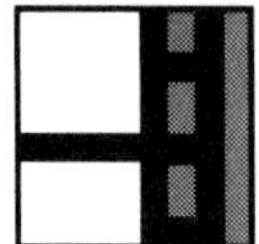

tip *During editing and authoring, regularly test the sound-and-image synchronization of your project on the slowest platform, as well as the fastest.*

Don't forget to evaluate your sound storage medium. How much RAM does your project need to run effectively? Some authoring and delivery packages will stream sound directly off the hard disk or CD-ROM; others require the sound to be loaded into memory from the hard disk before they play. Sometimes you will need to break a sound or a music file into smaller parts. Some 8-bit audio cards may choke on a 16-bit file. And MIDI files that sound terrific on a $400 General MIDI sound card during development will not have the same quality on a low-end FM-synthesis device at the end user's site.

In the world of professional film and video production, sound is incorporated during a postproduction, or *post* session after all the film and video footage has been assembled. Just so with multimedia—and don't give it short shrift because of time or budget constraints. The soundtrack can make or break your project!

Copyright Issues

Ownership rights are significant issues for multimedia producers who would love to use a few bars of Madonna's latest hit or a nostalgic background of Bach Suites played by Pablo Casals. Producers may rightfully fret about copyrights and permissions. Most developers play it safe by always making their own custom music from scratch in a sound studio, with synthesizers, or by using sounds that have a clear and paid-for ownership and permission trail. Others simply take a risk and break the law.

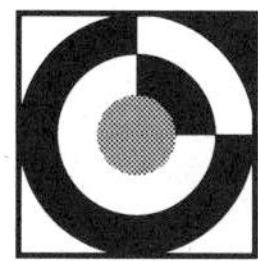

warning *You are breaking the law if you record and use copyrighted material without first securing the rights from the owner or publisher of the material.*

Over the coming years, as more and more multimedia is produced by more and more developers hungry for sound content, the copyright of sounds and images will become a major issue—not so much about who owns something, but how much of it they own. Because it is so easy to manipulate and edit a sound, just how much of someone's original work do you have to change before it then becomes your own? Copyright issues and methods of securing permission for use (equally relevant for sounds, still images, and motion video) are discussed in more detail in Chapter 16.

A number of software vendors have entered the multimedia marketplace by selling digitized clip sounds with an unlimited-use, royalty-free license. Among them are Passport Designs (MediaMusic), ProSonus (SoundBytes), and Voyetra (MusiClips). Some of these products include musical clips and some include only sound effects (doors closing, dogs barking, and water dripping); other products have a mixture of both. But beware of public domain sources that offer "Phaser" and "Beam-Me-Up" clips from such favorites as *Star Trek,* or one-liners from Humphrey Bogart movies; these sounds have likely been used without permission.

We needed some digital sound effects for the Dr. J and Larry Bird basketball game we were making. So we bought some Warriors tickets and took a tape recorder to the Oakland Coliseum and just recorded the sounds while we watched the game. It was a great tax deduction, and we got to go to the game for nothing!

Trip Hawkins, Chairman, Electronics Arts

Multi

[At the beginning of a project, the screen is a blank canvas, ready for you, the multimedia designer, to express your craft.]

visual connection

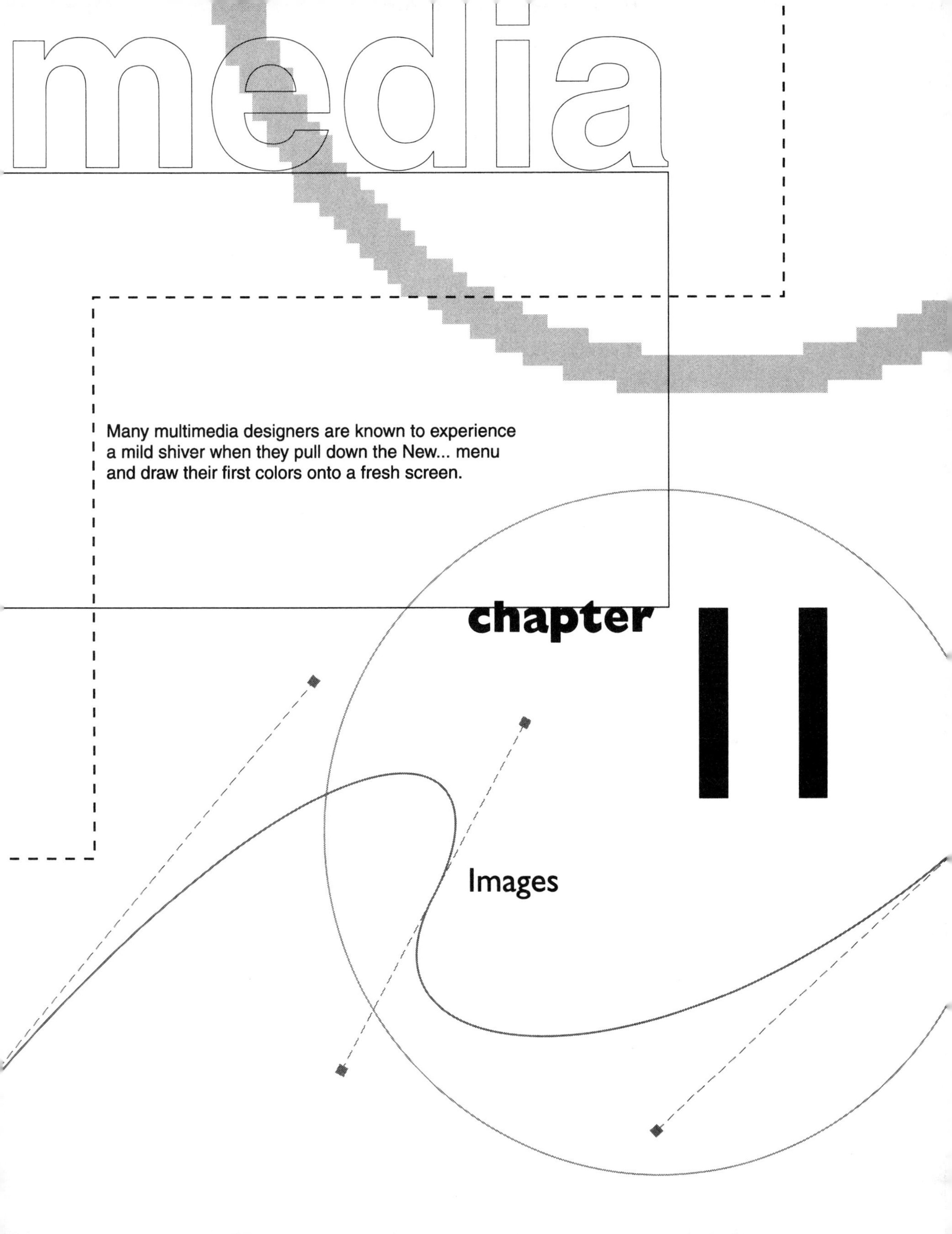

Many multimedia designers are known to experience a mild shiver when they pull down the New... menu and draw their first colors onto a fresh screen.

chapter 11

Images

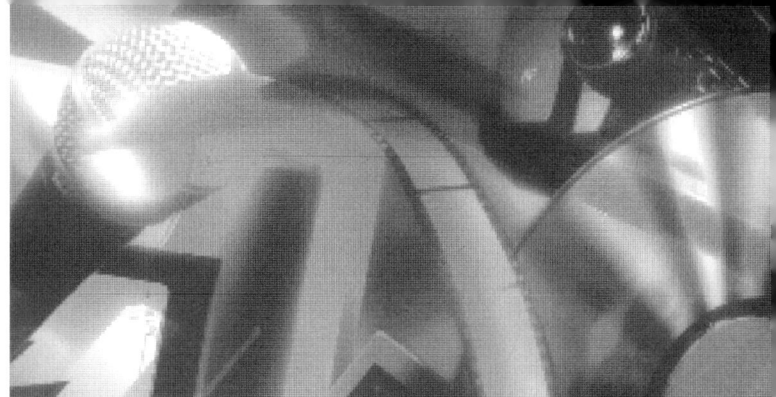

WHAT you see on a multimedia computer screen at any given time is a composite of elements: text, symbols, photograph-like bitmaps, vector-drawn graphics, three-dimensional renderings, distinctive buttons to click, and windows of motion video. Some parts of this image may even twitch or move so that the screen never seems still and tempts your eye. It may be a very colorful screen with gentle pastel washes of mauve and puce, or it may be brutally primary with splashes of Crayola red and blue and yellow and green. It might be stark black and white, full of sharp angles, or softened with gray-scale blends and anti-aliasing. It may be elegant or, by design, not. The computer screen is where the action is—it contains much more than your message; it is also the viewer's primary connection to all of your project's content.

This chapter will help you understand the visual elements that make up a multimedia screen. Graphic elements can usually be scaled to different sizes, colorized or patterned or made transparent, placed in front of or behind other objects, or be made visible or invisible on command. How you blend these elements, how you choose your colors and fonts, what tricks you use that catch the eye, how adept you are at using your tools—these are the signatures of your skill, talent, knowledge, and creativity that coalesce into the all-important visual connection to your viewers.

Before You Start to Create

At the beginning of a project, the screen is a blank canvas, ready for you, the multimedia designer, to express your craft. The screen will change again and again during the course of your project as you experiment, as you stretch and reshape elements, draw new objects and throw out old ones, and test various colors and effects—creating the vehicle for your message. Indeed, many multimedia designers are known to experience a mild shiver when they pull down the New... menu and draw their first colors onto a fresh screen. Just so; this screen represents a powerful and seductive avenue for channeling creativity.

warning *Multimedia designers are regularly lured into agonizingly steep learning curves, long nights of cerebral problem solving, and the pursuit of performance perfection. If you are fundamentally creative, multimedia may become a calling, not a profession.*

Plan Your Approach

Whether you use templates and ready-made screens provided by your authoring system; whether you use clip art or objects crafted by others; even if you simply clone the look and feel of another project—there will always be a starting point where your page is "clean." But even before reaching this starting point, be sure you have given your project a good deal of thought and planning. Work out your graphic approach either in your head or during creative sessions with your client or colleagues. There are strong arguments against drawing on a fresh screen without such foresight and preparation. See Chapter 14 for advice on organizing a multimedia project, and Chapter 15 for more about the design process.

Organize Your Tools

Most authoring systems provide the tools with which you can create the graphic objects of multimedia (text, buttons, vector-drawn objects, and bitmaps) directly on your screen. If one of these tools is not part of your authoring system, it usually offers a mechanism for importing the object you need from another application. When you are working with animated objects or motion video, most authoring systems include a feature for activating these elements, such as a programming language or special functions. You'll also usually have a library of special effects—zooms, wipes, and dissolves, for instance. Many multimedia designers do not limit their toolkits to the features of a single authoring platform, but employ a variety of applications and tools to accomplish many specialized tasks; see Chapters 6 and 8 for advice on gathering the tools you need.

Multiple Monitors

When developing multimedia, it is helpful to have more than one monitor, or a single high-resolution monitor with lots of screen real estate, hooked up to your computer. In this way, you can display the full-screen working area of your project or presentation and still have space to put your tools and other menus. This is particularly important in an authoring system such as Macromedia Director, where the edits and changes you make in one window are immediately visible in the presentation window—provided the presentation window is not obscured by your editing tool! During development there is a lot of cutting and pasting among windows and among various applications, and with an extra monitor you can open many windows at once and spread them out.

A few weeks of having to repeatedly bring windows to the front and then hide them again to see the results of your editing will probably convince you to invest in a second or larger monitor. A satisfactory second monitor may even be a simple black-and-white unit; you can use it for commands and menu activity.

Making Still Images

Still images may be small or large, or even full screen. They may be colored, placed at random on the screen, evenly geometric or oddly shaped. Still images may be a single tree on a wintry hillside; stacked boxes of text against a gray, tartan, or Italian marble background; an engineering drawing; a snapshot of your department manager's new BMW. Whatever their form, still images are generated by the computer in two ways: as *bitmaps* (or paint graphics), and as *vector-drawn* (or just plain *drawn*) graphics.

Bitmaps are used for photo-realistic images and for complex drawings requiring fine detail. Vector-drawn objects are used for lines, boxes, circles, polygons, and other graphic shapes that can be mathematically expressed in angles, coordinates, and distances. A drawn object can be filled with color and patterns, and you can select it as a single object. The appearance of both types of images depends on the display resolution and capabilities of your computer's graphics hardware and monitor. Both types of images are stored in various file formats, and can be translated from one application to another or from one computer platform to another. Typically, image files are compressed to save memory and disk space.

Still images may be the most important element of your multimedia project. If you are designing multimedia by yourself, put yourself in the role of graphic artist and layout designer. Take the time necessary to discover all the tricks you can learn about your drawing software. Competent, computer-literate skills in graphic art and design are vital to the success of your project. Remember—more than anything else, the user's judgment of your work will be most heavily influenced by the work's visual impact.

First Person

A few years ago a large corporation asked us and one other multimedia developer to bid on a long-term contract for computer-based training. Though busy with other active projects, we didn't want this possibly lucrative opportunity to slip by, so we spent a few days hastily putting together a demonstration of our technical skills for building nifty databases, designing tricky telecommunications systems, and integrating live video from videodisc into the computer. We even "wire-framed" a bit of a working multimedia database with real data we got from the corporation.

We showed our demo to about a dozen management and training executives, in a fancy boardroom that had a built-in projector and sound system with mixers and light dimmers–a place where we could knock the socks off anybody. But within 30 seconds, the disaster bells started tinkling: Most of our presentation was going way over their heads. Afterward, there were one or two vague questions and some thank-you's.

Our competitor's presentation, on the other hand, provided a slick series of finely rendered bitmapped screen images and elegant visuals. It was heavy on pretty menu screens and very light on how-it-is-done technology. We later learned that one of their graphic artists had worked for two solid weeks on the color bitmaps for that demo. In the follow-up phone call, we were told by our potential clients that the competition's "incredible artwork" had won out over our "excellent technology demonstration."

To cover our disappointment, we mumbled something to ourselves about not wanting to work with computer illiterates, anyway–people who could be taken to the cleaners by fresh paint. But we knew we'd missed a hefty piece of contract work because we hadn't invested serious graphic art talent in our demonstration. We decided that's why the real peas in the can are never the same bright green as the ones on the label. So we learned a marketing lesson.

Bitmaps

A *bitmap* is a simple information matrix describing the individual dots that are the smallest elements of resolution on a computer screen or other display or printing device. A one-dimensional matrix is required for monochrome (black and white); greater depth (more bits of information) is required to describe the more than 16 million colors the picture elements may have, as illustrated in Figure 11-1. These picture elements (known as *pels* or, more commonly, *pixels*) can be either on or off (the 1-bit bitmap, monochrome black and white), or can represent varying shades of color (4-bit, 16 colors; 8-bit, 256 colors; 16-bit, 32,768 colors; 24-bit, millions of colors). Together, the state of all the pixels on a computer screen (in about 1/60 second, which is about how often the screen is redrawn) make up the image seen by the viewer, whether it's combinations of black and white or colored pixels in a line of text, a photograph-like picture, or a simple background pattern.

FIGURE 11-1

A bitmap is a matrix that describes the characteristics of all the pixels making up an image

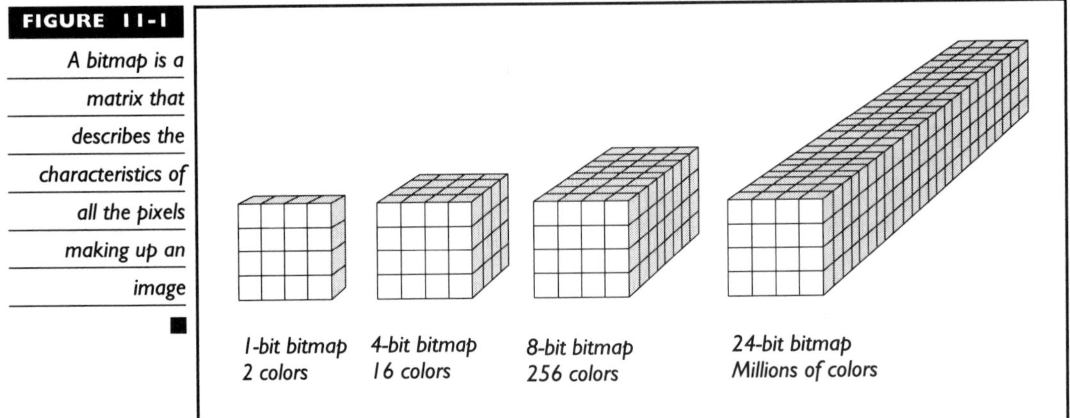

Not all pixels are created equal; pixel count does not equate to image quality.

Jon Barrett, founder of Dycam, home of the world's first digital still camera

You have three different ways to make a bitmap:

- Make a bitmap from scratch with a paint program.
- Grab a bitmap from an active computer screen with a screen capture program, and then paste it into a paint program or your application.
- Capture a bitmap from a photo, artwork, or a television image using a scanner or video capture device that digitizes the image.

Clip Art

If you do not want to make your own, you can get bitmaps from suppliers of clip art, and from photograph suppliers who have already digitized the images for you. Clip art is available on floppy disks, on CD-ROMs, and through some online services. Many graphics applications such as CorelDraw and Photostyler are shipped with CD-ROMs of clip art and useful graphics, or they will send you a collection when you register the product. A clip art collection may contain a random assortment of images, or it may contain a series of graphics, photographs, sound, and video related to a single topic. For example, Macromedia has ClipMedia collections covering "Business and Technology" and "Industry at Work."

Application: *ClipMedia*
Path: *Click on the ClipMedia icon in the Showcase CD.*

Figure 11-2 shows a page of thumbnails from a commercially available resource called PhotoDisc. Each CD-ROM contains about 400 full-color, high-resolution bitmaps with a license for unlimited use. Once you have a clip art bitmap, you can then manipulate and adjust many of its properties (such as brightness, contrast, color depth, hue, and size). You can also cut and paste among many bitmaps using specialized image editing or "darkroom" programs.

Bitmap Software

The abilities and features of paint programs for both the Macintosh and PC/Windows range from simple to complex. In the simple category are programs supplied at no cost with the systems themselves: HyperCard for the Macintosh (HyperCard version 2.2 offers color drawing facilities), and Paintbrush for Windows (with 16 colors). More sophisticated are elaborately featured programs such as SuperPaint from Aldus, Cricket Paint from Computer Associates, and Designer from Micrografx. And Fractal Design's Painter for both Macintosh and Windows provides astoundingly realistic classical art effects, using a complete palette of brushes and digital tools. Painter can work with millions of colors, depending upon your system's video card and monitor hardware (see Figure 11-3 and Color Plate 8). Chapter 6 provides a list of some painting programs commonly used to create images for multimedia projects.

tip *It is virtually impossible to paint a photo-realistic bitmap using a painting program. For photo-realism, use images that are first scanned and then pasted into your paint or image editing program. Use your paint program for drawing cartoons, text, icons, symbols, buttons, and abstract screens that have a refined "graphic" look.*

Capturing and Editing Images

The image you see on your monitor is a digital bitmap stored in video memory, updated about every 1/60 second or faster depending upon your monitor's scan rate. As you assemble images for your multimedia project, you may often need to capture and store an image directly from your screen. The simplest way to capture what you see on the screen at any given moment

FIGURE 11-2 A page of thumbnails from the index of a PhotoDisc CD-ROM

PhotoDisc™ Volume 2: People and Lifestyles

001

002

003

004

005

006

007

008

009

010

011

012

013

014

015

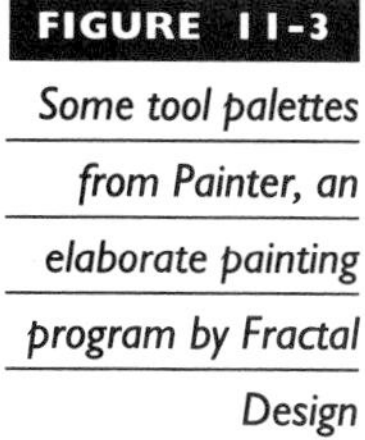

FIGURE 11-3 *Some tool palettes from Painter, an elaborate painting program by Fractal Design*

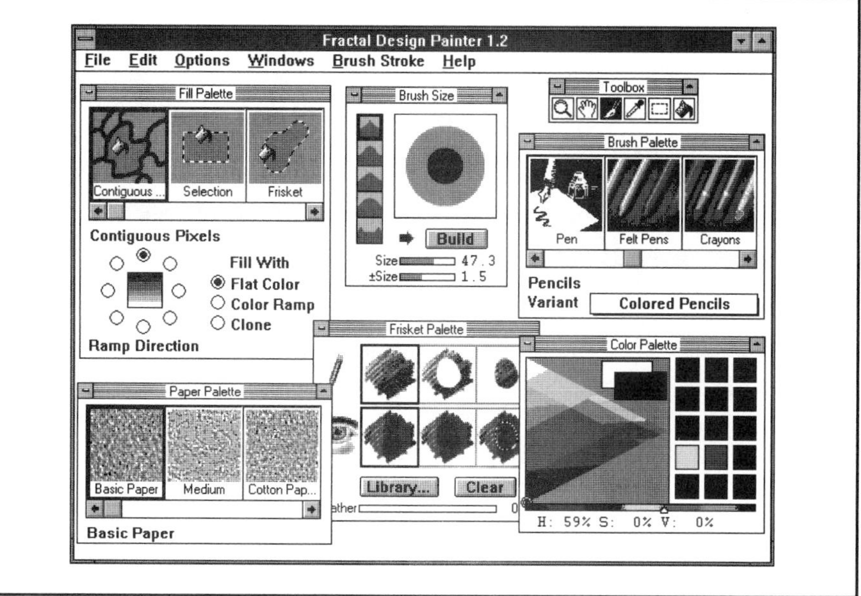

is to press the proper keys on your computer keyboard. This causes a conversion from the video bitmap to a bitmap in a format that you can use.

- On the Macintosh, the keystroke combination COMMAND-SHIFT-3 creates a readable PICT2-format file named Picture and places it in your active disk drive's root directory. You can then import this file's image into your multimedia authoring system or paint program.
- Both the Macintosh and Windows environments have a Clipboard, an area of memory where data such as text and images are temporarily stored when you cut or copy them within an application. In Windows, when you press PRINT SCREEN, a copy of your screen's image goes to the Clipboard. From the Clipboard you can then paste the captured bitmap into an application such as Paintbrush (the painting utility that comes with Windows), or you can save it as a CLP file using the Clipboard utility in the Main program group.

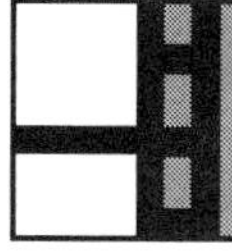

tip *When pasting full-screen Clipboard images into Window's Paintbrush accessory, you first need to maximize Paintbrush and then zoom out the working area. Then paste twice before zooming in again. Otherwise, your image will be clipped.*

The way to get more creative power when manipulating bitmaps is to use an image editing program. These are the king-of-the-mountain programs that let you not only retouch the blemishes and details of photo images, but do tricks like placing an image of your own face at the helm of a square-rigger or right at the sideline at last year's Super Bowl. Figure 11-4 shows just such a composite image, made from two photographs. It was deftly created by Russel Brown, one of the designers of Adobe's Photoshop, during a nationally broadcast live television show.

In addition to letting you enhance and make composite images, image editing tools allow you to alter and distort images. A color photograph of a red rose can be changed into a purple rose, or blue if you prefer. A small child standing next to her older brother can be "stretched" to tower over him.

Morphing is another effect that can be used to manipulate still images or to create interesting and often bizarre animated transformations. Morphing allows you to smoothly blend two images so that one image seems to melt into the next, often producing some amusing results. Color Plate 12 shows an example of a girl morphing into a boy that was created using Morph, a software application by Gryphon.

FIGURE 11-4

With image editing programs you can quickly add and delete elements, such as the person in the middle of this photo (courtesy of "The NBC Today Show")

Image editing programs may, indeed, represent the single most significant advance in computer image processing during the late 1980s, bringing truly amazing power to PC desktops. Color Plate 7 illustrates a few of the many special effects for manipulating bitmaps. Such tools are indispensable for excellent multimedia production. Look for, among others, the following programs: Photoshop from Adobe, Canvas from Deneba, Composer from Altamira, and Digital Darkroom from Aldus for the Macintosh; Picture Publisher from Micrografx and PhotoStyler from Aldus for Windows. You can find further discussion of these programs in Chapter 6.

cross platform *When you import a color or gray-scale bitmap from the Macintosh to Windows, the colors will seem darker and richer, even though they have precisely the same red, green, and blue (RGB) values. In some cases, this may improve the look of your image, but in other cases you will want to first lighten (increase the brightness and possibly lower the contrast) of the Macintosh bitmap before bringing it into Windows.*

Scanning Images

After pouring through countless clip art collections, you still haven't found the unusual background you want for a screen about gardening. Sometimes when you search for something too hard, you don't realize that it's right in front of your face. Common everyday objects can be scanned and manipulated using image editing tools, such as those described in the previous section, to create unusual, attention-getting effects. For example, to enliven a screen with a gardening motif, scan a mixture of seeds, some fall foliage, or grass-stained garden gloves. Open the scan in an image editing program and experiment with different filters, the contrast, and various special effects. Be creative and don't be afraid to try strange combinations—sometimes mistakes yield the most intriguing results.

Another alternative to computer-generated graphics is to create artwork using traditional methods: watercolors, pastels, and even crayons. You can then scan the image, make necessary alterations, and tweak pixels on the computer. Too many designers have fallen into the trap of trying to draw detailed sketches using a mouse, when a pencil or pen would have produced better results quicker. The main menu illustrated in Figure 11-5 was created by graphic artist Shirley Rafieetary at Medius IV on a drawing board with pastels and pen. Then it was scanned on a flatbed color scanner and enhanced using an image editing program.

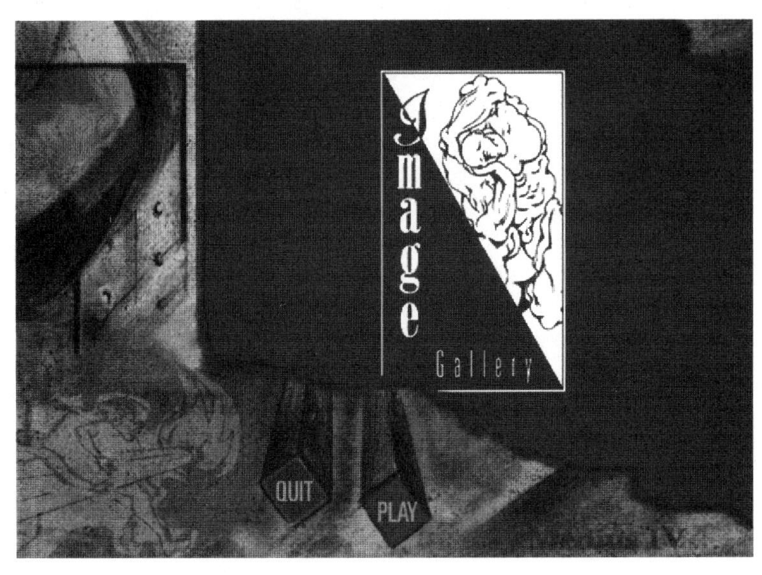

FIGURE 11-5 *This simple main menu graphic from Medius IV began as hand-drawn art*

Vector Drawing

Most multimedia authoring systems provide for use of vector-drawn objects such as lines, rectangles, ovals, polygons, and text.

- Computer-Aided Design (CAD) programs have traditionally used vector-drawn object systems for creating the highly complex and geometric renderings needed by architects and engineers (CAD tools are discussed in Chapter 6).
- Graphic artists designing for print media use vector-drawn objects because the same mathematics that put a rectangle on your screen can also place that rectangle (or the fancy Bézier curves of a good line-art illustration) on paper without jaggies. This requires the highest resolution of the printer, using a page description language such as PostScript.
- Programs for three-dimensional (3-D) animation also use vector-drawn graphics. For example, the various changes of position, rotation, and shading of light required to spin the extruded corporate logo shown in Figure 11-6 must be calculated mathematically. (Animation is discussed in Chapter 12.)

FIGURE 11-6 A few of the many still images required to "spin" a logo

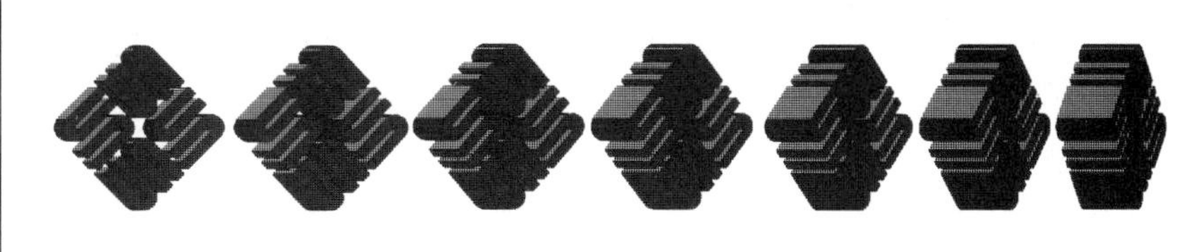

How Vector Drawing Works

Vector-drawn objects are described and drawn to the computer screen using a fraction of the memory space required to describe and store the same object in bitmap form. A *vector* is a line that is described by the location of its two endpoints. A simple rectangle, for example, might be defined as follows:

```
RECT 0,0,200,200
```

Using Cartesian coordinates, your software will draw this rectangle starting at the upper-left corner of your screen, going 200 pixels horizontally to the right, and 200 pixels downward. This rectangle would be a square, as all sides are identical lengths. For this description:

```
RECT 0,0,200,200,RED,BLUE
```

your software will draw the same square with a red boundary line and fill the square with the color blue. You can, of course, add other parameters to describe a fill pattern or the width of the boundary line.

Vector-Drawn Objects Versus Bitmaps

The concise description of the vector-drawn colored square described in the previous section contains less than 30 bytes of alphanumeric data (even less when the description is tokenized or compressed). On the other hand, the same square as an uncompressed bitmap image, in black and white (which requires the least memory, at 1-bit color depth per pixel) would take 5000 bytes to describe (200×200 / 8). Furthermore, an image made in 256 colors (8-bit color depth per pixel) would require a whopping 40K as a bitmap (200×200 / 8×8).

In terms of performance, when you draw many objects on your screen, you may experience a slowdown while you wait for the screen to be refreshed—the size, location, and other properties for each of the objects must be computed. Thus a single image made up of 500 individual line and rectangle objects, for example, may take longer for the computer to process and place on the screen than an image consisting of just a few objects.

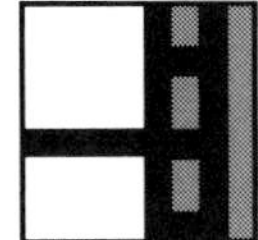

tip *Using a single bitmap for a complicated image may give you faster screen-refresh performance than using a large number of vector-drawn objects to make that same screen.*

Converting Between Bitmaps and Drawn Images

Most drawing programs offer several file formats for saving your work, and, if you wish, you can convert a drawing that consists of several vector-drawn objects into a bitmap when you save the drawing. You can also grab a bitmapped screen image of your drawn objects with a capture program.

Converting bitmaps to drawn objects is more difficult. There are, however, programs and utilities that will compute the bounds of a bitmapped image or the shapes of colors within an image and then derive the polygon object that describes the image. This procedure is called *autotracing*. It is available in some authoring systems that integrate both bitmapped and drawn objects (such as SuperCard), as well as in specialized packages such as Adobe's Streamline.

3-D Drawing and Rendering

Drawing in perspective or in 3-D on a two-dimensional surface takes special skill and talent. Dedicated software is available to help you *render* three-dimensional scenes, complete with directional lighting and special effects, but get ready for another steep learning curve! From making 3-D text with Pixar's Typestry (see Figure 9-17 in Chapter 9) to creating detailed walk-throughs of 3-D space with Virtus VR (see Figure 11-7), each application will demand study and practice before you are efficient and comfortable with its feature set and power. Macromedia offers several drawing packages (Three-D, Swivel 3D Professional, MacroModel, ModelShop II, and LifeForms), and each provides tools for rendering 3-D images as illustrated by LifeForms and Swivel 3D in Figure 11-8.

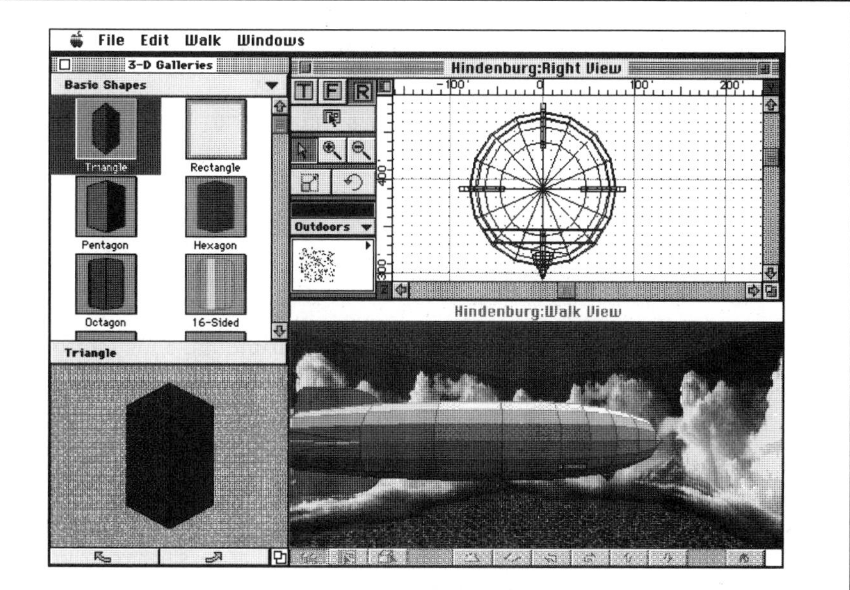

FIGURE 11-7 *Virtus VR for Macintosh and Windows lets you create 3-D virtual environments in which you can "walk" around and even through objects* ■

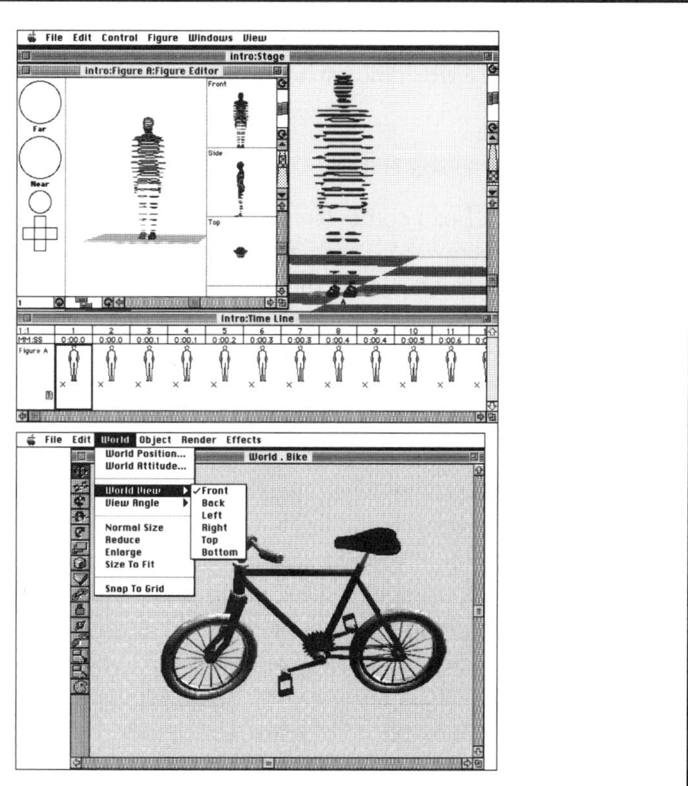

FIGURE 11-8 *3-D graphics tools can be complicated and difficult to learn, but they yield results proportional to the learning effort* ■

Application: *Swivel 3D Pro*
MacroModel
ModelShop
Life Forms
Three-D

Color

Color is a vital component of multimedia. This section explains where color comes from and how colors are displayed on a computer monitor.

Working with Color

Management of color is both a subjective and a technical exercise. Picking the right colors and combinations of colors for your project can involve many tries until you feel the result is right. But the technical description of a color may be expressed in known physical values (humans, for example, perceive colors with wavelengths ranging from 400 to 600 nanometers on the electromagnetic spectrum), and there are several methods and models to describe color space using mathematics and values.

Understanding Natural Light and Color

Light comes from an atom when an electron passes from a higher to a lower energy level; each atom produces uniquely specific colors. This explanation of light, known as the *quantum theory,* was developed by physicist Max Planck in the late 19th century. Niels Bohr, another physicist, later showed that an excited atom that has absorbed energy and whose electrons have moved into higher orbits will throw off that energy in the form of *quanta,* or *photons,* when it reverts to a stable state. This is where light comes from.

Color is the frequency of a light wave within the narrow band of the electromagnetic spectrum to which the human eye responds. The letters of the mnemonic ROY G. BIV, learned by many of us to remember the colors of the rainbow, are the ascending frequencies of the visible light spectrum: red, orange, yellow, green, blue, indigo, and violet. Light that is infrared, or below the frequency of red light and not perceivable by the human eye, can be created and viewed by electronic diodes and sensors, and it is used for TV and VCR remote controls and for night goggles used in the military. Infrared light is radiated heat. Ultraviolet light, on the other hand, is beyond the higher end of the visible spectrum and can be damaging to humans.

The color white is a noisy mixture of all the color frequencies in the visible spectrum. Sunlight and fluorescent tubes produce white light; tungsten lamp filaments produce light with a yellowish cast; sodium vapor lamps, typically used for low-cost outdoor street lighting, produce an orange light characteristic of the sodium atom. These are the most common sources of light in the everyday (or every night) world. The light these sources produce typically reaches your eye as a reflection of that light into the lens of your eye.

The cornea of the eye acts as a lens to focus light rays onto the retina. The light rays stimulate many thousands of specialized nerves called *rods* and *cones* that cover the surface of the retina. Receptors in the cones are sensitive to red, green, and blue light, and all the nerves together transmit the pattern of color information to the brain. The eye can differentiate among millions of colors, or *hues*, consisting of combinations of red, green, and blue.

As color information is sent to the brain, other parts of the mind massage the data en route to its point of cognitive recognition. Human response to color is complicated by cultural and experiential filters that cause otherwise straightforward color frequencies to carry pleasant, unpleasant, soothing, depressing, and many other special meanings. In western cultures, for example, red is the color of anger and danger; in eastern cultures, red is the color of happiness. Red is the traditional color for Chinese restaurant motifs, to make them attractive and happy places; western restaurants are often decorated in quieter pastels and earth tones.

Green, blue, yellow, orange, purple, pink, brown, black, gray, and white are the ten most common color-describing words used in all human languages and cultures.

Computerized Color

Because the eye's receptors are sensitive to red, green, and blue light, by adjusting combinations of these three *additive primary colors*, the eye and brain will interpolate the combinations of colors in between. This is the psychology, not the physics of color: what you perceive as orange on a computer monitor is a combination of two frequencies of green and red light, not the actual spectral frequency you see when you look at that namesake fruit, an orange, in sunlight. All these factors make computerized color pretty tricky to manage.

The reflected light that reaches your eye from a printed page is made up of tiny halftone dots of a few primary colors (printers use the *subtractive primary colors*, cyan, magenta, and yellow, with black). In contrast, computer monitor screens are, like the sun, sources of light. On the back of the glass face of a monitor are thousands of phosphorescing chemical color dots (red, green, and blue) that are bombarded by electrons that paint the screen at very high speeds. These dots are each about .30mm or less in diameter (the *dot pitch*) and are positioned very carefully and very close together.

The red, green, and blue dots light up when hit by the electron beam, and the eye sees the combination of red, green, and blue (RGB) light and interpolates it. When one of the primary colors is subtracted from this RGB mix, the subtractive primary color is perceived, as follows:

RGB Combination	Perceived Color
Red only	Red
Green only	Green
Blue	Blue
Red and green (blue subtracted)	Yellow
Red and blue (green subtracted)	Magenta
Green and blue (red subtracted)	Cyan
Red, green, and blue	White
None	Black

Monitors and Color

Most multimedia today is presented on color monitors that display a matrix of 640 pixels across and 480 pixels down (640×480), usually at about 72 dots or pixels per inch; each pixel may be one of 256 colors. With fewer colors, there is not enough range to make good photo-realistic images, although gray-scale pictures with 16 shades of gray often come out well. With more colors, your computer must work much harder to display the image on the screen, and performance takes a serious hit unless you boost it with faster, expensive processors and added memory devices.

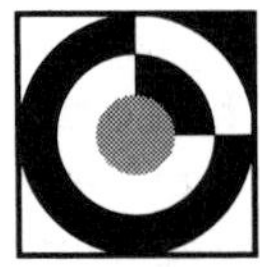

warning *Sometimes the term "video card" is used synonymously with "graphics adapter," which is the hardware that makes the monitor work. Do not confuse "video card" with "video capture card" or "video display card," which are the terms used for video (television) editing and display.*

The 640×480, 256-color (8-bit) setup is called VGA (for Video Graphics Array), and it is the default configuration for most Windows and Macintosh multimedia systems. Although Windows does support 16-color (4-bit) VGA graphics adapters, you will need to have at least a 256-color VGA graphics adapter card and a VGA monitor attached to your computer to create good multimedia. It will be a few years until the faster processors and adapters with 16 million colors become commonplace and inexpensive for Macintoshes and for PCs running Windows.

Computer Color Models

The color of a pixel on your computer monitor is typically expressed as an amount of red, green, and blue. It takes more computer memory and processing speed to digitally manage and display the greater combinations of red, green, and blue values that make more shades of color visible to the eye.

Models or methodologies used to specify colors in computer terms are RGB, HSB, HSL, CMYK, CIE, and others. Using the RGB (red, green, blue) model, you specify a color by setting the amount of red, green, and blue, in the range 0 to 65535. Color Plate 2 illustrates the RGB color cube, where the three dimensions represent the values of the three color channels that specify a color.

Red (R)	Green (G)	Blue (B)	Color
65535	65535	65535	White
65535	65535	0	Yellow
65535	0	65535	Magenta
0	65535	65535	Cyan
65535	0	0	Red
0	65535	0	Green
0	0	65535	Blue
0	0	0	Black

In the HSB (hue, saturation, brightness) and HSL (hue, saturation, lightness) models, you specify hue or color as an angle from 0 to 360 degrees on a color wheel, and saturation, brightness, and lightness as percentages. Lightness or brightness is the percentage of black or white that is mixed with a color. A lightness of 100 percent will yield a white color; 0 percent is black; the pure color has a 50 percent lightness. Saturation is the intensity of the color. At 100 percent saturation, the color is pure; at 0 percent saturation, the color is white, black, or gray. Color Plate 3 shows the location of colors on a color wheel, as defined in the following:

Color	Degrees
Red	0°
Yellow	60°
Green	120°
Cyan	180°
Blue	240°
Magenta	300°

The CMYK color model is less applicable to multimedia production. It is used primarily in the printing trade where cyan, magenta, yellow, and black are used to print process color separations.

Other color models include CIE, YIQ, YUV, and YCC. CIE describes color value in terms of frequency, saturation, and illuminance (blue/yellow or red/green, which in turn corresponds to the color receptors in the cones of the eye). CIE more closely resembles how human beings perceive color, but certain devices such as scanners are unable to replicate the process.

YIQ and YUV were developed for broadcast TV (composite NTSC, as explained in Chapter 13). They are based on luminance and chrominance expressed as the amplitude of a wave and the phase of the wave relative to some reference. Detail is carried by luminance (black and white), so reduction in color does not result in the loss of image definition detail. This analog process can be translated to a number value so that the computer can use a palette or CLUT (color lookup table) to assign a pixel a color.

The Photo YCC model has been developed by Kodak to provide a definition that enables consistent representation of digital color images from negatives, slides, and other high-quality input. YCC is used for Photo CD images, described in Chapter 18.

Color Palettes/Color Lookup Tables

Palettes are mathematical tables that define the color of a pixel displayed on the screen. On the Macintosh, these tables are called *color lookup tables* or CLUTs. In Windows, the term *palette* is used.

The most common palettes are 1, 4, 8, 16, and 24 bits deep:

Color Depth	Colors Available
1-bit	Black and white (or any two colors)
4-bit	16 colors
8-bit	256 colors (good enough for color images)
16-bit	Thousands of colors (excellent for color images)
24-bit	More than 16 million colors (photo-realistic)

For 256-color, 8-bit VGA systems, your computer uses a color lookup table or palette to determine which 256 colors out of the millions possible are available to you at any one time. Color Plate 1 shows the default Macintosh system palette as well as other combinations of 256 and 16 colors.

The default colors were statistically selected by Apple and Microsoft engineers (working independently) to be the colors and shades that are most "popular" in photographic images; the two palettes are, of course, different.

To generate a palette which is best for representing a particular image, we support Heckbert's median cut algorithm. This algorithm first builds a three dimensional table (a histogram cube) indicating how popular any given colour in the RGB cube is in the image being converted. It then proceeds to subdivide this histogram cube (by dividing boxes in half) until it has created as many boxes as there are palette entries. The decision as to where to divide a box is based on the distribution of colours within the box. This algorithm attempts to create boxes which have approximately equal popularity in the image. Palette entries are then assigned to represent each box. There are other methods of generating a palette from an image, but Heckbert's algorithm is generally regarded as the best tradeoff between speed and quality.

Allan Hessenflow of HandMade Software, makers of Image Alchemy, describing how an 8-bit palette is made

Paint programs provide a palette tool for displaying available colors. Most color pickers and selectors (see examples shown in Color Plate 3) also provide a mechanism for specifying a palette color numerically when precision is required. Palette display and color picking tools, however, are not uniform among applications or across platforms.

It would be great if we could give up the tricky business of palettes and mapping entirely and go full-bore with 24-bits and millions of colors. It would save a lot of hassle for a lot of software programmers, multimedia developers, and ISV's, and the screens would look great! But the cost curves and performance realities of this industry won't let that happen for some time. 8-bit is where it's at for now.

Glenn Morrisey, Asymetrix, Inc.

In 24-bit color systems, your graphics adapter works with three channels of 256 discrete shades of each color (red, green, and blue) represented as the three axes of a cube. This allows a total of 16,777,216 colors (256×256×256). Like the 44.1KHz sampled-sound standard for CD music on compact discs that was discussed in Chapter 10, the color range offered by 24-bit systems covers what the human eye can sense. Even though millions of colors can be painted on a computer screen in 24-bit mode, only 307,200 (640×480) actual pixels are available at any one time on typical Macintosh and Windows display monitors. This is, however, more than sufficient for excellent gradients and photo-realism. Other 16-bit SVGA boards provide 5 bits per channel, for a total of 32,768 different colors (32×32×32) that are quite realistic and smooth.

About Palette Flashing

When you work with the 256 colors of an 8-bit palette, only one combination of any 256 colors can be displayed on your monitor at any given moment. If you change the colors in the current palette by remapping, there will be an annoying flash of strange colors in your image while the computer remakes its color lookup table and the old colors change to the new. This *palette flashing* is a serious practical problem for multimedia designers. For example, it occurs when you show a series of images (an animation), each with its own optimal palette; when the new image replaces the old one, a flash occurs.

All techniques for handling the palette-flashing problem involve design solutions:

- The simplest solution is to map all images in your project to a single, shared palette. The disadvantage here is that you will trade the best 256 colors that show a single image for an "average" of 256 colors shared among all images.
- A less simple but more effective technique is to fade each image to white or black before showing the next image. Black and white are usually present in all palettes.

Most image editing, painting, and authoring applications let you remap, optimize, and customize palettes. When you input an image with a flat-bed color scanner or a video frame-grabber, the resulting image file will likely be three 8-bit channels of color information. Your images will be highly detailed, showing rich and subtle color variations, wood grain, and various lighting conditions. If you dither this image to 8 bits, you must weigh the compromises.

And here are some color techniques to avoid when the destination of your animation is a videotape:

- Avoid using a pattern or mosaic.

- Avoid extremely bright or intense colors that may flare up on a television screen; stick to pastels and earth colors.
- Avoid some reds that may turn brown on television.

Dithering

Dithering is a process where the color value of each pixel is changed to the closest matching color value in the target palette, using a mathematical algorithm. Often the adjacent pixels are also examined, and patterns of different colors are created in the more limited palette to best represent the original colors. Thus any given pixel might not be mapped to its closest palette entry, but instead to the average over some area of the image; this average will be closer to the correct color than a substitute color would be. Depending upon the algorithm used, dithering can render a very good approximation of the original. Color Plate 6 compares the same scanned image dithered from millions of colors to 256 colors, 16 colors, 16 shades of gray, and black and white.

Dithering concepts are important to understand when you are working with bitmaps that are derived from RGB information or are based upon different palettes or CLUTs. The palette for the image of a rose, for example, may contain mostly shades of red with a number of greens thrown in for the stem and leaves. The image of your pretty Delft vase, into which you want to electronically place the rose, may be mostly blues and grays. Your software will use a dithering algorithm to find the 256 color shades that best represent both images, generating a new palette in the process.

Multimedia is just another way to transform ambiguity. There were so many ambiguous colors in this scan, I decided to make them unambiguous. How do you like the purple?

Lars Hidde, explaining why he dithered a perfectly fine 8-bit image into a 16-color default palette

Dithering software is usually built into image editing programs and is also available in many multimedia authoring systems as part of the application's palette management suite of tools.

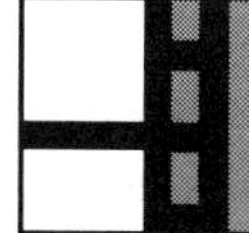

tip *Instead of trying to display a photo-realistic image using 16 colors, or if you are not satisfied with the colors of your image, consider dithering your photo to a gray-scale image. It will show extraordinary detail.*

warning *It is very difficult to create outstanding graphics with just 16 colors. Using various dithers will certainly improve the range of perceived colors, but you will need to double your graphics budget–optimizing the look of drawn and painted objects at this color depth is painstaking and time consuming.*

Image File Formats

As mentioned earlier in this chapter, there are many file formats used to store bitmaps and drawings. Developers of paint and draw applications continually create native file formats that allow their programs to load and save files more quickly or more efficiently. Most of these applications, however, offer a Save As option that lets you write files in other common formats. And third-party translators are now widely available, for files generated on the same platform as well as for going cross-platform between Macintosh and PC/Windows (and others).

If you are using a specialized application to make bitmaps or drawings, make sure your multimedia authoring package can import the image files you produce, and that your application can export such a file. You need a common format.

Macintosh Formats

On the Macintosh, just about every image application can import or export PICT files. PICT is a complicated but versatile format developed by Apple as a common format that is always available to Macintosh users. In a PICT file, both bitmaps and vector-drawn objects can live side by side, and programs such as SuperCard or Canvas make use of this feature. Many drawing programs for the Macintosh will allow you to import a bitmap but offer no facility for editing it. Authoring programs that can import PICT images may not utilize the drawn objects that are part of the file, but will usually convert them to bitmaps for you.

Windows Formats

Windows uses Device Independent Bitmaps (DIBs) as its common image file format. DIBs can stand alone or they can be buried within a Resource Interchange File Format (RIFF) file. A RIFF is actually the preferred file type for all multimedia development in Windows, because this format was designed to contain many types of files, including bitmaps, MIDI scores, and formatted text. In Windows, there is no provision for managing drawn

First Person

I needed to get about 40 bitmap files from the Macintosh to the Sun SparcStation. "Piece of cake," I said; "Give me a few minutes." The network hadn't gone down in three days, and we were connected at Ethernet speeds. Well, the files had been saved in native Photoshop format on the Macintosh. So I launched Photoshop, opened each file, and then saved it in PICT format. The translator program I wanted to use to convert Macintosh PICT files to Sun raster files was an MS-DOS application, so I renamed all the Macintosh files to fit the DOS eight-plus-three-character filename convention. Then I cranked up the 486, launched the translator, and batch-processed all of the files into .RAS files using the network. The 40 new files were now on the Macintosh, mixed in with the original PICTs. I collected the needed raster files into a single folder on the Macintosh and then sent the whole thing over to the Sun.

A few minutes? The process kept three chairs warm for about two hours.

objects in a common format, as is provided by Macintosh PICT files. The following table contains image file formats you might use in the Windows environment. These formats are translatable using CONVERT, a utility program installed with Microsoft's Multimedia Extensions.

Format	Extension
Microsoft Windows DIB	BMP, DIB, and RLE
Microsoft RLE DIB	DIB
Microsoft Palette	PAL
Microsoft RIFF DIB	RDI
Computer Graphics Metafile	CGM
Micrografx Designer/Draw	DRW
AutoCAD Format 2-D	DXF
Initial Graphics Exchange Standard	IGS
Encapsulated PostScript	EPS
CompuServe GIF	GIF
HP Graphic Language	HGL
PC Paintbrush	PCX
Apple Macintosh PICT	PIC
Lotus 1-2-3 Graphics	PIC
AutoCAD Import	PLT
Truevision TGA	TGA
TIFF	TIF
Windows Metafile	WMF
DrawPerfect	WPG

The image file formats used most often in Windows are DIB, BMP, PCX, and TIF. A BMP file is a Windows bitmap file. PCX files were originally developed for use in Z-Soft MS-DOS paint packages; these files can be opened and saved by almost all MS-DOS paint software and desktop publishing software. TIFF, or *Tagged Interchange File Format*, was designed to be a universal bitmapped image format and is also used extensively in desktop publishing packages.

Cross-Platform Formats

For handling drawn objects across many platforms, there are two common formats: DXF and IGS. DXF was developed by AutoDesk as an ASCII drawing interchange file for AutoCAD, but the format is used today by many computer-aided design applications. IGS (or IGES, for Initial Graphics Exchange Standard) was developed in an industry committee as a broader standard for transferring CAD drawings. These formats are also used in 3-D rendering and animation programs. Applications such as Equilibrium Software's DeBabelizer for the Macintosh (see Figure 6-12 in Chapter 6) and Handmade Software's Image Alchemy for the PC provide specialized image format translators.

Multi

[Animation is possible because of a biological phenomenon known as persistence of vision.]

Animation is a button actually moving across the screen...

dynamic action

media

chapter 12

Animation

- a spinning globe of our earth;
- a car driving along a line-art highway;
- a bug crawling out from under a stack of disks,
- with a screaming voice from the speaker telling you to "Shoot it, now!"

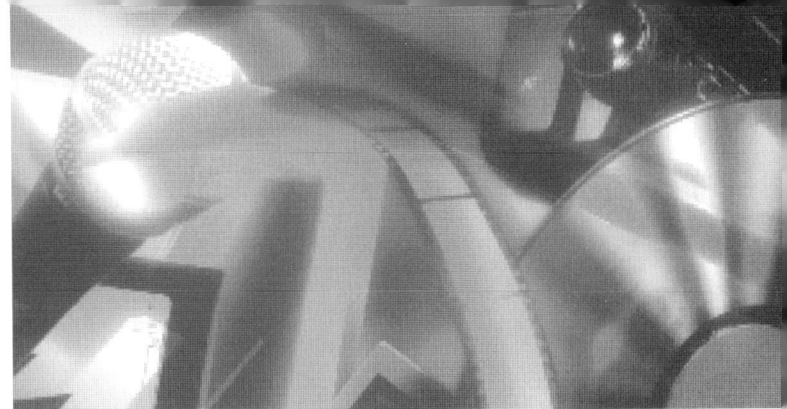

ANIMATION adds visual impact to your multimedia project. Many multimedia applications for both the Macintosh and Windows provide animation tools, but you should first understand the principles of how the eye interprets the changes it sees as motion.

The Power of Motion

You can animate your whole project, or you can animate here and there, accenting and adding spice. For a brief product demonstration with little user interaction, it might make sense to design the entire project as a movie and keep the presentation always in motion. For speaker support, you can animate bulleted text or fly it in, or you can use charts with quantities that grow or dwindle; then, give the speaker control of these eye-catchers. In a parts-assembly training manual, you might show components exploding into an expanded view.

Visual effects such as wipes, fades, zooms, and dissolves are available in most authoring packages, and some of these can be used for primitive animation. For example, you can slide images onto the screen with a wipe, or you can make an object implode with an iris/close effect. Figure 12-1 shows the many effects available in Macromedia Director.

But animation is more than visual effects. Animation is a button actually moving across the screen; a spinning globe of our earth; a car driving along a line-art highway; a bug crawling out from under a stack of disks, with a screaming voice from the speaker telling you to "Shoot it, now!" Until motion video became more commonplace, animation techniques were the primary source of dynamic action in multimedia presentations.

Tools for designing animated multimedia presentations are discussed in detail in Chapters 6 and 8.

FIGURE 12-1 *Macromedia Director offers many visual effects*

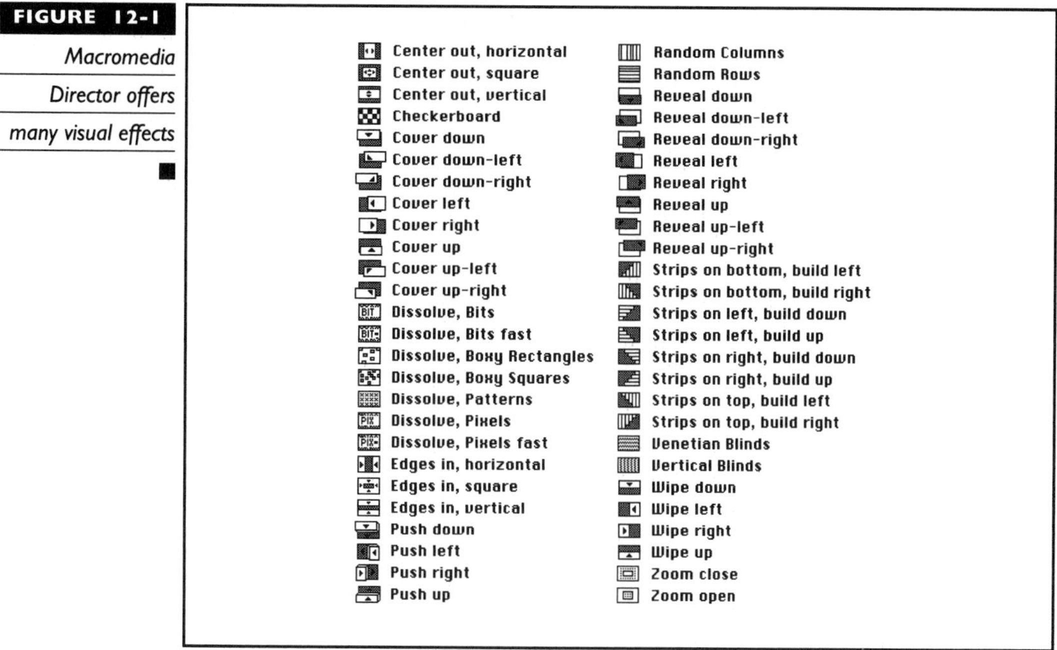

Principles of Animation

Animation is possible because of a biological phenomenon known as *persistence of vision*. An object seen by the human eye remains mapped on the eye's retina for a brief time after viewing. This makes it possible for a series of images that are changed very slightly and very rapidly, one after the other, to seemingly blend together into a visual illusion of movement. In other words, if you just change slightly the location or shape of an object rapidly enough the eye will perceive the changes as motion. The following shows a few cells or frames of a rotating logo. When the images are progressively and rapidly changed, the arrow of the compass is perceived as spinning.

Television video builds 30 entire frames or pictures every second; the speed with which each frame is replaced by the next one makes the images appear to blend smoothly into movement. Movies are shot at a shutter rate of 24 frames per second, but by using projection tricks (the projector's shutter flashes light through each image twice), the flicker rate is increased to 48 times per second, and the human eye thus sees a motion picture. Quickly changing the viewed image is the principle of an animatic, a flip-book, or a zoetrope. To make an object travel across the screen while it changes its shape, just change the shape and also move it a few pixels for each frame. Then, when you play the frames back at a faster speed, the changes blend together and you have motion and animation. (It's the same magic as when the hand is quicker than the eye, and you don't see the pea moving in the blur of the gypsy's cups.)

Animation Techniques

The animation techniques made famous by Disney use a series of progressively different graphics on each frame of movie film (which plays at 24 frames per second). A minute of animation may thus require as many as 1440 separate frames. The term *cel* derives from the clear celluloid sheets that were used for drawing each frame, which have been replaced today by acetate or plastic. Cels of famous animated cartoons have become sought-after, suitable-for-framing collector's items.

Cel Animation

Cel animation artwork begins with *keyframes* (the first and last frame of an action). For example, when an animated figure of a man walks across the screen, he balances the weight of his entire body on one foot and then the other in a series of falls and recoveries, with the opposite foot and leg catching up to support the body. Thus the first keyframe to portray a single step might be the man pitching his body weight forward off the left foot and leg, while his center of gravity shifts forward; the feet are close together and he appears to be falling. The last keyframe might be the right foot and leg catching the body's fall, with the center of gravity now centered between the outstretched stride, and the left and right feet positioned far apart.

The series of frames in between the keyframes are drawn in a process called *tweening*. Tweening an action requires calculating the number of frames between keyframes and the path the action takes, and then actually sketching onto a cel with pencil the series of progressively different outlines. As tweening progresses, the action sequence is checked by flipping through the frames. The penciled frames are assembled and then actually filmed as a pencil test to check smoothness, continuity, and timing.

When the pencil frames are satisfactory, they are permanently inked, and acrylic colors are painted on. In the hands of a master, cel paint applied to the back of acetate can produce beautiful and subtle effects, with feathered edges or smudges, or simply flat and perfectly even.

The cels for each frame of our example of a walking man—which may consist of a text title, a background, a left arm, a right arm, legs, shoes, a body, and facial features—are carefully registered and stacked. It is this composite that becomes the final photographed frame in an animated movie.

Computer Animation

Computer animation programs typically employ the same logic and procedural concepts as cel animation, using layer, keyframe, and tweening techniques, and even borrowing from the vocabulary of classic animators. On the computer, paint is most often filled or drawn with tools using features such as gradients and anti-aliasing. The word *inks,* in computer animation terminology, usually means special methods for computing RGB pixel values, providing edge detection, and layering so that images can blend or otherwise mix their colors to produce special transparencies, inversions, and effects.

You can usually set your own frame rates on the computer, but the rate at which changes are computed and screens are refreshed will depend on the speed and power of your hardware. Although your animations will probably never push the limits of your monitor's scan rate (about 60 to 70 frames a second), animation does put raw computing horsepower to task. If you cannot compute all your changes and display them as a new frame on your monitor within, say, 1/30 second, then the animation may appear jerky and slow.

tip *The smaller the object, the faster it can move. Bouncing a 10-pixel-diameter tennis ball on your screen provides far snappier motion than bouncing a 150-pixel-diameter beach ball.*

MORPHING Morphing is a popular effect in which one image transforms into another. Morphing applications like Morph from Gryphon, Elastic Reality from ASDG, and MetaFlo from the Valis Group can transition not only between still images, but between moving images as well. Color Plate 12 illustrates still images morphed one into the other.

Animation File Formats

Some file formats are designed to contain animations, which you can port among applications and platforms with the proper translators. Those formats include the following:

Director (MMM)
AnimatorPro (FLI and FLC)
SuperCard, Director, Super3D (PICS)
Windows Audio Video Interleaved Format (AVI)
Macintosh Time-Based Data Format (QuickTime)
Tempra Animation Editor (FLX)

Making Animations That Work

Animation catches the eye and makes things noticeable. But, like sound, animation quickly becomes trite if it is improperly applied. Unless your project has a backbone of movie-like animated imagery, use animation carefully and sparingly to achieve the greatest impact. Your screens will otherwise become busy and "noisy."

Multimedia authoring systems typically provide tools to simplify creating animations within that authoring system. And they often have a mechanism for playing the special animation files created by dedicated animation software. Today, the most widely used tool for creating multimedia animations for Macintosh and Windows environments is Macromedia's Director (see Chapter 8).

The following three sections will provide three examples of animation. The first section is a brief tutorial on making a textured spherical ball, using Photoshop and Kai's Power Tools, and rolling it across the screen. The second section is a step-by-step description of an animated scene created in Macromedia Director. The third section uses a series of characters as text to create an animation. These examples demonstrate that computer-generated animations actually consist of many bits and pieces carefully orchestrated to appear as one image, in motion—just like the many layers in classical cel animation.

A Rolling Ball

Billiard-ball spheres can be made quickly on a Macintosh using Photoshop and Kai's Power Tools, a set of graphic manipulation plug-ins. First, create a new, blank image file at 200×200 pixels, and fill it with a background using

Kai's Power Tools. In Photoshop, place some white text at the center of the image, and rotate the text:

Set the oval marquee to a fixed dimension of 200×200 pixels (double-click on the oval icon) so that a circle of "marching ants" (dotted outline of a circle) fills the square. Use the KPT Glass Lens Bright filter (under the Distort menu) applied to the selected circle to produce this result:

Then resize the image to a dimension of 100×100 pixels. Now select a full circle, comprised of the distorted (spherized) image, using the oval selection marquee set to a fixed size of 100×100 pixels:

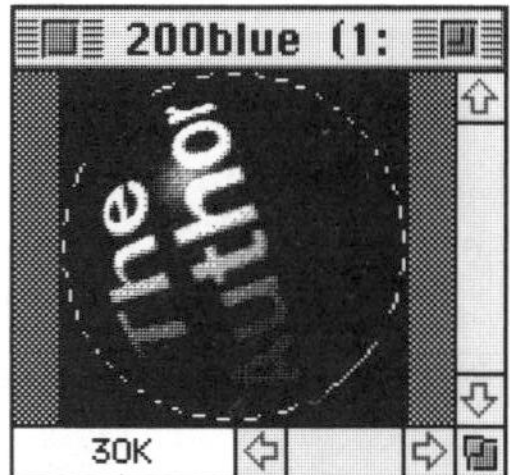

Cut out this circle and paste it where you want it:

To animate the sphere by rolling it across the screen, you first need to make a number of rotated images of the sphere. Rotate the image in 45-degree increments to create eight images including the original, rotating in a full circle of 360 degrees. When displayed sequentially, the sphere spins:

For a realistic rolling motion effect, the circumference (calculated at pi times 100, or about 314 pixels) is divided by eight (yielding about 40 pixels). As each image is successively displayed, the ball is moved 40 pixels along a line. This math applies when you roll any round object.

Creating an Animated Scene

The animation example presented here became a small piece of the roll-out presentation to developers and the press of Microsoft's Multimedia Extensions for Windows. The event is described in the "First Person" anecdote following.

A creative committee organized a brief storyboard of a gorilla chasing a man. From a CD-ROM containing many unlimited-licensed images, a photograph was chosen of Manhattan's Central Park where a bridge crossed a small river and high-rise apartments lined the horizon. The chase scene would occur across the bridge. To produce frames of the running man, an actor was videotaped running in place against an ultimatte blue background in a studio; a few frames of this were grabbed with a video capture board, and the blue background was removed from each image. The gorilla was difficult to find, so a toy model dinosaur about 25 centimeters tall was used; again, a few frames were captured and the background made transparent. That was all that was required for image resources.

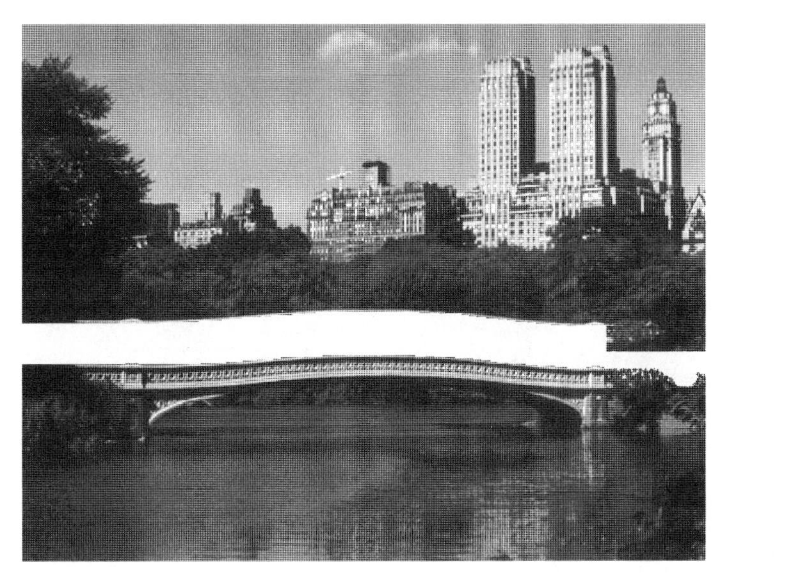

FIGURE 12-2 *The upper portion of this photo was placed behind the runners (see Figure 12-4) and the lower portion in front of them, to make them appear to run behind the bridge railing*

As illustrated in Figure 12-2, the background was carefully cut in half along the edge of the bridge, so the bridge railing could be placed in front of the runners.

The running man was organized in a series of six frames that could be repeated many times across the screen to provide the pumping motions of running. The same was done for the dinosaur, to give him a lumbering, bulky look as he chased the little man across the bridge (see Figure 12-3). The result, in Figure 12-4, was simple and quickly achieved.

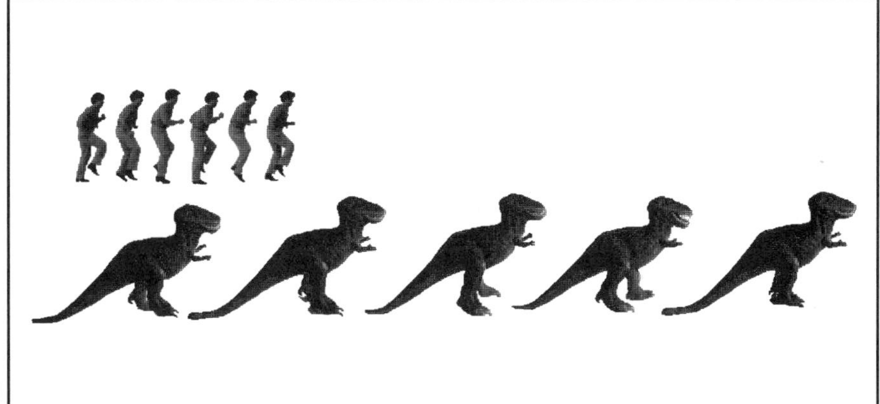

FIGURE 12-3 *Just a few images of a running creature are needed to make up an animation. The more in-between frames, the smoother the animation*

FIGURE 12-4

The combined elements of an animation

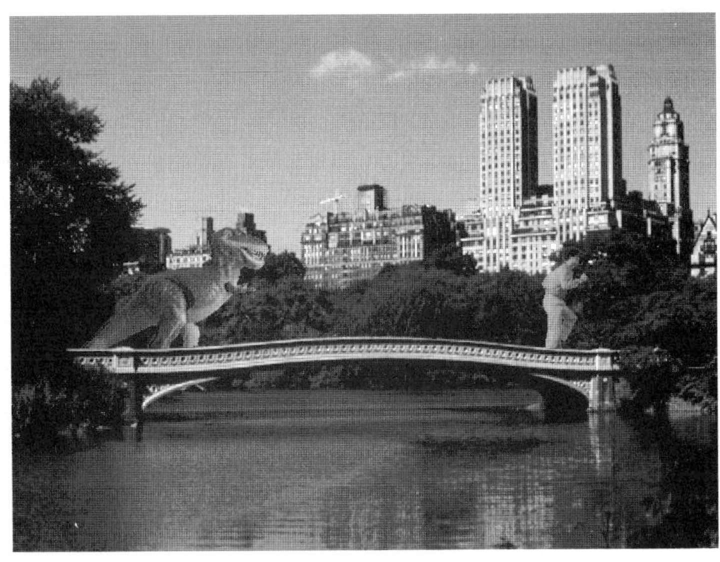

First Person

The animation storyboard called for a photo-realistic monster chasing a running man through a city park amid screams of terror. The man was already in Director, running in great strides across an arched footbridge in a woodsy scene with high rises in the background; he even looked over his shoulder a few times in panic. We were scouting around for an effective Godzilla when a friend dropped by with a motorized, 12-inch Tyrannosaurus Rex from Toys'R'Us. It was perfect, opening a toothy, gaping mouth every few steps as it lumbered along on C batteries.

I took the dinosaur and a video camera home to the delight and fascination of my three-year-old daughter, who helped rig a white sheet in front of the living room fireplace and a cardboard-box runway where Mr. TRex could strut his stuff before the camera. A couple of lamps gave him a sweaty sheen. We ran about five minutes of VHS tape as my daughter happily retrieved Mr. TRex each time he nosed off the "cliff" at the end of the stage.

Playing the tape on a VCR with a five-head, single-frame advance feature, I grabbed about every fourth frame with an old ColorSpace digitizing board on the Macintosh, and imported the resulting PICT files into Director as cast members. They needed a little cleanup and scaling, but the fellow looked really convincing when he was finally scored to run across the bridge. Next day, I mixed a bunch of sounds–singing birds, running footsteps, screams, roars, sirens, and gunshots–and it was done. We exported it from the Macintosh to Windows as an MMM file.

A few weeks later, in November, 1990, Mr. TRex helped introduce Bill Gates to a crowd of 600 at the opening of the first Microsoft Multimedia Developers Conference.

Font Animation

Computers manage text quickly and efficiently. By replacing specially made characters very rapidly in a text field, you can create excellent animations. You will need font editing tools (see Chapter 9 for product descriptions) to make your special characters. First, let's examine the process for spinning this turbine:

The largest-sized bitmapped font managed by the Macintosh is 127 points in height, and it can be wider. Our turbine image itself is about 180 pixels high, so the image is split into a top character and a bottom character. The font will have a total of eight characters. And remember, pixels and points are the same size in this environment.

To create the effect of spinning, the entire turbine image was rotated into four views, each one offset 90 degrees. Capital letters represent the top of the turbine, and small letters the bottom half of the turbine. Both characters are displayed 90 points high in a single field, one on top of the other without leading. The four views, top and bottom, will be combined to make a full picture:

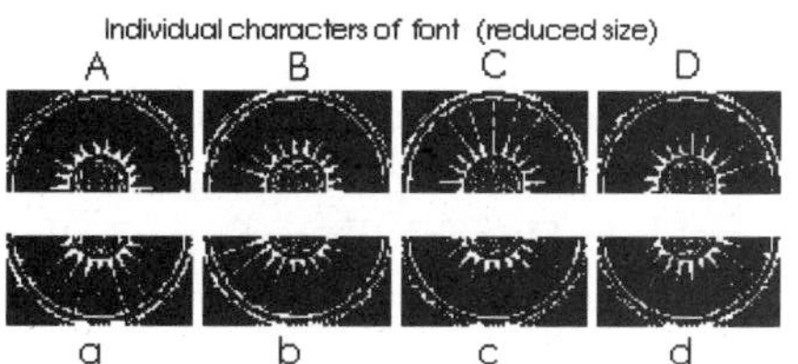

The character size and the line height of the text field where the character is displayed are both set to 90 points, so there is no blank space between the upper and lower characters.

Here is a step-by-step explanation of the process of creating the characters used to rotate the turbine blades in the previous illustration:

1. First, render the image. The turbine was scanned from a manufacturer's photograph of a real jet engine, to create an image approximately 180×180 pixels in size. The image could also have been drawn by hand. To "true" up the rough image, a center point was determined (notice the tiny cross at the precise center), and concentric rings were drawn. These rings and the hub were rendered to exactly symmetrical dimensions.
2. Capture and split the character images into 8 smaller images, 180 pixels wide and 90 pixels high.
3. Make each image a single character in a custom font. Using a font editor, you can make fine adjustments to the characters and precisely size and line them up, as shown here by using ResEdit's font editor:

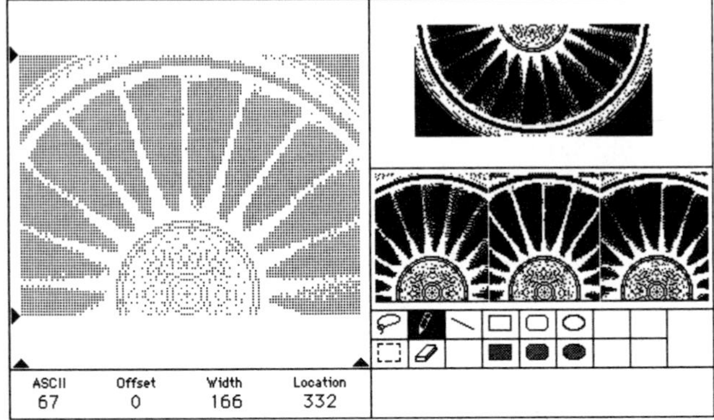

4. Install the font into your system.
5. Write appropriate script or program code to create the animation. Do this in a loop that continuously replaces the characters in the field. In HyperTalk or SuperTalk, the script for our turbine would look like this:

```
on mouseUp
  repeat 8 times
    put return & "D d" into card field "turbine"
    put return & "C c" into card field "turbine"
    put return & "B b" into card field "turbine"
    put return & "A a" into card field "turbine"
  end repeat
end mouseUp
```

Multi

[*Carefully planned, well executed video clips can make a dramatic difference in a multimedia project.*]

Digital video is the most **engaging** of multimedia venues

compelling

chapter 13

Video

it is a very **powerful** tool to bring computer users closer to the real world.

CAREFULLY planned, well executed video clips can make a dramatic difference in a multimedia project. A clip of John F. Kennedy proclaiming, "Ich bin ein Berliner" in video and sound is more compelling than a scrolling text field containing that same speech. Before deciding to add video to your project, however, it is essential to have an understanding of the medium, its limitations, and its costs. This chapter provides a basic foundation to help you understand how video works, the different formats and standards for recording and playing video, and the differences between computer and television video. The equipment needed to shoot and edit video, as well as tips for adding video to your project, are also covered.

Using Video

Since the first silent movie flickered to life, people have been fascinated with "motion" pictures. To this day, motion video is the element of multimedia that can draw gasps from a crowd at a trade show or firmly hold a student's interest in a computer-based learning project. Digital video is the most engaging of multimedia venues, and it is a very powerful tool to bring computer users closer to the real world. It is also a very effective method for delivering multimedia to an audience raised on television. With video elements in your project, you can effectively present your messages and reinforce your story, and viewers tend to retain more of what they see. But take care! Video that is not thought out or well produced can degrade your presentation.

Full-motion video on personal computers changes everything. It is like turning a ten-speed bicycle into a Harley-Davidson.

David Bunnell, Editor in Chief, *NewMedia* magazine

Standards and formats for digital text, imagery, and sound are well established and familiar. But video is the most recent addition to the elements of multimedia. And it is still being refined as transport, storage, compression, and display technologies take shape in laboratories and in the marketplace. Working with multimedia video today can be like a Mojave Desert camping trip: you may pitch your tent on comfortable high ground, and find that overnight the shifting sands have buried both your approach and your investment. Firm ground tends to shift rapidly in the 100-mph backdraft of the many silicon engineers, computer scientists, and start-up company salespeople driving in the fast lane of video overlay boards, compression schemes, and interleaving software.

Of all the multimedia elements, video places the highest performance demands on your computer and its memory. Consider that the still color image on a computer screen could require as much as one megabyte of memory. Multiply this by 30 (the number of times per second that the picture is replaced to provide the appearance of motion), and you need 30 megabytes of memory per second to play your video—1.8 gigabytes of memory per minute, or 108 gigabytes per hour. Just moving the picture data at that rate from computer memory to the screen challenges the processing capability of a super computer. These massive memory storage demands make the Library of Congress look like a magazine rack at your local grocery store. Some of the hottest and most arcane multimedia technologies and research efforts today deal with compressing this digital video image data into manageable streams of information.

If you have control over your project's delivery platform, such as a specially designed kiosk, you can get the highest video performance by specifying special hardware and software enhancements. A video compression board allows you to work with full-screen, full-motion video. A sophisticated audio board allows you to use CD-quality audio. You can install a super-fast disk array to support high-speed data transfer rates. You can include instructions in your authoring system that spools video into RAM for rapid playback.

Since multimedia gives you the ability to present information in a variety of ways, let the content drive the selection of media for each chunk of information to be presented. Use traditional text and graphics where appropriate; add animation when "still life" won't get your message across; add audio when further explanation is required; resort to video only when all other methods pale by comparison.

David A. Ludwig, Interactive Learning Designs

Obtaining Video Clips

If your project will include video, consider whether you should shoot new footage or acquire pre-existing content for your video clips. There are many sources for film and video clips: a friend's home movies may suffice, or you can go to a "stock" footage house or a television station or movie studio. But acquiring footage that you do not own outright can be a nightmare—it is expensive, and licensing rights and permissions may be difficult, if not impossible, to obtain. Each second of video could cost $50 to $100 or more to license. Even a "public domain clip" from the National Archives costs a minimum of $125 to copy the footage, with a turnaround time of up to six weeks.

On some projects, you will have no choice but to pay the price for required footage. If it is absolutely essential that your project include a clip of Elvis Presley crooning "You Ain't Nothing but a Hound Dog," and an Elvis impersonator just won't do, you will have to negotiate for rights to use the real thing. If your budget can't cover the cost of licensing a particular video clip, you may want to consider using other alternatives: locating a less expensive archival video source, using a series of still images rather than video, or shooting your own video. If you shoot your own video for a project, make sure you have releases from all persons who appear or speak, and you have permission to use the audio effects and music you weave into it. Licensing, permissions, and legal issues are discussed more fully in Chapter 16.

Before you head out to the field with your camcorder in hand, it is important to understand at least the basics of video recording and editing, as well as the constraints of using video in a multimedia project. The remainder of this chapter will help you to understand how video works and will provide practical guidelines for shooting your own videos.

How Video Works

When light reflected from an object passes through a video camera lens, that light is converted into an electronic signal by a special sensor called a *charge-coupled device*, or a CCD. Top-quality broadcast cameras may have as many as three CCDs to improve the resolution of the camera. The signal from the camera contains three channels of color information (red, green, and blue) and synchronization pulses (*sync*). If each channel of color information is transmitted as a separate signal, the signals are called *RGB*, which is the preferred method for higher-quality and professional video work. The video signal can also be split into two separate chroma channels and a brightness channel, to make *component* video. If the signals are mixed together and carried on a single cable, it is a *composite* of the three color

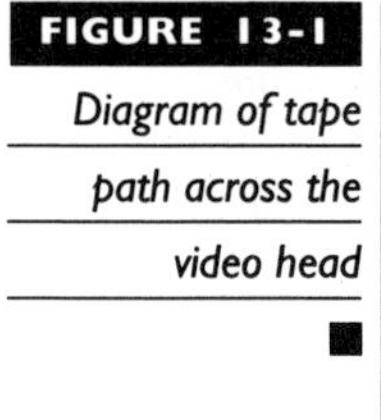
FIGURE 13-1
Diagram of tape path across the video head

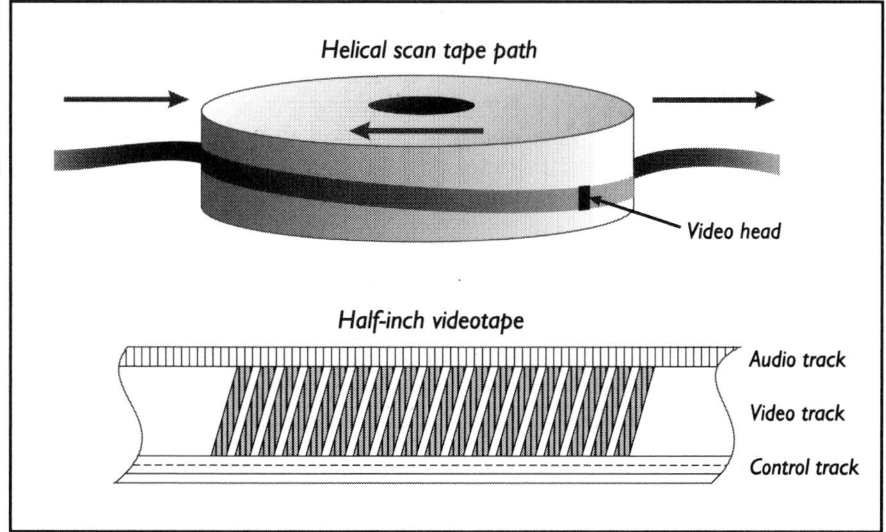

channels and the sync signal; this system yields less-precise color definition that cannot be manipulated or color corrected as much as an RGB signal.

The video signal is delivered to the Video In connector of a VCR, where it is recorded on magnetic videotape. One or two channels of sound may also be recorded on the tape. The video signal is written to tape by a spinning recording head that changes the local magnetic properties of the tape's surface in a series of long diagonal stripes. Because the head follows a helical path, this is called *helical scan recording*. As illustrated in Figure 13-1, each stripe represents information for one field of a video frame. A single video frame is made up of two fields that are interlaced.

Audio is recorded on a separate straight-line track at the top of the videotape, although with some recording systems (notably for 3/4-inch tape and for 1/2-inch tape with high-fidelity audio) sound is recorded helically between the video tracks. At the bottom of the tape is a control track containing the pulses used to regulate speed. *Tracking* is fine adjustment of the tape so that the tracks are properly aligned as the tape moves across the playback head.

A video cassette recorder (VCR) can also add the video and sound signals to a subcarrier and modulate them into a radio frequency in the FM broadcast band. This is the NTSC signal available at the Antenna Out connector of a VCR (NTSC is explained in the next section). Usually you

First Person

Surf Alligators live within the cusps of breaking technology waves. They can be snuffed with good knowledge, tools, and a network of colleagues willing to answer arcane questions. Catching these alligators requires the patience of Costa Rican beach children who cast unbaited three-barbed hooks into the incoming waves to yank out their surprised and luckless silver prey.

My 19-inch RGB monitor, a Hitachi re-branded by both SuperMac and Silicon Graphics, has BNC inputs for red, green, and blue and requires that horizontal sync be superimposed on the green channel. This is supported by SuperMac's and other NuBus video cards at 8-bit color depth. I wanted the Quadra 840AV's internal video support for 19-inch monitors at 16 bits, claimed in Apple's literature. But no way would my monitor work, and it took four days of calling around to discover why. Sorry, no sync on green from that Quadra, they said. Throw the monitor away. Get one with more BNC inputs.

Apple's User Assistance Center (usually busy, and not open at 1:00 a.m.) was of no help. My arcane questions were not in the annoying hierarchy of voice message help, and it took two days to get hold of a real person to tell me the answer wasn't in her data bank. I felt like trolling with those Costa Rican fish hooks across the many rows of phone- answering cubicles at the Assistance Center, and yanking real hard.

Real information was finally forthcoming when I contacted two guys on Apple's Quadra hardware team through AOL and AppleLink. They had documents that explained all and included the peculiar sensing codes (pins 4, 7, and 10 of the 15-pin monitor connector) used by the Quadra's built-in video to automatically adjust to most monitors. I felt 100 percent better when I knew the WHY of it, even though I had to buy a new monitor.

Every time you upgrade your computer hardware, and occasionally when you upgrade your software, you are likely to attract surf alligators. These perils aren't like the steep learning curves where with effort you can incrementally improve your skill; they are brutally mechanical and test you in other ways.

From "Alligators," a monthly column written by Tay Vaughan for *Morph's Outpost*, October, 1993

can choose between Channel 3 or Channel 4 frequencies, and the resulting signal or picture can be viewed on a television. Some television sets provide a separate composite signal connector to avoid the unnecessary step of modulating and demodulating the signal into the broadcast frequency bands.

Colored phosphors on the screen glow red, green, or blue when they are energized by the electron beam. Because the intensity of the beam varies as it moves across the screen, some colors glow brighter than others. Finely tuned magnets around the picture tube aim the electrons very precisely onto the phosphor screen while the intensity of the beam is varied according to the video signal. All of these electronic activities work in concert to yield a television picture.

Broadcast Video Standards

Three broadcast and video standards and recording formats are in use around the world: NTSC, PAL, and SECAM. Because these standards and formats are not easily interchangeable, it is important to know where your multimedia project will be used. A videocassette recorded in the United States does not play on a television set in any European country, even though the recording method and style of the cassette is "VHS." Likewise, tapes recorded in European PAL or SECAM formats do not play back on an NTSC video cassette recorder. Each system is based on a different standard that defines the manner in which information is encoded to produce the electronic signal that ultimately creates a television picture. Multiformat VCRs can play back all three standards, but typically cannot dub from one standard to another; dubbing between standards still requires high-end, specialized equipment.

NTSC

The United States, Japan, and many other countries use a system for broadcasting and displaying video that is based upon the specifications set forth by the 1952 National Television Standards Committee (NTSC). These standards define a method for encoding information into the electronic signal that ultimately creates a television picture. As specified by the NTSC standard, a single frame of video is made up of 525 horizontal scan lines drawn onto the inside face of a phosphor-coated picture tube every 1/30 of a second by a fast-moving electron beam. The drawing occurs so fast that your eye perceives the image as stable. The electron beam actually makes two passes as it draws a single video frame, first laying down all the odd-numbered lines, then all the even-numbered lines. Each of these passes (which happen at a rate of 60 per second, or 60 Hz) paints a field. The process of building a single frame from two fields is called *interlacing,* a technique that helps to prevent flicker on television screens. Remember that computer monitors draw the lines of an entire frame in one scan, without interlacing.

Sometimes we define "NTSC" as "Never The Same Color."

Richard Santalesa, R&D Technologies

"Super NTSC" and "16×9" are new forms of the NTSC standard currently under testing. These are interim steps to High Definition Television (described in the HDTV section below), which uses a 16:9 screen aspect ratio instead of the traditional 4:3 and twice the number of horizontal scan lines on the screen. Professional and some consumer video equipment that supports this screen ratio is already beginning to appear; regular use is yet to come.

PAL

The Phase Alternate Line (PAL) system is used in the United Kingdom, Europe, Australia, and South Africa. PAL is an integrated method of adding color to a black and white television signal that paints 625 lines at a frame rate of 25 frames per second. Like NTSC, the even and odd lines are interlaced, each field taking 1/50 of a second to draw (50 Hz).

SECAM

The Sequential Color and Memory (SECAM) system is used in France, Russia, and a few other countries. Although SECAM is a 625-line, 50 Hz system, it differs greatly from both the NTSC and the PAL color systems in its basic technology and broadcast method.

HDTV

High Definition Television (HDTV) is scheduled to be the next step in television technology. At this point in the development of this standard, it provides 1,200 lines of resolution in a 16:9 aspect ratio (see Figure 13-2). This aspect ratio allows the viewing of Cinemascope and Panavision movies. There are three competing HDTV standards, one each developed by the Japanese and the Europeans (both are analog formats), and one developed by the United States that is a digital format. The winner of the HDTV standard wars will take over the airwaves in the early 21st century.

warning *Today's multimedia typically uses a screen pixel ratio of 4:3 (640×480), but the new HDTV standard specifies a ratio of 16:9, much wider than tall (see Figure 13-2). There is no easy way to stretch and shrink existing graphics material to fit this new aspect ratio, so new multimedia design and interface principles will need to be developed for HDTV presentations.*

FIGURE 13-2 *Here you can see the difference between VGA and HDTV aspect ratios*

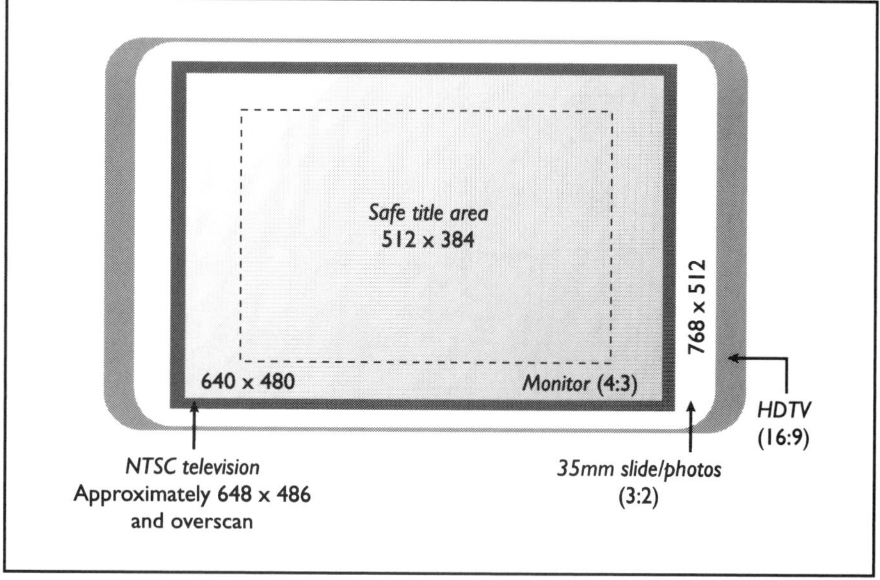

Integrating Computers and Television

There is some confusion of terms when discussing video in computer and television contexts. Bear in mind that television video is based on analog technology and fixed international standards for the broadcast and display of images. Computer video is based on digital technology and other, more extensible standards for displaying images. In the late 1990s these two technologies—television and computer-based video—will merge with the introduction of High Definition Television.

The First Step: Video Overlay Systems

The video/computer marriage began when computers were used simply to control analog video images from tape decks and videodisc players displayed on a television. In fact, the most common computer-based training (CBT) configuration is still a dual-monitor workstation, where one monitor shows computer-managed training material and a television displays supporting video from a source that is controlled by the computer (see Figure 13-3). Trainees using these systems move their heads in a rhythmic tennis-match tempo set by the application's design metronome. As you might imagine, there was early pressure from CBT developers and vendors alike to integrate both the digital and analog images onto a single monitor.

To display analog video (television) images on a computer monitor, the video signal must first be converted from analog to digital form. A special

FIGURE 13-3 Videodisc players can be controlled by a computer

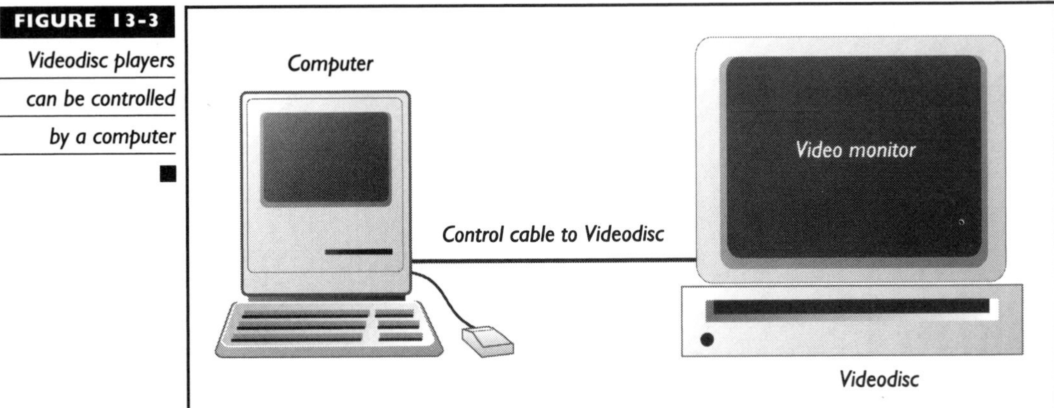

video digitizing overlay board must be installed in your computer to take the video signal and convert it to digital information. The analog video signal (converted to digital information) and the computer's own digital graphics are mixed, yielding either a full screen of motion video or a window of video cut into the computer's normal display (see Figure 13-4). Video overlay boards offer real advantages over today's fully digital systems: the video is of excellent quality and can be full-screen, full-motion, and full-color. On the other hand, the added cost of these boards and the videodisc players or tape decks required can double the price of your system.

Some video overlay boards simply let you display video images on your computer screen, usually with several choices of window size. Better and more expensive boards offer visual effects such as freezing, fades, spins, mirrors, and chroma keys. Chroma keys allow you to choose a color or range of colors that becomes transparent, allowing the video image to be seen "through" the computer image. Some boards can capture a single 1/30-second frame and save it as a digitized still image, and some, such as the DVA-4000 from VideoLogic (available for both Macintosh and PC), also provide control of stereo audio.

Speak92!, shown in Figure 13-5, is a videodisc (and QuickTime) English-language training program from OpenMind International that uses a video overlay board. It presents real-life encounters using video in a window; it expertly guides students' progress; and it provides statistics and tracking information for the instructor.

Commands such as play, forward, reverse, stop, rewind, and pause are sent over a serial cable connected between the computer and the videodisc player or tape deck. Videodisc players with serial communication ports (these are not the consumer variety) are most commonly used to supply the video image because these players provide "random access" to all the frames

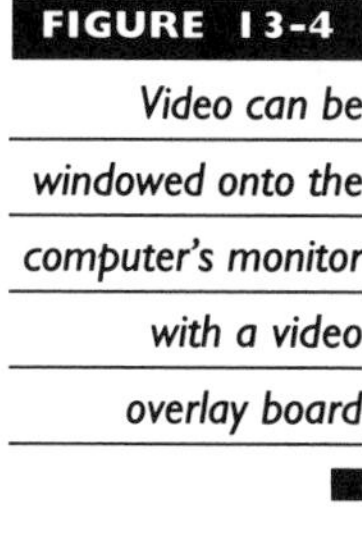

FIGURE 13-4 Video can be windowed onto the computer's monitor with a video overlay board

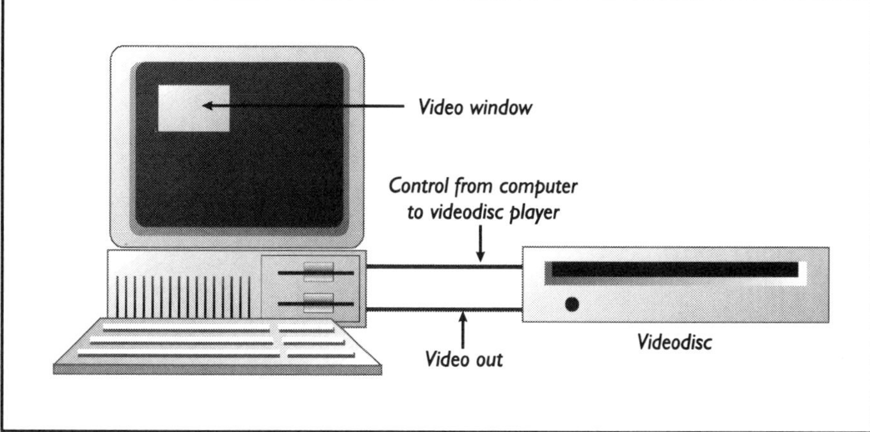

on the videodisc, allowing programmers to select with their software a video sequence to play at a given time and in a specific way. For example, a typical CAV (Constant Angular Velocity) format videodisc may contain as many as 54,000 individual frames of analog video. With the combination of video board special effects and the programmer's control of the videodisc player, multimedia designers have terrific power to mix eye-grabbing motion into their computer productions. Videodiscs can also be used to store many thousands of video-quality still images, and the computer can be programmed to display each image on demand using these same visual effects.

Video Capture Boards

Video overlay boards can often capture or digitize video frames as well as play them back from analog video sources, and they are commonly used for making QuickTime and AVI movies (see Chapter 6). Many video boards also incorporate audio input and sound management so that the audio portion of a video clip can be digitally interleaved and synced with the images during digitizing. You should be aware, however, that some video digitizing boards offer only 8-bit audio at a sampling rate of 22 KHz. This is not CD quality, but it is currently the most common sound quality used for CD-ROM-delivered multimedia. Audio technology and these terms are fully described in Chapter 10.

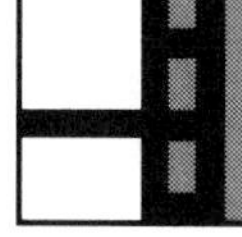

tip *Always import video and sound at the highest resolution available. You can reduce the resolution later according to your needs.*

FIGURE 13-5

Speak92! uses videos of real life situations to teach language skills

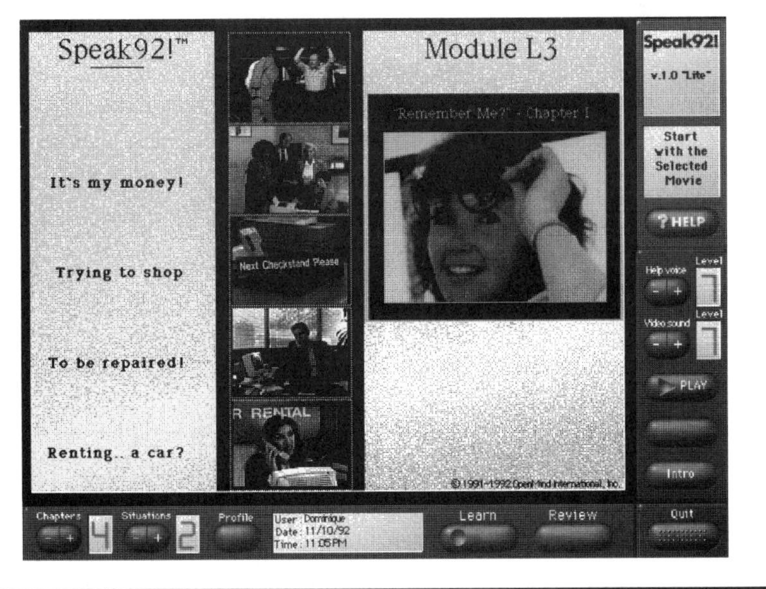

Some video overlay boards offer hardware compression. On even the fastest PCs or Macintoshes some frames are lost or dropped during digitizing because the computer is overwhelmed by the demands of managing the video data as it comes in. To relieve the processing bottleneck, some boards use specialized chips to speed up the digitizing process and can successfully digitize full-screen, full-motion video at 60 fields (or 30 frames) per second. The drawback of these hardware-dependent video systems, however, is that you typically require a playback system that has the same compression chips on board.

Some video overlay boards also support output of NTSC video so that you can record what you see on the computer monitor to videotape. Table 13-1 includes the names and manufacturers of selected video digitizing and capture boards.

The Next Step: Digitized Video Playback

The next step toward fully integrating motion video and digital computer graphics is to eliminate the analog television form of video from the multimedia delivery platform. If a video clip can first be converted from analog to digital, then stored as data on a hard disk, CD-ROM, or other mass-storage device, that clip can be played back on the computer's monitor without overlay boards, videodisc players, or second monitors. This play-

Name of Board	Manufacturer	Capture Sizes
SNAPplus	Cardinal Technologies	160×120, 320×240, 640×480
Video Blaster	Creative Labs	4 resolutions, 80×60 to 640×480
VideoSpigot for Windows	Creative Labs	5 resolutions, 80×60 to 640×480
ComputerEyes/RT	Digital Vision	4 resolutions, 64×50 to 512×480
ComputerEyes/RT SCSI Mac	Digital Vision	2 resolutions, 160×120, 320×240
ActionMedia II	IBM	Up to 256×240, motion
ProMotion	IEV International	160×120, 320×240, 480×360
Smart Video Recorder	Intel	160×120, 320×240, 640×480
MacVision SCSI Color	Koala	640×480
Pro MovieStudio	Media Vision	5 resolutions, 80×60 to 640×480
ClipIt!	New Media Graphics	320×240, 640×480
Super VideoWindows	New Media Graphics	320×240, 640×480
Eye-Q 2.0	New Video	320×240
VideoVision	Radius	640×480
VideoVision Studio	Radius	640×480
24STV	RasterOps	640×480
MediaTime	RasterOps	640×480
MoviePak	RasterOps	320×240
MovieMovie	Sigma Designs	160×120, 320×240
WinMovie	Sigma Designs	5 resolutions, 80×60 to 640×480
DigitalFilm	SuperMac	320×480, 640×240
Spigot & Sound	SuperMac	320×240
VideoSpigot	SuperMac	320×240
Bravado/16	Truevision	16 resolutions, 40×30 to 640×480
Bravado/24	Truevision	640×480
Captivator	Videologic	32×32 to 640×480
MediaSpace	Videologic	1024×768
XingIt!	Xing	160x120 to 320×240

TABLE 13-1 *Some Video Overlay Boards and Their Features* ■

back is accomplished using software such as QuickTime for the Macintosh or Video for Windows, which are explained in Chapter 6.

As a multimedia producer or developer you need to convert your video source material from its common analog form (videotape) to a digital form manageable by the end user's computer system. So an understanding of analog video and some special hardware must remain in your multimedia toolbox.

Analog to digital conversion of video can often be accomplished using the video overlay hardware described in the preceding section, but to repeatedly digitize a full-screen color video image every 1/30 second and store it to disk or RAM severely taxes both Macintosh and PC processing capabilities— special hardware, compression software, and massive amounts of digital storage space is required. And repeated reading from disk and displaying to the monitor the full-screen color images of motion video, at a rate of one frame every 1/30 second, taxes the computational and display power of both the Macintosh and the PC.

The final evolutionary step to fully digital video will not occur until the acquisition and recording of video becomes entirely a digital procedure, and analog videotape is removed from the process.

Differences Between Computer and Television Video

Although most computer screens have the same 4:3 aspect ratio as a television screen, a typical computer screen only scans 480 horizontal lines from top to bottom, not the 525 or 625 lines of NTSC or PAL television. Also, a computer monitor scans each line progressively, with no interlacing; the scan is full frame at a rate of typically 66.67 Hz or higher, compared to 60 Hz for a full television frame.

Overscan and the Safe Title Area

As illustrated in Figure 13-2, it is common practice in the television industry to broadcast an image larger than will fit on a standard TV screen so that the "edge" of the image seen by a viewer is always bounded by the TV's physical frame or bezel. This is called *overscan*. In contrast, computer monitors display a smaller image on the TV's picture tube (*underscan*). Consequently, when a digitized video image is displayed on an RGB screen, there is a border around the image; when a computer screen is converted to video, the outer edges of the image do not fit on a TV screen. Only about 360 of the 480 lines of the computer screen are visible.

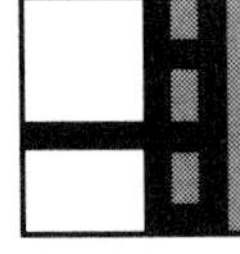

tip *Avoid using the outer 15 percent of the screen when producing computer-generated graphics and titles for use in television video. The safe title area, where your image will not be affected by overscanning, even in the worst conditions, is illustrated in Figure 13-2.*

Video Color

Color reproduction and display is different between televisions and computer monitors. Because computers use RGB component video (they split colors into red, green, and blue signals), their colors are purer and more accurate than those seen on a television monitor. Consequently, colors used in a graphic image created for computer video may display differently when that image is transformed into NTSC television video.

Indeed, NTSC television uses a limited color palette and restricted luminance (brightness) levels and black levels (the richness of the blacks). Some colors generated by your computer that display fine on an RGB monitor may be "illegal" for display on an NTSC television. These colors are particularly apparent in shades of red, and cause bleeding or noisy shimmering when displayed on a television. Most commercial broadcast facilities and TV studios refuse to run video programs that include illegal colors. Filters to convert illegal colors to legal colors are available in image editing and processing applications such as Photoshop, ColorSense, and JAG II.

When producing a multimedia project, you should consider whether it will be played back on an RGB monitor and/or on a conventional television set. If your work is destined, for example, for a set-top player such as SEGA, 3DO, CD-I, or Photo CD, choose your colors to meet the NTSC color specifications.

There are many variables in providing perfect colors on a television. End users can control hue and balance (an adjustment not available on most RGB monitors), and it is likely that few viewers of your project will have perfectly calibrated television sets. So you are fighting an uphill battle from the beginning.

It helps to do color corrections and editing on your computer, then view the corrected image on a real television screen, not just the RGB monitor. For this, you need a signal converter card that can provide NTSC output installed in your computer; video overlay cards often offer this feature.

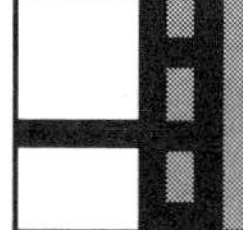

tip *A useful trick is to grab a standard broadcast color test bar using a video frame grabber, then save it as a PICT or TIFF image. When viewing the bar in Photoshop, for example, you can check the levels of each color by viewing red, green, and blue one at a time. The gradient of grays in the color bar should be smooth and even for each color channel.*

First Person

Captain's Log: We received some excellent design tips from Bernice T. Glenn:

As intermedia applications continue to proliferate, producers and designers need to know how to float between print and color pigment, digital color and RGB as viewed on a monitor, and analog color as viewed on a television screen. Color formulas for multimedia, especially when it is interactive, depend heavily on human factors.

Contrast, the degree of tonal difference between one color and another, is often more important when working with color on a computer screen. A combination of pure yellow with pure violet, or blue and orange, for example, will vibrate when viewed in RGB. On video, disturbing flickers, extraneous colors, and other artifacts usually appear on the borders between pure complementary colors. On top of that, colors that look great on your computer monitor may not even show up when transferred to video.

Important elements can be emphasized by using fully saturated colors against a neutral background, whose color may complement as a grayed-down tint of the color.

When readability is important, contrast in color saturation and value between the type and its background really works, using almost any color combination.

Red or green may need to be avoided as cue colors [for menu buttons and icons] because 8 percent of the population is color blind to some extent, and cannot see reds or greens in their true color value.

From "Ask the Captain," a monthly column written by Tay Vaughan for *NewMedia* Magazine, January, 1994

Interlacing Effects

In television, the electron beam actually makes two passes on the screen as it draws a single video frame, first laying down all the odd-numbered lines, then all the even-numbered lines; they are interlaced. On an RGB monitor, lines are painted one-pixel thick and are not interlaced. Single-pixel lines displayed on an RGB monitor look fine; on a television, these thin lines flicker brightly as they only appear in every other field. To prevent this flicker, make sure that your lines are greater than two pixels thick and that you avoid very thin or highly serifed typefaces. You can filter your completed image through a de-interlacing filter provided by image editing applications such as Photoshop or JAG II. With typefaces, interlacing flicker can often be avoided by anti-aliasing the type to slightly blur the edges of the characters.

Working with Text and Titles for Television

Titles for video productions can be created with an analog character generator, but your computer can do this digitally using video and image editing software. Here are some suggestions for creating good titles:

- Fonts for titles should be plain, sans serif, and bold enough to be easily read.
- When you are laying text onto a dark background, use white or a light color for the text.
- Use a drop shadow to help separate the text from the background image.
- Never use black or colored text on a stark white background or it will bleed; anti-aliasing can prevent bleeding.
- Do not kern your letters too tightly.
- If you use underlining or drawn graphics, always make your lines at least two pixels wide. If you use a one-pixel-wide line (or a width measured in an odd number of pixels), the line will flicker when transferred to video, due to interlacing.
- Use parallel lines, boxes, and tight concentric circles sparingly. When you use them, draw them large and with thick lines.
- Avoid colors that are too hot, like pure red.
- Neighboring colors should be markedly different in intensity. For example, use a light blue and a dark red, but not a medium blue and a medium red.
- Keep your graphics and titles within the safe area of the screen. Remember that televisions overscan computer output (see the earlier section, "Differences Between Computer and Television Video").
- Bring titles on slowly, keep them onscreen for a sufficient interval, then fade them out.
- Avoid making busy title screens; use more pages, instead.

Shooting and Editing Video

To add full-screen, full-motion video to your multimedia project, you need to invest in specialized hardware and software or purchase the services of a professional video production studio. In many cases, a professional studio will also provide editing tools and post-production capabilities that you cannot duplicate with your Macintosh or PC.

Expensive professional video equipment and services may not yield proportionately greater benefits than consumer-grade equipment. As with audio equipment (see Chapter 10), you need to make balancing decisions using Vaughan's Law of Multimedia Minimums. Most likely, your goal is to expend resources without diminishing returns—to produce multimedia that is adequate and does its job but doesn't break your bank. If you can, experiment with various combinations of video recording and playback devices hooked to your video digitizing hardware and test the results using your multimedia authoring platform. You can do a great deal of satisfactory work with consumer-grade video cameras and recording equipment if you understand the limitations of the technology.

Software tools for editing and working with digital video on the Macintosh and PC are described in detail in Chapter 6.

Recording Formats

There are a number of different recording formats to choose from when shooting video. These formats represent different means of putting the video signal onto tape. They range from formats that are relatively inexpensive (a few hundred dollars) using a cassette small enough to fit in a shirt pocket, to high-resolution digital recorders costing hundreds of thousands of dollars and needing a carrying case the size of a briefcase. The sections below describe common video recording formats.

S-VHS Video

S-VHS video keeps the color and luminance information on two separate tracks. The result is a definite improvement in picture quality. This standard is also used in Hi-8. Although basically oriented toward consumers, this format is gaining rapid acceptance among lower-end broadcasters. Still, if your ultimate goal is to have the project accepted by broadcast stations, S-VHS is not the best choice.

Component (YUV)

In the early 1980s, Sony began to experiment with a new portable professional video format based on Betamax. Called Betacam, it required speeding the tape up considerably (a two-hour tape was used up in 20 minutes), and laying the signal on the tape in three channels, one for red, one for blue, and one for luminance information. The resulting format (called "component") produced images that had none of the problems of traditional composite video, such as color shift and bleed and crawling edges on graphics. Betacam has evolved into Betacam SP, which features four channels of audio and is superior to one-inch and even some digital formats. Though Panasonic has developed its own standard based on a similar technology, called MII, Betacam SP has become the industry standard for professional video field recording.

This format may soon be eclipsed by a new digital version called "Digital Betacam." Featuring four channels of CD-quality audio, its video quality is almost equal to D-1 digital (the highest video quality available today, described in the following section).

Betacam SP is without a doubt THE choice for the broadcast industry. No format is so widely used and praised. Looking at a typical jerky, one-quarter screen QuickTime movie in a multimedia title, you may think shooting on Betacam SP is overkill. But you should start thinking ahead to the next wave, when full screen/full motion becomes a reality and the differences between S-VHS or Hi-8 and Betacam become apparent.

In addition, Sony has mounted a campaign to drop the cost of Betacam SP ever lower with their PVW and UVW lines of recorders. For the first time, Betacam SP is almost as cheap as industrial-grade 3/4-inch U-matic.

Component Digital

Around the same time Sony was developing Betacam, the company also began research in digital video, where the signal was converted to digital information before it was recorded as bits and bytes. The advantages were many, including better color and image resolution and an ability to make almost unlimited copies without loss of quality. The result of this research was D-1, or Component Digital. Using a 19-mm (3/4-inch) tape and recording the signal in a digital version of the component technology developed for Betacam, D-1 quickly proved itself as the format of choice for graphics. Although it is the oldest of digital video formats, D-1 is the standard by which all others are compared. It has most recently spawned DCT (from Ampex), D-5 (from Panasonic), and Digital Betacam (from Sony).

D-1 is at the pinnacle of NTSC video and is becoming the mastering standard of choice among high-end editing facilities. However, this quality comes with an extremely high price tag (a Quantel Henry editing system has a price of over $900,000 and can only work with 15 minutes of video). The result is that this format really only fits super-high-end broadcast projects and not your standard multimedia title.

Composite Digital

Although D-1 is a vastly superior recording format, its steep price scared away broadcasters: recording decks, for example, cost $110,000 or more. To reduce hardware costs, other less expensive formats were developed to record an NTSC composite signal in digital form: D-2 and D-3 (from Panasonic).

Though surpassed in quality by D-1, composite digital is still the most common digital standard for broadcast and editing facilities. Again, this format is more expensive to work with than is currently justified for multimedia.

Video Hardware Resolutions

Video horizontal resolution is the number of lines of detail a camera is able to reproduce; this aspect is not to be confused with the vertical scan lines on a TV set. The lens used, and the number, size, and quality of the CCDs, determine this resolution. Poor resolution and image quality when using consumer-grade equipment is usually the result of an inferior lens, cheaper circuit design, and shoddy video record heads.

The following table provides typical resolutions offered by various video recording hardware systems:

Video Type	Resolution
8 mm	230
VHS	240
3/4-SP	330
S-VHS	400
Hi-8	400
Betacam SP	550
MII	550
Broadcast-quality	1000

Consumer-Grade Equipment

Consumer-grade video equipment is designed for mass production and low manufacturing cost. In general, it is easier to use than industrial-grade or broadcast-quality equipment, but is not built to suffer wear and tear. The tape transport mechanisms are both fragile and imprecise. VCRs that incorporate special circuits to enhance sharpness provide a superior perceived picture image than do regular VCRs (some less expensive VCRs do not have these circuits). Both Beta- and VHS-type recorders are available with high-fidelity (hi-fi) sound with a dynamic range of up to 90 dB. Hi-fi sound is recorded diagonally on the tape between the video scans (but lower on the tape), so video and audio are recorded at the same time.

The High-Band 8 mm (known as Hi-8) and Super VHS (known as S-VHS) formats split the composite video signal into other components, to provide a higher-quality signal. Two additional channels are added, one containing luminance or brightness information (Y channel), and one containing chroma or color intensity information (C channel). Cameras and camcorders working in the Hi-8 and S-VHS formats use a four-pin DIN or S connector and produce pictures that are far superior to those of regular VHS and 8 mm systems, especially when viewed on a television or monitor designed for these formats.

Most S-VHS and 3/4-inch industrial equipment has built-in noise reduction circuitry to overcome the poor audio quality inherent to consumer-grade VHS decks. The regular 8 mm tape decks, however, employ a recording method similar to that used for digital audio tape (DAT). Audio is digitized and recorded on a track separate from the video signal, providing a dynamic range of about 88 dB.

Hi-8 is the most widely accepted tape format used for industrial and corporate video communications. One reason for this is the wide availability of Sony's Video System Control Architecture (VISCA), a platform-independent command language that lets you control up to seven video peripherals from a personal computer. With VISCA-compatible hardware, any 8 mm or VHS consumer deck or camcorder can be controlled through the computer's serial port. Working with video-capture and movie-making digitizer boards, video can be imported into a project, assembled and stored, and later printed to videotape. VISCA includes the V-Box, a computer/video interface for controlling playback and recording devices, and the V-Deck, a computer-controllable Hi-8 VCR. For video images that will be scaled to smaller windows than full-screen, standard VHS format recording works fine. Super VHS is better yet, and Hi-8 is probably the best you can do with consumer-grade equipment.

tip *When you shop for a new camcorder, exercise and test several camera/recorder combinations, then view the result on a good video monitor (not a television). You will see a difference.*

Signal Loss

If you ever plan to copy the tape you make during a production shoot to another tape (say, for a promotion or demo), use at least Super VHS, which will prevent your copies from bleeding colors and being disappointingly fuzzy. Better yet, use Hi-8, which will allow unlimited VHS copies to be made without degradation. If you plan to do video editing on tape (not on the computer), then Hi-8 is the consumer-grade option of choice.

Successful copying of video (*dubbing*) depends upon the format of the tape recording and the quality of equipment used. Copying from Hi-8 to VHS, for example, produces excellent results. Copying from Betacam SP to Super VHS gets good results as long as the Y/C connections are maintained. Dubbing from one-inch tape to other formats works well, copy after copy.

When copying from VHS to VHS, color smear and loss of image resolution are very noticeable. The bandwidth of the VHS signal is limited, and during dubbing much information is lost—even in a first generation dub from a Betacam SP edited master to a VHS submaster. A second generation dub (from a VHS master to a first copy) is proportionately worse. Yet another copy of the copy (a third generation) produces a tape that is practically unrecognizable.

Always dub in SP mode, never in LP or SLP, because the faster the video heads write on the tape, the better the recorded image will be. Always use the highest-quality tape to prevent clogging the video heads with loose magnetic particles.

Video Window Size

When you digitize a video image and shrink it to, say, half or quarter size, you will notice improvement in the perceived sharpness. This also happens when you switch from watching television on a 19-inch screen to watching a 12-inch screen. The image becomes crisper because the scan lines are physically much tighter. So VHS works fine in these circumstances. Super VHS and Hi-8 provide better full-screen images, but your digitizing video board must be able to utilize this resolution; in digitizing the video signal, the board dithers the image on the fly.

Editing with Consumer VCRs

Using two consumer-grade VCRs for editing results in glitches, picture noise, and rolling, because the VCRs are not in sync. You may also experience considerable loss in quality when dubbing, and possibly an audio lag. With consumer-grade decks, it is impossible to accurately preroll a tape prior to editing a scene.

To solve this problem, you have to use the tape counter on both the playback deck and the record deck, to reverse both tapes a given distance and then start them playing at exactly the same time. When they are both at speed and have reached the appropriate counter number for your edit, press the Record button on the recording machine (or release it from Pause mode). If your edit comes in too late, you must reverse both machines and try again; if you cut into the scene too soon, you have to repeat the entire edit of the previous shot and then try again. This can be tedious and time consuming—even if your decks have flying erase heads to avoid edit glitches—and the results may be disappointing.

To make fancy transitions, cross-fades, and wipes between scenes, you need two source players feeding into a switcher, all of which are in sync (see Figure 13-6). This is called *A/B roll editing*. For this you need a time base corrector (TBC) for each VCR. This device corrects timing errors present in all VCRs and replaces the sync with one generated by the TBC.

Two terms are often heard at editing facilities: offline editing and online editing. In *offline editing,* you spend most of your time making a *rough cut*—a quick assemblage of everything you decide to use. Then you make an *edit decision list* (EDL) of all the scenes on your rough cut, the name of the original cassette where the scene is located, and the times of your edit in-points and out-points, using time codes. You take this list and your original footage to an online post production facility with expensive equipment to auto assemble your tape according to the EDL, inserting transitions, wipes, graphics, titles, audio, and music segments as required. The result is an *edited master.*

Editing with two VCRs is less common today in multimedia production than editing with digital editing software designed specifically for use on Macintoshes and PCs, such as Premiere, After Effects, or VideoFusion (see Chapter 6). In either case, an edit decision list is useful.

Professional Video Equipment

Professional, broadcast-quality equipment includes Sony's Betacam SP and Panasonic's MII formats, both of which use half-inch tape in cassettes. These are component video systems with excellent picture and sound quality, but because they are component, the decks require complex and expensive cabling. Many videographers and production companies use Hi-8 as the image acquisition format, then transfer the content to Betacam SP for editing and mastering. Copies dubbed directly from Betacam SP, especially in component mode, differ little from the master in quality.

FIGURE 13-6

Desktop A/B roll-editing system

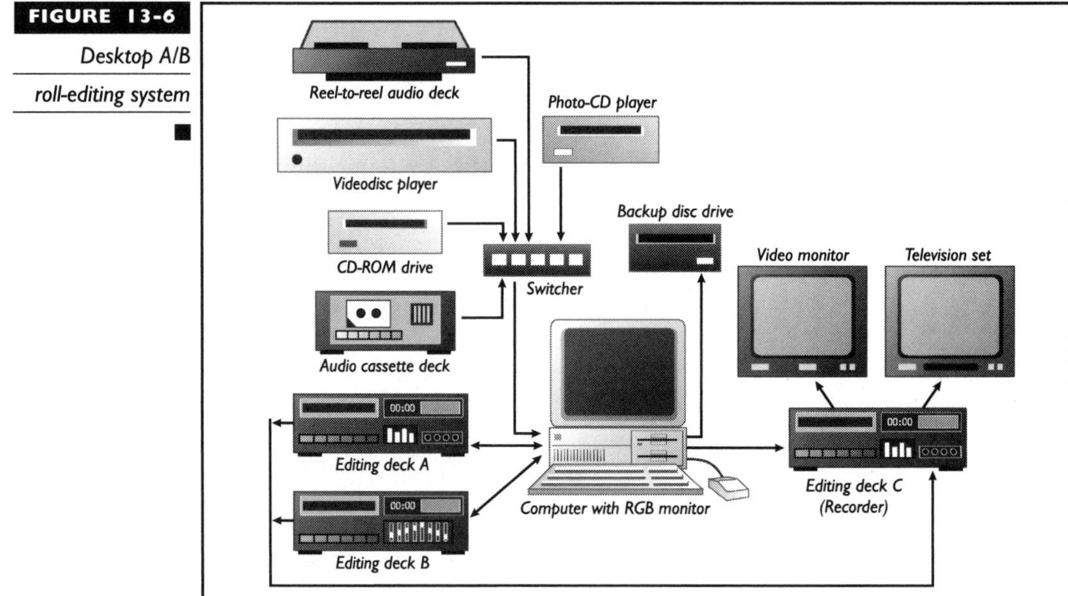

One-inch (Type C format), and D-1, D-2, and D-3 (the three digital formats) are used almost exclusively in broadcasting because of their size, weight, and very high cost. Type C is an analog composite format and is the workhorse of the television studios; it provides a superb image. Digital-format decks are used in great part for adding computer images over live video (for weather maps and video graphics) and for making multigeneration edits and dubs. These digital formats require massive amounts of data storage and are thus extremely expensive.

Differences in quality between consumer-grade and industrial equipment can be found in the technical specifications of the video equipment you consider. Following are brief discussions of some items to which you should pay attention.

Flying Erase Heads

Unlike the fixed erase heads in consumer-grade decks, flying erase heads are mounted in the same rotating drum as the recording video heads and can erase the tape completely prior to recording new material onto the tape. They can thus record new video without any glitches or picture breakup when you are adding a new video segment to a previously recorded scene (called *assemble editing*) or inserting a video segment between two prerecorded scenes (called *insert editing*). This way, both the first frame edit and the final frame edit are clean, without any video noise whatsoever.

Audio Dubbing

This feature allows you to dub new audio information on the audio track, without affecting the video that has been previously recorded on the tape. This is particularly valuable when you are using a voice-over narration, recording audio in another language, or adding a new audio track to the video.

External Sync

This input is necessary when working with professional equipment, especially time base correctors, switchers, and other cameras.

Professional Connectors

Most industrial-quality VCRs and camcorders have what are known as BNC connectors, instead of the popular RCA or phono connectors found on consumer-grade gear. BNC connectors are the standard connectors used in professional equipment; they are more secure and make better contact. Industrial-grade VCRs also have multiple input/output connectors to aid in editing. These allow you to choose from two different video and audio sources and monitor both as you edit, without having to frequently change cables. Consumer-grade equipment generally has only one set of audio and video input/output connectors.

Time Code Input/Output

This is an industry-standard audible time code established by the Society of Motion Picture and Television Engineers (SMPTE) as a universal synchronization standard used in video, audio, and film editing. SMPTE time code is based on hours, minutes, and seconds and, in the case of video, frames. This code gives each individual frame of video a unique number, to allow precise tape control and indexing. A typical SMPTE number reads 06:15:45:20 (representing hours:minutes:seconds:frames); this signal is recorded as a modulated audio signal on the audio track and as a visible digital signal in the picture area.

The better quality industrial editing decks are capable of addressing each frame by its time code and accurately accessing it during the editing process. If an editing deck can fast-forward or rewind to a specific frame number, it is referred to as being *frame accurate*, and only the top industrial decks can achieve accuracy of 1/30 second.

Zoom Lens

Perhaps the most important attribute of an industrial- or professional-model video camera (and even a camcorder) is its high-quality zoom lens. Most of these are made by Canon and Fujinon. Among lenses there are considerable differences in resolution and optical quality. Most professional units are equipped with either 10:1 or 12:1 zoom lenses, as compared with the average consumer-grade camera's 6:1 or perhaps 8:1 lens. This is extremely important in field work, for example in videotaping sports events, and when space constraints prevent the camera operator from getting close to a subject.

Most industrial cameras and some camcorders have removable zoom lenses with C-mounts, so that other high-quality optics such as still camera lenses can be utilized. Another feature is the speed of the zoom itself. Many quality zoom lenses have variable speeds that allow the camera operator to approach a subject very slowly or very quickly.

Signal-to-Noise Ratio

VCRs with a high signal-to-noise ratio produce clean pictures with lots of detail; VCRs with a lower signal-to-noise ratio (and especially consumer-grade camcorders) produce very grainy pictures with less detail. The ideal ratio should be in the range between 43 dB and 45 dB (the higher the number, the better the image quality). The audio track should also have a high signal-to-noise ratio, the norm being around 48 dB on high-quality VCRs, and 90 dB or higher for hi-fi units, 8 mm VCRs, and camcorders (the higher the number, the poorer the sound quality).

Number of Video Heads

A minimum of four rotary heads is a must. All industrial-grade VCRs have four heads; some have five. On decks with four heads, two are used to record video in the Standard Play (SP) mode, laying down a strong signal on the tape. The other heads are used to provide a glitch-free picture in fast-forward and freeze-frame modes.

Editing VCR

Editing VCRs have robust tape transport systems, good motors, and can stop precisely on a frame. All have at least four heads, and many have a shuttle search knob to fast-scan at variable speeds, both backward and forward. VCRs require a few seconds of preroll to get up to speed, usually from four to seven seconds. Both the source and record decks must stop, count backward the exact number of frames required for preroll, and begin playing simultaneously.

Video Tips

Listed below are some tips for shooting video for your multimedia project.

Shooting Platform

Never underestimate the value of a steady shooting platform. A classic symbol of "amateur home movies" is shaky camera work. Using a tripod or even placing the camera on a stable platform, such as a rolled-up sweater on the hood of a car, can improve a shot. With a little care, and careful adjustment of the lockdown screws, a sturdy conventional tripod can do wonders. If you must shoot hand-held, try to use a camera with an electronic image stabilization feature for static shots, a "steady-cam" balancing attachment, or try camera moves and a moving subject to mask your lack of steadiness.

Lighting

Perhaps the greatest difference between professional camcorders and consumer camcorders is their ability to perform at low light levels. With proper lighting, however, it may be difficult for uninitiated viewers to differentiate between shots taken with an expensive Betacam SP camcorder and a Hi-8 camcorder. Using a simple flood light kit, or even just being sure that daylight illuminates the room, can improve your image.

Onboard battery lights for camcorders can be useful, but only in conditions where the light acts as a "fill light" to illuminate the details of a subject's face. As in photography, good lighting techniques separate amateurs from professionals in video shoots.

Illustrated in Figure 13-7 is a screen from The Lighting Lab, a CD-ROM available from Robert Hone Productions. The standard lighting arrangement of a studio is displayed with fill, key, rim, and background lights. Changing any of these lights can make a dramatic difference in the shot. This Macromedia Director project uses a QuickTime movie containing several hundred single-frame images of the model as she is lighted by every permutation of lamp and intensity; clicking a light switch instantly shows the effect

FIGURE 13-7 *Good lighting is essential for quality video results*

of that combination. If you are not convinced that lighting is critical to the success of a photo or video shoot, it will become immediately clear with this exercise!

Chroma Key or Blue Screen

A useful tool easily implemented in most digital video editing applications is "blue screen," "Ultimatte," or "chroma key" editing. When Captain Picard of *Star Trek* fame walks on the surface of the moon, it is likely that he is actually walking on a studio set in front of a screen or wall painted blue. Actually placing Picard on the moon is, no doubt, beyond the budget of the shoot, but it can be "faked" using blue screen techniques. After shooting the video of Picard's walk against a blue background and shooting another video consisting of the desired background moonscape, the two videos are mixed together: any blue in the Picard shot is replaced by the background image, frame by frame.

Blue screen is a popular technique for making multimedia titles, because expensive sets are not required. Incredible backgrounds can be generated using 3D modeling and graphic software, and one or more actors, vehicles, or other objects can be neatly layered onto that background. Applications such as VideoShop and Premiere provide this capability on Macintoshes and PCs.

When you are shooting blue screen, be sure that the lighting of the screen is absolutely even; fluctuations in intensity will make this key appear choppy or broken. *Key* is the term used to describe the process of replacing the blue screen with a background image. Shooting in daylight and letting the sun illuminate the screen mitigates this problem. Also be careful about "color spill." If your actors stand too close to the screen, the reflecting colored light will spill onto them, and parts of their body will key out, or become transparent. While adjustments in most applications can compensate for this, the adjustments are limited. Beware of fine detail, such as hair or smoke, that wisps over the screen; this does not "key" well to the chroma key color.

Figure 13-8 shows frames from a video of an actor shot against blue screen on a commercial stage. The video was digitized, the blue background was removed from each frame, and the actor himself was turned into a photo-realistic animation that walked, jumped, pointed, and ran.

Composition

The general rules for shooting quality video for broadcast use apply to multimedia.

When shooting video for playback from CD-ROM in a small computer window, it is best to avoid wide panoramic shots. The effect of sweeping panoramas are lost in small windows. Use close-ups and medium shots,

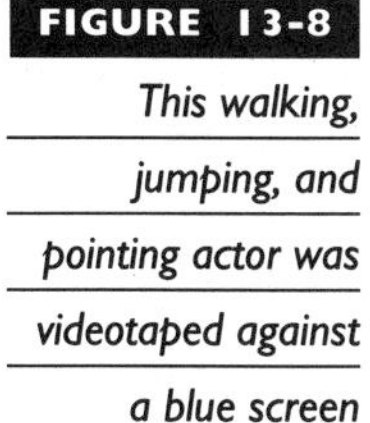

FIGURE 13-8 *This walking, jumping, and pointing actor was videotaped against a blue screen*

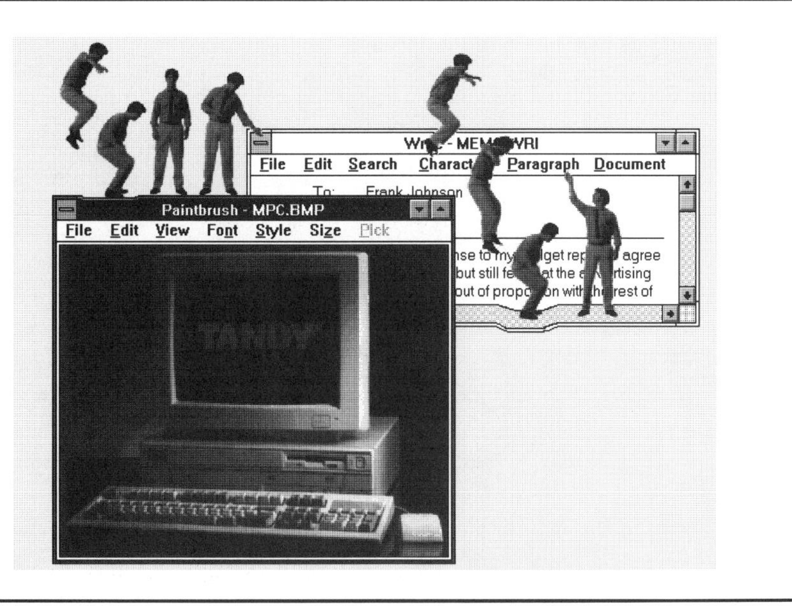

head-and-shoulders or even tighter. Depending on the compression algorithm used (see the following section on video compression), consider also the amount of motion in the shot: the more a scene changes from frame to frame, the more "delta" information needs to be transferred from the computer's memory to the screen, and the slower the playback speed. Keep the camera still instead of panning and zooming; let the subject add the motion to your shot by walking, turning, or talking.

Expand the apparent size of the scene. In many multimedia projects that display video, the screen interface is designed so that there is a small window in which video can play, but the video appears larger. In this way, a 160×120-pixel QuickTime video window is placed on a carefully designed background for the CD-ROM mystery, *Who Killed Sam Rupert,* by Shannon Gilligan; the video seems larger than it really is and provides a head shot (see Figure 13-9).

Video Compression

Digitizing and storing a 10-second clip of full-motion video in your computer requires transfer of an enormous amount of data in a very short amount of time. Reproducing just one frame of digital component video at 24 bits

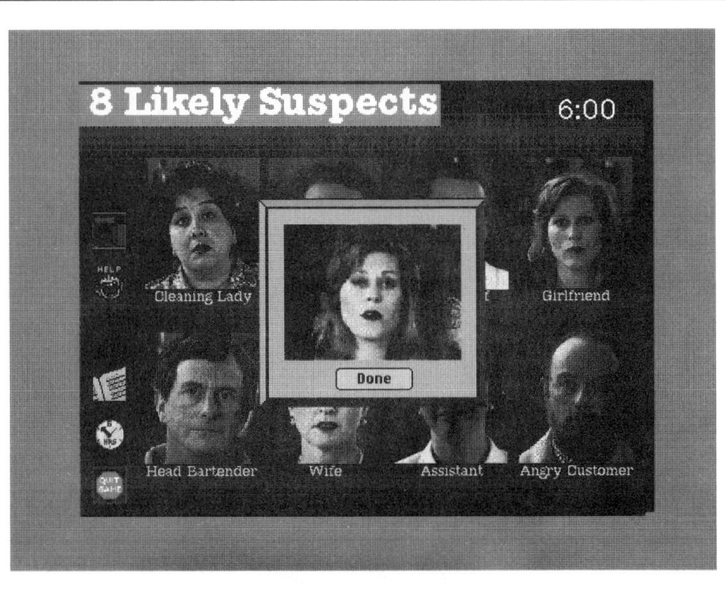

FIGURE 13-9 A tiny video window can be made to seem larger

requires almost 1MB of computer data; 10 seconds of video fills a 300MB hard disk. Full-size, full-motion video requires that the computer deliver data at about 30MB per second—this is simply more than Macintoshes and PCs can handle. The NuBus channel on a Macintosh, for example, can transfer data at about 13MB per second (still only about one-third the speed required). Typical hard disk drives transfer data at only about 1MB per second, and single-speed CD-ROM players at a paltry 150K per second. This overwhelming technological bottleneck is currently being overcome by digital image compression techniques. Real-time video compression algorithms such as JPEG, MPEG, P*64, DVI, and C-Cube are now available to compress digital video information at rates that range from 50:1 to 200:1. JPEG, MPEG, and P*64 compression schemes use Discrete Cosine Transform (DCT), an encoding algorithm that quantifies the human eye's ability to detect color and image distortion.

JPEG

The most popular of compression standards is JPEG (Joint Photographic Experts Group), developed for use with still images. It compresses about 20:1 before visible image degradation occurs. JPEG has become popular for compressing full-motion video on Macintosh, PC, and Amiga platforms, but at higher compression rates it is "lossy," sacrificing a lot of image data. When a compression ratio of 30:1 is applied to a full color frame of video, the image storage requirement is reduced from 1,000K to 33K, and the data transfer rate is reduced to about 1MB per second, well within the capabilities of most storage devices.

To compress an image with JPEG, the image is divided into 8×8 pixel blocks, and the resulting 64 pixels (called a *search range*) are mathematically described relative to the characteristic of the pixel in the top-left corner. The binary description of this relationship requires far less than 64 pixels, so more information can be transmitted in less time. JPEG compresses slowly—about one to three seconds for a 1MB image—depending upon computer speed, but JPEG can compress images as much as 75:1 with loss of some picture information.

The images in Figure 13-10 are 24-bit, 72-dpi PICT files shown at 3× magnification (so you can see the pixels). The image on the left is uncompressed. The image on the right was compressed in Photoshop using the "JPEG - low quality" setting. The uncompressed file is 60K in size, the compressed file 16K in size. While the compressed image is about one-quarter the size of the uncompressed image, there is a penalty, and it is lossy.

MPEG

The MPEG standard, from the Moving Picture Experts Group, is used to encode motion images. The MPEG scheme allows compression of audio, its compression speeds are fast, and decompression occurs in real time. MPEG delivers decompressed data at 1.2 to 1.5MB per second. This allows CD players to play full-motion color movies at 30 frames per second. MPEG compresses at about a 50:1 ratio before degradation of the image occurs, but compression ratios as high as 200:1 are attainable with observable degradation of the image. MPEG, like JPEG, is a symmetrical system, which means it compresses and decompresses images at the same speed.

DVI

DVI is a proprietary, programmable compression/decompression technology based on the Intel i750 chip set. This hardware consists of two VLSI (Very Large Scale Integrated) components to separate the image processing and display functions.

Two levels of compression and decompression are provided by DVI: Production Level Video (PLV) and Real Time Video (RTV). PLV is a proprietary asymmetrical compression technique for encoding full-motion color video; it requires that compression be performed by Intel at its facilities or at licensed encoding facilities set up by Intel. RTV provides image quality comparable to frame-rate (motion) JPEG and uses a symmetrical, variable-rate compression. PLV and RTV both use variable compression rates.

FIGURE 13-10 *Compression schemes save disk space, but can degrade an image*

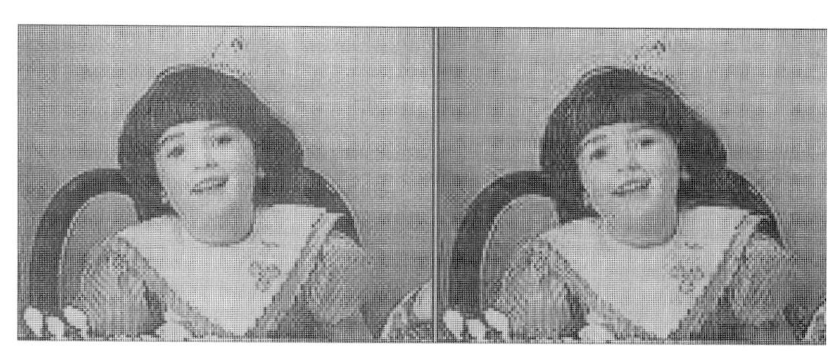

DVI's algorithms can compress video images at ratios between 80:1 and 160:1. DVI plays back video in full-frame size and in full color at 30 frames per second, whereas JPEG provides only an acceptable image in a small picture window on the computer screen. When tied in with a mainframe computer, DVI playback approaches the quality of broadcast video.

Other Compression Methods

P*64 (pronounced "pee star sixty-four") is a video telephone conferencing standard for compressing audio and motion video images, from the Consultative Committee on International Telegraph and Telephone (CCITT). P*64 complies with CCITT's recommendation H.261 and incorporates multiplexing, demultiplexing, framing of data, transmission protocol and bandwidth congruence, and call setup and teardown. Encoder products from telephone service providers such as AT&T and Northern Telecom use P*64 to deliver wide-spectrum telecommunication capabilities incorporating high-speed and very-high-throughput data transmission over both copper and fiber optic digital telephone networks.

P*64 encodes real-time motion video and audio for transmission over copper or fiber optic telephone lines at 30 frames per second, at a bandwidth between 40 kilobits per second to 4 megabits per second.

Other compression systems are being developed by companies including Kodak, Sony, Storm Technology, SuperMac, Iterated Systems, and C-Cube Micro-systems, and rapid progress is being made in this field.

Optimizing Video Files for CD-ROM

CD-ROMs provide an excellent distribution medium for computer-based video: they are inexpensive to mass produce and they can store great quantities of information. CD-ROM players offer, however, very slow data transfer rates (see Chapter 18). Adequate video transfer can be achieved from a CD-ROM, but you need to spend great care to properly prepare your digital video file.

- Limit the amount of synchronization required between the video and audio. With Microsoft's AVI files, the audio and video data are already interleaved, so this is not a necessity; but with QuickTime files, you should "flatten" your movie. *Flattening* means you interleave the audio and video segments together.

- Use regularly spaced key frames, 10 to 15 frames apart, and temporal compression can correct for seek time delays. *Seek time* is how long it takes the CD-ROM player to locate specific data on the CD-ROM disc.
- The size of the video window and the frame rate you specify dramatically affect performance. In QuickTime, 20 frames per second played in a 160×120 pixel window is equivalent to playing 10 frames per second in a 320×240 window. The more data that has to be decompressed and transferred from the CD-ROM to the screen, the slower the playback.
- While interleaving CD-quality audio into your video production theoretically yields highest-quality sound, the volume of data required may be too great to transfer from the CD-ROM in real time. Try a lower sampling rate and sample size to reduce the quantity of audio data.
- The software compression algorithm you specify will make a dramatic difference in performance. The Cinepack algorithm, available within both AVI and QuickTime, is optimized for CD-ROM playback. But take care: it can take many hours of computation to compress just a few minutes of digital video.
- If you are working with QuickTime, consider using a specialized application such as MovieShop to automatically optimize your digital video file for playback from CD-ROM.

Recording Computer Output

You may wish to transfer your project to videotape. To do this, you need an add-on board with a digital/analog encoder. This hardware converts the high-quality RGB signal of the computer into a lower-quality NTSC signal that can be recorded on a VCR. Some boards provide a genlock feature for superimposing computer graphics (such as titles and logos) over the video image.

Boards such as NewTek's Video Toaster, VideoLogic's DVA4000, and Fast's VideoMachine (see Figure 13-11), as well as other boards from Mass Micro Systems, Radius, Computer Friends, SuperMac, New Media, Creative Labs, and RasterOps, all produce excellent video with graphics overlay for consumer/industrial applications. Most can also digitize movies for QuickTime or AVI. From TrueVision, the Targa board for PCs and the NuVista+

First Person

We are developing an application for a Tandy VIS system that will be viewed on TV. We prepare menu screens and clean up our 24-bit images on our Mac RGB monitors, but would like to see them as they will look on TV, before we have pressed the CD. Are there particular problems we need to look out for when moving to TV, and what's the best way to output the image?

Eve Montague,
Phoenix, Arizona

There are some "gotchas" to keep in mind when creating computer images that will be shown on television, and developers for VIS, CD-I, 3DO, and Kodak's Photo CD should test for them. Among other things, avoid thin one-pixel horizontal lines and fine serifed type. This is because a computer monitor paints the screen in a single pass while televisions paint the same image in two interlaced passes, first drawing the odd lines, then the even lines. This interlacing causes moiré effects, and can turn a handsome striped shirt or fine-lined background into an annoying shimmering of light. Also avoid small-size text and intense or "hot" colors like bright red displayed in small areas.

You need an encoder or scan converter to translate the RGB signal of computer monitors into the composite signal required for a television. These devices are finally becoming affordable! For a Macintosh solution, try Lapis Technologies' $349 L-TV (800/435-2747), Radius' $1,999 VideoVision (408/434-1010), or RasterOps' $699 VideoExpander (408/562-4200). For PCs try Cardinal's $1295 SnapPlus card (800/233-0187) or RGB Spectrum's $9495 RGB/Videolink 1500 (510/814-7000). Some of these solutions provide more video editing features than others, and prices vary greatly according to feature set, but all will let you view your monitor output on a television. If you can view it on television, you can also record it to videotape!

From Tay Vaughan's "Ask the Captain" column, *NewMedia* magazine, May, 1993

board for the Macintosh have inputs and outputs for both NTSC and PAL signals and also provide Y/C connectors for use with S-VHS and Hi-8 VCRs.

Taking Care of Your Tapes

- Always fast-forward new tapes to the end and then rewind them, a technique known as *packing*, to make sure that tape tension is even from beginning to end. Unequal tape tension can cause timing and editing problems.
- *Black-stripe* your tape by running it through the recorder once with the lens cap on and the audio turned off. Only black and a uniform control track is recorded. Later, during editing, blank spots in your video program will be a quiet black instead of snowy noise.

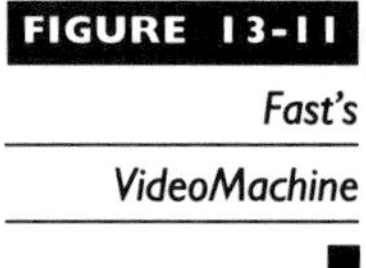

FIGURE 13-11 *Fast's VideoMachine*

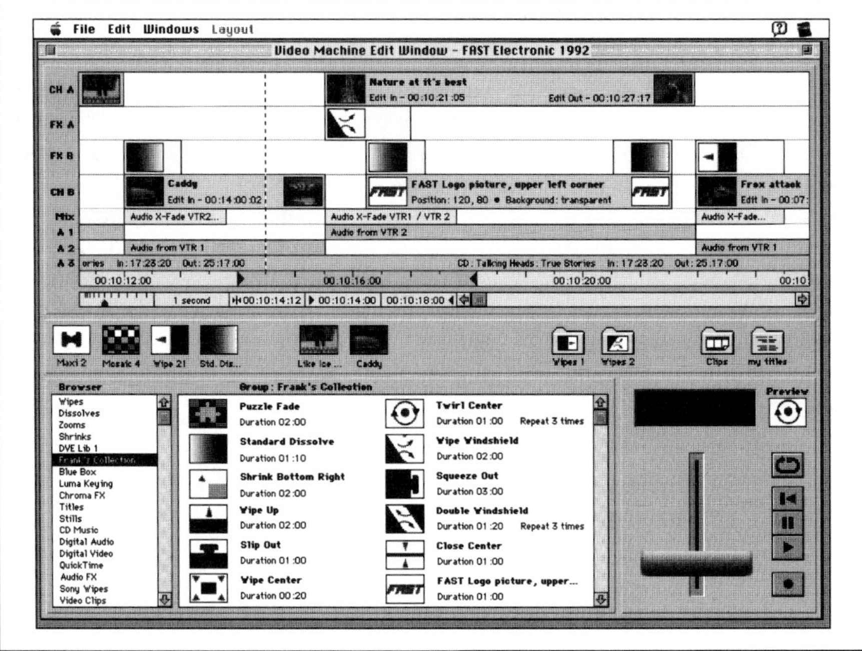

- Before you begin editing, always remove the break-off tab on the back of your original video cassettes, to avoid accidental erasure or overwriting.
- Editing videotape requires a lot of shuttling backward and forward, which can deform the tape. For best results, do not reuse 8 mm video cassettes.

warning *Your original videotapes are irreplaceable, so always make a backup copy of these tapes before you begin editing–tapes can break, be erased, or be eaten up by machinery.*

Multi

[*Plan for the whole process, beginning with your first ideas and ending with completion and delivery of a finished product.*]

You must develop an organized outline

experience

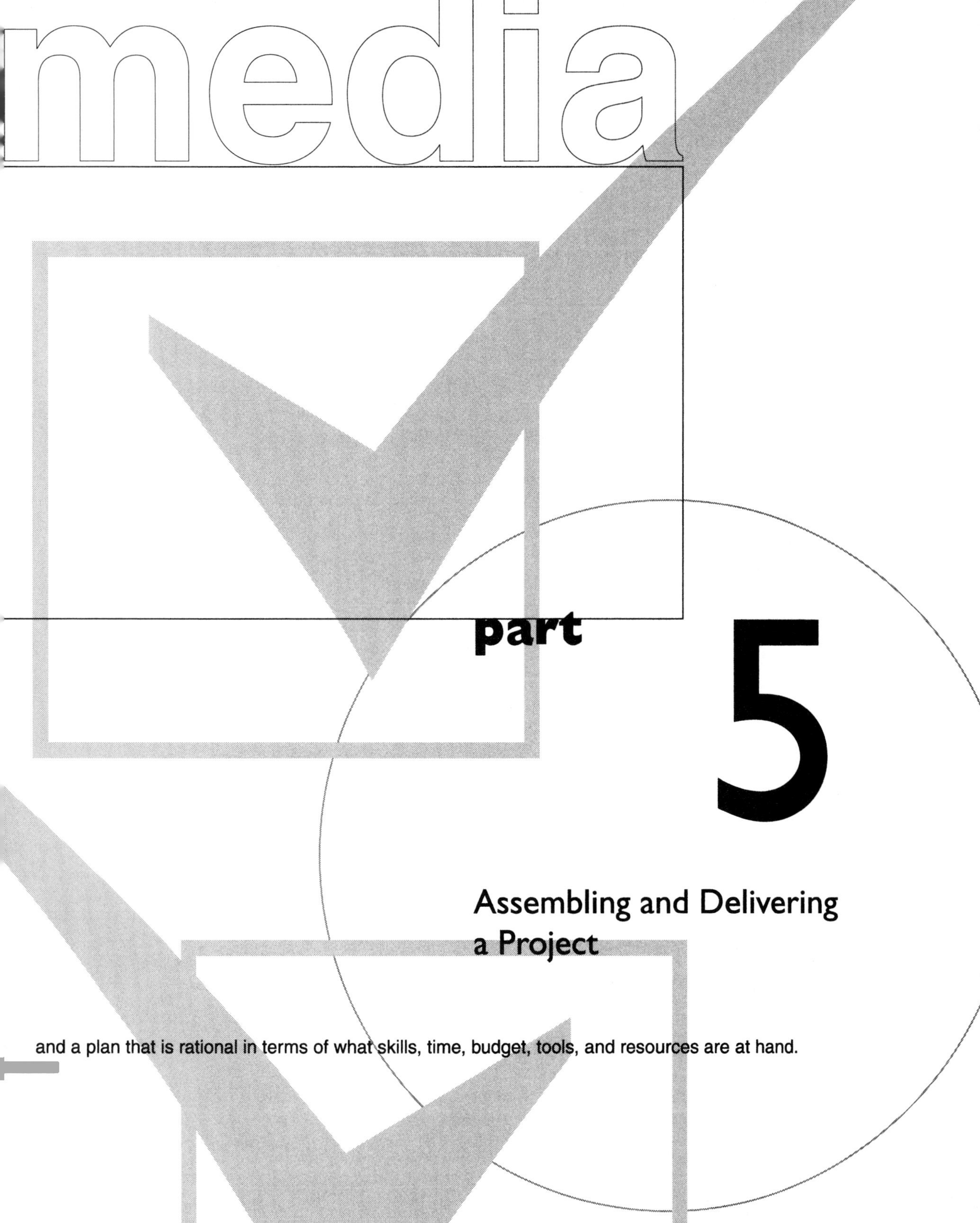

part 5

Assembling and Delivering a Project

and a plan that is rational in terms of what skills, time, budget, tools, and resources are at hand.

Multi

Before you begin a multimedia project, you must first develop a sense of its scope and content.

You must develop an organized outline

experience

chapter 14

Planning and Costing

and a plan that is rational in terms of what skills, time, budget, tools, and resources are at hand.

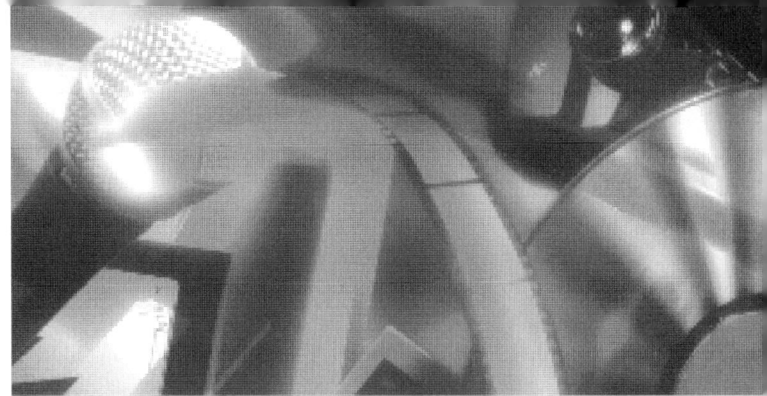

BEFORE you begin a multimedia project, you must first develop a sense of its scope and content, letting the project take shape in your head as you think through the various methods available to get your message across to your viewers.

Then you must develop an organized outline and a plan that is rational in terms of what skills, time, budget, tools, and resources are at hand. Proper project planning is as important as planning the layout and content. Your plans should be in place before you start to render graphics, sounds, and other components, and they should continue to be monitored throughout the project's execution.

First Person

When I was nine, my father told me about China. He brought the big spinning globe into the kitchen and used a fork to point out where we were and where China was. He explained that if we dug a hole deep enough in the backyard, eventually we would come out in someplace called "Peking." After school the next day, I began, unannounced, trenching a pit into the rocky soil of our New England backyard: the first layer was tough sod, then there was some topsoil and loam, and then a thick stratum of moist pea gravel. I was knee-deep into the next layer–hard-packed clay–when my father discovered the work site at the end of his day. He was pleased I had missed the septic tank by several feet, and sternly suggested that more study would be required before I dug any further.

This was my first lesson in project planning, not to mention my first experience with project abandonment. Be sure you analyze the requirements of your multimedia project before you go to the tool shed.

Project Planning

Planning for multimedia projects is like cellular fission: the big picture of your idea is divided into production phases and then divided again into smaller and more manageable tasks and items spread over a given amount of time. These are the building blocks of project management. Some tasks are prerequisites and must be completed before others begin, so planning ahead is important. Allocate an estimated amount of time to each task, and place each one along a calendar-based time line. This is your project plan.

tip *The end of each phase is a natural place to set a milestone–that is, a time to deliver work-in-progress, to invoice based on real work done, to assess or test progress, and/or to solicit and receive constructive feedback. Depending on the complexity of the project, you may wish to place these milestones at the end of each task as well.*

It is, of course, easiest to plan a project using the experience you have accumulated in similar past projects. Over time, you can maintain and improve your multimedia planning format like a batch of sourdough starter. Just keep adding a little rye and water every time you do a project, and the starter for your next job gets a bit more potent as your estimates become tempered by experience.

Plan for the whole process, beginning with your first ideas and ending with completion and delivery of a finished product. Think in the overview; this step-wise process of making multimedia is illustrated in Brian Blum's chart shown in Figure 14-1; use this chart to help you get your arms around the phases of a project. Note the loop-backs for revisions based on testing.

The Idea

Usually something will click in your mind or in the mind of a client that says "Hey, this would make a great multimedia project!" Your visions of sound and music, flashy images, and perhaps some video will solve a business need, provide an attention-grabbing product demo, or yield a slick front-end to an otherwise drab computer database. You might want to spark a little interest or a laugh in an otherwise dull meeting, build an interactive photo album for Christmas greetings to your family, or distribute your company's annual report on disk to 40,000 shareholders. Here are a few purposes where multimedia has been successfully applied:

- Desktop presentations
- Videoconferencing

FIGURE 14-1

The process of making multimedia. Chart created by Brian Blum, a Multimedia Producer at The Software Toolworks and President of the International Interactive Communications Society (IICS)

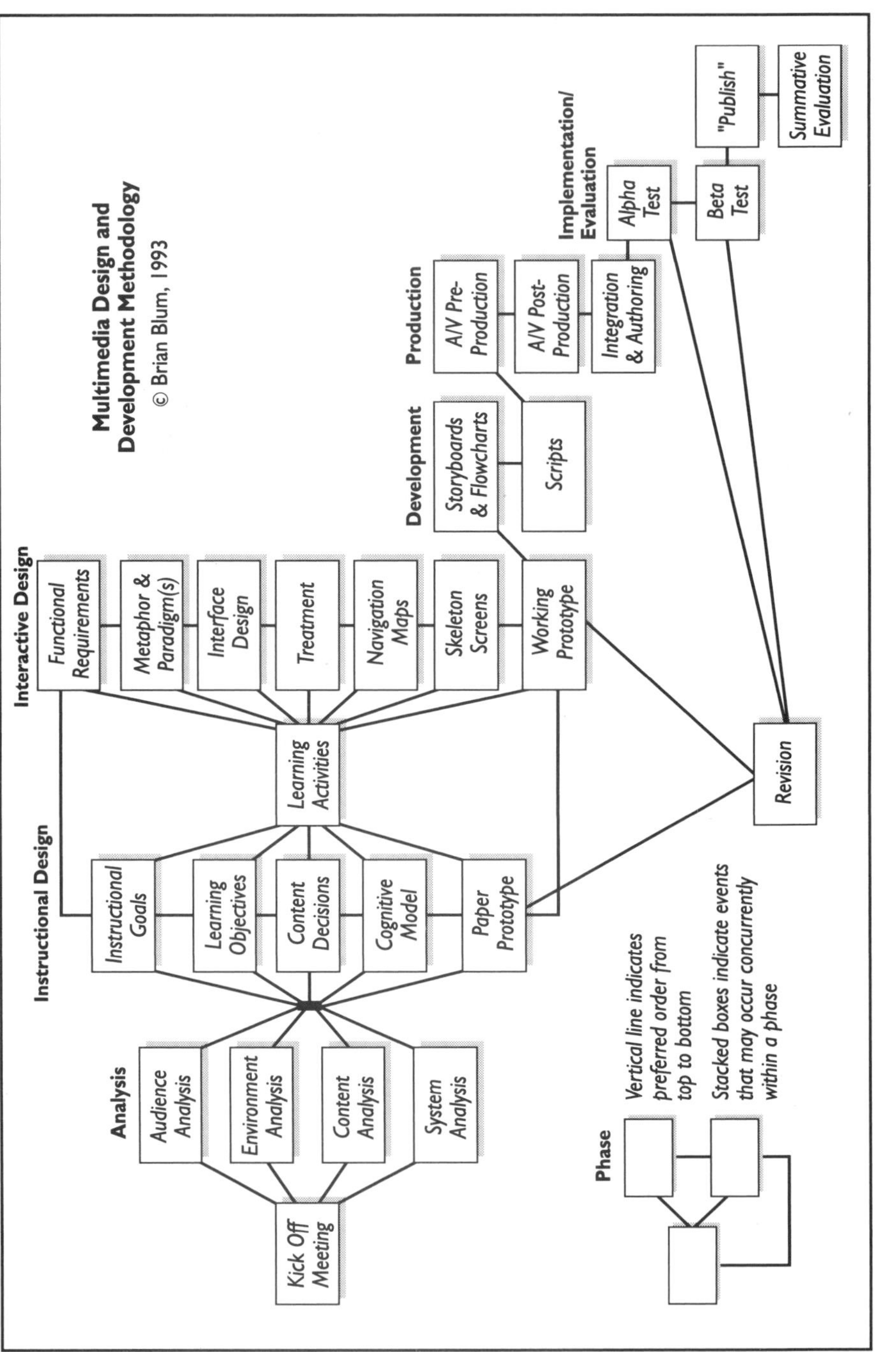

- Product marketing, advertising, and sales demonstrations
- Encyclopedias, reference materials, musical works, and other digital data-on-demand retrieval systems
- Fine arts, museum, and zoo presentations
- Voice and video-annotated documents
- Interactive information kiosks and point-of-sale retailing systems
- Storage systems for documents and images and other data management systems
- Personal information managers and personnel identification and security systems
- Games, children's stories, and interactive entertainment
- Shopping services delivered online or distributed on compact disc
- Interactive computer-based training
- Interactive help systems and guided tours
- Architectural and engineering 3-D renderings and walk-throughs, process modeling and simulation, and scientific data visualizations

The important thing to keep in mind during the idea stage is balance. As you think through your idea, you must continually weigh your purpose against the feasibility and cost of production and delivery.

We locked eight people in a room with pizza and out popped a design...

Mike Duffy, Chief Technical Officer, The Software Toolworks, describing how the design for the *20th Century Almanac* was developed

Fleshing Out the Idea

Use note paper and scratch pads as you flesh out your idea, or use a note taking or outlining program on your computer. Start with broad brush strokes, then think through each constituent multimedia element. Ultimately, you will generate a plan of action that will become your road map for production. It will be in balance if you have considered and weighed the proper elements:

- What is the essence of what you want to do? What is your purpose and message?
- How can you organize your project?
- What multimedia elements (text, sounds, and visuals) will best deliver your message?
- Do you already have content material with which you can leverage your project, such as videotape, music, documents, photographs, logos, advertisements, marketing packages, and other artwork?
- Is your idea derivative from an existing theme that can be enhanced with multimedia, or will you create something totally new?
- What hardware is available for development of your project? Is it enough?
- How much storage space do you have? How much do you need?
- What hardware will be available to your end users?
- What multimedia software is available to you?
- What are your capabilities and skills with both the software and the hardware?
- Can you do it alone? Who can help you?
- How much time do you have?
- How much money do you have?
- How will you distribute the final project?

You can maintain balance between purpose and feasibility by dynamically adding and subtracting multimedia elements as you stretch and shape your idea. You can start small, then build from minimum capabilities toward a satisfactory result in an additive way. Or you can shoot the moon with a heavy list of features and desired multimedia results, then discard items one by one because they are just not possible. Both additive and subtractive processes can work in concert. In the end, this process will yield very useful cost estimates and a production road map.

Consider the following scenario: You have a videotape with four head-and-shoulders testimonials that will be perfect for illustrating your message.

So add motion video to your list. You will need to purchase a video digitizing board and digitizing software, so add those items and their cost to your list as well. But you will distribute your software on two floppy disks, which means not enough storage for both your message and lengthy digitized video. Subtract motion video, but add tiny framed still images of the four talking heads (captured with your new video equipment) using short, one-sentence voice-overs of the speakers (recorded from the video tape). Subtract two of the four testimonials because you are again running out of storage space. Add a more efficient animation instead. Subtract. Add. Subtract. In this manner, you will flesh out your idea, adding and subtracting elements within the constraints of the hardware, software, and your budget of time and cost.

tip *Treat your multimedia idea like a business venture. As you visualize in your mind's eye what you want to accomplish, balance the project's profit potential against the investment of effort and resources required to make it happen.*

Hardware

Hardware is the most common limiting factor for realizing a multimedia idea: no videodisc player, then no random access analog video; no sound board, then no sound effects; no synthesizer, then no MIDI composed by you on site; no CD-ROM player, then no broad distribution of large projects; no high resolution color display, then no pretty pictures.

Begin by listing the hardware capabilities of the end user's computer platform (not necessarily the platform on which you will develop the project). If the elements are not enough, then examine the cost of enhancing the delivery platform and balance those results against your purpose and resources.

Available Skills and Software

You should also list the skills and software capabilities available to you. This list is not as limiting as the hardware list because you can always budget for new and more powerful software and for the learning curve (or consultant fees) required to make use of it. Indeed, the software is usually necessary only for development of the project, not its delivery, and should not be a cost or learning burden passed on to end users.

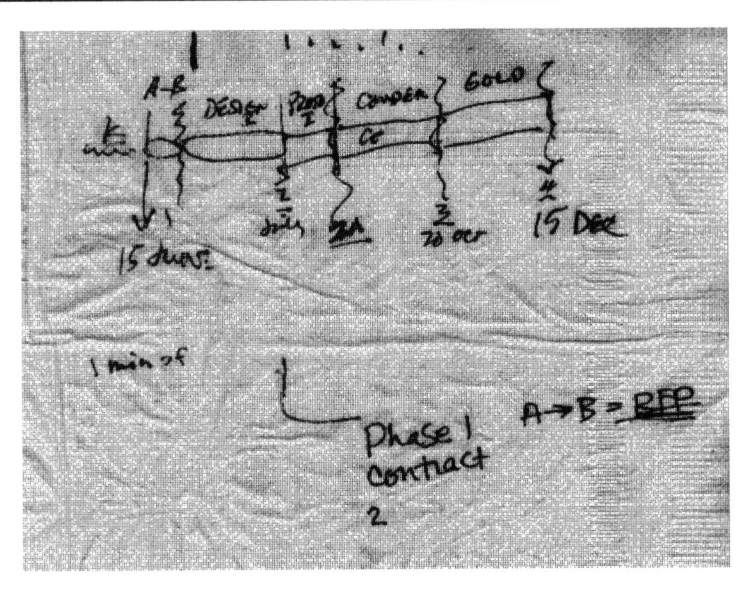

FIGURE 14-2 The ideas on this luncheon napkin evolved into an animated guided tour for Lotus' Multimedia 1-2-3

The Paper Napkin

The very early idea processing and preliminary planning sketched on the working-lunch paper napkin shown in Figure 14-2 evolved into a complex

First Person

Last time I took the redeye home, the fat guy behind me was pretty ill, sneezing and hawking incessantly over my headrest on the full hot plane. My glasses blurred with misty droplets and I wiped the fog away with the damp cocktail napkin under my Coke. That trip cost me four days sick in bed, and I promised I would never fly night coach again to make a meeting, no matter how important.

Then I broke my promise, and, after a sleepless night on the plane, found myself sitting in the muggy summer air on the bank of the Charles River, having lunch with Rob Lippincott and his multimedia team from Lotus. I pretended to be alert, but residual white noise from the plane ride beat in my ears, and my dry eyes wouldn't focus in the umbrella sunlight. Rob made intelligent notes with a ballpoint pen on a paper napkin while my own input to the creative process was reduced to grunts and short sentences. The smartest thing I did was slip the paper napkin with its notes into my briefcase as we left the table. After some sleep, I was able to retrieve the napkin and craft those luncheon thoughts into the backbone of a rational project proposal and action plan. We launched the venture and about ten months later it went gold, shipping with Lotus's new Multimedia 1-2-3 product.

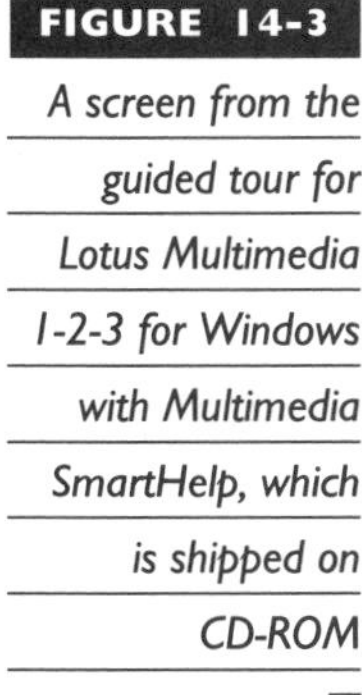

FIGURE 14-3 A screen from the guided tour for Lotus Multimedia 1-2-3 for Windows with Multimedia SmartHelp, which is shipped on CD-ROM

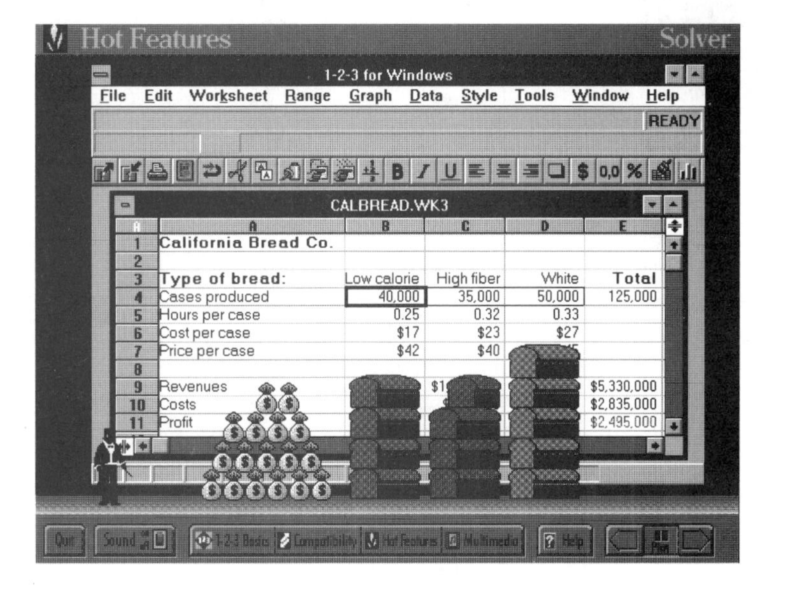

multimedia project of many months' duration (see also the "First Person" account of this project).

First, the idea was discussed, refined, and cultivated as a preliminary project plan. Then work began with the building of a prototype, shown as the A-B portion of the napkin notes, which quite literally answered the question "How do we get from A to B with this idea?" The prototype was then carefully examined in terms of projected work effort and the technology required to implement a full-blown version of the prototype. Based on experience, a more complete plan and cost estimate for full implementation was then developed, and the project was launched in earnest. Figure 14-3 shows a screen from the final product.

Idea Management Software

Software such as Inspiration (see Figure 14-4), MacProject, Microsoft Project (see Figure 14-5), outlining programs such as MORE, and spreadsheets such as Lotus 1-2-3 or Excel can be useful for arranging your ideas and the many tasks, work items, employee resources, and costs required of your multimedia project. Project management tools provide the added benefit of built-in analysis to help you stay within your schedule and budget during the rendering of the project itself.

FIGURE 14-4

Inspiration allows you to organize ideas in interrelated structures

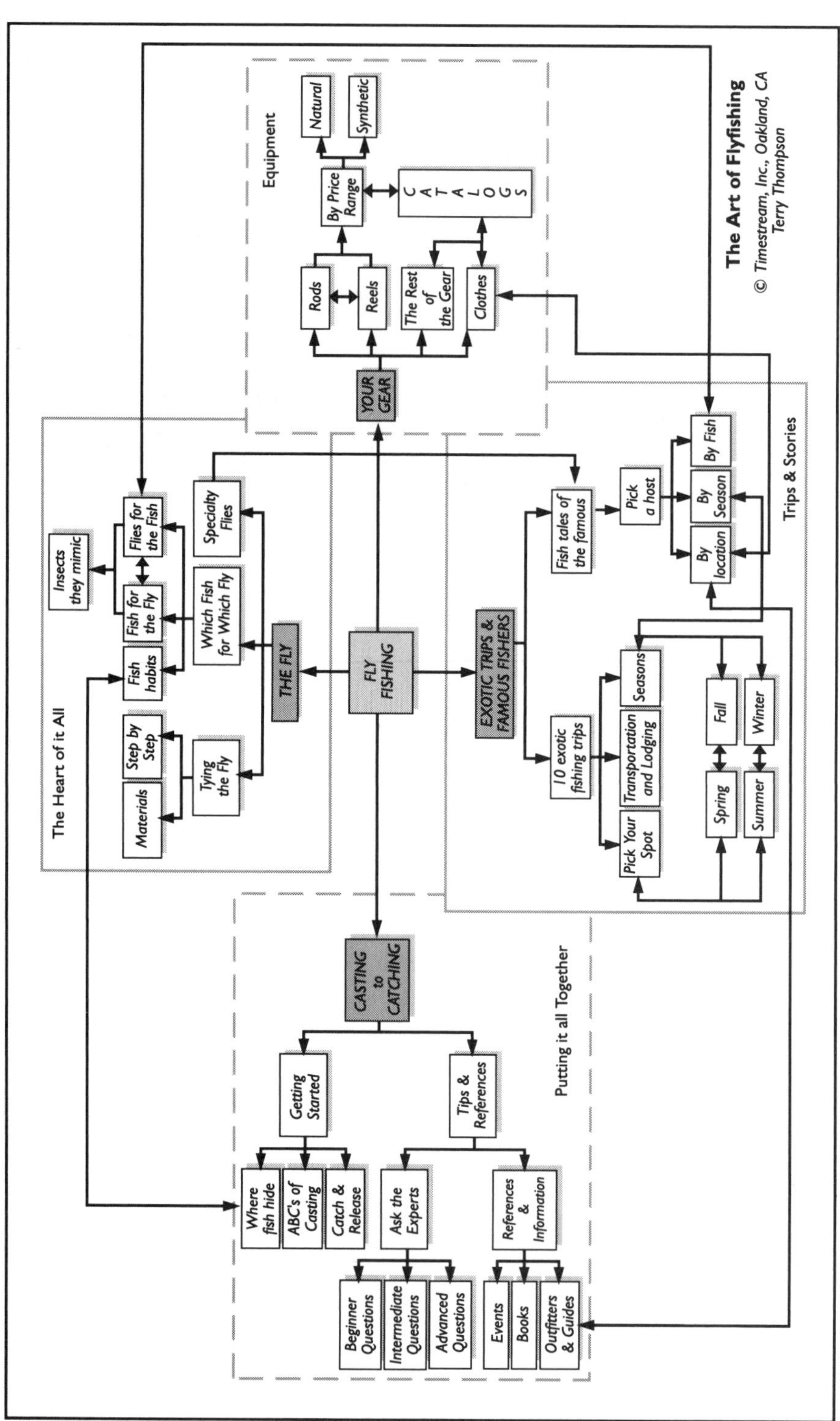

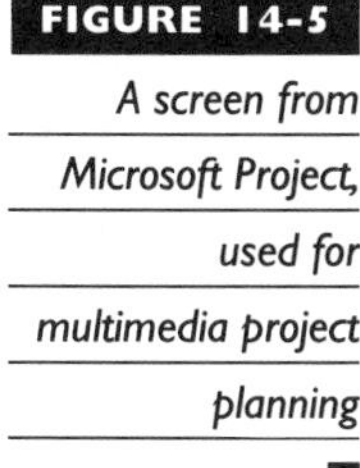

FIGURE 14-5

A screen from Microsoft Project, used for multimedia project planning

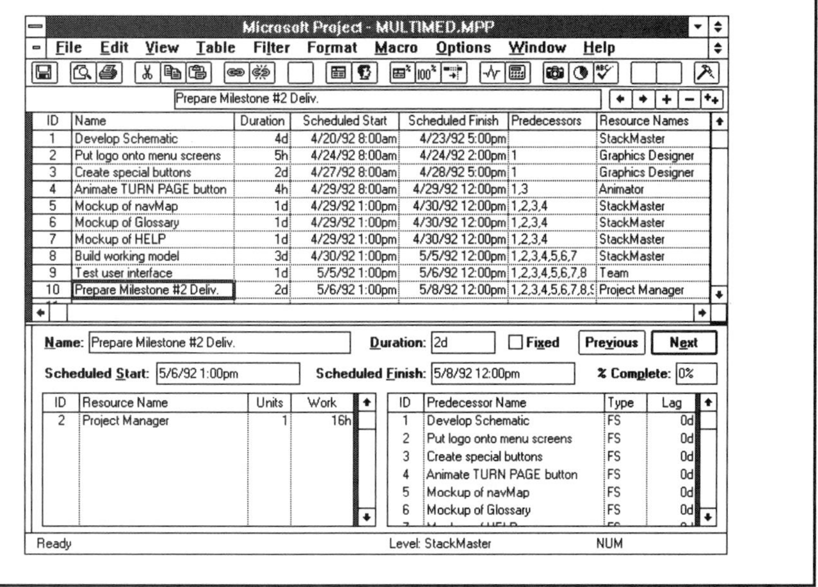

warning *Budget your time if you are new to project management software. It may be difficult to learn and to use effectively.*

Project management software typically provides Critical Path Method (CPM) scheduling functions to calculate the total duration of a project based on each identified task, earmarking tasks that are critical and that, if lengthened, result in a delay in project completion. Program Evaluation Review Technique (PERT) charts provide graphic representations of task relationships, showing what tasks must be completed before others can commence. Gantt charts depict all the tasks along a time line (see Figure 14-6).

Building a Team

Multimedia is an emerging technology requiring a set of skills so broad that multimedia itself remains poorly defined. Players in this technology come from all corners of the computer and art worlds as well as from a variety of other disciplines, so if you need to assemble a team, you need to know what people and skills it takes to make multimedia (refer to Chapter 3 for a description of the various skills and talents needed).

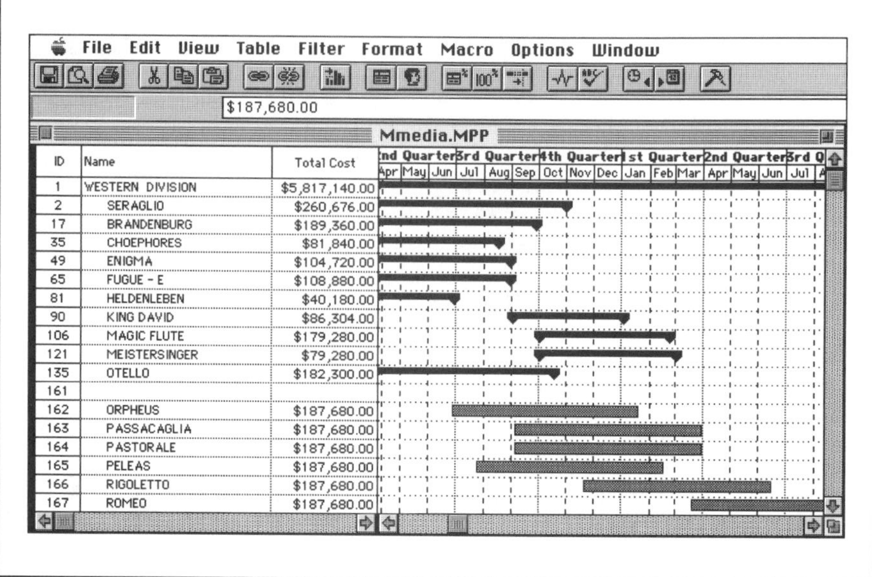

FIGURE 14-6 A Gantt chart made with Microsof Project showing production of many projects over time

In a business where success and failure often depends on our ability to monitor and anticipate emerging technology, job recruiters see multimedia as very challenging. Not only does the fledgling multimedia industry incorporate some of the hottest computer technology tools, it draws on talent that comes from outside the traditional boundaries of data processing and MIS recruitment. The ill-defined but very technical skills needed for multimedia provide us, the industry recruiters, an exceptional opportunity for creativity. Our clients, too, need to be open minded and flexible about the talent and skills required of multimedia developers.

Heinz Bartesch, Director of Sales and Marketing,
The Search Firm, San Francisco

Staying at the leading edge is important. If you remain knowledgeable about what's new and expected, you will be more valuable to your own endeavors, to your team, and to your employer or prospective clients. But be prepared for steep learning curves and difficult challenges in keeping your own skills and those of your employees current and in demand. And don't neglect team morale as hours grow long, deadlines slip, and tempers flare.

tip *If you are looking for multimedia talent, try placing a Help Wanted ad in one of the special-interest group forums on CompuServe, America OnLine, AppleLink, or a local or national bulletin board such as that operated by the Boston Computer Society (BCS) or the Berkeley Macintosh Users Group (BMUG). Job seekers will also find these forums valuable.*

Pilot Projects and Prototyping

When organizing your multimedia project, it may be advisable to incorporate a proof-of-concept or pilot project phase. During this phase you can test ideas, mock up interfaces, exercise the hardware platform, and develop a sense about where the alligators live. These alligators are typically found in the swampy edges of your own expertise, in the dark recesses of software platforms that almost-but-not-quite perform as advertised and in your misjudgment of the effort required for various tasks. The alligators will appear unexpectedly behind you and nip at your knees, unless you explore the terrain a little before you start out.

Persuade the client to spend a small amount of money and effort up front to let you build a skeletal version of the project, including some artwork, interactive navigation, and performance checks. Indeed, there may be some very specific technology issues that need thorough examination and proof before you can provide a realistic estimate of the work and cost required. The focused experience of this proof will allow both you and the client to assess the project's goals and the means to achieve them.

Build in your experimental pilot as the first phase of your project. At the pilot's conclusion, prepare a milestone report and a functional demo. You will be paid for the work so far, and the client will get real demonstration material that can be shown to bosses and managers. If your demo is good, it will be a very persuasive argument within the client's management hierarchy for completing the full-scale project. Figure 14-7 is excerpted from trial calculations that were the result of a prototype five-language Photo CD project. In the prototype, office staff read the voice-over script as a "scratch track," similar to using a stand-in for the real thing; later, professional talent was used in the recording studio. As a result of building a prototype, accurate estimates of required storage space on the disc were possible.

As part of your delivery at the end of the pilot phase, reassess your estimate of the tasks required and the cost. Prepare a written report and analysis of budgets and anticipated additional costs. This is also the proper time to develop a revised and detailed project plan for the client. It allows the client some flexibility and provides a reality check for you. At this point you can also finalize your budget and payment schedule for the continuation of the project, as well as ink a contract and determine overrun procedures.

FIGURE 14-7

Trial calculations are possible after prototyping

Calculation Sheet

Photo CD Project

Allocation of Disc Space

Note 1: The following trial calculations are based upon the file sizes yielded by an early voice rendering of the Project's English script.

Note 2: File sizes for base resolution images of 640×480 and 768×512 pixel dimensions are estimated at 768K each.

Note 3: File sizes for full imagePacs may range from 3.7MB to 4.5MB, depending upon image complexity and compression rates. The conservative figure of 4.5MB per imagePac is used in these estimates.

Note 4: More accurate real estate estimates will be available following finalization of the script and recording of the English version narration.

Note 5: Firm count of base resolution images and their pixel dimensions will be calculated upon script freeze.

SUMMARY: There is adequate room on the disc for both sound and images if each language recording is limited to no more than 9 minutes.

Scratch Track File (English)	Duration	Scractch Track File (English)	Duration
SNDE01A	18.369	SNDE10A	5.658
SNDE01B	9.180	SNDE11A	23.856
SNDE01C	9.295	SNDE12A	14.314
SNDE02A	17.609	SNDE13A	14.193
SNDE03A	17.932	SNDE14A	7.487
SNDE04A	11.156	SNDE15A	16.172
SNDE05A	18.035	SNDE16A	19.450
SNDE06A	8.050	SNDE17A	5.830
SNDE07A	12.790	SNDE18A	21.443
SNDE08A	16.218	SNDE19A	12.295
SNDE09A	27.468		
		Total	306.800 Seconds
			5.113 Minutes
		plus	
		Intro Fanfare	30.0 Seconds
		(Shared by all languages)	

Task Planning

Your multimedia project may contain many tasks. Here is a brief check list of action items for which you should plan ahead as you think through your project:

- ☐ Design Instructional Framework
- ☐ Hold Creative Idea Session(s)
- ☐ Determine Delivery Platform
- ☐ Determine Authoring Platform
- ☐ Assay Available Content
- ☐ Draw Navigation Map
- ☐ Create Storyboards
- ☐ Design Interface
- ☐ Design Information Containers
- ☐ Research/Gather Content
- ☐ Assemble Team
- ☐ Build Prototype
- ☐ User Test
- ☐ Revise Design
- ☐ Create Graphics
- ☐ Create Animations
- ☐ Produce Audio
- ☐ Produce Video
- ☐ Digitize Audio and Video
- ☐ Take Still Photographs
- ☐ Program and Author
- ☐ Test Functionality
- ☐ Fix Bugs
- ☐ Beta Test
- ☐ Create Golden Master
- ☐ Replicate
- ☐ Prepare Package
- ☐ Deliver
- ☐ Award Bonuses
- ☐ Throw Party

FIGURE 14-8 *A portion of an Excel spreadsheet used to schedule manpower and project costs*

PROJECT CALC SHEET						1					2	
C. 5 5	$112,000		MARCH				APRIL					MAY
		SALARY	1	2	3	4	5	6	7	8	9	10
1 CONTEN	ORIGINATION FEE		5									
	DIRECTOR	40	0.1	0.1	0.1	0.1	0.1	0.1	0.1	0.1	0.1	0.1
		cost	0.22	0.22	0.22	0.22	0.22	0.22	0.22	0.22	0.22	0.22
	EDITOR	20					1	1				
		cost	0.00	0.00	0.00	0.00	1.12	1.12	0.00	0.00	0.00	0.00
	WRITER A	40	1	1	1	1	1					
		cost	2.24	2.24	2.24	2.24	2.24	0.00	0.00	0.00	0.00	0.00
	RESEARCHER	16										
		cost	0.00	0.00	0.00	0.00	0.00	0.00	0.00	0.00	0.00	0.00
	subtotal number personnel		1.1	1.1	1.1	1.1	2.1	1.1	1.1	0.1	0.1	0.1
		cost	2.46	2.46	2.46	2.46	3.58	1.34	0.22	0.22	0.22	0.22
2 ART												
	DIRECTOR	35	1	1	1	1	1	1	1	1	1	1
		cost	1.40	1.40	1.40	1.40	1.40	1.40	1.40	1.40	1.40	1.40
	ART 1	18								1	1	1
		cost	0.00	0.00	0.00	0.00	0.00	0.00	0.00	1.01	1.01	1.01
	ART2	13										
		cost	0.00	0.00	0.00	0.00	0.00	0.00	0.00	0.00	0.00	0.00
	subtotal number personnel		1	1	1	1	1	1	1	2	2	2
		cost	1.40	1.40	1.40	1.40	1.40	1.40	1.40	2.41	2.41	2.41
3 TECHNICAL												
	DIRECTOR	35								1	1	1
		cost	0.00	0.00	0.00	0.00	0.00	0.00	0.00	1.40	1.40	1.40

Scheduling

When you have worked up a plan that encompasses the phases, tasks, and work items you feel will be required to complete your project, you need to lay out these elements along a time line. To do this, you must estimate the total time required for each task and then allocate this time among the number of persons who will be asynchronously working on the project (see, for example, Figure 14-8). Again, the notion of balance is important: if you can distribute the required hours to perform a task among several workers, completion should take proportionally less time.

First Person

Many times we have heard about the Feedback Alligator. *Its mottled skin boasts an Escher-like pattern of lines and marks, showing apparently clear definition along the head and neck, but converging to a brown muddled wash at the tail. When the tail wags on this alligator, all hell breaks loose, and multimedia contracts can be severely strained or lost altogether.*

Feedback Alligators can appear when you throw a client into the mix of creative people... when necessary-for-client-satisfaction approval cycles can turn your project into an anorexic nightmare of continuing rework, change, and consequently diminished profit. These alligators typically slink out from the damps after you have locked down a contract and scope of work, when the creative guys are already being well paid to ply their craft.

For client protection, multimedia creative artists should be hired with a cap on budget and time. They should be highly skilled, efficient, and should have a clear understanding of what a project's goals are, and they should be allowed to accomplish these goals with as much freedom as possible. But good multimedia artists should come close to the mark the first time.

They don't always. For example, you agree to compose background theme music to play whenever your client's logo shows on the screen. You master up a sample cassette tape and pass it to the client. She doesn't quite like the sound, but is not sure why. You go back to the MIDI sequencer and try again. The client still isn't sure that's it. Again, you make up a tape and pass it to her for review. No, maybe it needs a little more Sgt. Pepper... this is our logo, remember?

The process of client feedback can go on and on forever in a resonance of a desire to please and creative uncertainty unless you have developed rules for limiting these cycles. While your client might always be right, you will still go broke working unlimited changes on a fixed budget.

So do two things to ward off the Feedback Alligator. First, make it clear up front (in your contract) that there will be only a certain number of review cycles before the client must pay for changes. Second, invite the client to the workstation or studio where the creative work is done. For sound, tickle the keyboard until the client says "that's it!" Make 'em sign off on it. For artwork and animation, let the client spend an afternoon riding shotgun over the artist's shoulder, participating in color and design choices. Get the client involved.

If your client contact isn't empowered to make decisions but simply carries your work up to the bosses for "management approval," you are facing the unpleasant Son of Feedback Alligator. Demand a client contact who has budget and design authority.

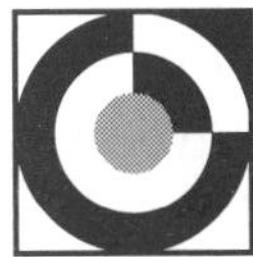

warning *Assigning twice as many people to work on a task may not cut the time for its completion precisely in half. Consider the administrative and management overhead of communication, networking, and necessary staff meetings required when additional staff is added.*

Scheduling can be very difficult for multimedia projects because so much of the making of multimedia is artistic trial and error. A recorded sound will need to be edited and perhaps altered many times. Animations need to be run again and again and adjusted so that they are smooth and properly placed. A QuickTime or AVI movie may require many hours of editing and tweaking before it works in sync with other screen activities. Scheduling multimedia projects is also difficult because the technology of computer hardware and software is in constant flux, and upgrades while your project is underway may drive you to new installations and concomitant learning curves. The general rule of thumb when working with computers and new technology under a deadline is that everything will take longer to do than you think it will.

In scheduling for a project that is to be rendered for a client, remember that the client will need to approve or sign off on your work at various stages. This approval process takes time and may also require revision of your submitted work. These client feedback loops are dependent on factors beyond your control, and they can wreck havoc with your schedule.

tip *When you negotiate with your client, you should limit the number of revisions allowed (each revision costs time and money) before you rename the revisions as change orders and bill extra.*

Estimating

In production and manufacturing industries, estimating costs and effort is a relatively simple matter. To make chocolate-chip cookies, for example, you need ingredients such as flour and sugar and equipment such as mixers, ovens, and packaging machines. Once the process is running smoothly, you can turn out hundreds of cookies, each tasting the same and each made of the same stuff. You then control your costs by fine-tuning known expenses, negotiating deals on flour and sugar in quantity, installing more efficient ovens, and hiring personnel at a more competitive wage. In contrast, making multimedia is not a repetitive manufacturing process. Rather, it is by its very nature a continuous research and development effort characterized by creative trial and error. Each new project is somewhat different from the last, and each may require application of many different tools and solutions.

In the area of professional services, consider some typical costs in the advertising community. Production of a storyboard for a 30-second commercial spot costs about $50,000. Postproduction editing time in a professional video studio runs upwards of $500 per hour. An hour of professional acting talent costs $350 or more at union scale. The emerging multimedia industry, on the other hand, does not have a track record long enough to have produced "going rates" for its services. A self-guided tour distributed with a software product, for example, may cost $15,000 for one client and $150,000 for another, depending on the tour's length and polish. A short original musical clip may cost $50 or $500, based on the talent used and the nature of the music. A graphical menu screen might take 2 or 20 hours to develop, depending on its complexity and the graphic art talent applied. Without available going rates for segments of work or entire projects, you must estimate the costs of your multimedia project by analyzing the tasks that it comprises and the people who build it.

The first time you accomplish a multimedia task, it will demand great effort as you learn the software and hardware tools and the techniques required. The second time you do a similar task, you will already know where the tools are and how they work, and the task will require less effort. On the third take, you should be quite proficient.

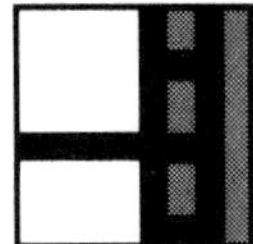

tip *To recoup learning-curve costs when you first perform a task, you must factor extra time into your budget; later you can increase your billing rate to reflect your improved skill level.*

Be sure you include the hidden costs of administration and management. It takes time to speak with clients on the telephone, to write progress reports, and to mail invoices. In addition, you may have many people in your work force who represent specialized skills, for example, a graphic artist, musician, instructional designer, and writer. In this case, you'll need to include a little extra buffer of time and expense in your estimate to pay for these artists' participation in project meetings and creative sessions.

As a general rule, three elements can vary in project estimates: time, money, and people. As illustrated here, if you decrease any one of these elements, you'll generally need to increase one or both of the others.

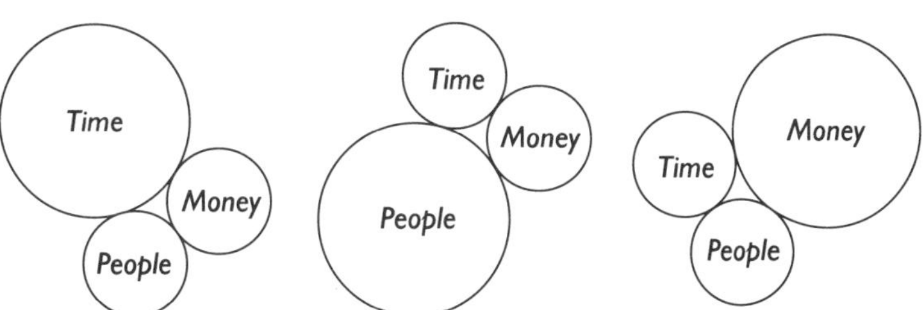

For example, if you have very little time to do a project (an aggressive schedule), it will cost more money in overtime and premium sweat, and it may take more people. If you have a good number of people, the project should take less time. By increasing the money spent, you can actually decrease the number of people required by purchasing efficient (but costly) experts; this may also reduce the time required.

First Person

We were asked by a large institution to complete a project that had fallen on the floor. It was really worse than that–the project had actually slipped through the cracks in that floor. The single known copy of work–representing about $30,000 in paid billings–had been copied to 19 high-density floppy disks and stored in a file cabinet. Here they were discovered by the secretarial pool and formatted, to be used for WordPerfect documents. The secretaries remembered the whole thing because the stored backups contained protected files, so the disks were unusually difficult to erase! Luckily, bits and pieces of the project were unearthed on the hard disk of a computer that had been disconnected and stored in the basement. We were able to reconstruct much of the artwork, but not the interactive links.

As we studied the leavings of the embarrassed progenitors, we discovered a trail of mistakes and errors. It became clear that the institution made a bad decision in hiring a well qualified engineering firm at great expense (standard billing rates) to construct a difficult multimedia presentation. CAD/CAM drawings and finite element analysis were the forte of these engineers–not animated icons and colorful bitmaps with sound tracks. Furthermore, the engineering firm erred in selecting software that performed on the target hardware platform at about the speed of snails chasing a dog. Money had been spent, the product didn't work, and everyone involved was in gray limbo, slinking around, looking for a solution.

We determinedly pulled together the bits and pieces we could find, designed a snappy navigational structure we were proud of, and quickly fixed the big problem for a small fee (based on our own standard billing rate). The institution, of course, was delighted and became a client of long standing.

Do your best to estimate the amount of time it will take to perform each task in your plan. Multiply this estimate by your hourly billing rate. Sum up the total costs for each task, and you now have an estimate of the project's total time and cost. Though this simple formula is easy, what is not so easy is diligently remaining within the budgeted time and money for each task. For this, you need good tracking and management oversight.

Billing Rates

Your billing rate should be set according to your cost of doing business plus a reasonable profit margin. Typical billing rates for multimedia production companies range from $55 to $170 per hour, depending on the work being done and the person doing it. If consultants or specialists are employed on a project, the billing rate can go much higher. You can establish a rate that is the same for all tasks, or you can specify different rates according to the person assigned to a task.

Everyone who contributes to a project should have two rates associated with their work: the employee's cost to the employer (including salary and benefits), and the employee's rate billed to the customer. The employee's cost, of course, is not included in your estimate, but you need to know this as part of your estimate—because your profit margin is the difference between the rate you charge the client and the cost to your company, less a proportion of overhead expenses (rental or leasing of space, utilities, phones, shared secretarial and administrative services, and so forth). If your profit margin is negative, you should reconsider both your project plan and your long-term plan.

Multimedia production companies with high billing rates claim that their rates allow them to accomplish more work in a given amount of time, expertly, thus saving money, time, and enhancing the finished quality and reliability of a project; this is particularly the case with larger-scale, complex projects. Smaller and leaner companies that offer lower billing rates may claim to be more streamlined, hungry, and willing to perform extra services. Lower rates do not necessarily mean lower quality work but rather imply that the company either supports less overhead or is satisfied with a reduced margin of profit. As more and more multimedia producers enter this marketplace, the competition is increasing and the free hand of supply and demand is driving prices.

Purchasers of multimedia services must, however, thoroughly examine the qualifications of a prospective contracting company to ensure that the work required can be accomplished on time and within budget. There isn't a more difficult business situation than a half-completed job and an exhausted budget.

Contractors and consultants can bring specialized skills such as graphic art, C programming, database expertise, music composition, and video to your project. If you use these experts, be sure your billing rate is higher than theirs. Or, if you have a task the client has capped with a not-to-exceed cost, be sure your arrangement with the contractor is also capped. Contractors place no burden on your overhead and administration other than a few cups of coffee, and they should generate a generous profit margin for you during the course of your project. Be sure that contractors perform the majority of their work off site, using their own equipment; otherwise, federal tax regulators may reclassify these free-lancers as employees and require you to pay employee benefits.

Example Cost Sheets

Figure 14-9 contains groups of expense categories for producing multimedia. If you use these in your own work, be sure to temper your guesses with experience; if you are new to multimedia production, get some qualified advice during this planning stage.

Proposals and Bids

A multimedia proposal will be passed through several levels of a company so that managers and directors can evaluate the project's quality and its price. The higher a proposal goes in the management hierarchy, the less chance it has of being read in detail. For this reason, you always want to provide an executive summary or overview as the first page of your proposal, briefly describing the project's goals, how the goals will be achieved, and the cost.

In the body of the proposal, include a section dealing with creative issues and describe your method for conveying the client's message or meeting the graphic and interactive goals of the project. Also incorporate a discussion of technical issues, in which you clearly define the target hardware platform. If necessary, identify the members of your staff who will work on the project, and list their roles and qualifications.

The backbone of the proposal is the estimate and project plan that you have created up to this point. It describes the scope of the work. If the project is complicated, prepare a brief synopsis of both the plan and the timetable; include this in the overview. If the project has many phases, you can present each phase as a separate section of the proposal.

FIGURE 14-9

The many costs associated with producing multimedia

PROJECT DEVELOPMENT COSTS
Salaries
Client Meetings
Acquisition of Content
Communications
Travel
Research
Proposal & Contract Prep
Overhead

PRODUCTION COSTS
Management
- Salaries
- Communications
- Travel
- Consumables

Content Gathering
- Salaries
- Research Services
- Licenses

Graphics Production
- Salaries
- Hardware/Software
- Fees for Content Use
- Animation
- Consumables

Audio Production
- Salaries
- Hardware/Software
- Studio Fees
- Licenses
- Consumables
- Data Storage
- Talent Fees

Video Production
- Salaries
- Hardware/Software
- Equipment Rental
- Talent Fees
- Location Fees
- Studio Fees
- Digital Capture & Editing
- Consumables

Authoring
- Salaries
- Hardware/Software
- Consumables

TESTING COSTS
Salaries
Focus Groups
Editing
Beta Program

DISTRIBUTION COSTS
Salaries
Documentation
Packaging
Manufacturing
Marketing
Advertising
Shipping

Cost estimates for each phase or deliverable milestone, as well as payment schedules, should follow the description of the work. If this section is lengthy, it should also include a summary.

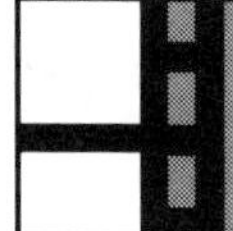

tip *Make the proposal look good–it should be attractive and easy to read. You might also wish to provide an unbound copy so that it can be easily photocopied. Include separate, relevant literature about your company and qualifications. A list of clients and brief descriptions of projects you have successfully completed are also useful for demonstrating your capabilities.*

First Person

I was downbound from Puget Sound to San Francisco, and the weather was up, with seas running heavy and winds gusting to 80 knots in our face. The master and the first mate were on the bridge, the old man sitting curled up in his upholstered highchair on the darkened starboard wing, the first mate pacing on the rubber mat behind the helmsman. The third mate was on watch, leaning over the radar screen and making fluorescent notes with a grease pencil. As I was a guest with no duties, I mostly hung out in the chart room while white water broke over the bows and the shuddering propeller cavitated out of the sea; wind screamed in the vents on the roof of the bridge. There wasn't much conversation that night, but the master slowed us to 5 knots, concerned about the containers lashed to the forward deck.

When the young third mate came into the chart room, I asked "Where are we," and he took a sharp pencil, made a fine point on the chart, and drew a tiny circle around the point; he smiled, proud to have good radar bearings. The first mate came in about a half hour later, and, when I asked the same question, he circled an area about the size of a walnut. As the master left the bridge for his cabin, I asked him, too, where we were. He took his thumb and rubbed it on the chart in a rough oval about the diameter of his fist, saying "somewhere in here," and grinned at me as the ship heaved suddenly and we grabbed for the handholds.

The more experience these professionals had, the larger the circle they drew, and the less they relied on pinpoint navigation. You should be prudent when costing a multimedia production; precision estimating can wreck your project.

Finally, include a list of your terms. Contract terms may become a legally binding document, so have your terms reviewed by legal counsel. An example is shown in Figure 14-10. Terms should include the following:

- A description of your billing rates and invoicing policy.
- Your policy for billing out-of-pocket expenses for travel, telephone, courier services, and so forth.
- Your policy regarding third-party licensing fees for run-time modules and special drivers (the client pays).
- Specific statements of who owns what on completion of the project. You may wish to retain the rights to show parts of the work for your own promotional purposes and to reuse in other projects segments of code and algorithms that you develop.
- An assurance to the client that you will not disclose proprietary information.
- Your right to display your credits appropriately within the work.
- Your unlimited right to work for other clients.
- A disclaimer for liability and damages arising out of the work.

FIGURE 14-10

Sample contract terms adapted from language developed by the HyperMedia Group, Inc. (do not use without appropriate legal counsel)

Sample Terms:

We will undertake this assignment on a time-and-expenses basis at our current hourly rate of $___ per hour for __job title__, $___ per hour for __job title__, $___ per hour for __job title__ , plus applicable taxes and reimbursement of authorized out-of-pocket expenses. Reasonable travel, express, freight, courier and telecommunication expenses incurred in relation to the project, will be considered pre-authorized. [Client] will be responsible for all licensing fees of third-party products incorporated (with [Client]'s knowledge and approval) into the final product. We will invoice [Client] either upon [Client]'s acceptance of the specified deliverables for each work phase specified above, or monthly, whichever is more often. [Client]'s authorization, either written or verbal, to commence a work phase will constitute acceptance of the previous phase's deliverables. Invoices are due and payable upon presentation. To commence work, we require a retainer in the amount of $________, which will be deducted from the final invoice for the project.

Upon our receipt of final payment, [Client] shall own all rights, except those noted below, to the completed work delivered under this agreement, including graphics, written text, and program code. [Client] may at [Client]'s sole discretion copyright the work in [Client]'s name or assign rights to a third party. Ownership of material provided by third parties and incorporated in our work with [Client]'s knowledge and approval shall be as provided in any license or sale agreement governing said materials. We reserve the right to use in any of our future work for ourselves or any client all techniques, structures, designs and individual modules of program code we develop that are applicable to requirements outside those specified above. Further, our performance of this work for [Client] shall in no way limit us regarding assignments we may accept from any other clients now or at any time in the future.

We shall be allowed to show [Client]'s finished work, or any elements of it, to existing and prospective clients for demonstration purposes. If such demonstration showings would reveal information [Client] has identified to us as proprietary or confidential, we shall be allowed to create a special version for demonstrations which omits or disguises such information and/or [Client]'s identity as the client. We shall also be allowed to include a production credit display, e.g. "Produced by [Our Name]" or equivalent copy, on the closing screen or other mutually agreeable position in the finished work. Following [Client]'s acceptance of this proposal we shall also be allowed to identify [Client] as a client in our marketing communications materials.

In the event it is necessary in the course of this assignment for us to view or work with information of [Client]'s that [Client] identify to us as proprietary and confidential (possibly including customer lists, supplier data, financial figures and the like), we agree not to disclose it except to our principals, associates and contractors having confidentiality agreements with us.

We make no warranty regarding this work, or its fitness for a particular purpose, once [Client] accepts it following any testing procedures of [Client]'s choice. In any event, our liability for any damages arising out of this work, expressly including consequential damages, shall not exceed the total amount of fees paid for this work.

It is a significant task to write a project proposal that creatively sells a multimedia concept, accurately estimates the scope of work, and provides realistic budget costs. The proposal often becomes a melting pot—you develop the elements of your idea during early conversations with a potential client, then add in the results of discussions on technique and approach with graphic artists and instructional designers. You blend what the client wants done with what you can actually do, given the client's budgetary constraints, and when the cauldron of compromise cools, your proposal is the result.

The Cover and Package

You have many options for designing the look and feel of your proposal. And though one is often warned to avoid judging a book by its cover, the reality is that executives take about two seconds to assess the quality of the document they are holding. Sometimes, they decide before even touching it. Size up the people who will read your proposal and ferret out their expectancies; tailor your proposal to these expectancies.

If your client judges from the cover of your proposal that the document inside is amateurish rather than professional, you are already fighting an uphill battle. You have two strategies for avoiding this negative first impression:

- Develop your own special style for a proposal cover and package, including custom fonts, cover art and graphics, illustrations and figures, unique section and paragraph styles, and a clean binding. Do your proposal first class.
- Make the entire package plain and simple, yet businesslike. The "plain" part of the approach means not fussing with too many fonts and type styles. This austerity may be particularly successful for proposals to government agencies, where 10-point Courier Elite or 12-point Pica may be not just a de facto standard but a required document format. For the "simple" part of the approach, a stapled sheaf of papers is adequate. Don't try to dress up your plain presentation with Pee-Chee folders or cheap plastic covers; keep it lean and mean.

Table of Contents

Busy executives want to anticipate a document and grasp its content in very short order. A table of contents or index is a straightforward way to present the elements of your proposal in condensed overview.

Executive Summary

Always include an executive summary—a prelude containing no more than a few paragraphs of pithy description and budget totals. The summary should be on the cover page or immediately following the table of contents.

Needs Analysis and Description

In many proposals, it is useful to describe in some detail the reason the project is being put forward. A needs analysis and description is particularly common in proposals that must move through a company's executive hierarchy in search of approval and funding.

Target Audience

All multimedia proposals should include a section that describes the target audience and target platform. When the end user's multimedia capabilities have a broad and uncertain range, it is very important to describe the hardware and software delivery platform you intend to provide. For instance, if your project requires a compact disc player but the end user platform has none, you will need to adjust your multimedia strategy by revising the design or by requiring the end user to acquire a player. Some clients will clearly control the delivery platform, so you may not need to provide detail regarding system components.

Creative Strategy

A creative strategy section—a description of the look and feel of the project itself—can be important to your proposal, especially if the executives reviewing your proposal were not present for creative sessions or did not participate in preliminary discussions. If you have a library of completed projects that are similar to your proposed effort, including them with your proposal is helpful, pointing the client to techniques and presentation methods that may be relevant. If you have designed a prototype, describe it here, or create a separate heading and include graphics and diagrams.

Project Implementation

A proposal must describe the way a project will be organized and scheduled. Your estimate of costs and expenses will be based on this description. The project implementation section of your proposal may contain a detailed calendar, PERT and Gantt charts, and lists of specific tasks with associated completion dates and work hours (see the earlier section "Idea Management Software"). This information may be general or very detailed, depending on the demands of the client. The project implementation section is not just about how much work there is, but how the work will be managed and performed. You may not need to specify time estimates in work hours but rather in the amount of calendar time required to complete each phase.

Budget

The budget relates directly to the scope of work which you have laid out in the project implementation section. Distill your itemized costs from the project implementation description and consolidate the minute tasks of each project phase into categories of activity meaningful to the client.

Multi

> Feedback loops and good communication between the design and production effort are critical to the success of a project.

strengths and limitations

media

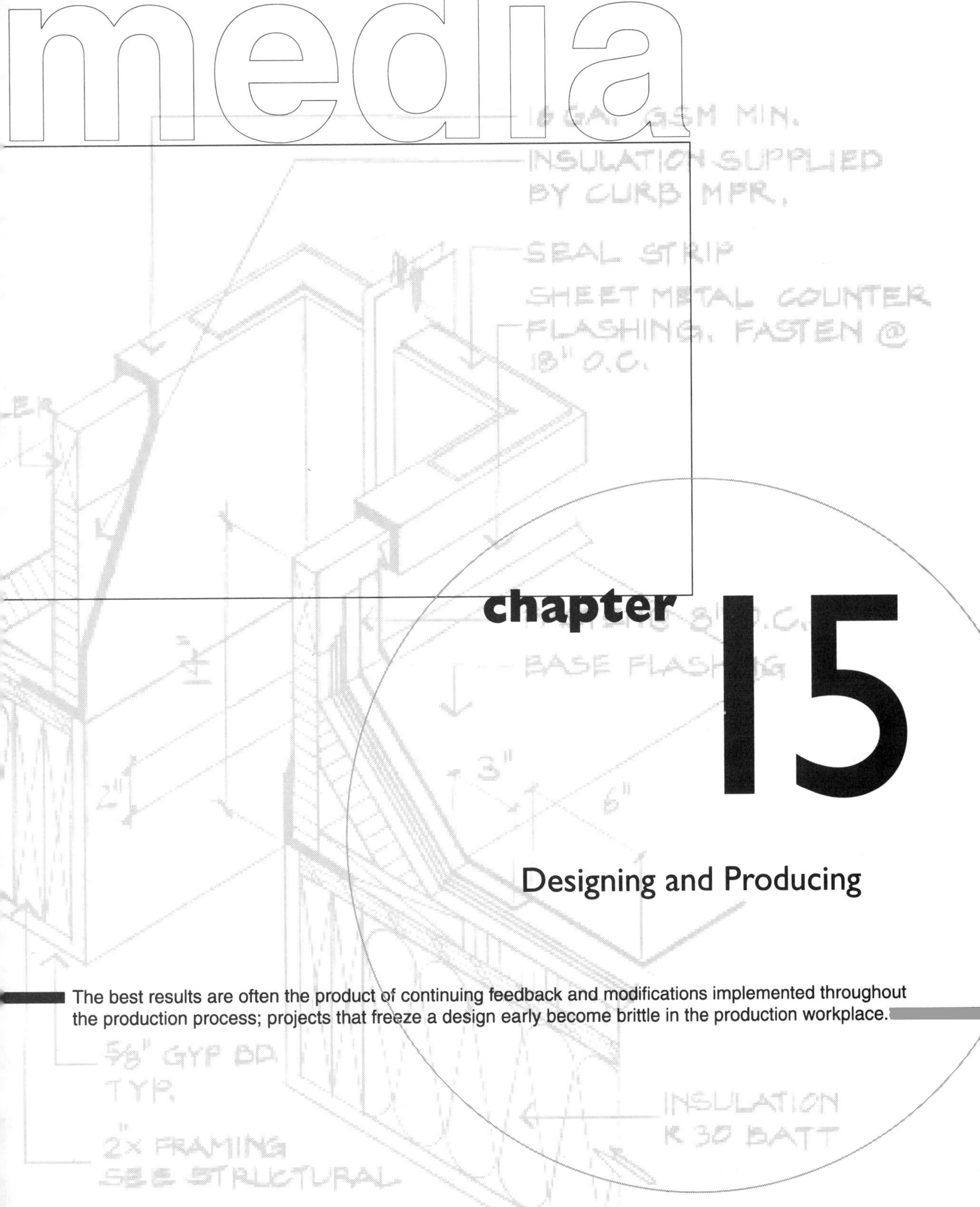

chapter 15

Designing and Producing

The best results are often the product of continuing feedback and modifications implemented throughout the production process; projects that freeze a design early become brittle in the production workplace.

DESIGNING and building multimedia projects go hand-in-hand. Indeed, design input to a project is never over until the product is actually frozen and shipped. The best results are often the product of continuing feedback and modifications implemented throughout the production process; projects that freeze a design early become brittle in the production workplace, losing the chances for incremental improvement.

Just as the architect of a high-rise office tower must understand how to utilize the materials with which he or she works (lest the construction collapse on top of trusting clients), designers of multimedia projects must also understand the strengths and limitations of the elements that will compose their project. It makes no sense, for example, to design the audio elements of a multimedia project in memory-consuming 16-bit, 44.1KHz stereo sound when the delivery CD-ROM will not have sufficient room for it; or to produce lengthy full-screen QuickTime movies to play at 30 frames per second when end user platforms can't handle the throughput; or to design 24-bit color graphics for elementary schools when that environment can hardly support 8-bit graphics. Architects don't design inner-city parking garages with 14-foot ceilings and wide turning radii for 18-wheel big rigs, and they don't build them using wood or mud laid on a swampy foundation.

Designers must work closely with producers to ensure that their ideas can be properly realized, and producers need to confirm the results of their work with the designers. "These colors seem to work better, what do you think?" "It plays faster now, but I had to change the animation sequence..." "Doing the index with highlighted lines slows it down, can we eliminate this feature?" Feedback loops and good communication between the design and production effort are critical to the success of a project.

This is so crazy it just might work!

Brian Snook, Producer, Visual In-Seitz, Inc., ...
the night before the first review

The idea processing (described in Chapter 14) of your multimedia project will have resulted in a detailed and balanced plan of action, a production schedule, and a timetable. Now it's time for implementation!

Designing

The design part of your project is where your knowledge and skill with computers; your talent in graphic arts, video, and music; and your ability to conceptualize logical pathways through information are all focused to create the real thing. Design is thinking, choosing, making, and doing. It is shaping, smoothing, reworking, polishing, testing, and editing. When you design your project, your ideas and concepts are moved one step closer to reality. Competence in the design phase is what separates amateurs from professionals in the making of multimedia.

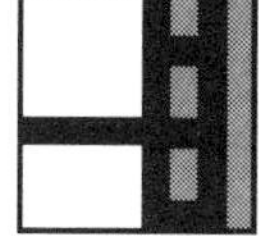

tip *Never begin a multimedia project without first outlining its structure and content.*

Depending on the scope of your project and the size and style of your team, you can take two approaches to creating an original interactive multimedia design. You can spend great effort on the *storyboards*, or graphic outlines, describing the project in exact detail—using words and sketches for each and every screen image, sound, and navigational choice, right down to specific colors and shades, text content, attributes and fonts, button shapes, styles, responses, and voice inflections. Or you can use the storyboards as a rough schematic guide, exerting less design sweat up front and more effort actually rendering the product at a workstation.

Both these approaches require the same thorough knowledge of the tools and capabilities of multimedia, and both demand a storyboard or a project outline. The first approach is often favored by clients who wish to tightly control the production process and labor costs. The second approach gets you more quickly into the nitty-gritty, hands-on tasks, but you may ultimately have to give back that time because more iterations and editing will be required to smooth the work in progress.

Designing the Structure

A revolution is taking place today in the way humans access, learn, and interact with information. Indeed, the nature of information itself is changing in ways more complex and socially powerful than the liberation of the printed word that occurred 500 years ago. That last revolution, led by Johann Gutenberg, Jean Grolier, Aldus Manutius, and others, yielded powerful and long-lasting changes, many of which certainly exceeded the imagination of that time. Today, creative and engineering talents are emerging to invent new ways to marry fresh ideas with enabling technology, to set the standards for the "new literature" and truly alter the human condition! The way resources are structured and organized into an information space, and the way users then get at that information through a human interface, are the essence of this contemporary multimedia revolution.

On the face of it, a multimedia project is no more than an arrangement of text, graphic, sound, and video elements (or *objects*). But the way you compose these elements makes each project different, shaped by the project's purpose and the messages it contains.

Navigation

Mapping the structure of your project is a task that should be started early in the planning phase. A *navigation map* (or *navMap*) outlines the connections or links among various areas of your content and helps you organize your content and messages. A navMap also provides you with a table of contents as well as a chart of the logical flow of the interactive interface. It describes your multimedia objects and shows what happens when the user interacts.

Just as eight story plots might account for 99 percent of all literature ever written (boy meets girl, protagonist meets antagonist, etc.), a few basic structures for multimedia projects will cover most cases: linear, hierarchical, nonlinear, and composite. Figure 15-1 illustrates the four fundamental organizing structures used in multimedia projects, often in combination:

- *Linear:* Users navigate sequentially, from one frame or bite of information to another.
- *Hierarchical:* Users navigate along the branches of a tree structure that is shaped by the natural logic of the content.
- *Nonlinear:* Users navigate freely through the content of the project, unbound by predetermined routes.
- *Composite:* Users may navigate freely (nonlinear) but are occasionally constrained to linear presentations of movies or critical information and/or to data that are most logically organized in a hierarchy.

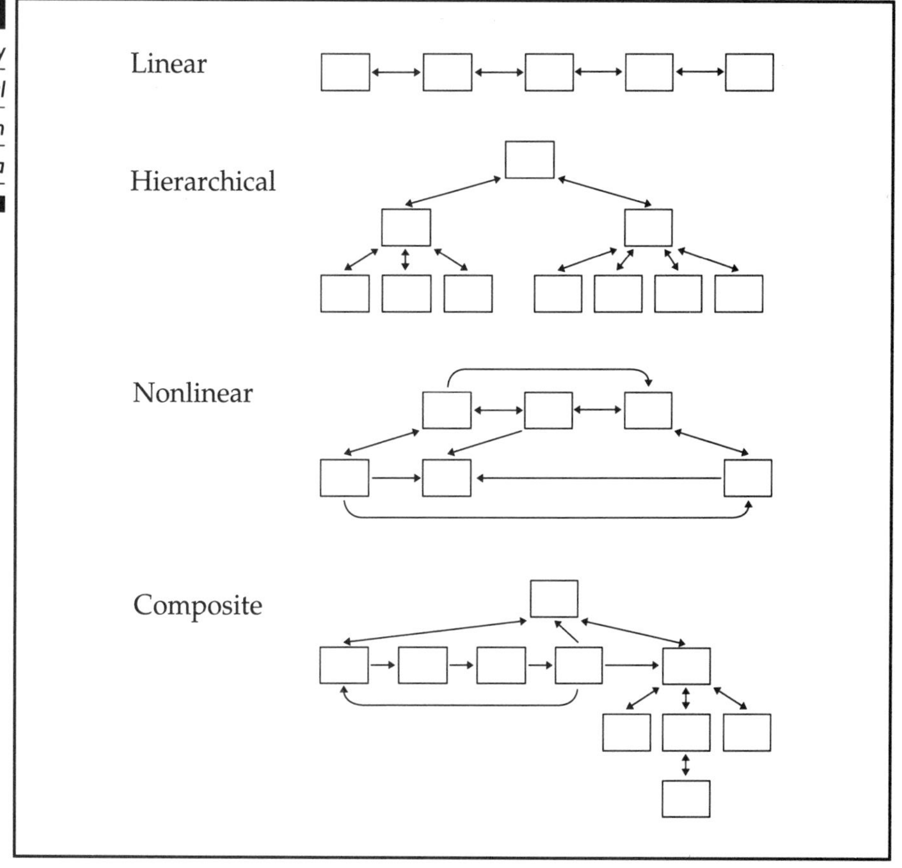

FIGURE 15-1 *The four primary navigational structures used in multimedia*

First Person

With regard to the creation of interactive fiction, what kinds of software engineering strategies would you recommend for creating stories that maintain a strong sense of cumulative action (otherwise known as plot) while still offering the audience a high frequency of interaction? In other words, how do you constrain the combinatoric explosion of the narrative pathways while still maintaining the Aristotelian sense of a unity of plot?

—Patrick Dillon, Atlanta, GA

One and one-half T-shirts to Patrick Dillon! Would have been two for your invocation of a famous Greek philosopher, but then I couldn't find "combinatoric" in Webster's. Aristotle himself would have been pleased by the harmonious balance of your reward: you have asked a really good question.

As multimedia and the power of computers begin to change our approach to literature and storytelling, new engineering strategies do need to be implemented.

(continued)

First Person

When fiction becomes nonlinear, and users can choose among alternative plot lines, the permutations can become staggering. To an author, this means each new plot pathway chosen by user interaction requires its own development, and one story may actually become several hundred or more. To constrain this fearsome explosion of narrative pathways yet retain a high frequency of interaction, try designing your fiction around a single core plot that provides the cumulative action, and use arrays of returning branches for detail and illustration. In this way you can entirely avoid the permutations of alternative universes and still offer the adventure of interactive exploration.

Dear Tay: I just read your answer to Patrick Dillon's question about interactive fiction in your column for March, 1993. My response is difficult to contain: "Aaarrrrggghhhh!!!! You Ignorant Slut!" OK, perhaps I am overreacting, but you are refusing to let go of linearity. Why ever do you want to "constrain the combinatoric explosion of narrative pathways"? Good Lord, that's what makes the gametree bushy. This is exactly the kind of work that's well-suited for a computer to perform–grinding out three billion story variations!
– Chris Crawford, San Jose, CA.

Chris, I've been called a lot of things over the years (like Fay and Ray), and it's with a smile that I add your gift to my collection. Playing Jane Curtin to your Dan Aykroyd, I'll be happy to counter your counterpoint.

Your challenge represents a serious subject for multimedia designers today. I agree that interactive stories with too few branches are disappointingly flat and shallow. When a plot is broadly non-linear, however, the permutations of events and possible outcomes become staggering, and the story as a whole becomes difficult to visualize and manage. Producing such work is also an intellectual challenge and costly in time and effort.

A truly open-ended "hypermedia" navigation system for consumer consumption risks death by shock caused by open arterial branches and loss of story pressure, where plot lines become too diffuse and users founder in trivia. Most users may, indeed, prefer a structured, organized, and well-defined story environment.

The argument for simplicity is voiced by Steven Levy, the author of Hackers *and* Artificial Life*, who says, "There's really something to be said for documents with a beginning, middle, and end."*

The shape of this new literature made possible by multimedia computers and wide-bandwidth cable and telephone delivery systems is being born in the working designs of developers. The final test for successful multimedia design is the marketplace, where consumers will decide.

From correspondence in "Ask the Captain," a monthly column by Tay Vaughan in *NewMedia* magazine (March & July, 1993).

The method you provide for navigating from one place to another in your project is part of the user interface. The success of the user interface depends not only on its general design and graphic art implementations but also on myriad engineering details—such as the position of interactive buttons or hot spots relative to the user's current activity, whether these buttons "light up," and whether you use standard Macintosh or Windows pull-down menus.

Many navMaps are essentially nonlinear. In these navigational systems, viewers are always free to jump to an index, a glossary, various menus, Help or About... sections, or even to the navMap itself. It is often important to give viewers the sense that free choice is available; this empowers them within the context of the subject matter.

The architectural drawings for your multimedia project are the storyboards and navigation maps. *Storyboards* are the sketches and notes that describe in great detail each image, animation, movie segment, sound, text, and navigation cue. The storyboards are married to the navigation maps during the design process

Because all forms of information—including text, numbers, photos, video and sound—can exist in a common digital format, they can be used simultaneously as people browse through an information stream, just as people use their various senses simultaneously to perceive the real world.

Bill Gates, Chairman of Microsoft Corporation, in his keynote address to the International Conference on Multimedia and CD-ROM, March 10, 1992

A simple hierarchical navigation map is illustrated in Figure 15-2, where the subject matter of a small project is organized schematically. The items in boxes are not only descriptions of content but also active buttons that can take users directly to that content. At any place in the project, users can call up this screen and then navigate directly to their chosen subject.

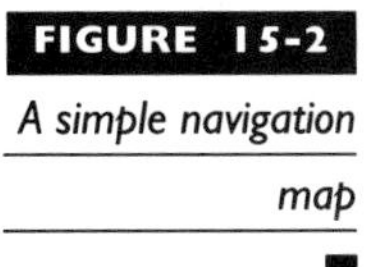

FIGURE 15-2 *A simple navigation map*

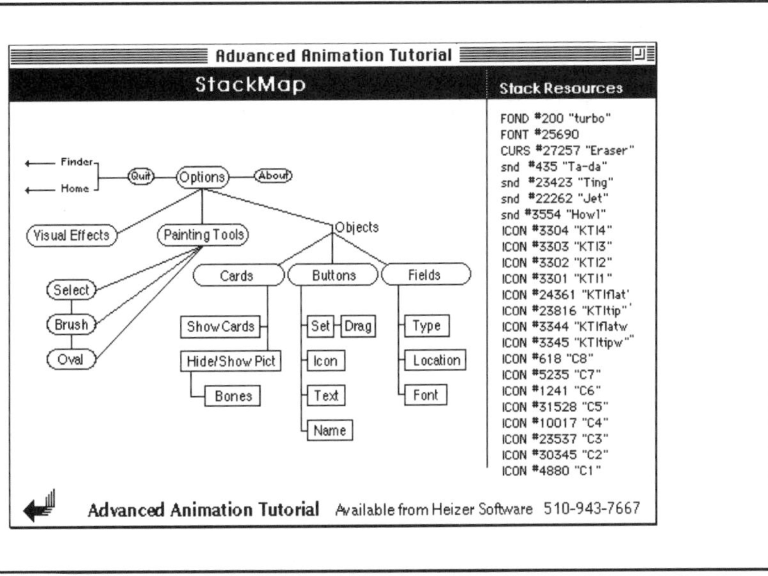

A storyboard for this same project is organized sequentially, screen by screen, and each screen is sketched out with design notes and specifications before rendering. At the left of Figure 15-3 is part of the storyboard for this project; at the right are corresponding finished screens.

Multimedia provides great power for jumping about within your project's content. And though it is important to give users a sense of free choice, too much freedom can be disconcerting and viewers may get lost. Try to keep your messages and content organized along a steady stream of the major subjects, letting users branch outward to explore details. Always provide a secure anchor, with buttons that lead to expected places, and build a familiar landscape to which users may return at any time.

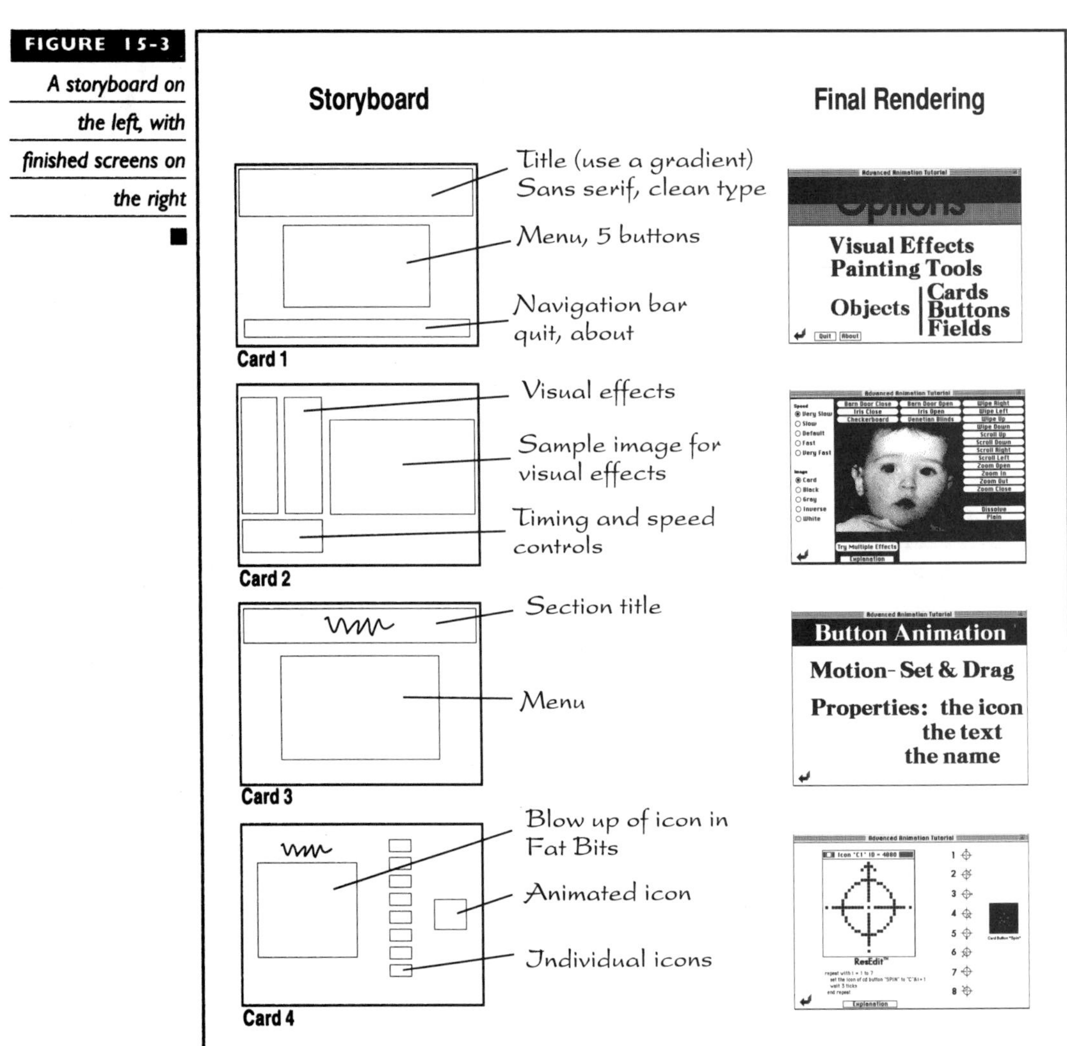

FIGURE 15-3 *A storyboard on the left, with finished screens on the right*

Really good software products should be simple, hot, and deep. People need to get into your software in about 20 seconds and get immediate positive feedback and reward; then they are smiling and having a good time and they want to go further. Hot means that you've got to be fully cooking the machine, with all its graphics and sound capabilities, conveying something dynamic and exciting that competes with what people are used to seeing in a movie or on TV. In terms of deep, it's kind of like the ocean where there are people of all ages: some kids will just wade out in a foot of surf, other guys with scuba gear go way out and way deep. Make it possible for me to go as deep as I want but don't force it on me. Just let the depth of your product unfold to me in a very natural way.

Trip Hawkins, Chairman, Electronic Arts

Your content may not always be an assembly of discrete subjects as illustrated in Figure 15-2. If your material deals with a chronology of events occurring over time, for example, you may wish to design the structure as a linear sequence of events, and then send users along that sequence, allowing them to jump directly to specific dates or time frames if desired (see Figure 15-4).

Even within a linear, time-based structure, you may still wish to sort events into categories regardless of when they occur. There is no reason you can't do this and offer more than one method of navigating through your content.

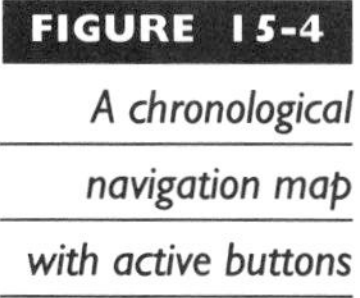

FIGURE 15-4 A chronological navigation map with active buttons

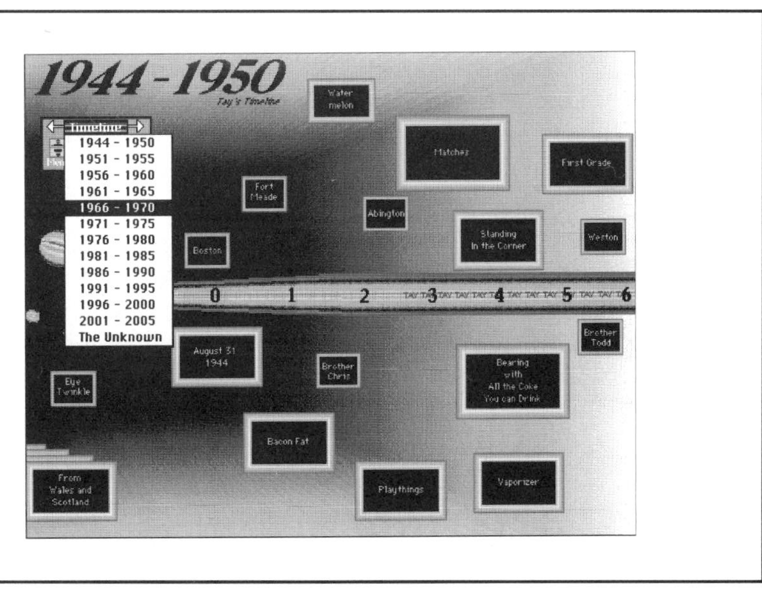

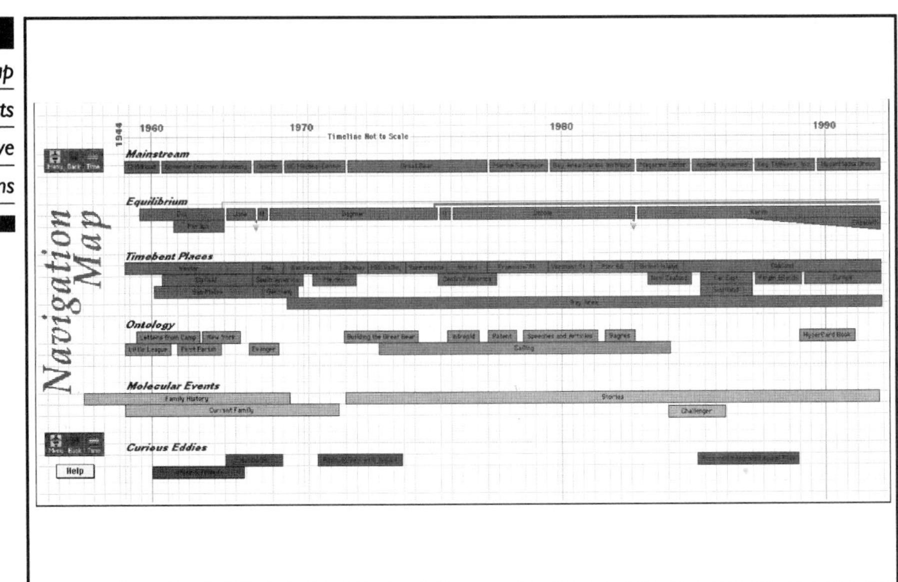

FIGURE 15-5 A navigation map based on events that are active buttons

Figure 15-5, for instance, illustrates a navigation map that accesses the same events from the time-line form of Figure 15-4, but arranged here instead into meaningful groups of events.

Hot Spots and Buttons

Most multimedia authoring systems allow you to make any part of the screen, or any object, into a button or "hot spot." When you click a button at that location, something happens—this makes multimedia not just interactive, but exciting. Your navigation design must provide buttons that make sense, so their actions will be intuitively understood by means of their icon or graphic representation or via text cues. Do not force your viewers to learn many new or special icons; keep the learning curve to a minimum. It's also important to include buttons that perform basic housekeeping tasks, such as quitting the project at any given point, or canceling an activity.

There are three general categories of buttons: text, graphic, and icon. Text buttons and their fonts and styles are described in Chapter 9. Graphic buttons can contain graphic images or even parts of images—for example, a map of the world where each country is color coded, and a mouse click on a country yields further information. Icons are graphic objects designed specifically to be meaningful buttons and are usually small (although size is, in theory, not a determining factor). Icons are fundamental graphic objects symbolic of an activity or entity. Figure 15-7 shows a selection of clip-art

First Person

One day I launched an application named Disk Formatter on my Macintosh, just to see what it was about. Suddenly I was in a pretty scary user-interface predicament (Figure 15-6 is what I saw). I could tell from its name that the software erased and formatted hard disks and cartridges; my mounted hard disks were listed on the screen by SCSI number, and I was being prompted to select one of them. I looked over at the CPU and was pleased that the disk drive access light wasn't ticking away at sector-length intervals. I didn't know what the software was doing because I hadn't read the manual; I did know, however, what I wanted to do–back out and quit. Too much at stake to be fooling around here!

Well, there was no CANCEL button and no QUIT button, and OK was too risky with the radio button for my 200MB internal hard disk turned on. Did OK mean "OK, start formatting," or did it mean "OK, thanks for selecting that drive, now on to further options"? As a dialog box, the Disk Formatter application limited my choices, and I didn't like any of them. I figured I would do an emergency power-down by pulling the plug on the CPU, and then I could restart. But before employing that ultimate solution for sticky-cursors, I tried ⌘-Q. This is the conventional Macintosh keyboard method to quit an application, and it worked. The screen went away.

I was pretty unhappy with the application's design, though, because there was no clear route to back out of the formatting activity, and OK implies going forward in most user interactions.

icon buttons available to users of ToolBook and Figure 15-8 shows buttons supplied with Passport Producer. Most authoring systems provide a tool for creating text buttons of various styles (radio buttons, check boxes, push buttons, animated buttons, and spin buttons), as well as graphic and icon buttons.

FIGURE 15-6

A user interface with no CANCEL or QUIT provision

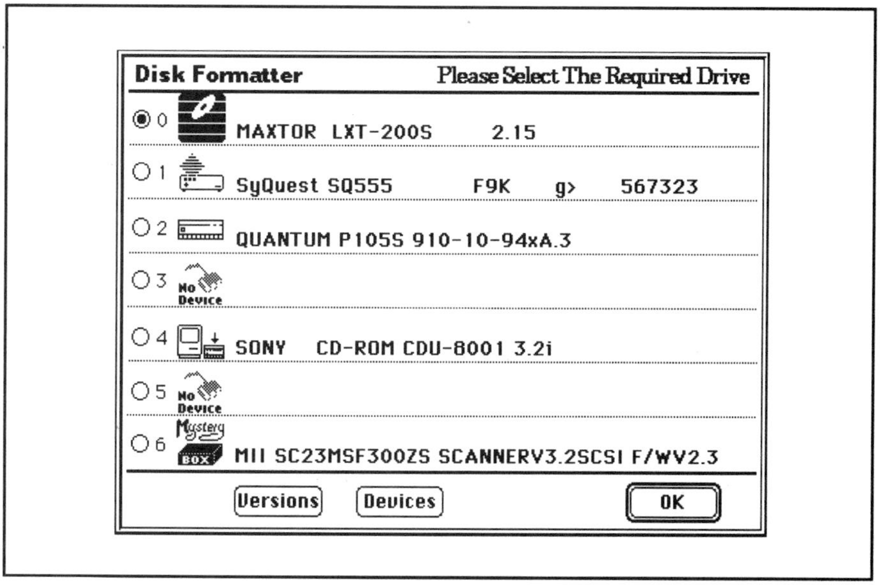

FIGURE 15-7 *Sample icons from ToolBook's clip-art library*

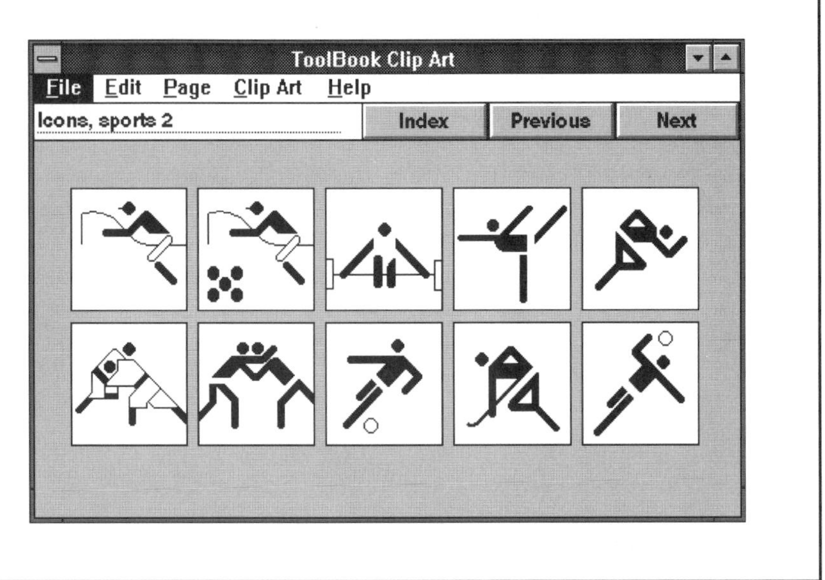

cross platform *Windows does not manage icon resources in the same manner as Macintosh. Each Windows multimedia authoring tool allows for the construction and use of graphic buttons in its own way. If you are bringing Macintosh icons into a Windows tool, export them from the Macintosh as bitmaps, import them into your Windows authoring tool, and create appropriate mouse-clicking activities for highlighting and other effects.*

Highlighting a button or object is the most common method of distinguishing it as the object of interest when single-clicking. When a button is double-clicked, it should be highlighted before the intended activity occurs, to let the user know that the button was, indeed, clicked. Highlighting is usually accomplished by reversing the object's colors: changing black to white or vice versa, or otherwise altering its colors. Drop shadows placed slightly below and to the right of a button can give it a 3-D look and, depending on how you arrange the highlighting, can make a button appear out (not pressed) or in (pressed). In Microsoft Word for Windows, when the Help button is pressed (clicked or selected), the perimeter shading is changed and the icon is offset to the right, as illustrated here:

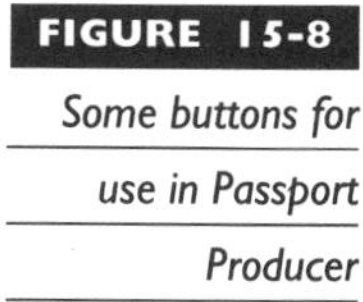

FIGURE 15-8

Some buttons for use in Passport Producer

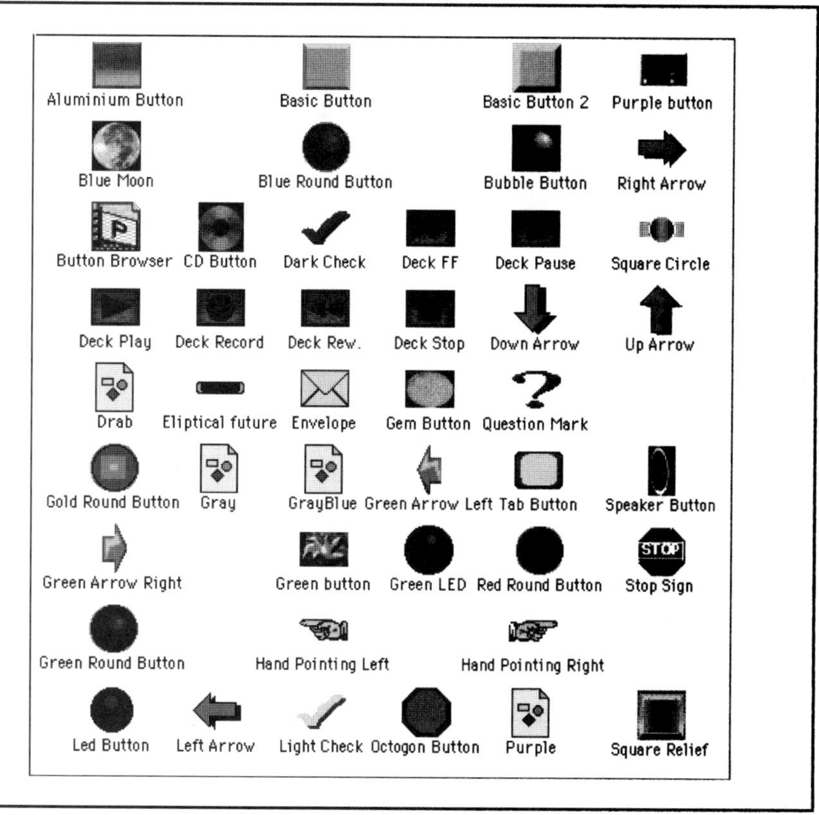

If you ever show computer software to somebody who's not really accustomed to computers, you'll find that they look at the screen the way they look at TV. I'm talking about people who can't set the time on their VCR. It's not quite as bad as when your cat watches TV because the cat luckily can't figure out what's going on. But every single pixel on a computer screen could be the all-important key pixel. Maybe it's the cursor. So designers will build screens where there are tiny little things going on all over it at different places, and everything has momentous significance. And then the user is supposed to be able to find these momentous things. So people just glaze over. If you want them to hit a button, put a big button right in the middle of the screen.

Trip Hawkins, Chairman, Electronic Arts

Icons

On the Macintosh, icons have a special meaning; they constitute a suite of image resources that can be linked to the Finder and used to identify an application or project. They are small (16×16 pixels) or large (32×32 pixels), they may be colored, and they may have a text label attached, as shown here:

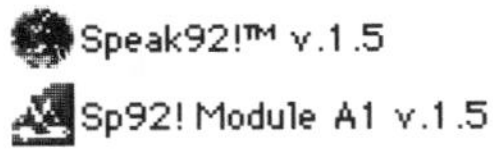

ResEdit, the resource editing tool from Apple, allows you to create and edit Finder icons. Some authoring systems, such as SuperCard, let you make stand-alone or executable projects (see Chapter 8), and you can then customize the Finder icons as you wish.

Icons can be embedded within a Macintosh application or project for use as buttons, but these icons are limited in size to 32×32 pixels. To make larger icon buttons, you can group several into a single object and program the whole element to respond when any element is clicked. This is a useful trick in HyperCard, for example, where changing the icon resource of a button in HyperTalk will provide very fast graphical changes suitable for animation (much faster than going to another card in the HyperCard stack), as shown by these eight different icons:

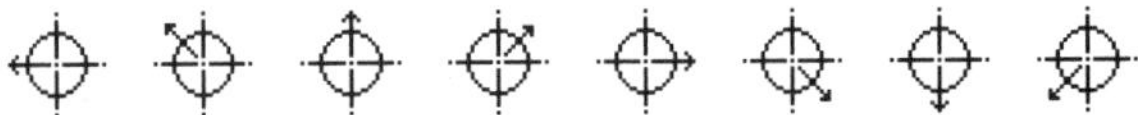

In Windows, icons are typically embedded in program and document files. You can view the available icons from within Program Manager by selecting (highlighting) a file, choosing Properties under the File menu, and selecting the Change Icon option. You'll see this dialog box:

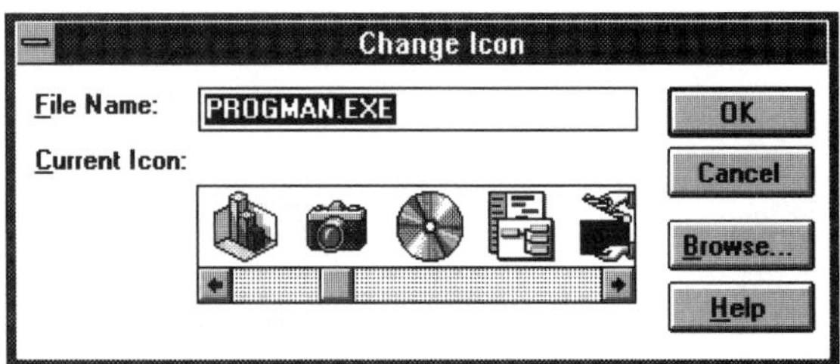

Icons (and .ICO files that contain icons) are created using an icon editor such as IconDraw (available in the Microsoft Resource Kit) or another editor utility. Many icon editing utilities can also be found on electronic bulletin boards (BBSs). Icons in Windows, however, relate to the Windows operating system and to Program Manager (as do Finder icons on the Macintosh), and these icons are typically not available for use within an authoring tool.

tip *Designing a good navigation system and creating original buttons appropriate for your project is not a trivial artistic task. Be sure you budget sufficient time in your design process for many trials, so you'll be able to get your buttons looking and acting just right.*

Designing the User Interface

The user interface of your multimedia product is a blend of its graphic elements and its navigation system. If your messages and content are disorganized and difficult to find, or if users become disoriented or bored, your project may fail. Poor graphics can cause boredom. Poor navigation aids can make viewers feel lost and unconnected to the content; or, worse, they may sail right off the edge and just give up and quit the program.

The breakthrough of multimedia computing is that for the first time information can be presented in human terms instead of requiring the user to adapt to the delivery of information in computer terms.

Glenn Ochsenreiter, from opening remarks at the Multimedia PC Introduction, Museum of Natural History, New York, NY, October 12, 1991

Novice/Expert Modes

Be aware that there are two types of end users: those who are computer literate and those who are not. Creating a user interface that will satisfy both types has been a design dilemma since the invention of computers. The simplest solution for handling varied levels of user expertise is to provide a *modal interface*—one where the viewer can simply click a NOVICE/EXPERT button and change the approach of the whole interface, to be either more or less detailed or complex. Modal interfaces are common on bulletin boards, for example, allowing novices to read menus and select desired activities, while experts can altogether eliminate the time-consuming download and display of menus and simply type an activity code directly into an executable command line.

Unfortunately, in multimedia projects, modal interfaces are not a good answer. It's best to avoid designing modal interfaces because they tend to confuse the user. Typically, only a minority of users are expert, and so the majority are caught in between and frustrated. The solution is to build your multimedia project to contain plenty of navigational power, providing access to content and tasks for users at all levels, as well as a Help system to provide some hand holding and reassurance. Present all this power in easy-to-understand structures and concepts, and use clear textual cues. Above all, keep the interface simple! Even experts will balk at a complex screen full of tiny buttons and arcane switches, and they will appreciate having neat and clean doorways into your project's content.

Two readers didn't notice the screen had changed in different circumstances. This happened when the button they clicked on took them to a visually similar screen, and there was no visual effect as the screens changed. One reader was looking at the details of a hostel and clicked on the left-hand "NEXT" arrow. He arrived at a screen with details about another hostel, but did not notice he was looking at a different screen. He tried the right-hand "NEXT" arrow as well, and the screen changed back to the one he had been viewing initially, but again he did not notice the change and concluded the "NEXT" buttons did nothing. A visual effect or animation here would have provided a cue to make the screen changes more noticeable.

Lynda Hardman of the Scottish HCI Centre, after focus group testing the "Glasgow Online" hypertext system

GUIs

The Macintosh and Windows graphical user interfaces (GUI, pronounced "gooey") are successful partly because their basic point-and-click style is simple, consistent, and quickly mastered. Both these GUIs offer built-in Help systems, and both provide standard patterns of activity that produce standard expected results. The following actions, for example, are consistently performed by similar keystrokes when running most programs on the Macintosh or in Windows:

Action	Macintosh Keystroke	Windows Keystroke
New File	⌘-N	ALT-F-N
Open File	⌘-O	ALT-F-O
Save File	⌘-S	ALT-F-S
Quit	⌘-Q	ALT-F-X
Undo	⌘-Z	ALT-E-U or CTRL-Z
Cut	⌘-X	ALT-E-T or CTRL-X
Copy	⌘-C	ALT-E-C or CTRL-C
Paste	z-V	ALT-E-P or CTRL-V

For your multimedia interface to be successful, you, too, must be consistent in designing both the look and the behavior of your human interface. Multimedia authoring systems provide you with the tools to design and implement your own graphical user interface from scratch. Be prudent with all that flexibility, however. Unless your content and messages are bizarre or require special treatment, it's best to stick with accepted conventions for button design and grouping, visual and audio feedback, and navigation structure.

Vaughan's General Rule for Interface Design

The best user interface demands the least learning effort

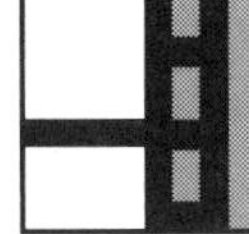

tip *Most multimedia authoring systems include tutorials and instructions for creating and using buttons and navigation aids. Typically, they also supply templates or examples of attractive backgrounds and distinctive buttons that serve as an excellent starting place.*

Stick with real-world metaphors that will be understood by the widest selection of potential end users. For example, consider using the well-known trash can for deleting files, a hand cursor for dragging objects, and a clock or an hourglass for pauses. If your material is time oriented, develop metaphors for past, present, and future. If it is topic oriented, choose metaphors related to the topics themselves. If it is polar (the pros and cons of an issue, for example), choose relevant contrasting images.

In a large project, you might want to use a different metaphor as the backbone of each major section, to provide a helpful cue for users to orient themselves within your content. For the Travel section, for example, you could use icons that are sailing ships with various riggings; for the Finance section, buttons that are coins of different denominations; and for the buttons of the International Business section, you could use colorful flags from various countries.

Throw out your tried and true training or software development methodologies, and pretend that you're Spielberg or Lucas: think of what the viewer sees and hears and how the viewer interacts with the system you deliver. Create an "experience" for the viewer.

David A. Ludwig, Interactive Learning Designs

Users like to be in control, so avoid hidden commands and unusual keystroke/mouse click combinations. Design your interface with the goal that no instruction manual or special training will be required to move through your project. Users do not like to have to remember keywords or special codes, so always make the full range of options easily available as interactive buttons or menu items. And finally, users do make mistakes, so allow them a chance to escape from inadvertent or dangerous predicaments ("Do you really want to delete? DELETE/ESCAPE"). Keep your interface simple and friendly.

Graphical Approaches

Designing excellent computer screens requires a special set of fine art skills, and not every programmer or graduate in fine arts may be suited to creating computer graphics. Like programmers who must keep up with current operating systems and languages, computer graphic artists must also stay informed about the rapidly changing canvas of new features, techniques, applications, and creative tools.

Computer graphics is more left- and right-brained—and not so spontaneous as doing it by hand. The ramp time is tedious; I am used to instant gratification with my fine artwork.

Cornelia Atchley, a fine artist creating multimedia art with computers, Washington, DC

The artist must make broad design choices: cartoon stick figures for a children's game, rendered illustrations for a medical reference, scanned bitmaps for a travel tour of Europe. The graphic artwork must be appropriate not only for the subject matter, but for the user, as well. Once the approach is decided, then the artist has to put real pixels onto a computer screen and do the work. A multimedia graphic artist must always play the role of the end user during the design and rendering process, choosing colors that look good, specifying text fonts that "speak," and designing buttons that are clearly marked for what they do.

THINGS THAT WORK Here are some graphical approaches that get good results:

- Neatly executed contrasts: big/small, heavy/light, bright/dark, thin/thick, cheap/dear (see Figure 15-9)
- Simple and clean screens with lots of white space (see Figure 15-10)
- Eye-grabbers such as Initial Caps, or a single brightly colored object alone on a gray-scale screen
- Shadows and drop shadows in various shades

FIGURE 15-9

Contrasts will attract the eye. Bud Knight, PGA Junior Champion at the turn of the century, was made thick by stretching him in an image editing program

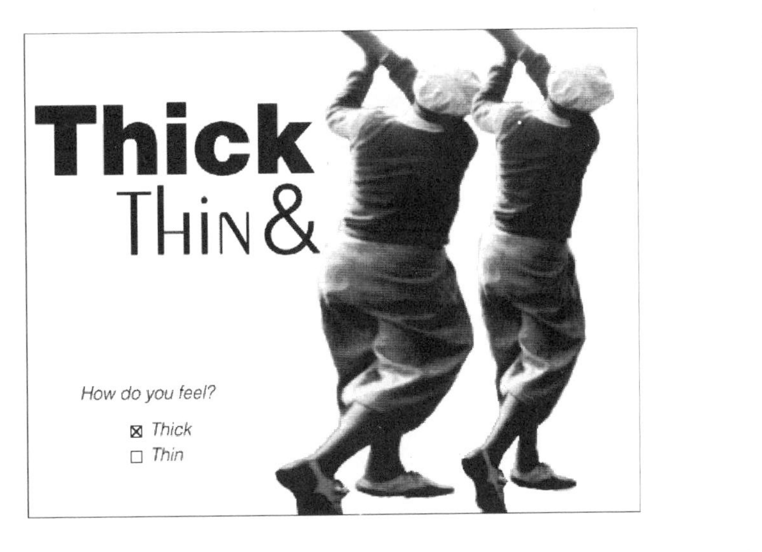

- Gradients
- Reversed graphics to emphasize important text or images
- Shaded objects and text in 2-D and 3-D

Arrows may not be universal, but they work for me.

Mark Edwards, Multimedia Developer, San Francisco, CA

THINGS TO AVOID Here are some mistakes you will want to avoid in creating computer graphics:

- Clashes of color
- Busy screens (too much stuff)
- Trite humor in oft-repeated animations
- Clanging bells or squeaks when a button is clicked
- Frilly pattern borders
- Cute one-liners from famous movies
- Requiring more than two button clicks to quit

FIGURE 15-10 *Use plenty of white space ("noninformation areas") in your screens*

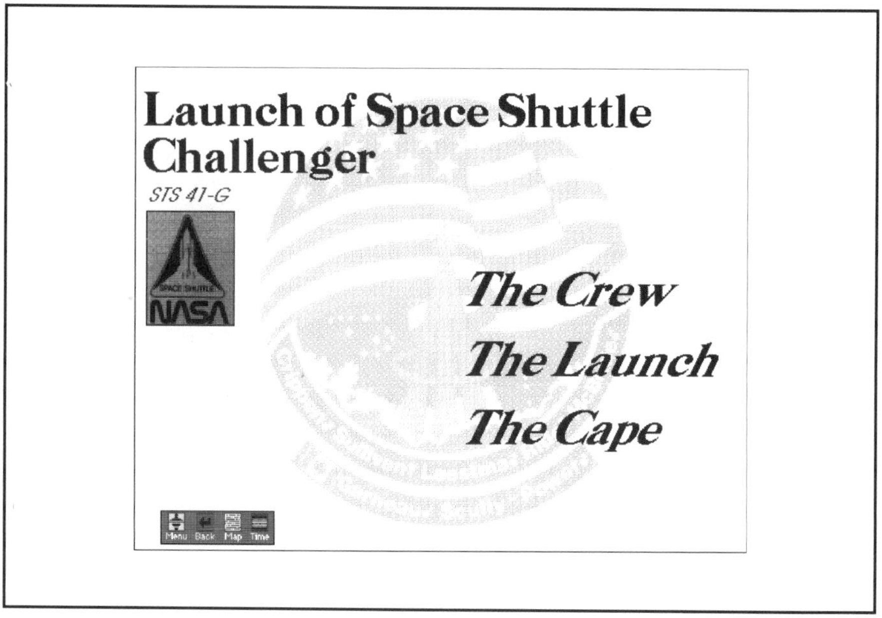

- Too many numbers (limit charts to about 25 numbers; if you can, just show totals)
- Too many words (don't crowd them; split your information into bite-sized chunks)
- Too many substantive elements presented too quickly

Most graphic artists will tell you that design is an "intuitive thing," but they will be hard pressed to describe the rules they follow in their everyday work. They know when colors are not "working" and will change them again and again until they're right, but usually won't be able to explain why the colors work or don't work. A project with a good navigation design, though it may have been developed with good planning and storyboarding, is indeed more often the result of many hours of crafty finagling with buttons and editors.

We never throw water balloons in the office.

Lars Hidde, Multimedia Producer

A Multimedia Design Case History

This section presents an example of the design process for a simple multimedia project about the construction and launch of a 31-foot ocean-going sailboat. While this project was initially crafted in SuperCard, the project was later ported to Director on the Macintosh so that it could then be ported to the PC using Director's Windows Player (see Chapter 8).

Storyboarding a Project

The source material (all that was available) practically sorted itself into logical groups: a pile of old photographs, a magazine article and newspaper clippings, engineering drawings, official documents, and some cassettes with recorded sounds. The first storyboard was a simple hierarchical structure with branches to each subject area, as shown in Figure 15-11.

Putting It Together

The most eye-catching photograph was chosen as a background for the main menu, and, as shown in Figure 15-12, the main menu was planned to contain clearly labeled buttons navigating to linear presentations of each topic area. From every screen in the project, users would be able to return to the main menu. Where sound bites were appropriate, sounds would be

FIGURE 15-11

The first storyboard

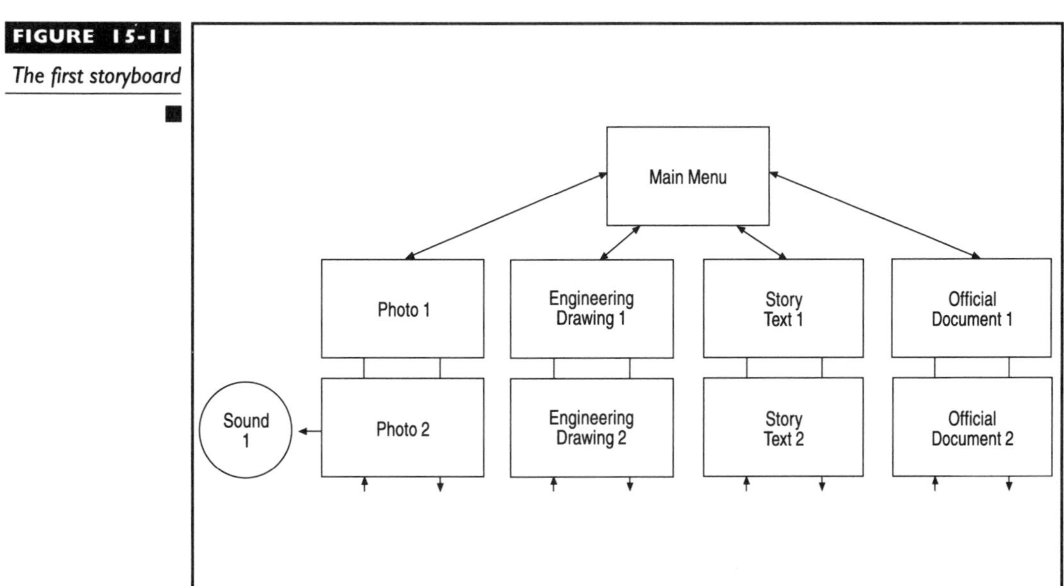

FIGURE 15-12 Main menu screen with relevant artwork as background

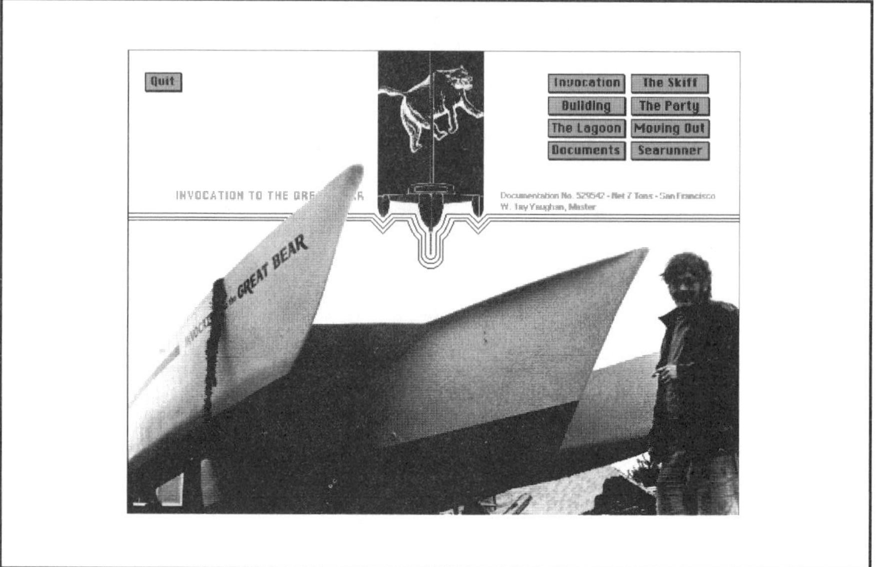

played by buttons to be clicked on screens. And a QUIT button was necessary, also on the main menu, so that users would never be more than two button clicks from exiting the project (back to the main menu, and then quit).

The 50 or so 4×5 photographs were old color prints that offered poor contrast and faded colors (due to a saltwater dunking in a storm off the Central American coastline). Digitized on a flat-bed scanner in gray-scale, however, they worked fine, and an image manipulation program was available to improve contrast. All the prints were scanned, cropped to the same dimension, optimized, and stored as bitmapped objects within SuperCard. While at the scanner, merchant marine licenses and documents were also digitized, and the magazine article was scanned using OCR software to bring it into ASCII format. The story text was placed into a SuperCard text field.

After all the content was on cards in the computer (see Chapter 8 for more about SuperCard cards), and work on the navigation system was under way, several issues emerged. First, it is terrifically boring to read a 3,000-word story by scrolling a long text field. Second, the photos were too small to be placed alone on a single card. So it made sense to combine the story line with the images, even though they were not directly related; the story about launching the boat would progress from beginning to end as the boat was slowly built in the pictures. The storyboard changed to that shown in Figure 15-13.

FIGURE 15-13

The second storyboard

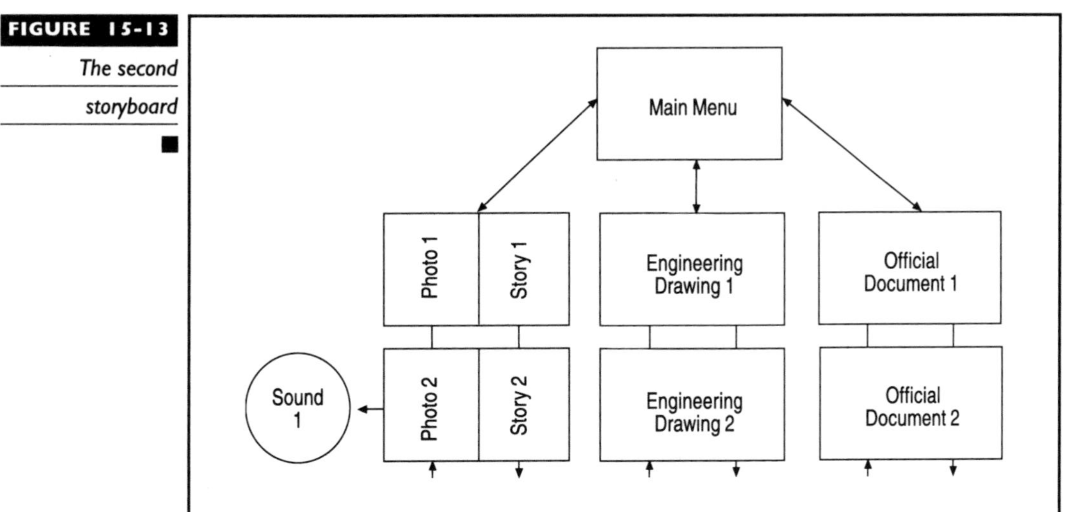

The photo-essay-and-story combination worked out to 28 screens. The photos were placed, and the text was cut and pasted to fit into text fields (see Figure 15-14). After reworking the basic navigation pattern for this new model, it became clear that users might want to rapidly scan through the photographs to watch the boat being built, ignoring the text of the story. So a special button was programmed to scan through the images until the mouse was clicked; the program for scanning through the stack is provided here:

```
on mouseUp
  repeat                              --Begin endless loop
    set cursor to busy                --Cursor prompt for busy
    if the mouse is down then         --Test for mouse click
      exit to superCard               --Escape from loop
    end if                            --End of test
    put the number of this cd into cN --Get num of current cd
    if cN = 28 then                   --If last, start again
      visual barn door open           --Use visual effect
      go to cd 2                      --Start again with card 2
    else                              --If not last card then
      visual barn door open           --Use visual effect
      go next                         --Go to next card in series
    end if                            --End of test
  end repeat                          --End of loop
end mouseUp                           --End of handler
```

FIGURE 15-14 *Snapshots are combined with text to form a 28-screen story line*

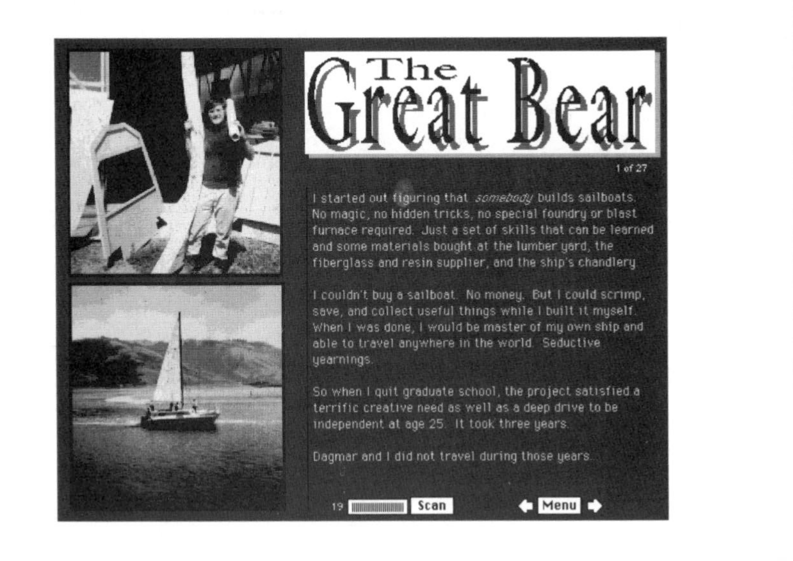

Images that did not fit into the photo essay about building the boat—for instance, the launching party with its roast pig, the long haul to the beach by trailer, and setting the mooring—were withdrawn from the pile of construction photographs; but because they were interesting, they were attached as separate branches accessible by button from the main menu. This was the third time the navigation changed, proving that you can continue to hang elements on a menu until the menu screen is too busy (and then you use submenus), or until you run out of material, as shown in Figure 15-15.

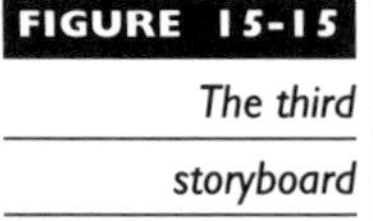

FIGURE 15-15 *The third storyboard*

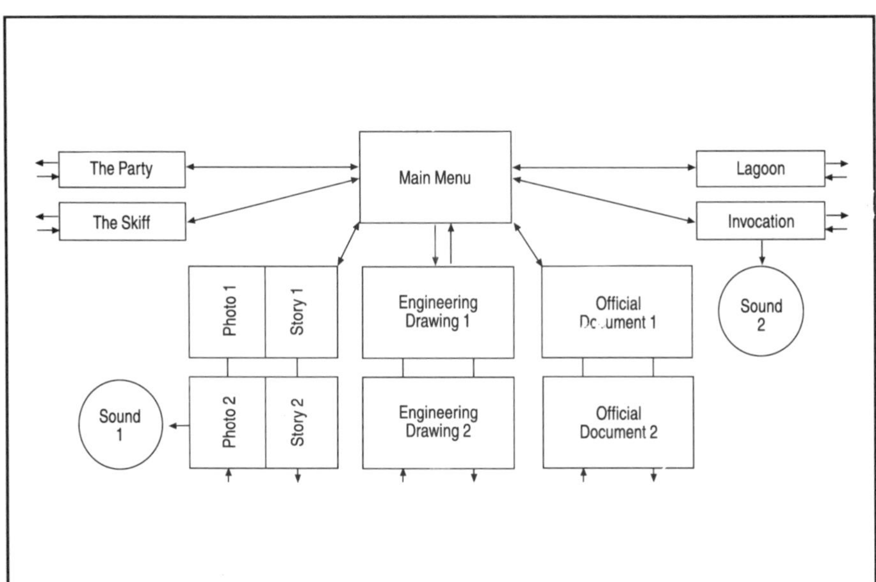

Next, the sound bites were recorded, digitized, and added to the project. Figure 15-16, the screen where the sounds were to play, shows the special button installed to play sound bites. It's simply a picture of a loudspeaker with this simple programming:

```
on mouseUp
  playSound "Great Bear"
end mouseUp
```

The documents for the project included engineering drawings, highway permits, and licenses. The highway permit, for example, was 8 1/2×11 inches (portrait; but after some experimentation, once it was scaled to 480 pixels in height at 72 dpi, it was (barely) readable and acceptable for this project. The licenses and drawings were in landscape orientation, and fit more easily on the 640×480-pixel screen (see Figure 15-17).

Reworking

The buttons on the main menu were the wrong color, so they were changed a few times until the color worked. Helvetica title text wasn't fancy enough, so it was reworked and a drop shadow was laid in. A special slider

FIGURE 15-16 *Sound is played when the loudspeaker icon is clicked*

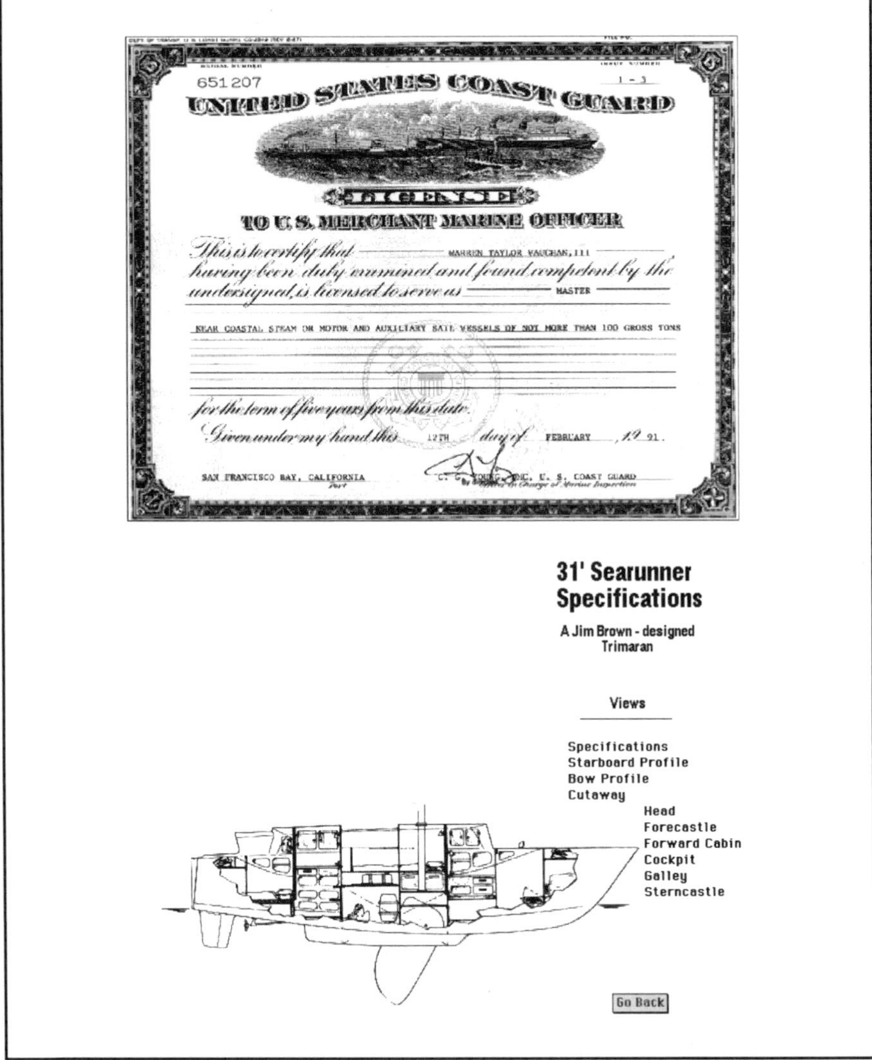

FIGURE 15-17 *The larger fonts of some scanned documents can be read at 72 dpi resolution, and engineering drawings in landscape orientation can be resized to fit* ■

button was built to allow the construction sequence to go immediately to any of the pictures in the sequence. The backgrounds were tweaked a little, and the order of images changed somewhat. A small red car was animated to drive along the edge of the lagoon.

The project described above was a straightforward one. With the exception of designing a few custom buttons for autoscanning through some of the images and designing the animations, the entire project was a simple progression of screens of information, with links activated by clicking buttons.

Producing

Now you're ready to start building your multimedia project. Remember, you should already have taken care to prepare your plan and to get organized. The project plan (see Chapter 14) is your step-by-step instruction manual for building the product. For many multimedia developers, following this plan and actually doing the construction work—being down in the trenches of hands-on creation and production—is the fun part of any project.

Developing multimedia can be like taking a joy ride in a washer/dryer. When it's all over you feel like you've been washed, rinsed, spun, and tumble dried.

Kevin McCarthy, Director of Business Development, Medius IV

Production is the phase when your multimedia project is actually rendered. During this phase you will contend with important and continuing organizing tasks. There will be times in a complex project when graphics files seem to disappear from the server, when you forget to send or cannot produce milestone progress reports, when your voice talent gets lost on the way to the recording studio, or when your hard disk crashes. So it's important to start out on the right foot, with good organization, and to maintain detailed management oversight during the entire construction process. This rule applies to projects large and small, projects for yourself or for a client, and projects with a one- or twenty-person staff. Above all, provide a good time-accounting system for everyone working on the project. At the end of the week, it's hard to remember how much time you spent on tasks done on Monday.

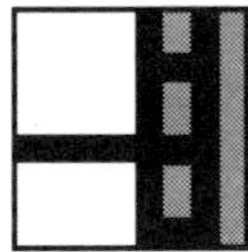

tip *If your project is to be built by more than one person, establish a management structure in advance that includes specific milestones and production expectations for each contributor.*

Starting Up

Before you begin your multimedia project, it's important to check on your development hardware and software and review your organizational and administrative setup, even if it involves you working alone. This is a serious last-minute task. It prevents you from finding yourself halfway through the project with nowhere to put your graphics files and digitized movie segments when you're out of disk space, or stuck with an incompatible version of a critical software tool, or with a network that bogs down and quits every two days. Such incidents can take many days or weeks to resolve, so try to head off as many potential problems as you can before you begin.

- Desk and mind clear of obstructions?
- Fastest CPU and RAM you can afford?
- Time accounting and management system in place?
- Biggest (or most) monitors you can afford?
- Sufficient disk storage space for all work files?
- System for regular backup of critical files?
- System for naming your working files and managing source documents?
- Latest version of your primary authoring software?
- Latest versions of software tools and accessories?
- Communication pathways open with client?
- Breathing room for administrative tasks?
- Financial arrangements secure (retainer in the bank)?
- Expertise lined up for all stages of the project?
- Kick-off meeting completed?

First Person

At 18, I used to hang around with people who drove fast cars, and I once volunteered to help an acquaintance prepare his Ferrari Berlinetta for a race at Watkins Glen. My job was to set the valves while my friend went over the suspension, brakes, and later, the carburetor. The car boasted 12 cylinders and 24 valves, and adjusting the clearance between tappet and rocker arm seemed to me akin to a jeweler's fine work. It required special wrenches and feeler gauges and an uncommon touch to rotate the high-compression engine so the cam was precisely at its highest point for each valve. I was blown away by the sheer quantity of moving parts under the Ferrari's long and shiny valve covers–my own fast car had only 4 cylinders and 8 simple valves. It took me about seven exhausting hours (including double-checking) to get it right. As the sun came up, though, the engine sounded great!

Tuning up and preparing, I learned, is as important to the race as the race itself. My friend, however, learned a much tougher lesson: he spun out and rolled his Ferrari at the hairpin turn in the seventh lap. He crawled unhurt from the twisted wreckage, but all he was able to salvage was the engine.

Working with Clients

Making multimedia for clients is a special case. Be sure that the organization of your project incorporates a system for good communication between you and the client as well as among the people actually building the project.

Client Approval Cycles

Provide good management oversight to avoid endless feedback loops—in this situation the client is somehow never quite happy and you are forced to tweak and edit many times. Manage production so that your client is continually informed and formally approves artwork and other elements as you build them. Develop a scheme that specifies the number and duration of client approval cycles, and then provide a mechanism for change orders. For change orders, remember that the client should pay extra. Client feedback loops and "Feedback Alligators" are also discussed in Chapter 14; they can be dangerous.

Data Storage Media and Transportation

It's important that the client be able to easily review your work. Remember that both you and the distant site need to have matching data transfer systems and media. Organize your system before you begin work, as it may take some time for both you and the client to agree on an appropriate system and on the method of transportation. For storage media, you can use floppy disks, external hard disks, SyQuest removable cartridges, Bernoulli disks, or optical disks. See Chapter 5 for more about peripherals.

Because multimedia files are large, your means of transporting the project to distant clients is particularly important. Unless both you and the client are connected to a high-speed network, the most cost- and time-effective method for transporting your files is by an overnight courier service (Federal Express, DHL, Airborne Express, or U.S. Postal Service Express Mail). Material completed in time for an afternoon pickup will usually be at the client's site by the next morning. Sending an overnight letter-size package (with floppies or cartridges inside) costs from $10 to $16.

Modems are becoming a more viable option for telephone transfer of multimedia data files, because baud rates are increasing and modem costs are decreasing.

First Person

We made up two sample musical tracks to play in the background and sent them off by overnight courier to the client. Four days later, the client phoned to say that both were good, but couldn't we make it sound a little more like Windham Hill. So we redid the music and sent two more samples. Five days later, the client said the samples were great, but the boss wanted something with a New Orleans feel. So we sent a fifth creation, this time with a note that they would have to either settle on one of the five styles submitted, supply the music themselves, or pay us more money to keep up the creative composition work. They chose the music the boss liked, but we wound up more than two weeks behind schedule and had spent significantly more money and effort on this task than originally budgeted.

Several months later, in the next job requiring original music composition, we specified a maximum of two review/feedback cycles and added a clause for cost overrun beyond that. The first sound we submitted to this new client was approved, and we stayed ahead of schedule and budget.

Tracking

Organize a method for tracking the receipt of material that you will incorporate into your multimedia project. Even in small projects, you will be dealing with many digital bits and pieces.

Develop a file-naming convention specific to your project's structure. Store the files in directories or folders with logical names. If you are working across platforms, develop a file identification system that uses the DOS file-naming convention of eight characters plus a three-character extension. Use this convention on files for the Macintosh as well as the PC; otherwise, files transferred from the Macintosh to the PC will receive default names with strange characters and extensions that are difficult to remember. You may also need to set up a database with filenames as eight-character codes matched to lengthier descriptive names, so you know what the codes mean.

Version control of your files (that is, tracking editing changes) is critically important, too, especially in large projects. If more than one person is working on a group of files, be sure that you always know what version is the latest, and who has the current version. If storage space allows, archive all file iterations, in case you change your mind about something and need to go back to a prior rendering.

Open Code

HyperCard, SuperCard, Macromedia Director, ToolBook, and other commonly used authoring platforms may allow access to the software programming code or script that drives your particular project.

In such an open-code environment, are you prepared to let others see your programming work? Is your code neat and commented? Perhaps your mother cautioned you to wear clean underclothing in case you were suddenly among strangers in a hospital emergency room—well, apply this rule to your code. You can insert a copyright statement in your project that clearly (and legally) designates the code as your intellectual property (see Figure 15-18), but the code, tricks, and programming techniques remain accessible for study, learning, and tweaking by others.

Hazards and Annoyances

Even experienced producers and developers commonly run into at least some light chop and turbulence during the course of a project's development. The experts, however, never crash when their vehicle shudders or loses some altitude. You can expect the going to get rough when you're negotiating the following points in the multimedia plan:

- Designing the perfect user interface
- Writing low-level custom programs
- Solving hardware performance challenges
- Working long strings of 18-hour days
- Testing, testing, and more testing

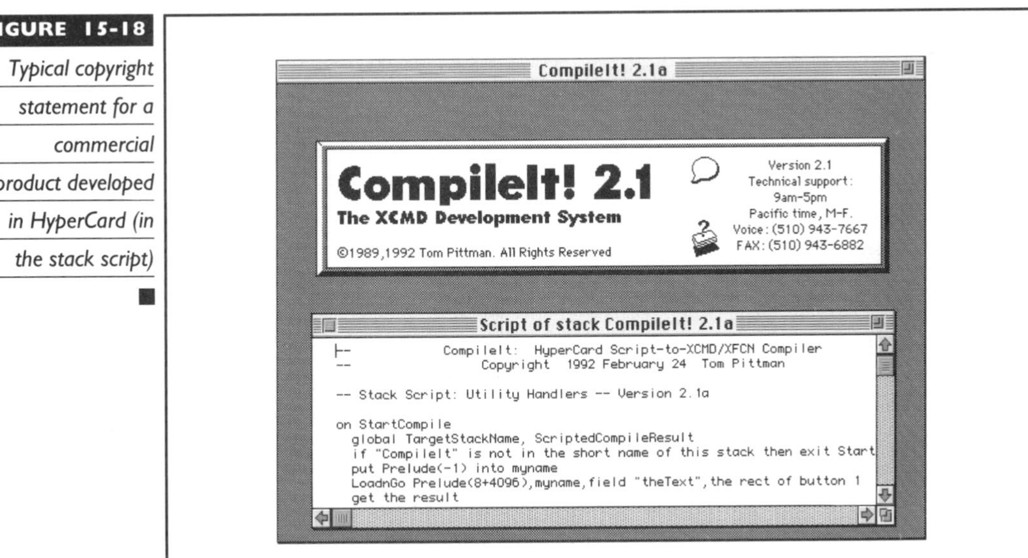

FIGURE 15-18 Typical copyright statement for a commercial product developed in HyperCard (in the stack script)

- Navigating client sign-off loops
- Facing delayed payments (the check's in the mail...)
- Handling events beyond your control

Things are normal over here—the Quadra 700 keeps crashing, Jim (the client) spilled water into his FX (the cover was off). The audio inputs on the video decks are low impedance and the CPUs are high impedance. One of the MicroTouch touchscreen monitors is busted, the SuperMac 20" monitor got trashed in shipping...I'll be around all night programming so call if [you] can help.

AppleLink to Ikonic SF from Ikonic support team on arriving onsite in Hawaii to install interactive kiosks for an international conference, February 1992

Small annoyances, too, can become serious distractions that are counterproductive. The production stage is a time of great creativity, dynamic intercourse among all contributors, and, above all, hard work. The following common irritants can be avoided or at least alleviated by proper planning and execution:

- Creative co-workers who don't handle criticism well
- Clients who cannot or are not authorized to make decisions

First Person

In 1975, I was hired to deliver a 41-foot cruising sailboat from Fort Lauderdale to the British Virgin Islands for the charter trade. In three days I assembled a crew of strangers, provisioned the boat, and checked all the equipment. Then we took off across the Gulf Stream and into the Bermuda Triangle.

After two days it was clear that the cook was a bad apple. It wasn't just that she couldn't cook–she whined about everything: the stove wouldn't light, the boat heeled too much, her socks were wet, her sleeping bag tore on a cleat, her hair was tangled, she couldn't get her favorite radio station (now a few hundred miles astern). It was unending.

The whining began to envelop her in a smog-colored, onion-like layering, each new complaint accreting to the last one, like growing coral. By the fifth day, her unpleasant aura saturated the entire main cabin; the rest of us sought sanctuary in the cockpit or the small aft cabin. Efforts were made to solve this bizarre situation, but by then, nobody could get near her (or wanted to).

When we pulled into tiny Caicos Island for water and fresh stores, I paid her off and arranged for a room at the quaint waterfront hotel, where she could wait three days for the weekly airplane back to Florida. Everyone felt badly about her disappointment and how it all turned out–for about an hour. The rest of the voyage was jubilant.

- More than two all-nighters in a row
- Too many custom-coded routines
- Instant coffee and microwaved corn dogs
- Too many meetings; off-site meetings
- Missed deadlines

If your project is a team effort, then it is critical that everyone works well together—or can at least tolerate one another's differences—especially when the going gets tough. Pay attention to the mental health of all personnel involved in your project, and be aware if the dynamics of the group are being adversely affected by individual personalities. If problems arise, deal with them before they become hazardous; the mix of special creative talents required for multimedia can be volatile.

Multi

[*Content is the information and material that forms the heart of your project...*]

Content comes from somewhere.

balance

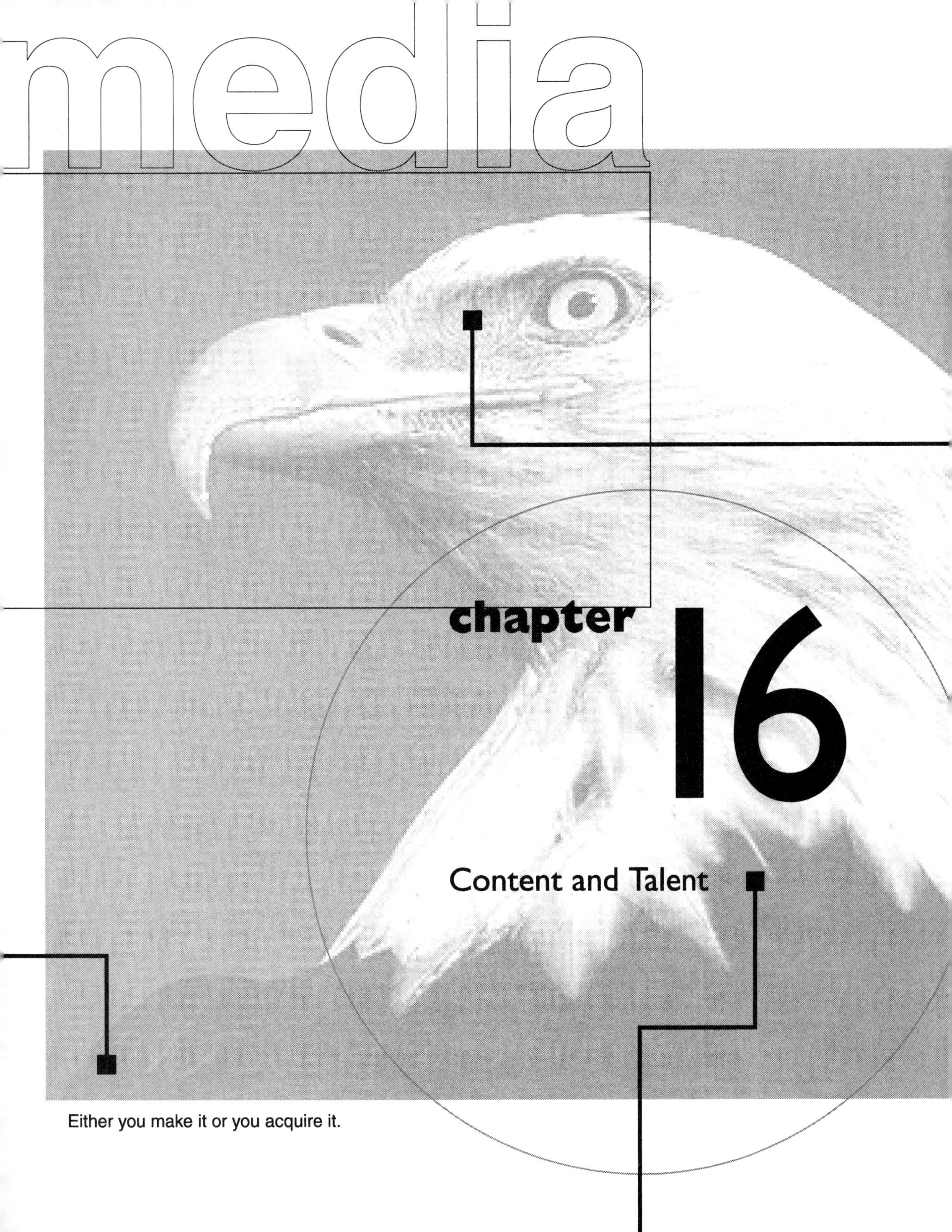

chapter 16

Content and Talent

Either you make it or you acquire it.

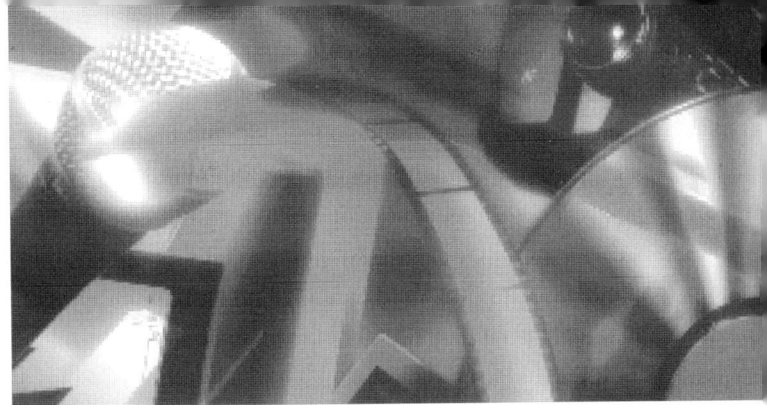

CONTENT is many things: the narration and motion video of a training program that teaches people to speak English; a compilation of photographs and essays about Winston Churchill organized on a CD-ROM; a library of musical hits in a store kiosk; the information built into an intelligent system for advising triage nurses in a hospital emergency room.

Every multimedia project includes content. It is the "stuff" from which you fashion your messages. It is also the information and material that forms the heart of your project—that defines what your project is about.

Practically, content can be any and all of the elements of multimedia. You might use your collection of wedding photographs and video tapes to create a special multmiedia newsletter for family and relatives. Or you might edit just portions of the audio track from these videotapes and capture still images to build a multimedia database of aunts, uncles, and cousins. This material is your project's content.

Content can have low and high *production value*. If you hire a team of professionals to shoot your wedding video and then they digitize images and audio clips at broadcast quality, your content will have high production value. If you persuade Hillary Clinton to record the voice-over and Charles Schultz, the *Peanuts* artist, to retouch the images, it will have yet higher production value.

You must always balance the production value of your project against your budget and the desired result. For aerial photographs of the wedding reception, you would not likely commission the private launch of a spy satellite from Kennedy Space Center to achieve highest production value. Instead, you could rent a helicopter with paparazzi and still achieve good production value. Or you could photograph the wedding yourself from a neighboring rooftop, and be satisfied with the lower production value. The production value of your project is a question of balance (see "Vaughan's Law of Multimedia Minimums" in Chapter 10).

Content comes from somewhere. Either you make it or you acquire it. Whether you make it, borrow it, or buy it depends upon your project's needs, your time constraints, and your pocketbook. Content that is destined for sale to the public is also wrapped in numerous legal issues. Who owns the content? Do you have the proper rights to use it? Copyright laws, for example, protect literary works; musical works; dramatic works; pictorial, graphic, and sculptural works; motion pictures and other audio visual works; and sound recordings. Do you have licenses and signed releases?

This chapter discusses some of the legal issues surrounding content and the use of talent in multimedia projects. It provides examples of contract terms, and introduces you to some of the sources and providers of content and talent. Needless to say, always consult an attorney versed in intellectual property law when you negotiate the rights and ownership of content.

Though I am a McLuhanist by nature, late in life I've begun to realize that content actually matters.

David Bunnell, Editor in Chief, *New Media* magazine

Acquiring Content

One of the most expensive and time-consuming tasks in organizing a multimedia project can be the acquisition of its content. You must plan ahead, allocating sufficient time (and money) for this task. Consider the following examples:

- If your project describes the use of a new piece of robotic machinery, will you need to send a photographer to the factory for the pictures? Or can you digitize existing photographs?
- Suppose you are working with 100 graphs and charts about the future of petroleum exploration. Will you begin by collecting the raw data from reports and memos, or start with an existing spreadsheet or database? Perhaps you have charts that have already been generated from the data and stored as TIFF or PICT files?
- Or perhaps you are developing an interactive guide to the trails in a national park, complete with video clips of the wildlife that hikers might encounter on the trails. Will you need to shoot original video footage, or are there existing tapes for you to edit?

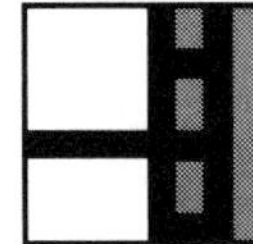

tip *Be sure to specify in your project plan the format and quality of content and data to be supplied to you by third parties. Format conversion and editing takes real time.*

This is how you do things on a shoe string. Almost ten years ago, we created a basketball product starring Dr. J and Larry Bird. The first thing we knew we had to do was sign a contract with Dr. J. So we found a guy that knew his agent and we made a side deal with him to pay him to convince Julius to do it. And then we went to Julius and we made a deal where we gave him some stock in the company, rather than writing a huge check. And we convinced him of the educational value of what we were doing, instead of just trying to get it to be an arms-length financial deal. So we were able to sign him up with an advance of only $20,000. And he was quite easily the biggest name in basketball and one of the top two or three regarded professional athletes at the time. We got him for a royalty rate of 2-1/2 percent (not what you hear today in a lot of cases), so you don't have to do things that have really high royalty rates and advances. By the way, he made a killing on the stock!

Trip Hawkins, Chairman, Electronics Arts

Using Content Created by Others

Since the late 1980s, investors in the multimedia marketplace have been quietly purchasing electronic rights to the basic building blocks of content—films, videos, photographic collections, and textual information bases—knowing that in the future these elements can and perhaps will be converted from their traditional form to computer-based storage and delivery. This is smart, but not easy; the many union-supported contract restrictions, and performer and producer rights are not only complicated and difficult to trace, but also very expensive to acquire.

warning *If you negotiate ownership or rights to someone else's content, be sure to get the advice of a skilled copyright and contracts attorney.*

Obtaining the rights to content is not, however, a hopeless undertaking. For example, Amaze, Inc. acquired rights from several sources to produce a series of computer-based daily planners with a cartoon-a-day from Gary Larson's "The Far Side" or Cathy Guisewite's "Cathy"; a word-a-day from Random House; or a question-a-day from the Trivial Pursuit game. Random

House and Brøderbund's Living Books Division negotiated the rights to the Dr. Seuss books for multimedia use. Multimedia rights to Elvis Presley historical material, to the movie *Jurassic Park*, and to a myraid of other content have been acquired by multimedia developers and publishers.

Depending on the type and source of your content, the negotiations for usage rights can be simple and straightforward, or they may require complicated contracts and a stack of release forms. Each potential content provider you approach will likely have his or her own set of terms that you need to look at carefully so that the terms are broad enough not to constrain the scope of your multimedia project.

Locating Preexisting Content

Preexisting content can come from a variety of sources: from a trunk of old photographs in your neighbor's attic or from a stock house or image bank offering hundreds of thousands of hours of film and video or still images, available for licensing for a fee.

If your needs are simple and fairly flexible, you may be able to use material from collections of clip art. Such collections of photographs, graphics, sounds, music, animation, and video are becoming widely available from many sources, for anywhere from fifty to several hundred dollars. Part of the value of many of these packages is that you are granted unlimited use, and you can be comfortable creating derivative versions tailored to your specific application.

Carefully read the license agreement that comes with a collection before assuming you can use the material in any manner. In the six-point italicized type on the back of the agreement, you may discover that the licensor offers no guarantee that the contents of the collection are original works. Thus, the licensor bears no responsibility to indemnify you for inadvertently infringing on the copyrights of a third party. You may also discover that the collection comes with severe restrictions on the way material can be used, or that a royalty is required for use.

If your content needs are more specific or complex, a good place to start your search for material might be at a still photo library, a sound library, or a stock footage house. These resources may be public or private and may contain copyrighted works as well as materials that are in the public domain, meaning that its copyright protection has expired over time and not been renewed; you can use the material without a license.

The National Archives in Washington D.C. is a rich source of content, both copyrighted and in the public domain. Other public sources include the Library of Congress, NASA, U.S. Information Agency, and the Smithsonian

Institution, all in Washington D.C. You cannot, however, safely assume that all material acquired from a public source is in the public domain. You remain responsible for ensuring that you do not infringe on a copyright.

In addition to public sources, there are many other repositories of content material. Commercial stock houses offer millions of images, video and film clips, and sound clips, and often own the works outright—so you don't have to worry about copyright infringement. Some stock sources also specialize in special subjects. For example, if you want a video clip of a shark, you might contact a stock footage house that specializes in underwater footage, such as Al Giddings/Images Unlimited in Pray, Montana or Sea Studios in Monterey, California.

Copyrights

Copyright protection applies to "original works of authorship fixed in any tangible medium of expression." The Copyright Act of 1976, as amended (17 U.S.C.A. §101 et. seq.) protects the legal rights of the creator of an original work. Consequently, before you can use someone else's work in your multimedia project, you must first obtain permission from the owner of the copyright. If you do not do this, you may find yourself being sued for copyright infringement (unauthorized use of copyrighted material).

Works come under copyright protection as soon as they are created and presented in a fixed form. Works do not have to be registered with the U.S. Copyright Office to be protected. There are limited "fair use" exceptions in which copyrighted material can be used without permission, but you should consult an attorney before assuming this exception.

Owning a copy of a work does not entitle you to reproduce the work unless you have the permission of the copyright owner. If you buy a painting from an artist, the artist retains the copyright unless it is assigned to you. You do not have the right to reproduce the painting in any form, such as in postcards or a calendar, without permission.

For additional discussion about copyrights as they apply to original works created for a project, see "Using Content Created for a Project," later in this chapter.

Obtaining Rights

You should license the rights to use copyrighted material before you develop a project around it. You may be able to negotiate outright ownership of copyrighted material. If the owner does not wish to give up or sell ownership rights, however, you may still be able to *license* the rights to use that material.

There are few guidelines for negotiating content rights for use in multimedia products. If you are dealing with content providers who are professionals familiar with electronic media, you may be given a standard rate card listing licensing fees for different uses, formats, and markets. Other content providers or owners may be less familiar with multimedia and electronic uses, and you will need to educate them.

Explaining multimedia technology to people can be a challenge. Michelle, an 8th grader, wanted to scan some 1920's photographs to use in the San Rafael Community Express, a multimedia magazine done for kids by kids. When Michelle asked the 80 year old docent at the local museum if she could use the photographs for a computer project, the woman responded in horror that these were priceless pictures and that they couldn't be put in a computer—they'd be ruined. The team spent another 15 minutes explaining scanning to the woman by comparing a scanner to a copy machine and assuring her that the original photographs would be returned unharmed.

John MacLeod, Publisher and Chief Pizza Provider for the "San Rafael Community Express," a HyperStudio-based interactive magazine created by seventh- and eighth-graders at Davidson Middle School, San Rafael, California

Some licensing agreements may be as simple as a signed permission letter or release form describing how you may use the material. Other agreements will specify in minute detail how, where, when, and for what purpose the content may be used. Ideally, you would seek rights to use the content anytime, anywhere, and in any way you choose; more likely, however, the final license would contain restrictions about how the material may be used. Try to retain the option to renegotiate terms in case you want to broaden the scope of use at a later date.

The following items are but a few of the issues you need to consider when negotiating for rights to use preexisting content:

- How will your product be delivered? If you limit yourself to CD-ROMs, for example, you may not be able to distribute your product over cable or telephone lines without renegotiation.
- Is the license for a set period of time?
- Is the license exclusive or nonexclusive? In an exclusive use arrangement, no one else would be able to use the material in the manner stipulated.
- Where will your product be distributed? There may be different rates for domestic and international distribution.
- Do you intend to use the material in its entirety, or just a portion of it?

- What rights do you need? You need to be sure you have the right to reproduce and distribute the material. In addition, you may wish to use the material in promotions for your product.
- Does the content owner have the authority to assign rights to you? It is important to ensure you will not be held liable if a third party later sues for copyright infringement.
- Do you need to obtain any additional rights to use the content? For example, if you use a clip from a movie, do you need to get separate releases from actors appearing in the clip or from the director or producer of the movie?
- Will the copyright owner receive remuneration for the license? If so, what form will it take? A one-time fee? Royalty? Or a simple credit attribution?
- In what format do you wish to receive the content? Specifying formats is particularly important with video dubbed from a master.

Derivative Works

Any text taken verbatim, or any image or music perfectly copied, clearly requires permission from its owner to incorporate it into your work. But there are some other, less clear-cut issues. For example, as a starter for your work, you may wish to incorporate but a tiny portion of an image owned by someone else, altering the image until the original is no longer recognizable. Is this legal? Indeed, how much of the original must you change before the product becomes yours? There are no simple answers to these tough questions.

Figure 16-1 shows an original photograph taken by Mark Newman, along with some artwork derived from it. Newman sold certain rights to 21st Century Media, Inc., which packages and sells assortments of stock photographs on CD-ROM to computer graphics and multimedia developers. The CD-ROM product contains these instructions:

> You may make copies of the digitized images contained on the Product for use in advertisements, public or private presentations, business communications, multimedia presentations, and other uses as long as the images are not used to create a product for sale. For example, you may not use the images to create calendars, posters, greeting cards, or books of image collections for sale. You may not use, in whole or in part, or alter a digitized image in any manner for pornographic use.

FIGURE 16-1

The original photograph by Mark Newman was clipped and manipulated for use in a multimedia project. Who owns the resulting image?

Suppose, however, that the image in Figure 16-1 were scanned from the pages of *National Geographic* or *Time*—what then? If you change 51 percent of the pixels, is the image yours? These questions of ownership will undoubtedly be resolved eventually in the courts.

There is a serious issue facing multimedia developers. Now that they have tools to creatively modify things, how much of someone else's image, music, or video clip needs to be modified before ownership changes? This is up for grabs. There is a law called "fair use" which comes into play in a very limited way here. But I think there needs to be a law called "fair modification." We need something like that because otherwise multimedia is not going to get anywhere.

Trip Hawkins, Chairman, Electronics Arts

Use of images, sounds, and other resources from stock houses such as 21st Century Media, Inc. is perhaps the safest way to go, because ownership and your rights to use the material are clearly stated.

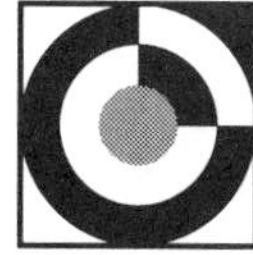

warning *Beware of clip media claiming to be public domain (where no copyrights apply) that includes sounds from popular television shows or motion pictures.*

Permission must also be obtained to use copyrighted text. Figure 16-2 provides sample language for requesting permission to reprint copyrighted text material and sample terms that you might expect from the copyright owner.

At the Multimedia/CD-ROM conference last spring we brought our usual cast of characters to promote MusicBytes. Our featured performer was Scott Page, who is currently recording and touring as Pink Floyd's saxophonist.

After his morning performance, Scott decided to walk around and look at some of the new toys being exhibited. He wandered into a booth with a huge projection TV system. This company (which shall remain nameless) was using the Pink Floyd movie The Wall *to demonstrate their product. Scott was intrigued by this and stood there for a few minutes and watched himself perform with the Berlin Wall in the background.*

Suddenly a member of the booth staff recognized Scott and did a very animated double-take. "Hey, hey, you're him... he's you... that's you on TV," the man nervously stammered.

Well, Scott's about the nicest rock star you'll ever meet. So he hung around, rapped with the staff and signed autographs. He also informed them that what they were doing was illegal and in violation of about a million copyright laws.

It was ironic that Scott would stumble upon that particular situation during a show where he was promoting license-free/copyright-free music. It really drove home the point that most corporations are not familiar with copyright laws, and may be subject to litigation. And certainly stressed the importance of license-free music.

Marty Fortier, Vice President, Prosonus, Inc.

Using Content Created for a Project

In the process of developing your multimedia project, interfaces will be designed, text written, lines of code programmed, and original artwork, photographs, animations, musical scores, sound effects, and video may be produced.

Each of these elements is an original work. If you are creating a project single-handedly, you own the copyright outright. If other persons who are not your employees also contribute to the final product, they may own copyright of the element created by them or may share joint ownership of the product unless they assign or license their ownership rights to you.

The ownership of a project created by employees in the course of their employment belongs solely to the employer if the work fits the requirements of a "work made for hire." To meet the definition of a work made for hire, several factors must be weighed to determine if the individual is legally an

FIGURE 16-2

Sample permission request to and terms from a publisher to use a copyrighted text or images

Typical request to a large publishing company:

Dear Sirs:

I am currently producing a computer-based multimedia presentation with a working title of TITLE. My publisher is PUBLISHER, PUBLISHER'S ADDRESS. The anticipated completion date of the work is MONTH/YEAR. It will be used for USE.

This letter is to request your permission to incorporate into this work a brief passage from: TITLE, AUTHOR, EDITION, ISBN, PAGE.

The text I wish to reproduce is: TEXT.

Please process this request at your earliest convenience and use this letter or your own form to return your approval by mail or fax to: YOUR NAME/ADDRESS

The undersigned, having full authority, hereby grants permission to YOUR NAME to copy and reproduce the referenced text for use in the work cited above.

Typical terms from a large publishing company:

1) To give full credit in every copy printed, on the copyright page or as a footnote on the page on which the quotation begins, or if in a magazine or a newspaper, on the first page of each quotation covered by the permission, exactly as "Reprinted with the permission of PUBLISHER from TITLE by AUTHOR. Copyright YEAR by PUBLISHER."

2) To pay on publication of the work, or within 24 months of the date of granting the permission, whichever is earlier, a fee of: $______.

3) To forward one copy of the work and payment on publication to the Permissions Department of PUBLISHER.

4) To make no deletions from, additions to, or changes in the text, without the written approval of PUBLISHER.

5) That the permission hereby granted applies only to the edition of the work specified in this agreement.

6) That permission granted herein is nonexclusive and not transferable.

7) That this permission applies, unless otherwise stated, solely to publication of the above-cited work in the English language in the United States, its territories and dependencies and throughout the world. For translation rights, apply to the international rights department of PUBLISHER.

8) That unless the work is published within two years from the date of the applicant's signature (unless extended by written permission of PUBLISHER) or if published, it remains out of print for a period of six months, this permission shall automatically terminate.

9) This permission does not extend to any copyrighted material from other sources that may be incorporated in the books in question, nor to any illustrations or charts, nor to poetry, unless otherwise specified.

10) That the work containing our selection may be reproduced in Braille, large type, and sound recordings provided no charge is made to the visually handicapped.

11) That unless the agreement is signed and returned within six months from the date of issue, the permission shall automatically terminate.

employee or an independent contractor. Among these factors are where the work is done, the relationship between the parties, and who provides the tools and equipment.

If the individual contributing to a project is not an employee, the commissioned work must fall within one of the following "work made for hire" categories: a contribution to a collective work, a work that is part of a motion picture or other audiovisual work, a translation, a supplementary work, a compilation, an instructional text, a test, answer material for a test, or an atlas (1976 Copyright Act, 17 U.S.C. §201(b)). Even if the work falls within one of these categories, be sure to get an agreement assigning ownership in writing from every individual contributing to the work that it is being created as a work for hire.

The copyright ownership of works created in whole or in part by persons who fall under the definition of independent contractor may belong to that contractor unless the work is specially ordered or commissioned for use and qualifies as a work made for hire, in which case the copyright belongs to the entity commissioning the work.

A copyright can belong to a single individual or entity, or it may be shared jointly by several entities. Make sure that copyright ownership issues have been resolved, in writing, before people contribute to your project.

Using Talent

After you have tested everybody you know and you still have vacant seats in your project, you may need to turn to professional talent. Getting the perfect actor, model, or narrator's voice is critical. You don't want to settle for a voice or an actor who is not quite polished or is ill suited to the part, or your whole project may have an amateurish feel.

Professional voice-over talents and actors in the United States usually belong to a union or guild, either AFTRA (American Federation of Television and Radio Artists) or SAG (Screen Actors Guild). They are usually represented by a talent agent or agency that you can find in the Yellow Pages.

Locating the Professionals You Need

Before you can safely put a professional in front of a camera or a microphone, you have to find the talent first, and then deal with hiring and union contracts. Begin by calling a talent agency; explain what you need. The agency will probably suggest several clients who might fit your needs and send you a collection of video tapes or cassettes as samples of the actors'

First Person

We put out a call for a multimedia acting job (male, mid-30s, credible voice, earnest smile), and 18 men showed up for tryouts at a local studio—17 were nonunion and one belonged to AFTRA. We videotaped each applicant as he read a prepared script, chatted with all of them, and asked them to walk around and jump up and down. The best choice by far, we thought at the end of a long day, was Dave Kazanjian, the union member.

"Oooh," we said to ourselves, "real union talent! This is going to cost us." So we got together with the client and ran tapes of half a dozen of the better actors trying out, without saying which was our favorite. The client's choice was the same as ours, because Dave was very polished and professional and simply perfect for the part. Paying union-scale wages to the actor would double what we had estimated in our original budget; we had naively assumed we could quickly and easily find the right talent from the nonunion pool. We ran the new numbers past the client, implying that the second-choice actor was more affordable, even if he wasn't quite perfect. Then we showed Dave's clip next to the other guy, and repeated it a few times, until the difference was really apparent. The comparison was persuasive, and in the end, the client supported the extra cost.

We all learned again that you get what you pay for: Dave did a terrific job. In future proposals, we used union scale in estimating cost, whether we hired a union actor or not.

work. After reviewing the tapes, you can arrange auditions of the best candidates, at your office or at a studio. You can also get in touch with several agencies and put out a casting call for screen or audio auditions. Furthermore, you are not limited to using union talent, and if your call is posted on bulletin boards in public places (in the theater department of a local university, for example), you may find yourself with many applicants, both union and nonunion, who are eager for the work.

If you run your own audition, be sure you are organized for it. You will need sign-up sheets for names and phone numbers, a sample script for applicants to read, a video camera or tape recorder, tracking sheets so you can coordinate actors' names with their video or audio clips, and hospitable coffee and donuts.

Working with Union Contracts

The two unions, AFTRA and SAG, have similar contracts and terms for minimum pay and benefits. AFTRA recently approved an Interactive Media Agreement to cover on- and off-camera performers on all interactive media platforms. Figure 16-3 shows some AFTRA definitions related to interactive media.

The AFTRA and SAG contracts are lengthy and detailed. Both share language and job descriptions (such as principal, voice-over performer,

FIGURE 16-3

From the 1994 AFTRA Interactive Media Agreement (reprinted courtesy of AFTRA, 260 Madison Avenue, New York, NY 10016)

DEFINITIONS

"Material": includes all products (audio or visual) derived from the recordation of the live-action performances of performers, whether or not such performances are incorporated into the final version of the fully-edited Interactive Program produced hereunder by Producer.

"Interactive": Interactive describes the attribute of products which enables the viewer to manipulate, affect or alter the presentation of the creative content of such product simultaneous with its use by the viewer.

"Interactive Media" means: any media on which interactive product operates and through which the user may interact with such product including but not limited to personal computers, games, machines, arcade games, all CD-interactive machines and any and all analogous, similar or dissimilar microprocessor-based units and the digitized, electronic or any other formats now known or hereinafter invented which may be utilized in connection therewith.

"Performers": Persons whose performances are used as on or off-camera, including those who speak, act, sing, or in any other manner perform as talent in material for Interactive Media.

extra, singer, and dancer). Also, both unions have approximately the same wage scales for these jobs. In 1994, AFTRA's minimum wage for an on-camera principal performer for interactive media was $504 for one 8-hour day, $1,276 for three days, or $1,752 for a week. The minimum wage for a voice-over performer doing up to three voices in a 4-hour day was $504, each additional voice would be $168 more. Of course, an actor can always negotiate more than minimum wage.

If your talent needs are simple, then you can usually get good contract advice directly from the union representative in your area or from the actors themselves. If your needs are elaborate or undefined, you may wish to consult an attorney or agent who specializes in this area and who can oversee the many required clauses and details of the contract.

Talent contracts are filled with quirky details and complicated formulas. Consider, for example, Article I.17.A.4(c)(i) of the AFTRA 1994 Interactive Media Agreement, which reads:

> If a solo or duo is called upon to step out of a group to sing up to fifteen (15) cumulative bars during a session, the solo/duo shall be paid an adjustment of fifty percent (50%) of the solo/duo rate in addition to the appropriate group rate for that day.

Although the concept of *stepping out* may be more in keeping with an MTV video project than with your own multimedia work, you need to keep an eye out for buried clauses that do apply to your project.

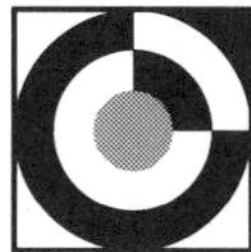

warning *If you create a multimedia product that incorporates union talent under contract, you will be restricted to using the material only for its initial primary use. Later, if you wish to spin off bits and pieces for other purposes (such as a commercial or as part of a product for sale to the public), you must then negotiate again with the talent and the union and pay for this expanded and supplemental use.*

Acquiring Releases

A union talent contract explicitly states what rights you have to the still and motion images and voices you make and use. If, however, your talent is nonunion (a co-worker in your office, perhaps, or a neighbor's child, student actor, waitress, or tugboat captain), be sure to require the person to sign a release form. This form grants to you certain permissions and specifies the terms under which you can use the material you make during a recording session.

Sometimes it is very difficult to do certain things because of previous rights that have been given out. For example, not too long ago I asked an executive from a media company if it would be possible to take some of his film footage and put it into a copyright library, to have something available for multimedia software developers to freely use in their interactive products. He said, "Well, we couldn't use a single frame of any film that was ever shot by a director who was a member of the Directors Guild of America." The bottom line is that there are so many rights attached to so many of these things, with so many different people involved, that it is very complicated even to figure out if you have the right to use it in any way, and that's too bad because again, that is just going to slow us down.

Trip Hawkins, Chairman, Electronics Arts

Figure 16-4 is a sample release form that covers most situations in a multimedia project and provides nearly perfect rights to the producer. Because such forms are legal documents, always consult an attorney to be sure that the specific language of your own release document meets your requirements.

warning *Do not include in your multimedia project any images or voices of people–even if you yourself recorded and edited the material–unless you have their written consent to use it, it is in the public domain (copyrights expire after 75 years), or it is work unarguably made for hire.*

FIGURE 16-4

Sample release form; consult an attorney when preparing your own legal document

Release Form

This is a release and authorization to use the name, voice, sounds, image and likeness, and writings of the undersigned ("Model"), as obtained in the photography / filming / video / audio session / creative session taking place

__________ at, __________________________ ("the Session"), for commercial purposes
(Date) (Place)
by _______________ and his respective successors and assigns (collectively, "Producer").

For valuable consideration, Model hereby authorizes the unlimited use in perpetuity by Producer of all recorded images, likenesses, voice and recorded sounds, and writings of Model obtained during the Session, and of Model's name in connection with such use. Model grants Producer the rights to use such sounds, images, and likenesses in any and all media and forms now known or hereafter devised throughout the universe without limitation as to territory or term, including but not limited to advertising, literature, computer demonstrations, and packaging, whether in the form of photography, magnetic or electronic data storage, or any other form, both as obtained and as modified at Producer's sole discretion to suit business purposes of Producer. The compensation stated above shall be the sole compensation for all such use, and no further compensation, including but not limited to royalties, residuals or use fees, shall be payable at any time.

Model further transfers and assigns all copyrights and all other rights in the recordings, sounds, images and likeness and writings obtained at the Session to Producer. Producer shall have the right to register the copyright to these in the name of its choice and shall have the exclusive right to dispose of these in any manner whatsoever. This agreement constitutes the sole, complete, and exclusive agreement between Model and Producer.

Name: ____________________ SIGNATURE: ____________________________
Address: ____________________ SOCIAL SECURITY NO.: __________________
____________________ DATE: ________________________________
Phone: ____________________

Multi

Test it, then test it again; that's the unavoidable rule.

It's critical that you take the time to thoroughly exercise your project and fix both big and little problems...

test and review

media

Alpha...

chapter 17

Delivering

...in the end,
you will save yourself
a great deal of agony!

...Beta

TEST it, then test it again; that's the unavoidable rule. You must test and review your project to ensure that it is bug free and accurate, operationally and visually on target, and that the client's requirements have been met.

Do this before the work is finalized and released for public or client consumption. A bad reputation earned by premature product release can destroy an otherwise excellent piece of work representing thousands of hours of effort. If you need to, delay the release of the work to be sure that it is as good as possible. It's critical that you take the time to thoroughly exercise your project and fix both big and little problems; in the end, you will save yourself a great deal of agony!

One of the major difficulties you face in testing the operation of your multimedia project is that its performance depends on specific hardware and system configurations. If you cannot control the end user's platform, or if the project is designed to be shown in many different environments, you must fully test your project on as many platforms as possible.

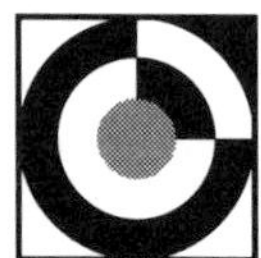

warning *Remember to budget for obtaining the hardware test platforms, as well as for the many hours of effort that testing will require.*

Few computer configurations are identical. Even identical hardware configurations may be running dissimilar software that can interact with your program in unexpected ways. The Macintosh environment is well known for its sensitivity to certain INITs (drivers and other parts of system software) that conflict with some software applications. The WIN.INI and SYSTEM.INI files in Windows contain custom information that may be different for each installation. If your project depends upon the Windows Multimedia Extensions, you will discover a great variety of options and implementations.

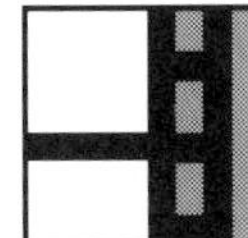

tip *If you are working for a client, clearly specify the intended delivery platform and its hardware and software configuration, and provide a clause in your agreement or contract that you will test only to that platform.*

As any element of a computer's configuration may be the cause of a problem or a bug, you will spend a good portion of testing time configuring platforms, and additional time reproducing reported problems and curing them. It is very difficult for even a well-equipped developer to test every possible configuration of computer, software, and third-party add-on boards. With this in mind, Apple Computer, for example, makes available to developers an elaborate testing facility at its corporate offices in Cupertino, California, where all of Apple's computer models and most variations of hardware and software are available.

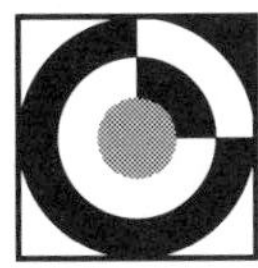

warning *Not everyone can test software. It takes a special personality to slog through this process. Every feature and function must be exercised, every button clicked. Then the same tests must be repeated again and again with different hardware and under various conditions.*

Testing

The terms alpha and beta are used by software developers to describe levels of product development when testing is done and feedback is sought. *Alpha* releases are typically for internal circulation only, and are passed among a selected group of mock users. These versions of a product are often the very first working drafts of your project, and are expected to have problems or be incomplete. *Beta* releases, on the other hand, are sent to a wider but still select audience with the same caveat: This software may contain errors, bugs, and unknown alligators that slither out of the swamp at day's end to bite startled designers from behind. Because your product is now being shown and used outside the privacy of its birth nest, its reputation will begin to take form during beta phase; thankfully, beta-level bugs are typically less virulent than alpha bugs.

Alpha Testing

Remain flexible and amenable to changes in both the design and the behavior of your project as you review the comments of your alpha testers. Beware of alpha testing groups made up of kindly friends who can provide positive criticism. Rather, you need to include aggressive people who will attack all aspects of your work. The meaner and nastier they are, the more likely they will sweat out errors or uncertainties in your product's design or navigation system. In the testing arena, learn to skillfully utilize friend and enemy alike. You will undoubtedly discover aspects of your work that, despite even the most insightful planning, you have overlooked.

Beta Testing

The beta testing group should be representative of real users, and should not include persons who have been involved in the project's production. Beta testers must have no preconceived ideas. You want them to provide commentary and reports in exchange for getting to play with the latest software and for recognition as part of this "inside" process.

Managing beta test feedback is critical. If tester comments are overlooked or ignored, the testing effort is a waste. Ask your beta testers to include a very detailed description of the hardware and software configuration at the time the problem occurred, and a step-by-step recounting of the problem, so that you can re-create it, analyze it, and repair it. You should also solicit general comments and suggestions. Figure 17-1 presents a sample bug reporting form used for beta testing.

From a letter with enclosed disk, delivered by overnight courier to 240 testers around the world: "We had a bit of a scare on this Beta. Here is the replacement copy for the infected B5 program disk. For your info, the virus that got past me was a strain of nVir. It was dormant and fooled Virus Detective, Virex, and Interferon. Virex 1.1 listed it as a harmless 'Stub' that was left over from a previous clean up. It wasn't until late yesterday that we discovered that it was real. I must apologize for letting this slip past me and thank the people in our tech support department for their help in calling all the members of the Beta test team and alerting them to this problem. If they didn't get a hold of you, it was certainly not for lack of trying."

Ben Calica, letter author and SuperCard product manager who claims this product shortened his life span by two years

Polishing to Gold

As you move through alpha and beta testing, then through the debugging process toward a final release, you may want to use terms that indicate the current version status of your project: bronze when you are close to being finished, gold when you have determined there is nothing left to change or correct and are ready to reproduce copies from your golden master. Some software developers also use the term *release candidate* (with a version

FIGURE 17-1

A typical bug reporting form for beta testing

Bug Reporting Form

Please fax or mail completed forms to:

Jane Researcher
Market Research Group
Large Computer Company
Industrial Park
Near A Major City, CA 94567
Phone: 555 - 555 - 1234
Fax: 555 - 555 - 5678

Beta program contact:

Name: ______________________
Title: ______________________
Company: ______________________
Address: ______________________
City: _____State: ________Zip:_____
Phone: ______________________
Fax: ______________________

System configuration:

CPU: _____ Clock speed: _____ MHz Manufacturer: ______________________
Hard disk capacity: ________ Currently available: ______________ RAM: _______
System software: ____________________ Monitor: ______________________

Summary of the problem:

____

____

____

____

Description of the bug:

____

____

____

____

____

Replication steps:

If the bug is reproducible, please describe how to do so:

____

____

____

____

First Person

We beat on the bronze version of the program right up to the last day, when we had to send a golden master to the duplicator by overnight courier. They were prepared to make 40,000 disks in a matter of hours and then courier them directly to a trade show.

Like kids with sticks at a piñata birthday party, we did everything we could to make all the bugs tumble out of the program. Every time a bug appeared, we killed it. As we pounded and tested, fewer and fewer bugs fell out, until none appeared for about six hours straight, under every condition we could dream up. As the deadline for the courier's airport facility neared, we were ready to sew up the product and stamp it gold. One of the guys waited in his car with engine running, ready for the sprint through commuter traffic to the airport.

We were saving the program every three minutes and nervously backing it up on different media about every ten minutes. We had built in a hidden software routine for debugging this project, and when the product manager pressed SAVE for the last time, he forgot to reset the program for normal use–we didn't know the master was flawed. Handling the disk like a uranium fuel rod traveling through heavy water, we packed it up and got it to the waiting car. An hour later, our postpartum celebration was interrupted by a painful cry from down the hall–someone had discovered the flaw. By then the courier flight had departed.

We fixed it. Faced with the appalling possibility of 40,000 bad disks being invoiced to us instead of the client, we sent the exhausted product manager out on the midnight flight, without a chance to even go home and clean up. He had a golden master disk in his briefcase, one in his shirt pocket, one in his pants pocket, and one in a manila envelope that would never see an airport x-ray machine.

number) as they continue to refine the product and approach a golden master. *Going gold*, or announcing that the job is finished and then shipping, can be a scary thing. Indeed, if you examine the file creation time and date for many software programs, you will discover that many went gold at two o'clock in the morning.

Preparing for Delivery

If your completed multimedia project will be delivered to consumers or to a client who will install the project on many computers, you will need to prepare your files so they can be easily transferred from your media to the user's platform. Simply copying a project's files to the user's hard disk is often not enough for proper installation; frequently you will also need to install special system and run-time files. You may need to provide a single program that acts as an installation routine, so that end users can easily and automatically set up your project or application on their own computers.

warning *The task of writing a proper installation routine is not a trivial one. Be sure you set aside adequate time in your schedule and money in your programming budget for writing and testing the installation program for your project platform.*

It is important to provide good written documentation about the installation process so that users have a clear step-by-step procedure to follow. That documentation must include a discussion of potential problems and constraints related to the full range of your target platforms. Because you likely will not have control over the specification and configuration of the user's platform, it is critical that you include appropriate warnings in your installation document, like these examples:

- Must have at least 8MB of RAM
- Will not run unless QuickTime is installed
- For running under Windows, Multimedia Extensions must be installed
- Disable all screensavers before running
- Back up older versions before installing this update

Often a file named README.TXT or ReadMeFirst is a good thing to include on the distribution disk of your project. This file can be a simple ASCII text file accessible by any text editor or word processing application. It should contain a description of changes or bugs reported since the documentation was printed, and may also contain a detailed description of the installation process.

The clearer and more detailed your installation instructions are, the fewer frustrated queries you will receive from your project's users. If your project is designed for wide distribution, installation problems can cause you many headaches and a great deal of time and expense in providing answers and service over the telephone.

That's it! I'm re-designing my reset button. I want it big, I want it yellow, and I want it padded!

Sharon Klocek, Producer, Visual In-Seitz, Inc., while restarting during a day long turned night

Compressing and Joining Files

When your project is small and simple and not dependent upon other applications or files, installing the project may be a matter of simply copying the software from a floppy disk to the user's hard disk, and you won't need to write an installation routine. If any of your project's files is too large to reside on a single floppy disk, however, you may need to compress or pack that file so that it will fit on the floppy. Packed files require less disk storage space and generally take less time to copy, because the CPU usually decompresses faster than the disk drive can transfer the original file. This lets you use fewer disks—an especially important feature that decreases installation time when you have many large data files. If your file, even when compressed, is still too large to fit on a single floppy disk, you must then split it into segments that can later be joined together on the user's hard disk.

Floppy disks for the Macintosh are the 3.5-inch size and provide either 800K storage on a double-density (DD) disk or 1.4K storage on a high-density (HD) disk. For DOS-based Windows computers, disks may be either 5.25-inch or 3.5-inch, and provide 360K, 720K, 1.2K, 1.4K or 2.88MB of storage.

The most common disk medium used for distribution to Windows platforms is the high-density 1.44MB 3.5-inch floppy disk, although it is not uncommon for developers to ship two sets of disks—the 1.44MB 3.5-inch and the 1.2MB 5.25-inch sizes—in the same package with their product for use in the Windows environment. More recently, many developers are shipping only the 1.44MB disks, with instructions to the user to call and ask for overnight shipment of the older format if it is required.

For products to be used on the Macintosh, both 800K and 1.44MB disks are distributed, but the 800K size is most common for applications. For multimedia projects in color, however, 1.44MB disks make the most sense. With the exception of the earliest Macintosh II, all color-capable Macintoshes can read these higher-density disks (beginning with the Macintosh IIx).

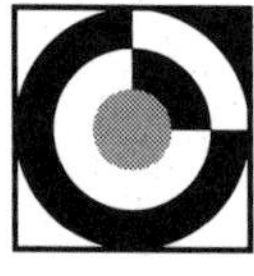

warning *There are still a great many older Macintoshes and DOS machines in use that can only read the older-format disks.*

File Archives

Shareware and commercial utility programs for compressing and decompressing files have been in wide use in both the Macintosh and DOS environments for some time. These have been particularly popular with users of bulletin boards (BBSs) and online services such as CompuServe, AppleLink, America OnLine, and GEnie, because compressed files take less time to transmit by modem than do uncompressed files. Files are typically uploaded and downloaded in compressed form to and from libraries and forums on the BBS or online service, so you need the proper decompressor to read the file. AppleLink software, for example, automatically packs files into compressed packages unless instructed not to, as shown in AppleLink's File menu:

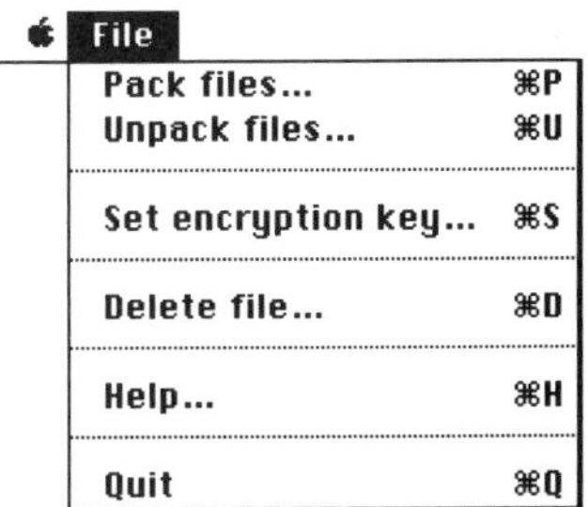

One or more of the files in your project can be compressed into a single file, called an *archive*. When that archive is then decompressed, or the files are expanded or extracted, each file in the archive is "reconstituted." Figure 17-2 shows the Translate menu of a StuffIt archive, containing options for converting several archive types. Archives are usually identified by filename

FIGURE 17-2

An archive can contain many compressed files

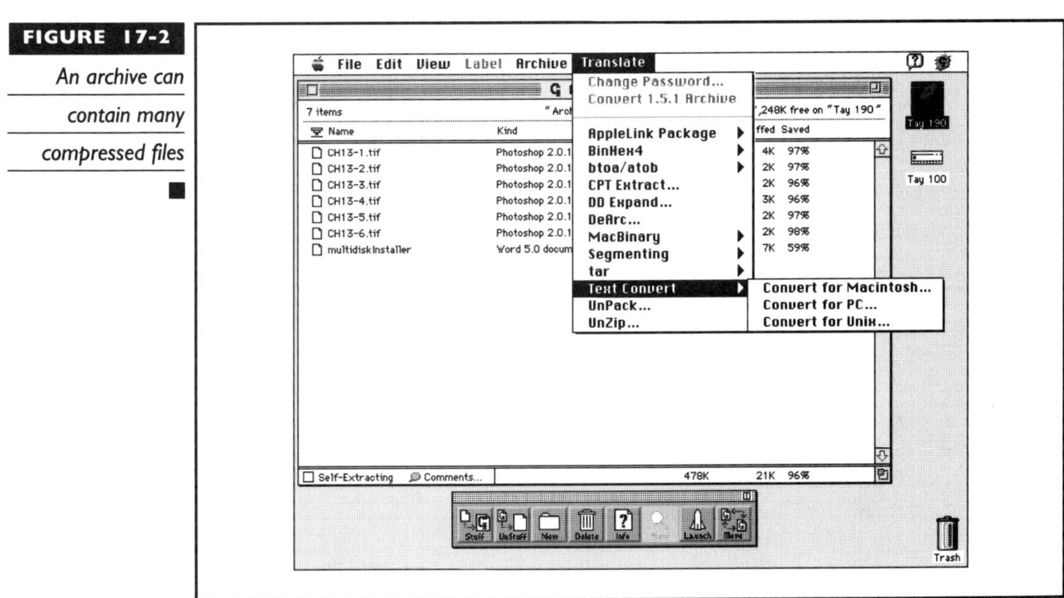

Compression Software	Extension	Platform
PKZIP	.ZIP (standard) or.EXE (self-extracting)	DOS
ARC	.ARC	DOS
PAK	.PAK	DOS
Windows Install	.xx__	Windows
StuffIt	.SIT	Macintosh
PackIt	.PIT	Macintosh
DiskDoubler	.DD	Macintosh
CompactPro	.CPT	Macintosh
AppleLink	.PKG	Macintosh
Self-extracting	.SEA	Macintosh

TABLE 17-1 *Common Compression Software Filename Extensions* ■

extensions representing the compression software that was utilized, as shown in Table 17-1.

Self-extracting archives are useful for delivering projects on disks in compressed form. On the Mac, these files typically carry the DOS-like filename extension, .SEA. On DOS platforms, these archives are executable files with an .EXE filename extender. With self-extracting archives, the user simply runs the executable archive, and the compressed files are automatically decompressed and placed on the hard disk. DiskDoubler and StuffIt Deluxe both create self-extracting archives on the Macintosh; PAK and PKZIP both create them in DOS environments (PKZIP has a command that will turn a .ZIP file into a self-extracting .EXE file). StuffIt Deluxe, while running on the Macintosh (as shown in Figure 17-2), also decompresses .ARC, .PAK, and .ZIP files, and converts text that was originally created on a PC.

Some compression applications allow you to compress, split, and store large files on several disks; the segments from these disks are then automatically joined during installation. Most compression utilities also provide an encryption or security feature, so that people who have access to disks containing private archive files cannot read them without authorization. This helps hide classified data.

For more information about applications for file compression and creating self-extracting archives, contact any of these publishers:

PKWARE, Inc. (PKZIP)
7545 N. Port Washington Rd.
Glendale, WI 53217

Aladdin Systems, Inc. (StuffIt)
165 Westridge Drive
Watsonville, CA 95076

NoGate Consulting (PAK)
P.O. Box 88115
Grand Rapids, MI
49518-0115

Symantec (DiskDoubler)
10201 Torre Avenue
Cupertino, CA 95014

First Person

I recently discovered a group of computer scientists and programmers fully dedicated to exploring and improving the techniques and algorithms used for compression of digital data. These folks are from around the world and hang out on bulletin boards, where they have long and arcane electronic conversations. Programmers and mathematicians such as Huffman, Lempel, and Ziv have been made famous on these services.

The greatest contribution this group has made to computer technology may not be in the area of information condensation, but in the creative spin-off of peculiar new words such as freshen, pack, crunch, squash, shrink, crush, implode, distill, squeeze, stuff, and garble. When you throw a few atoms and bestGuesses into this potpourri of words, the language of data compression joins that of modern physics, with its own quarks, gluons, and happy and sad particles. It's a creative and inventive place in the day-to-day forward motion of human endeavor, this place of strange and beautiful compression algorithms...

Designing Installation Programs

A typical installation procedure for your project will include processes for checking the user's environment to see if it is capable of running your project; decompressing compressed files; transferring the necessary files from your media to the user's media (without destroying existing files, directories, or folders); and installing any required system software. Often the user's computer must be restarted after the project is installed, so that the system software required by the project will work. Some installer programs (such as Apple's Installer), allow you to set up new software on many computers from a single network server.

Before you create the procedure, answer the following questions:

- What is the target platform?
- Will the installation routine need to verify that the target computer is a compatible platform?
- What changes, if any, can the installation routine make to the user's operating environment? How will the user answer prompts to verify decisions about implementing these changes?
- How much disk space will your project files require?
- Will your project include optional modules to be installed based on the user's configuration or available disk space?

Both Macintosh and Windows systems may require that special files be made accessible to the operating system in order to enable multimedia features used by your project. On the Macintosh, such files might include the QuickTime extension for movies, extensions for playing MIDI music, and special fonts. In Windows, you may need to put Dynamic Link Libraries (DLLs), fonts, and custom drivers for video hardware in the \WINDOWS\SYSTEM directory.

Many authoring systems (see Chapter 8) provide an "engine" for running your finished project on the target platform. Such engines allow playback and user interaction, but typically do not include the editing and construction facilities of the full-bore authoring tool. So the last step in developing your project process may be to create this run-time or stand-alone version. The application to run this run-time version must then be installed on the end user's computer.

warning *If your project includes special files or executable run-time files that are required by your authoring system, be sure you have the proper permissions and licenses for distribution of these files.*

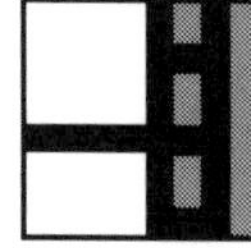

tip *Always provide users the option to install on any hard disk or media, not just "C:" drive or the system disk.*

Installation on a Windows Platform

Microsoft's Setup Toolkit for Windows gives multimedia authors great flexibility and power in building installation routines. The Setup Toolkit's robust scripting language lets you thoroughly examine the operating environment and control the details of the installation process. This and other similar tools demand serious programming effort and development time. Simpler installation utilities, however, are available for building installation routines in Windows.

An INSTALL.EXE file installs Windows applications using a file named INSTALL.INF to provide the details of where to put files and what files to alter or delete on the end user's own drive. The INSTALL.EXE file prompts users for information, creates proper directories, copies files to be installed, creates Program Manager group items, modifies other .INI files, and displays README.TXT files. Often, other files will also be required by the INSTALL.EXE installer, such as for installing icons (.ICO files) or displaying bitmaped background images (.BMP) during the process.

EDI Install for Windows

Unlike Microsoft's Setup Toolkit for Windows, with EDI Install Pro no programming is required. It is a complete installation utility that you can use "right out of the box" so end users can copy and set up applications on their system according to your instructions. It uses a simple interface, INF Maker, to create the .INF file for you. INF Maker scans your disks for files and allows you to enter components, .INI file entries, and Program Manager items.

INF Maker's main window (see Figure 17-3) allows you to open and save INF files, scan your disks, and enter information specific to your desired installation. The window itself contains the four primary pieces of information required for a Windows installation: application name, installation title, default directory, and the default Program Manager group. Other information can be entered through the Section menu.

When you are done with INF Maker, the end user can follow a simple instruction like "INSERT DISK AND RUN INSTALL FROM WINDOWS."

You can place files in normal, compressed, stored, or split format (requiring more than a single disk). If you use split files, you will want to order them so users will not need to swap back and forth between disks when accessing normal files between split files.

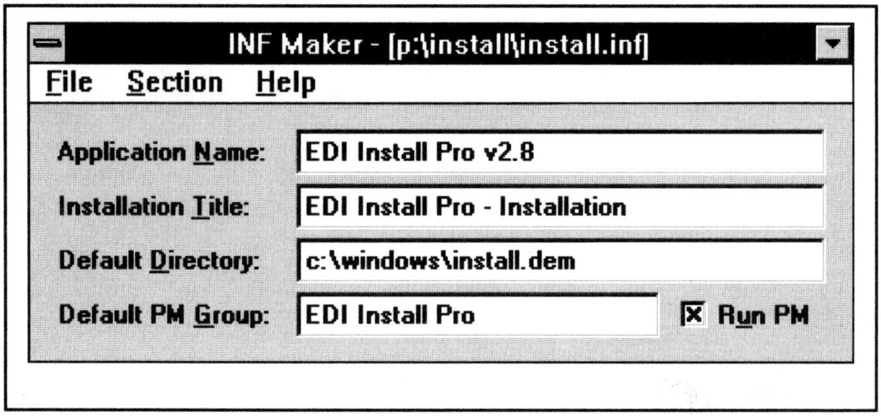

FIGURE 17-3 INF Maker's main window

INF Maker - [p:\install\install.inf]

File Section Help

Application Name: EDI Install Pro v2.8

Installation Title: EDI Install Pro - Installation

Default Directory: c:\windows\install.dem

Default PM Group: EDI Install Pro [X] Run PM

EDI Install Pro supports *.xx$* file compression. The Windows naming convention uses a dollar sign as the last character of the filename extension for a file in compressed form (for example, MONDO.EX$, ISLIP01.DL$, or DIRSTART.DL$). The original filename extension, however, is saved in the compressed file, and the last character is restored during decompression.

EDI Install Pro includes a special utility, NETSETUP.EXE, to allow installations through e-mail. This will work with any e-mail system that supports file attachments. The only requirement is that all the client stations use the same path to the server.

When you have completed the .INF file and created your distribution disks, you will need to copy INSTALL.EXE, INSTALL.BIN, your INSTALL.INF, and optionally EDI3D.BIN and EXTRACT.EXE, to the first disk in your package. EDI3D.BIN adds the standard Microsoft 3D look to EDI Install Pro (as well as any dialogs you display in a custom DLL). EXTRACT.EXE allows users to extract a compressed file without using EDI Install Pro. This file is not required for EDI Install Pro to work, but is provided to let users extract files in case of an emergency, such as when a single file on a disk is corrupted.

For information on EDI Install Pro:

Eschalon Development, Inc.
24-2979 Panorama Drive
Coquitlam
British Columbia
V3E2W8 CANADA
604-945-3198

Installation on a Macintosh Platform

Apple provides Multidisk Installer to software developers so that the human interface and the process of installing or updating software on a Macintosh will be familiar to users, time after time, no matter what software is being installed (see Figure 17-4). Unless your installation is very simple, Apple recommends that you use the Multidisk Installer to install your software.

Among its features, Apple's Multidisk Installer provides

- Easy Install, where you can specify an installation based upon examination of the target environment. Easy Install provides the user with one-button installation.
- Custom Install, where power users can customize the installation.
- Live Install, which installs to the currently booted and active System, so it is not necessary to ship the Installer on a bootable disk with a System Folder.
- Network Install, which lets you install from an AppleShare server.
- Installation from multiple source disks.
- Installation of software to folders other than the System Folder, as well as creation of new folders as necessary.

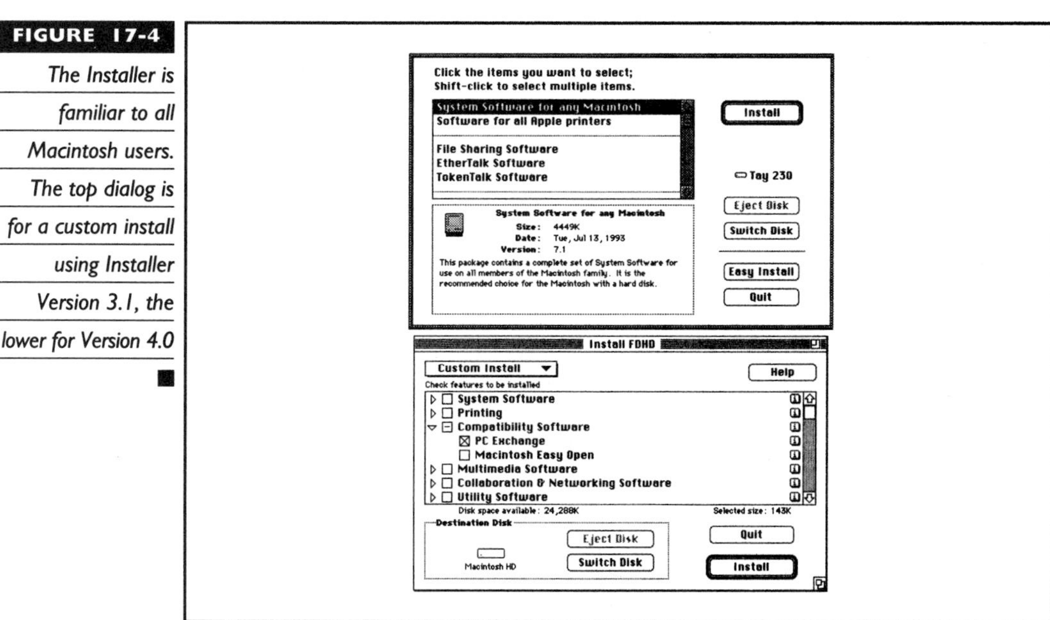

FIGURE 17-4 *The Installer is familiar to all Macintosh users. The top dialog is for a custom install using Installer Version 3.1, the lower for Version 4.0*

- User Function support, to provide linkage to developer-defined code segments during Easy Install. You can customize the process of determining what software to install and how to install it.
- Action Atom support, to provide linkage to developer-defined code segments that are called before or after the installation takes place. You can use this feature to extend the capabilities of the Installer.
- Audit Records, a feature that lets you record details about an installation so that future installations of the software can be more intelligent.

Successfully using Apple's Installer, however, requires advanced programming and scripting skills.

Using StuffIt InstallerMaker

Unlike Apple's Installer, no scripting is required to create powerful installers with StuffIt InstallerMaker. Installation conditions, destinations, and "packages" can be defined using a point-and-click interface (see Figure 17-5). You can, however, further customize installers by adding your own

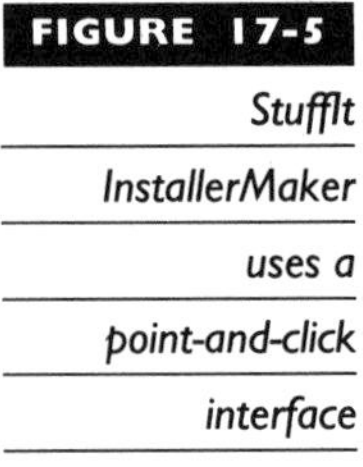

FIGURE 17-5 *StuffIt InstallerMaker uses a point-and-click interface*

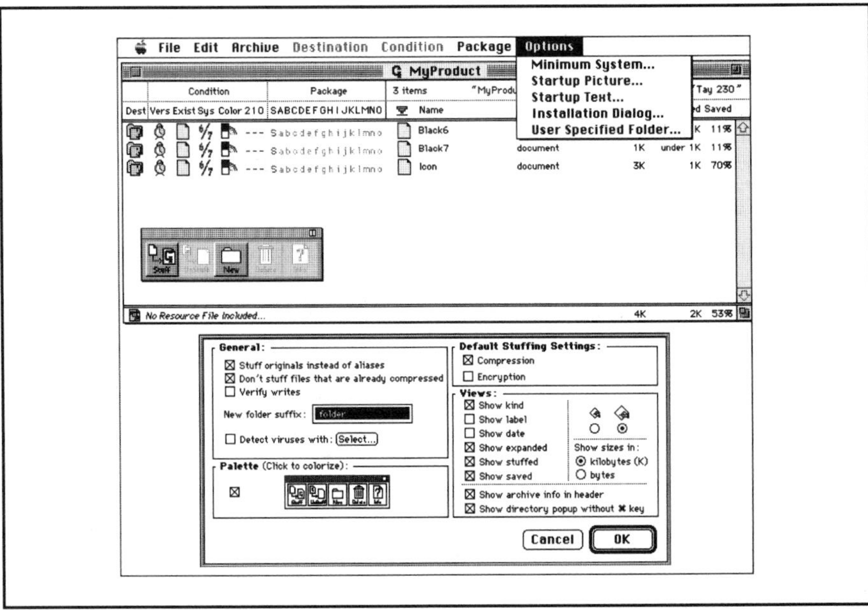

custom code during startup, installation, and at the end of installation. Because of its built-in features, most developers will find that they will not need to write any custom code or use ResEdit, Apple's resource editor, when using InstallerMaker. InstallerMaker supports the Macintosh PowerPC.

Here is a summary (provided by Aladdin Systems) of significant features and benefits of InstallerMaker:

- Integrated Compression—allows developers to ship their products on fewer disks, thus saving money.
- Combine files into a single Integrated Installer Application—all the files in a product can also be uploaded as a single file for distribution of online updates. Since the file is compressed, it will take less time for end users to download.
- Destination Support—developers can easily choose where the installer should place any file in the product. For example, the System Folder, Control Panels folder, or any pre-designated folder.
- Condition Support—developers can place simple "IF...THEN" rules on any file in the product. For example, a developer can state, "Only install this file if running on a 68000 machine without Color QuickDraw."
- Startup Splash Screen and Text—developers can paste their own images into their installer to give the installer the same look as their program. They can also have "licensing" or "Read-Me" text displayed for the end user before the user installs the software.
- Standard and Custom Install—developers can give their end users a choice of what to install. For instance, the end user can be given the option to install an application, but not its help file.
- Super-Checksums—the files that are installed have checksums so that bad media and duplication errors are caught when the end user tries to install from a defective disk, thus eliminating end user problems at a later time due to bad data.
- Correct Installation—the user does not have to manually drag files to their correct location. The Installer will place all files as the developer specified, thus eliminating any error due to improper installation. In addition, since all files have been checksummed, there is no chance of installing a corrupted file due to bad floppy disks or a bad download.

- End users get only the files that are correct for their specific hardware/software configuration. Since the developer can specify which files should be installed based on the end user's machine, there is no need for the end user to throw away unusable files (for example, color art, if they have a monochrome machine).
- End users can be given a choice of groups of files to install. They do not need to install everything, unless the developer requires that everything be installed. Most developers will give the user the choice of not installing groups of files, such as Read Me files, Help files, etc.

For information on StuffsIt InstallerMaker, contact:

Aladdin Systems
165 Westridge Drive
Watsonville, CA 95076
(408) 761-6200

Multi

[By the end of 1991, more than three million CD-ROM players were installed around the world...]

technology

media

With multimedia capability increasing,
more new CD titles are being published in the areas of

education,
TRAINING,
and
Entertainment

chapter 18

CD-ROMs and Software Packaging

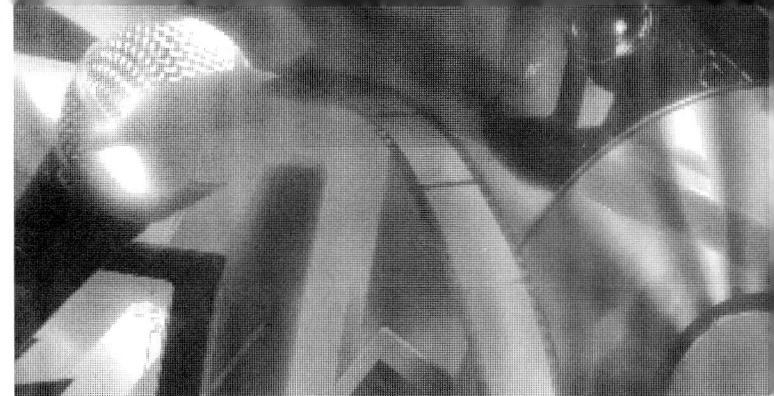

THE majority of multimedia products sold into retail and business channels during the 1990s will be delivered on CD-ROM (compact disc, read-only memory). This chapter discusses CD-ROM technology and then the methods for packaging your product for delivery.

CD-ROM

By the end of 1991, more than three million CD-ROM players were installed around the world, and more than three thousand commercial CD-ROM titles were published. These numbers are expected to double every year as CD-ROM players penetrate the marketplace and even more software titles drive sales upward. CD-ROM players are the chickens, and the titles are the eggs—you can't have one without the other. As more chickens produce eggs, more chickens will emerge to produce even more eggs that yield yet greater numbers of chickens...and so forth in geometrically increasing progression.

The first users of CD-ROMs were owners of large databases: library catalogs, reference systems, and parts lists. In 1992, it was estimated that some 60 percent of existing CD-ROMs contained text-based databases. With multimedia capability increasing, however, more new CD titles are being published in the areas of education, training, and entertainment. Consumer-oriented CD titles generally fall into these categories:

Agriculture
Bibliography
Business
Dictionaries
Directories
Education
Encyclopedias
Games
Geography
Graphics
Health
History
Leisure
Life Sciences
Literature
Music and Sound
Science and Technology
Travel

The extremely low cost of data storage and delivery using compact discs is a major economic justification for investing in this technology. Following is a list of costs per megabyte of project delivery on various media:

Media	Capacity	Cost per Megabyte
Online service	$6/hour for download at 2400 baud	More than $8
Hard disk	100MB	About $7
Paper	2K per page	About $5
Magnetic tape	60MB	Less than $1
Floppy disk	1.44MB	Less than $.50
CD-ROM	650MB	About $.01

The largest number of CD-ROM players are connected to computers. The installed base of multimedia-equipped computers in U.S. households at the end of 1993 was 3.8 million: 2.5 million MPCs and 1.3 million Macintoshes. The installed base of CD-ROM players grew 300 percent from the end of 1992 to the end of 1993, and it is expected to triple again in 1994. Some CD-ROM players are sold for dedicated and special purposes and do not represent purchasers or consumers of CD-ROM-based multimedia titles. The *available installed base* is that fraction of the projected installed base into which consumer/mass market and business titles might be sold. Figure 18-1 illustrates the estimated installed base of CD-ROM players in the United States in 1993 as well as predicted growth rates through 1998.

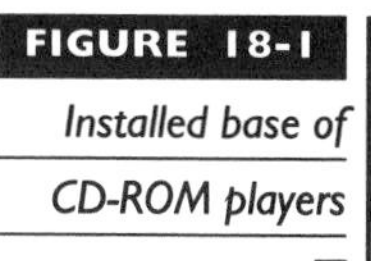

FIGURE 18-1

Installed base of CD-ROM players

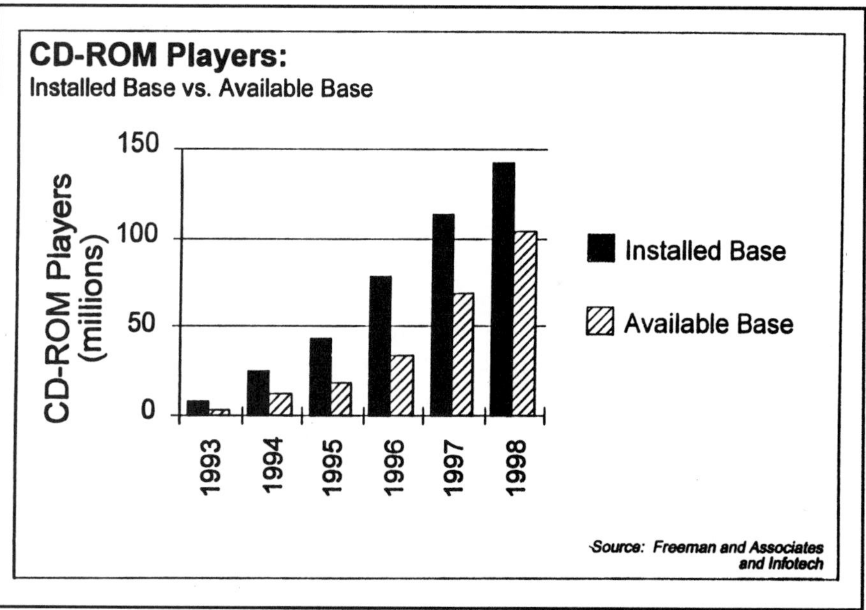

Compact Disc Technology

A *compact disc,* or CD, is a thin wafer of clear polycarbonate plastic and metal measuring 4.75 inches (120mm) in diameter, with a small hole, or *hub,* in its center (see Figure 18-9). The metal layer is usually pure aluminum, sputtered onto the polycarbonate surface in a thickness measurable in molecules. As the disc spins in the CD player, the metal reflects light from a tiny infrared laser into a light-sensitive receiver diode. These reflections are transformed into an electrical signal, and then further converted to meaningful bits and bytes for use in digital equipment.

Pits on the CD, where the information is stored, are 1 to 3 microns long, about 1/2 micron wide, and 1/10 micron deep (by comparison, a human hair is about 18 microns in diameter). A CD can contain as many as 3 miles of these tiny pits wound in a spiral pattern from the hub to the edge. A layer of lacquer is applied to protect the surface, and artwork from the disc's author or publisher is usually silkscreened on the back side.

Compact discs are made in what is generally referred to as a *family* process. The glass master is made using the well-developed photolithographic techniques created by the microchip industry: First an optically ground glass disc is coated with a layer of photoresist material 1/10 micron thick. A laser exposes (*writes*) a pattern of pits onto the surface of the chemical layer of material. The disc is developed (the exposed areas are washed away) and is silvered, resulting in the actual pit structure of the finished master disc. The master is then electroplated with layers of nickel one molecule thick, one layer at a time, until the desired thickness is reached. The nickel layer is separated from the glass disc and forms a metal negative, or *father.*

In cases where low runs of just a few discs are required, the father is used to make the actual discs. Most projects, though, require several *mothers,* or positives, to be made by plating the surface of the father.

In a third plating stage, *sons* or stampers are made from the mother, and these are the parts that are used in the injection molding machines. Plastic pellets are heated and injected into the mold or stamper, forming the disc with the pits in it. The plastic disc is coated with a thin aluminum layer for reflectance and protective lacquer for protection, given a silkscreened label for marketing, and packaged for delivery. Most of these activities occur in a particle-free cleanroom, because one speck of dust larger than a pit can ruin many hours of work. The mastering process alone takes around 12 hours.

CDs produced in this manner may cost less than $2 each, depending on the size of the run. Mastering may cost between $800 and $1500. Additional expenses include premastering, or arranging your files and data into CD-ROM format (about $250); multicolor silkscreen setup charges (about $400); packaging (for example, $.35 per plastic-wrapped jewel box); and the costs of designing and manufacturing printed booklets to be included in the jewel boxes.

Compact Disc Standards

In 1986, Philips and Sony together launched CD technology as a digital method of delivering sound and music (audio) to consumers (see Chapter10). This collaboration resulted in the Red Book standard (named for the color of the document's jacket), officially called the Compact Disc Digital Audio Standard. The Red Book standard defines the audio format for CDs available in music stores today; the Yellow Book is for CD-ROM; the Green Book is for CD-I (Interactive); and the Orange Book is for write-once, read-only (WORM) CD-ROMs. These and other CD formats are discussed in this section.

The Red, Yellow, Green, and Orange Books

Red Book remains the basis for recent standards that define more elaborate digital data formats for computers and other digital devices. Audio CDs can provide up to 76 minutes of playing time, which is enough for a slow-tempo rendition of Beethoven's Ninth Symphony. This was reported to be Philips's and Sony's actual criterion during research and development for determining the size of sectors and ultimately the physical size of the CD itself.

A CD may contain one or more tracks. These are areas normally allocated for storing a single song in the Red Book format. CDs also contain lead-in information and a table of contents. Each track on the CD may use a different format; this allows you to create a mixed mode disc that combines, for example, high-quality CD-Audio with Macintosh HFS (Hierarchiacal Filing System) CD-ROM or ISO 9660 data formats. Figure 18-2 illustrates the track layouts for Red Book, Yellow Book, Green Book, mixed mode, and for Kodak Photo CD's Orange Book layout, discussed later.

cross platform *Both Macintosh and Windows support commands to access both Red Book Audio and data tracks on a CD, but you cannot access both at the same time.*

Though a CD contains tracks, the primary logical unit for data storage on a CD is a *sector,* which is 1/75 second in length. Each sector of a CD contains 2352 bytes of data. After every sector are another 882 bytes consisting of two layers of error detecting and error correcting information (EDC and ECC) and timing control data. A CD actually requires, then, 3234 bytes to store 2352 bytes of data. EDC and ECC allow a scratched or dirty data sector to be reconstructed by software fast enough to avoid drop-out of music. Timing codes are used to display song-playing time on an audio CD player.

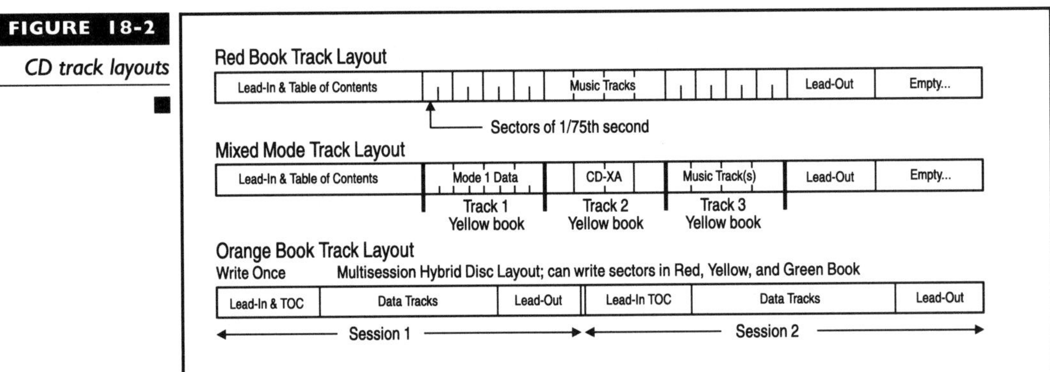

FIGURE 18-2

CD track layouts

The disc spins at a constant linear velocity (CLV), so data can be read at a constant density and spacing. This means the rotational speed of the disc may vary from about 200 rpm (revolutions per minute) when the read head is at the outer edge, to 530 rpm when it is reading near the hub. This translates to about 1.3 meters (51 inches) of travel along the data track each second. CD players use very sensitive motors so that no matter where the read head is on the disc, approximately the same amount of data is read in each second.

The CD's rotational speed and the density of the pits and lands on the CD allow data to be read at a sustained rate of 150K per second. This is sufficient for good audio, but it is very slow for large image files, motion video, and other multimedia resources, especially when compared to the high data-transfer rates of hard disk drives. New drives that spin twice as fast (300K transfer rate) or even three, four or six times as fast when reading computer data, and slower for Red Book Audio, have been designed specifically for computers and other devices and are currently entering the marketplace. But CD access speed and transfer rate from CD-ROM is much slower than from a hard disk.

A major multimedia technology issue has to do with CD-ROM performance: CD-ROM systems are incredibly slow and have neither the transfer rate of information coming off the disk that you'd like nor the access speed to find the data on the disk that you want. This is going to improve over the years through compression technology, by spinning the disk faster, and by going to different types of lasers. But in the meantime, we're going to have to suffer with it the way it is. It's still a huge storage device, so it's wonderful for storing digital anything. But it's slower than the hard disk drive, so anybody accustomed to a personal computer will be unhappy with it. And it's slower than a video game system with a cartridge, so it's going to be real challenge to software designers to be very clever so their stuff doesn't put the consumer to sleep. These consumers are very impatient, no matter their age.

Trip Hawkins, Chairman, Electronics Arts

Philips and Sony developed the Yellow Book to provide an established standard for data storage and retrieval. Yellow Book adds yet another layer of error checking to accommodate the greater reliability required of computer data, and provides two modes: one for computer data and the other for compressed audio and video/picture data.

The most common standard currently used for CD-ROM production evolved from the Yellow Book, with Microsoft joining the collaboration, and it was approved by the International Standards Organization as ISO 9660 (see the next section). Later, other standards were developed to deal with specific user requirements, such as synchronized interleaving of compressed audio and visual data in interactive digital movies (Green Book), and with formats for write-once and magneto-optical CD technologies (Orange Book).

The Red, Yellow, Green, and Orange books describe the types of compact discs listed in Table 18-1.

Within each standard there are variations called modes, forms, and levels (see Figure 18-3). These variations pertain to the method used to allocate the 2352 bytes available in a CD data sector and how the player reads them. Figure 18-4 shows the most common data layouts within sectors.

Each track on a CD can be one and only one of the following formats: CD-Audio, CD-ROM Mode 1, CD-ROM Mode 2, CD-ROM/XA, or CD-I. The whole track must be the same type. When you combine different types of tracks on the same disc, the disc is called a *mixed mode* disc—for example, track 1 might be CD-ROM Mode 1 data, and all subsequent tracks might

Format Name	Description	Application
CD-Audio or CD-DA	Digital audio	Consumer audio discs
CD-ROM High Sierra	Read-only memory	Vestigial standard, seldom used
CD-ROM ISO 9660	Read-only memory	MS-DOS and Macintosh files
CD-ROM HFS	Read-only memory	Macintosh HFS files
CD-ROM/XA	Read-only memory	Extended Architecture
CD-I or CD-RTOS	Interactive	Philips Interactive motion video
CD-I Ready	Interactive/Ready	CD-Audio with features for CD-I player
CD-Bridge	Bridge	Allows XA track to play on CD-I player
CD-MO	Magneto-optical	Premastered area readable on any CD player
CD-WO or WORM	Write-once	May use multiple sessions to fill disc
CD+G	Mixed mode	CD+Graphics, MTV on disc
Photo CD	Compressed images	Kodak multisession XA system
CDTV	ISO 9660 variant	Commodore proprietary system

TABLE 18-1 *Compact Disc Formats*

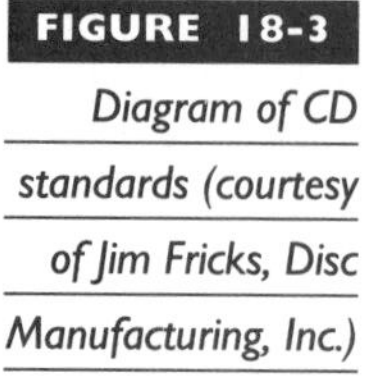

FIGURE 18-3 *Diagram of CD standards (courtesy of Jim Fricks, Disc Manufacturing, Inc.)*

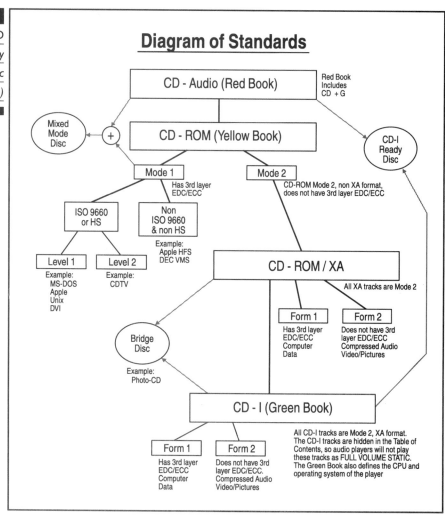

be audio data. This is the most common layout for CD-ROM Mode 2, CD-ROM/XA, or CD-I, but each whole track must be the same type.

Note that the CD-ROM/XA format uses an additional subheader that tells the reading software what type of data to expect in that sector: either computer data, or compressed audio data interleaved with picture data. (CD-ROM/XA is discussed further in a later section.) Additional hardware is required to play a CD-ROM/XA disc, but these XA-capable players, and players that can read Kodak's Photo CD multisession XA discs, may be the CD-ROM players of choice for multimedia in the 1990s. These players can also play Red Book and Yellow Book formats.

FIGURE 18-4

The sectors on a CD may store data in various ways

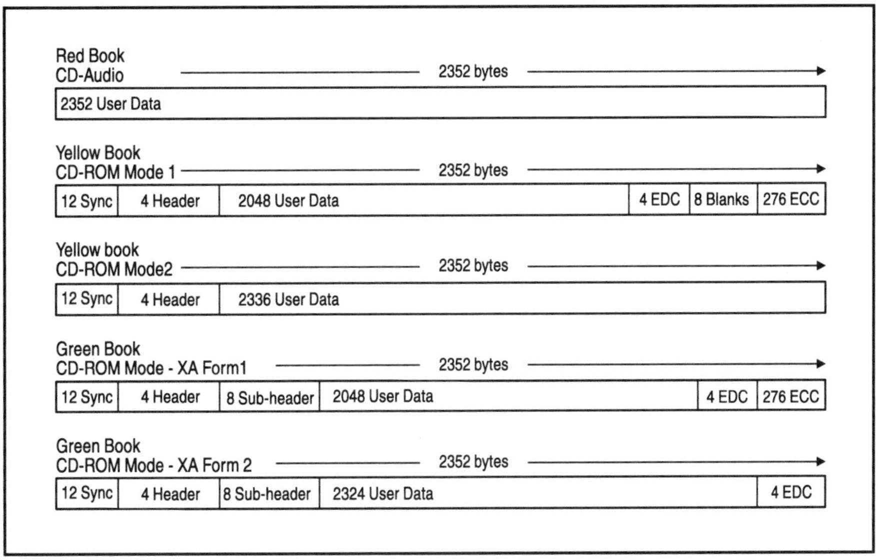

Red Book CD-Audio — 2352 bytes

2352 User Data

Yellow Book CD-ROM Mode 1 — 2352 bytes

12 Sync | 4 Header | 2048 User Data | 4 EDC | 8 Blanks | 276 ECC

Yellow book CD-ROM Mode2 — 2352 bytes

12 Sync | 4 Header | 2336 User Data

Green Book CD-ROM Mode - XA Form1 — 2352 bytes

12 Sync | 4 Header | 8 Sub-header | 2048 User Data | 4 EDC | 276 ECC

Green Book CD-ROM Mode - XA Form 2 — 2352 bytes

12 Sync | 4 Header | 8 Sub-header | 2324 User Data | 4 EDC

ISO 9660

The most widely utilized format for storing digital data in files on CDs is ISO 9660. This standard had its origin at a famous meeting of industry representatives at Del Webb's High Sierra Hotel & Casino in Reno, Nevada. At that meeting, a common file structure for CDs specifically used by computers was defined. By the time it was processed as an international standard many months later, enhancements had been added, and the "High Sierra" format became outdated. Some popular discs produced during the hiatus still require the High Sierra drivers on MS-DOS, Macintosh, and UNIX systems.

ISO 9660 file-naming conventions follow the MS-DOS style of eight characters, a period, and three extender characters. Directory names are limited to eight characters. Acceptable characters for names are the capital letters A–Z, the digits 0–9, and the underscore character.

An executable program file designed for the PC will not run on a Macintosh (and vice versa). You can, however, access all files on the CD from either platform. On the Macintosh you need the Apple CD-ROM extension, and the files named Foreign File Access and ISO 9660 File Access must be in the System Folder. On MS-DOS computers, a device driver supplied by the player manufacturer must be called from the CONFIG.SYS file, and the file MSCDEX.EXE (the Microsoft CD-ROM Extensions) or equivalent (such as Corel's CDX Extension) must be run during boot-up.

The ISO 9660 CD-ROM is viewed by either operating system as just another storage device containing directories or folders, and files.

Many multimedia developers place both Macintosh files and PC files on the same CD in a hybrid format, letting the user launch the proper applications for the appropriate platform.

cross platform *Graphics, text, and data files written in common formats such as DOC, TIF, PIC, DBF, and WKS can be read from an ISO 9660 CD and imported into your application, whether the file was generated on a Macintosh or a PC.*

Macintosh HFS

The Hierarchical File System (HFS) is Apple's method for managing files and folders on the Macintosh desktop. Apple has developed its own drivers for Yellow Book Mode 1 CDs, and the HFS driver for CD-ROMs (the default driver built into Apple CD-ROM) provides Macintosh users with the expected comfort of the familiar Apple desktop, complete with 32-character, mixed-case filenames. HFS does not, however, comply with the international ISO 9660 standard. If your project is destined only for Macintosh platforms, the HFS format is the preferred choice.

It is easy to produce a Macintosh HFS-formatted CD. Just organize all your files and folders on a hard disk, test that all paths are correct and your software works, and submit the disk to a CD-ROM manufacturing house. They will copy your disk contents to an HFS CD-ROM with no muss or fuss. When you then mount the disk on a Macintosh, it will look just like the submitted hard disk.

CD-ROM/XA (Sony)

A standard of great interest to multimedia developers is CD-ROM/XA (Extended Architecture), which is an extension to the Yellow Book standard. XA defines a new sector format to allow computer data (Form 1), as well as compressed audio data and video/image information (Form 2) to be read and played back apparently simultaneously. Computer data can be interleaved or mixed with audio and images. In effect, XA provides audio synchronization, similar to QuickTime or AVI.

Special enabling hardware is required on board a CD-ROM/XA player because the audio must be separated from the interleaved data, decompressed, and then output to speakers—while the computer data is sent onward to the computer. XA audio can be digitized and played back at two quality levels (A and B); though it falls short of Red Book quality, it is still adequate, as shown below:

Level	Sample Size	Sampling Rate
CD-ROM/XA Level B	4 bits	37.8 kHz mono, music quality
CD-ROM/XA Level C	4 bits	18.9 kHz mono, voice quality

Production of a CD-ROM/XA disc requires extensive premastering, because the data and audio/video information must be properly interleaved from your original material. You can still have high-quality Red Book tracks on your XA disc.

Photo CD

In the summer of 1992, Eastman Kodak Company pioneered a well-planned and heavily financed effort to establish early market share in worldwide electronic photo-imaging systems for consumers. Designed to protect Kodak's investment in the photoprocessing industry, its vast sales and technology infrastructure, and to allow gradual consumer transition from film-based cameras to digital cameras over the next decades, the new technology is a marriage of silver halide wet processing and digital processing and display techniques. Kodak has named this venture Photo CD.

We consider the Kodak Photo CD System to be a pivotal point in the history of photography. It builds on our core business and brings high-quality silver-halide imaging into the realm of electronic imaging at low cost for both home and commercial use. Our belief that the Photo CD system will win overwhelming acceptance is based on three elements. First, it responds to strong consumer demands. Second, it is a high-quality product that delivers remarkable results. And finally, it offers exceptional profit potential to all of our customers—the stores that sell Photo CD players and the wholesale and retail operations that offer finishing services.

Leo Thomas, Group Vice President and President, Imaging, Eastman Kodak Company

Customers present an exposed 35mm roll of color film for wet processing, and purchase a Photo CD for an additional charge of about $20 for 24 images. The source images (negatives) are then processed by a technician who scans each image at an imaging workstation. The images (a *session*) are written onto Photo CD write-once media, a color index of thumbnails of all the images is printed, and the Photo CD is returned to the consumer in a CD jewel case with the index sheet inserted as an attractive cover. The customer may return that same Photo CD to have more images written onto it, creating a multisession disc. A Photo CD can contain 125 or more high-resolution images.

Photo CD images may be viewed using a Kodak Photo CD player connected to a television at the customer's home or business. The player can also play Red Book Audio consumer CDs, as well as Red Book tracks that may be associated with any Photo CD image. Photo CD images can also be viewed using a CD-ROM/XA player connected to a computer. In this way, desktop publishing and multimedia production houses have access to images and libraries of images distributed on Photo CD.

Multimedia developers should investigate Photo CD both as a tool and as a delivery platform. Using Kodak's own Photo CD Access software, or plug-ins for image manipulation software such as Photoshop, or programs such as Fetch from Aldus, you can import a Photo CD image and convert it to a TIFF or PICT file. This can be a very inexpensive method for turning negatives or 35mm slides into multimedia artwork. As a delivery platform, you can deliver Portfolio format Photo CD projects that users can play on their television sets.

The recent Orange Book standard used for Kodak's Photo CD format is described in Figure 18-5. Photo CD is a multisession, Mode 2, Form 1 disc using an ISO 9660 file and directory structure. A Photo CD can also be mixed mode, providing Red Book Audio tracks.

IMAGE PACS An Image Pac is a Photo CD file containing five separate forms (components) of the image stored in that file, as outlined in Table 18-2.

The smaller-resolution Image Pac files are stored without compression. The larger files need to be decompressed and recomposed using proprietary Kodak software or appropriate plug-ins and drivers. The larger files may take many seconds to display.

Component	Size (Pixels)	Description
Base/16	128×192	Overview pac, also thumbnails 64×96
Base/4	256×384	Quickly accessed
Base	512×768	Most useful for 640×480 multimedia
4Base	1024×1536	Compressed, base luma interpolated
16Base	2048×3072	Compressed, base luma interpolated

TABLE 18-2 *Image Pac Components*

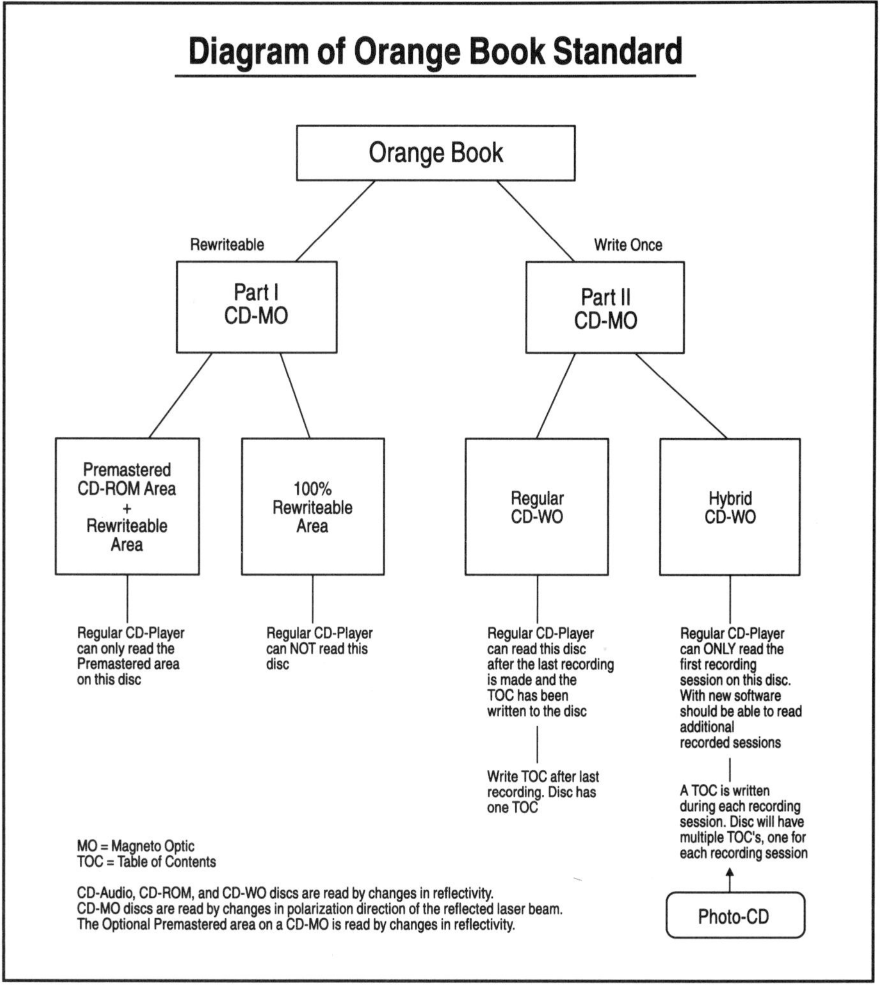

FIGURE 18-5 *Diagram of the Orange Book standards for write-only CDs (courtesy of Jim Fricks, Disc Manufacturing, Inc.)*

Philips CD-I

The Green Book, published in 1988, specifies an Extended Architecture format and operating system (CD-RTOS) for Philips's proprietary CD-I (CD-Interactive) environment. Like Photo CD, CD-I discs are designed to play on a consumer-grade player connected to a television set. To prevent users from playing a CD-I track on an audio player (which produces maximum-volume noise and can damage eardrums), the CD-I tracks are not listed in the disc's table of contents. CD-I uses XA Form 1 and Form 2 data formats.

CD-I ready discs are Red Book Audio discs with special information stored just ahead of track 1, in an area called the *pregap*. These discs are designed specifically to work with Philips CD-I players, allowing special pictures and text to be loaded into the player's memory before the Red Book Audio tracks begin to play. The disc can also be played on a standard CD-Audio player without interference from the additional information stored on the disc.

CD-Bridge discs are also designed to accommodate the Philips CD-I proprietary player system, and conform to both the CD-I and CD-ROM/XA specifications. This format—which assigns two separate disc label locations, one for each format—allows a CD-ROM/XA track to be played on a CD-I player. Kodak Photo CD discs are playable on Philips CD-I players because they are Bridge discs.

During the early 1990s, Philips, Kodak, Commodore, Tandy, Sega, NEC, Nintendo, Panasonic, and Sony entered the consumer electronics marketplace with television-based systems that allow users to dynamically interact with sound and displayed graphical information. The Commodore CDTV and Tandy VIS ventures never caught on in the retail marketplace of the United States, however, and were abandoned by 1994.

We just finished an entire CD-I title in six weeks and needed serious time off to recuperate. I can relate to your being tired of all-nighters.

Cornelia Atchley, graphic artist, after the fact

3DO

In early 1993, the 3DO Company introduced a new platform for interactive multimedia in the consumer mass market. It uses new hardware incorporating fast interactive processing, lifelike graphics, complex real-time animation, and full audio and video capabilities. The 3DO Interactive Multiplayer features a 32-bit Reduced Instruction Set Computer (RISC) architecture and a double-speed CD-ROM player, and can display 16 million colors simultaneously. A custom Digital Signal Processor (DSP) chip allows mixing of CD-quality sound, and video compression technology displays full-screen images at a rate of 30 frames per second.

To encourage widespread acceptance of the 3DO format, 3DO licenses its technology so that other manufacturers and publishers can produce 3DO-compatible hardware and software titles. Panasonic was the first company to market a 3DO Interactive Multiplayer.

Producing a CD

Before you begin a CD-ROM project, get in touch with a disc manufacturer. Most are prepared to answer your questions, give you cost estimates, and hold your hand through the whole process. Packaging and layout considerations for CD-ROMs will be discussed in the next section. You will find that producing a CD-ROM is a very straightforward, if somewhat technical process. Some CD manufacturers are listed below:

Disc Manufacturing, Inc.
1409 Foulk Road #200
Wilmington, DE 19803

Discovery Systems
7001 Discovery Blvd.
Dublin, OH 43017

3M Optical Recording
Building 223-5
S-01/3M Center
St. Paul, MN 55144

Nimbus Information Systems
SR 629, Guildford Farm
Ruckersville, VA 22968

DADC
1800 North Fruitridge Avenue
Terre Haute, IN 47804

When producing a CD, you will need to do the following:

- Research and analyze the user's hardware and software environment.
- Design a good interface (see Chapter 15).
- Build a prototype and, before pressing, test a "one-off" made on a compact disc writer such as the Philips CDD-521 or Sony CDW-900E.
- Optimize for speed, determine what files should be moved to the local hard disk, and consult with the disc premasterer.
- Be prepared to get technical.
- Study your production costs.
- Use a search engine.
- Include installation and user documentation with the CD itself.

- Provide at least one gigabyte of local storage for development, and be prepared to ship a hard disk, cartridges, or DAT to the disc premasterer or manufacturer.

Packaging Your Project

Just like a book, many people will first judge your work based on its cover, and then later by what's inside. Sales, marketing, and packaging considerations will influence your multimedia project if it is aimed at consumers. If your product is for your own use, however, you may not need any of the amenities: the pretty cover, a cardboard box, and the shrink-wrap that is required for over-the-counter software. If your product is for a client, you may only need to deliver it on a disk, a removable cartridge, or some other storage medium. But if your project is headed for wider distribution within a large organization, or into retail channels, you will need to pay attention to packaging.

If your project will be sold in the consumer retail channel, then you have made a *title*. Software application titles are most often distributed on floppy disk, multimedia projects on CD-ROM. And your project may be only one item (the most important one) in a package that also includes a user's manual, a registration card, quick reference guides, hardware adapters, and collateral marketing material from you or other parties.

Consumers typically relate the packaging of a product to its quality and price. The fancier, bigger, and heavier the package, the higher its perceived value. Vendors understand this when they set their price points. Many software boxes are shipped with plenty of air or air-filled plastic popcorn inside, shaped by tricky internal die-cut folds and perforated cardboard or open-cell foam to hold fragile disks in place. All this empty space allows the vendor's marketing people some flexibility when setting product price.

Package Covers

The art for your cover should reflect the content and function of the enclosed product; it should also follow the rules for good design layout. Your company's logo should be prominent, of course. And if this is one of a series of titles, the artwork should be coordinated with the style you are using throughout that series or product line. Use photo-quality images and high-caliber artwork for the front face, because this is the most visible face of your package.

When your product reaches the retail channel, it may be displayed on shelves or racks, in kiosks, or it may be hung on brackets. So be sure to put the title's name on the spine as well as the front face of the package. You might also want to put the title's name on the lower part of this front face, so that it will be clearly visible if the package is displayed on angled shelving. If yours is a Multimedia PC (MPC) title, the MPC mark should be displayed on the front in the lower-right corner, on the spine at the bottom, and on the back next to the system requirements (see the section "Multimedia PC Packaging Standards" later in this chapter).

Most retail products are shrink-wrapped in thin plastic to protect the package from fingerprints, damage, and pilferage at the retail outlet. But don't forget that even after the shrink-wrap is on your package, there is still room for additional artwork: Bright stickers can be effective eye-catchers. Some vendors apply special holographic stickers to identify their product and to prevent unauthorized bootleg copies from reaching the marketplace. Figure 18-6 shows some examples of stickers and holograms.

Package Shapes

Some truly unique packaging shapes have been developed to make a product really stand out. Fractal Design Painter, for example, is packaged in a metal paint can with a colorful paper wrapper (see Figure 18-7). In the most typical situation, however, package size and shape options are limited by the constraints of the floor and shelf space found in retail outlets, as well as by the expense of fabricating a nonstandard container.

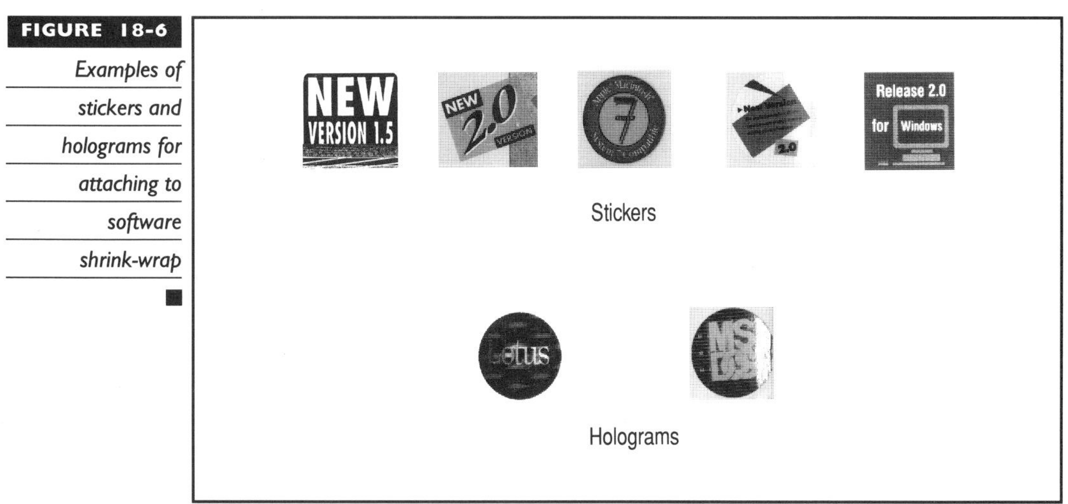

FIGURE 18-6 *Examples of stickers and holograms for attaching to software shrink-wrap*

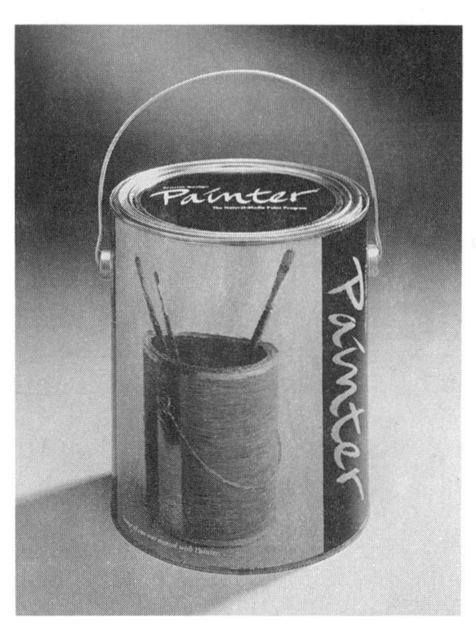

FIGURE 18-7 *Some software comes in interesting packages*

Basic Packaging

Most industrial cities in the United States boast more than one packaging specialist with whom you can consult. These outfits can supply cardboard and plastic boxes, printing, cutting, folding, and wrapping services.

Basic shipping options are as follows:

- Manual and disks shrink-wrapped together
- Cardboard envelope with disks and manual inside
- Cardboard box with disks and manual inside, with or without air filler to make box bigger, and shrink-wrapped
- Cardboard box as described above, enclosed in a slipcover and shrink-wrapped
- Open-ended cardboard box with sliding tray insert containing manual and disks, with or without slipcover
- Open-ended cardboard box with a ring binder containing manual and disks (in plastic sleeves)

Packaging costs can range from about $5 per unit for simple shrink-wrapping (this includes printing costs for a manual and single disk) to more than $50 per unit for elaborate boxes and materials. Be sure to consider the weight and bulk of your package, because even one ounce of extra weight over that allowed for shipping to a certain zone or destination can increase your costs significantly. The outside wrap for shipping should be plain, to discourage pilferage, especially when your product is bound for international destinations where it must clear customs.

Environmentally responsible packaging, especially for compact discs, is becoming popular, and special sleeves and cardboard containers are available. You may find, however, that although the packaging looks rougher and more "natural," there may be no significant cost savings in using these packaging materials over the industry standard jewel box.

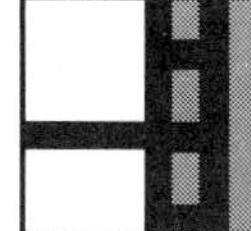

tip *Always ask your packager and shipper about volume discounts and price breaks.*

Multimedia PC Packaging Standards

In addition to establishing and encouraging a standard multimedia computing platform, the Multimedia PC Marketing Council provides guidelines for consistent packaging of MPC software. The Council licenses a special trademark to vendors whose products comply with MPC standards.

The MPC licensing program ensures that consumer-purchased software and hardware products bearing this mark are compatible with the MPC platform and will "plug and play" with no installation hassles. The Multimedia PC Trademark License Agreement defines the permitted uses of the mark with hardware and software products; the Multimedia PC Mark Guidelines clarify the permitted uses of the mark with hardware and software products; and the Multimedia PC Specification defines the minimum MPC hardware configuration. For more information about these standards, contact

Glenn Ochsenreiter
Managing Director
Multimedia PC Marketing Council, Inc.
1730 M Street, Suite 707
Washington, D.C. 20036

MPC Recommended Packaging

The MPC guidelines recommend the following packaging standards:

- **Traditional Software Packaging:** Software priced at or above $59.95 (typically information and productivity titles) should be in traditional software boxes.
- **CD Packaging:** Titles priced below $59.95, especially entertainment titles, should be in CD boxes. Education and consumer information titles, such as shopping catalogs and street maps, should also use this type of packaging.

Traditional software boxes should be 9 to 9.5 inches tall, because standard retail shelves best accommodate this height. The width of the box should be between 6.75 and 6.85 inches; this allows up to seven packages to be displayed face-front on standard shelves that are 48 inches across. The depth of the software box will depend on both the price of the title and the extent of its supporting documentation and other materials. Software titles costing more than $200 should be in boxes that are at least 2 inches deep. All of the above boxes should use a board stock.

Tall CD boxes, usually about 12.25 inches high, are not well suited to display on some types of retail shelves. To overcome this difficulty and still maintain a positive association with the audio CD format, the MPC Council recommends a short CD box about 9 to 9.75 inches tall—approximately the same height as the software box that contains disks and manuals. The height of a standard CD-Audio jewel case is approximately 4.875 inches, making 9.75 inches exactly twice the height of the jewel case. Standard CD box width (5.75 to 6 inches) should be used, with the CD itself housed in the lower part of the package.

CD Packaging

Serious multimedia publishers often use CDs for delivery of their products to end users, leaning heavily upon the successful track record of consumer audio titles. Figure 18-8 shows three common types of CD packages used for consumer audio titles:

- *The long box* (also known as the "6-by-12 box" because of its approximate size) is a thin cardboard box that contains a jewel-cased CD. The box is usually printed with graphics similar to those used on the booklet inside the jewel case, and is usually windowless with glued flaps.

- *The blister pack* is a clear plastic version of the long box. The top half of the package displays the booklet, and the bottom half displays the jewel-boxed compact disc. The long box and blister packs are seldom used for multimedia titles.
- *The poly-overwrapped jewel box* (also called a *cigarette pack* because of the resemblance) is especially popular for mail-order and overseas sales.

These packages are suitable for CD-ROMs, with two qualifications: First, if your title requires more written documentation than can fit in the standard description booklet, then you will need to insert your jewel case into a box that can also accommodate a manual and other paper materials. (Booklets are discussed in an upcoming section.) Second, if you wish to enhance the perceived value of your software on the retail shelf, you will want to distinguish it from less-expensive audio titles.

A popular box size for CDs is 8.5×5.25×1.25 inches, with a glued partition inside. This size accommodates your jewel case as well as a single-folded 8.5×11-inch document up to .75 inch thick. Even products without the extra document often are shipped in boxes this size to clearly define the product as software rather than an audio disc.

Unless a publisher chooses alternative environmentally responsible packaging, most CDs are packaged in a jewel case. Retail furniture and organizing shelves are designed to accommodate libraries of these cases.

FIGURE 18-8

Typical packaging for audio CDs

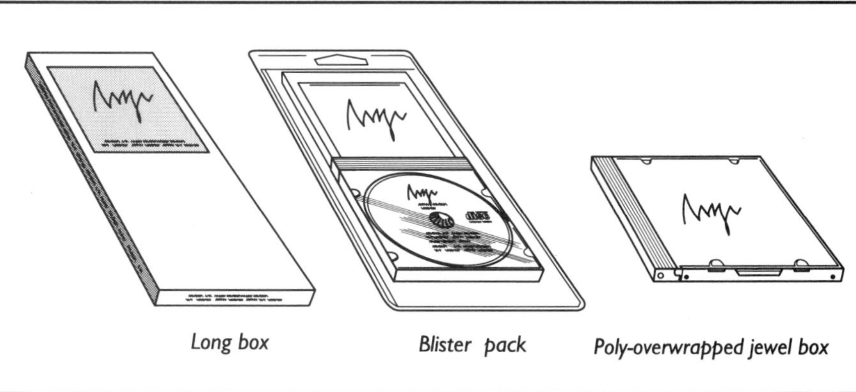

For the disc manufacturer, who usually assembles your entire package, you will need to prepare disc label artwork for silkscreening, printed booklets, and printed inlay cards.

The Disc Label Artwork

The artwork that the disc manufacturer will silk-screen onto the actual disc must be designed to precise dimensions (see Figure 18-9). The white ring in Figure 18-9 shows an area near the hub that cannot be printed; usually the inner hub is left clear as well. The manufacturer will typically place its logo or name and a serial number in very tiny mirrored type between the hub and your artwork. Bear in mind that, because this is a silk-screen process,

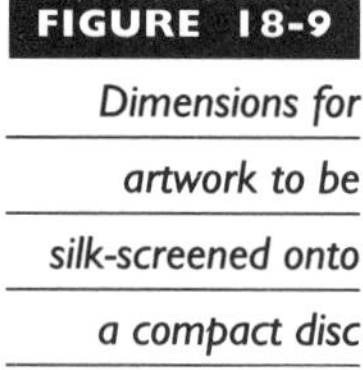

FIGURE 18-9 *Dimensions for artwork to be silk-screened onto a compact disc*

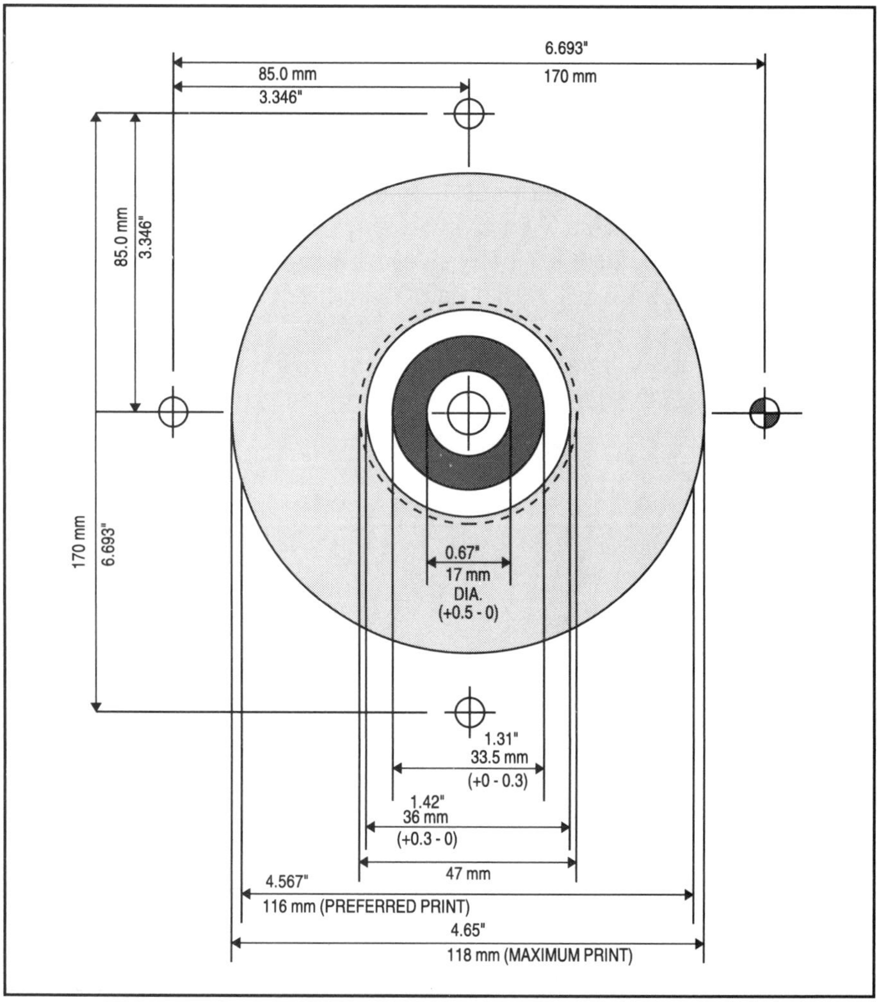

thin lines and spaces, and type smaller than about six points, do not reproduce very well.

The Booklet

Figure 18-10 shows the booklet—the printed material seen through the front of the jewel case. It should show your graphic art, company logo, the product's title, and other information you decide is important. Remember that the booklet cover is what first meets the public's eye, even through the shrink-wrap, and may be as important to your market as any other packaging detail.

The thickness of the booklet must not be greater than 1.5 millimeters (.06 inch) when closed, or it will not fit into the jewel case. Many disc manufacturers recommend using 100-pound opaque, wood-free, text paper that is coated on both sides. The booklet should be folded and stapled with a noncorrosive staple, and should open to the left.

tip *To avoid the cost of a second printing, order a 10 percent overrun of the booklets you order, because printers usually deliver about 10 percent over or under the number of most printed materials ordered.*

FIGURE 18-10

Dimensions for the booklet inserted into the jewel case (the front graphics)

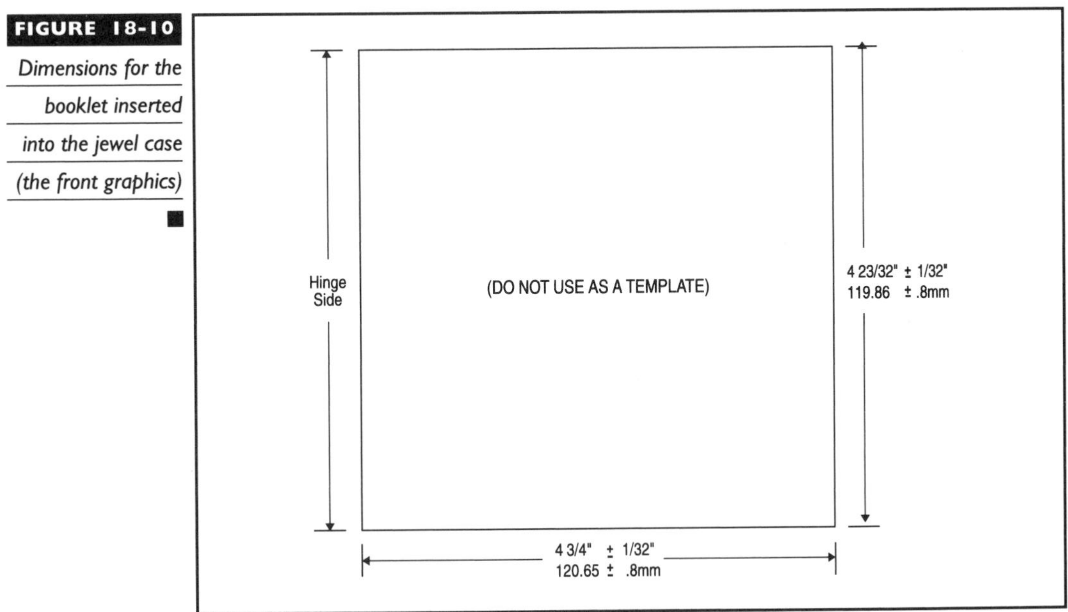

The Inlay Card

The inlay card (see Figure 18-11) is placed in the back of the jewel case. It is printed only on one side, and is folded so that one edge becomes the "spine." When CDs in jewel cases are shelved side by side, it is important for the disc's title to be visible on the spine. On the inlay card you can place technical information such as system requirements or a table of contents.

Displaying System Requirements

To avoid customer confusion and possible disappointment in performance (resulting in complaints, costly service, and product returns), you need to accurately describe the minimum system requirements for your software on the box. Typically these requirements are placed on the back of the package, to conserve the front face of the box for important marketing statements and banners.

Typical system requirements for a Multimedia PC title might be these:

- MS-DOS or PC-DOS operating system version 3.1 or later
- Microsoft Windows 3.1
- Microsoft MS-DOS CD-ROM extensions (MSCDEX) version 2.2 or later
- Multimedia PC or equivalent (includes 80386SX or higher, 2MB RAM, 30MB hard disk, CD-ROM drive, VGA display, audio board, and mouse); or PC with Multimedia PC upgrade kit (CD-ROM drive and audio board)

Typical system requirements for the Macintosh might read as follows:

- Macintosh Plus, Classic, Portable, SE, LC, PowerBook, Quadra, or II family (SE30, LC, II, or Quadra family are recommended)
- 40MB hard disk
- 2MB RAM (4MB with System 7 or for millions of colors)
- System software 6.0.5 or later (System 7 for full use of AppleEvents, publish-and-subscribe, and QuickTime features)
- Support for Apple LaserWriter and other PostScript printers

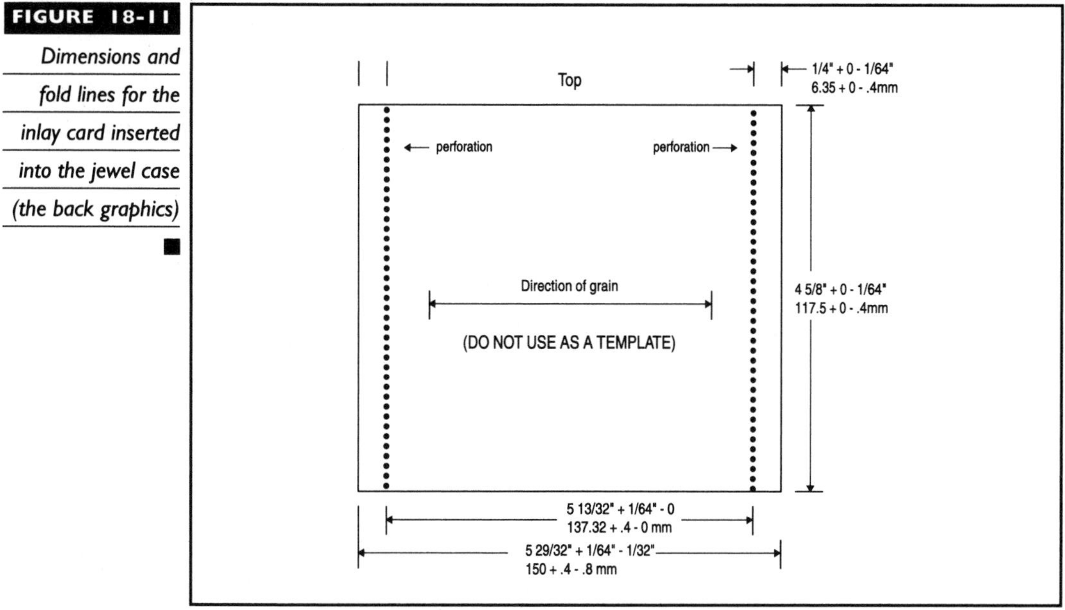

FIGURE 18-11 *Dimensions and fold lines for the inlay card inserted into the jewel case (the back graphics)*

Above all, in stating system hardware requirements, you want to avoid confusing or disappointing the customer. So if you want to recommend higher-performance hardware for improved performance of your product, identify this hardware by including the text "Additional Hardware Recommended" in your system requirements statements. If additional hardware or software is required, clearly state this as "Additional Hardware Required." And if your product requires or takes advantage of special hardware (such as a videodisc player, MIDI interface, or video overlay or compression board), be sure to clearly identify this additional hardware.

Multi

Font libraries are available through retail channels or directly from the manufacturers.

digital typography

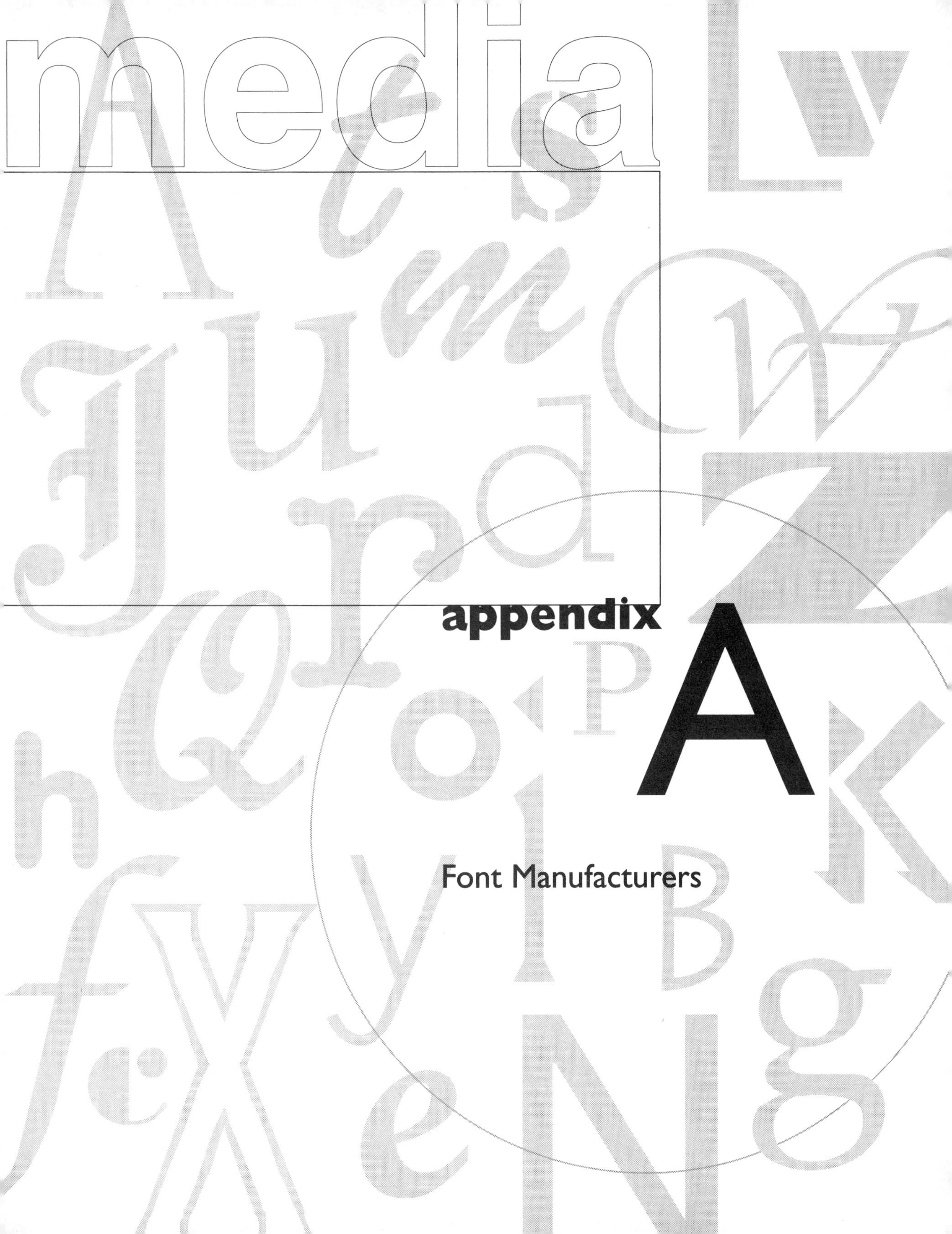

media

appendix

A

Font Manufacturers

FONT libraries are available through retail channels or directly from the manufacturers. The following is a partial list of font manufacturers with descriptions of their collections. For more information about fonts and typefaces, refer to Chapter 9.

Agfa Compugraphic

Agfa Compugraphic
200 Ballardvale Street
Wilmington, MA 01887
(800) 424-TYPE

Agfa Compugraphic is an electronic and photographic pre-press company that creates fonts and font scaling technologies. Agfa's fonts are available on floppy disk, as well as on the AgfaType CD-ROM, a single compact disc containing Agfa's extensive library of fonts along with relevant third-party software applications.

Alphabets & Images, Inc.

Alphabets & Images, Inc.
2620 Central Street
Evanston, IL 60201
(708) 328-7380

Alphabets & Images supplies Ed Benguiat's Personal Collection of fonts. Benguiat is one of the more prolific and successful contemporary type designers, with credits such as *Star Wars* and James Bond movie titles, and with corporate clients including AT&T. The Personal Collection series of fonts comprise 1875 display fonts in volumes of 10 fonts each, for about $100 per volume.

Altsys Corporation

Altsys Corporation
269 W. Renner Road
Richardson, TX 75080
(214) 680-2060

Altsys Corporation provides software solutions for graphic artists, designers, typographers, and publishers. The Metamorphosis Professional (Meta Pro) application from Altsys produces TrueType fonts from existing font formats. Meta Pro and Altsys's Fontographer, a font design application, provide a complete TrueType font development environment and were discussed in Chapter 9.

Ares Software

Ares Software
P.O. Box 4667
Foster City, CA 94404
(415) 578-9090

FontMonger software from Ares Software converts existing Macintosh fonts into TrueType fonts. It also allows you to exchange character outlines with graphics applications. FontMonger offers a unique range of capabilities, including access to unencoded characters, true small capitals, superscript and subscript characters, and fractions. Type transformations can be rendered on a single character, multiple characters, or the entire font.

Bitstream, Inc.

Bitstream, Inc.
215 First Street
Cambridge, MA 02142-1270
(800) 237-3335

The Bitstream Type Treasury offers over 1000 typefaces in PostScript Type 1 format for the Macintosh, and a selection of 40 TrueType faces, all on one CD-ROM disc. With a phone call, users can purchase the codes to unlock the faces. The suggested U.S. list price for this disc is $69; you get the CD and can choose six typefaces to unlock, free, from a group of 20. You can unlock additional typefaces from the disc for about $30 each.

Casady & Greene, Inc.

Casady & Greene, Inc.
22734 Portola Drive
Salinas, CA 93908
(408) 484-9228

Casady & Greene offers over 100 Type 1 typefaces. The Fluent Laser Fonts Library includes 81 Postscript Type 1 typefaces and comprises a variety of display and text faces. On the Macintosh, the Library includes TrueType versions of the faces. On the IBM PC–compatible version, the Library includes ATM by Adobe for Windows.

Emigre Fonts

Emigre Fonts
4475 D Street
Sacramento, CA 95819-2840
(800) 944-9021

Emigre has been developing high-quality, original typefaces since 1985 and is a pioneer in the areas of graphic design and digital typography. Emigre offers 80 original typefaces available in PostScript Type 1 and TrueType formats for Macintosh and PC computers. Emigre Fonts have been seen in the opening titles of *Batman Returns,* in Nike television commercials, the *New York Times,* the *Boston Globe,* and *Esquire,* and on MTV.

FontBank

FontBank
2620 Central Street
Evanston, IL 60201
(708) 328-7370

FontBank specializes in display typefaces in PostScript and TrueType for use as headlines and titles and for other large, attention-grabbing type. The collection includes traditional, novelty, decorative, specialty, brush, calligraphic, and script typefaces. Currently, FontBank has 325 typefaces in two libraries. The basic library costs about $95.

Image Club Graphics, Inc.

Image Club Graphics, Inc.
1902 Eleventh Street Southeast, Suite 5
Calgary, Alberta, T2G 3G2
Canada

Image Club Typeface Library for the Macintosh contains 635 fonts in Type 1 and Type 3 PostScript, and TrueType. These fonts are very expensive, and they are available on disk, in FontPaks, and on the LetterPress CD-ROM.

International Typeface Corporation

International Typeface Corporation
866 Second Avenue
New York, NY 10017
(212) 371-0699
Fax (212) 752-4752

International Typeface Corporation (ITC) is a leading source of new typeface designs. The more than 550 text and display typefaces in ITC's typeface library are available today from more than 125 licensed manufacturers of typeface fonts (for both Macintosh- and PC-compatible platforms); laser printers; desktop publishing software; typesetting, video, and sign-making equipment; and dry transfer letterform sheets. ITC is a subsidiary of Esselte Letraset.

Kingsley/ATF Type Corporation

Kingsley/ATF Type Corporation
2559-2 E. Broadway
Tucson, AZ 85716
(800) 289-8973

Kingsley/ATF offers a large digital font library in PostScript and TrueType formats. Each font package includes the outline, kerning, and metric data, and selected bitmaps. If you want to design your own fonts, Kingsley/ATF offers ATF Type Designer I, a fully integrated type design system that supports standard font formats.

Letraset

Letraset
40 Eisenhower Drive
Paramus, NJ 07653
(800) 343-TYPE

Letraset provides TrueType and other fonts. They also distribute a powerful typographer's tool, FontStudio, for making your own fonts and special typographic effects. FontStudio is described and illustrated in Chapter 9.

Linotype-Hell Company

Linotype-Hell Company
425 Oser Avenue
Hauppauge, NY 11788
(516) 434-2684

Linotype-Hell is one of the world's leading manufacturers of typesetting equipment and publishing systems and solutions. The Linotype Library consists of more than 2000 typefaces, including original designs and licensed faces from leading designers and foundries around the world. Faces such as Frutiger, Helvetica, Palatino, Optima, Times, and Univers are part of the Linotype Library. Many Linotype fonts are available in Type 3 PostScript and TrueType formats.

Monotype Typography

Monotype Typography
53 W. Jackson Blvd., Suite 504
Chicago, IL 60604
(800) 666-6897

The Monotype Typeface Library is a comprehensive font collection, including Times New Roman (the original font designed by Monotype for the *London Times* in 1931), Bembo, Gill Sans, Plantin, and Rockwell. Monotype typefaces are also available on a single CD-ROM—the Monotype FoneFonts CD-ROM—which contains over 1450 typefaces, including fonts from Adobe and Font Bureau. The fonts are "locked" and can be purchased with a phone call to Monotype or a selected type reseller. The FoneFonts disk has a suggested list price of $49.99, which includes your choice of eight fonts from a selected list of 32 typefaces. Monotype fonts are sold in other packages, too, at various prices, and some include an illustrated design guide, publishing guide, glossary, and two type specimen booklets.

U-Design Type Foundry

U-Design Type Foundry
270 Farmington Avenue
Hartford, CT 06105
(203) 278-3648
Fax (203) 278-3003

U-Design Type Foundry (UTF) specializes in Picture Fonts, historic revivals, and original display fonts. Some fonts, reminiscent of New York's Great White Way in the Gatsby era, include Bill's Brushed Broadway (a sign-painterly display face), and Bill's Broadway DECOrations in Type 1 PostScript format. There are also characters, symbols, and border elements drawn from the New York Moderne school of art deco design, with a theatrical theme. Included in the symbols are showgirls, musicians, bon vivants, masks, spotlights, taxis, East Hampton speedboats, luxury liners, marquee borders, and architectural finials. UTF fonts cost about $30 each.

Multimedia resources

[...many new training programs are being developed in response to the increasing popularity and definition of multimedia.]

appendix B

Multimedia Training Providers

Khalsa Productions, Phoenix, Arizona

(602) 678-0713

Khalsa Productions specializes in video and QuickTime, with training and consulting performed on a project basis.

Mac Training Consortium, Raleigh, North Carolina

(919) 833-7161

Mac Training Consortium provides "high-end" Macintosh applications training in intensive workshop formats with a hands-on training approach.

OmniCom Associates, Ithaca, New York

(607) 272-7700

OmniCom Associates provides custom workshops, executive briefings, and consultation on multimedia development and management.

Preston Media Associates, Oakland, California

(510) 482-4509

Preston Media offers workshops and consulting support to schools, businesses, and nonprofits in all aspects of multimedia design, implementation, and networking.

SGI Technologies Group, North Haven, Connecticut

(800) 852-8111

SGI Technologies Group provides training in all forms of professional, industrial, and corporate digital communications.

THIS appendix provides names and descriptions of some of the colleges and organizations offering courses or curriculums related to multimedia. This is by no means a complete survey of multimedia training resources; many new programs are being developed in response to the increasing popularity and definition of multimedia.

College Multimedia Programs

The following list includes some academic programs in multimedia tools and technology that are available from universities and colleges.

The Georgia Institute of Technology, Atlanta, Georgia
(404) 894-8556

Georgia Tech offers about a dozen courses through its Continuing Education program covering design, theory, production, and applications. A Certificate in Multimedia can be earned.

New York University, Tisch School of Arts, Manhattan
(212) 998-1880

As part of its Telecommunications Program, NYU offers a two-year master's program that integrates some multimedia elements.

Massachusetts Institute of Technology, Media Lab, Cambridge, Massachusetts
(617) 253-5114

MIT offers a 12-month graduate program in Media Arts and Sciences geared more toward theoretical than applied multimedia issues.

Columbia College, Chicago, Illinois
(312) 663-1600

Columbia College is one of the first schools in the country to offer undergraduates a multimedia major.

Bloomsburg University, Bloomsburg, Pennsylvania
(717) 389-2094

Bloomsburg University operates the Institute for Interactive Technologies for master's degree candidates interested in instructional design and multimedia authoring tools.

Florida State University, Tallahassee, Florida
(904) 644-8742

Florida State University offers a master's degree program in Interactive Communication that provides experience in the design, production, and marketing of multimedia products and online services.

San Francisco State University, Extended Education, Multimedia Studies Program, San Francisco, California
(415) 904-7700

The Multimedia Studies Program at the San Francisco State University Extension Division offers over 50 classes in multimedia: from writing and design to business and marketing.

Stanford University, Stanford Media Integration Lab for Education (SMILE), Stanford, California
(415) 329-1316

SMILE consists of a computer classroom, a curriculum development lab, and a public computer cluster intended to serve as a crucible where faculty, students, and staff can receive individual instruction in multimedia and also collaborate in developing media-based curriculum materials.

University of California Extension: Berkeley, Los Angeles, Santa Cruz
(510) 642-4111, (213) 343-3000, (408) 427-6600

These three University of California Extension programs offer some multimedia classes and developer-specific multimedia programs.

Other Multimedia Training Providers

The following list contains the names of a fraction of the more than 500 training providers that provide highly focused, specialized instruction on a variety of multimedia tools.

The Acacia Group, Long Beach, California
(310) 437-7690

The Acacia Group offers custom courseware and instructor-led training in graphics, information management, media integration, telecommunications, and more.

American Film Institute, Advanced Technology Programs, Los Angeles, California
(213) 856-7600

AFI offers "Computer Media Salons" consisting of classes and workshops for professionals in film, television, and new media arts.

Center for Creative Imaging, Camden, Maine
(207) 236-7490

CCI offers classes in multimedia design, production and authoring, desktop video tools, and desktop video post-production.

Diversified Media Design, East Chatham, New York
(518) 766-5940

Diversified Media Design offers training in audio recording for multimedia, video production, and all aspects of Macromedia Director.

Emerging Technology Consultants, St. Paul, Minnesota
(612) 639-3973

Emerging Technology Consultants provides multimedia support and training for educational institutions and companies, focusing on interactive videodisc and related products.

Khalsa Productions, Phoenix, Arizona
(602) 678-0743

Khalsa Productions specializes in video and QuickTime, with training and consulting performed on a project basis.

Mac Training Consortium, Raleigh, North Carolina
(919) 833-7161

Mac Training Consortium provides "high-end" Macintosh applications training in intensive workshop formats with a hands-on training approach.

OmniCom Associates, Ithaca, New York
(607) 272-7700

OmniCom Associates provides custom workshops, executive briefings, and consultation on multimedia development and management.

Preston Media Associates, Oakland, California
(510) 482-4599

Preston Media offers workshops and consulting support to schools, businesses, and nonprofit organizations in all aspects of multimedia design, implementation, and networking.

SGI Technologies Group, North Haven, Connecticut
(800) 852-8441

SGI Technologies Group provides training in all forms of professional, industrial, and corporate digital communications.

Tech Museum of Innovation, San Jose, California
(408) 279-7174

The Tech Museum provides multimedia training for teachers. It takes a hands-on approach to learning technology and to the integration of technology into the classroom curriculum.

Wheeler Multimedia Consulting, Chicago, Illinois

(312) 728-9714

Wheeler Multimedia Consulting offers customized training and consulting services, with product support services designed to help finish projects on time and add extra features or effects.

Multi

In time, multimedia will pervade all aspects of our lives.

revolutionizing

appendix C

Macromedia Product Reference

Macromedia's tools power the ideas that are revolutionizing the way people learn and communicate.

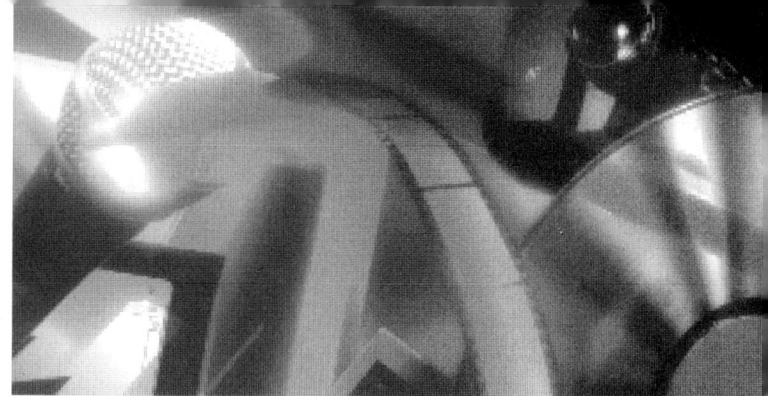

MACROMEDIA develops and markets leading software tools for creating multimedia applications. Offered on both Windows and Macintosh platforms, these products are used by organizations to create and deliver interactive programs that utilize a full range of media—from text and graphics to animation, video, and sound. Macromedia's tools power the ideas that are revolutionizing the way people learn and communicate. These tools and demonstrations of their use are available on the Macromedia Product Showcase CD-ROM included with this book. This Appendix includes case-history and "insider" material about Macromedia as a business, Macromedia's market strategy, and its line of products for the multimedia industry.

Macromedia—The Company

Macromedia was formed in April, 1992, by the merger of Authorware and MacroMindParacomp. MacroMind was founded in 1984 and merged with Paracomp in 1991. Authorware began operations in 1987. Macromedia's strategic equity grew from a shared vision across these companies that computers would have a strong impact on the art of communication. This vision was supplemented by extensive research of the creative process across a broad range of disciplines, including choreography, opera, painting, architecture, and music.

The results of this research powered the development of a family of software tools used by more than 100,000 professional developers and enthusiasts, and by more than one million business users and enthusiasts today. Macromedia's animation, authoring, and presentation strengths are evident in industry-leading products Director and Action!. Innovative 3-D graphics and animation technologies are the hallmark of very popular desktop visualization and design products such as Swivel 3D and MacroModel. And Authorware Professional's breakthrough authoring and media management tools enable nonprogrammers to create sophisticated training and education programs. Today, more than 50 percent of the leading Macintosh CD-ROM multimedia titles and a growing number of Windows titles are made with Macromedia tools.

In addition to developing and marketing multimedia software, Macromedia provides its customers with valuable technical support services; and its authorized domestic network of more than 200 value-added resellers, 100 trainers, and 300 developers offer customers expertise in the design and development of multimedia applications that are being enjoyed by millions of people around the world.

Macromedia has enjoyed significant growth in the last three years with revenues increasing at two times the PC software industry average. The company is profitable, employing more than 150 people worldwide, and is traded on NASDAQ under the symbol MACR. Based in San Francisco, California, Macromedia has more than 50 distribution partners in Asia, Canada, Latin America, Europe, and the Middle East.

Market Opportunity

Multimedia is revolutionizing the way we work, learn, and play. By combining text, sound, animation, and images, it engages multiple senses and enables people to interact with information in a richer, more natural way. In time, multimedia will pervade all aspects of our lives: we will communicate with our co-workers through voice and video mail messages; our home or office computers will scan wire services, newspapers, and television programs to create personalized news; and companies and schools will offer interactive courses that allow students to explore learning material at their own pace.

The fundamental hardware technologies for multimedia—including fast processors, audio support, high-resolution color displays, CD-ROM drives, high speed networks, and fiber-optic cable—exist today. New system software extensions, such as Apple's QuickTime and Microsoft's Video for Windows, provide built-in interfaces, digital media support, and compression capabilities to the general computing environment. Effective authoring, presentation, and media creation software takes advantage of these capabilities and allows the user to create quality interactive content.

In addition, the leading systems vendors—Apple, IBM, Microsoft, and Intel—are providing multimedia technologies for both professional and personal users on all major computing platforms. Multimedia systems are becoming widely available for business, education, and home use. Approximately 3.5 million MPC-compatible personal computers and two million multimedia-capable Macintosh computers were installed in 1993; by the end of 1995, more than 15 million Windows and Macintosh-based PCs will be capable of playing multimedia titles.

As multimedia gains consumer acceptance, and organizations realize performance and cost savings, the opportunity for interactive software continues to grow. Already, simple and effective authoring programs and quality titles in the form of shrink-wrapped interactive books, games, and lessons are becoming high-volume items. Approximately 1,000 titles are available today on Windows and Macintosh, and GISTICS (a market research company) estimates that more than 3,000 titles are now under development. By conservative estimates, more than 5,000 titles will be available by 1995. At the same time, total unit sales of CD-ROM titles are expected to climb from 2.5 million in 1992 to 37.2 units million by 1995.

Dataquest, a market research group in San Jose, California, reports the market for Windows and Macintosh multimedia authoring software was $40 million in 1992, and projects its growth to $150 million by 1995. Macromedia estimates the market for multimedia 3-D graphics tools on Macintosh and Windows will grow from $38 million to $80 million by 1995.

Macromedia's Business Strategy

Macromedia's business strategy leverages the evolving opportunities for multimedia software, for professional and personal use. By initially focusing on the need for professional multimedia software to build corporate learning applications and presentations, the company exploited a market segment and established a strong international reputation with leading corporate, independent, and educational customers. Its flagship authoring tools—Authorware Professional and Macromedia Director—are far and away the market leaders in their categories. And its premier 3-D graphics tool—MacroModel—is the most comprehensive 3-D design tool available for Windows and Macintosh-based computers.

To meet the needs of a more general market, Macromedia continues to adapt its products and services as opportunities for multimedia broaden to personal use. For example, the company released Action!—software for creating business presentations with sound, motion, and interactivity. Awarded Editors' Choice by *PC Magazine* (September 12, 1993) in the desktop presentations category, Action! has enjoyed great success with more than one million units shipped.

Macromedia has also built international strategic alliances with leading systems providers to gain broad distribution and establish its products as the standard for creating interactive productions. More than 25 strategic alliances were signed in 1993 and 1994, including Apple Computer, 3DO, Paramount Publishing/Prentice Hall, Bell Labs, Bell Atlantic, Brøderbund, Kaleida, HyperMedia Communications, Macmillan/McGraw-Hill, Jostens Learning, LifeTouch Learning, and others.

In order to build strong brand awareness of Macromedia and its products, the company encourages titles publishers to carry the "Made with Macromedia" seal of excellence on their commercial titles. This seal identifies products created with the most advanced multimedia technology available, and enables publishers to benefit from Macromedia's extensive comarketing efforts.

Macromedia has strong authorized programs for value-added resellers, trainers, and developers and continues to build a preferred channel for professional multimedia software solutions. For personal technologies, the company works closely with retail distribution, mail order, and mass merchants to bring its products to mainstream users.

Macromedia also enjoys a high level of direct communication with its end users. The annual Macromedia International User Conference draws top developers and publishers demonstrating and discussing the latest in multimedia technology. Macromedia also offers world-class technical training, consulting, and support services and has active user communication via online bulletin boards.

Technological Leadership

Macromedia focuses its product development efforts on creating a family of multiplatform authoring software for creative and learning professionals, and multiplatform playback software for personal computers and consumer players. Its products are distinguished by four key design strategies:

- *Power:* Broad feature sets combined with high performance provide the efficiency necessary for both professional and personal use.
- *Platform Independence:* Software is available on the leading desktop platforms, for maximum flexibility in both creation and distribution.
- *Interoperability:* A family of products whose interfaces are well designed to directly share both media and structure.
- *System Savviness:* Software supports extensions for digital media compression, device control and inter-application control.

Currently, Macromedia offers the only off-the-shelf authoring tools that support cross-platform playback on both Macintosh and Windows personal computers—and that is just the beginning. As the multimedia industry growth expands, Macromedia will continue to support platform leaders including Windows, Macintosh, 3DO, and other consumer and set-top platforms. Macromedia's multimedia software will continue to provide a standard that ensures maximum playback options for multimedia developers.

The company's principal product development efforts include developing enhanced versions of its existing authoring tools, integrating its 3-D technology into its authoring tools to meet the anticipated demand for such capabilities, adapting its products to support new operating systems, and developing players for delivery of applications on new playback platforms. To support the engineering of its products on multiple platforms in an efficient manner, Macromedia has developed core software components that can be shared across the different platforms.

Macromedia Products

Macromedia provides award-winning multimedia software for personal and professional use on a range of hardware platforms. These tools have been recognized by the press as leaders in their categories. According to a recent study by GISTICS, Macromedia products are being used by more than 60 percent of today's multimedia developers.

Authorware Professional for Macintosh and Windows (Authoring)

The premier multimedia authoring tool for interactive learning gives nonprogrammers the power to create, deliver, and maintain applications on Macintosh and Windows platforms without scripting. Its powerful object-oriented programming and media management features have made it an enterprise standard.

Application: *Authorware*
Macintosh Pathname: *MACROMEDIA :Product Demonstrations :APM Demo :Authorware Professionsl*
Windows Pathname: *After installing the Showcase CD, click on the appropriate icon in the Windows*

Macromedia Showcase CD Program Group for Newton's Apple APW Demo, City of Novato APW Demo, and Authorware Working Model Demo.

Macromedia Director for Macintosh and Windows (Authoring)

The most powerful authoring tool for multimedia production, Director is the program-of-choice for more than 100,000 multimedia developers. Director offers complete control over animation, high-fidelity sound, QuickTime movies, video, text, and graphics and provides a complete scripting language for extensive interactivity and maximum flexibility.

Application: *Director*
Macintosh Pathname: *MACROMEDIA :Product Demonstrations :Director Demo :MacroMind Director 3.1.1 (SD)*
Macintosh Pathname: *MACROMEDIA :Director 4.0 Save Disabled :Director 4.0 Demo*
Windows Pathname: *After installing the Showcase CD, click on the Showcase CD Version 2 icon in the Windows Macromedia Showcase CD Program Group.*

MacroModel for Macintosh and Windows (3-D Graphics)

The most comprehensive 3-D modeling program for the Macintosh, MacroModel enables users to intuitively create 3-D models from 2-D reference objects with a click of the mouse. Its wide range of capabilities makes it suitable for creating 3-D illustrations for desktop publishing and CAD-accurate product prototyping as well as for the everyday needs of multimedia production artists.

Application: *MacroModel*
Macintosh Pathname: *MACROMEDIA :Product Demonstrations :MacroModel Demo ::MacroModel DEMO 1.0.0.*
Windows Pathname: *After installing the Showcase CD, click on the Showcase CD Version 2 icon in the*

Windows Macromedia Showcase CD Program Group.

Action! for Macintosh and Windows (Presentation)

This revolutionary application lets business computer users create dazzling multimedia presentations. Action! makes it easy to combine sound, video, text, graphics, animation, and interactivity to produce professional-quality, high-impact presentations.

Application: *Action*
Macintosh Pathname: *MACROMEDIA :Product Demonstrations :Action Demo :Action demo disk :Action! Demonstration*
Windows Pathname: *After installing the Showcase CD, click on the Action! Working Model Demo icon in the Windows Macromedia Showcase CD Program Group.*

SoundEdit 16 and SoundEdit 8 (Sound)

The premier sound editing tools for multimedia production as well as educational and engineering markets.

Application: *SoundEdit*
Macintosh Pathname: *MACROMEDIA :Product Demonstrations :SoundEdit Pro SD*
Windows Pathname: *N/A—Macintosh only*

Swivel 3D Pro, Three-D, ModelShop II, Life Forms (3-D Graphics)

Breakthrough technologies that combine a simple user interface with powerful capabilities to foster creativity, increase productivity, and maximize the impact of your designs.

Application: *Swivel 3D Pro*
Macintosh Pathname: *MACROMEDIA :Product Demonstrations :Other 3D Demo App's :Swivel 3D Pro*
Windows Pathname: *N/A—Macintosh only*

Application: *ModelShop*
Macintosh Pathname: *MACROMEDIA :Product Demonstrations :Other 3D Demo App's :ModelShop II :ModelShop II 1.2 C DEMO*
Windows Pathname: *N/A—Macintosh only*

CD-ROM

Application: *Life Forms*
Macintosh Pathname: *MACROMEDIA :Product Demonstrations :Other 3D Demo App's :Life Forms Demo*
Windows Pathname: *N/A—Macintosh only*

ClipMedia for Macintosh and Windows (Content)

High-quality media without royalty or license restrictions that can be used and modified over and over again in multimedia presentations and productions.

Macromedia Users

Macromedia's interactive software is used by major corporations, government agencies, educational institutions, leading publishers, and independent producers worldwide, including

CORPORATE American Airlines, Australia Funds Management, Procter & Gamble, 3M, Nike, Tokyo Gas, Marriott Corp., Northern Telecom, Steelcase, Mitsubishi, Ernst & Young, Levis, Boeing Company, Mercury Telecom, Deutsches Bank, Kobe Steel, Chiat/Day Advertising;

GOVERNMENT U.S. Department of Defense, Federal Aviation Administration, Central Intelligence Agency, NASA, German Bundespost, French Army, Australian Submarine Corp., Singapore Defense Agency;

EDUCATION University of Nottingham, The Ohio State University, New York University, The University System of Georgia, Sendai Group of Japan, University of Alberta, TAFE;

PUBLISHING Jostens Learning, LifeTouch Learning, IDG Publications, Macmillan/McGraw-Hill, Brøderbund, Porcupine, Viacom International, Houghton-Mifflin, Voyager Company;

INDEPENDENT Aaron Marcus & Associates, Against All Odds, Reactor Corporation, Printz Electronic Design, Roger East Design, Clement Mok Designs, Magnum Designs, Drew Pictures, Timestream, ICONOS, The Human Element, and many more.

Here are some other examples of how customers are using Macromedia tools:

- American Airlines, the world's leading airline, uses Authorware Professional to educate and train 50,000 of its 90,000 employees annually. Authorware applications replaced 300 hours of training with 147 hours of interactive multimedia.
- Kobe Steel, Ltd., a Japanese steel manufacturer, used Director, Swivel 3D, and SoundEdit to develop a sales presentation (see Figure 1-2) to overcome the communication barriers of international business. The presentation incorporates extensive animation to explain the steel production process, takes prospects on a "guided tour" of the factory, and even calculates the cost of a new factory on the spot.

Application: *Director / Authorware*
Macintosh Pathname: *MACROMEDIA :SltnDems :KbeStl :KbeDem*
Windows Pathname: *SHOWCASE_CD \MACROMED \ATHWRDEM \NEWTONS \NEWTONLE.EXE*

- The United States Central Intelligence Agency (CIA) uses Authorware Professional to create language learning courses for its employees. The agency teamed up with Analysas Corp. in Washington D.C. to make these state-of-the-art courses available to the public.
- Brøderbund Software, Inc., uses Director to design and author its popular line of CD-ROM–based Living Books. These titles, including Just Grandma and Me (see Figure 1-4), Arthur's Teacher Trouble, and The Tortoise and the Hare have won critical acclaim, and are frequently cited as examples of quality multimedia titles.
- The Cincinnati Art Museum used Authorware Professional to create Interactions, an interactive multimedia kiosk. The kiosk takes the visitor through more than 70 of the museum's 19th century European and American paintings, providing details about the artists' lives as well as information about the historical and cultural milieu of the period.

- Drew Pictures, Inc., a developer of interactive CD-ROM titles, used Director, MacroModel, Swivel 3D, and SoundEdit to produce Iron Helix, a photo-realistic adventure in full-motion 3-D. The application combines the fast-paced arcade style of a video game with cinematic graphics and the original score of a movie.

Authorware and Director are registered trademarks, and Macromedia, Authorware Professional, Action!, ClipMedia, MacRecorder, Three-D, MacroModel, MediaMaker, SoundEdit and Star are trademarks of Macromedia, Inc. Swivel 3D and Swivel 3D Professional are trademarks of VPL Research, Inc. Life Forms is a trademark of Kinetic Effects, Inc., with exclusive license to Macromedia, Inc. All other trademarks or registered trademarks are the property of their respective holders.

Multi

The Showcase is an excellent way to experience the power of multimedia...

hands-on
product overview

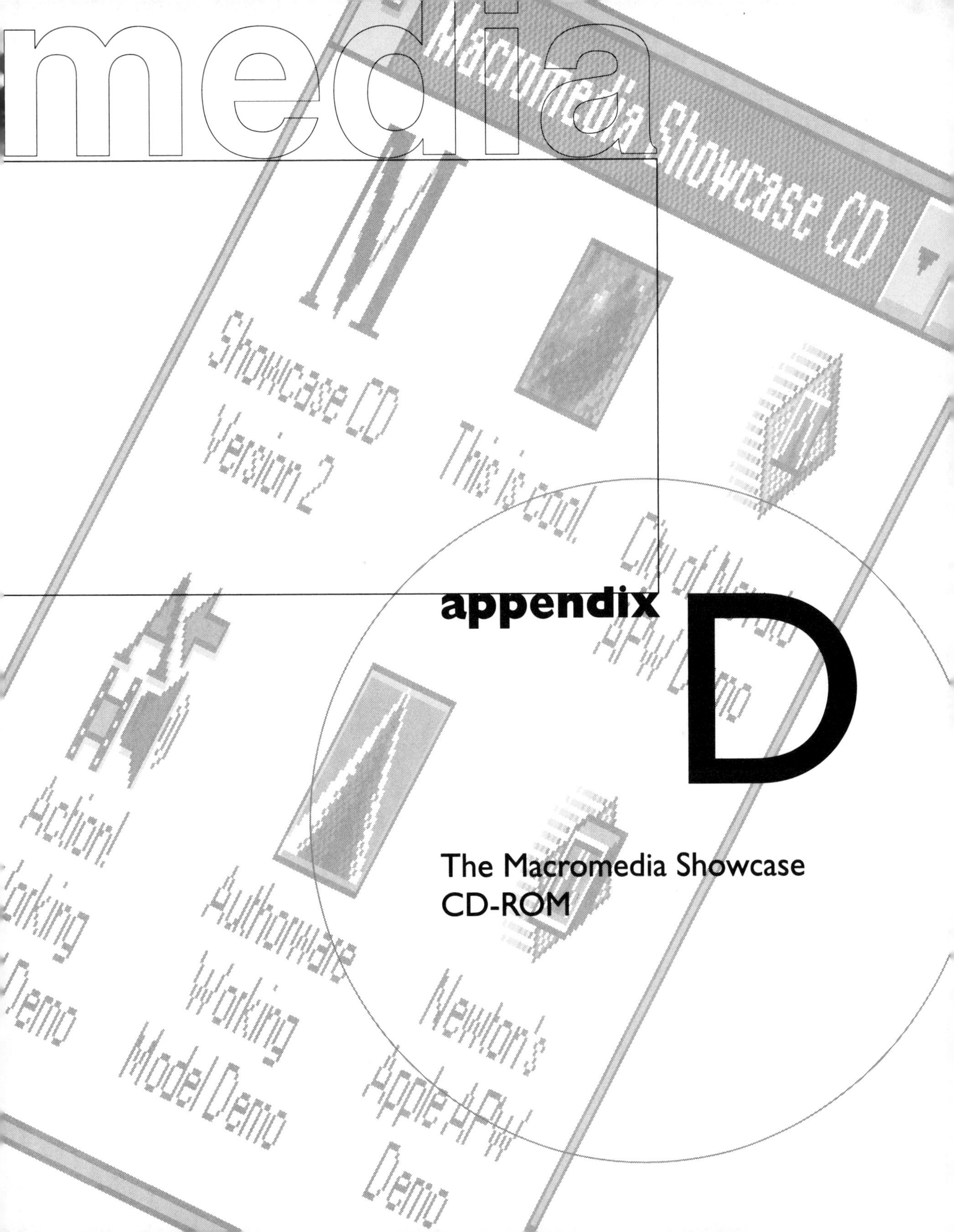

appendix D

The Macromedia Showcase CD-ROM

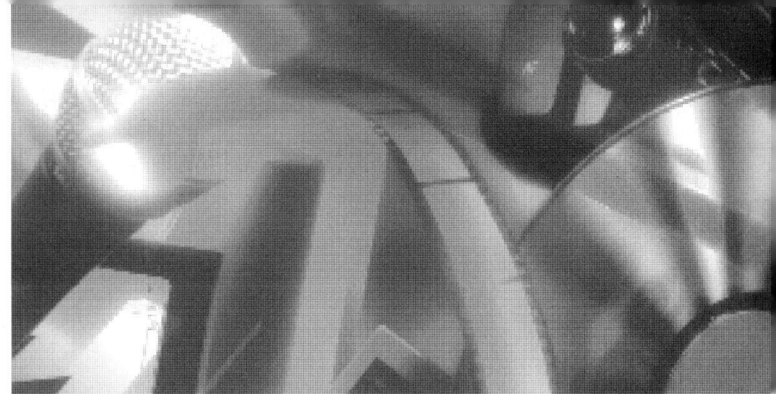

THE Product Showcase CD-ROM from Macromedia is an eye-catching interactive multimedia vehicle ready to transport you through hands-on product and solution overviews, digital-video success stories from star developers, working models of Macromedia software, product ordering and compatibility information, and demo versions of titles made with Macromedia tools. The Showcase is simple enough for customers to use on their own, powerful enough to be used as a reseller sales-support tool, and flexible enough to be used by retailers as a stand-alone multimedia kiosk. The Showcase is an excellent way to experience the power of multimedia and the many ways you can apply it to your needs.

The Showcase provides a detailed interactive road map to Macromedia's products and services as well as many product demonstration files that take you step by step through the most popular programs including Action!, Authorware Professional, Director, and MacroModel. The Showcase CD also includes an interactive catalog (in a Macromedia Director file named *mmWork*) containing all of Osborne/McGraw-Hill's computer books and title ordering information.

Application: *Director*
Subject: *Osborne/McGraw-Hill Catalog*
Macintosh Pathname: *MACROMEDIA :SHOWCASE :mmWork*
Windows Pathname: *After installing the Showcase CD, click on the Showcase CD Version 2 icon in the Windows Macromedia Showcase CD Program Group.*

Version 2 of the Showcase, included in this second edition of Tay Vaughan's *Multimedia: Making It Work,* was developed for the Macintosh platform in two months' time by Macromedia with the help of outside contractors. In just 15 days, this complex project was then converted to the Windows platform using Director Player for Windows. The Macintosh and the Windows versions share space on the same hybrid-format CD-ROM, so you can launch applications for either platform from the same disc.

Macromedia maintains that the Showcase CD-ROM is the most efficient way to provide customers with detailed information and examples about Macromedia's extensive line of multimedia software. The Showcase application, claims Macromedia, cost $25,000 to develop, and less than $2 for each disc replicated thereafter.

How to Use the Showcase CD-ROM

The Showcase disc is an interactive Director presentation. The CD-ROM has been partitioned for both Apple Macintosh and Microsoft Windows operating systems.

Hybrid CD-ROMs

Macintosh CD-ROMs use Apple's HFS (Hierarchical File Structure) format for laying out the table of contents and data files. CD-ROMs for DOS and Windows use the International Standards Organization format (ISO 9660). Both formats are simply different methods of organizing the digital information contained on the CD-ROM. For example, ISO 9660 limits users to filenames with eight characters and a three-character extender (standard DOS convention); HFS allows filenames as long as 32 characters (standard Macintosh convention). Hybrid CD-ROMs are made with two separate partitions, one that is ISO 9660, another that is Mac HFS. They will play on both PCs and Macs. The Macromedia Showcase2 CD-ROM enclosed with this book is a hybrid disc.

For Macintosh Users

Double-click on the START HERE file icon in the Showcase folder, and you're off and running!

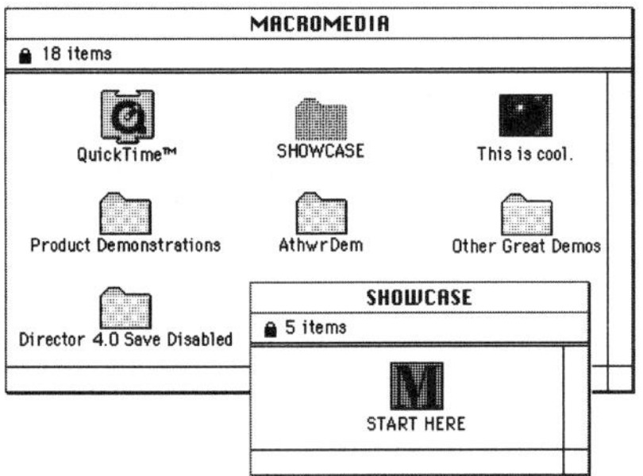

Performance Improvement for Macintosh

Showcase has been optimized for playback from CD-ROM. However, to further improve performance, choose one of the following options:

FIRST OPTION Copy the showcase folder to your hard disk (requires about 8.7MB of free disk space) by following these steps:

1. Copy only the SHOWCASE FOLDER to your hard drive (other folders remain on the CD-ROM).
2. Double-click on the START HERE projector in the SHOWCASE FOLDER (now on your hard drive) to begin.

SECOND OPTION Copy the entire contents of the Showcase CD-ROM to the root level of your hard disk (requires about 250MB of free disk space) by following these steps:

1. Copy all files from the Showcase CD-ROM to the root level of your hard disk.
2. Eject the CD-ROM.
3. Rename your hard disk to MACROMEDIA (Required!).
4. Double-click on the START HERE projector to begin.

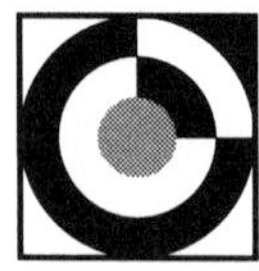

warning *This CD-ROM requiires that your color depth is set to 8-bit. Open your monitor's control panel and choose 256 colors.*

QuickTime Users

To run Showcase on a Macintosh, the QuickTime 1.5 extension must be installed in your system (System 6.07 or higher). The QuickTime extension is included on this CD-ROM. To install QuickTime, just drag the QuickTime extension into your System Folder and restart your computer.

For Windows Users

The Showcase is an interactive Director Player for Windows 3.1 presentation. To run this presentation on your PC, the QuickTime for Windows 1.0 drivers and the DPW.INI file must be installed in your system. You can do this automatically by opening the File Manager application and running the SETUP.EXE program found on the root directory of the Showcase CD-ROM. The setup program will examine your system and install the required software (after asking your permission). It will also create a Program Group and Windows Icons for the Showcase, product demonstrations, and working models. Make sure that you reboot your system (after running the SETUP program) before proceeding.

After you have successfully installed the Showcase CD-ROM, you can start the Showcase by double-clicking on the "Showcase CD Version 2" icon.

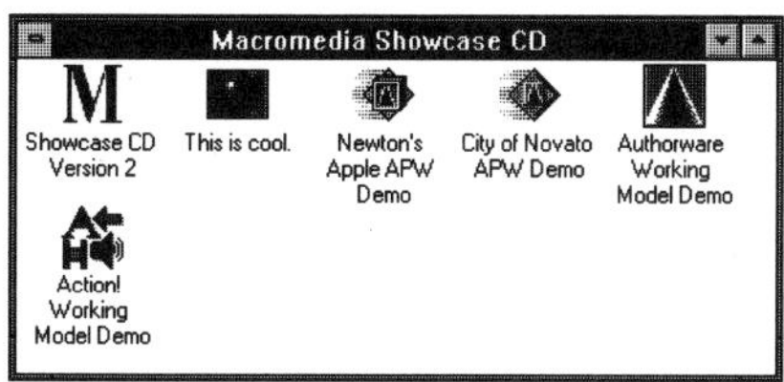

QuickTime for Windows 1.1 or Later Users

QuickTime for Windows 1.0 is included on the Showcase CD-ROM. Use of QuickTime for Windows 1.1 or later versions should work OK, but these later versions were not fully tested at the time this CD-ROM was pressed. If you experience QuickTime movie playback problems while running QuickTime for Windows 1.1 or later, try installing version 1.0 from the Showcase CD-ROM.

Performance Improvement in Windows

This presentation has been designed and optimized for playback from CD-ROM. However, to further improve performance, you can

- Disable unnecessary drivers and boot-up applications to free up additional memory for Showcase.
- Use a 640 ∀ 480 pixel resolution video display driver at 8-bit color depth (256 colors). Higher resolution drivers and more colors will slow down performance.

- Run Showcase from a double-, triple-, or quad-speed CD-ROM drive.
- Copy the entire contents of the CD-ROM to your hard disk and run the Setup program. If you do this, you do not need to copy the contents of the directory named "\MACROMED\ATHWRDEM" because these files are not accessed directly by the interactive portion of Showcase.

Video Drivers and Board Compatibility

When it starts up, the Showcase application performs a capability analysis of your video board and your currently installed display driver. If the video board or driver is found to be unsupported, you will be returned to the Windows desktop. Some video boards and drivers do not properly support all of the graphics display functions required by Windows and are therefore not supported by the Showcase application. Here is a list of video boards and display drivers running at 640 ∀ 480 resolution and 8-bit color depth that have been tested with the Showcase presentation:

Video Card/Manufacturer	Driver Name	Driver Date
ATI	W31-626.DRV	4/20/92
Diamond Viper VLB	VIPER_08.DRV	4/27/93
Headland Technology	V7256.DRV	5/15/92
Orchid Prodesigner II	VGA448.DRV	3/1/92
Orchid Fahrenheit	ORCHIDF.DRV	8/10/92
Trident	WSPDR480.DRV	4/10/92
Video 7	n/a	n/a
Western Digital	WSPDR480.DRV	4/10/92

If you receive an error message informing you that your video board or display driver is not capable of running the Showcase presentation, you can try the following:

- Make sure you are running the appropriate and latest version of your video board display driver (contact your video board's manufacturer for more information).
- Make sure you are using a 640 ∀ 480 pixel driver at 256 colors.

- Make sure you have the line "Optimize=driver" in the QTW.INI file located in your QuickTime for Windows directory. The QTW.INI file supplied on the Showcase CD-ROM contains this line of code.
- Use a supported video board.

What's on the Product Showcase Disc

The Macromedia Product Showcase CD-ROM is a well-integrated interactive application, not a scattered collection of stand-alone files. You will have the best experience, therefore, if you launch the Showcase application and follow its paths. Installing and launching Showcase is described in the preceding section.

Multimedia Solution Demos

Macromedia's eleven multimedia tools deliver solutions in five multimedia areas:

- Interactive learning
- Multimedia production
- Business presentations
- Visualization and design
- Media creation and editing

At the main menu of the Showcase (see Figure D-1), click on the text of a solution—for example, click on "Interactive Learning." As you can see in Figure D-2, a new menu offers a tour about how others have solved interactive learning multimedia needs (such as American Airlines). A digital video overview of each product (click on the Authorware product icon—the result is Figure D-3) and text from that product's data sheet (click on the Product Info button—the result is Figure D-4) are available. If you are using a Macintosh, the product data sheet can be printed. Other demos are included in the *Product Demonstration* and the *Other Great Demos* folders.

Interactive Learning

- American Airlines (training) (Macintosh only)
- Newton's Apple (educational CD-ROM title prototype)
- Electronic City Hall (Kiosk for city of Novato) (Windows only)

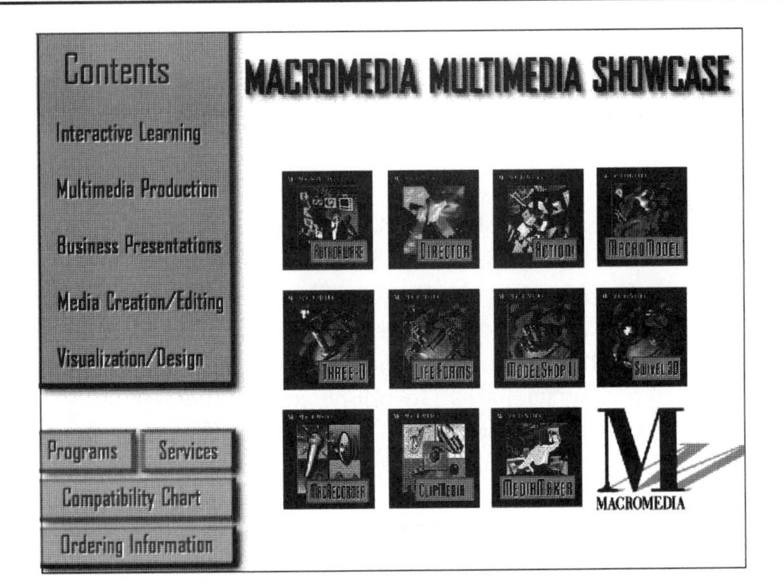

FIGURE D-1 The main menu of the Showcase application

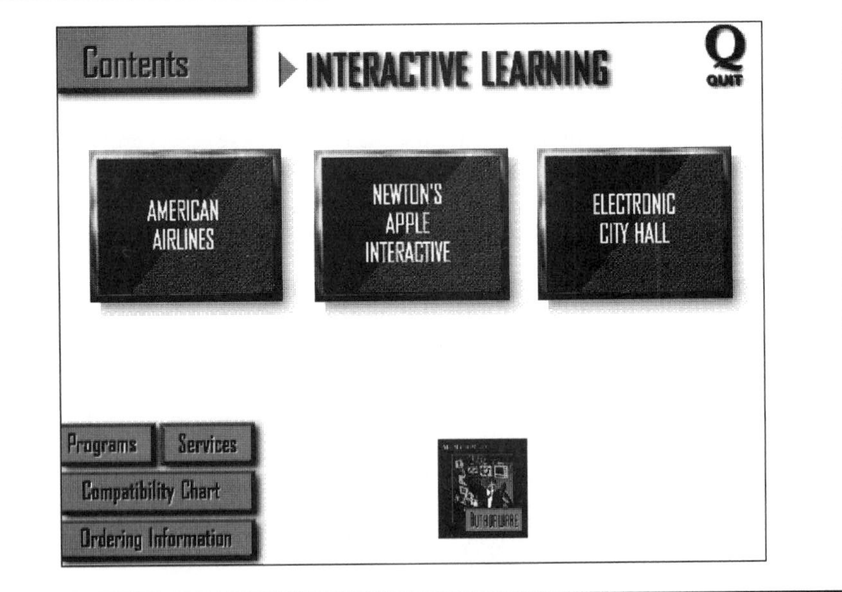

FIGURE D-2 The Interactive Learning menu branches off the main menu

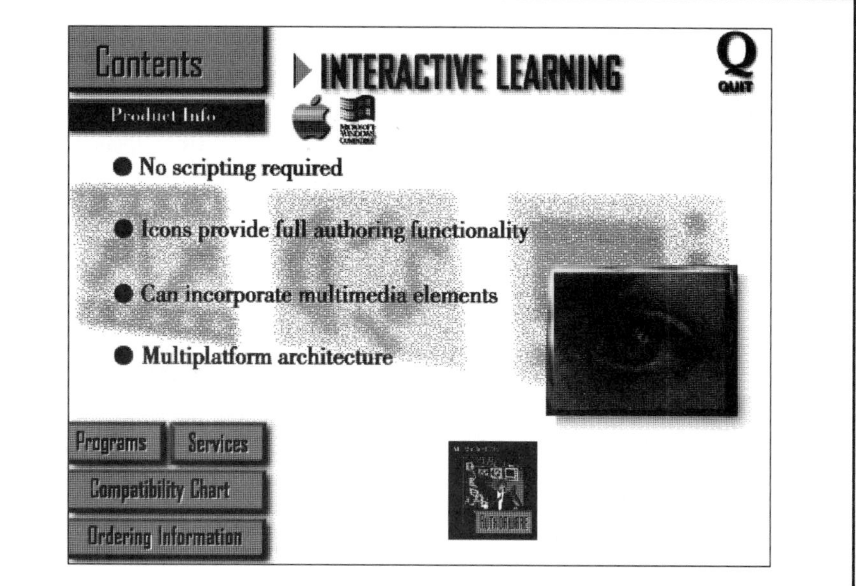

FIGURE D-3 The Authorware product description menu is available from the Interactive Learning menu

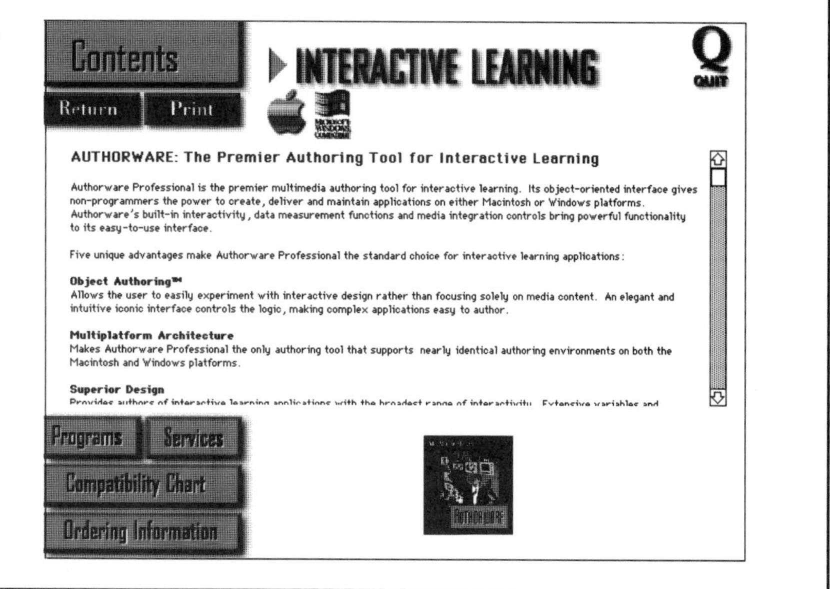

FIGURE D-4 Data sheets are available for all Macromedia products

Multimedia Production

- Kobe Steel (presentation /calculation tool for steel manufacturers)
- From Alice to Ocean (CD-ROM title packaged with a book)
- Bell Atlantic Intelligent Home (fiber optic interactive services prototype)

Business Presentations

- Rockwell International testimonial (QuickTime movie)

Media Creation/Editing

- Product Manager's testimonial (QuickTime movie)

Visualization/Design

- Donald Grahame (MacroModel and 3-D medical illustrations)
- Klitsner Industrial Design (Swivel Pro for toy design)

Macromedia Programs

General information is available about the Macromedia VAR, Publisher, OEM, Developer, and Training programs.

Macromedia Services

General information is available about the Macromedia User Conference, User Group, Technical Support, Training, and Online Communication services. Highlights include a User Conference commercial shot at last year's conference, John Sculley's comments about the conference, and a morphing video clip of the tech support staff. Also, the Online Communications section contains Macromedia bulletin board addresses for Applelink, AOL, Compuserve, and Internet.

Ordering Information

The ordering information section is an interactive directory that lists all Macromedia worldwide distributors as well as North American mail order, educational, commercial, and government distributors.

Compatability Information

This section provides detailed file input and output compatability information and demonstrates how Macromedia products work together. It now also includes Windows product information.

Working Models

Working models, demos, and save-disabled versions are available for these products:

For the Macintosh

Action!
Authorware
Director Version 3.1.3
Director Version 4.0
MacroModel
SoundEdit
Life Forms
Swivel Pro
ModelShop II

For Windows

Action!
Authorware

GNS Demo

The GNS demo (Macintosh only) was created in Director and used at MacWorld Expo in 1992 as a solutions-oriented example of how Macromedia products could be used to develop, prototype, and demonstrate a fictitious Global Navigation System device. Very cool! Looks great! If possible, move this demo to your hard drive for better performance.

Other Great Demos

Macromedia had some leftover space, so they added Director, Authorware, and 3-D examples:

Director

- Clinton Portrait of Victory
- Total Distortion
- Wonder Windows (includes a free copy of Data Shorts—a $10.00 value)
- Peanuts Yearn to Learn
- Japanese and English QuickTime commercial

Authorware

MacWorld Interactive

MacroModel and 3-D:

More of Donald Grahame's illustrations (PICT files)

Directory: Macintosh Partition

The following is a list of all directories and files in the Macintosh partition:

```
MACROMEDIA
|    DeskTop
|    1.IntLearning
|    |    IntLearning.moovs
|    |    |    1.3IntLrng Other
|    |    Authorware.MOOVS
|    |    |    1a.1Authorware.intro
|    |    |    1a.2Authorware
|    |    JoyKpp1.mov
|    |    JoyKpp2.mov
|    |    LncBbbe1.mov
|    |    LncBbbe3.mov
|    |    RckBenn1.mov
|    |    RckBenn2.mov
|    2.MultimediaProd
|    |    MultimediaProd.moovs
|    |    |    2.3MM Prod Other
|    |    Accelerator.moovs
```

```
|    |    |    2b.1Accelerator intro
|    |    |    2b.2Accelerator
|    |    BllWht1.mov
|    |    BllWht2.mov
|    |    Director.moovs
|    |    |    2a.1Director intro
|    |    |    2a.2Director
|    |    EllnWht1.mov
|    |    EllnWht2.mov
|    |    Smoln1.mov
|    |    Smoln2.mov
|    |    Windows.moovs
|    |    |    2c.1Windows intro
|    |    |    2c.2Windows
|    3.BusinessPres
|    |    BusinessPres.moovs
|    |    |    3.2BusPres Solutions Final
|    |    |    3.3BusPres other
|    |    Action.moovs
|    |    |    3a.1Action intro
|    |    |    3a.2Action
|    |    ClipMedia.moovs
|    |    |    3b.1ClipMedia intro
|    |    |    3b.2ClipMedia
|    4. MediaCreat
|    |    MediaCreat.Moovs
|    |    |    4.1MediaCreat intro.AIFF copy
|    |    |    4.2MediaCreat Solutions
|    |    |    4.3MediaCreat Other
|    |    MacRecorder.Moovs
|    |    |    4c.1MacRecorder intro
|    |    |    4c.2MacRecorder
|    |    MediaMaker.Moovs
|    |    |    4a.1MediaMaker intro
|    |    |    4a.2MediaMaker
|    5.VisDesign
|    |    VisDesign.moovs
|    |    |    5.3VisDesign.Other
|    |    DnGrhm1.mov
|    |    DnGrhm2.mov
|    |    DnKlt1.mov
|    |    DnKlt2.mov
```

```
|    |    LifeForms.moovs
|    |    |    5e.1LifeForms intro
|    |    |    5e.2LifeForms
|    |    Macromodel.moovs
|    |    |    5d.1MacroModel intro
|    |    |    5d.2MacroModel
|    |    ModelShop.Moovs
|    |    |    5c.1ModelShop intro
|    |    |    5c.2ModelShop
|    |    Swivel.moovs
|    |    |    5a.1Swivel intro
|    |    |    5a.2Swivel
|    |    SwivelArt.moovs
|    |    |    5f.1SwivelArt intro
|    |    |    5f.2SwivelArt
|    |    ThreeD.moovs
|    |    |    5b.1ThreeD intro
|    |    |    5b.2ThreeD
|    AIFFsounds
|    |    002.AIFF
|    |    005.AIFF
|    |    007.AIFF
|    |    009.AIFF
|    |    BlltLoop
|    |    Button 2
|    |    Button 8
|    |    GooDMusic
|    |    goodMusic2
|    |    inbetwnSegShort
|    |    Intro.AIFF
|    |    MapPrompt
|    |    Programs
|    |    |    1 programs
|    |    |    10 when you purchase...
|    |    |    11 authorized developer
|    |    |    12 macromedia's authorized...
|    |    |    2 click on..
|    |    |    3 authorized var
|    |    |    4 macromedia's authorized...
|    |    |    5 oems
|    |    |    6 through oem...
```

```
|    |    |    7 publisher program
|    |    |    8 the macromedia publishers
|    |    |    9 authorized training
|    |    services
|    |    |    1 services
|    |    |    10 each of these
|    |    |    11 training seminars
|    |    |    12 mm offers..
|    |    |    2 click on 1
|    |    |    3 macromedia international user
|    |    |    4 the 4th annual...
|    |    |    5 technical support
|    |    |    6 mm's technical...
|    |    |    7 mm user forum
|    |    |    8 mm's user group prog...
|    |    |    9 authorized training
|    |    |    9 on line comm
|    |    |    9a mm administers
|    |    ZigZagZing
|    AthwrDem
|    |    AA demo
|    |    |    AA de concept titles
|    |    |    AA demo.pkg
|    |    |    flift7.moov
|    |    |    QuickTime™ Movies
|    |    |    rampp.moov
|    |    Newton's Apple
|    |    |    Assem1.mov
|    |    |    David.mov
|    |    |    Newton's Apple Demo.pkg
|    |    |    QuickTime™ Movies
|    CD summary
|    Desktop
|    Desktop DB
|    Desktop DF
|    Director 4.0 Save Disabled
|    |    Behind the Scenes
|    |    Director 4.0 Demo
|    |    Director 4.0 Help
|    |    Director 4.0 Help Settings
|    Icon
|    Intro
```

```
|    |    LogoANim.shop
|    |    M Logo w Sound.moov
|    Other Great Demos
|    |    Clinton Folder
|    |    |    Clinton.Projector
|    |    |    Dogepur
|    |    |    eAssi
|    |    |    eAssi.ss1
|    |    |    eAssi.vid
|    |    |    Exit
|    |    |    ExitM.aif
|    |    |    Main Menu
|    |    |    open.aif
|    |    |    PFStory.aif
|    |    |    Shared Cast
|    |    MacroModel/Three-D images
|    |    |    Donald Grahame
|    |    |    |    back sat 2
|    |    |    |    best back copy
|    |    |    |    combined guit piano matt
|    |    |    |    foot.rib Pict rt
|    |    |    |    full demo final copy
|    |    |    |    hamstring sat
|    |    |    |    headache rt
|    |    |    |    knee sat
|    |    |    |    Lotus easter
|    |    |    |    neck final rt
|    |    |    |    obj rib Pict rt 2
|    |    |    |    packard matt frnt 640 by 480
|    |    |    |    shoulder rib Pict rt 2
|    |    |    |    thigh pict later
|    |    |    |    thigh render 1
|    |    MacWorld
|    |    |    Articles
|    |    |    |    3D.app
|    |    |    |    Commentary.app
|    |    |    |    Memory.app
|    |    |    Macworld Interactive Demo
|    |    |    MWI Movie Lib 1.1
|    |    |    |    3D
|    |    |    |    |    Bump Map_QT
```

```
|    |    |    |    |    Procedural_QT
|    |    |    |    |    Reflec.map_QT
|    |    |    |    |    tex. mapping_QTM
|    |    |    |    CD
|    |    |    |    Commentary
|    |    |    |    |    INDN1
|    |    |    |    |    INEH1
|    |    |    |    Memory
|    |    |    |    |    INRW1.QTM
|    |    |    |    |    Mac2_S1
|    |    |    |    |    Mac2_S2
|    |    |    |    |    Mac2_S3
|    |    |    |    |    Mac2_S4
|    |    |    |    |    Mac2_S5
|    |    |    |    |    Mac2_S6
|    |    |    |    TOC
|    |    |    |    |    3D_Preview
|    |    |    |    |    CD_Preview
|    |    |    |    |    Comment_Preview
|    |    |    |    |    Memory_Preview
|    |    |    QuickTime™ Movies
|    |    Peanuts
|    |    |    1 minute Demo
|    |    |    |    Y-2-L Demo
|    |    |    |    Yearn 2 Demo.VOICE OVER
|    |    |    Crippled Version
|    |    |    |    PEANUTS
|    |    |    |    _Data Files
|    |    |    |    |    *Bowling Game
|    |    |    |    |    *Coloring Book
|    |    |    |    |    *Flying Ace 1
|    |    |    |    |    *Geography Game
|    |    |    |    |    *Pumpkin Patch
|    |    |    |    |    *Woodstock Numbers
|    |    |    |    |    Coloring Pictures
|    |    |    |    |    HOME
|    |    |    |    |    Intro Animation
|    |    |    |    |    OVERVIEW Comic
|    |    |    |    |    OVERVIEW Math Games
|    |    |    |    |    OVERVIEW Mouse Games
|    |    |    |    |    Shared Cast
|    |    |    |    |    Strips
```

```
|    |    |    |    |    |    •2-3-5 Strip
|    |    |    English QT Movie
|    |    |    Japanese QT Movie
|    |    Total Distortion
|    |    |    1
|    |    |    2
|    |    |    26
|    |    |    28
|    |    |    29
|    |    |    30
|    |    |    31
|    |    |    34
|    |    |    36
|    |    |    37
|    |    |    38
|    |    |    AlienBomb.1
|    |    |    BlockPump.3
|    |    |    CE
|    |    |    COE.clip
|    |    |    d
|    |    |    LetsRock
|    |    |    mvag.anim
|    |    |    Promosity
|    |    |    |    Icon
|    |    |    |    PopLogo.III.clr.bitmap
|    |    |    |    PopLogo.III.v3.clr
|    |    |    |    TD Logo.III.v2
|    |    |    |    TD.CrzyPromo.TEXT
|    |    |    S 26.1
|    |    |    S 27.1
|    |    |    S 28.1
|    |    |    S 28.2
|    |    |    S 28.3
|    |    |    S 29.1
|    |    |    S 30.1
|    |    |    S 30.2
|    |    |    S 31.1
|    |    |    S 31.2
|    |    |    S 31.3
|    |    |    S 31.4
|    |    |    S 32.1
```

```
|   |   |   S 32.2
|   |   |   S 32.3
|   |   |   S 32.4
|   |   |   S 32.5
|   |   |   S 32.6
|   |   |   S 32.8
|   |   |   S 32.9
|   |   |   S 33.1
|   |   |   S 33.2
|   |   |   S 33.3
|   |   |   S 34.1
|   |   |   S 34.2
|   |   |   S 35.1
|   |   |   S 35.2
|   |   |   S 35.3
|   |   |   S 36.1
|   |   |   S 36.2
|   |   |   S 37.1
|   |   |   S 37.2
|   |   |   S 38.1
|   |   |   S V
|   |   |   s1.qt
|   |   |   s11.qt
|   |   |   S43.qt
|   |   |   Shared Cast
|   |   |   TD CD Demo!
|   |   |   TDTitle.CD Demo
|   |   |   Total Distortion Start Here!
|   |   WonderWindow
|   |   |   CheapRodneyDemo
|   |   |   DataShorts
|   |   |   FunIntroDem
|   |   |   FunMenuDem
|   |   |   Shared Cast
|   |   |   The Credits
|   |   |   WonderFaces
|   |   |   |   1derFace#01
|   |   |   |   1derFace#02
|   |   |   |   1derFace#03
|   |   |   |   1derFace#04
|   |   |   |   1derFace#05
|   |   |   |   1derFace#06
```

```
|    |    |    |    1derFace#07
|    |    |    |    1derFace#08
|    |    |    |    1derFace#09
|    |    |    |    1derFace#10
|    |    |    |    1derFace#11
|    |    |    |    1derFace#12
|    |    |    |    1derFace#13
|    |    |    |    1derFace#14
|    |    |    |    1derFace#15
|    |    |    |    1derFace#16
|    |    |    |    StartZapped
|    |    |    WonderWindow demo
|    |    |    WWindow Demo
|    Product Demonstrations
|    |    Action! Demo
|    |    |    Action! demo disk
|    |    |    |    <- copy to hard disk 1st ->
|    |    |    |    Action! Demonstration
|    |    |    |    Action! Player
|    |    |    |    Action! Player Readme
|    |    |    Action! GNS demo files
|    |    |    |    Action! GNS demo script
|    |    |    |    Action! Player
|    |    |    |    GNS Background
|    |    |    |    GNS Bullet template
|    |    |    |    GNS complete presentation
|    |    |    |    GNS QuickTime template
|    |    |    |    Golden Gate At Sunset.QT
|    |    |    |    Mirage.AIFF
|    |    |    Action! Help
|    |    |    Action! Help.note
|    |    |    Action! Mac 1.0 (SD)
|    |    |    Action! templates
|    |    |    |    2/Bullet
|    |    |    |    2/Chart
|    |    |    |    2/Introduction
|    |    |    |    2/Paragraph
|    |    |    |    2/Picture
|    |    |    |    2/Table
|    |    |    |    Golden Gate At Sunset.QT
|    |    APM Demo
```

```
|    |    |    Authorware Professional™
|    |    |    Authorware—GNS
|    |    |    |    Fonts
|    |    |    |    READ ME before using Demo!
|    |    |    |    APM 2.0 Demo Script
|    |    |    |    Benefits
|    |    |    |    Direction 2000
|    |    |    |    Direction 2000.MooV
|    |    |    |    Introduction
|    |    |    |    Map Movie
|    |    |    |    On The Money.sound
|    |    |    |    sample
|    |    |    |    Simulation
|    |    |    |    Testing
|    |    |    Camera
|    |    |    Direction 2000
|    |    |    Direction 2000 ƒ
|    |    |    |    Direction 2000 ƒ
|    |    |    |    Direction 2000.MooV
|    |    |    |    Map Movie2
|    |    |    |    On The Money.sound
|    |    |    Director
|    |    |    QuickTime™ Movies
|    |    |    ScrollEdit
|    |    |    Welcome ƒ
|    |    |    |    Author.mov
|    |    |    |    Bird.PICS
|    |    |    |    Cartoon Walk
|    |    |    |    Roulette Wheel.QT
|    |    |    |    Welcome Library
|    |    |    Welcome! (click me first)
|    |    |    Where to Buy
|    |    Director demo
|    |    |    Device.PICT
|    |    |    Director 3.1 Demo Script
|    |    |    Director Demo
|    |    |    Earth.QT
|    |    |    MacroMind Director 3.1.1 (SD)
|    |    |    On The Money.sound
|    |    |    Stars.PICT
|    |    GNS Demo
|    |    |    GNS Demo
```

```
|    |    |    Hard Rock Cafe.moov
|    |    |    Macromedia Products
|    |    |    Projector
|    |    |    Spinning Logo.moov
|    |    MacroModel Demo
|    |    |    Final Demo Model
|    |    |    MacroModel 1.0.0 READ ME!
|    |    |    MacroModel Demo
|    |    |    MacroModel DEMO 1.0.0
|    |    |    MM Demo Script
|    |    |    MM logo small.QT
|    |    |    MM/3D Demo.QT
|    |    |    MoviePlayer
|    |    |    Scripts
|    |    |    |    cmarble.pst
|    |    |    |    glass.pst
|    |    |    |    MacroModelDefault
|    |    |    |    MacroModelPrefs
|    |    |    |    spatter.pst
|    |    |    |    stippled.pst
|    |    |    TeachText
|    |    Other 3D Demo App's
|    |    |    Life Forms
|    |    |    |    Life Forms Demo
|    |    |    |    Sample Animations
|    |    |    |    |    intro
|    |    |    |    |    tumble
|    |    |    |    Sample Shape Palettes
|    |    |    |    |    jump
|    |    |    |    |    tricks
|    |    |    |    Sample Swivel 3D Files
|    |    |    |    |    Simple Body
|    |    |    |    |    tumble.cmd
|    |    |    ModelShop II
|    |    |    |    ModelShop II 1.2 C DEMO
|    |    |    |    ModelShop II V.1.2 DEMO
|    |    |    |    MS II Demo Script
|    |    |    |    Sample Models
|    |    |    |    |    Final Demo File
|    |    |    |    |    Library Items
|    |    |    |    |    |    Big Table
|    |    |    |    |    |    Conference Table
```

```
|    |    |    |    |    |    Office Desk
|    |    |    |    |    San Francisco II
|    |    |    Other 3D App's  READ ME!
|    |    |    Swivel 3D Pro
|    |    |    |    Sample Environment Maps
|    |    |    |    |    Chrome
|    |    |    |    Sample Models
|    |    |    |    |    Bike
|    |    |    |    |    Chair.cow
|    |    |    |    |    Kenneth and Barbara
|    |    |    |    |    Mac Portable
|    |    |    |    |    T.V. w/Stand
|    |    |    |    |    Woodman
|    |    |    |    Swivel Pro 2.0.4 Demo
|    |    SoundEdit Pro SD
|    |    |    ClipMedia™ music & effects
|    |    |    |    Applause
|    |    |    |    Light And Easy
|    |    |    |    Phone ring
|    |    |    |    Read Me First
|    |    |    |    Robotic Bang
|    |    |    |    The Harvest
|    |    |    MacRecorder® Driver 1.0.2
|    |    |    SoundEdit™ Pro Demo
|    Programs/Services
|    |    Applause-concertMono
|    |    Conference Text
|    |    Credits
|    |    OEM's
|    |    OEMS
|    |    Online Text
|    |    tchSprt.mov
|    |    Training Sem Text
|    |    User Forum Text
|    |    UserConf.mov
|    QuickTime™
|    SHOWCASE
|    |    FINAL PROJECTOR
|    |    Icon
|    |    introloop
|    |    Showcase V2
```

```
|    |    START HERE
|    SltnDems
|    |    AlicDem
|    |    |    Alice.*GR.BG Sidebar Index
|    |    |    Alice.*GR.credits1
|    |    |    Alice.*GR.Main Map GreyDK.8
|    |    |    Alice.*GR.MainMapBg.NoLine
|    |    |    Alice.*GR.MainMapStart
|    |    |    Alice.*GR.MainTitle
|    |    |    Alice.*GR.PT index foregrnd.8
|    |    |    Alice.*GR.SB index foregrnd.8
|    |    |    Alice.GR.Map2.8
|    |    |    Alice.PH.A 0093.8
|    |    |    Alice.PH.A 0094.8
|    |    |    Alice.PH.A 0095.8
|    |    |    Alice.PH.B 0017.8
|    |    |    Alice.PH.C 0021/RobinRain.8
|    |    |    Alice.PH.C 0053.8
|    |    |    Alice.PH.D 0047.8
|    |    |    Alice.PH.D.AyersAbove.8
|    |    |    Alice.PH.G.AyersPool.8
|    |    |    Alice.PT.3.Rob&rain
|    |    |    Alice.QT.Camels
|    |    |    Alice.QT.Intro.B
|    |    |    Alice.QT.Intro.C
|    |    |    Alice.QT.Kangaroos
|    |    |    Alice.QT.LogoAnim3
|    |    |    Alice.SB.Camel 1
|    |    |    Alice.SB.Camel 2
|    |    |    Alice.SB.camel 3
|    |    |    Alice.SB.camel 4
|    |    |    Alice.SB.camel 5
|    |    |    Alice.TH.2.seeolgas
|    |    |    Alice.TH.RickPrologue
|    |    |    Alice.Traveling.2.10s
|    |    |    Alice.VO.2E.1
|    |    |    Alice.VO.2E.2
|    |    |    Alice.VO.2E.3
|    |    |    Alice.VO.intro.1Mix
|    |    |    alicMov
|    |    |    From Alice to Ocean.DEMO
|    |    |    VO.RobynPrologue
```

```
|    |    DGrhm
|    |    |    Grhm1
|    |    |    Grhm2
|    |    |    Grhm3
|    |    |    Grhm4
|    |    DKltsnr
|    |    |    bckt.mov
|    |    |    swng.mov
|    |    IntlgntH
|    |    |    Cascades CD Demo
|    |    |    |    Cascades Animation
|    |    |    |    Cascades Shell
|    |    |    |    CS
|    |    |    |    |    health bites
|    |    |    |    |    |    Health Confirm
|    |    |    |    |    |    Health Pin PIN
|    |    |    |    |    MMCDROM 1
|    |    |    |    |    MMCDROM 2
|    |    |    |    |    MMCDROM 3
|    |    |    |    |    MMCDROM 3 a
|    |    |    |    |    MMCDROM 3 b
|    |    |    |    |    MMCDROM A
|    |    |    |    |    MMCDROM B a
|    |    |    |    |    MMCDROM B b
|    |    |    |    |    music
|    |    |    |    |    shop bites
|    |    |    |    |    |    delivery
|    |    |    |    |    |    done
|    |    |    |    |    |    swipe
|    |    |    |    |    travel bites
|    |    |    |    |    |    01
|    |    |    |    |    |    02
|    |    |    |    |    |    03
|    |    |    |    |    |    04
|    |    |    |    |    |    05
|    |    |    |    |    |    06
|    |    |    |    Grocery Demo
|    |    |    |    Health Demo
|    |    |    |    Kesler.moov
|    |    |    |    Raw Cursor
|    |    |    |    Seaworld small
```

```
|    |    |    |    Travel Demo
|    |    KbeStl
|    |    |    KbeDem
|    |    |    KobeQT.mov
|    TeachText
|    This is cool.
```

Directory: DOS/Windows Partition

The following is a list of all directories and files in the DOS/Windows partition:

```
SHOWCASE_CD
|    DPW.INI
|    INSTALL.EX$
|    INSTALL.INS
|    MMSCCD.LIS
|    PATHFIND.DLL
|    SETUP.EXE
|    SHOWCASE.BMP
|    EXTRA!
|    DPWDEMO.EXE
|    MACROMED
|    |    AIFFSNDS
|    |    |    002AIFF
|    |    |    005AIFF
|    |    |    007AIFF
|    |    |    009AIFF
|    |    |    009AIFF.MOV
|    |    |    BLLTLOOP
|    |    |    BUTTON2
|    |    |    BUTTON8
|    |    |    GOODMUS
|    |    |    GOODMUS2
|    |    |    INTAIFF
|    |    |    MAPPRMPT
|    |    |    SEGSHORT
|    |    |    ZIGZAGZ
|    |    |    PRODUCTS
|    |    |    |    AWARE1
|    |    |    |    AWARE2
```

```
|    |    |    |    CLIPMED1
|    |    |    |    CLIPMED2
|    |    |    |    DIRECTR1
|    |    |    |    DIRECTR2
|    |    |    |    MMODEL1
|    |    |    |    MMODEL2
|    |    |    |    THREED1
|    |    |    |    THREED2
|    |    |    |    WINIRIS1
|    |    |    |    WINIRIS2
|    |    |    PROGRAMS
|    |    |    |    10WHEN
|    |    |    |    11AUTHD&
|    |    |    |    12MMAUTH
|    |    |    |    1PROGS
|    |    |    |    2CLICK
|    |    |    |    3AUTHVAR
|    |    |    |    4MMAUTH
|    |    |    |    5OEMS
|    |    |    |    6THRUOEM
|    |    |    |    7PUBPROG
|    |    |    |    8MMPUB
|    |    |    |    9AUTHTRA
|    |    |    SERVICES
|    |    |    |    10EACHOF
|    |    |    |    11TRASEM
|    |    |    |    12MMOFF
|    |    |    |    1SERVS
|    |    |    |    2CLICK
|    |    |    |    3MMINTL
|    |    |    |    4THE4TH
|    |    |    |    5TECHSUP
|    |    |    |    6MMTECH
|    |    |    |    7MMUSER
|    |    |    |    8USERGRP
|    |    |    |    9AMMADM
|    |    |    |    9AUTHTRA
|    |    |    |    9ONLINE
|    |    |    SLUGS
|    |    |    |    10LIFE
|    |    |    |    11RECORD
|    |    |    |    12ACTION
```

```
|     |     |     |     2AUTHOR
|     |     |     |     3DIRECTR
|     |     |     |     4DIRPLAY
|     |     |     |     5MMODEL
|     |     |     |     6SWIVEL
|     |     |     |     7SWIVELM
|     |     |     |     83D
|     |     |     |     9MODEL
|     |     ATHWRDEM
|     |     |     NEWTONS
|     |     |     |     APMMM.VDR
|     |     |     |     APQT.VDR
|     |     |     |     ASSEM1.MOV
|     |     |     |     DAVID.MOV
|     |     |     |     MMPLAYER.DLL
|     |     |     |     NEWTONLE.APW
|     |     |     |     NEWTONLE.EXE
|     |     |     NOVATO
|     |     |     |     12HELP.WAV
|     |     |     |     2WELCOME.WAV
|     |     |     |     403CITYF.WAV
|     |     |     |     4064PUBL.WAV
|     |     |     |     4082SCHO.WAV
|     |     |     |     502NEIGH.WAV
|     |     |     |     504CHILD.WAV
|     |     |     |     506SENIO.WAV
|     |     |     |     8024PARK.WAV
|     |     |     |     8032SEAS.WAV
|     |     |     |     8033REGI.WAV
|     |     |     |     8041MARI.WAV
|     |     |     |     8042NOVA.WAV
|     |     |     |     902BUILD.WAV
|     |     |     |     903BUILD.WAV
|     |     |     |     904START.WAV
|     |     |     |     CALEND.TXT
|     |     |     |     CCAGENDA.TXT
|     |     |     |     DID.TXT
|     |     |     |     JOBS.TXT
|     |     |     |     MAYOR.WAV
|     |     |     |     NOVATO.APL
|     |     |     |     NOVATO.APR
```

```
|    |    |    |    NOVATO.APW
|    |    |    |    NOVATO.EXE
|    |    |    |    PCAGENDA.TXT
|    |    |    |    RUNAPW2.EXE
|    |    BUSPRES
|    |    |    ACTMOVS
|    |    |    |    3A1ACT.MOV
|    |    |    |    3A2ACT.MOV
|    |    |    BUSPMOVS
|    |    |    |    32BUSP.MOV
|    |    |    |    33BUSP.MOV
|    |    |    CLIPMOVS
|    |    |    |    3B1CLIP.MOV
|    |    |    |    3B2CLIP.MOV
|    |    INTRO
|    |    |    BOXTITLE.MOV
|    |    |    LOGOANIM.MOV
|    |    |    MLOGOWS.MOV
|    |    LEARNING
|    |    |    |    JOYKPP1.MOV
|    |    |    |    JOYKPP2.MOV
|    |    |    |    LNCBBBE1.MOV
|    |    |    |    LNCBBBE3.MOV
|    |    |    |    RCKBENN1.MOV
|    |    |    |    RCKBENN2.MOV
|    |    |    AWMOVS
|    |    |    |    1A1AW.MOV
|    |    |    |    1A2AW.MOV
|    |    |    INTLMOVS
|    |    |    |    13INTL.MOV
|    |    MEDCREAT
|    |    |    MACRMOVS
|    |    |    |    4C1MACR.MOV
|    |    |    |    4C2MACR.MOV
|    |    |    MEDCMOVS
|    |    |    |    41MEDC.MOV
|    |    |    |    42MEDC.MOV
|    |    |    |    43MEDC.MOV
|    |    |    MMAKMOVS
|    |    |    |    4A1MMAK.MOV
|    |    |    |    4A2MMAK.MOV
|    |    MMPROD
```

```
|    |    |    |    BLLWHT1.MOV
|    |    |    |    BLLWHT2.MOV
|    |    |    |    ELLNWHT1.MOV
|    |    |    |    ELLNWHT2.MOV
|    |    |    |    SMOLN1.MOV
|    |    |    |    SMOLN2.MOV
|    |    |    ACCLMOVS
|    |    |    |    2B1ACCL.MOV
|    |    |    |    2B2ACCL.MOV
|    |    |    DIRMOVS
|    |    |    |    2A1DIR.MOV
|    |    |    |    2A2DIR.MOV
|    |    |    PRODMOVS
|    |    |    |    23MMPROD.MOV
|    |    |    WINMOVS
|    |    |    |    2C1WIN.MOV
|    |    |    |    2C2WIN.MOV
|    |    PRODDEMS
|    |    |    ACTIONPC
|    |    |    |    ACTDEMO.ACP
|    |    |    |    MMPLAYER.DLL
|    |    |    |    PLAYACT.EXE
|    |    |    |    README.TXT
|    |    |    AUTHORWR
|    |    |    |    APBRAVO.VDR
|    |    |    |    APDIB.IMP
|    |    |    |    APEPSF.IMP
|    |    |    |    APFLCFLI.IMM
|    |    |    |    APMACPNT.IMP
|    |    |    |    APMETA.IMP
|    |    |    |    APMMM.VDR
|    |    |    |    APMMOTN.VDR
|    |    |    |    APMVE.IMM
|    |    |    |    APPCX.IMP
|    |    |    |    APPICT.IMP
|    |    |    |    APPIONER.VDR
|    |    |    |    APQT.VDR
|    |    |    |    APSONY.VDR
|    |    |    |    APTIFF.IMP
|    |    |    |    APVBLAST.VDR
|    |    |    |    APVLOGIC.VDR
```

```
|    |    |    |    APVSVW.VDR
|    |    |    |    APW2WM.EXE
|    |    |    |    APW2WM.ZIP
|    |    |    |    APWMME.UCD
|    |    |    |    APWPCM.IMS
|    |    |    |    APWWAV.IMS
|    |    |    |    AUTHOR.MOV
|    |    |    |    CAMERA.APW
|    |    |    |    DIB.UCD
|    |    |    |    DIRECT.APL
|    |    |    |    DIRECT.APW
|    |    |    |    DIRECT.MOV
|    |    |    |    DIRECT1.APL
|    |    |    |    MAPMOVI2.MMM
|    |    |    |    MMPLAYER.DLL
|    |    |    |    PALETTE.UCD
|    |    |    |    WELCOME.APL
|    |    |    |    WELCOME.APW
|    |    |    |    WELCOME1.APL
|    |    |    |    WHEEL.MOV
|    |    PROGSERV
|    |    |    APPLAUSE.AIF
|    |    |    CONF.PIC
|    |    |    OEMS.PIC
|    |    |    OEMS2.PIC
|    |    |    ONLINE.PIC
|    |    |    TCHSPRT.MOV
|    |    |    TRAINSEM.PIC
|    |    |    USERCONF.MOV
|    |    |    USERFOR.PIC
|    |    SHOWCASE
|    |    |    DPWAVI.DLL
|    |    |    DPWQTW.DLL
|    |    |    FILEIO.DLL
|    |    |    FNLPRJCT.MMM
|    |    |    INTROLOP.MMM
|    |    |    LINGO.INI
|    |    |    SHOWCASE.EXE
|    |    |    SHOWCASE.ICO
|    |    |    SHOWCSV2.MMM
|    |    |    WAYCOOL.ICO
|    |    |    WAYCOOL.WRI
```

```
|       |       SLTNDEMS
|       |       |       ALICDEM
|       |       |       |       0017.PIC
|       |       |       |       0021.PIC
|       |       |       |       0047.PIC
|       |       |       |       0053.PIC
|       |       |       |       0093.PIC
|       |       |       |       0094.PIC
|       |       |       |       0095.PIC
|       |       |       |       ALICMOV.MMM
|       |       |       |       AYERPOOL.PIC
|       |       |       |       AYERSAB.PIC
|       |       |       |       CAMEL1.PIC
|       |       |       |       CAMEL2.PIC
|       |       |       |       CAMEL3.PIC
|       |       |       |       CAMEL4.PIC
|       |       |       |       CAMEL5.PIC
|       |       |       |       CAMELS.MOV
|       |       |       |       CREDITS1.PIC
|       |       |       |       INTROB.MOV
|       |       |       |       INTROC.MOV
|       |       |       |       INTROMIX.AIF
|       |       |       |       KANGAS.MOV
|       |       |       |       LOGOANIM.MOV
|       |       |       |       MAINMAP.PIC
|       |       |       |       MAINMAPG.PIC
|       |       |       |       MAINMPBN.PIC
|       |       |       |       MAINTIT.PIC
|       |       |       |       MAP2.PIC
|       |       |       |       PT3ROBRA.MOV
|       |       |       |       PTINDEX.PIC
|       |       |       |       RICKPROL.MOV
|       |       |       |       SBINDEX.PIC
|       |       |       |       SEEOLGAS.MOV
|       |       |       |       SIDEBAR.PIC
|       |       |       |       TRAVELNG.AIF
|       |       |       |       VO2E1.AIF
|       |       |       |       VO2E2.AIF
|       |       |       |       VO2E3.AIF
|       |       |       |       VOROBYN.AIF
```

```
|     |     |     DGRHM
|     |     |     |     GRHM1
|     |     |     |     GRHM2
|     |     |     |     GRHM3
|     |     |     |     GRHM4
|     |     |     DKLTSNR
|     |     |     |     BCKT.MOV
|     |     |     |     SWNG.MOV
|     |     |     INTLGNTH
|     |     |     |     CASCADES
|     |     |     |     |     CSCDSNMT.MMM
|     |     |     |     |     CSCDSSHL.MMM
|     |     |     |     |     CURSOR.PIC
|     |     |     |     |     GROCRYDM.MMM
|     |     |     |     |     HEALTHDM.MMM
|     |     |     |     |     KESLER.MOV
|     |     |     |     |     SEAWORLD.MOV
|     |     |     |     |     TRAVELDM.MMM
|     |     |     |     CS
|     |     |     |     |     CDROM1.AIF
|     |     |     |     |     CDROM2.AIF
|     |     |     |     |     CDROM3.AIF
|     |     |     |     |     CDROM3A.AIF
|     |     |     |     |     CDROM3B.AIF
|     |     |     |     |     CDROMA.AIF
|     |     |     |     |     CDROMBA.AIF
|     |     |     |     |     CDROMBB.AIF
|     |     |     |     |     MUSIC.AIF
|     |     |     |     BITES
|     |     |     |     |     O1.AIF
|     |     |     |     |     O2.AIF
|     |     |     |     |     O3.AIF
|     |     |     |     |     O4.AIF
|     |     |     |     |     O5.AIF
|     |     |     |     |     O6.AIF
|     |     |     |     HEALTHBS
|     |     |     |     |     HEALTHC.AIF
|     |     |     |     |     HEALTHP.AIF
|     |     |     |     SHOPBITS
|     |     |     |     |     DELIVERY.AIF
|     |     |     |     |     DONE.AIF
|     |     |     |     |     SWIPE.AIF
```

```
|    |    |    KBESTL
|    |    |    |    KBEDEM.MMM
|    |    |    |    KOBEQT.MOV
|    |    VISDSIGN
|    |    |    DNGRHM1.MOV
|    |    |    DNGRHM2.MOV
|    |    |    DNKLT1.MOV
|    |    |    DNKLT2.MOV
|    |    3DMOVS
|    |    |    5B1THRED.MOV
|    |    |    5B2THRED.MOV
|    |    LIFEMOVS
|    |    |    5E1LIFE.MOV
|    |    |    5E2LIFE.MOV
|    |    MACMMOVS
|    |    |    5D1MMOD.MOV
|    |    |    5D2MMOD.MOV
|    |    MSHPMOVS
|    |    |    5C1MSHOP.MOV
|    |    |    5C2MSHOP.MOV
|    |    SARTMOVS
|    |    |    5F1SWIVA.MOV
|    |    |    5F2SWIVA.MOV
|    |    SWIVMOVS
|    |    |    5A1SWIV.MOV
|    |    |    5A2SWIV.MOV
|    |    VDMOOVS
|    |    |    53VISD.MOV
|    QTW
|    |    QCMC.DLL
|    |    QTCVID.DLL
|    |    QTIM.DLL
|    |    QTIMCMGR.DLL
|    |    QTJPEG.DLL
|    |    QTNOTIFY.EXE
|    |    QTRAW.DLL
|    |    QTRLE.DLL
|    |    QTRPZA.DLL
|    |    QTSMC.DLL
|    |    QTW.INI
```

Index

A

A/B roll editing, 341-342
Accessories (software), 102, 122-123
Acoustics, 240
Action!, 11, 27, 168-170, 508
Actors
  in Animation Works Interactive, 171
  in PROmotion, 182
Adaptive Delta Pulse Code Modulation (ADPCM), 260
ADB (Apple Desktop Bus), 81
AddDepth, 228
AddImpact, 120
Additive primary colors, 293
Adobe Type Manager (ATM), 210-211
AFTRA (American Federation of Television and Radio Artists), 432-435
Agfa Compugraphic, 486
Alchemy, 111
Alpha releases, 441-442
Alpha testing, 441-442
Alphabets, 217-220
Alphabets & Images Inc., 486
Altsys Corporation, 487
Ami Pro, 133-134
Amplifiers, 87
Analog-to-digital conversion, 331-332
Andersen, Kurt, 39-40
Animation, 111-112, 305-316
  dinosaur scene, 312-314
  font, 315-316
  power of, 306
  principles of, 307-310
  rolling ball, 310-312
  techniques, 308-309
  text, 208
Animation Compressor (Apple), 115
Animation file formats, 310
Animation files, 112
Animation programs, 309
Animation Works Interactive, 170-172
ANSI standard characters, 216-217
Anti-aliasing, 202
Apple Desktop Bus (ADB), 81
AppleEvents, 127-128
AppleLink File menu, 447
Archive, 447
Archiving files, 446-449
Ares software, 487
Art. *See* Images
Art (clip art), 282-283
ASCII character set, 215-216
Aspect ratios, HDTV vs. VGA, 327
Assemble editing, 342
Astound, 139
Atchley, Cornelia, 404, 472
ATM (Adobe Type Manager), 210-211
ATypI organization, 220-221
Audio. *See* Digital audio; MIDI; Sound
Audio CD packaging, 479. *See also* CDs
Audio devices, 86-88
Audio dubbing, 343
Audio editing, 272-273
Audio file formats, 259-260
Audio recording, 271-275
Audio specialist, 46-47
Audio Visual Connection (AVC), 87
Authoring tools, 6, 147-188
  card- and page-based, 153-162
  cross-platform, 183-188
  delivery features, 153
  editing features, 150
  icon-based, 162-168
  interactivity features, 152
  organizing features, 151
  performance tuning features, 153
  playback features, 153
  programming features, 151-152

time-based, 168-183
types of, 148-153
Authorware Professional, 163-166, 506-507
Autotracing, 290
AVC (Audio Visual Connection), 87
AVI files, 112, 118

B

Baird, Patricia, 232
Barcoding, 84-85
Barrett, Jon, 282
Bartesch, Heinz, 370
Base-level MIDI devices, 264
BASIC. *See* Visual Basic
Baud, 92
Bell, Bob, 49-50
Bergstein, Andrew, 268
Beta releases, 441-442
Beta testing, 442-443
Bezier curves, 209
Bids, multimedia project, 379-383
Billing rates, multimedia project, 378-379
Binary-compatible file, 183
Bitmap software, 283
Bitmapped fonts, 212
Bitmaps, 280-290
Bitstream Inc., 487
Black-striping (videotape), 353
Blankenhorn, Dana, 63
Blister pack, 479
Blue screen, 346-347
Blum, Brian, 362
Booklet (with compact disc), 481
Boolean searches, 229
Booting, 77
Branching features of authoring tools, 152
Broadcast video standards, 325-326
Bronze version (multimedia project), 442
Buddrus, Ann Marie, 25
Building a project. *See* Multimedia projects
Bunnell, David, 320, 423
Burger, Jeff, 36
Business, multimedia in, 10-13
Buttons (navigation), 203-205
Buttons (user interface), 396-399

C

CA-Cricket Presents, 142
CAD tools, 101, 104-106
Calica, Ben, 442
Cameras, digital, 85-86
Canvas (Deneba), 142
Capture, 122
Capturing images, 283-287
Card-based authoring tools, 149, 153-162
Cards (HyperCard), 155
Carrigan, Tim, 272
Casady & Greene Inc., 488
Case insensitivity, 197
Cases, upper- and lower, 197
Cast feature (Macromedia Director), 174-175
CAV (Constant Angular Velocity) format, 329
CBT (computer-based training), 327
CCITT P*64 standard, 351
CD-Bridge, 472
CD-I (Philips), 471-472
CD-ROMs, 7-9, 78-79, 460-474
hybrid, 515
installed base, 58, 461
video files for, 351-352
CD-ROM/XA, 466, 468-469
CDs (compact discs), 462
artwork for the label, 480-481
booklet for, 481
categories of consumer titles, 460
formats, 465, 467-468
inlay card for, 482-483
packaging for, 478-483
producing, 473-474
sectors, 463
standards, 463, 465-466
technology, 462-474
tracks, 464
Cel animation, 308-309
Channel mapping (MIDI Mapper), 265-266
Character Map, 216-217
Character sets, 215-220
Charge-coupled device (CCD), 322
Charisma (Micrografx), 143
Chroma key, 346
Cinemania application, 36-37
Cinemation, 36-37, 172-174
Cinepak Compressor (Apple), 116
Client approval cycles, 415
Clients, working with, 415
Clients and servers, 129
Clip art, 282-283
ClipMaker feature (MediaBlitz!), 178
ClipMedia, 283, 509
Clipping a sound wave, 247-248
Cloning, 58

CLV (constant linear velocity), 464
CMYK color model, 296
Codecs (coder-decoders), 115
Cold link, 129
College multimedia programs, 494-495
Collier, David, 226
Color
 computerized, 293-296
 and monitors, 294
 primary, 293
 video, 333
 working with, 292-300
Color channels (RGB), 322
Color lookup tables, 296-299
Color models, 295-296
Color palettes, 296-299
Color spill, 347
Communication devices, 91-94
Compact discs. *See* CDs (compact discs)
Component Manager (QuickTime), 114
Component (YUV) video, 116, 296, 322, 336-338
Composite project organizing structures, 390
Composite video, 322, 338
Composition, 347-348
Compressing files, 446
Compression ratio, 121
Compression schemes (QuickTime), 115-116
Compression software filename extensions, 448
Compression software publishers, 449
Compression (video), 120-122, 348-354
 DVI, 350-351
 and image quality, 121
 JPEG, 349
 MPEG, 350
 and speed, 122
Computer-aided design (CAD), 101, 104-106
Computer-based training (CBT), 327
Computerized color, 293-296
Conditional branching, 152
Conferencing, 94
Connections (hardware), 70-74, 343
Consistent interfaces, keystroke guide for, 402
Constant Angular Velocity (CAV), 329
Constant Linear Velocity (CLV), 464
Consumer-grade video equipment, 338-341
Container file, 129
Content (multimedia project), 422-432
 acquiring, 423-424
 finding preexisting, 425-426
 obtaining rights to, 424-432,435-436
Contract terms, 381-382
Controls (Visual Basic), 162
Conversion (between applications), 129
ConvertIt!, 188
Copyright issues, 426, 432
 acquiring releases, 435-436
 copyright statement, 417
 permissions request for material, 431
 for sounds, 275
 for typefaces, 220-221
Cost sheet example, 379-380
Costing multimedia projects, 375-380, 461
Courier services, 415
Courier typeface, 199
Covers, for multimedia projects, 383
Crawford, Chris, 392
Creativity, 27-29
Credit Alligator, 28-29
Critical Path Method (CPM), 369
Cross-platform authoring tools, 183-188
Cue Sheets
 in Animation Works Interactive, 171
 in Producer, 179-180
Cues (media elements), 180, 182

D

Da Vinci, Leonardo, 34
DAT (digital audio tape), 271-272, 339
Database text searches, 231-236
Databases, 136-138
DDE (Dynamic Data Exchange), 128-129, 161
DeBabelizer, 123
Decibels (dB) scale, 241
Degradation (video), 340
Delivery features of authoring tools, 153
Delivery (multimedia project), 444-449
Delta, 121
DeltaGraph Professional, 141
Densities, disk, 76-77
Derivative works, 428-430
Design and development methodology, 362

Design tools for fonts, 221-228
Designing installation programs, 449-450
Designing project structure, 389-400
Designing with text, 200-201
Desktop A/B roll editing, 341-342
Developers, multimedia, 6
Device Independent Bitmaps (DIBs), 160, 300
Digital audio, 246-253 (*See also* Sound)
  on the Macintosh, 262-263
  vs. MIDI, 243-246
  under Windows, 267
Digital audio files, preparing, 247-253
Digital audio tape (DAT), 271-272, 339
Digital cameras, 85-86
Digital recordings, editing, 251-252
Digital signal processing (dsp), 88, 253
Digital Video Interactive (DVI), 113, 350-351
Digital video movies, 111-122. *See also* Video
Digitized video playback, 330-332
Dillon, Patrick, 391
Direction 2000, 11
Director (Macromedia), 18, 174-177, 507
  Authorware, 12
  visual effects, 307
  Windows Player, 187-188
Disks
  defragmenting and optimizing, 120
  densities of, 76-77
  formatting, 76-77
  storage on, 76-77
  tracks and sectors on, 76
Dithering, 299-300
DLLs (Dynamic Link Libraries), 160
D-1 video format, 337-338
Dot pitch, 294
Downsampling sound, 252
Drawing
  3-D, 290-292
  vector-drawn objects, 288-290
Drawing tools, 101-104
Drawn graphics, 280
Drivers, video, 518-519
Dubbing, 340, 343
Duderstadt, Hank, 45
Duffy, Mike, 363
DVA4000, 352
DVI (Digital Video Interactive), 113, 350-351
Dynamic Data Exchange (DDE), 128-129, 161
Dynamic Link Libraries (DLLs), 160

E

EDI Install Pro, 451-452
Edit decision list (EDL), 341
Edited master, 341
Editing
  audio, 272-273
  using authoring tools, 150
  digital recordings, 251-252
  fonts, 221-228
  images, 283-287
  a QuickTime movie, 119-121
  sound, 101, 109-111
  sound waveforms, 272
  text, 108-109
  with VCRs, 340-341, 344-345
  video, 335-345, 354
Editing VCRs, 344-345
Edition file, 128
Edwards, Mark, 405
Embedded object, 129
Emigre Fonts, 488
End user, 5
Environment, multimedia, 7
Epstein, Jonathan, 8
Equalization (EQ), 253
Erase heads, flying, 342
Escapes from the Zoo, 15
Estimating multimedia project cost, 375-380
Ethernet, 93
Event-driven programming, 162
Excel, 136
  linking to Word, 132
  using for project task planning, 373
Expert mode, 401
Extended character set, 216-217
Extended-level MIDI devices, 265
External sync, 343
Eye rods and cones, 293

F

Fade-ins and fade-outs (audio), 252-253
Family process of CD manufacture, 462
Fathers (in CD manufacture), 462
Feedback Alligator, 374

Fellowships, 50-51
Fields, 205
File compression, 446. *See also* Compression (video)
File format converters, 123
File formats
  animation, 112, 310
  audio, 259-260
  HIFF, 188
  image files, 300-302
  QuickTime movies, 116-122
  sound, 110-111
  video, 112-113
FileMaker Pro, 137
Filmstrips (Cinemation), 172-173
Filtering images, 108
Flattening a movie, 351
FlexCam application, 13
FLI and FLC files, 112
Floppy disk formats, 77
Floppy disks, 76-77
Flying erase heads, 342
Font animation, 315-316
Font manufacturers, 485-491
FONT resources, 212-213
Font Software Anti-Piracy Initiative, 221
Font styles, 196
Font wars, 209-210
FONTastic Plus, 222-223
FontBank, 488-489
Fontographer, 223-224
Fonts, 196-200
  choosing, 201-202
  editing and design tools, 221-228
  hints for designing, 210
  installed Windows and System 7, 213-214
  Macintosh bitmapped, 212
  on Macintosh vs. PC monitors, 197
  managing, 214-215
  and platforms, 215
  PostScript, 209-210, 212
  printer, 211
  selecting for buttons, 205
  TrueType, 210, 212
FontStudio, 225-226
Format converters, 123
Formats, file. *See* File formats
Formatted disk, 76-77
Forms (Visual Basic), 162
Fortier, Marty, 430
Frame accurate time, 343
Frames (graphics scenes), 111

G

Gallery Effects, 107-108
Gantt chart, 370
Gates, Bill, 122, 393
General MIDI Instrument Sounds, 254-257
General MIDI standards, 266-267
Glenn, Bernice T., 334
Going gold, 442, 444
Gold version (multimedia project), 442, 444
Graphic elements, creating, 277-302
Graphical user interface (GUI), 81, 402-406
Graphics adapter, 294
Graphics Compressor (Apple), 115
Graphics tablets, 83-84
Green Book standard, 463, 465-466, 471
GUIs (graphical user interfaces), 81, 402-406

H

Hard disks, 77
Hardman, Lynda, 402
Hardware, 25-26
  displaying requirements for, 482-483
  MPC Level 2 specifications, 64-66
  multimedia, 53-94
  peripherals, 69-94
  and project design, 365
Harris, Chip, 46
Hawkins, Trip, 14, 275, 395, 399, 424, 429, 464
HDTV (High Definition Television), 326-327
Helical scan recording, 323
Helical scan tape path, 323
Hessenflow, Allan, 297
HFS (Hierarchical File System), 468
Hidde, Lars, 299, 406
Hi-8 tape format (High-Band 8 mm), 339
Hierarchical project organizing structures, 390
HIFF (Hypermedia Interchange File Format), 188
High Definition Television (HDTV), 326-327
Highway, multimedia, 8-9
Hints (for designing fonts), 210
Hiring talent, 432-436
Hits (database search), 231
Home-use multimedia, 16-17
Hot link, 129
Hot spots (user interface), 396-398
Hot words, 229

HSB and HSL color models, 295
HSC Interactive, 167-168
Hub (compact disc), 462
Hues, 293
Human interface, 6
Hybrid CD-ROMs, 515
Hypercard, 61, 154-158
Hypermedia, 6, 228-236
Hypermedia Interchange File Format (HIFF), 188
Hypermedia structures, 234-235
HyperTalk, 155
Hypertext, 228-236
  links and nodes, 234-235
  power of, 231-232
  searching, 231-236
  tools, 236
  using, 232-233
HyperWriter!, 235

I

IAC (InterApplication Communication), 127
ICM (QuickTime), 114
IconAuthor, 166-167
Icon-based authoring tools, 149, 162-168
Icons, 206-208, 398-400
Idea management software, 367-369
Ideas for projects, 361, 363-367
Image Club Graphics Inc., 489
Image compression. *See* Compression (video)
Image editing programs, 286
Image editing tools, 101, 105-108
Image file formats, 300-302
Image Pac, 470
Images
  capturing and editing, 283-287
  creating, 277-302
  filtering, 108
  having multiple monitors, 279
  making still images, 280-292
  organizing your tools, 279
  planning your approach, 279
  scanning, 287
Indexing (hypermedia), 231-236
INF Maker, 451-452
Infrared remotes, 85
Inglesby, Tom, 35
Inks (in animation), 309
Inlay card (with compact disc), 482-483
Input devices, 80-86
Insert editing, 342
Inspiration package, 367-368
Installation
  Macintosh platform, 453-456
  Windows platform, 451-452
Installation programs
  designing, 449-450
  writing, 445
Installed base of CD-ROM players, 461
Instant multimedia, 125-145
Interactive multimedia, 6, 152, 228
Interactive programmer, 48
InterApplication Communication (IAC), 127
Interface designer, 40-42
Interlacing, 325, 334-335
Interleaving, 113
International Typeface Corporation, 489
Internships, 50-51
ISO 9660 standards, 467-468

J

Jaggies, 210
Joining files, 446
JPEG video compression, 349
Just Grandma and Me, 14-15

K

Kai's Power Tools, 310
Kerning text, 201
Key mapping (MIDI Mapper), 266
Keyboards, 80
KeyCaps, 216-217
Keyframes, 308
Keying color images, 347
Keystroke guide for consistent interfaces, 402
Keystroke macros, 80
Kingsley/ATF Type Corporation, 489-490
Kiosks, 18
Klocek, Sharon, 17, 250, 445
Kodak's Photo CD, 16-17, 466, 469-470

L

Label artwork (compact disc), 480-481
Landscape vs. portrait orientation, 206

Languages (scripting), 151-152, 176, 217-220, 269
LANs (local area networks), 92-94
Laserdiscs, 16
Lazzaro, Nicole, 40-42
Leading (type spacing), 196, 198
Letraset, 490
Levitus, Bob, 113
Levy, Steven, 194
Libraries, font, 485-491
Licensing rights to material, 426. *See also* Copyright issues
Life Forms, 509
Light levels, for video shooting, 292, 345-346
Light (natural), working with, 292, 345-346
Linear multimedia project, 6
Linear project organizing structures, 390
Linear Pulse Code Modulation, 260
Lingo (Macromedia Director), 176
Link anchor (hypertext system), 234
Link end (hypertext system), 234
Linked objects, 127-129
Linking Excel and Word, 132
Links (hypertext system), 234-235
Linotype-Hell Company, 490
Local area networks (LANs), 92-94
Localization, 218
LocalTalk, 93
Long box packaging, 478-479
Lookup tables, color, 296-299
Lossy vs. lossless compression, 121, 349
Lotus 1-2-3 for the Macintosh, 135
Lotus 1-2-3 for Windows, 135
Lowercase, 197
Ludwig, David A., 321, 403

M

Macintosh desktops, 61-63
Macintosh HFS, 468
Macintosh Performas, 62
Macintosh platform, 59-63
  installation on, 453-456
  vs. PC platform, 57-59
  system requirements, 482
Macintosh PowerBooks, 63
Macintosh PowerPC, 60
Macintosh Quadras, 61-62
Macintosh Showcase CD-ROM, 515-516
MacLeod, John, 427
Macromedia (*See also* Showcase CD-ROM)
  business strategy, 504-505
  the company, 502-503
  market opportunity, 503-504
  product reference, 506-509
  technological leadership, 505-506
  users, 509-511
Macromedia Director, 18, 174-177, 507
  Authorware, 12
  visual effects, 307
  Windows Player, 187-188
MacroModel, 507-508
Macros, 80
Magnetic (mag) card setups, 82
Magneto-optical (MO) drives, 78
Marker cues (Producer), 181
May, Robert, 6, 67
McCabe, Georgia, 7
McCarthy, Kevin, 413
McConathy, Charles, 59
Media Control Interface (MCI), 72-74, 113
Media Player, 118-119
MediaBlitz!, 177-179
Medius IV, 288
Memory, 74-76
Menus, 202-203
Metamorphosis Professional, 224-225
Mice, 81
Microsoft Project, 369-370
Microsoft Video for Windows, 111, 117-118
Microsoft Word for the Macintosh, 130-131
Microsoft Word for Windows, 131-132
Microsoft Works Multimedia Edition, 134
MIDI devices, 264-265
MIDI files, preparing, 257-259
MIDI (Musical Instrument Digital Interface), 243
  channel and polyphony assignments, 266
  vs. digital audio, 243-246
  General Instrument Sounds, 254-257
  on the Macintosh, 261-262

making MIDI audio, 253-259
mapping, 265-266
playing back sounds, 259
under Windows, 264-267
MIDI sound files, 110-111
Midiscan, 273
Midisoft Studio for Windows, 254
MiniCad+, 106
Mixed mode compact disc, 465
MMM file format, 112
MO (magneto-optical) drives, 78
Modal interface, 401-402
ModelShop, 509
ModelShopII, 20
Modeming, 415
Modems, 92
Monitors, 88-90, 294
Monotype Typography, 490
Montague, Eve, 353
Morphing, 286, 309
Morrisey, Glenn, 297
Mothers (in CD manufacture), 462
Movie editors/editing. *See* QuickTime
Movie file formats. *See* File formats
Movie files, compressing. *See* Compression (video)
Movie players (QuickTime), 118-119
Movie Toolbox (QuickTime), 114
Movies. *See* Video
MPC (multimedia PC)
platform, 7, 64-67
Level 2 specifications, 64-67
memory use, 76
recommended packaging, 477-478
system requirements, 482
MPEG video compression, 350
Multidisk Installer (Apple), 453-454
Multimedia authoring tools. *See* Authoring tools
Multimedia designer, 38-40
Multimedia developers, 6
Multimedia environments, 7
Multimedia hardware. *See* Hardware
Multimedia highway, 8-9
Multimedia objects, linking, 127-129
Multimedia programmer, 47-48
Multimedia projects
adding sound, 267-269
assembly and delivery, 357-483
bids and proposals, 379-383
billing rates, 378-379
budget, 385
building a team, 369-371
content, 422-432
costing for various media, 461
cover and package, 383
creative strategy, 27-29, 384
design case history, 407-412
designing, 389-412
estimating, 375-380
hazards, 417-419
ideas for, 361, 363-367
implementation, 384-385
linear and nonlinear, 6
navigation, 390-396
needs analysis, 384
organization, 30
packaging, 474-483
planning, 361-375
planning and costing, 359-385
preparing for delivery, 444-449
production, 413-419
prototyping, 371-372
requirements, 25-30
resources for, 365
scheduling, 374-375
stages of, 24
storyboarding, 407-410
table of contents, 383
target audience, 384
task planning, 373
testing, 440-444
tracking, 416
user interface, 396-406
working with clients, 415
Multimedia Resource Kit (MMRK) for ToolBook, 160
Multimedia skillset, 34
Multimedia software. *See* Software
Multimedia team, 35-49
Multimedia title, 6, 474
Murray, Philip, 231

N

National Information Infrastructure (NII), 8
Navigable Movies, 117
Navigation map (navMap), 390, 393, 395-396
Navigation (multimedia project), 390-396
Navigation symbols, 208
Networks, 92-94

NFNT resources, 212
Nodes (communications), 93
Nodes (hypertext system), 234-235
Nonlinear multimedia project, 6
Nonlinear project organizing structures, 390
Novice/expert modes, 401-402
NTSC (National Television Standards Committee), 325
NTSC video and recording standard, 325, 333

O

Object-oriented programming systems (OOPs), 127
Objects, 111, 127-129, 390
Ochsenreiter, Glenn, 5, 401
OCR, 25
 devices, 84-85
 software, 101, 108-109
Offline editing, 341
OLE (Object Linking and Embedding), 128-129
OmniPage Pro, 109
Open-code environment, 416-417
OpenScript, 155
Optical character recognition (OCR), 25
 devices, 84-85
 software, 101, 108-109
Orange Book standard, 463, 465-466, 471
Organizing structures, project, 390
Output hardware, 86-91
Overscan, 332

P

Packaged CD-ROM. *See* Showcase CD-ROM
Packaging (CD), 478-483
Packaging (multimedia project), 383, 474-483
 covers, 474-475
 shapes for, 475-476
 shipping, 476-477
 standards for, 477-478
Packing (videotape), 353
PACo Producer, 184-187
Page orientation, portrait vs. landscape, 206
Page-based authoring tools, 149, 153-162
Paint graphics, 280
Painter (Fractal Design), 285
Painting tools, 101-104
PAL video and recording standard, 325-326
Palette flashing, 298
Palettes, color, 296-299
Paper napkin idea planning, 366
Passport's Producer, 179-181, 399
Patch mapping (MIDI Mapper), 265
PatchBay utility (Apple), 262
Pels (pixels), 281
Performas (Macintosh), 62
Peripherals, 69-94
Permissions and rights
 obtaining, 322, 424-432, 435-436
 sample request, 431
Persistence of vision, 307
Personal Digital Assistants (PDAs), 85
Personnel, hiring and using, 432-436
Persuasion (Aldus), 140
PERT (Program Evaluation Review Technique), 369
Philips CD-I, 471-472
Photo CD (Kodak), 16-17, 469-470
Photo CD-compatible players, 466
Photo YCC color model, 296
PhotoDisc CD-ROM thumbnails, 284
Photo-JPEG Compressor (Apple), 115
Photons, 292
Photoshop, 310
PICS file format, 112
PICT file format, 117, 300
Pilot projects, 371-372
Planning a multimedia project, 361-375
Platforms (multimedia), Macintosh vs. PC, 57-59
Playback features of authoring tools, 153
Players, for QuickTime movies, 118-119
PLV (Production Level Video), 350
Pointing (and linking), 129
Points (type size), 196
Poly-overwrapped jewel box, 479
Polyphony, 265
Polyphony assignments (MIDI), 266
Popcorn, 118
Portrait vs. landscape orientation, 206
Post (postproduction) session, 274
Posters (movie frames), 117
PostScript fonts, 209-210, 212

PowerBooks (Macintosh), 63
PowerPC, 60
PowerPoint, 140-141
Pregap (compact disc), 472
Premiere (Adobe), 111-112, 121
Presentation tools, 138-145
Primary colors, 293
Printer fonts, 211
Producer (Passport), 179-181, 399
Producing a CD, 473-474
Producing a multimedia project, 413-419
Producing sound, 270-271
Production Level Video (PLV), 350
Production value of content, 422
Professional connectors, 343
Professional video equipment, 341-345
Professionals, hiring and using, 432-436
Program Evaluation Review Technique (PERT), 369
Programmer, multimedia, 47-48
Programming features of authoring tools, 151-152
Project management software, 367-370
Project manager, 36-38
Project organizing structures, types of, 390
Projectors, 90-91, 187
Projects, multimedia. *See* Multimedia projects
PROmotion, 181-183
Properties of multimedia objects, 127
Proposals, multimedia project, 379-383
Prototyping, multimedia project, 371-372
P*64 (CCITT) standard, 351
Public-place multimedia, 17-19
Publishing, 127-128
Publish-and-subscribe, 127-128

Q

Q+E Database/VB, 138
Quadras (Macintosh), 61-62
Quanta, 292
Quantizing sound, 247-248
Quantum theory, 292
QuickTime, 111, 113, 517
  audio technology, 263
  building blocks, 114
  compression schemes, 115-116
  with Macromedia Director, 176-177
  movie editors, 119-120
  movie file compression, 120-122
  movie file format, 116-122
  movie players, 118-119
  system software, 114
  and Video for Windows, 117-118
Quicktime player (WordPerfect for Macintosh), 133

R

RAM configurations, 75-76
Rasterizing text, 197
Rate sample size, 246
Real Time Video (RTV), 350
Recording computer output, 352-353
Recording formats, video, 336-345
Recording sound, 271-275. *See also* Sound
Red Book standard, 269-270, 463, 465-466
Registering software, 100
Release candidate (multimedia project), 442
Release of rights, acquiring, 435-436
Rendered 3-D images, 105, 290-292
Rendering, 105, 290-292
Resampling sound, 252
ResEdit, 222, 400
Resolution (sound), 248
Resolution (video), 338
Resource Interchange File Format (RIFF), 300
Reversing sounds, 253
RGB color channels, 322
RGB color model, 294-295, 322
Rights and permissions, 322, 424-432, 435-436
Rolling ball animation, 310-312
Rough cut, 341
RTV (Real Time Video), 350
Run Length Encoding (RLE), 115

S

Safe title area, 332
SAG (Screen Actors Guild), 432-435
Sampled sound, 246
  samples, 244
  sampling, 246, 252

sampling rates, 248-250
Santalesa, Richard, 325
Scanners, 84, 109
Scanning images, 287
Scheduling (multimedia project), 374-375
Schools, multimedia in, 13-16
Score feature (Macromedia Director), 175-176
ScoreMaker feature (MediaBlitz!), 179
Screen Actors Guild (SAG), 432-435
Screen grabbers, 122-123
Scriabin's colors, table of, 19
Scripting, 6
Scripting languages, 151-152, 176, 217-220, 269
SCSI (Small Computer System Interface) devices, 71-72
Search range in JPEG, 349
Searching for text, 231-236
SECAM video and recording standard, 325-326
Sectors (compact disc), 463
Sectors (floppy disk), 76
Self-extracting archives, 448-449
Seppala, Karl, 139
Serif vs. sans serif typefaces, 197-200
Servers and clients, 129
Shipping packages, 476-477
Shooting and editing video, 335-345
Showcase CD-ROM, 513-546
compatibility, 523
data sheets, 521
demos, 523-524
directory (DOS/Windows), 538-546
directory (Macintosh), 524-538
GNS demo, 523
how to use, 515-519
interactive learning, 519-522
Macromedia programs, 522
Macromedia services, 522
main menu, 520
multimedia production, 522
multimedia solution demos, 519, 522
ordering, 522
working models, 523
Signal loss (video), 340
Signal-to-noise ratio (VCR), 344
Simple branching, 152
SimplePlayer, 118
Sixteen colors, working with, 299-300
Skills, categories of multimedia, 35
Skills availability, and project design, 365
Skillset, multimedia, 34
Small Fonts (Windows), 211-212
SmarText, 236
SMPTE time code, 343
SnapPRO!, 122
SND file format, 262
Snook, Brian, 388
Software, 26-27, 97-188
accessories, 102, 122-123
basic toolset, 99-123
CAD and 3-D, 104-106
drawing and painting, 103-104
image editing, 105-108
MPC Level 2 specifications, 66-67
OCR, 108-109
and project design, 365
registering, 100
sound editing, 109-111
toolset list, 101-102
Software boxes, 478
Sound, 239-275 (*See also* Sampled sound)
adding to a project, 267-269
copyright issues of, 275
keeping track of, 273-274
on the Macintosh, 260-263
multimedia system, 242-243
power of, 240-242
production, 270-271
in QuickTime, 263
reversing, 253
in Windows, 263-267
Sound control panels, 243
Sound editing software, 101, 109-111
Sound files, 110-111
Sound Recorder, 110
Sound recording, 271-275 (*See also* Sound)
determining recording size, 248-250
editing, 250-251
setting levels, 250-251
splicing and assembly, 251-252
trimming dead air, 251
Sound waveforms, 247-248
SoundEdit, 272, 508
Speak92!, 328, 330

SPEAKER.DRV file, 242
Speakers, 87
Speed Disk (Norton), 120
Spitzer, David, 102
Splicing (audio), 251-252
Spreadsheets, 132, 134-136
Sprites (animation), 111, 175
Stacks (HyperCard), 155
Stage (Producer), 181
Standards
    broadcast video, 325-326
    CCITT P*64, 351
    compact disc (CD), 463, 465-466
    General MIDI, 266-267
    for packaging, 477-478
    Red Book, 269-270
Stansberry, Domenic, 43-44
Stepping out, 434
Stewart, Ann, 203
Still images, making, 280-292
Stock video footage, 322
Storage devices, 74-80
Storyboarding, 6, 389, 393-394, 407-410
Storyboards, 389, 393-394
Structured languages, 152
StuffIt InstallerMaker, 454-456
Subtractive primary colors, 293
Super NTSC, 325
Superbase, 137
SuperCard authoring system, 154, 158-159, 268
Surf Alligators, 324
S-VHS (super-VHS) video format, 336, 339
Swivel 3D Pro, 292, 508
Symbols, 206-208
Sync (synchronization pulses), 322
SyQuest drives, 78
SYSTAT, 143-145
System requirements (Macintosh and MPC), 482
System software, QuickTime, 114
System sounds, 242-243
SYSTEM.INI, 73-74

T

Tagged Interchange File Format (TIFF), 302
Take Control application, 42
Talent
    searching for or selling, 371
    using, 432-436
Tape path across video head, 323
Tapes, video, 323, 352-354
Task planning (multimedia project), 373
Team, multimedia project, 35-49, 369-371
Team-building, 48
Television, integrating computers with, 327-335
Testing a project, 440-444
Text, 193-236
    animating, 208
    designing with, 200-201
    editing, 108-109
    making artwork of, 226-228
Text searches, 229, 231-236
Text tools, 101
Thomas, Leo, 469
3-D drawing, 290-292
3-D images, rendered, 105
3-D tools, 101, 104-106
3DO, 472
Thumbnails, PhotoDisc CD-ROM, 284
TIFF (Tagged Interchange File Format), 302
Time code input/output, 343
Time-based authoring tools, 149-150, 168-183
Titles, multimedia, 6, 335, 474. *See also* Multimedia projects
TMS Inner View, 230
ToolBook authoring system, 154-155, 160-161, 398
Toolset, basic software, 99-123. *See also* Authoring tools
Toolset, list, 101-102
TouchMate, 82-83
Touchscreens, 82-83
Track layouts (compact disc), 464
Trackballs, 81-82
Tracking projects, 416
Tracking (video), 323
Tracks
    disk, 76
    videotape, 323
Training
    opportunities, 49-51
    providers, 51, 493-498
Translating into other languages, 218
Trimming dead air, 251
TrueType fonts, 210, 212
Tweening, 308
Type C video format, 342
Type measurement, 196
Type sizes, 196
TypeAlign, 108, 228
Typefaces, 196-200
    design protection for, 220
    serif vs. sans serif, 197-200

Typestry, 229

U

U-Design Type Foundry, 491
Underscan, 332
Underwhelming multimedia, 27
Unicode, 219-220
Union contracts for personnel, 433-435
Uppercase, 197
User interface
  designing, 401-406
  hot spots and buttons, 396-399
  icons, 398-400

V

Vasquez, David, 35
Vaughan's General Rule for Interface Design, 403
Vaughan's Law of Multimedia Minimums, 271
Vaughan's One-Way Rule, 61
Vaughan's Rule of Capacity, 75
Vaughan's Rule for Keeping Up, 57
VCRs, 323, 325-326, 339 (*See also* Video)
  editing with, 340-341, 344-345
  signal-to-noise ratio, 344
  stereo audio, 271
  video heads, 344
  zoom lenses, 344
V-Deck, 339
Vector drawing, 288-290
Vector-drawn graphics, 280
Vector-drawn objects, vs. bitmaps, 289-290
VGA (Video Graphics Array), 294
Video, 319-354
  digital video movies, 111-122
  file formats, 112-113
  how it works, 322-324
  light levels, 345-346
  shooting and editing, 335-345
Video capture boards, 329-330
Video capture cards, 294
Video cards, 294
Video cassette recorders. *See* VCRs
Video color, 333
Video compression. *See* Compression (video)
Video Compressor (Apple), 115
Video devices, 90
Video display card, 294
Video drivers, 518-519
Video editing, 335-345, 354
Video equipment
  consumer-grade, 338-341
  professional, 341-345
Video files for CD-ROMS, optimizing, 351-352
Video Graphics Array (VGA), 294
Video hardware resolutions, table of, 338
Video heads, 323, 344
Video overlay boards, table of, 331
Video overlay systems, 327-330
Video playback, digitized, 330-332
Video production titles, 335
Video recording formats, 336-345
Video shooting platforms, 345
Video signal, 322
Video specialist, 44-45
Video standards, 325-326
Video System Control Architecture (VISCA), 339
Video Toaster, 352
Video windows, 340, 348
Video for Windows, 111, 117-118
Videodisc players, 79-80, 328
VideoMachine, 352, 354
Videotapes
  backing up, 354
  taking care of, 353-354
  tracks on, 323
  transferring from computer to, 352-353
Virtual reality, 19-21
Virtus VR, 291
Visual Basic, 138, 162-163
Visual programming, 151
VLSI (Very Large Scale Integrated) hardware, 350
Voice recognition systems, 85
Volume adjustment (audio editing), 252
Von Bargen, Sally, 21
VRAM (video RAM), 89

W

Waldman, Helayne, 35, 51
WAV sound files, 110, 260
Wave audio, 263
WaveEdit, 87, 110
Waveform editing, 272
Waveforms, sound, 247-248

White space, 406
Who Killed Sam Rupert, 348
Wide area networks (WANs), 92-94
Wild Magic, 119
Williams, Mark, 36
WindowBase, 137
Windows MCI, 72-73
Windows multimedia architecture, 72
Windows platform installation, 451-452
Windows Player (Director), 187-188
Windows Showcase CD-ROM, how to use, 517-519
Windows, video, 340, 348
Wine, Hal, 47-48
Word for the Macintosh (Microsoft), 130-131
Word processors, 129-134
Word for Windows (Microsoft), 131-132
WordPerfect for Macintosh, 131-133
WordPerfect for Windows, 133
Work made for hire, 430, 432
World Intellectual Property Organization (WIPO), 220
Writer, multimedia, 42-44

X

X-height (type size), 196

Y

Yalonis, Chris, 26
YCC color model, 296
Yellow Book standard, 463, 465-466
YIQ color model, 296
YUV (component) video, 116, 296, 322, 336-338

Z

Zoom lenses, 344

Limited Warranty

Osborne/McGraw-Hill warrants the physical compact disc enclosed herein to be free of defects in materials and workmanship for a period of sixty days from the purchase date. If Osborne/McGraw-Hill receives written notification within the warranty period of defects in materials or workmanship, and such notification is determined by Osborne/McGraw-Hill to be correct, Osborne/McGraw-Hill will replace the defective disc. Osborne/McGraw-Hill, 2600 Tenth Street, Berkeley, CA 94710-2586. Toll free 1-800-227-0900 (Mon-Fri, 8:30-4:30, Pacific Time)

The entire and exclusive liability and remedy for breach of this Limited Warranty shall be limited to replacement of defective disc and shall not include or extend to any claim for or right to cover any other damages, including but not limited to, loss of profit, data, or use of the software, or special, incidental, or consequential damages or other similar claims, even if Osborne/McGraw-Hill has been specifically advised of the possibility of such damages. In no event will Osborne/McGraw-Hill's liability for any damages to you or any other person ever exceed the lower of the suggested list price or actual price paid for the license to use the software, regardless of any form of the claim.

OSBORNE, A DIVISION OF McGRAW-HILL, INC., SPECIFICALLY DISCLAIMS ALL OTHER WARRANTIES, EXPRESS OR IMPLIED, INCLUDING BUT NOT LIMITED TO, ANY IMPLIED WARRANTY OF MERCHANTABILITY OR FITNESS FOR A PARTICULAR PURPOSE. Specifically, Osborne/McGraw-Hill makes no representation or warranty that the software is fit for any particular purpose, and any implied warranty of merchantability is limited to the sixty-day duration of the Limited Warranty covering the physical disc only (and not the software), and is otherwise expressly and specifically disclaimed.

This limited warranty gives you specific legal rights; you may have others which may vary from state to state. Some states do not allow the exclusion of incidental or consequential damages, or the limitation on how long an implied warranty lasts, so some of the above may not apply to you.

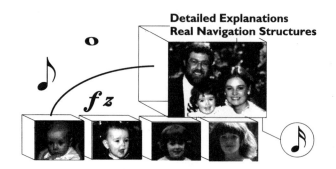